STREET ATLAS
Northamptonshire

Contents

III Key to map symbols

IV-V Key to map pages

VI-VII Route planning

VIII Administrative and post code boundaries

1 Street maps

240 Town maps of Banbury and Buckingham

241 Town maps of Rugby and Stamford

242 Index of hospitals, industrial estates, railway stations, schools, shopping centres, street names and universities

PHILIP'S

First colour edition published 1999

Ordnance Survey® and George Philip Ltd, a division of
Romsey Road Octopus Publishing Group Ltd
Maybush 2-4 Heron Quays
Southampton London
SO16 4GU E14 4JP

ISBN 0-540-07745-3 (hardback)
ISBN 0-540-07746-1 (spiral)

To the best of the Publishers' knowledge, the information in this atlas was
correct at the time of going to press. No responsibility can be accepted
for any errors or their consequences.

The representation in this atlas of a road, track or path is no evidence
of the existence of a right of way.

**The mapping between pages 1 and 241 (inclusive) in this atlas is
derived from Ordnance Survey® OSCAR® and Land-Line® data and
Landranger® mapping.**

Ordnance Survey, OSCAR, Land-line and Landranger are registered trade
marks of Ordnance Survey, the national mapping agency of Great Britain.

Printed and bound in Spain by Cayfosa

Digital Data

The exceptionally high-quality mapping
found in this book is available as digital
data in TIFF format, which is easily
convertible to other bit-mapped (raster)
image formats. The data can be provided
as pages or, in some regions, as larger
extracts of up to 200 sq km. The larger
extracts can also be supplied on paper.

The index is also available in digital form
as a standard database table. It contains
all the details found in the printed index
together with the National Grid reference
for the map square in which each entry is
named.

For further information and to discuss
your requirements, please contact
Philip's on 0171 531 8440 or
george.philip@philips-maps.co.uk

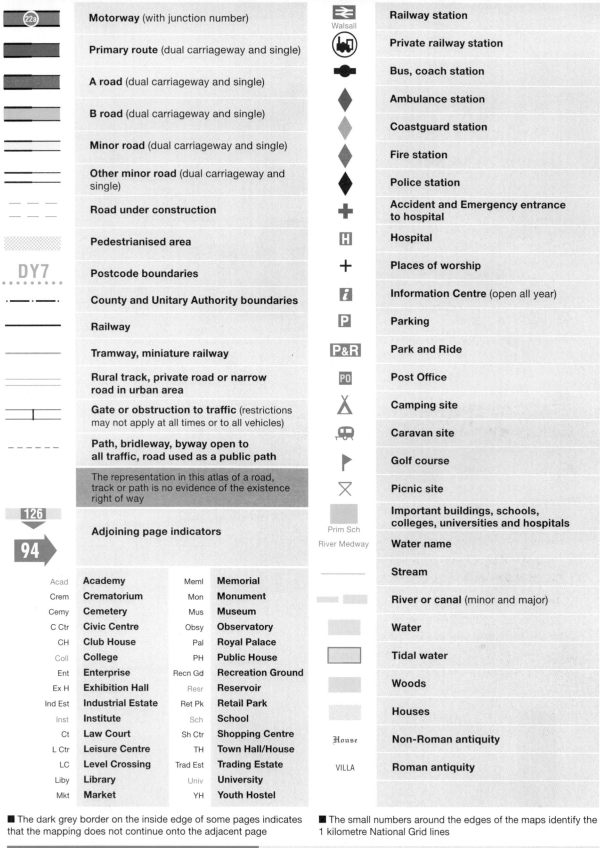

	Motorway (with junction number)
	Primary route (dual carriageway and single)
	A road (dual carriageway and single)
	B road (dual carriageway and single)
	Minor road (dual carriageway and single)
	Other minor road (dual carriageway and single)
	Road under construction
	Pedestrianised area
DY7	**Postcode boundaries**
	County and Unitary Authority boundaries
	Railway
	Tramway, miniature railway
	Rural track, private road or narrow road in urban area
	Gate or obstruction to traffic (restrictions may not apply at all times or to all vehicles)
	Path, bridleway, byway open to all traffic, road used as a public path
	The representation in this atlas of a road, track or path is no evidence of the existence right of way
126 / 94	**Adjoining page indicators**

Acad	**Academy**	Meml	**Memorial**
Crem	**Crematorium**	Mon	**Monument**
Cemy	**Cemetery**	Mus	**Museum**
C Ctr	**Civic Centre**	Obsy	**Observatory**
CH	**Club House**	Pal	**Royal Palace**
Coll	**College**	PH	**Public House**
Ent	**Enterprise**	Recn Gd	**Recreation Ground**
Ex H	**Exhibition Hall**	Resr	**Reservoir**
Ind Est	**Industrial Estate**	Ret Pk	**Retail Park**
Inst	**Institute**	Sch	**School**
Ct	**Law Court**	Sh Ctr	**Shopping Centre**
L Ctr	**Leisure Centre**	TH	**Town Hall/House**
LC	**Level Crossing**	Trad Est	**Trading Estate**
Liby	**Library**	Univ	**University**
Mkt	**Market**	YH	**Youth Hostel**

Walsall	**Railway station**
	Private railway station
	Bus, coach station
	Ambulance station
	Coastguard station
	Fire station
	Police station
	Accident and Emergency entrance to hospital
H	**Hospital**
	Places of worship
i	**Information Centre** (open all year)
P	**Parking**
P&R	**Park and Ride**
PO	**Post Office**
	Camping site
	Caravan site
	Golf course
	Picnic site
Prim Sch	**Important buildings, schools, colleges, universities and hospitals**
River Medway	**Water name**
	Stream
	River or canal (minor and major)
	Water
	Tidal water
	Woods
	Houses
House	**Non-Roman antiquity**
VILLA	**Roman antiquity**

■ The dark grey border on the inside edge of some pages indicates that the mapping does not continue onto the adjacent page

■ The small numbers around the edges of the maps identify the 1 kilometre National Grid lines

The scale of the maps is 5.52 cm to 1 km
(3½ inches to 1 mile)

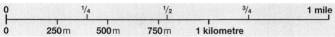

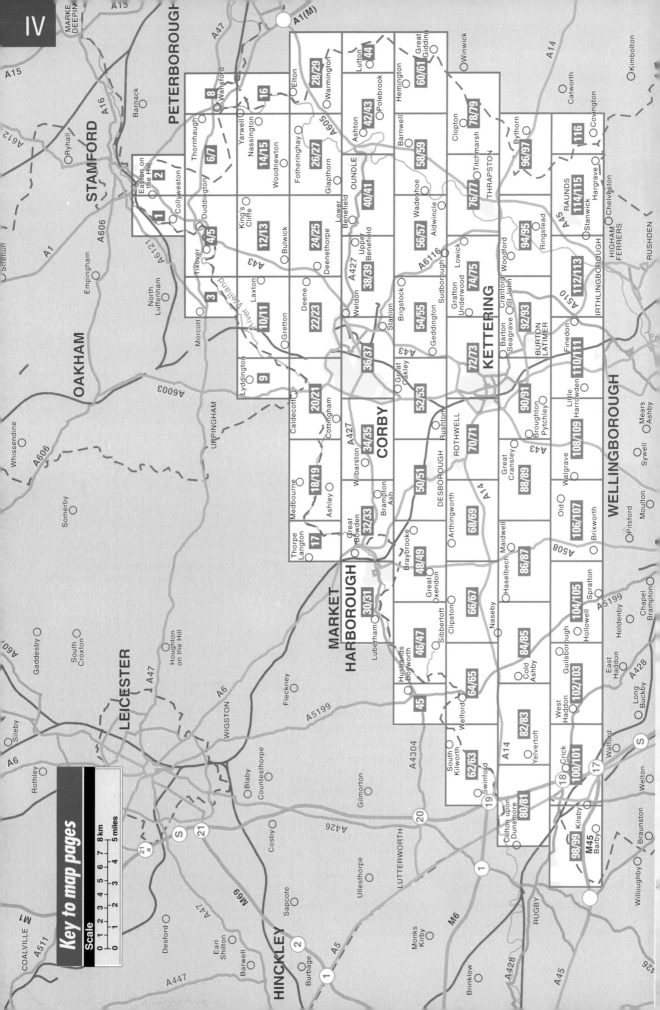

Key to map pages

Scale

0 1 2 3 4 5 6 7 8 km
0 1 2 3 4 5 miles

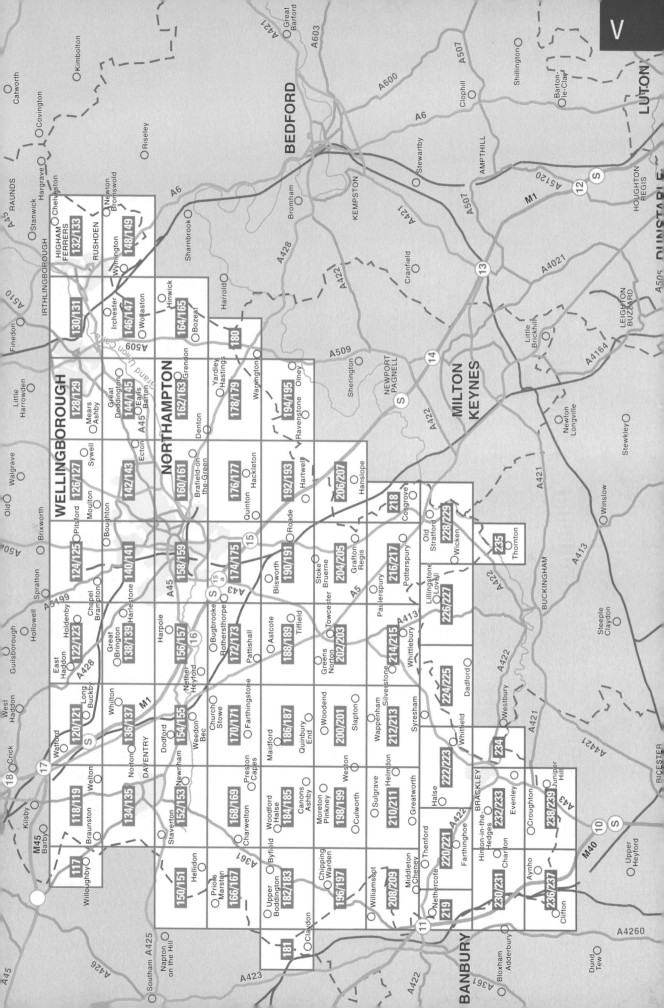

Route planning

Scale

0 1 2 3 4 5 6 7 8 km
0   1   2   3   4   5

Major administrative and Postcode boundaries

County and Unitary Authority boundaries

District boundaries

Postcode boundaries

Area covered by this atlas

Scale

0   5   10   15 km

0   5   10 miles

SK / TF

Lincolnshire

SK / SP

Rutland

City of Peterborough

Leicestershire

Easton on the Hill

PE9

Thornhaugh

Wansford

LE15

Wakerley

LE15

Elton

Rockingham

NN17

Deene

Fotheringhay

PE7

LE16

Corby

Corby

PE8

Oundle

Cottingham

Market Harborough

NN18

Great Oakley

LE16

East Northamptonshire

LE17

Desborough

Kettering

Geddington

PE17

Husbands Bosworth

Braybrooke

Rothwell

NN16

NN14

Thrapston

Stanford on Avon

Sibbertoft

Harrington

Kettering

Welford

NN14

NN15

Keyston

Lilbourne

Naseby

Burton Latimer

PE18

CV21

CV23

Yelvertoft

Northamptonshire

Cambridgeshire

CV22

West Haddon

Creaton

NN9

Irthlingborough

Raunds

CV23

Kilsby

NN6

Brixworth

NN9

Warwickshire

Daventry

NN6

Wellingborough

Rushden

Great Brington

NN8

Wellingborough

NN10

Daventry

NN2

NN3

Wollaston

MK44

Priors Marston

NN11

Northampton

NN5

NN1

Castle Ashby

NN29

Podington

Charwelton

Weedon Bec

Northampton

Bozeat

MK43

NN4

NN7

CV33

Farthingstone

Blisworth

Horton

Claydon

Canons Ashby

South Northamptonshire

Eakley Lanes

MK46

Olney

Culworth

Weston

NN12

Towcester

Tathall

MK16

Milton Keynes

Bedfordshire

OX17

Sulgrave

MK19

Middleton Cheney

Helmdon

Silverstone

Cosgrove

OX16

NN13

MK18

MK19

MK12

Stony Stratford

Farthinghoe

Lillingstone Lovell

MK11

OX17

Brackley

Clifton Deddington

Aynho

Croughton

Thornton

MK17

OX15

Souldern

OX6

Oxfordshire

Buckinghamshire

Herts

Luton

SP / TL

SP / TL

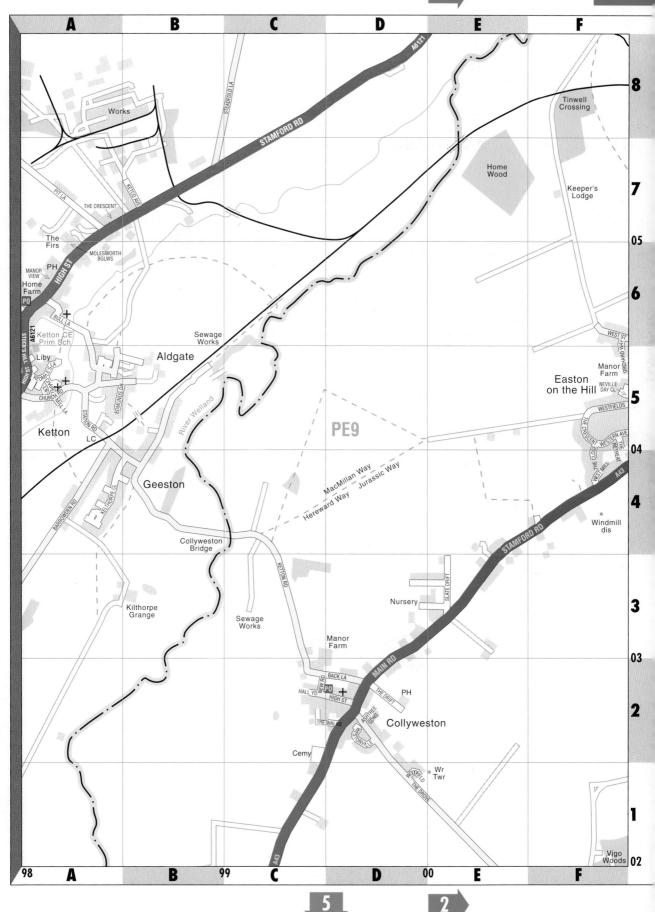

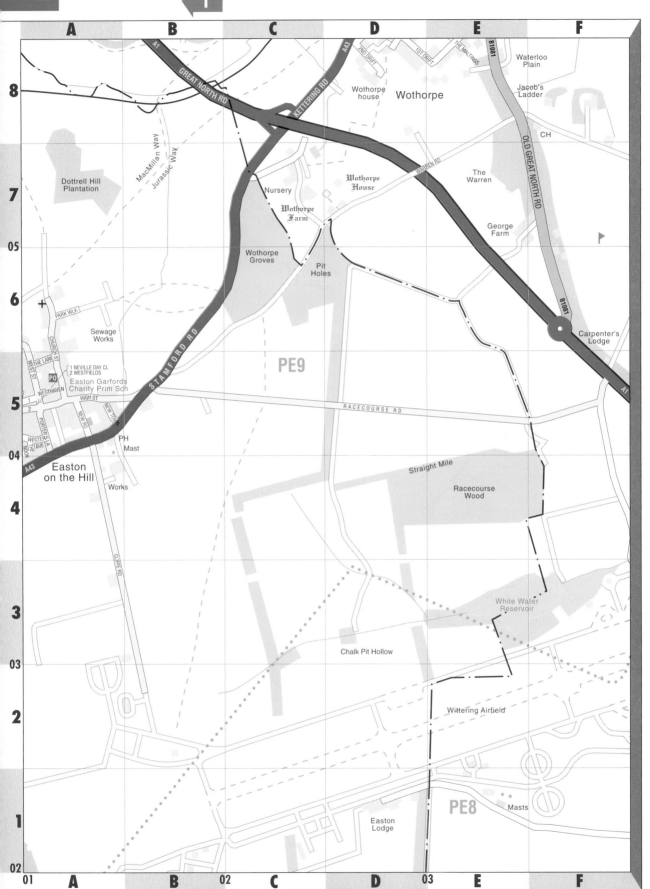
A B C D E F

8 Wothorpe house Wothorpe Waterloo Plain Jacob's Ladder

GREAT NORTH RD KETTERING RD A43 2ND DRIFT 1ST DRIFT THE MALTINGS B1081 CH

A1 OLD GREAT NORTH RD

7 Dottrell Hill Plantation MacMillan Way Jurassic Way Nursery Wothorpe House WARREN RD The Warren George Farm

Wothorpe Farm

05 Wothorpe Groves Pit Holes

6 PARK WLK Sewage Works Carpenter's Lodge B1081

CHURCH ST THE LANE WEST ST 1 NEVILLE DAY CL 2 WESTFIELDS PO WESTHAVEN Easton Garfords Charity Prim Sch PE9 STAMFORD RD

5 HIGH ST 1 2 NEW RD NEW TOK RACECOURSE RD

PORTER'S LA WESTERN AVE PH Mast

04 THE NOOK A43 Easton on the Hill Works Straight Mile Racecourse Wood

4 CLIFFE RD

3 White Water Reservoir

03 Chalk Pit Hollow

2 Wittering Airfield

PE8

1 Easton Lodge Masts

02 A B 02 C D 03 E F

01 A

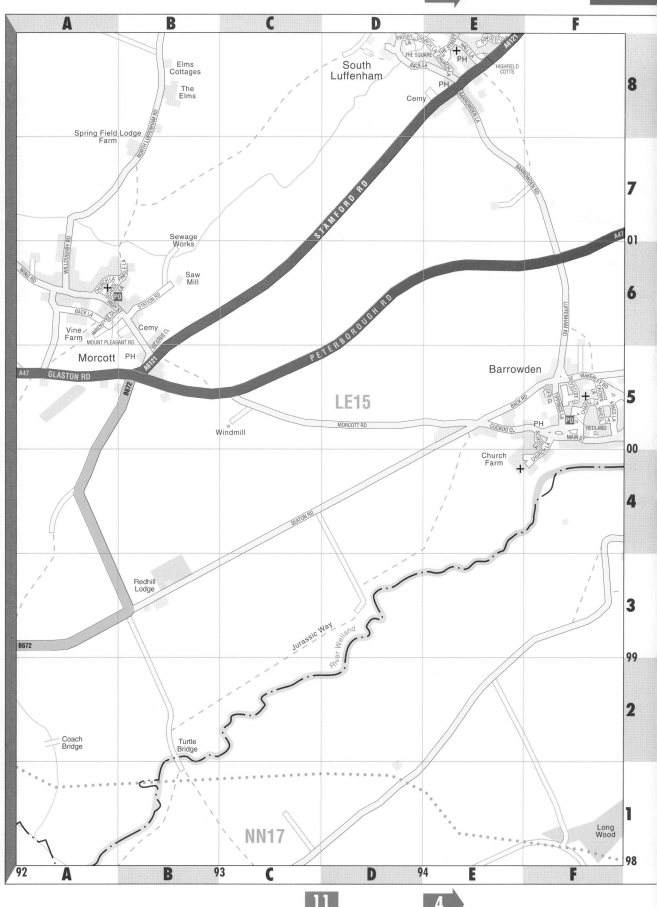

A B C D E F

8
7
01
6
5
00
4
3
99
2
1
98

Elms
Cottages

The
Elms

South
Luffenham

FRISBY LA
CHURCH LA
THE SQUARE
BACK LA
CHURCH LA
THE STREET
MILL LA
PH
PINFOLD CL
A6121

HIGHFIELD
COTTS

PH

Cemy

BARROWDEN LA

BARROWDEN RD

A47

01

Spring Field Lodge
Farm

NORTH LUFFENHAM RD

STAMFORD RD

PETERBOROUGH RD

LUFFENHAM RD

Sewage
Works

Saw
Mill

WILLOUGHBY RD

WING RD

CHURCH LA
SCHOOL LA
PINFOLD LA
HIGH ST
PO
STATION RD

BACK LA

WRENDYKE CL

Vine
Farm

Cemy

VICAR'S CL

MOUNT PLEASANT RD

Morcott

PH

A6121

A47
GLASTON RD

B672

Barrowden

CIDER CL
BACK RD
DOVECOTE CL
TIPPINGS LA
CHAPEL LA
CROWN
WAKERLEY RD
WHEEL
KINGS LA
PO
REDLAND
CL
PH
CUCKOO CL
MAIN ST
SCHOOL LA
CHURCH LA

LE15

Windmill

MORCOTT RD

Church
Farm

SEATON RD

Redhill
Lodge

B672

Jurassic Way

River Welland

Coach
Bridge

Turtle
Bridge

NN17

Long
Wood

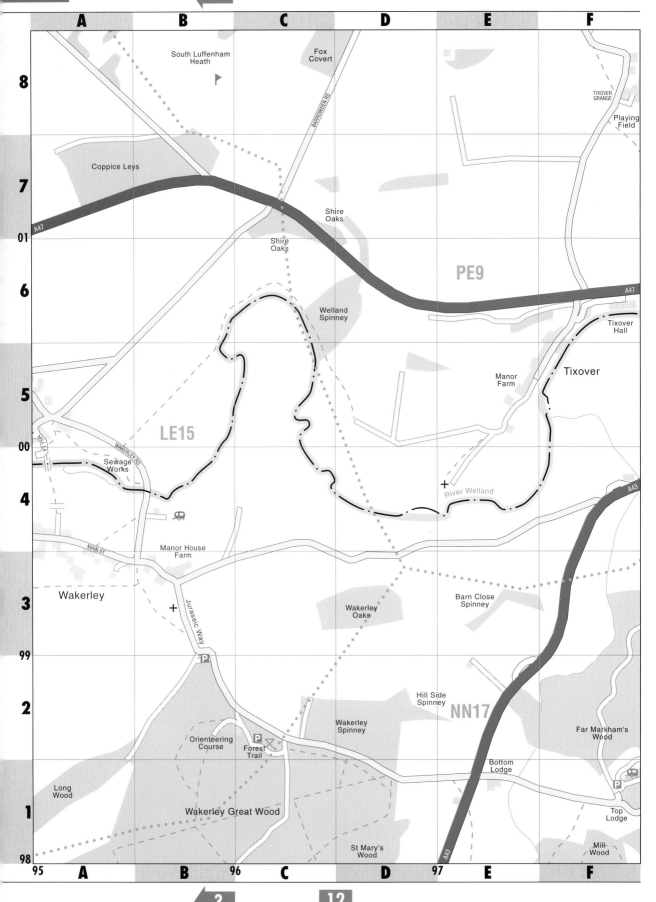

South Luffenham Heath

Fox Covert

BARROWDEN RD

TIXOVER GRANGE

Playing Field

Coppice Leys

A47

Shire Oaks

Shire Oaks

PE9

A47

Welland Spinney

Tixover Hall

Manor Farm

Tixover

LE15

MULLA

WAKERLEY RD

Sewage Works

River Welland

A43

Main St

Manor House Farm

Wakerley

Jurassic Way

Wakerley Oaks

Barn Close Spinney

P

Hill Side Spinney

NN17

Far Markham's Wood

Orienteering Course

Forest Trail

Wakerley Spinney

Bottom Lodge

Long Wood

Wakerley Great Wood

St Mary's Wood

A43

Top Lodge

Mill Wood

P

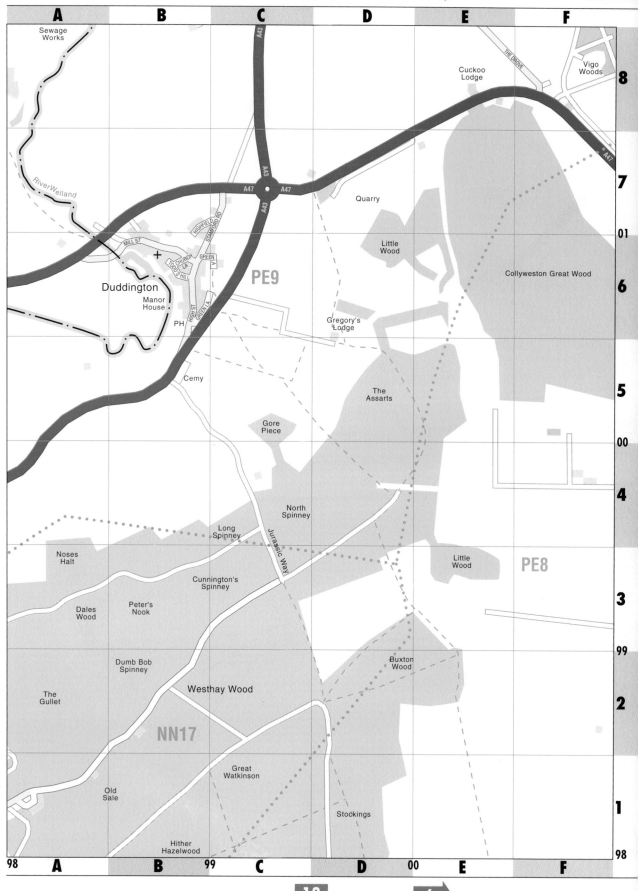

Sewage Works

Cuckoo Lodge

Vigo Woods

THE DROVE

8

RiverWelland

A43

A47

A47

A43

01

Quarry

HIGHFIELD

STAMFORD RD

GREEN LA

Little Wood

Collyweston Great Wood

7

MILL ST

TO CHURCH LA

TOAD'S HILL

+

Duddington

PE9

6

Manor House

HIGH ST

GREEN LA

PH

Gregory's Lodge

Cemy

The Assarts

5

Gore Piece

00

North Spinney

4

Long Spinney

Jurassic Way

Noses Halt

Little Wood

PE8

Cunnington's Spinney

Dales Wood

Peter's Nook

3

Buxton Wood

Dumb Bob Spinney

99

The Gullet

Westhay Wood

2

NN17

Great Watkinson

Old Sale

Stockings

1

Hither Hazelwood

98

5
2

A B C D E F

8

PE9

7

A47

01

Rogue
Sale

COLLYWESTON
CROSS ROADS

6

Wittering
Lodge

A47

5

Easton Hornstocks

Wittering
Coppice

Westhay
Cottages

00

PE8

Westhay
Farm

4

Cross Leys
Farm

Upper
Moiseys

Upper
Forty Acres

Cromwell
Sink Sale

3

Westhay
Lodge

Pebblegate
Sale

99

Law's
Lawn

St John's Wood
Farm

2

Rose
lodge

1

98

01 A B 02 C D 03 E F

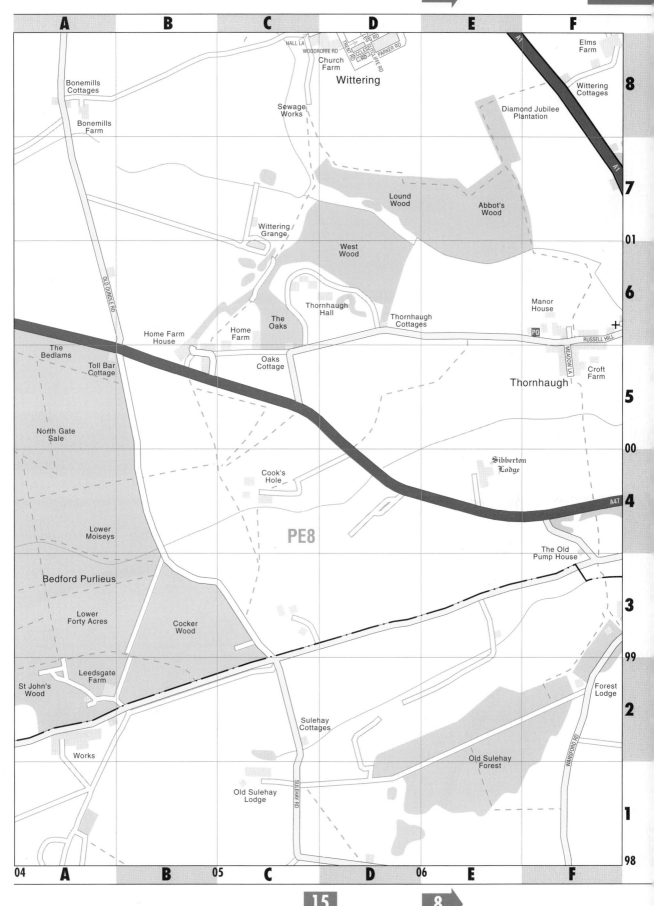

A B C D E F

8

Hotel

Manor
Farm

7

COLLEY RISE

PO

Lyddington

MAIN ST

MAIN ST

Prestley
Hill

97

STOKE RD

THE GREEN

Bede
House

LE15

BLUECOAT LA

PH

CHURCH LA

WINDMILL WAY

Bee
Hill

6

THORPE RD

GRETTON RD

Sewage
Works

5

B672

96

4

LE16

3

Middle
Bridge

95

UPPINGHAM RD

LYDDINGTON RD

MILL RD

2

The Old
Vicarage

River Welland

NN17

1

A6003

B672

94

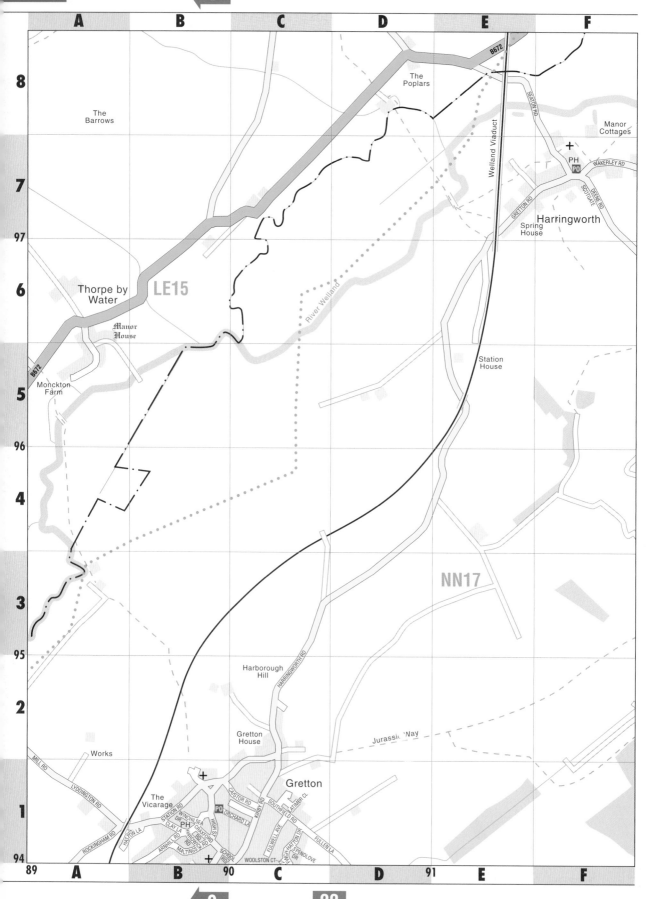

The Barrows

The Poplars

B672

Welland Viaduct

Manor
Cottages

PH
PO

WAKERLEY RD

SEATON RD

Harringworth

Spring
House

GRETTON RD

DEENE RD

SCOTGATE

Thorpe by
Water

LE15

River Welland

Manor
House

B672

Monckton
Farm

Station
House

NN17

Harborough
Hill

HARRINGWORTH RD

Jurassic Way

Works

Gretton
House

Gretton

MILL RD

LYDDINGTON RD

ROCKINGHAM RD

The
Vicarage

PH

HAXTON LA

STATION RD

WINCHILSEA

CLAY LA

ARNHILL RD

CRAYFORD RD

HARDWICK RD

MALTINGS

HIGH ST

SCHOOL RD

CAISTOR RD

PO

ORCHARD LA

KIRBY RD

FILWELL AVE

SOUTHFIELD RD

LATIMER CL

FINCH DR

HAT SPENDLOVE

FULLEN LA

WOOLSTON CT

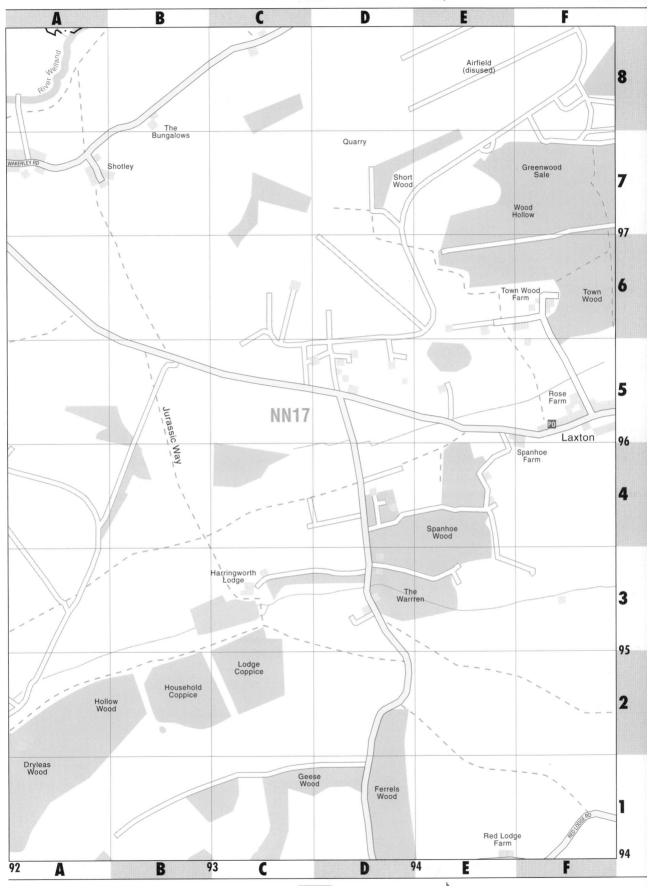

A   B   C   D   E   F

8

7

97

6

5

96

4

3

95

2

1

94

River Welland

The
Bungalows

WAKERLEY RD

Shotley

Airfield
(disused)

Quarry

Short
Wood

Greenwood
Sale

Wood
Hollow

Town Wood
Farm

Town
Wood

Jurassic Way

NN17

Rose
Farm

PO

Laxton

Spanhoe
Farm

Spanhoe
Wood

Harringworth
Lodge

The
Warrren

Lodge
Coppice

Household
Coppice

Hollow
Wood

Dryleas
Wood

Geese
Wood

Ferrels
Wood

Red Lodge
Farm

RED LODGE RD

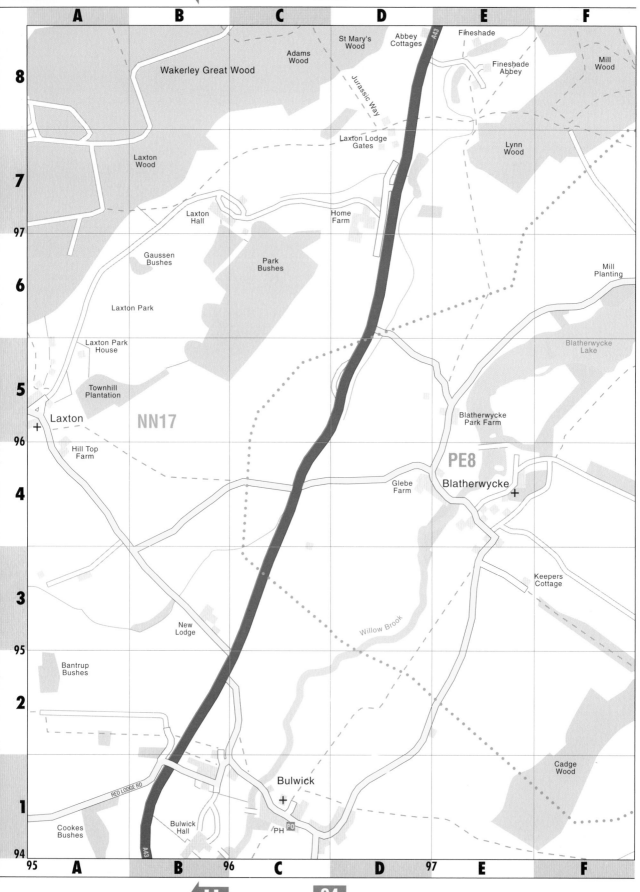

A	B	C	D	E	F

Far Hazelwood
Hither Hazelwood
Little Watkinson
Hollow Wood

NN17

Far Miers
Jurassic Way

Westhay Wood

Hither Miers

WOOD LA

8

Britain Sale

Kit Spinney

Oundle & King's Cliffe Mid Sch

KINGSMEAD

King's Cliffe

WILLOW LA
WOOD RD
FINESHADE CL
FOREST APP
KING'S FOREST
PARK ST
WALK FIELD
STATION RD
HOWARDS LA

King's Cliffe Endowed Prim Sch

7

MAZEWOOD GATE
BLATHERWYCKE RD
WEST ST
PH
ORCHARD LA

PO
DEANS LA
BRIDGE ST A
MOREHAY LA

97

Cemy

MOREHAY LA

6

Willow Brook

Alders Farm

5

PE8

96

The Spa (Chalybeate)

Calvey Wood

Spa Farm Cottages

4

Spa Farm

Brickhill Pond

Briary Wood

3

95

Tomlin Wood

Hostage Wood

2

NN17

Crayley Wood

Morehay Lawn

1

Bushey Wood

94

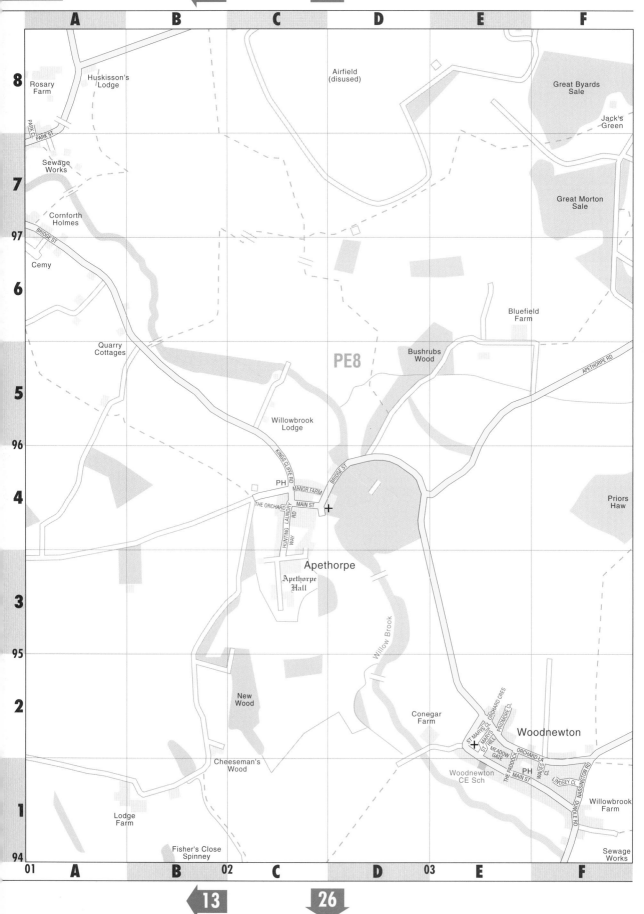

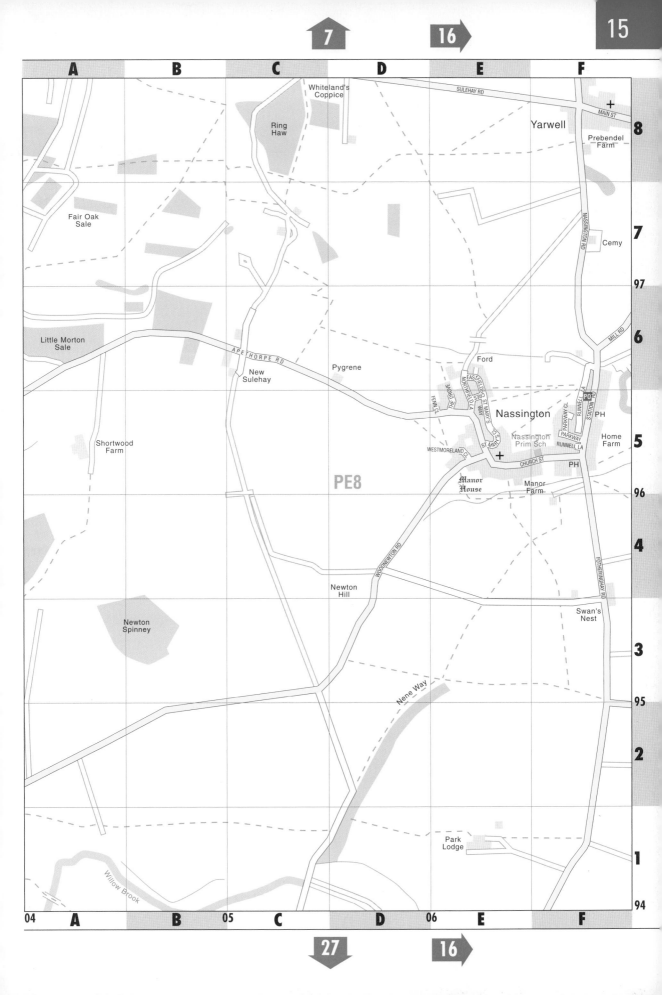

A B C D E F

SULEHAY RD

Whiteland's
Coppice

Ring
Haw

Yarwell

MAIN ST

Prebendel
Farm

Fair Oak
Sale

NASSINGTON RD

Cemy

MILL RD

Little Morton
Sale

APETHORPE RD

Ford

New
Sulehay

Pygrene

EASTFIELD
NORTHFIELD LA
ST MARY'S
THE DRIFT
FENN CL

Nassington
Prim Sch

Nassington

PARKWAY CL
RUNNELL LA
STATION RD

PO

PH

PARKWAY

RUNNELL LA

Home
Farm

PE8

Shortwood
Farm

WESTMORELAND CL

ST MARY'S

CHURCH ST

PH

Manor
House

Manor
Farm

WOODNEWTON RD

FOTHERINGHAM RD

Swan's
Nest

Newton
Hill

Newton
Spinney

Nene Way

Park
Lodge

Willow Brook

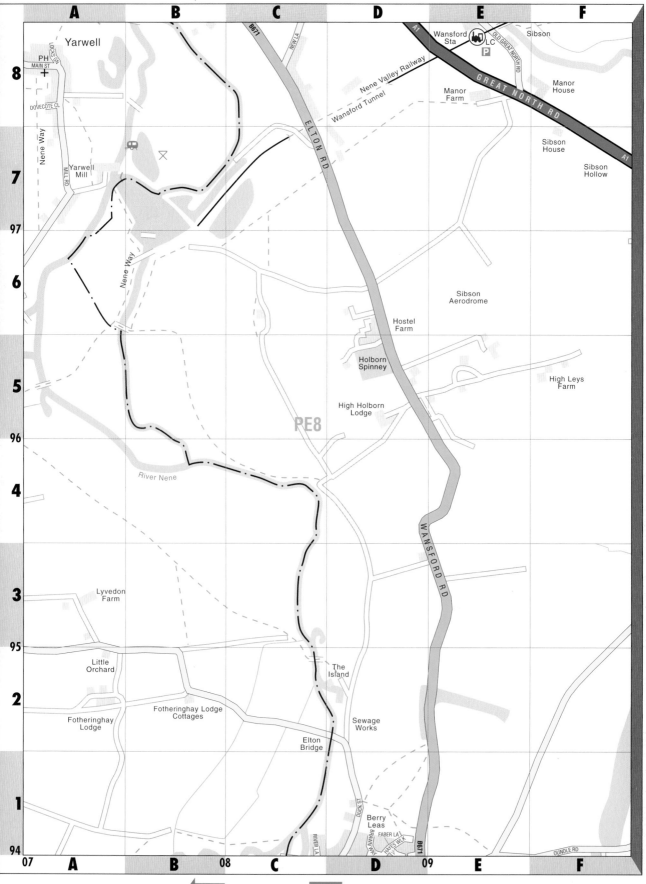

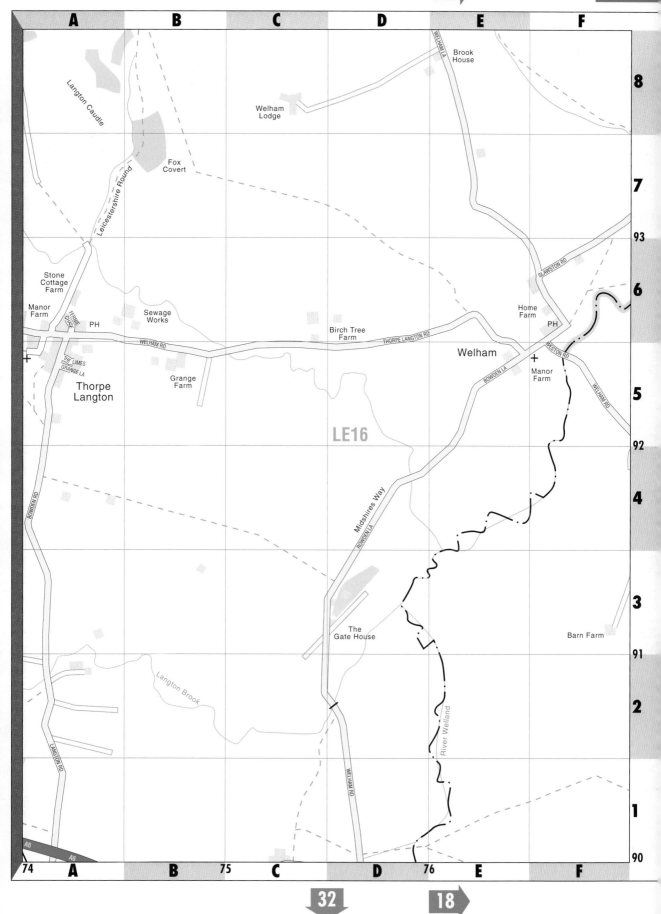

18

A B C D E F

8
7
93
6
5
92
4
3
91
2
1
90

Langton Caudle

Fox Covert

Welham Lodge

Brook House

WELHAM LA

SLAWSTON RD

Leicestershire Round

Stone Cottage Farm

Manor Farm

FERNIE CHASE

PH

Sewage Works

WELHAM RD

Birch Tree Farm

THORPE LANGTON RD

Welham

Home Farm

PH

WESTON RD

BOWDEN LA

Manor Farm

WELHAM RD

THE LIMES
GRANGE LA

Thorpe Langton

Grange Farm

LE16

BOWDEN RD

Midshires Way

BOWDEN LA

Langton Brook

The Gate House

River Welland

Barn Farm

WELHAM RD

LANGTON RD

A6 A6

74 A B 75 C D 76 E F

18

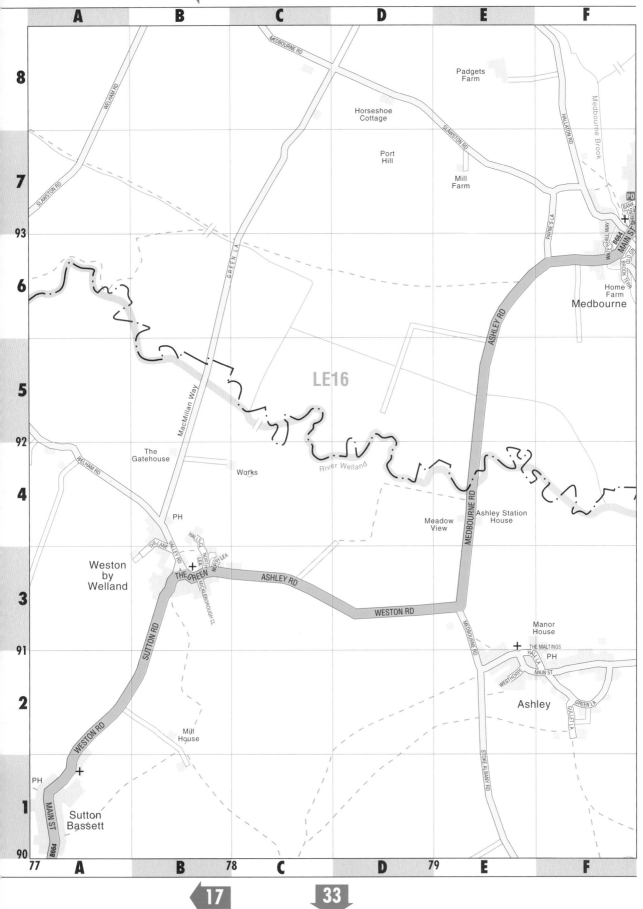

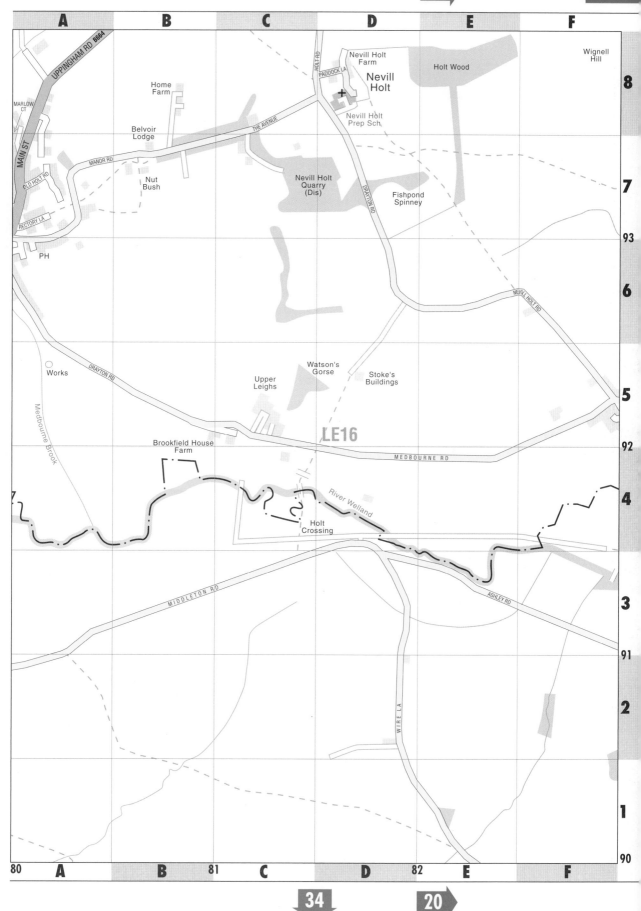

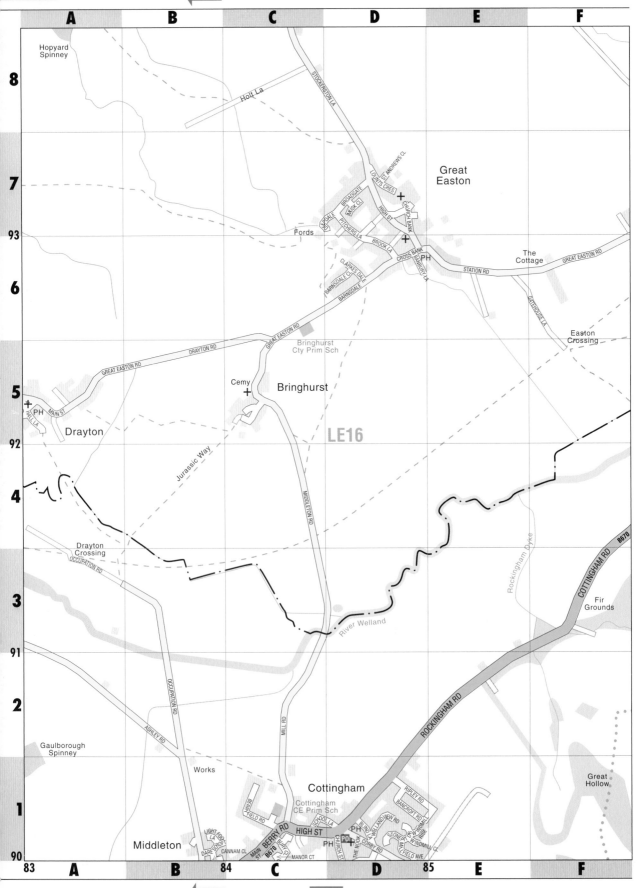

A B C D E F

8

Hopyard Spinney

Holt La

Great Easton

7

STOCKERSTON LA

ST ANDREWS CL

LOWTS CRES

BROADGATE

MASK CL

HIGH ST

CHURCH BANK

93

Fords

SAPCOTE

PITCHERS LA

BROOK LA

CLARKES DALE

CROSS BANK

BANBURY LA

PH

The Cottage

GREAT EASTON RD

6

BARNSDALE CLOSE

BARNSDALE

STATION RD

GATEHOUSE LA

Easton Crossing

Bringhurst Cty Prim Sch

GREAT EASTON RD

DRAYTON RD

5

GREAT EASTON RD

MAIN ST

Cemy

Bringhurst

LE16

92

PH

HALL LA

Drayton

Jurassic Way

MIDDLETON RD

Rockingham Dyke

4

Drayton Crossing

OCCUPATION RD

B670

COTTINGHAM RD

3

Fir Grounds

River Welland

91

ROCKINGHAM RD

OCCUPATION RD

2

ASHLEY RD

Gaulborough Spinney

Works

Great Hollow

RIPLEY RD

BANCROFT RD

1

Cottingham

Cottingham CE Prim Sch

BERRY FIELD RD

WELLAND VIEW RD

PH

Middleton

LIGHT FOOT LA

DARE CROFT

MAIN ST

B670

BERRY RD

HIGH ST

SCHOOL LA

BURY RD

MANOR CT

CANNAM CL

CHURCH ST

PO

PH

CORBY RD

THE NOOK

STONEY FIELD AVE

WINDMILL CL

JW RISE

90

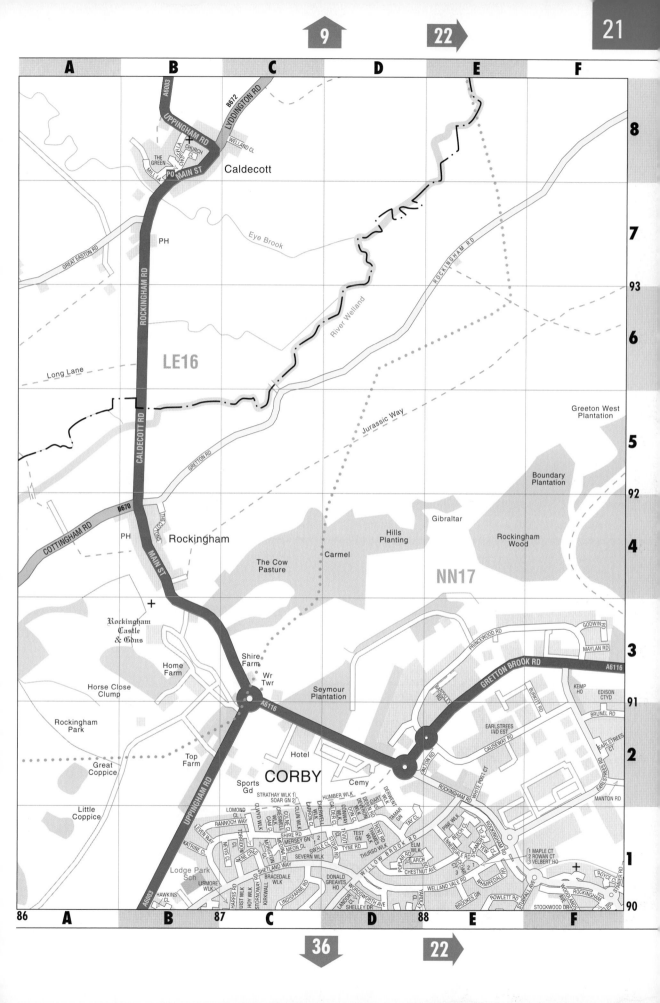

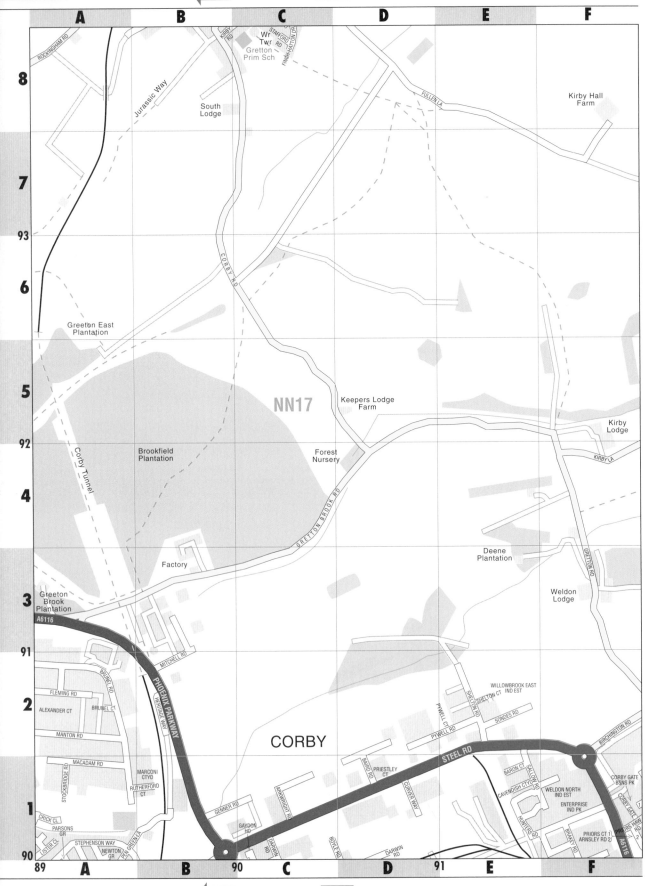

A   B   C   D   E   F

8

7

93

6

5

92

4

3

91

2

1

90

89   A   B   90   C   D   91   E   F

ROCKINGHAM RD

Jurassic Way

KIRBY RD

STAFFORD RD

FINCH-HATTON DR

Wr
Twr
Gretton
Prim Sch

Gretton

South
Lodge

FULLEN LA

Kirby Hall
Farm

CORBY RD

Greeton East
Plantation

NN17

Keepers Lodge
Farm

Kirby
Lodge

KIRBY LA

Corby Tunnel

Brookfield
Plantation

Forest
Nursery

GRETTON BROOK RD

Deene
Plantation

GRETTON RD

Weldon
Lodge

Factory

Greeton
Brook
Plantation

A6116

Mitchell Rd

PHOENIX PARKWAY

HERITAGE WAY

WILLOWBROOK EAST
IND EST

SHELTON CT

PYWELL CT

SHELTON RD

BRUNEL RD

FLEMING RD

Alexander Ct

BRUNEL CT

PYWELL RD

SONDES RD

CORBY

MANTON RD

MACADAM RD

STOCKBRIDGE GR

MARCONI
CTYD

RUTHERFORD
CT

GENNER RD

BARD RD

ARKWRIGHT RD

Priestley
CT

CURVER WAY

STEEL RD

BARON CT

SALLOW

CAVENDISH CTYD

Weldon North
Ind Est

Corby Gate
Bsns Pk

BIRCHINGTON RD

CORBY GATE

CRICK CL

PARSONS
GR

LISTER CL

NEW GREEN LA

STEPHENSON WAY

NEWTON
GR

GAYDON
HO

DARWIN

BOYLE RD

DARWIN
RD

HUNTER RD

Enterprise
Ind Pk

PRIORS LAW

Priors Ct 1
Arnsley Rd 2

A6116

21   37

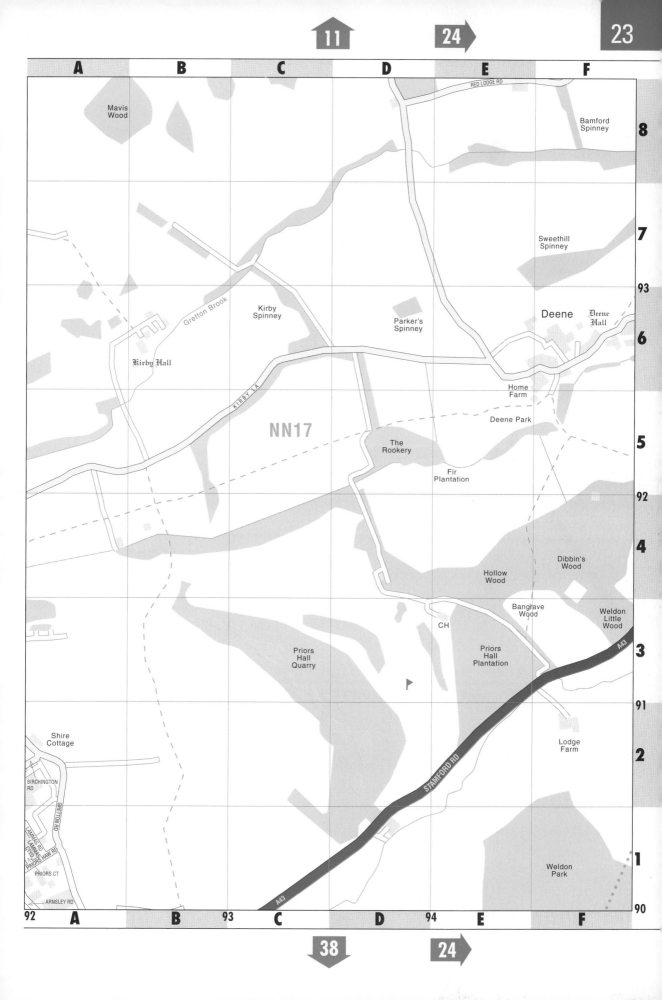

A B C D E F

8 7 93 6 5 92 4 91 3 2 1 90

Mavis Wood

Bamford Spinney

RED LODGE RD

Sweethill Spinney

Gretton Brook

Kirby Spinney

Parker's Spinney

Deene

Deene Hall

Kirby Hall

KIRBY LA

Home Farm

NN17

Deene Park

The Rookery

Fir Plantation

Dibbin's Wood

Hollow Wood

Bangrave Wood

Weldon Little Wood

CH

Priors Hall Quarry

Priors Hall Plantation

A43

Shire Cottage

Lodge Farm

BIRCHINGTON RD

GRETTON RD

STAMFORD RD

LAMMAS RD

PRIORS HAW RD

PRIORS CT

Weldon Park

ARNSLEY RD

A43

92 93 94

A B C D E F

8

Kennel
Coppice

Gretton Brook

7

Great
Spinney

Bulwick
Lodge

NN17

Glebe
Farm

93

6

+

The
Lake

Barratt's
Coppice

Rough
Close

5

DEENETHORPE LA

92

OSIER BED LA

Forest
Lodge

Deenethorpe

4

BENEFIELD RD

Burn
Coppice

A43

3

Home
Farm
Lodge

91

Langley
Coppice

2

Airfield
(dis)

PE8

1

90

95 A B 96 C D 97 E F

A B C D E F

8

7

93

6

5

92

4

91

2

1

90

Holey Brookes

Boar's Head Cottage

Boar's Head Farm

Shire Hill Lodge

Blackmore Thick Farm

NN17

Stone Hill

Great Old Sale

Little Old Sale

New Hall

Frere Hill Wood

Frere Hill

Crossway Hand Farm

Vicarage Farm

Crossway Hand Cottages

PE8

Wymond Hill

Tottenhoe Lodge

Westwood Lodge

Provost Lodge

Glapthorn Cow Pasture

Sandy Forth Lodge

98 A B 99 C D 00 E F

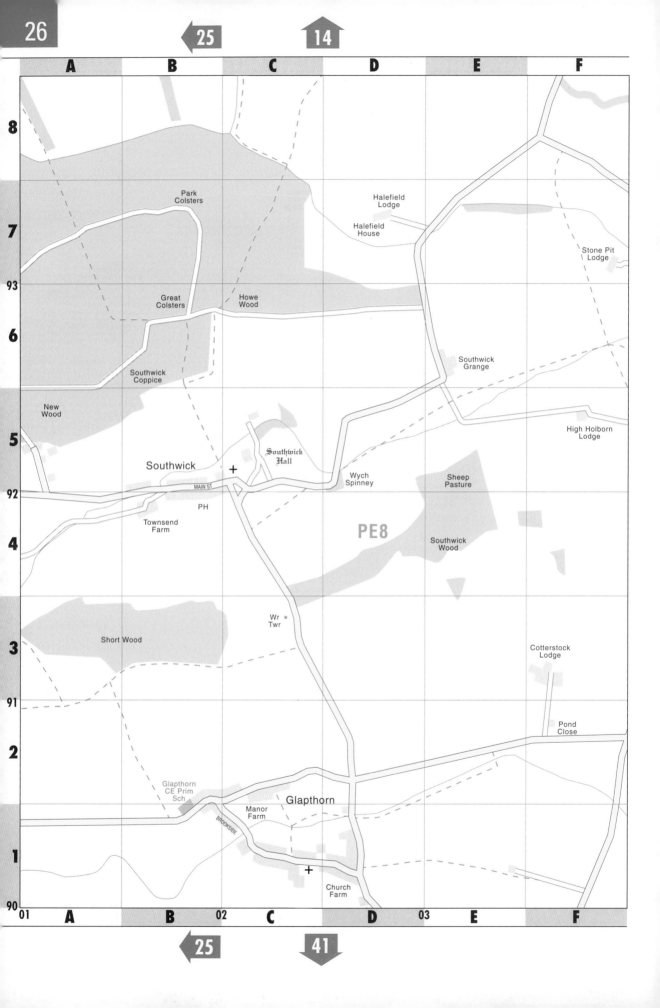

A   B   C   D   E   F

8

7

93

6

5

92

4

3

91

2

1

90

Park
Colsters

Halefield
Lodge

Halefield
House

Stone Pit
Lodge

Great
Colsters

Howe
Wood

Southwick
Grange

Southwick
Coppice

New
Wood

High Holborn
Lodge

Southwick
Hall

Southwick

Wych
Spinney

Sheep
Pasture

MAIN ST

PH

Townsend
Farm

PE8

Southwick
Wood

Short Wood

Wr
Twr

Cotterstock
Lodge

Pond
Close

Glapthorn
CE Prim
Sch

Glapthorn

BROOKSIDE

Manor
Farm

Church
Farm

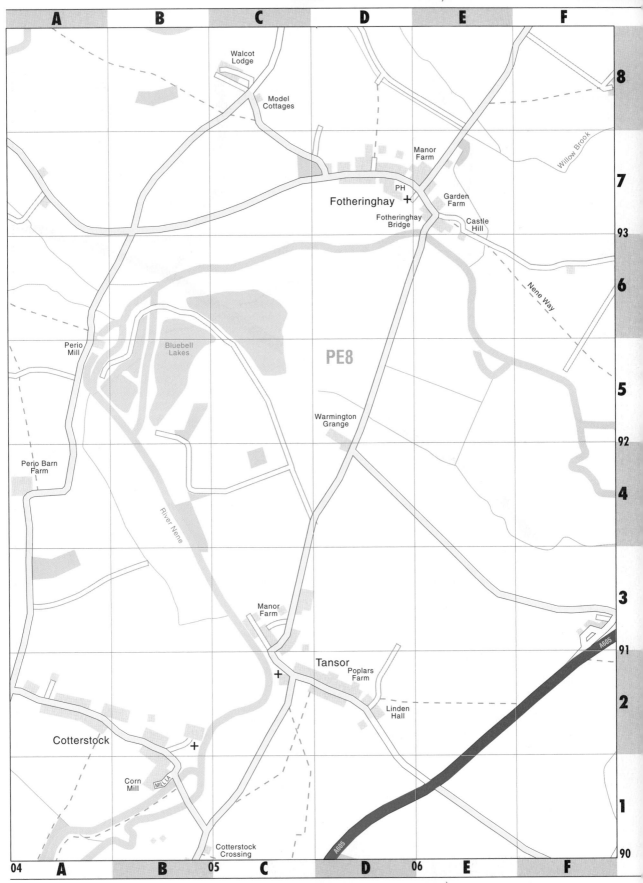

A B C D E F

8

Walcot Lodge

Model Cottages

Manor Farm

Willow Brook

7

PH

Fotheringhay

Garden Farm

Fotheringhay Bridge

Castle Hill

93

6

Nene Way

Perio Mill

Bluebell Lakes

PE8

92

Warmington Grange

5

Perio Barn Farm

River Nene

4

3

Manor Farm

91

Tansor

Poplars Farm

A605

2

Linden Hall

Cotterstock

Corn Mill

MILL LA

1

Cotterstock Crossing

A605

90

04 A B 05 C D 06 E F

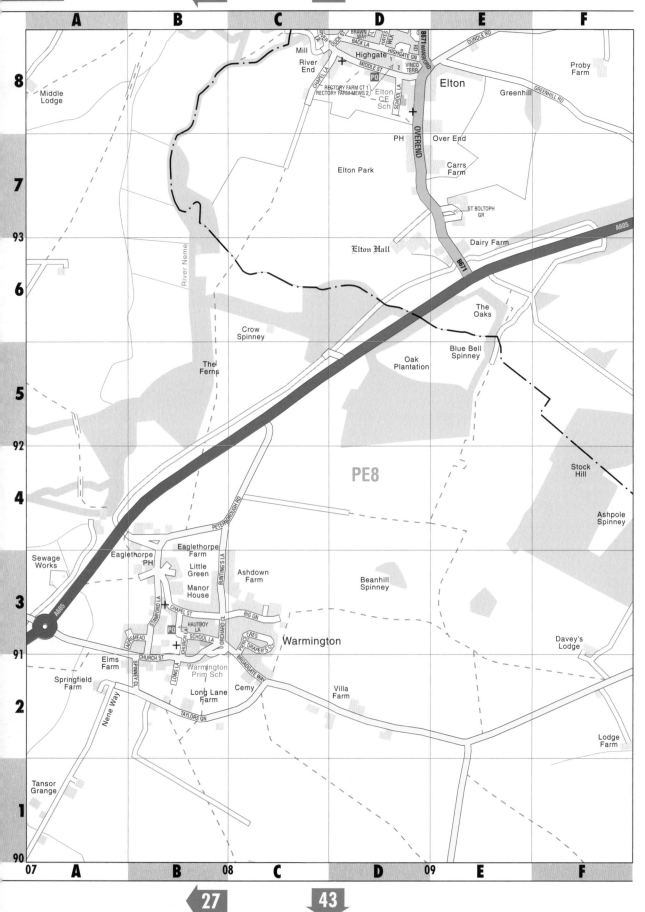

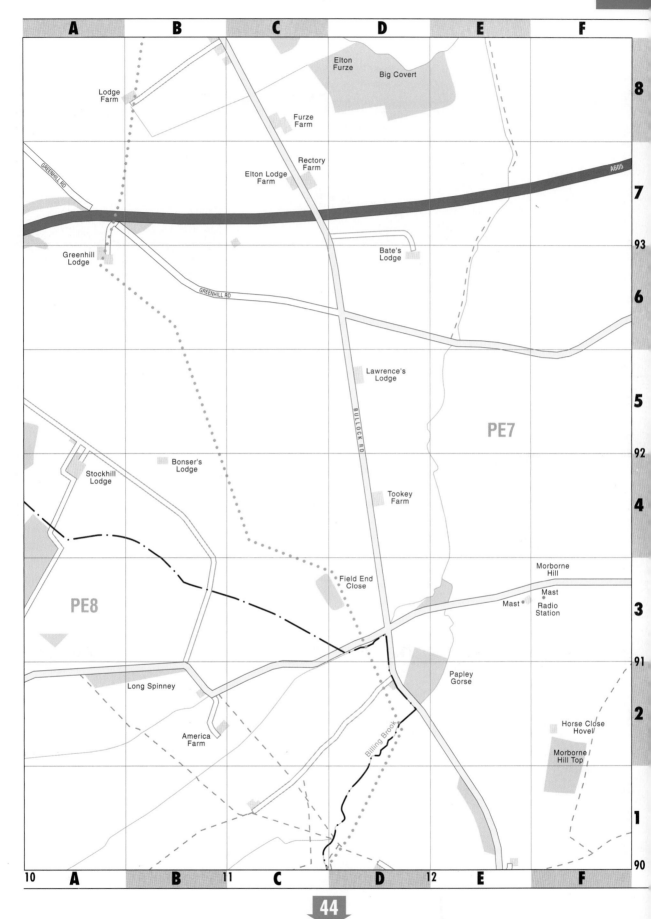

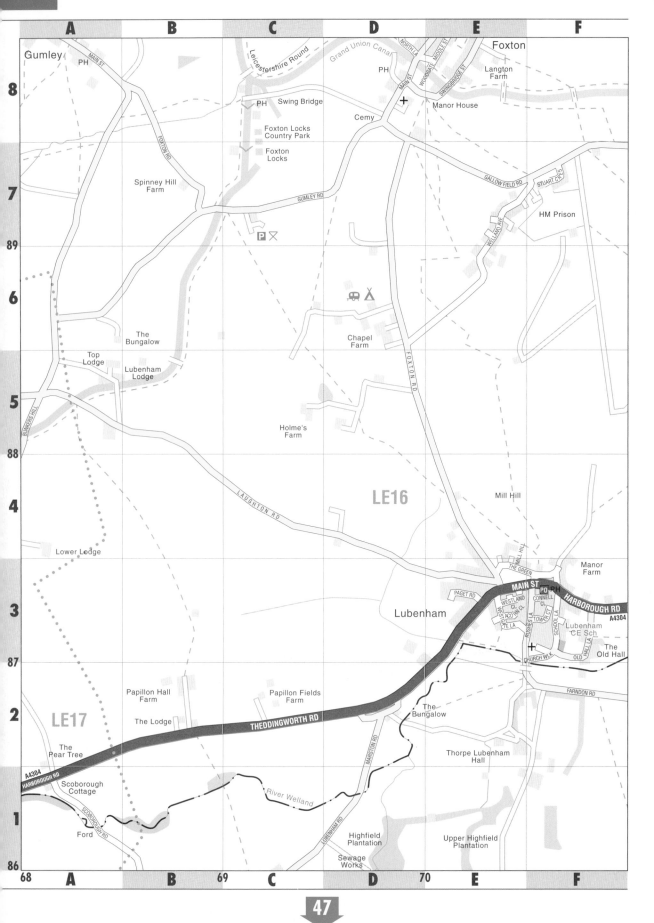

Gumley

Foxton

PH

PH   Swing Bridge

Leicestershire Round

Grand Union Canal

NORTH LA

MAIN ST

WOODGATE

MIDDLE ST

SWINGBRIDGE ST

Langton Farm

Cemy

Manor House

Foxton Locks Country Park

Foxton Locks

GALLOW FIELD RD

STUART CRES

HM Prison

Spinney Hill Farm

FOXTON RD

GUMLEY RD

WELLAND AVE

P

The Bungalow

Chapel Farm

FOXTON RD

Top Lodge

Lubenham Lodge

BUNKERS HILL

Holme's Farm

LE16

Mill Hill

LAUGHTON RD

Lower Lodge

MILL HILL

THE GREEN

Manor Farm

PAGET RD

MAIN ST

PH

HARBOROUGH RD

A4304

WESTLAND CL

ACORN CL

CONNELL CL

Lubenham
CE Sch

LE17

Lubenham

WESTGATE LA

RUSHES LA

TOWER CT

SCHOOL LA

The Old Hall

CHURCH WLK

OLD HALL LA

Papillon Hall Farm

Papillon Fields Farm

FARNDON RD

The Lodge

THEDDINGWORTH RD

The Bungalow

MARSTON RD

Thorpe Lubenham Hall

The Pear Tree

A4304

HARBOROUGH RD

Scoborough Cottage

SCOBOROUGH RD

River Welland

Ford

LUBENHAM RD

Highfield Plantation

Upper Highfield Plantation

Sewage Works

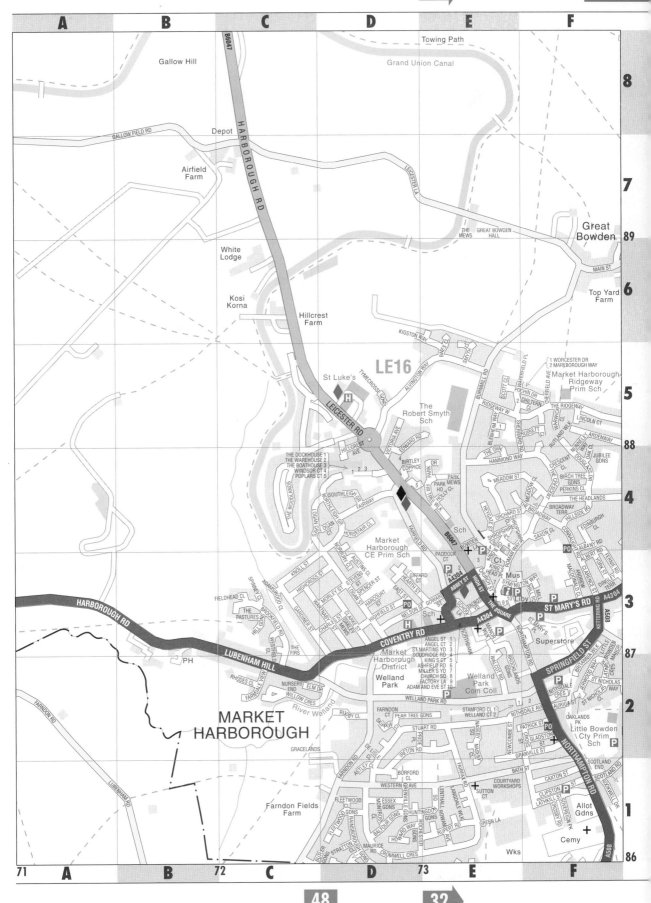

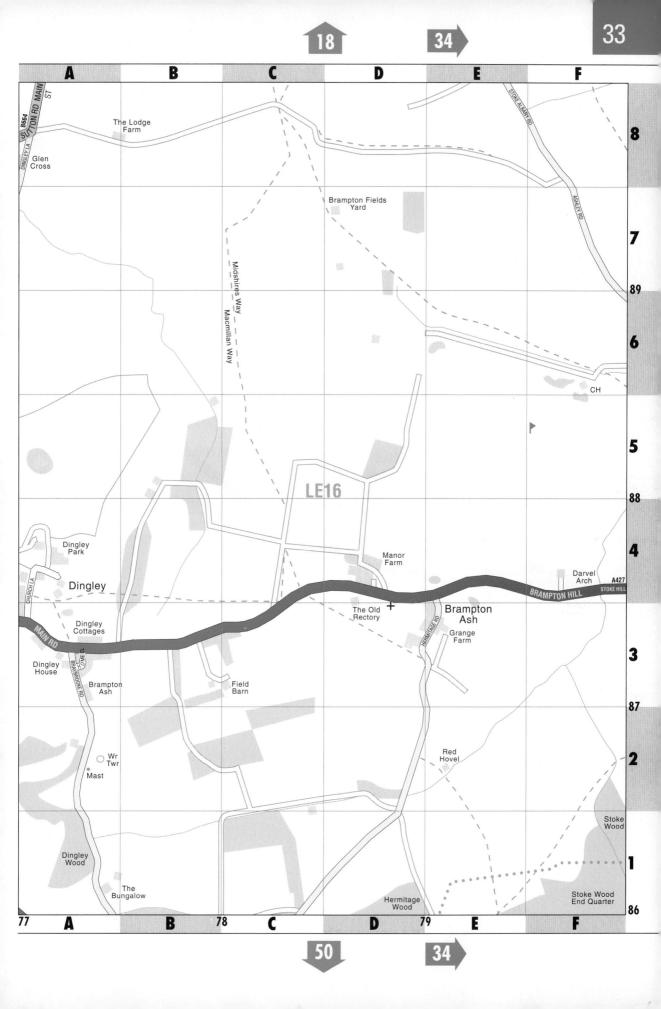

A | B | C | D | E | F

8

7

89

6

5

88

4

3

87

2

1

86

Wire Lane
Spinney

East Carlton
Grange

Brig Lane

Lower Lodge
Farm

Sewage
Works

LE16

A427

Dale
Farm

Jurassic Way

Redlands
Spinney

ASHLEY RD

LOWER RD

CHURCH ST

WENMAR CL

Wilbarston
CE Prim Sch

PH

PO

CARLTON RD

Windmill
Farm

Wilbarston
Lodge

Long
Plantation

SCHOOL LA

Liby

QUEENS CL

QUEENS RD

SCOTTS LA

DALLS CL

B669

ORCHARD CL

RUSHTON RD

HOLME

WILBARSTON RD

BOTTOM LA

CHAPEL LA

MIDDLE LA

CLWS LA

CHAPEL LA

Wilbarston

Stoke
Albany

HARBOROUGH RD

GREEN LA

D'ALBINI CL

DALLACRE RD

WINDSOR CL

SPRINGFIELD RD

ASHLEY RD

PH

A427

B669 HARBOROUGH RD

DENMAN CL

STOKE HILL

B669

PO

DESBOROUGH RD

Park
Farm

Stoke
House

Walter
Wood

Bowd Lane
Wood

B669

Stoke
Wood

Airfield
(abandoned)

NN14

Foxhole
Wood

Little Haws
Wood

80 | A | B | 81 | C | D | 82 | E | F

Shoulder of Mutton Plantation

Middleton

Jurassic Way

Motel

Water La

Lodge Coppice

Lodge

Corby Rd

8

Cottingham Quarry

Blackthorn Wood

Ashley Rd

Main St

B670

The Hill

School Hill

S Camsdale Wlk

PH

East Carlton Park

Countryside Park

East Carlton Hall

CH

A427

Home Farm

New Coppice

7

Wire La

Almshouses

B670

Great Cottage Wood

PO

The Glade

East Carlton

Church La

Darnell's Lodge

89

Forest Lodge

LE16

6

Pipewell Rd

East Carlton Lodge

Middleton Lodge Farm

NN17

5

88

4

A6003

Ash Coppice

Carlton Purlieus

Pipewell Rd

Wood Farm

Broad Angle

Daneshholme Rd

3

Denmark Cl

Oldenburg Rd

87

Askershaw Wood

Swinawe Barn Plantation

NN18

Viking Way

Brandenburg Rd

Oslo Gdns

Brunswick Gdns

Uppingham Rd

2

Bar Coppice

Woodlands Farm

Swinawe Wood

Herford Cl

Dresden Cl

Minden Cl

Copenhagen Rd

NN14

Barrowdykes Wood

Shieling Ct

Saxons W Way

1

Pipewell Wood

Monks Arbour Wood

Rawshaw Wood

Hedgerow Spinney

Great Folds Rd

North Folds Rd

A6003

86

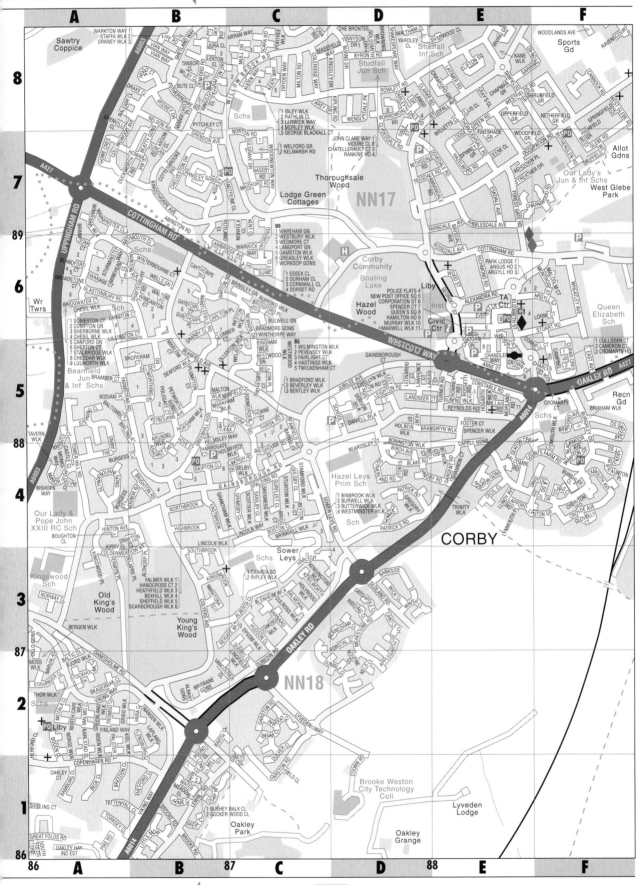

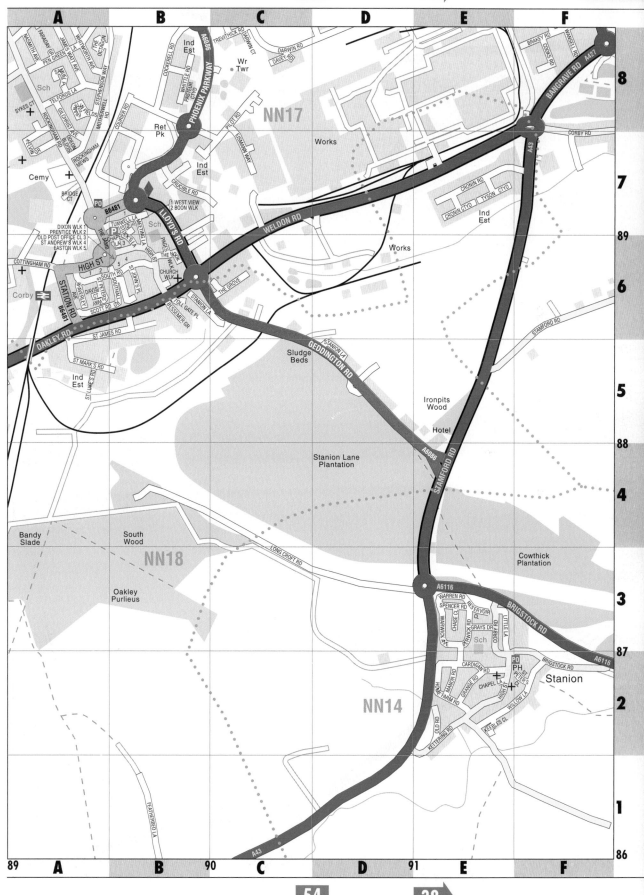

37
23

A427
ARNSLEY RD
LARRATT RD
GRETTON RD
Ind Est
HALL'S
Chapel Rd
WATER LA
DASH FARM CL
Weldon CE Prim Sch
GANDER CL
CORBY RD
HILLSIDE CRES
HILLSIDE CRES
ROSE AVE
ORCHARD CL
BRIDGES CT
DUBBIN CL
ROMAN CL
DEENESIDE
HIGH ST
KETTERING RD
CHURCH WLK
CHURCH ST
STAMFORD RD A427
A43
EAST CK
BEECH END
WOOD LANDS RD
SPINNEY RD

8

Weldon

Manor House

Allot Gdns

7

Weldon Stone Quarry

STAMFORD RD

89

OUNDLE RD
A427

PE8

6

NN17

5

88

Harry's Wood

4

Upper Laundimer Wood

Harry's Park Wood

Middle Laundimer Wood

Meadow Leys

3

Bushylawn Lodge

87

A6116
BRIGSTOCK RD

Nether Laundimer Wood

Old Dry Hills

NN14

2

Wks

Old Dry Bushes

STANION RD

Brigstock Camp

OLD DRY LA

1

Stanion Lodge

Red Piece

STANION RD

Maltley Farm

A6116

86

92   A   B   93   C   D   94   E   F

A B C D E F

8

Yoke
Hill

Meml

The
Grange

Middle
Farm

TOWNSEND CT

GIBSON DR

CORONATION CRES

A427

7

Upper
Benefield

Lammas
Farm

89

PE8

6

Yokehill
Farm

Sheepwalk
Spinney

5

Spring
Wood

88

Blackthorns

CAUSIN WAY

4

Cockendale
Wood

Blackthorn
Lodge

Springwood
House

Bocase
Farm

The
Cottages

Lodge
Cottages

Springwood
Lodge

3

Fermyn
Woods
Hall

Deer
Park

87

BENEFIELD RD

2

Stubby
Stiles

Samby
Skyes

Luscote's
Lodge

Tresham
Lodge

1

86

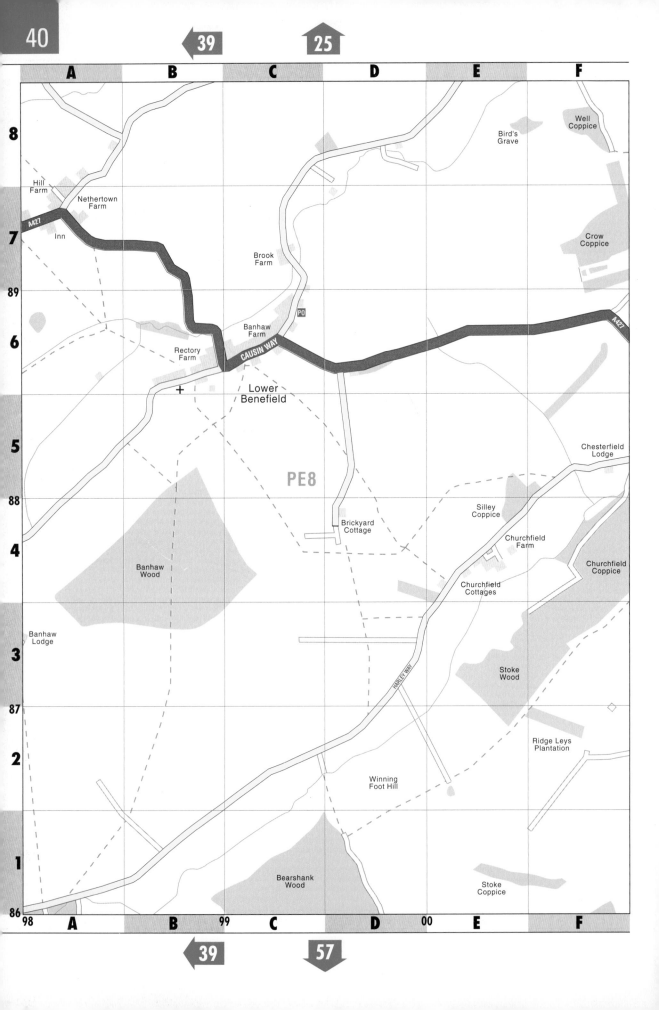

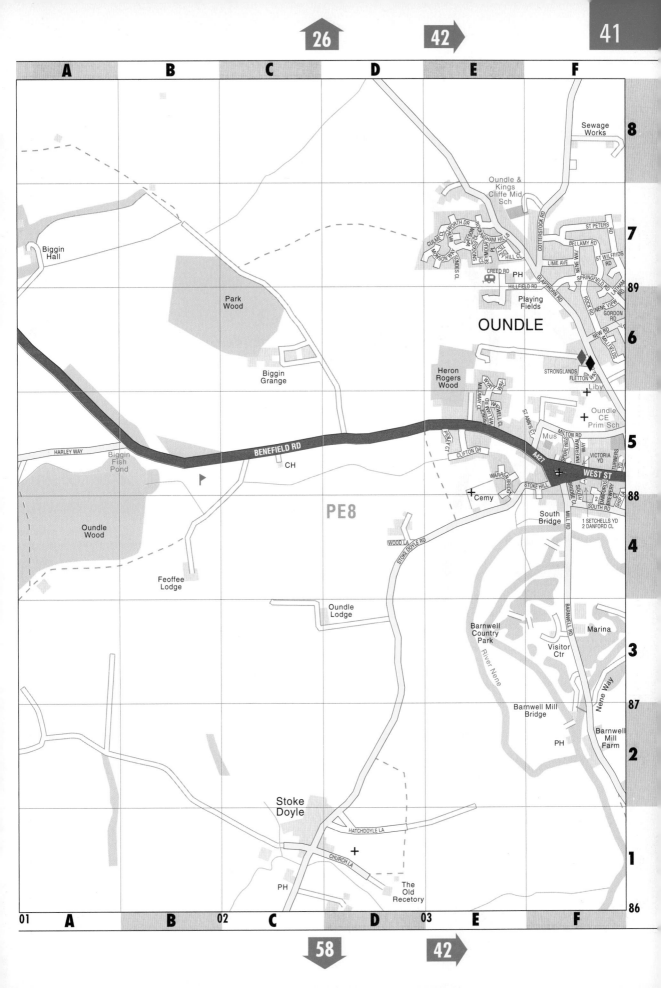

A B C D E F

8

Tansor Lodge

A605

Elmington
Lodge

Elmington

7

Elmington
Top Lodge

Rifle Range

89

1 DERWENT HO
2 SEVERN HO
3 TYNE HO
4 MEDWAY HO
5 GRANTA HO

SPRINGFIELD RD
ST PETERS RD
Oundle Wharf

STATION RD
A427

NEW RD
GORDON RD
MALTINGS
RIVERSIDE

6

North
Bridge

OUNDLE

VICTORIA RD
KING RD
VINE CL
BLACKPOT LA
CLAPTON RD
EASTWOOD RD
NORTH ST
A427

Oundle
Sch

Entrance
Lodge

Chapel
Farm

Ashton

Nene Way

The
National
Dragonfly
Mus

Brickyard
Wood

5

DRUMMING WELL LA
NEW ST
CHURCH
WEST ST
PO ST
MARKET

HAVELOCK
COTTS
EAST RD
DUCK LA
ASHTON RD
MASON CT
NENE VALLEY
BSNS PK
WEBB CL

PH

Ashton Green
Farm

CROWN CT
DRS LA
PL
Sch
TANEY
CT

SILVER ST
GLOWELL WAY
ST CHRISTOPHER'S DR

Manor
House

88

Herne
Lodge

BRAMSTON CL

BASSETT PL

PE8

4

SOUTH RD
BASSETT FORD RD
RIVERSIDE CL

Prince William
Upper
Sch

HERNE RD

River Nene

3

New Lodge
Farm

HIGHFIELDS

Red Lodge Farm

PH

KINGS ARMS LA
DUKE ST
MAIN ST
POLEBROOK
CT
CHURCH ST

87

HEMINGTON RD

2

Sands
Barn

1

Nene Way

Sewage
Works

Horse Close
Spinney

86

A605
Sweetley
Spinney

04 A B 05 C D 06 E F

A B C D E F

8
7
89
6
5
88
4
3
87
2
1
86

Rectory Farm

Tansor Wold Farm

Tansor Wold

Miriam's Cover

Stamford Hovels

Stamford Cover

Toll Bar Gate

The Gorse

Warmington Spinney Plantation

PE8

Ashton Wold Farm

West Lodge

Ashton Wold House

Greenhouse Corner

Ashton Wold

The Common

Lutton Hovels

Allard's Home

Water Gap Field

Lake Fields

Bluestone Covert

Polebrook

FERGUSON'S CL
MORGANS CL
MAIN ST
HALL GDNS
Polebrook CE Prim Sch

Lutton Road Cottages

Polebrook Airfield Nature Reserve

Polebrook Lodge

LUTTON RD

Rectory Farm

Airfield (disused)

43
29

A   B   C   D   E   F

8

7

89

6

5

88

4

87

3

2

1

86

10   A   11   B   C   12   D   E

Cold Harbour

New Farm

Ongutein Manor Farm

PE7

Lodge Farm

Field Farm

Papley Cottages

Papley

WASHINGLEY LA

Papley Coppice

Ringmoor Spinney

Papley Farm

BULLOCK RD

Grange Farm

Lutton Farm

Chapel End

MILTON TERR

Woodbine Farm

Lutton

The Old Rectory

Manor Farm

PE8

Lutton Lodge Farm

High Holborn Farm

Long Plantation

PE17 →

Top Lodge

43
61

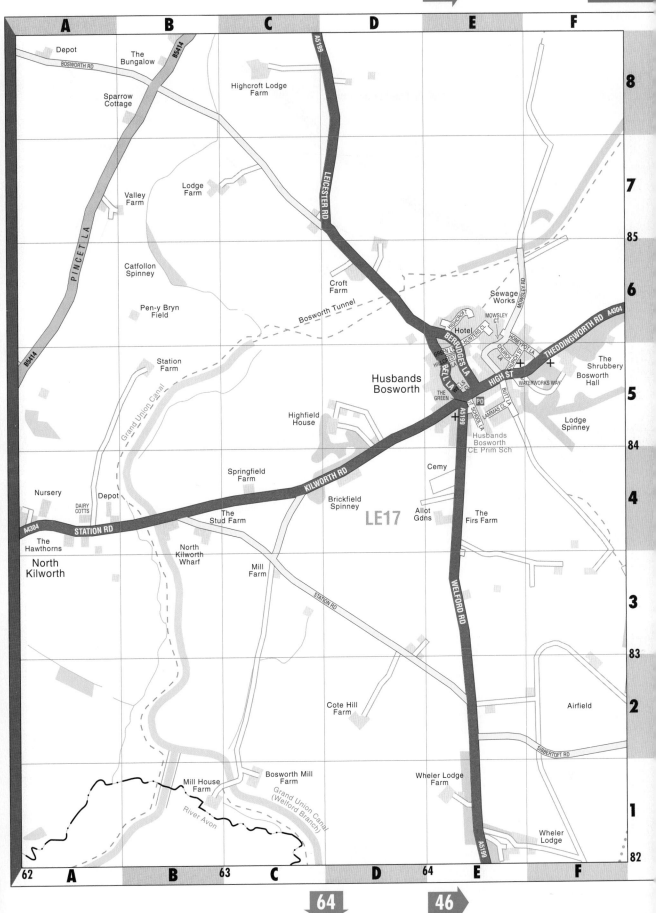

A   B   C   D   E   F

Depot
Bosworth Rd
The Bungalow
B5414
Sparrow Cottage
Highcroft Lodge Farm
Leicester Rd
A5199
Pincet La
Valley Farm
Lodge Farm
Catfollon Spinney
Pen-y Bryn Field
Croft Farm
Bosworth Tunnel
Sewage Works
Mowsley Ct
Mowsley Rd
B5414
Station Farm
Grand Union Canal
Highcroft
Hill Crest
Green La
Berridges La
Bell La
Hotel
Church St
Honey Pot La
Church St
Theddingworth Rd
A4304
High St
The Shrubbery
Bosworth Hall
Husbands Bosworth
Wells St
The Green
Waterworks Way
Highfield House
PO
Butt La
Lammas Cl
Lodge Spinney
School La
A5199
Husbands Bosworth CE Prim Sch
Cemy
Springfield Farm
Kilworth Rd
Brickfield Spinney
LE17
Allot Gdns
The Firs Farm
Nursery
Depot
Dairy Cotts
The Stud Farm
A4304
Station Rd
The Hawthorns
North Kilworth
North Kilworth Wharf
Mill Farm
Station Rd
Welford Rd
Cote Hill Farm
Airfield
Sibbertoft Rd
Mill House Farm
Bosworth Mill Farm
Grand Union Canal (Welford Branch)
River Avon
Wheler Lodge Farm
Wheler Lodge
A5199

45

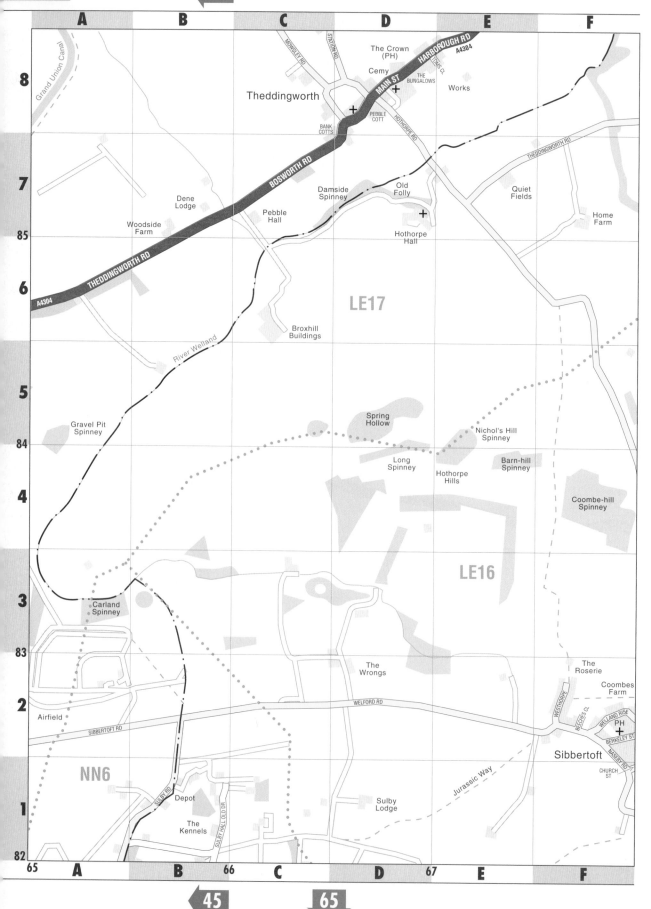

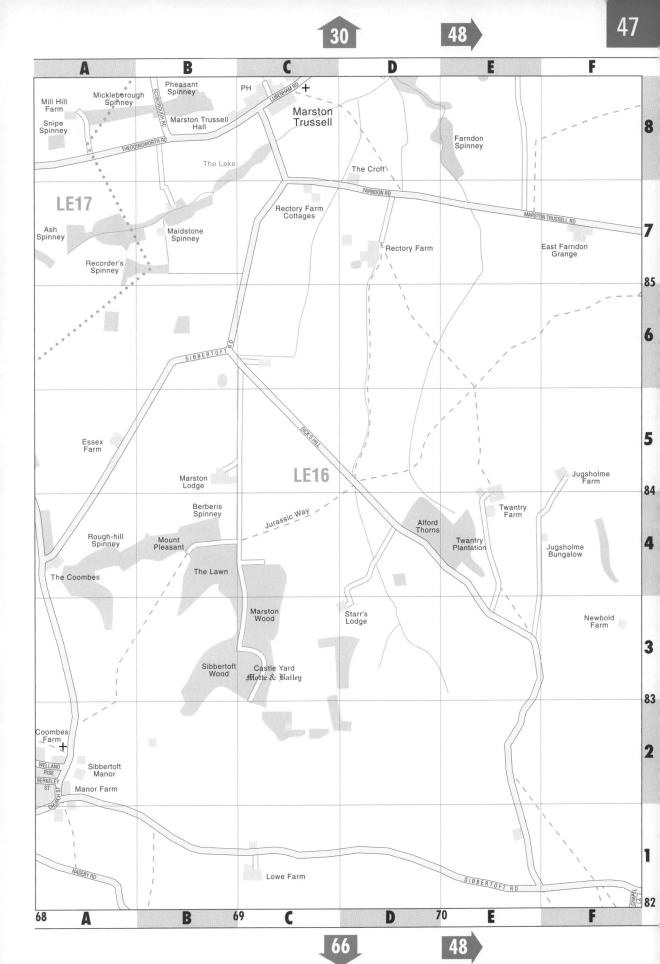

A B C D E F

Mill Hill Farm
Mickleborough Spinney
Pheasant Spinney
PH
Marston Trussell
Snipe Spinney
Marston Trussell Hall
LUBENHAM RD
THEDDINGWORTH RD
SCHOROUGH RD
Farndon Spinney

The Lake

LE17

The Croft
FARNDON RD
MARSTON TRUSSELL RD

Ash Spinney
Maidstone Spinney
Rectory Farm Cottages
Rectory Farm
East Farndon Grange

Recorder's Spinney

SIBBERTOFT RD

Essex Farm

DICK'S HILL

Jugsholme Farm

Marston Lodge
LE16
Twantry Farm

Berberis Spinney
Jurassic Way
Alford Thorns
Twantry Plantation
Jugsholme Bungalow

Rough-hill Spinney
Mount Pleasant
The Lawn

The Coombes

Marston Wood
Starr's Lodge
Newbold Farm

Sibbertoft Wood
Castle Yard
Motte & Bailey

Coombes Farm

WELLAND RISE
Sibbertoft Manor
BERKELEY ST
Manor Farm
CHURCH ST

NASEBY RD
Lowe Farm
SIBBERTOFT RD
CHAPEL LA

47
31

A B C D E F

8

7

85

6

5

84

4

3

83

2

1

82

71 A B 72 C D 73 E F

LUBENHAM RD

HARBOROUGH RD

THE LEALAND

COMMON S/H S

MAIN ST

MARSTON TRUSSELL RD

Brierley Farm

New House Farm

The Dales

East Farndon Hall

East Farndon

Jurassic Way

Farn Wood

Allot Gdns

CLIPSTON RD

OXENDON RD

Jurassic Way

The Lodge

Little Oxendon

LE16

FARNDON RD

West End

Oxendon House

Great Oxendon

The Spinney

MEWS COTTS

OXENDON HALL

Main St

PH

BRAYBROOKE RD

Sewage Works

HARBOROUGH RD

CLIPSTON RD

HARBOROUGH RD

Waterloo House

Station Cottage

OXENDON RD

Midshires Way

A508

WATSON AVE

MAURICE RD

BARNARD GDNS

HARRISON CL

GERRARD GDNS

LINDSEY GDNS

CROWN FIELDS

RAINSBOROUGH GDNS

RITCHIE PK

MONSON CL

BISHOP

ARGYLE PK

DIGBY CL

DALLISON CL

VAUGHAN CL

Market Harborough Farndon Fields Prim Sch

Leisure Ctr

NORTHAMPTON RD A508

Oxendon Lodge Farm

Oxendon Lodge Cottages

JUSTIN PARK

CH

SIBBERTOFT RD

OXENDON RD

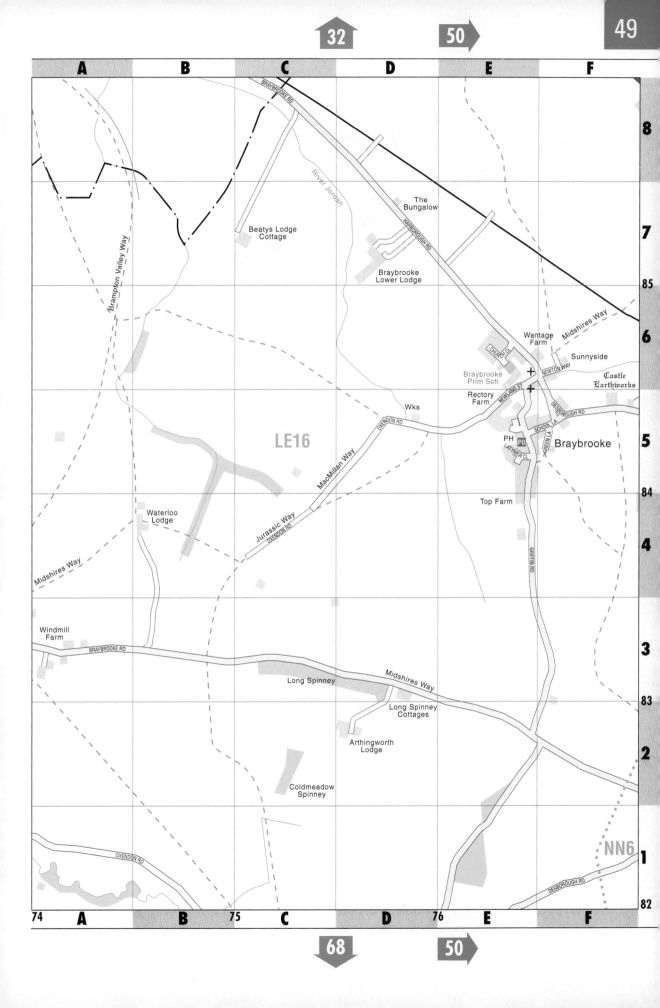

A B C D E F

8

BRAYBROOKE RD

River Jordan

The Bungalow

7

85

Beatys Lodge Cottage

HARBOROUGH RD

Braybrooke Lower Lodge

Brampton Valley Way

6

Wantage Farm

Midshires Way

CHURCH CL

Sunnyside

NEWTON WAY

Castle Earthworks

Braybrooke Prim Sch

NEWLAND ST

Rectory Farm

Wks

OXENDON RD

DESBOROUGH RD

LE16

PH

SCHOOL LA

PO

GREEN LA

Braybrooke

5

LATYMER CL

MacMillan Way

84

Top Farm

Waterloo Lodge

Jurassic Way

OXENDON RD

GRIFFIN RD

Midshires Way

4

Windmill Farm

BRAYBROOKE RD

3

Long Spinney

Midshires Way

83

Long Spinney Cottages

Arthingworth Lodge

2

Coldmeadow Spinney

NN6

1

OXENDON RD

DESBOROUGH RD

82

74 A B 75 C D 76 E F

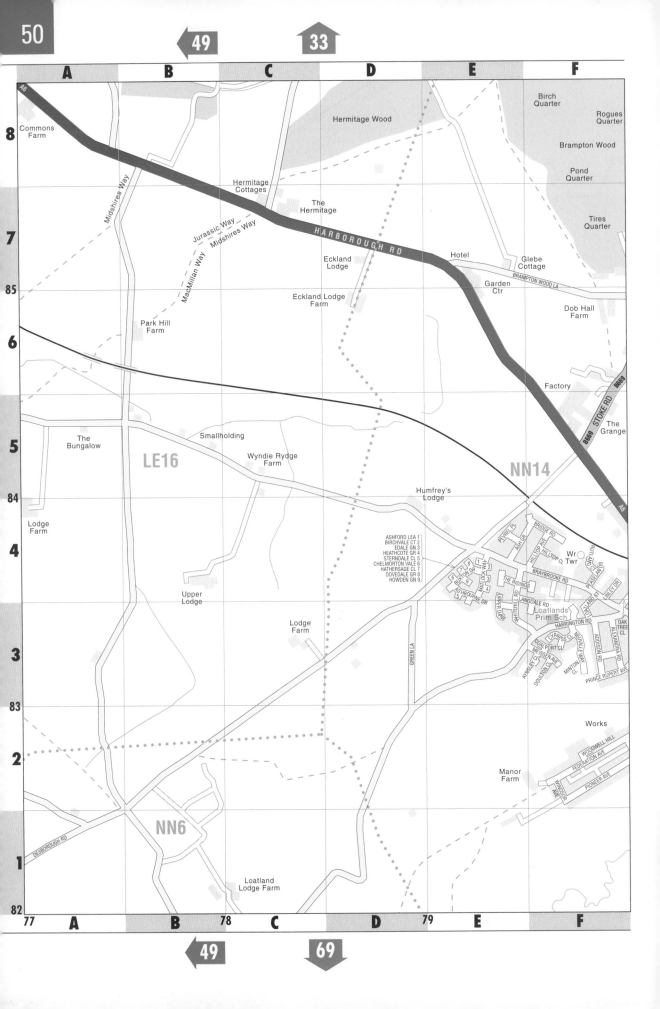

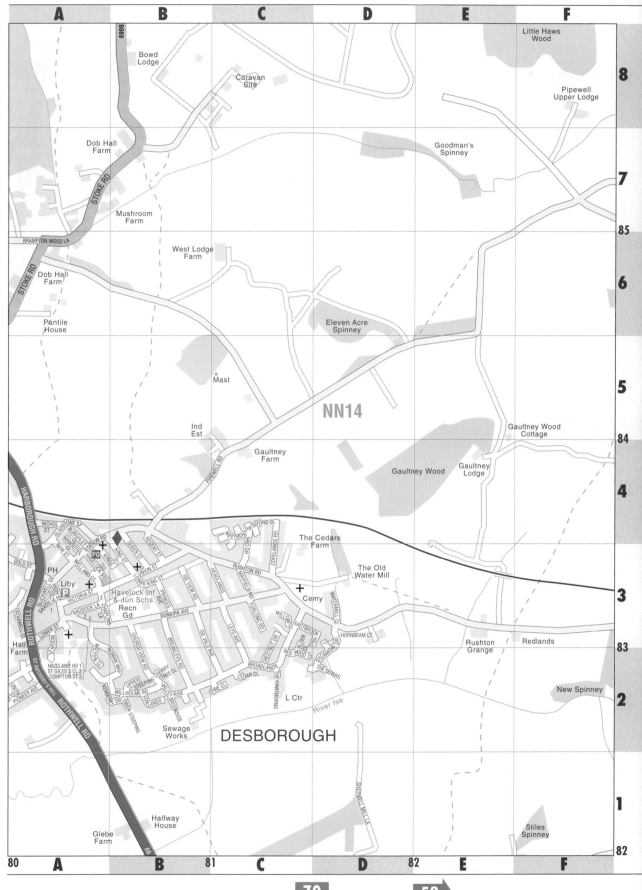

Little Haws
Wood

Pipewell
Upper Lodge

Bowd
Lodge

Caravan
Site

Goodman's
Spinney

Dob Hall
Farm

STOKE RD

B669

Mushroom
Farm

West Lodge
Farm

BRAMPTON WOOD LA

85

Dob Hall
Farm

STOKE RD

Eleven Acre
Spinney

Pantile
House

Mast

Gaultney Wood
Cottage

NN14

Ind
Est

84

PIPEWELL RD

Gaultney
Farm

Gaultney Wood

Gaultney
Lodge

HARBOROUGH RD

The Cedars
Farm

NICHOL ST
GLADSTONE ST
BURCHILL ST
STATION RD
HAVELOCK ST
MARGARET ST
NEW ST
GOLD ST

WOTMORE DR
HEREFORD CL
COPELANDS RD

WELLAND ST
PO
KINGS CT
KING ST
QUEEN ST
UNION ST
REGENT ST

RUSHTON RD
MAYFIELD RD
FURLONG RD

The Old
Water Mill

PH
BUCKWELL ST
HIGH ST
LOWER KING ST

PADDOCK LA
VICTORIA ST
CHAPEL PAS
PRINCES
HEADLANDS
ISE VIEW RD

ISE VIEW RD

Cemy

WATERMILL CL

Liby
P

ROTHWELL RD
CROMWELL RD
LOWER ST
BEECH CL

HAZELAND HO 1
ST GILES'S CL 2
COMPTON ST 3

CHURCH VIEW RD
ROMAN WAY
MILTON CT
SAXON CL

Havelock Inf
& Jun Schs
Recn
Gd

DUNKIRK AVE

BREAKLEYS RD

CHERRY
TREE CL

LEYS AVE
ISE DALE AVE

CEDAR CL

WILLOW CL
EASTBROOK
CHESTNUT DR
RED WOOD CL
ALDER
SYCAMORE DR
THE OSIERS

HORNBEAM CT

3

Rushton
Grange

Redlands

83

Hall
Farm

ST ANTHONY'S HILL

PIONEER AVE
UNITY

KENMORE DR
UPPER STEEPING
LOWER STEEPING
MILLHOLME RD
VALLEY RISE
BROADSIDE
ROWLANDS

BROADLANDS

THE HAWTHORNS

L Ctr

New Spinney

River Ise

DESBOROUGH

SHOTWELL MILL LA

Sewage
Works

ROTHWELL RD
A6

Halfway
House

Glebe
Farm

Stiles
Spinney

82

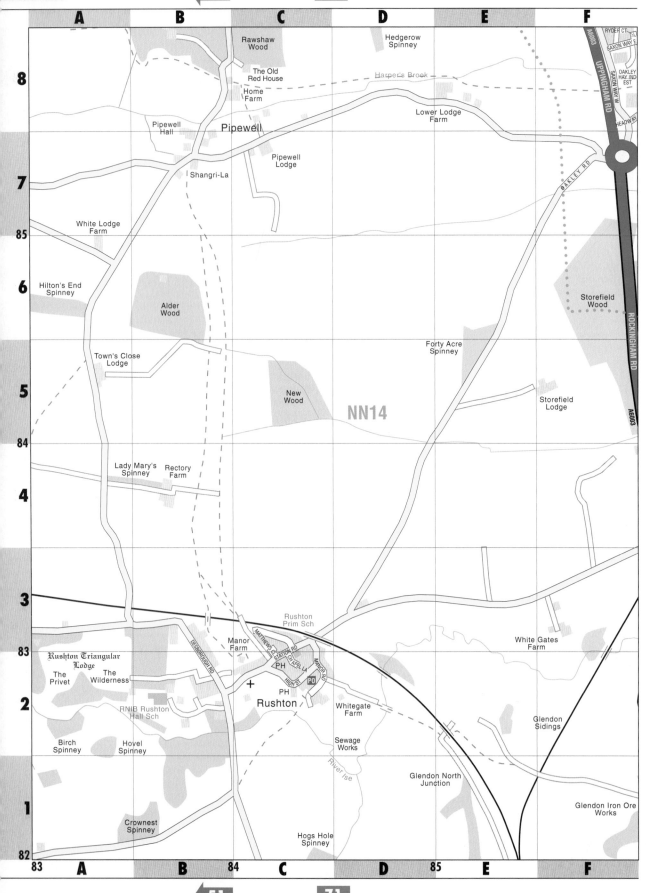

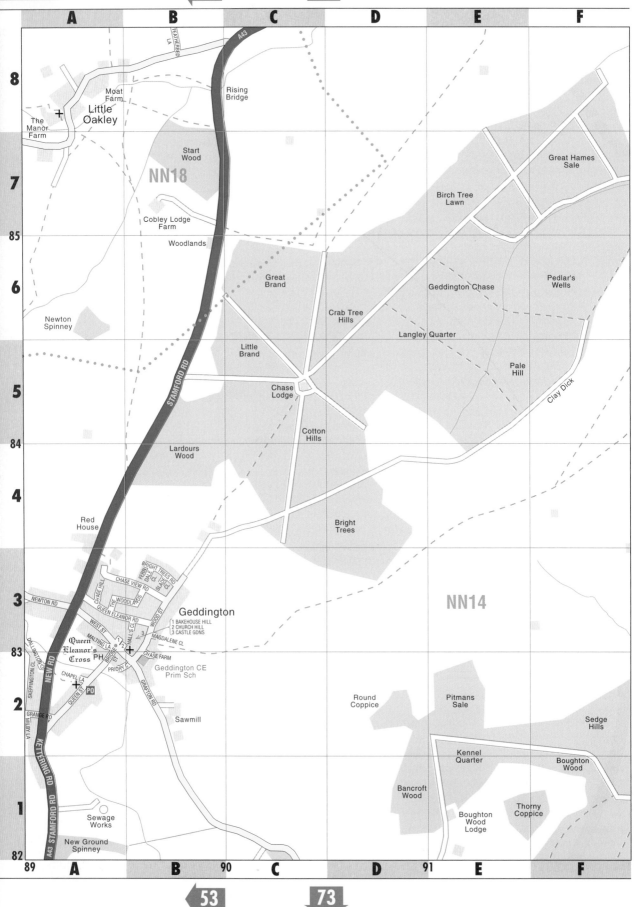

A   **B**   **C**   **D**   **E**   **F**

A43

8

The Manor Farm

Little Oakley

Moat Farm

Rising Bridge

Start Wood

Great Hames Sale

NN18

7

Birch Tree Lawn

Cobley Lodge Farm

85

Woodlands

Great Brand

Geddington Chase

Pedlar's Wells

6

Newton Spinney

Crab Tree Hills

Langley Quarter

Little Brand

Pale Hill

Clay Dick

5

Chase Lodge

STAMFORD RD

84

Lardours Wood

Cotton Hills

4

Red House

Bright Trees

NN14

NEWTON RD

BRIGHT TREES RD

CHASE VIEW RD

CHASE HILL

THE WOODLANDS

QUEEN ELEANOR RD

WOOD ST

FERN DALE

3

Geddington

1 BAKEHOUSE HILL
2 CHURCH HILL
3 CASTLE GDNS

WEST ST

HALL'S CL

MAGDALENE CL

Round Coppice

Pitmans Sale

Sedge Hills

MALTING LA

83

Queen Eleanor's Cross PH

CHASE FARM

PRIORY CL

Geddington CE Prim Sch

BRIDGE ST

GRAFTON RD

Kennel Quarter

Boughton Wood

SKEFFINGTON CL

DALLINGTON CL

CHAPEL LA

PO

QUEEN ST

2

GRANGE RD

Sawmill

Bancroft Wood

Boughton Wood Lodge

Thorny Coppice

MILBY LA

KETTERING RD

1

Sewage Works

New Ground Spinney

82

A43 STAMFORD RD

89   **A**   **B**   **90**   **C**   **D**   **91**   **E**   **F**

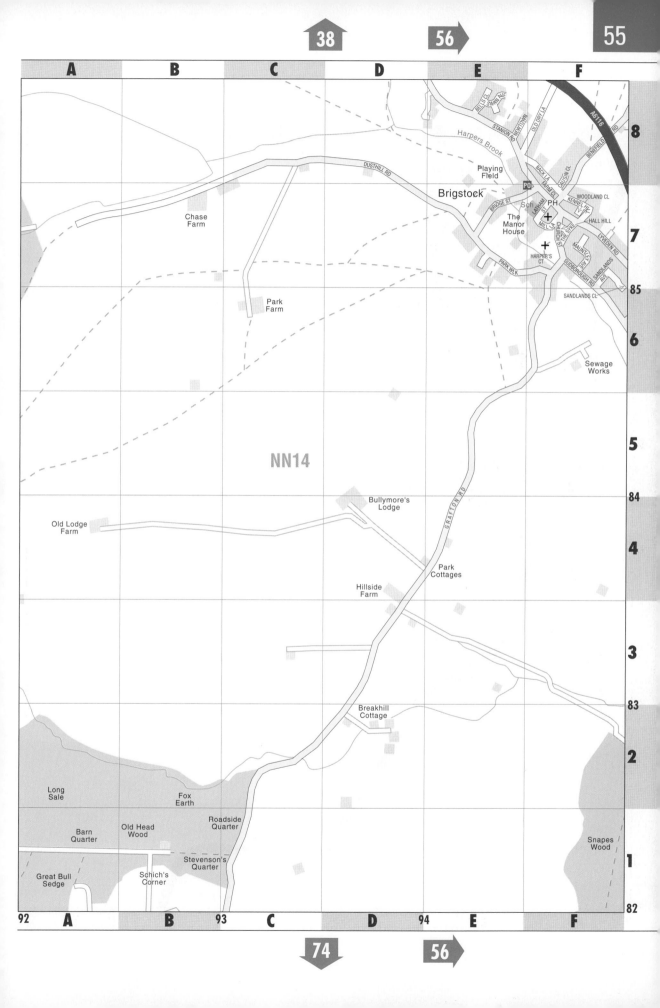

Brigstock

NN14

Chase Farm

Park Farm

Dusthill Rd

Harpers Brook

Playing Field

The Manor House

Harper's Ct

Sewage Works

Bullymore's Lodge

Old Lodge Farm

Park Cottages

Hillside Farm

Grafton Rd

Breakhill Cottage

Long Sale

Fox Earth

Roadside Quarter

Barn Quarter

Old Head Wood

Stevenson's Quarter

Snapes Wood

Great Bull Sedge

Schich's Corner

Bells Cl
Swan Ave
Station Rd
Old Dry La
Benefield Rd
A6116
Woodland Cl
Back La
Farm Cl
Cousin Cl
Kennel La
Hall Hill
Bridge St
Sch
PH
Latham St
Mill
Church St
Shelts Syke
Lyveden Rd
Maunt La
Sandlands Ave
Sudborough Rd
Sandlands Cl
Park Wlk
Newtown
PO

8
7
85
6
5
84
4
3
83
2
1
82

A B C D E F

8

7

85

6

5

84

4

3

83

2

1

82

95 A B 96 C D 97 E F

Mounterley
Wood

HARLEY WAY

Luscote
Lodge

Harley Way
Lodge

Stephen Oak
Riding

Cherry
Lap

Royal
Coppice

Fermyn
Woods

Sling's
Nook

BENEFIELD RD

A6116

LYVEDEN WAY
BARNARD'S RD

SUDBOROUGH RD

Brigstock
Country Park

P

Tresham
Coppice

Assart's
Coppice

Lady Wood
Head

Lady
Wood

PE8

Manor
Farm

Sudborough Green
Lodge

Souther
Wood

SUDBOROUGH RD

Cat's Head
Wood

NN14

Cat'shead
Farm

Green Side
Wood

Titchmarsh
Wood

Harper's Brook

Belle
Vue

Green
Lodge

Snapes
Lodge

Snapes
Wood

Sudborough

Grange
Farm

PH

A6116

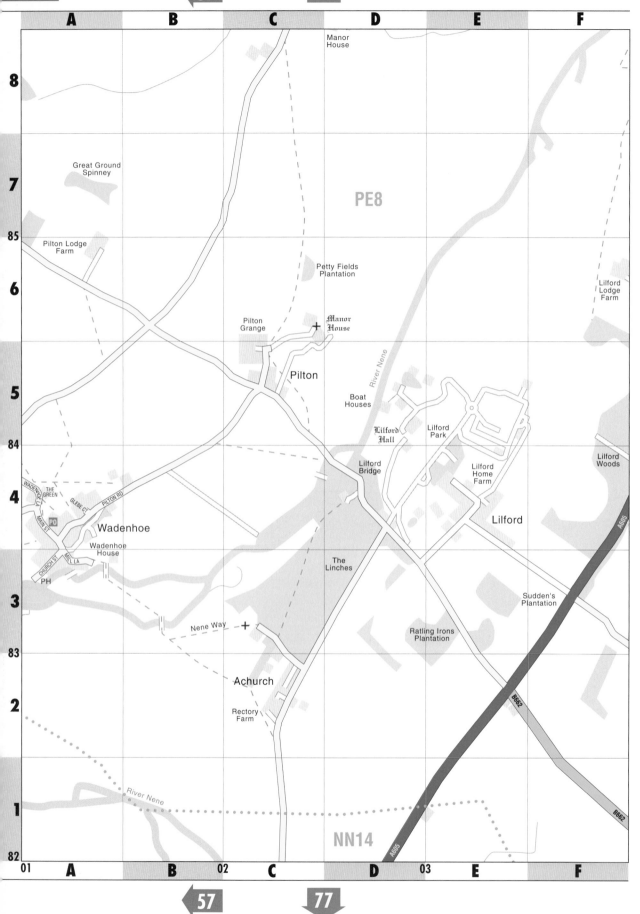

A **B** **C** **D** **E** **F**

Armston

Wks

Burray
Spinney

White
Lodge

New Fox
Convert

Armston
Grove

Empty
Spinney

Blind
Spinney

8

Barnwell
Castle

Barnwell
Manor

7

Fox
Convert

CASTLE VIEW LA

85

Barnwell
CE Prim Sch

CHURCH LA CHURCH HILL

PH

Barnwell
St Andrew

PO
LATHAM'S
HQSPL

PH

6

Barnwell

Castle
Farm

MONTAGU TERR

Barnwell
All Saints

CHANCEL TERR

MAIN ST

Nene Way

5

Friars Close
Farm

Lower
Farm

Broadway
Corner

84

PE8

Barnwell Brook

4

West
Lodge
Farm

Bright Pitts
Farm

Barnwell
Lodge
Farm

3

83

Wigsthorpe

2

South
Lodge
Farm

Hall
Farm

1

B662

82

04 **A** **B** **05** **C** **D** **06** **E** **F**

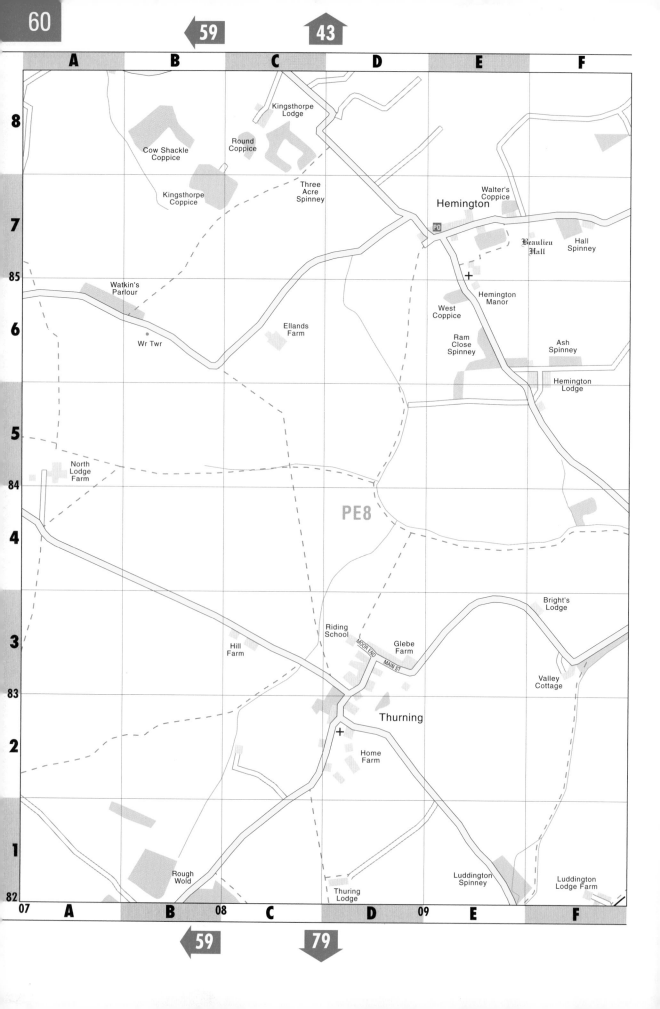

A B C D E F

8

Kingsthorpe
Lodge

Round
Coppice

Cow Shackle
Coppice

Three Acre
Spinney

Walter's
Coppice

Hemington

Kingsthorpe
Coppice

7

PO

Beaulieu
Hall

Hall
Spinney

85

Watkin's
Parlour

West
Coppice

Hemington
Manor

6

Ellands
Farm

Ram
Close
Spinney

Ash
Spinney

Wr Twr

Hemington
Lodge

5

North
Lodge
Farm

84

PE8

4

Bright's
Lodge

Hill
Farm

Riding
School

3

MOOR END

Glebe
Farm

MAIN ST

Valley
Cottage

83

Thurning

2

Home
Farm

Rough
Wold

1

Luddington
Spinney

Luddington
Lodge Farm

82

Thurning
Lodge

07 A B 08 C D 09 E F

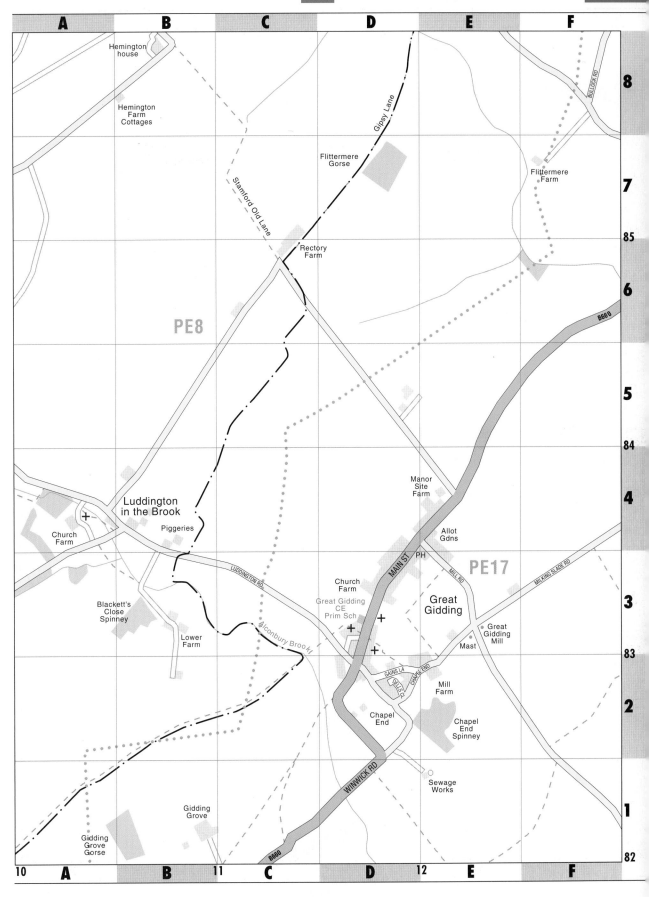

Hemington house

Hemington Farm Cottages

Gipsy Lane

Flittermere Gorse

Flittermere Farm

Stamford Old Lane

Rectory Farm

PE8

B660

Manor Site Farm

Luddington in the Brook

Piggeries

Allot Gdns

Church Farm

PH

MAIN ST

MILL RD

PE17

Blackett's Close Spinney

Church Farm

Great Gidding CE Prim Sch

Great Gidding

MILKING SLADE RD

Lower Farm

Alconbury Brook

Mast

Great Gidding Mill

GAINS LA

DELL'S CL

CHAPEL END

Mill Farm

Chapel End

Chapel End Spinney

WINWICK RD

Sewage Works

Gidding Grove

B660

Gidding Grove Gorse

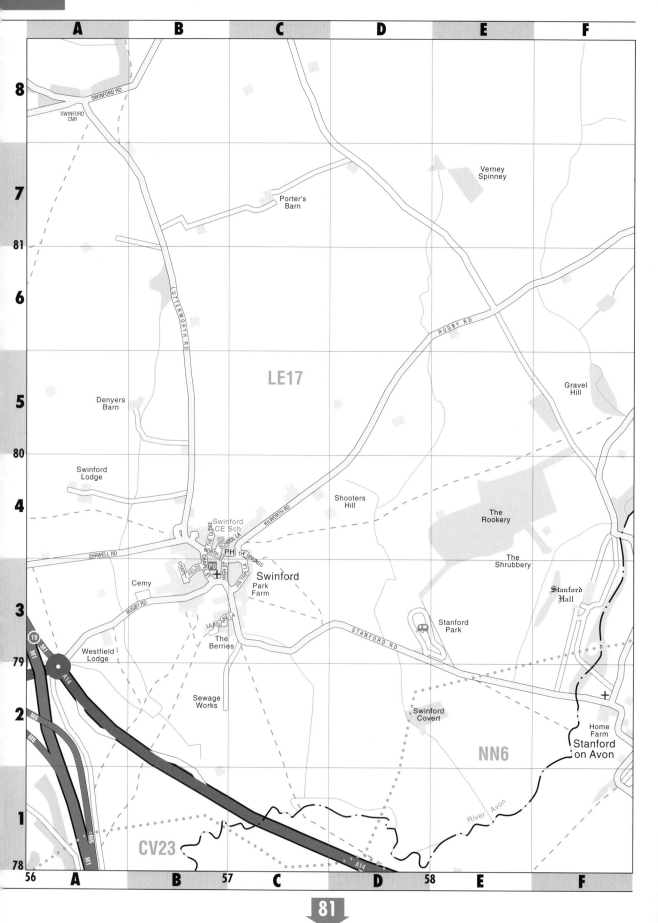

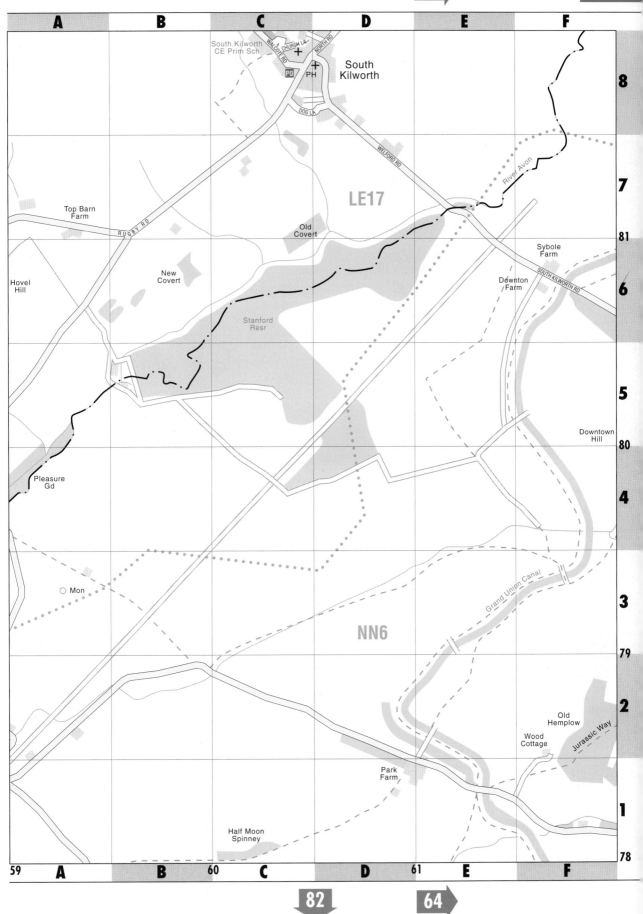

	A	B	C	D	E	F

LE17

Grand Union Canal

Grand Union Canal (Welford Branch)

Glebe Farm

River Avon

Lodge Farm

Sybolds Spinney

Hill House

Welford Resr

HALL LA

Hotel

Sewage Works

Grange Lodge

Welford Grange Farm

NASEBY RD

SULBY RD

A5199

WELFORD RD

Allot Gdns

THE SQUARE

Sulby Lodge Farm

WAKEFIELD CRES

ORCHARD TERR

WEST ST

SALFORD RD

AVON FIELDS

HIGH ST

Welford Sibbertoft & Sulby Sch

PH

Welford

Hallfield Cottage

SOUTH KILWORTH RD

PO

WAKEFIELD DR

CHURCH LA

THE LEYS

WOODFORD GLEBE

NEWLANDS RD

WEST END

Jurassic Way

Court Lane Farm

COURT LA

NORTHAMPTON RD

Fish Pond Covert

Hemplow Hills

HEMPLOW DR

West Hill Farm

Hemploe Lodge Farm

NN6

The Glebe

A5199

Dark Spinney

Prince of Wales Spinney

Watts Lodge Farm

Welford Lodge Farm

A14

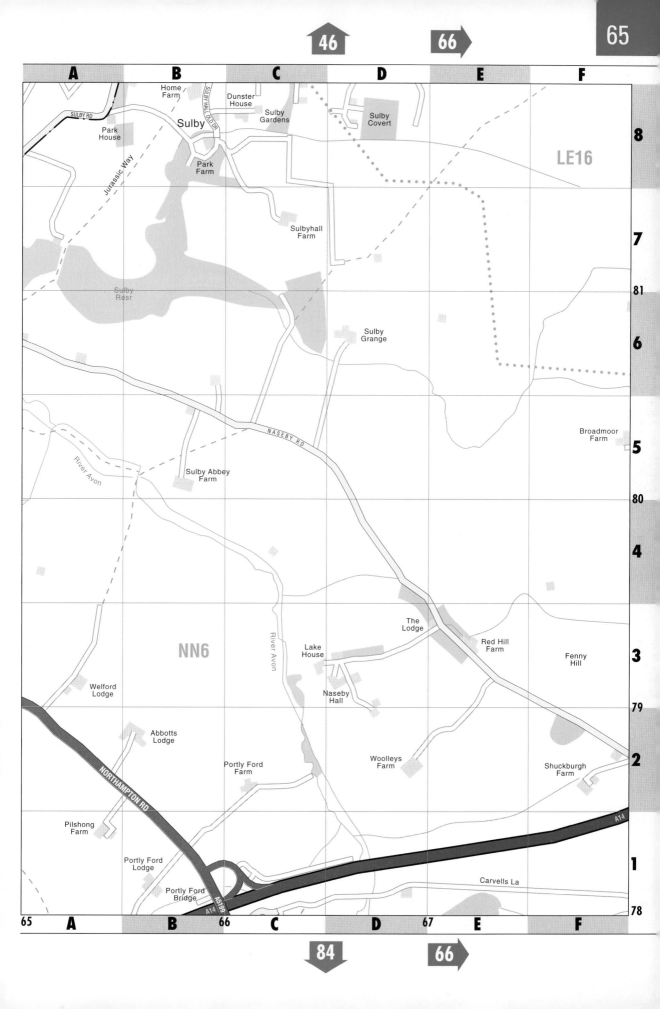

A   B   C   D   E   F

8

The
Paddocks

Clipston
The Old Manse
NGBOLD CT
PEG'S LA
The Chestnuts

LE16

Longhold
Lodge

7

81

Prince Rupert's
Farm

Long Hold
Spinney

6

Dust
Hill

Dust Hill
Farm

5

Mon

P

The
Plantation

80

Naseby
Covert

4

Paisnell
Spinney

Naseby
Field

Mill
Hill

3

New-House
Farm

A14

NN6

Mill Hill
Farm

79

Mast

2

Clothill
Spinney

A14

Obelisk

1

Naseby
PH
Naseby CE
Prim Sch
NEWLANDS
CHURCH ST
HIGH ST

78

68   A   B   69   C   D   70   E   F

A B C D E F

Newbold
Farm

Playing
Field

Kelmarsh Field
Farm

PH

HARBOROUGH RD

CHURCH CL

Sewage
Works

Wormslade
Farm

8

CHESTNUT
GR

NASEBY RD

HIGH ST

Clipston
Prim Sch

CHURCH LA

BASSETT WAY

WESKERS CL

Kelmarsh Field
Farm

A508

Macmillan Way

Midshires Way

KELMARSH RD

LE16

7

81

Lodge Ground
Spinney

6

Grasslands
Farm

Shipley
Wood

5

Hill Top
Farm

80

HARBOROUGH RD

Clipston
Grange

Shipley
Wood

Kelmarsh
Hall

4

Wilderness
Farm

Hall
Farm

Kelmarsh

The
Dales

3

Church
Spinney

79

Tallyho
Covert

River Ise

Rectory
Farm

2

A14

NN6

Scotland
Wood

A508

1

78

71 A B 72 C 73 D E F

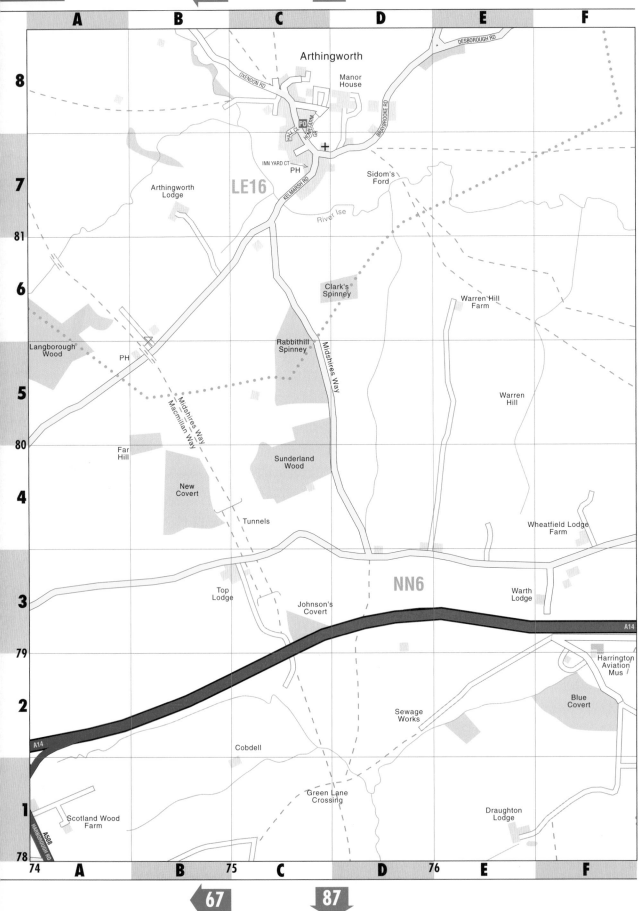

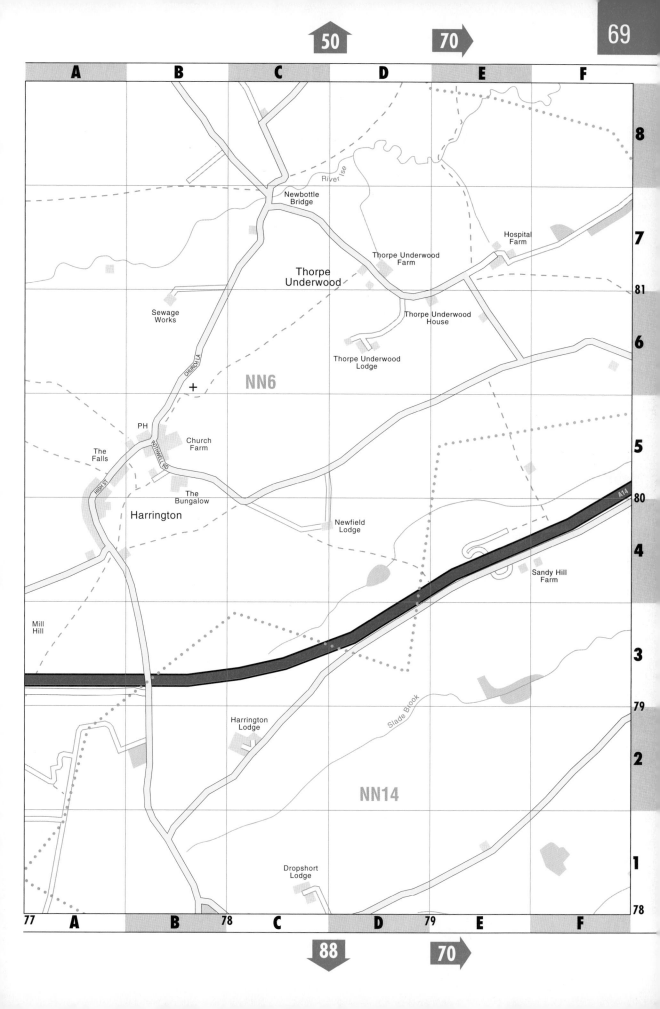

69 51

| A | B | C | D | E | F |

ROTHWELL

Grange Farm

Hospital Farm

Styles Lodge

SHOTWELL MILL LA

RUSHTON RD

Suffolk Villa

Allot Gdns Wr Twr

DESBOROUGH RD

Montsaye Sch

Rothwell Jun Sch

Cambridge St

SPENCER ST

OXFORD ST

SCOTT AVE

TEBBUTT CL

NUNNERY AVE

GREENING RD

KINGSLEY RD

TENNYSON RD

Rothwell Inf Sch

GLADSTONE ST

VICTORIA ST

CASTLE HILL

CECIL ST

CROSS ST

MADAMS GDN

MADAMS HILL

THE AVENUE

BUSWELL RISE

LITTLEWOOD ST

DRAKE CL

UPTON RD

NELSON RD

CONNOLLY DR

The Maltings 1
WHITEMAN LA 2
NEWHAM CL 3

BARLOW CL

LEWIN CL

BUTLIN CL

ADAMS DR

MAUNSELL RISE

MOORFIELD RD

BEVERLEY CL

COGAN CRES

MOORFIELD GDN

MATSON CL

TRINITY RD

MANOR RD

HIGH HILL AVE

DAISY BANK AVE

CROWN LA

WA ST

DRUCE CT

PO

Liby

BRIDGE ST

BELL HILL

MARKET HILL

THRESHER ST

NEW ST

ST

ROCK HILL

CORONATION AVE

POWDER ST

CRISPIN ST

STANLEY RD

RAGSDALE

NORTON ST

LANCASTER RD

JOHN SMITH AVE

LIVINGSTONE CL

GIBBONS DR

BALFOUR DR

CATESBY RD

SHARMAN CL

SLADE VALLEY AVE

TEABURY WAY

PLAYFORD WAY

KIPTON CL

GLENDON RD

RALEIGH CL

CHICHESTER

BURDITT CL

FOX ST

B576

HARRINGTON RD

UNDERWOOD RD

ROBERTS ST

GLOUCESTER CT

ELIZABETH RD

CRESCENT

EVANS ST

SUN HILL

PLOUGH CL

KETTERING RD A6

GORDON ST

JUBILEE ST

Wheelwright Ho
2 Forge Ho
3 Austin Ho

Spring

MVH

BAFFIN

GRENVILLE CL

COOK CL

COLUMBUS CRES

BLYTHE CL

VICKERS CL

MAGELLAN CL

MEADOW RD

Edinburgh CL

JOHN BEVERLY MEWS 1
HOBBS HILL 2
CLIPSTONE CT 3

Factory

TASMAN WAY

JANSEN CL

Nunnery Farm

A576

A14

KETTERING RD

Cemy

Rothwell Lodge

A14

NN14

Thorpe Malsor Resr

Slade Brook

Orton

Bay House Farm

Manor Farm

MAIN ST

Orton Lodge

The Cedar House

Three Chimneys

ORTON RD

Loddington

Uplands Farm

Loddington Hall

STERLING CT

MAIN ST

HALL GDNS

MANSIBLE RD

RICHARDSONS LA

PARK RD

NUS CL

Loddington CE Prim Sch

HARRINGTON RD

PO

CRANSLEY RD

MAWSLEY LA

Nus Hill Lodge

Cransley Resr

69 89

8

7

81

NN16

6

Glenn
Spinney

Glendon Hall
Cottages

Glendon
Hall

GLENDON RD

Oddstones | Bunkers Hill
Farm

Glen Hill
Farm

Woodfield
Farm

New
Wood

Glendon
Wood

Brookside Spinney
Slade Brook

Hill
Spinnies

VIOLET LA

Rothwell Lodge
Farm

Middle
Lodge

Top
Lodge

Rothwell Grange
Farm

5

A43

FURNACE LA

KETTERING RD

ROTHWELL RD

Furnace
Farm

80

The
Woodland H

Rothwell
Grange

Sewage
Works

Wyatt's
Plantation

Pottedbrig
Spinney

GLEN BAULK RD

Potted
Brig

Glebe
Farm

A43

Motel

Crem

Ind
Est

WYNDHAM WAY

HENSON WAY

RILEY RD

TORBRIDGE CL

LINNELL WAY

HENSON CL

ADAM
BSNS PK

TELFORD WAY

ROBINSON WAY

ENTERPRISE CL

4

Kingsthorne
Distribution Pk

A6
BSNS PK

BARTLEY
DR

ENTERPRISE
CENTRE
2000

A4300

KETTERING

Thorpe
Malsor

Allot
Gdns

THE SQUARE

SHORT LA

CHURCH WAY

NN14

BARON AVE

WARREN HILL

B5323

GARRARD WAY

BUSHACRE

EXPRESS
PK

ROTHWELL RD
A4300

3

1
2
3
HAWESWATER RD

BUTTERMERE CL

LANGSETT CL 1
CARSINGTON CL 2
LADYBOWER CL 3
THIRLMERE CL 4
THIRLMERE FLATS 5

4
5
CRES

H

79

Thorpe Malsor
Hall

Breakmill
Spinney

EAGLE LA

Brooklands
Farm

GIPSY LA

ULLSWATER RD

STAFF
HOS

Kettering
General

CONISTON RD

WINDERMERE RD

DERWENT CRES

GRASMERE RD

2

Northfield
Farm

NORTHFIELD RD

Wren Spinney
Sch

BOWHILL

WESTOVER RD

Prim
Sch

WEST FURLONG

WESTHILL
CL

B5323
A6013

NN15

1

Brocks
Spinney

Cransley
Resr

Bottom Lodge
Homestead

Bottom Lodge
Farm

A14

WESTWAY

NORTHAMPTON RD

A6013

THALL LA

GREENFIELD AVE

Prep
Sch

78

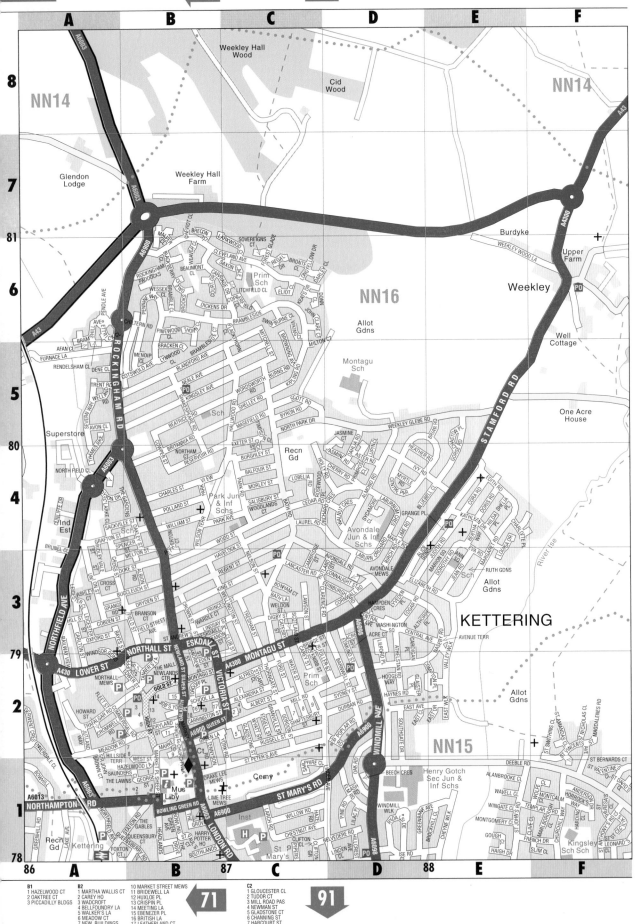

A   B   C   D   E   F

8

NN14

NN14

Weekley Hall
Wood

Cid
Wood

7

Glendon
Lodge

Weekley Hall
Farm

Burdyke

Upper
Farm

81

Weekley

6

NN16

Well
Cottage

Allot
Gdns

Montagu
Sch

One Acre
House

5

Superstore

80

Recn
Gd

Park Jun
& Inf
Schs

Avondale
Jun & Inf
Schs

4

Ind
Est

KETTERING

Avenue Terr

Allot
Gdns

3

Allot
Gdns

79

A430   LOWER ST

NORTHALL ST   ESKDALE ST   MONTAGU ST

2

NN15

Cemy

Henry Gotch
Sec Jun &
Inf Schs

1

A6013
NORTHAMPTON

ST MARY'S RD

Recn
Gd

Kettering

St
Mary's

Windmill
Wlk

Kingsley
Sch Sch

78

86   A   B   87   C   D   88   E   F

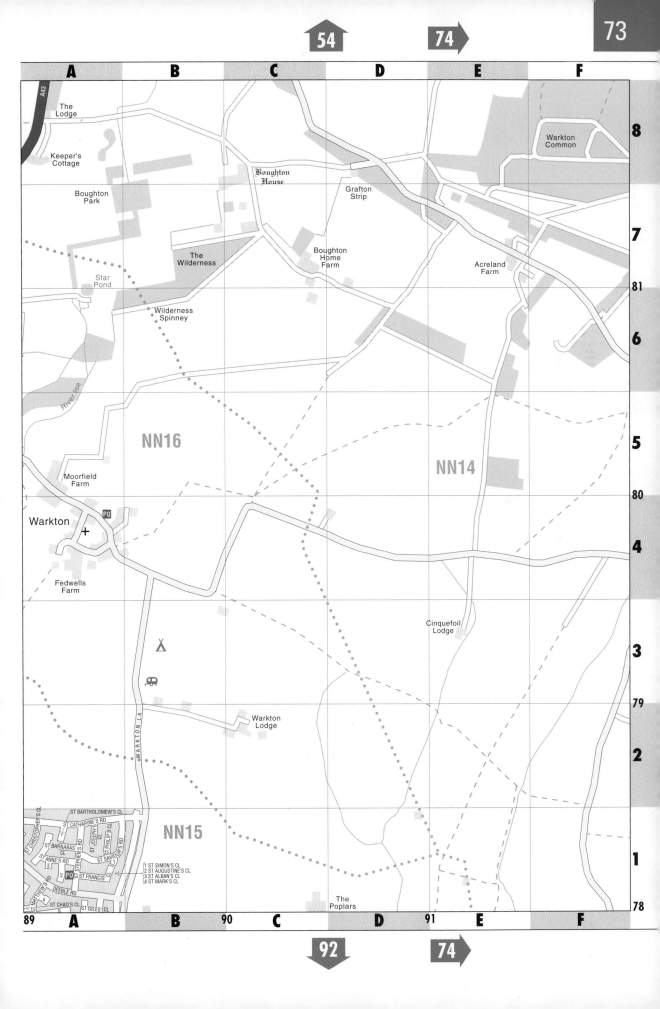

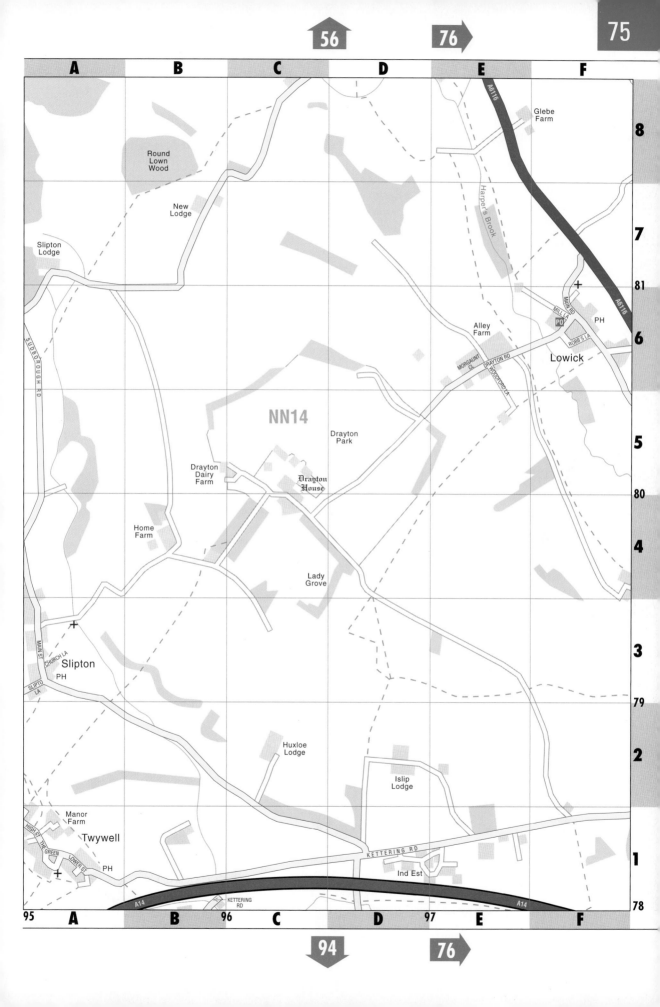

A B C D E F

8
Oxen Wood
FULLERS CL
Aldwincle
Aldwincle Trinity CE Lower Sch
Manor Farm
DAINTREE CT
MAIN ST

7
Aldwincle Lodge Farm
LOWICK RD
LOWICK LA

81
Bullicks Wood

6
ALDWINCLE RD
Rectory Farm
A6116

5
NN14
Nene Way

80
RIDGE RD
River Nene

4
Colpman's Farm
Sewage Works
A605

3
NENE VIEW
LOWICK RD
JUBILEE CL
ACORN CL
DRAYTON
RUSHMERE CL
ST NICHOLAS WAY
PO
Islip
MILL LA
Islip Mill
ACORN IND EST
HIGH ST
THE COURTYARD
MILL RD
LAKESIDE CL
POPPYFIELD CL
SWAN CL
GREEN LA
SPRINGFIELD AVE
HERON CL
GREBE
Cemy
HILLCREST
DUNDLE RD
NAVISFORD CL
NAVISFORD
MALLARD CL
WASHINGTON CL
ROMAN WAY
PARK LA
CLARE DR
Nene Cottage
Springfield Farm
TOP CL
ST MARYS CL
DUNDLE RD

79

2
SCHOOL LA
WELLINGTON TERR
Rectory Farm
CHAPEL HILL RD
RIVERSIDE WAY
TOLL BAR RD
PH
BRIDGE ST
BRIDGE CT
Ind Est
Liby
Hotel
PO
COTTINGHAM WAY
BASLER GDNS
THE MANOR HO
FERY LA
MANOR CL
DE VERE RD
WREN CL
SACK...
MONTAGUE CT
CRES
CHARLES RD
JOHN'S
QUEENS
WINDING WAY
FARADAY CT
P
HIGHFIELD RD
FOTHERINGHAM RD
PEMBROKE CT
WINDSOR DR
SHERBORNE RD
WARWICK GDNS
LEICESTER DR
ROCKINGHAM CL
RENBURN
HARLECH CT

1
KETTERING RD
GRANGE RD
MIDLAND RD
HALEGRD ST
GROVE RD
CEDAR DR
King John Sch
CORDWAINER GR 1
CHANDLERS GDNS 2
Thrapston Prim Sch
COOPER CT
BRAMBLESIDE
OAKLEAS RISE
HAWTHORN DR
SPINNEY CL
HORT
PARK VIEW
MARKET RD
HUNTINGDON RD
WAINWRIGHT AVE
FLETCHERS GDNS
FISHER CL
FORRESTER GR
MASON
MILLER CL
BAKER CL
ASH CT
ORCHARD CT
DAMSON WAY
CRAB APPLE WAY
Service Area
New Farm
THRAPSTON
A14
A6116
A605

78
98 A B 99 C D 00 E F

A B C D E F

PE8

Brook
Farm

Brancey
Bridge

Thorpe
Waterville

PH

Cricket
Gd

THORPE CT

A605

Thorpe Fox
Covert

8

7

81

Marina

Titchmarsh
Mill

Thorpe Brook

6

NN14

5

80

Islington

CHURCH ST

Titchmarsh
CE Prim Sch

MANOR
FARM CT

Sewage
Works

DRYDEN'S CL

PARK RD

SCHOOL LA

THE GREEN

CHAPEL ST

NORTH ST

Titchmarsh

4

Rectory
Farm

PH

HIGH ST

TOFTS CL

ST ANDREWS LA

ST ANDREW'S
CL

Newbrook
Farm

LONDON END

Polopit

ST LORRY CL

3

79

Townhill
Coppice

2

The
Bungalow

1

Castle Manor
Farm

A14

78

01 A B 02 C D 03 E F

PE8

A B C D E F

PE8

8

Towcester Hill
Spinney

Bull Nose
Coppice

Alvaston

Long Thong
Coppice

7

Long Thong
Farm

81

Blackthorn
Coppice

6

PO

BERRY GREEN PK

Ash Pole
Coppice

Clopton

NN14

5

Clopton
Manor

Skulking Dudley
Copse

80

+

B662

4

Ringdales
Wood

Crows
Nest
Farm

Bidwell
Farm

3

79

Foxholes
Farm

Fayway

2

WARREN LA

Chequer
Hill
Coppice

1

Warren
Lodge
Farm

78

04 A B 05 C D 06 E F

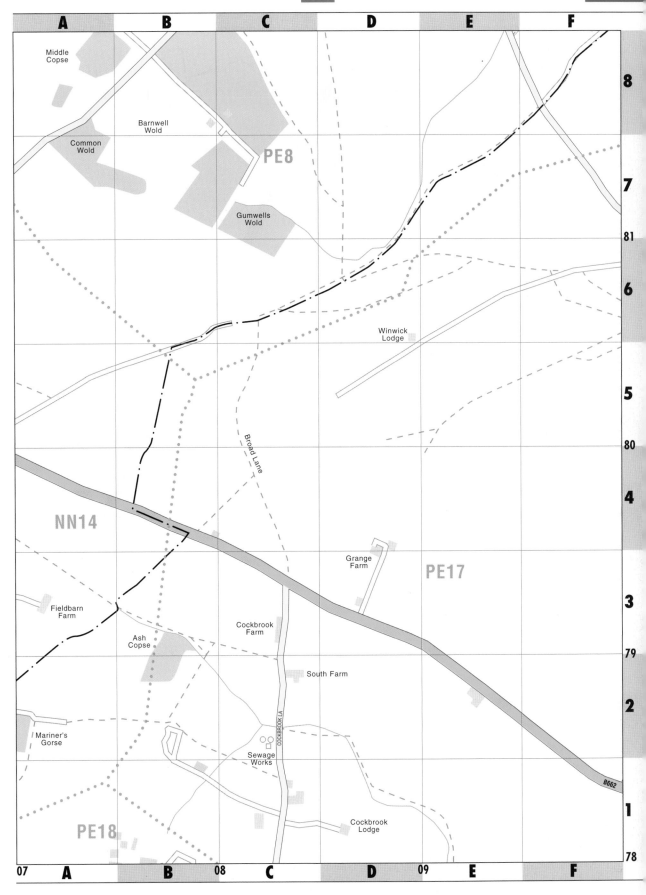

A   B   C   D   E   F

Middle
Copse

Barnwell
Wold

Common
Wold

PE8

Gumwells
Wold

Winwick
Lodge

81

6

Broad Lane

5

80

NN14

4

Grange
Farm

PE17

3

Fieldbarn
Farm

Cockbrook
Farm

Ash
Copse

79

South Farm

2

Mariner's
Gorse

COCKBROOK LA

Sewage
Works

B662

1

PE18

Cockbrook
Lodge

78

07   A   B   08   C   D   09   E   F

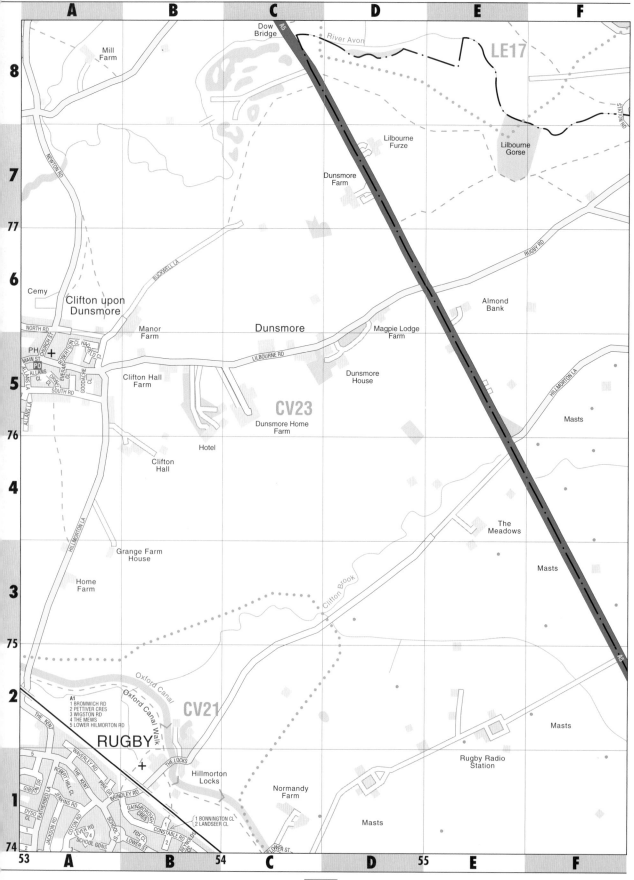

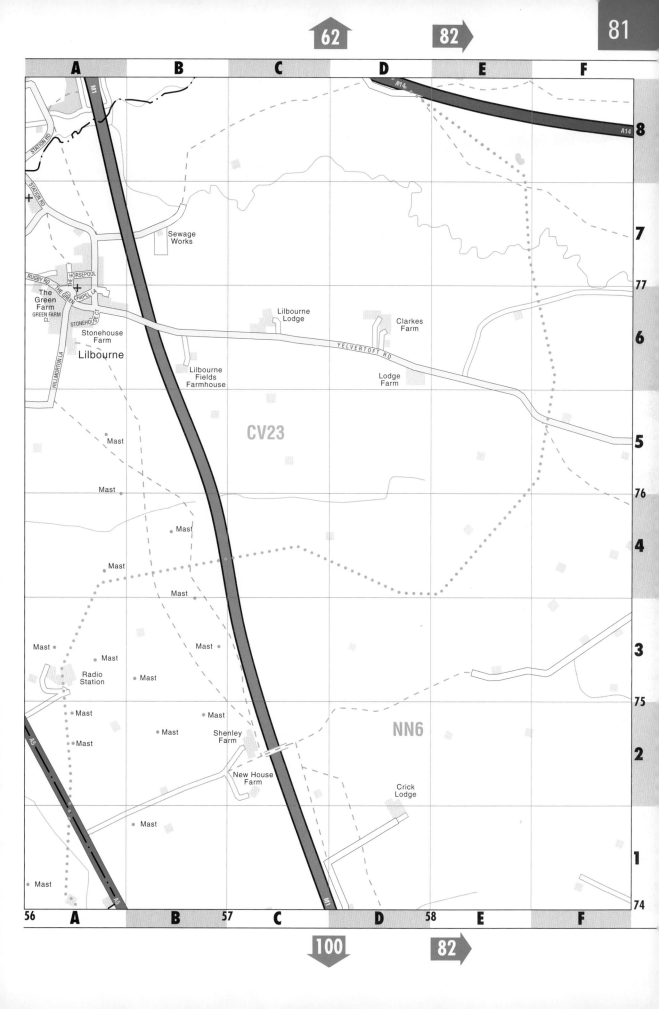

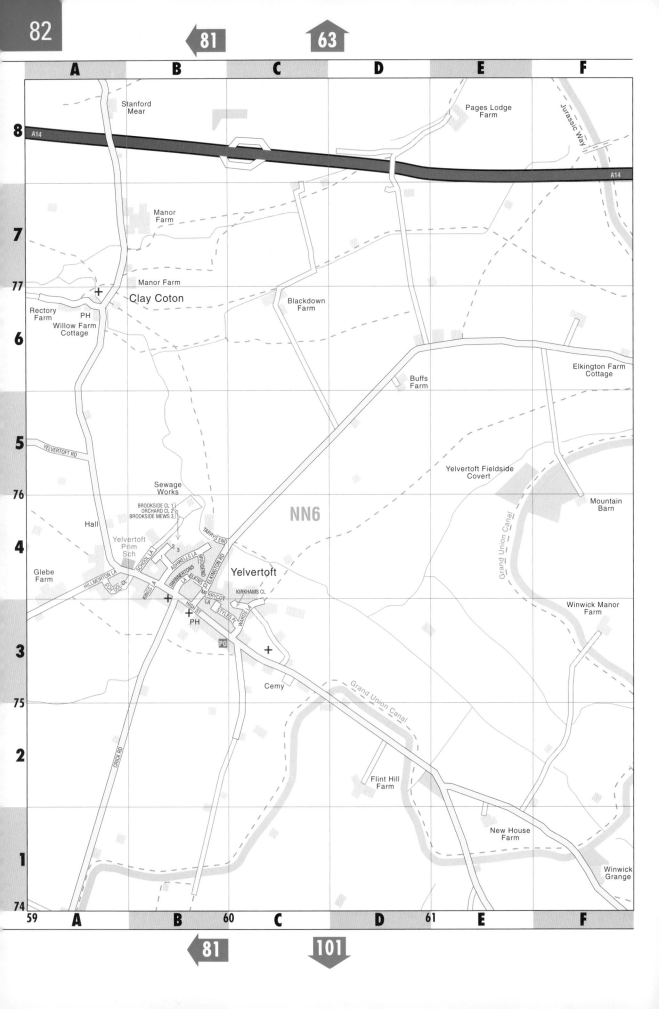

A14

Stanford
Mear

Manor
Farm

Manor Farm

Clay Coton

Rectory
Farm
PH
Willow Farm
Cottage

YELVERTOFT RD

Blackdown
Farm

Buffs
Farm

Pages Lodge
Farm

Jurassic Way

A14

Elkington Farm
Cottage

Mountain
Barn

Grand Union Canal

Sewage
Works

NN6

Yelvertoft Fieldside
Covert

BROOKSIDE CL 1
ORCHARD CL 2
BROOKSIDE MEWS 3

Hall

TARRYS END

Yelvertoft
Prim
Sch

SCHOOL LA

KINGS LA

HILLMORTON LA

SCHOOL CL

Glebe
Farm

ASHWELLS LA

SWINNERTONS

ELKINS LA

BRIDGEND CL

ELKINGTON RD

Yelvertoft

KIRKHAMS CL

MERRYCOT
LA

STYLES PL

WARDS LA

HIGH ST

PH

PO

CRICK RD

Cemy

Grand Union Canal

Winwick Manor
Farm

Flint Hill
Farm

New House
Farm

Winwick
Grange

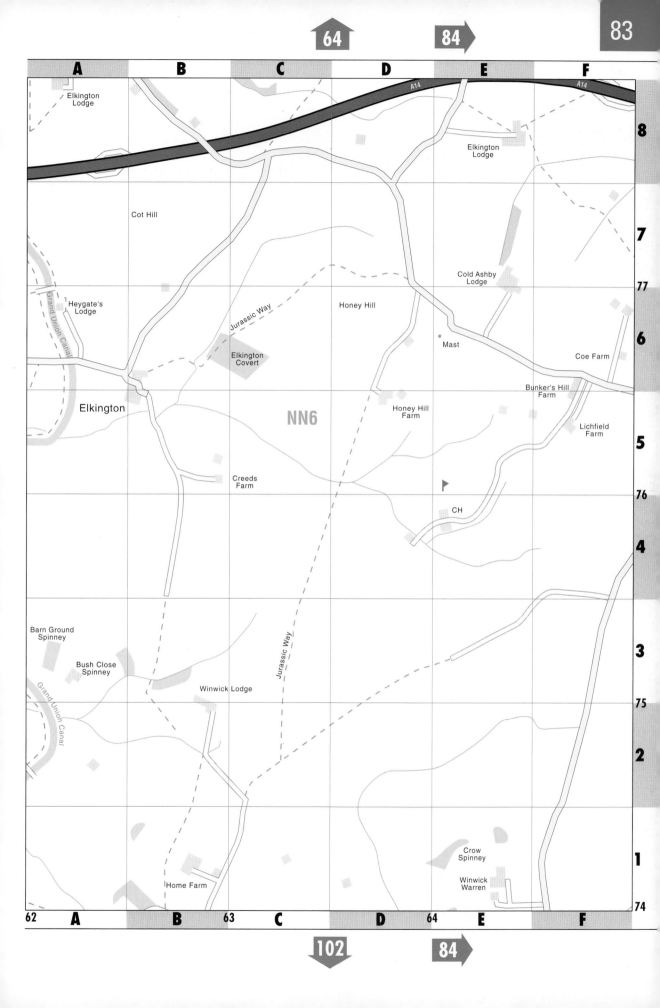

A   B   C   D   E   F

Elkington Lodge

A14

Elkington Lodge

8

Cot Hill

7

Grand Union Canal

Heygate's Lodge

77

Jurassic Way

Honey Hill

Cold Ashby Lodge

6

Elkington Covert

Mast

Coe Farm

Elkington

NN6

Honey Hill Farm

Bunker's Hill Farm

Lichfield Farm

5

Creeds Farm

76

CH

4

Barn Ground Spinney

3

Bush Close Spinney

Jurassic Way

Winwick Lodge

Grand Union Canal

75

2

Crow Spinney

1

Home Farm

Winwick Warren

74

A B C D E F

8

7

77

6

A14

A14

A5199

Naseby
Resr

Fulbrook
Farm

Reservoir
Farm

5

STANFORD RD
STANFORD CL
WEST HADDON RD
BRIDLE LA
CRABTREE LA
MAIN ST
PH
CHURCH LA
PARK
SPINNEY CL
THORNBY RD

NN6

Lodge Farm

Cold Ashby

WELFORD RD

76

Park
Spinney

4

Thornby House
Farm

COLD ASHBY RD

ST HELENS CL

Thornby
Hall

PH

NASEBY RD

STONE HOUSE
MEWS

Thornby

Doebank
Spinney

3

Lovells
Lodge

Firetail
Covert

Firetail

75

Thornby
Grange

2

Grange
Farm

Rabbit
Spinney

Nortoft
Lodge

Ashbylane
Farm

1

West Lodge

A5199

74

65 A B 66 C D 67 E F

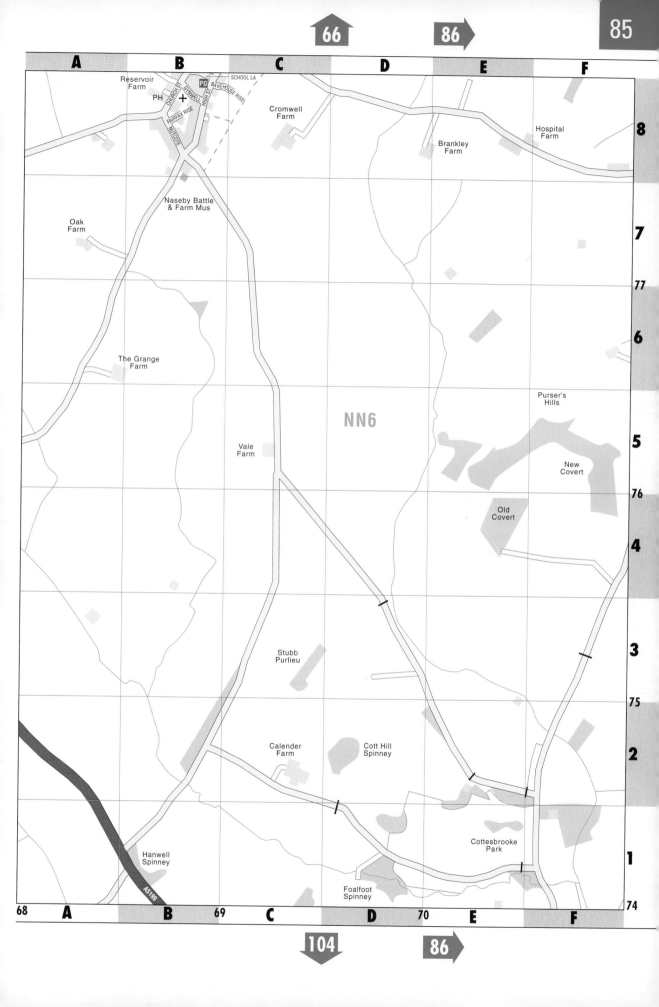

66
86
104
86

Reservoir Farm

PH

Cromwell Farm

SCHOOL LA

PO

BAKEHOUSE RISE

CHURCH ST

STIRWELL

HIGH ST

FAIRFAX RISE

NUTCOTE

Brankley Farm

Hospital Farm

Oak Farm

Naseby Battle & Farm Mus

The Grange Farm

Purser's Hills

NN6

Vale Farm

New Covert

Old Covert

Stubb Purlieu

Calender Farm

Cott Hill Spinney

Cottesbrooke Park

Hanwell Spinney

A5199

Foalfoot Spinney

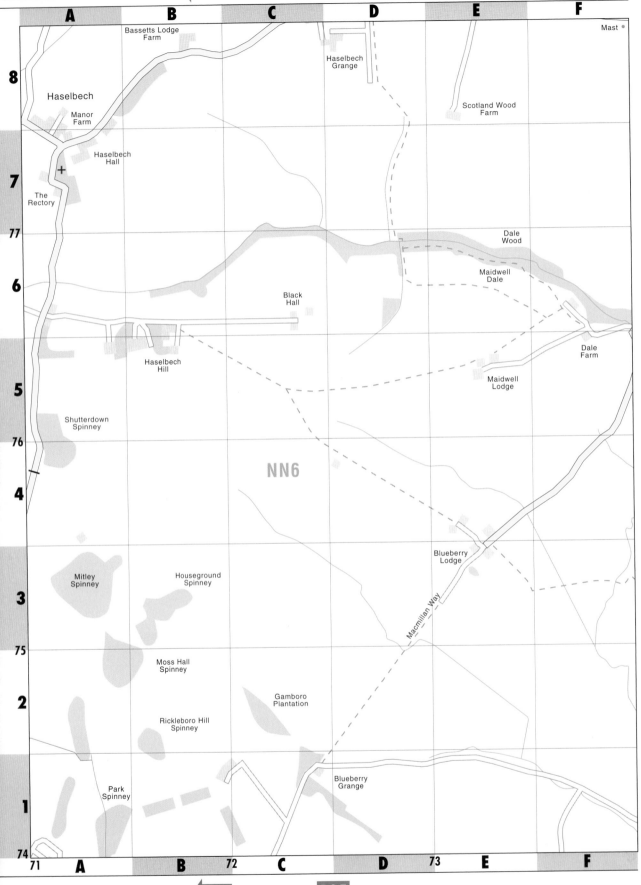

A   B   C   D   E   F

Mast •

Bassetts Lodge
Farm

Haselbech
Grange

8

Haselbech

Scotland Wood
Farm

Manor
Farm

Haselbech
Hall

7

The
Rectory

77

Dale
Wood

6

Maidwell
Dale

Black
Hall

Dale
Farm

Haselbech
Hill

Maidwell
Lodge

5

Shutterdown
Spinney

76

NN6

4

Mitley
Spinney

Houseground
Spinney

Blueberry
Lodge

3

Macmillan Way

75

Moss Hall
Spinney

2

Gamboro
Plantation

Rickleboro Hill
Spinney

Blueberry
Grange

Park
Spinney

1

74

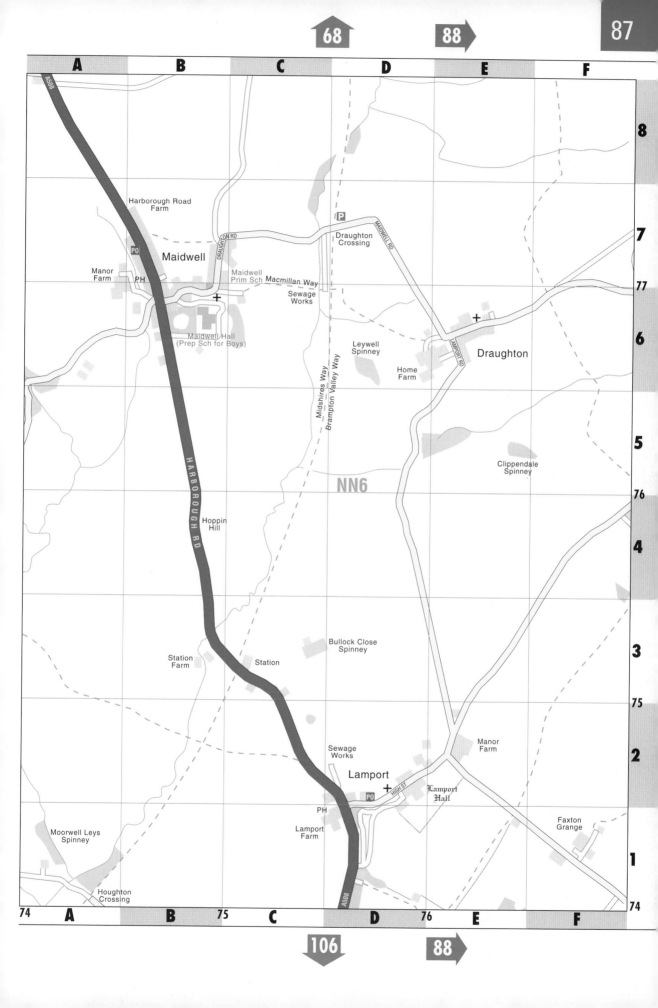

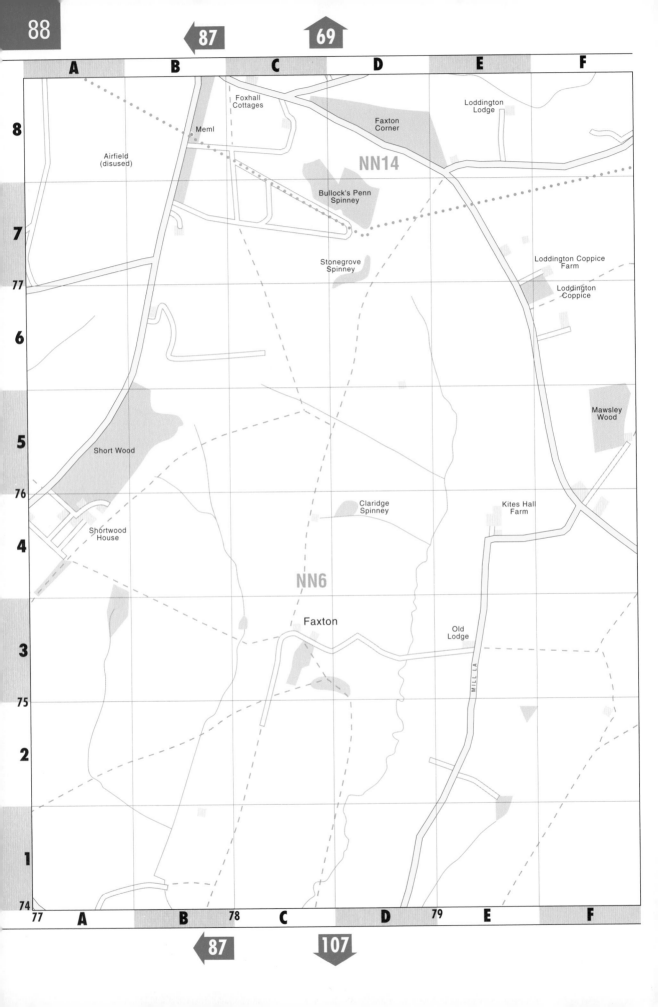

A B C D E F

8

Foxhall
Cottages

Loddington
Lodge

Faxton
Corner

Meml

NN14

Airfield
(disused)

Bullock's Penn
Spinney

7

Loddington Coppice
Farm

Stonegrove
Spinney

77

Loddington
Coppice

6

Mawsley
Wood

5

Short Wood

76

Claridge
Spinney

Kites Hall
Farm

Shortwood
House

4

NN6

Faxton

Old
Lodge

3

MILL LA

75

2

1

74

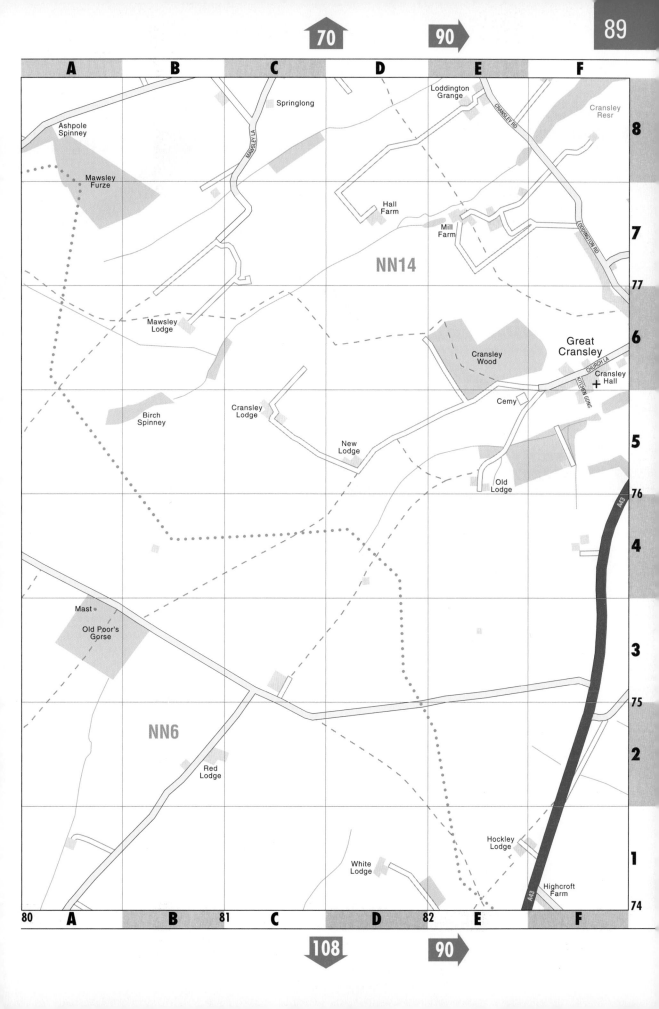

A B C D E F

8

White Hill
Lodge

Allotment
Spinney

Works

NORTHAMPTON RD

A14
A6013
BIGNAL CT
HALL CL
HALL LA
MOOREHOUSE WAY
FOSTER CL
LONSBOROUGH DR
BILLINGHAM
THOMPSON WAY
OWEN CL
WELL CL
CHRISTIE WAY
INKPEN CL
RIDGEWELL CL
WELLS
LAKE AVE
BRAITHWAITE CL
JACKSON CL
REDGRAVE CL

7

The
Gorse

A43

NN15

77

Broughton Hill
Bridle Way
Church La
Holly La

Sewage
Works

6

Broughton
Grange

Allot
Gdns

Sewage
Works

Little
Cransley

5

Grange Rd
Thurburns Rd
Kettering Rd
Crane Cl
The Banks

Allot
Gdns

76

Cox's La
West La
Silver St
Ivydene Terr
Cransley Hill
High St
Gate La
Brookdownhall
St Andrews Cl

Manor
Farm

Recn
Gd

Cemy

A43

Broughton
Prim Sch

Rathmine
Farm

4

St Andrews Way 1
Church View 2
Dawkins Ct 3

PO
3
2
1

St Andrew's Ct

Church St

Pytchley
Lodge

Broughton

Oak Cl
Glebe Ave
Line Cl
Hutchinson Ave

Wellingborough Rd

Baker Rd
Thedon Cl
Biggall Cl

NN14

Northampton Rd
Meacham Cl
Podmore Way
Carter Ave
Donaldson Cl
Kerby
Lenton Cl

3

Headlands
Farm

New
Covert

Underwood's Hill
Spinney

75

Manor
Farm

2

Pytchley New
Covert

Pytchley

Blacksmith's
La
Manor La
Snaggs Rd
Top End
High St
Orchard
Stringers Hill
Butcher's La
Pytchley
CE Sch

Stud
Farm

Broughton Rd

Orlingbury Rd

1

Spencer
Lodge

74

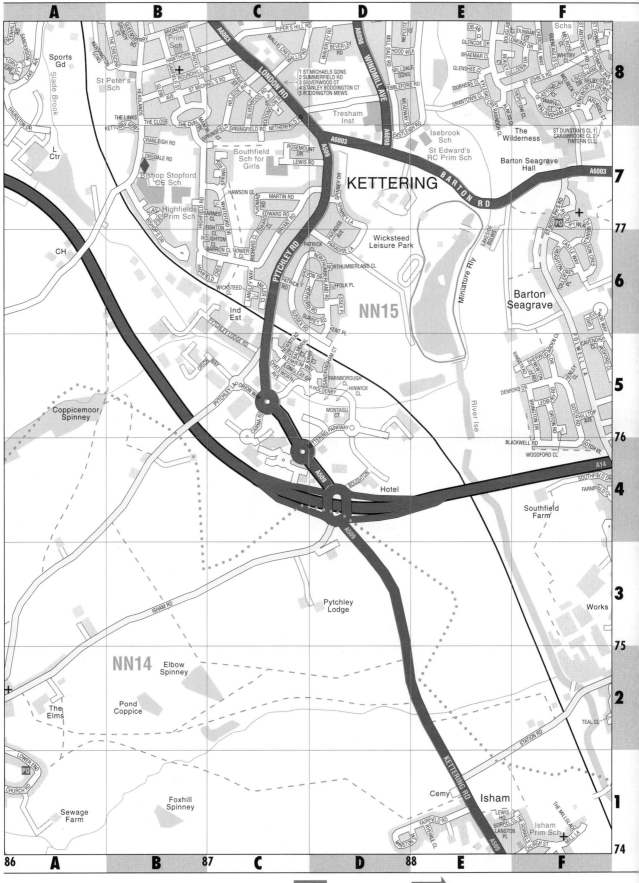

A B C D E F

8
77
7
6
5
76
4
3
75
2
74

KETTERING

NN15

NN14

Sports Gd

Slade Brook

L Ctr

St Peter's Sch

Broadway Prim Sch

PIPER'S HILL RD

Bishop Stopford CE Sch

Highfields Prim Sch

Southfield Sch for Girls

LONDON RD

A6003

A6003

A6098

WINDMILL AVE

Tresham Inst

Isebrook Sch

St Edward's RC Prim Sch

The Wilderness

Barton Seagrave Hall

BARTON RD

A6003

PO

Barton Seagrave

Wicksteed Leisure Park

Miniature Rly

Ind Est

A509

PYTCHLEY RD

River Ise

KETTERING PARKWAY

A509

A14

Hotel

Southfield Farm

Works

Coppicemoor Spinney

PYTCHLEY LODGE RD

ORION WAY

Pytchley Lodge

ISHAM RD

Elbow Spinney

Pond Coppice

The Elms

Sewage Farm

Foxhill Spinney

LOWER END

PO

CHURCH RD

Cemy

KETTERING RD

A509

Isham

Isham Prim Sch

STATION RD

TEAL CL

1 ST MICHAELS GDNS
2 SUMMERFIELD RD
3 SILVERWOOD CT
4 STANLEY BODDINGTON CT
5 BODDINGTON MEWS

ST DUNSTAN'S CL 1
CARISBROOKE CL 2
TINTERN CL 3

91 73

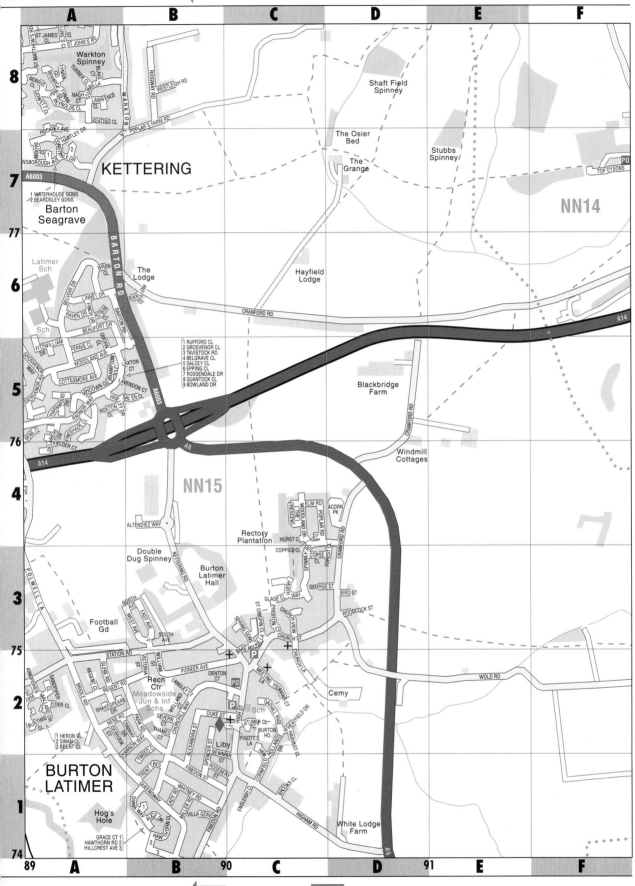

91 111

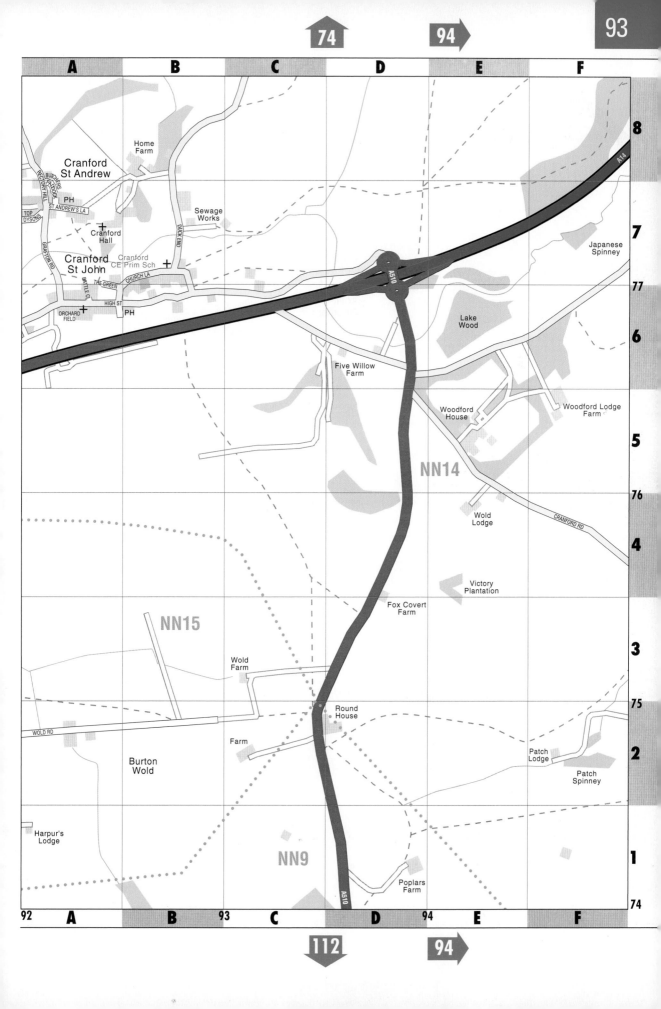

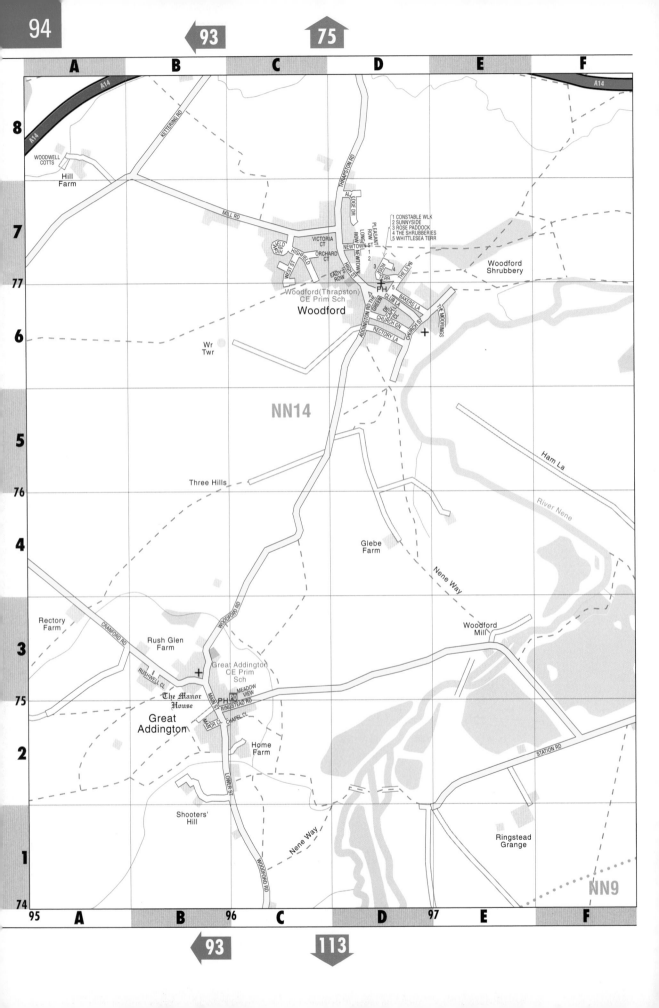

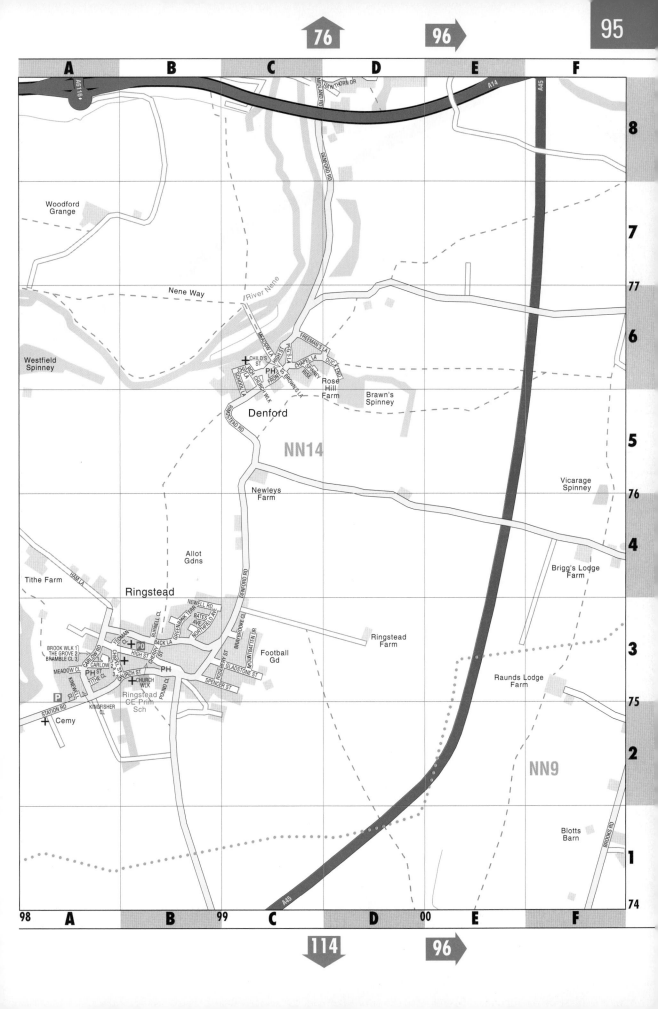

A B C D E F

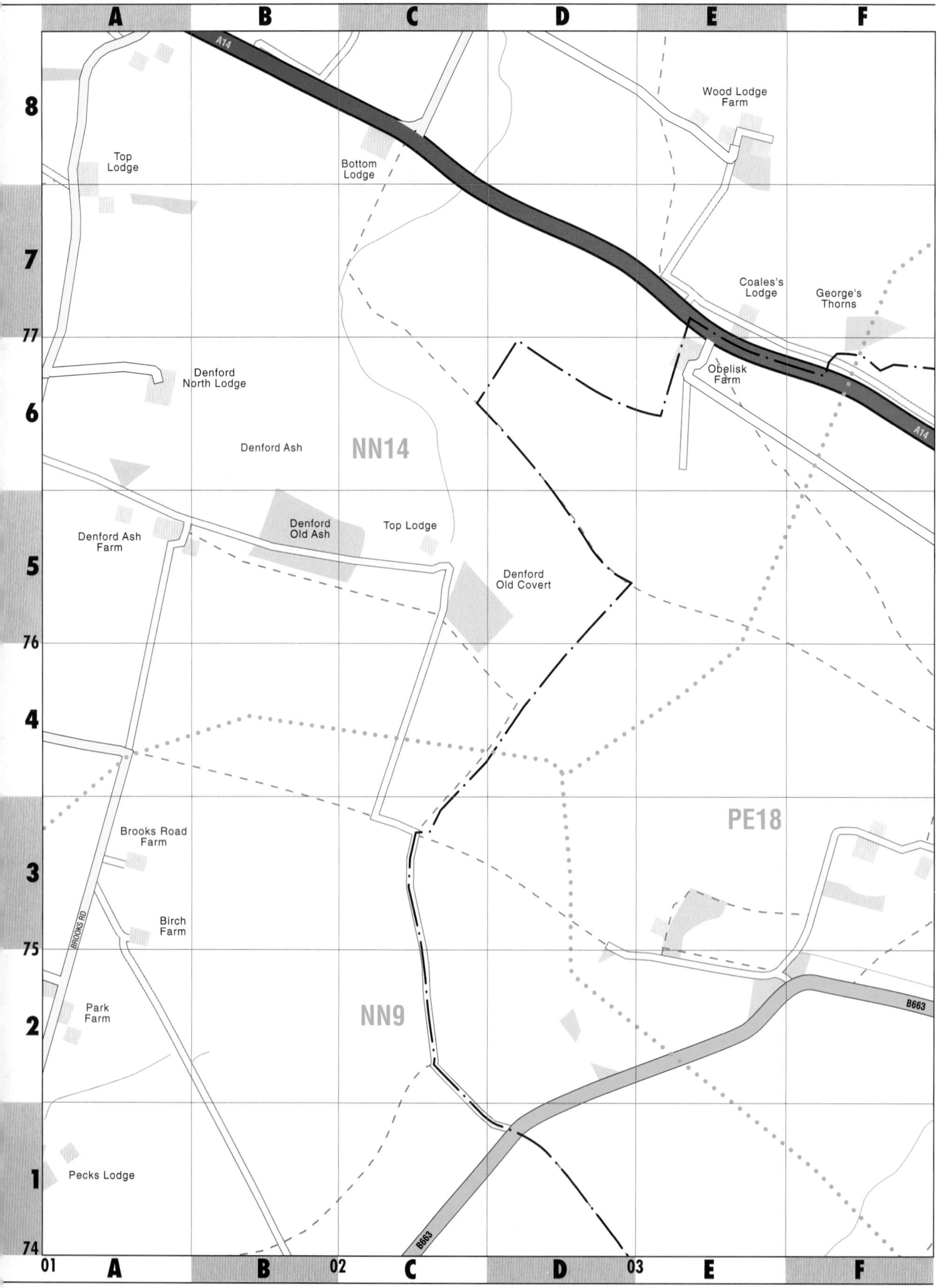

8 Top Lodge

Wood Lodge Farm

Bottom Lodge

A14

7 Coales's Lodge George's Thorns

77 Denford North Lodge

Obelisk Farm

6 Denford Ash NN14

A14

Denford Ash Farm

Denford Old Ash Top Lodge

5

Denford Old Covert

76

4

PE18

Brooks Road Farm

3

Birch Farm

75

Park Farm

2 NN9

B663

1 Pecks Lodge

74 01 A B 02 C D 03 E F

BROOKS RD

B663

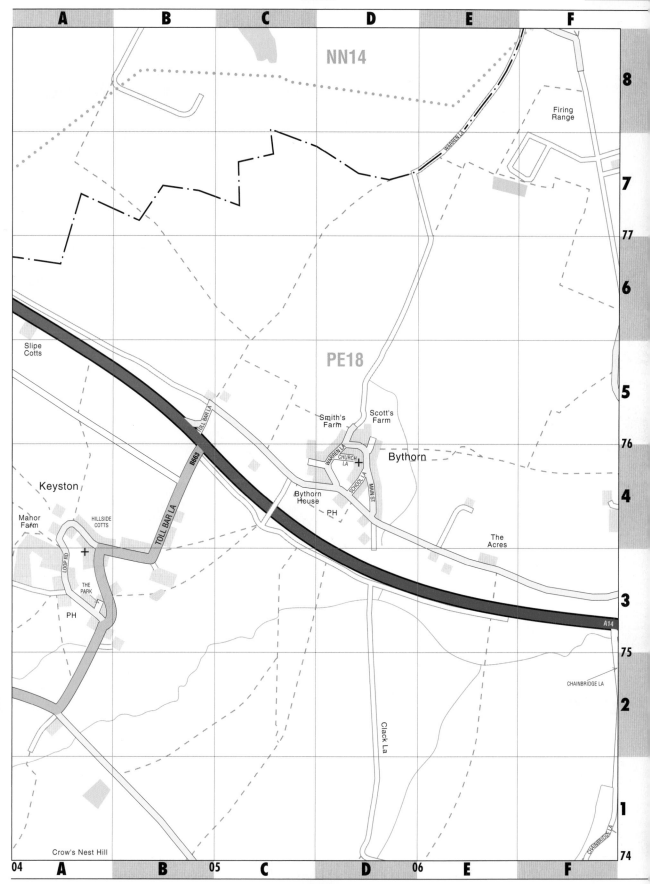

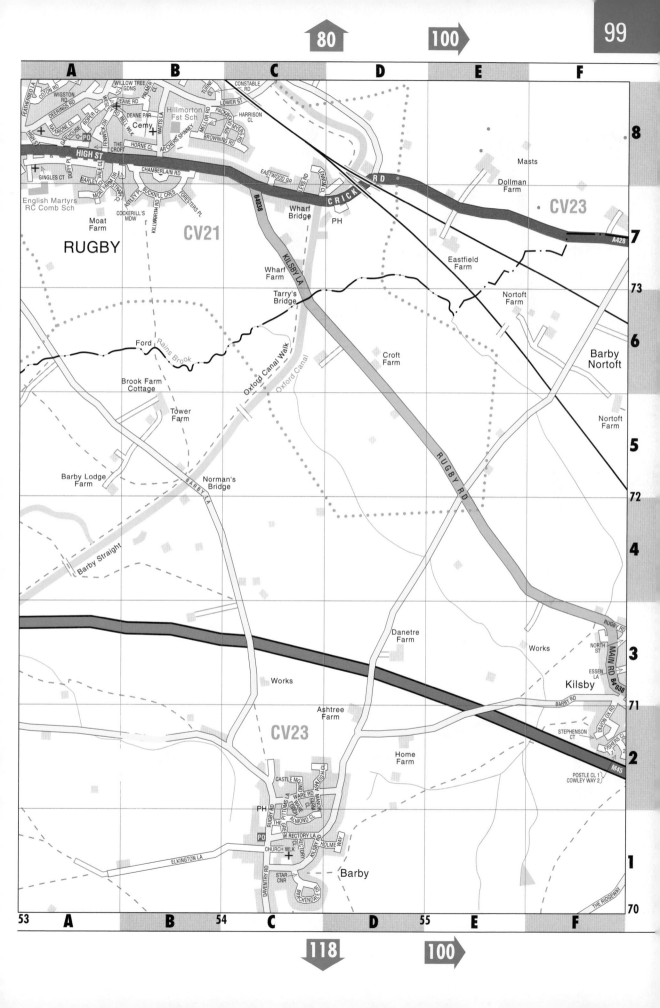

A B C D E F

8

Crick
Covert

Haythog
Farm

Sewage
Works

Covert
Lodge

Garage

Abbatoir

7

A428

PH

Hotel

NN6

73

A428

A5

18

A428

BARLEY CROFT

DRAYSON LA

OAK LA

PH

6

Nortoft Lodge
Farm

KING STY CL

PORTLOW LA

CHURCH ST

COLEMAN

Crick
Prim
Sch

ELLEN CL

BUCKNILLS LA

RECTORY CL

PH

ELDON WAY

ELDON CL

Ind
Est

Sewage
Works

MAIN RD

A428

HIGH ST

THE DERRY

THE PADDOCK

5

MARSONS DR

WELL HILL CL 1

ASHBY DR 2

1

2

THE HIGH LEYS

72

WATFORD RD

4

CV23

Field House
Farm

3

RUGBY RD

MIDDLE ST

PADDOX CL

HALL CL

WATLING ST

STATION RD

SMARTS
EST

Kilsby
CE
Prim
Sch

Kilsby

Tunnel
Farm

MONTAGUE DR

ESSEN LA

PO

MANOR RD

71

BARBY RD

MAIN RD

CHAPEL ST

A5

A361

MALT MILL LA

B4038

Bungalow
Farm

KILSBY RD

FISHERS

THE LAWNS

SPRING CL

THE BANKS

ARMIC

2

M45

Hall
Farm

Kilsby Grange

1

DAVENTRY RD

THE RIDGEWAY

M45

M1

A5

17

70

A361

56 A B 57 C D 58 E F

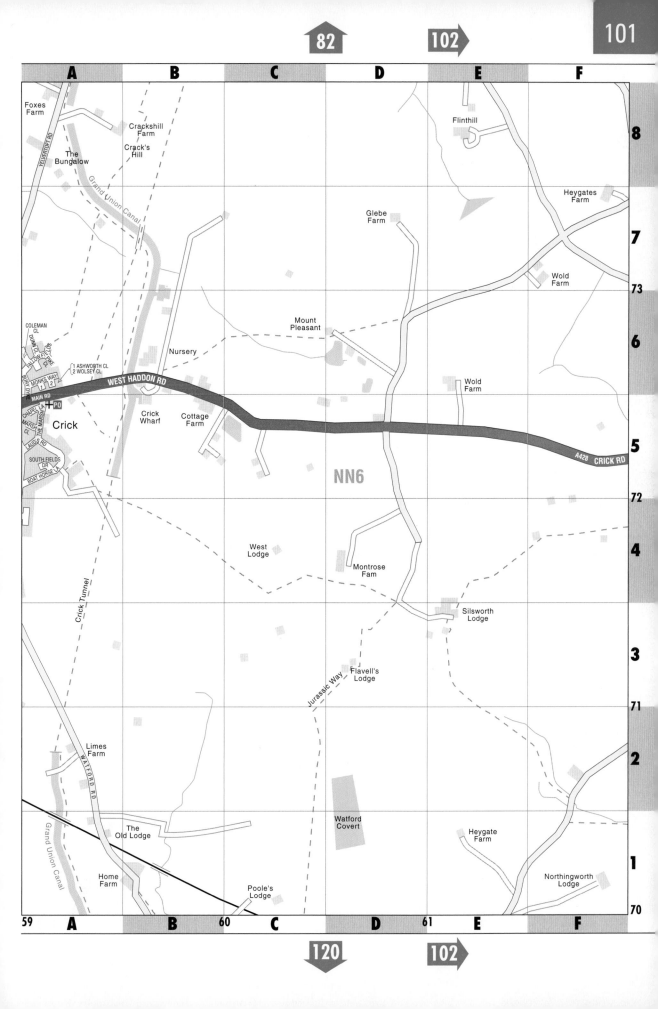

A · B · C · D · E · F

8

Foxes Farm
Flinthill
Crackshill Farm
Crack's Hill
The Bungalow
Heygates Farm
7
Grand Union Canal
Glebe Farm
Wold Farm
73
COLEMAN CL
Mount Pleasant
6
DUNN CL
TALLOW FIELDS
Nursery
Wold Farm
1 ASHWORTH CL
2 WOLSEY CL
MONKS WAY
WEST HADDON RD
BURN CL
MAIN RD
PO
Crick Wharf
Cottage Farm
CHAPEL LA
MARSH CL
THE MARSH
Crick
AUDIO RD
A428 CRICK RD
5
SOUTH FIELDS DR
BOAT HORSE LA
NN6
72
West Lodge
Montrose Fam
4
Silsworth Lodge
Crick Tunnel
3
Jurassic Way
Flavell's Lodge
71
Limes Farm
2
WATFORD RD
Grand Union Canal
The Old Lodge
Watford Covert
Heygate Farm
1
Home Farm
Poole's Lodge
Northingworth Lodge
70

59 · A · B · 60 · C · D · 61 · E · F

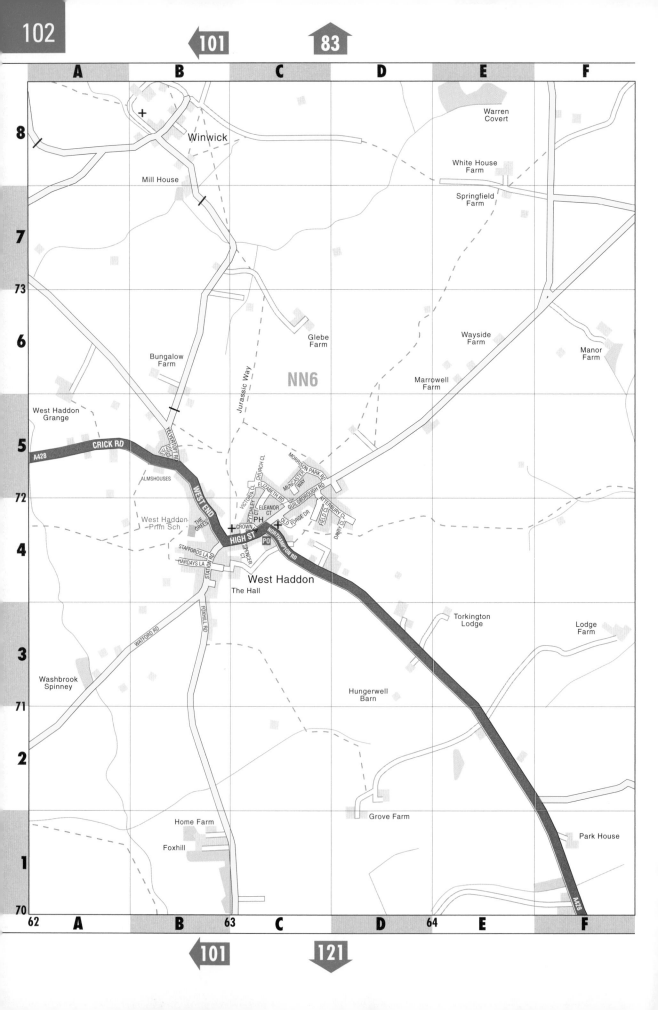

101
83

A   B   C   D   E   F

8

Warren Covert

Winwick

White House Farm

Mill House

Springfield Farm

7

73

6

Glebe Farm

Wayside Farm

Manor Farm

Bungalow Farm

Jurassic Way

NN6

Marrowell Farm

West Haddon Grange

5

CRICK RD

A428

WEST END

ALMSHOUSES

72

West Haddon Prim Sch

THE GREEN

CHURCH CL

ELIZABETH RD

MUNCASTER WAY

MORRISON PARK RD

GUILSBOROUGH RD

VICTORIA CL

PYTCHLEY CT

ELEANOR CT

OLD FORGE DR

ATTERBURY CL

FIELD CL

DARBY CL

CROWN

PH

HIGH ST

PO

STAFFORDS LA RD

HARDAYS LA

STATION RD

SPENCER CT

NORTHAMPTON RD

4

West Haddon

The Hall

FOXHILL RD

WATFORD RD

3

Torkington Lodge

Lodge Farm

Washbrook Spinney

71

Hungerwell Barn

2

Grove Farm

Home Farm

Foxhill

1

Park House

A428

70

62   A   B   63   C   D   64   E   F

84
104

A **B** **C** **D** **E** **F**

8

Lodge Farm

Nortoft
Grange

Guilsborough
Sch

7

Wildlife
Park

West Haddon Rd

Cold Ashby Rd

Council
Hos

Nortoft

Guilsborough Lodge
Farm

Lindow
Spinney

Thorneycroft
Spinney

Press Cl

Wills
Cl

Ashby Ct

The Poplars

PO

The Old Grammar
School

73

Gaytail
Lodge

Grange Farm

Guilsborough
CE Prim Sch

Guilsborough

High St

Well La

PH

6

NN6

Church Mount

Coton Lodge

Coton Rd

Teeton Rd

Upper Coton
Farm

5

72

Coton

Coton
Manor

4

Botany
Farm

Coton Park

Coton Mill

Water
Works

Coton Manor
Gardens

Causeway

3

71

Ravensthorpe
Resr

2

Chorley
Cop

West Haddon Rd

Hawtoft
Farm

Guilsborough Rd

The Orchards

Paddock Cl

Little La

Scott

PO

The High St

Cheruford

Church Hill

Coton Rd

Bittycroft Cl

The Hollow

Church
Gdns

Teeton Rd

Dairy Field

Ravensthorpe

1

70

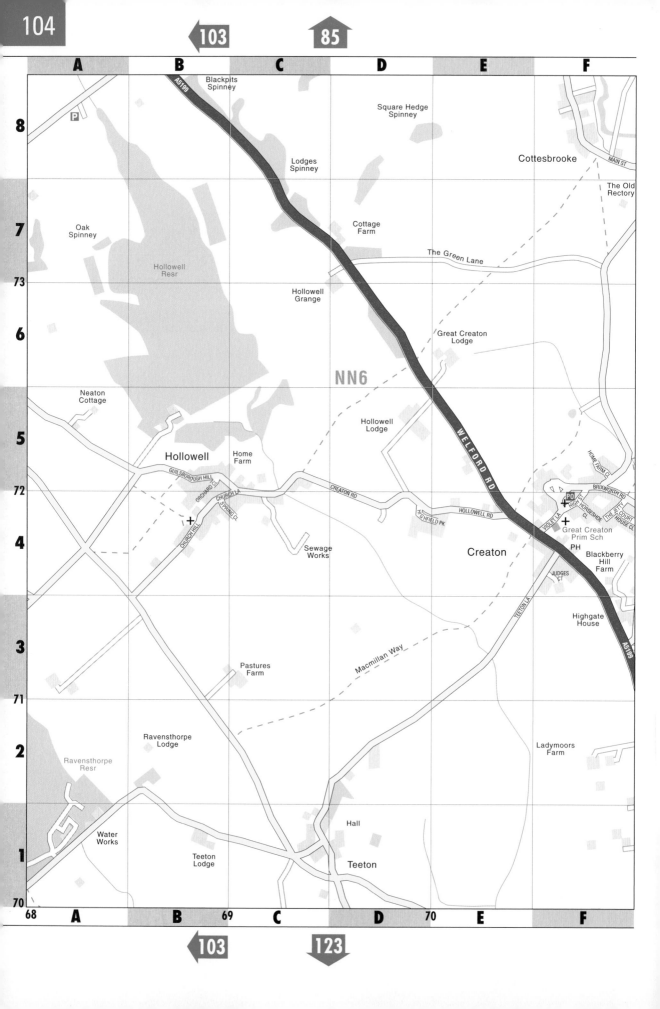

A B C D E F

8

7

73

6

5

72

4

3

71

2

1

70

Blackpits
Spinney

Square Hedge
Spinney

Cottesbrooke

The Old
Rectory

MAIN ST

Lodges
Spinney

Oak
Spinney

Cottage
Farm

The Green Lane

A5199

Hollowell
Resr

Hollowell
Grange

Great Creaton
Lodge

NN6

Neaton
Cottage

Hollowell
Lodge

WELFORD RD

HOME FARM CL

Hollowell

Home
Farm

Guilsborough Hill

Orchard Cl

Church La

Spring Cl

Creaton Rd

Hollowell Rd

BRIXWORTH RD

PO

HIGH ST

HORSESHOE
CL

THE JETTY

COURT
HOUSE CL

Church Hill

Highfield Pk

Great Creaton
Prim Sch

Violet La

Sewage
Works

Creaton

PH

Blackberry
Hill
Farm

JUDGES
CT

Teeton La

Highgate
House

A5199

Ravensthorpe
Resr

Pastures
Farm

Macmillan Way

Ravensthorpe
Lodge

Ladymoors
Farm

Water
Works

Hall

Teeton
Lodge

Teeton

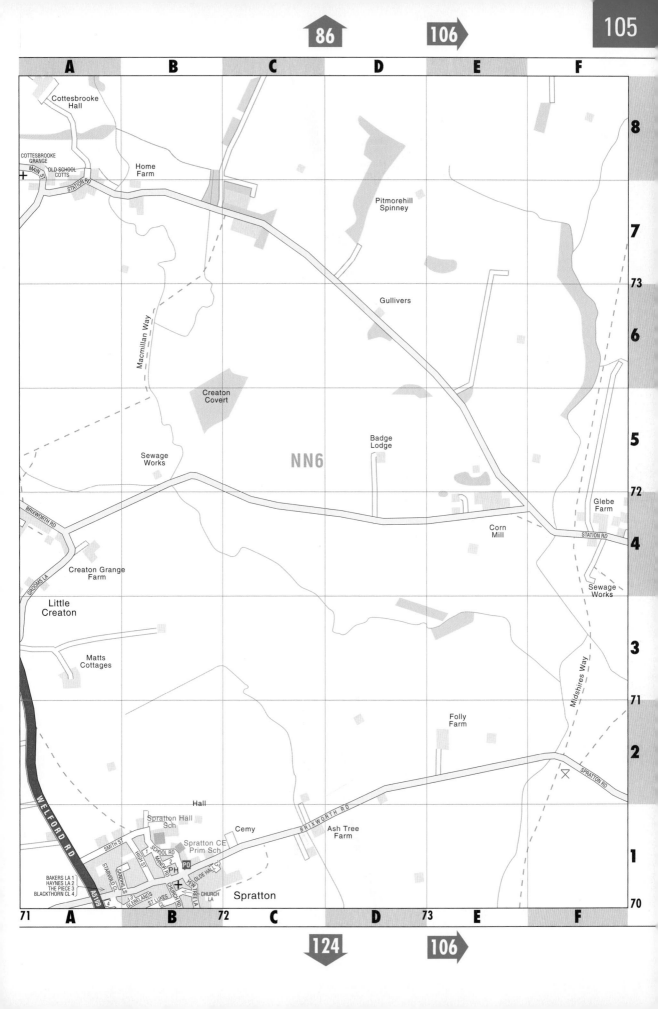

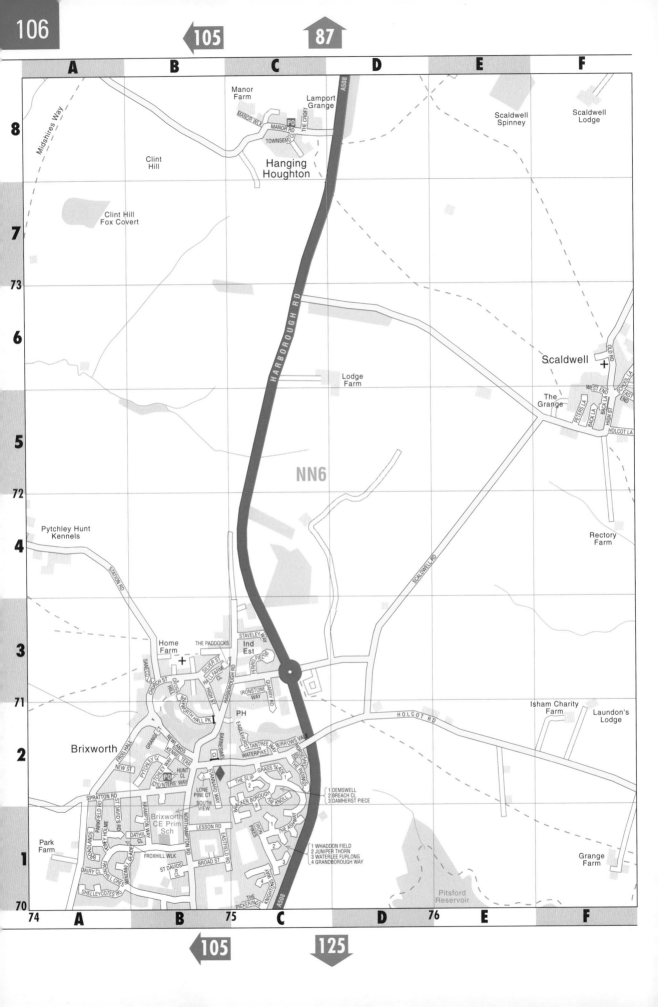

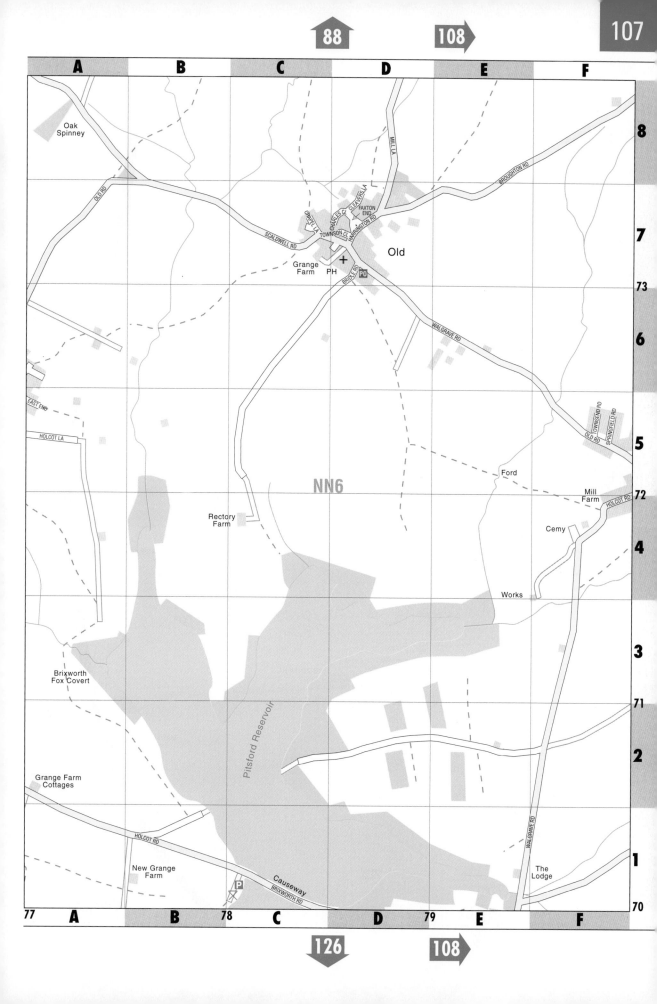

A B C D E F

8

Oak
Spinney

OLD RD

SCALDWELL RD

CHAPEL LA

CHARLES CL

TOWNSON CL

CLEAVERS LA

FAXTON
END

HARDINGTON RD

MILL LA

BROUGHTON RD

7

Grange
Farm

PH

Old

BRIDLE RD

PO

73

WALGRAVE RD

6

EAST END

HOLCOT LA

OLD RD

TOWNSEND RD

SPRINGFIELD RD

5

NN6

Ford

Mill
Farm

72

Rectory
Farm

HOLCOT RD

Cemy

4

Works

3

Brixworth
Fox Covert

71

Pitsford Reservoir

2

Grange Farm
Cottages

WALGRAVE RD

Holcot Rd

New Grange
Farm

P

Causeway

BRIXWORTH RD

The
Lodge

1

70

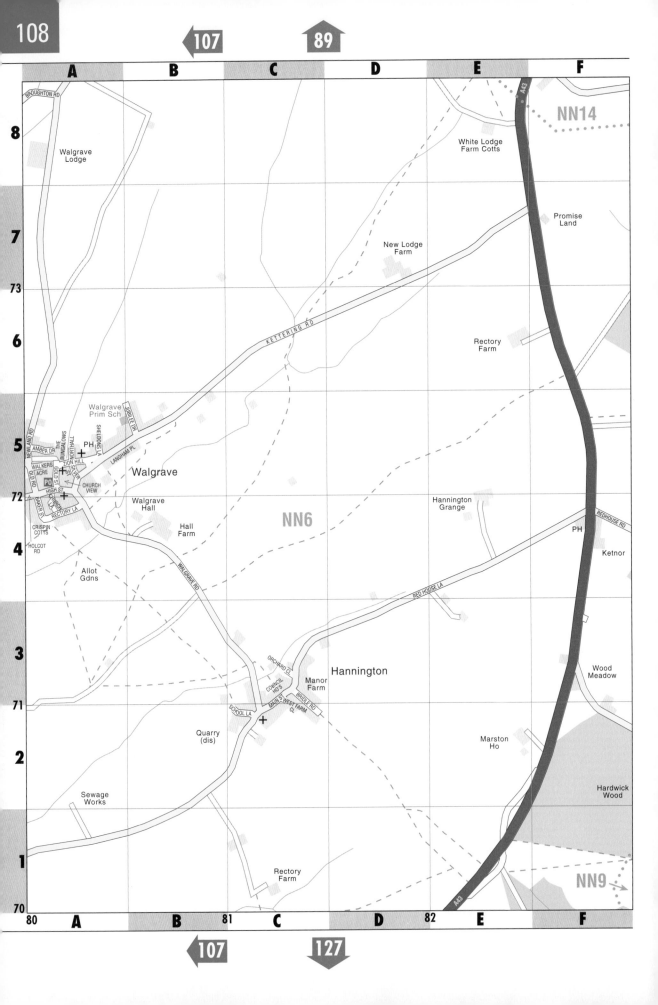

A B C D E F

8

7

73

6

5

72

4

3

71

2

1

70

80 A B 81 C D 82 E F

NN14

Promise Land

White Lodge Farm Cotts

New Lodge Farm

Rectory Farm

NN6

Hannington Grange

PH

Ketnor

Redhouse Rd

Red House La

Wood Meadow

Walgrave Lodge

Broughton Rd

Kettering Rd

Walgrave Prim Sch

Jubilee Dr

Sheldons La

Langham Pl

Walgrave

Walkers Acre

The Bungalows

Amber Dr

Northall

PH

Zion Hill

Silver St

Newland Rd

Old Rd

Church View

High St

PO

Baker St

Church La

Rectory La

Crispin Cotts

Holcot Rd

Walgrave Hall

Hall Farm

Allot Gdns

Walgrave Rd

Orchard Cl

Council Ho's

School La

Main St

West Farm Cl

Bridle Rd

Manor Farm

Hannington

Quarry (dis)

Sewage Works

Rectory Farm

Marston Ho

Hardwick Wood

NN9

A43

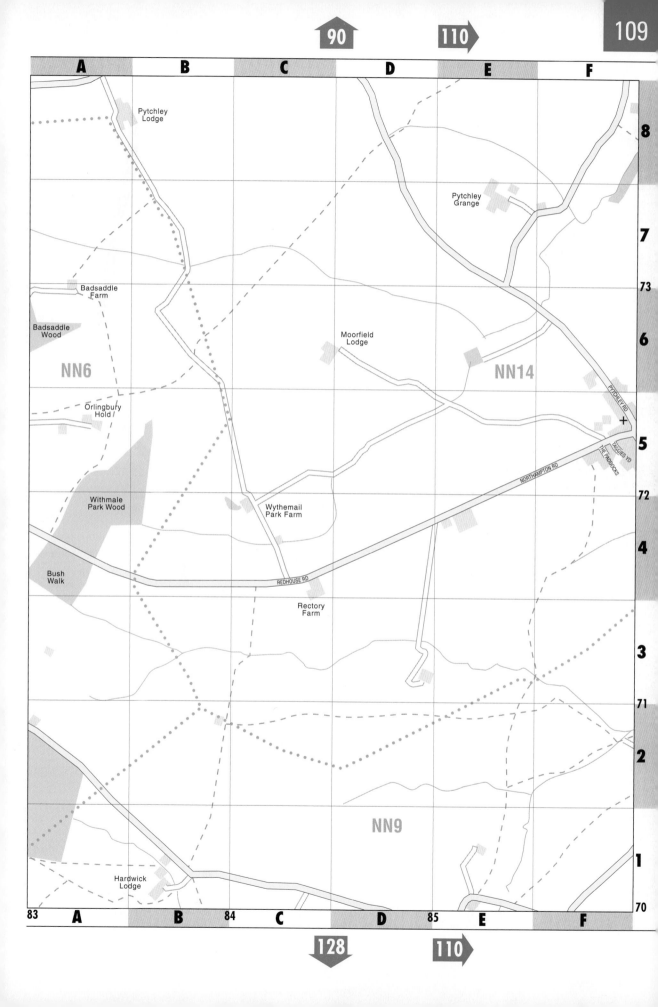

A   B   C   D   E   F

8

Pytchley
Lodge

Pytchley
Grange

7

73

Badsaddle
Farm

Badsaddle
Wood

6

Moorfield
Lodge

NN6

NN14

Orlingbury
Hold

PYTCHLEY RD

+

FAGGIES YD

5

THE PADDOCKS

NORTHAMPTON RD

Withmale
Park Wood

72

Wythemail
Park Farm

4

Bush
Walk

REDHOUSE RD

Rectory
Farm

3

71

2

NN9

1

Hardwick
Lodge

70

83   A   B   84   C   D   85   E   F

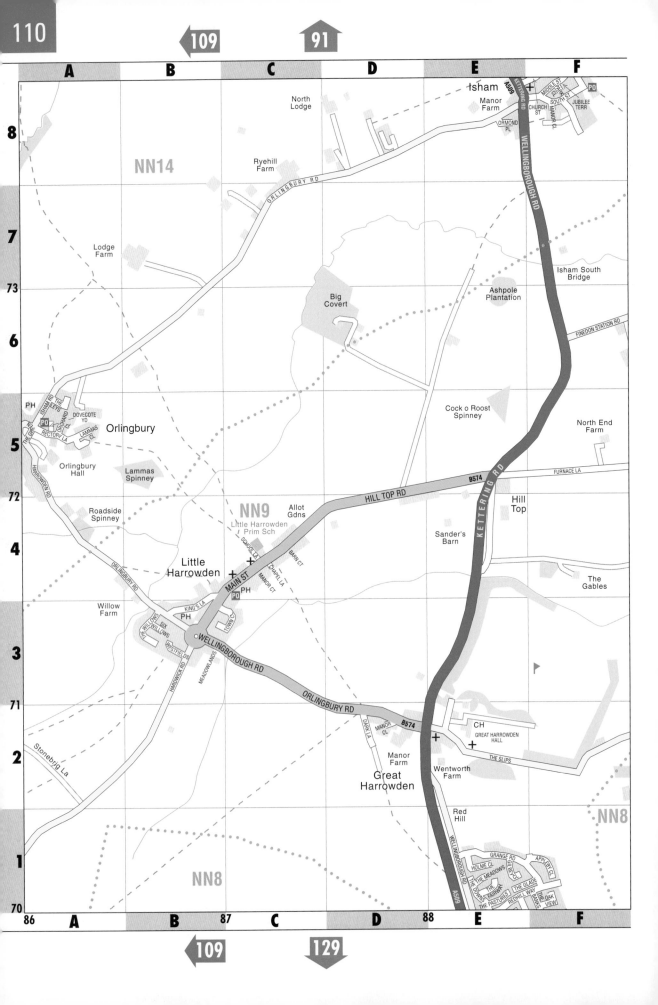

A   B   C   D   E   F

Isham

North
Lodge

Manor
Farm

MIDDLE ST

SOUTH ST

JUBILEE
TERR

CHURCH
ST

MANOR
CL

PO

ORMOND
PL

NN14

Ryehill
Farm

ORLINGBURY RD

8

A509

KETTERING RD

WELLINGBOROUGH RD

Lodge
Farm

7

Isham South
Bridge

73

Big
Covert

Ashpole
Plantation

FINEDON STATION RD

6

PH

ISHAM RD

THE
LEYS

ORCHARD
PL

DOVECOTE
YD

PO

RECTORY LA

LAMMAS
CL

Cock o Roost
Spinney

North End
Farm

Orlingbury

5

THE ELMS

HARROWDEN RD

Orlingbury
Hall

Lammas
Spinney

B574

FURNACE LA

Hill
Top

72

Roadside
Spinney

NN9

Little Harrowden
Prim Sch

Allot
Gdns

Sander's
Barn

KETTERING RD

The
Gables

4

ORLINGBURY RD

**Little
Harrowden**

SCHOOL LA

MAIN ST

CHAPEL LA

MANOR CT

BARN CT

PO PH

Willow
Farm

KING'S LA

PH

THE WILLOWS

SIX
WILLOWS

WELLINGBOROUGH RD

TOWN CL

3

HARROWICK RD

WESTFIELDS

MEADOWLANDS

ORLINGBURY RD

CH

GREAT HARROWDEN
HALL

71

B574

DARK LA

MANOR
CL

THE SLIPS

2

Stonebrig La

Manor
Farm

Wentworth
Farm

**Great
Harrowden**

Red
Hill

NN8

1

NN8

A509

WELLINGBOROUGH RD

GRANGE RD

GILBEY CL

APPLETREE CL

HOLME CL

THE MEADOWS

THE DOWNS

THE
FAIRWAY

THE GLADE

THE
OAK

REDHILL WAY

THE
BANKS

THE
VIEW

THE PASTURES

70

86   87   88

A   B   C   D   E   F

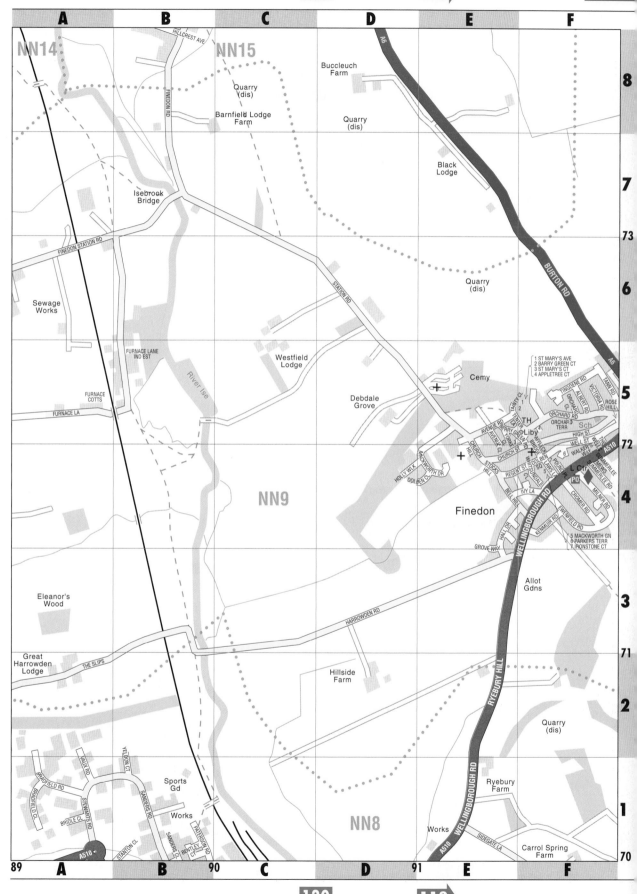

NN14

NN15

HILLCREST AVE

Quarry
(dis)

Barnfield Lodge
Farm

Buccleuch
Farm

Quarry
(dis)

Black
Lodge

FINEDON RD

Isebrook
Bridge

BURTON RD

A6

FINEDON STATION RD

STATION RD

Sewage
Works

FURNACE LANE
IND EST

Westfield
Lodge

Cemy

1 ST MARY'S AVE
2 BARRY GREEN CT
3 ST MARY'S CT
4 APPLETREE CT

FURNACE
COTTS

River Ise

Debdale
Grove

ROSE
HILL

FURNACE LA

TH
Liby

Sch

NN9

HOLLY WLK

MACKWORTH DR

DOLBEN CL

IVY LA

A510

L Ctre

PO

Finedon

5 MACKWORTH GN
& PARKERS TERR
X IRONSTONE CT

GROVE WAY

WELLINGBOROUGH RD

Allot
Gdns

Eleanor's
Wood

HARROWDEN RD

RYEBURY HILL

Great
Harrowden
Lodge

THE SLIPS

Hillside
Farm

Quarry
(dis)

BRADFIELD RD

VAUX RD

YELDON CT

SANDERS RD

Sports
Gd

NN8

Ryebury
Farm

WELLINGBOROUGH RD

BRADFIELD CL

STEWARTS RD

BRIDLE CL

STANTON CL

BENTLEY CT

SANDERS CL

PATERSON RD

Works

Works

A510

SIDEGATE LA

Carrol Spring
Farm

A510

A　B　C　D　E　F

NN14

8

Finedon
Poplars

Poplar's
Bungalow

Finedon
Lodge

Poplar
Lodge

7

THRAPSTON RD

A510

73

6

Burrows
Barn

Allot
Gdns

Bank
Farm

Finedon

MILLER'S CL
ROCKLEIGH
HYDE DR
A6 BURTON RD
ALINGTON RD
HIGH ST
EASTLANDS RD
POPLAR RD
WENTWORTH
CRES
CASTFIELD
ALLEN RD
HIGHFIELD ST
HAYDEN AVE
FREEMAN WAY
ROCK RD

NN9

Knightlands

5

A510
OBELISK RD
ROSE
HILL
MULSO RD
HAWTHORNE RD
WILLS RD
UNION ST
SIBLEY CL
CREES
OXFORD ST

72

Finedon
Mulso
CE Jun
Sch

Wr
Twr

Garrow Close
Spinney

4

Townside
Farm

IRTHLINGBOROUGH RD

Poplar Barn
Farm

By Pass
Farm

3

FINEDON RD

B5348
SCOTS
MERE

A6

B5348

LONG ACRES DR
O RD
MIDDLE
GRASS
BRISTOW RD
MOUNTROD
DRAYTON RD
PURLAND RD
DRAY
KNIGHTLANDS RD
FITZWILLIAM
B571

MEREFIELDS

FINEDON RD

Irthlingborough
Huxlow
Sch

GARROW CL
SCHARPWELL
PIPERS CL
HIGHFIELD RD
SPRING TERR
ALLEY TERR
ADDINGTON RD

71

Nevilles
Lodge

Irthlingborough
Cty Jun & Inf
Schs

NURSERY GDNS
SPENCER ST

Market
Cross
B571
LIME
KILN
Liby

IRTHLINGBOROUGH

EXCELSIOR
CT
SCARBOROUGH ST
WARREN ST

HIGH ST

B5348
STATION RD
/12
LIME ST
NENE
VIEW
THE
FLATLETS

2

MANTON RD
MUSSON CL
QUEEN ST
LEES ST
BAKER ST
JUBILEE ST
PETER'S WAY
OAK ST
SPINNEY RD
CHURCH ST
ST PETER'S WAY
MEADOW WAY
10

Cricket
Gd

Liby

Nene Way

1

NN8

WINDMILL RD
GEORGE ST
VICTORIA ST
WHITE'S RISE
CHERRY ST
CHERRY RD
JOHN PKE RD
PARK RD
MEADOW WAY
CLOUGH RD
NICHOLAS LA
NICHOLAS
LA
SHERIFF
HO

Factory

F2
1 BROOK TERR.
2 ARCHFIELD TERR
3 EASTFIELD RD
4 SPRING ST
5 CHURCH WLK
6 OAK TERR
7 THE LOUISA LILLEY HOMES
8 SPINNEY TERR
9 MEADOW WLK
10 GORSEHOLM CT
11 THE LIMES
12 LOVELL CT

COWPER CL 1
MARRIOTT CL 2

B571
WELLINGBOROUGH RD
EBBW VALE RD
ALLEN RD

70

92　A　B　93　C　D　94　E　F

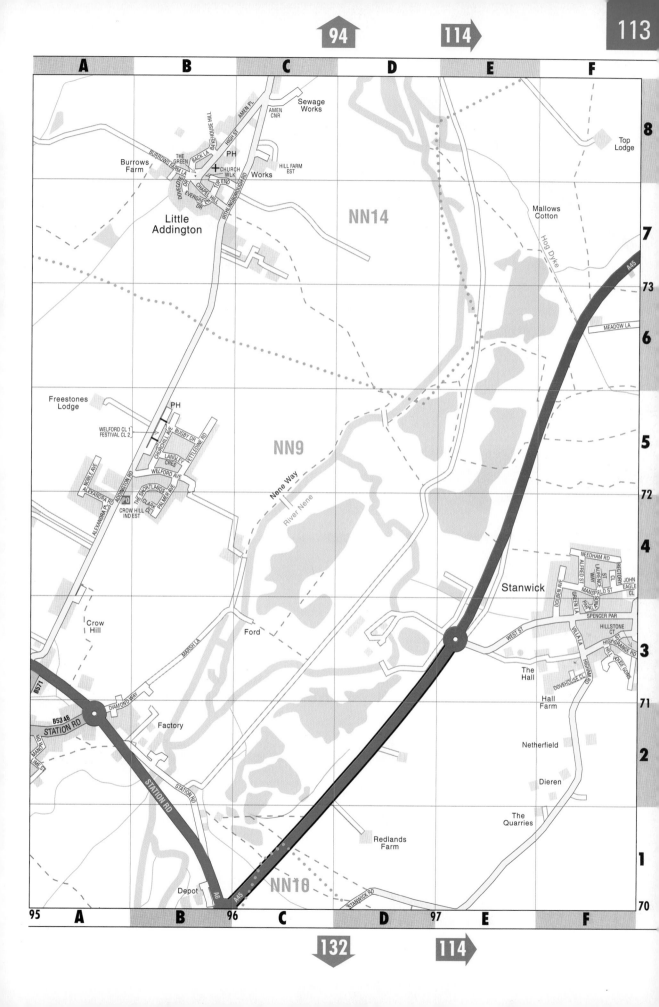

A B C D E F

8

New Barn
Farm

BRICK KILN RD

Northdale
Farm

Brooks
Farm

Scalley
Farm

Kepwick

St Crispin
Cemy
NICHOLS WAY
WHITTAM CL
WEBB RD
ELLISON CL
POPHAM CL
WINDMILL LA
CATLOW CL
WELLA RD
ORWELL CL
MALLOWS DR
NENE CL
IACINNES WAY
LUNDIE CL
DE FERNEUS DR
RUGBY WAY
EAST
LANGHAM RD
LANGHAM RD
CHURCH
VIEW
WINDMILL AVE
MILLER'S
NOTTON ROW
ENTERPRISE RD
WEBSTER RD
SPENCELLS

Ind
Est

NORTH ST

B663

MIDLAND RD

1 PENNY LA
2 BRIDGE ST
3 TITHE BARN CL
4 DOVECOTE CL
3
BIRSTEAD RISE
HERITAGE
WHEELWRIGHT
RICHARDSON WAY
WATSON CT
4
BERRI

7

YORK WAY
FAIROAKS DR
RAMSAY CL
WHITFIELD
GARDNER CL
OAKLEIGH
LEE CL
HARRIS

TWYFORD AVE
Windmill
Prim
Sch
WELBOURNE CL
THE DEVLES
MARSHALL'S RD
POPLARS RD
MILL CL

73

Scalley
Farm

MEADOW LA

LONDON RD
CARTRILL ST
WEST ST
THE SQUARE
ST PETERS
CT
WESLEY
CT
PORTS CL
MANOR ST
PARK RD
MANORHOUSE
GDNS
DERLING DR
BUTTS RD
ROMAN WAY
HOLMFIELD DR
VICEROY CL
KINGSMITH DR
MOUNT
SAXON WAY
BROAD LANDS

6

RAUNDS

P

SPINNEY ST
SHELMERDINE
RISE
BELMONT GDNS
GROMARD AVE
ASHFIELD
RISE
ASHFIELD AVE
RED ROW
DRYDEN ST
SMITHFIELD PL
MACKENZIE RD
GROVE ST
PO
GLADSTONE ST
LAWSON ST
CLARE ST
HARCOURT ST
SACKVILLE
SPENCER
ST
HOLLINGHAM RD
PRIMROSE
PARK RD
Schs

COLEMAN
ST

Manor
Farm

Sewage
Works

Hog Dyke

TITTY HO
CHERRY WLK
KESTON WAY
ORCHARD RD
CHAMBERLAIN WAY
SHEFFIELD CT
STREATHER CT
SMITH
CT
THE
FORESTERS
WARWICK PL
THORPE ST
HOLMES AVE
NORTHWOODS CL
NEW TOWN CL
PINDS WAY

WELLINGTON RD

5

SIDDLERS WAY
ANDREWS WAY
MILES CL
HARVEY
CL
MAPLETOFT
ST

Thorpe House
Farm

FRANCIS
TERR
STANWICK RD
LAWRENCE
CL
ANTONA DR
THE
PADDOCK

S WGW
CASTERTON CL
COTTINGHAM CL
COTTMAN RD

72

MANNINGHAM
LOVELL CL
WHITEWALL RD
CUMBERLAND AVE
RAUNDS RD
ANTONA
CL
WESTFIELD DR
ANTONA
GDNS
WESTFIELD AVE

NN9

Darsdale
Farm

4

Stanwick

Stanwick
Cty Prim Sch
PO
MANOR
GDNS
COURTWOOD
CHELVESTON RD

SHELTON RD

CHURCH ST
NEWBRIDGE
LA
THE AVENUE
BROOKSIDE
EAST ST
GRANGE RD
MARKS CL

3

CHELVESTON RD

Cemy

71

2

Pastures Lodge
Farm

Pastures
Cottage

New Covert

1

Pasture
Barn

B663

Stanwick
Pastures

70

98 A B 99 C D 00 E F

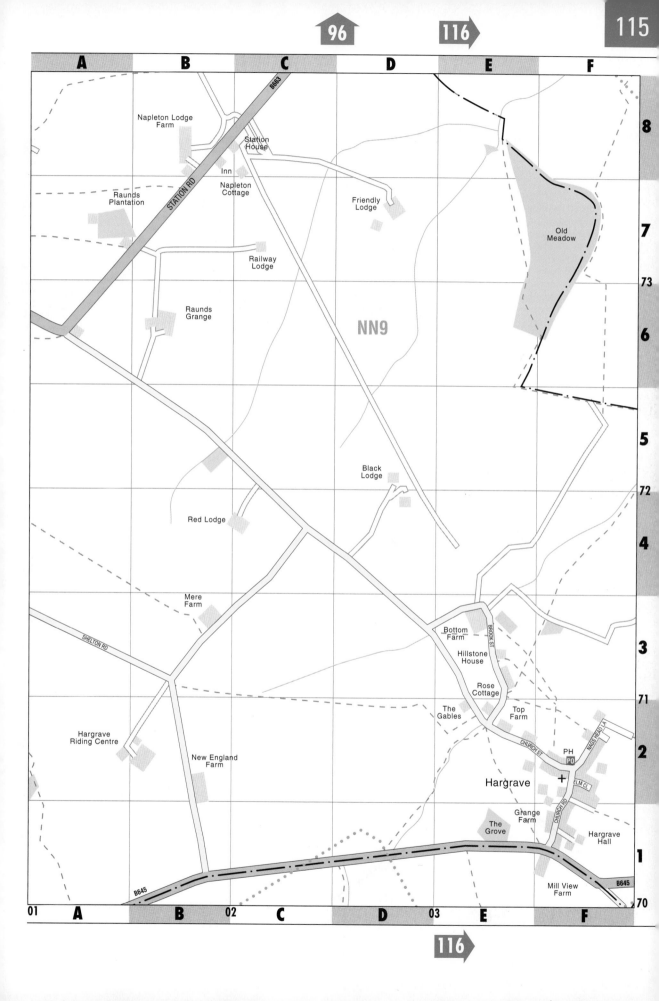

115
97

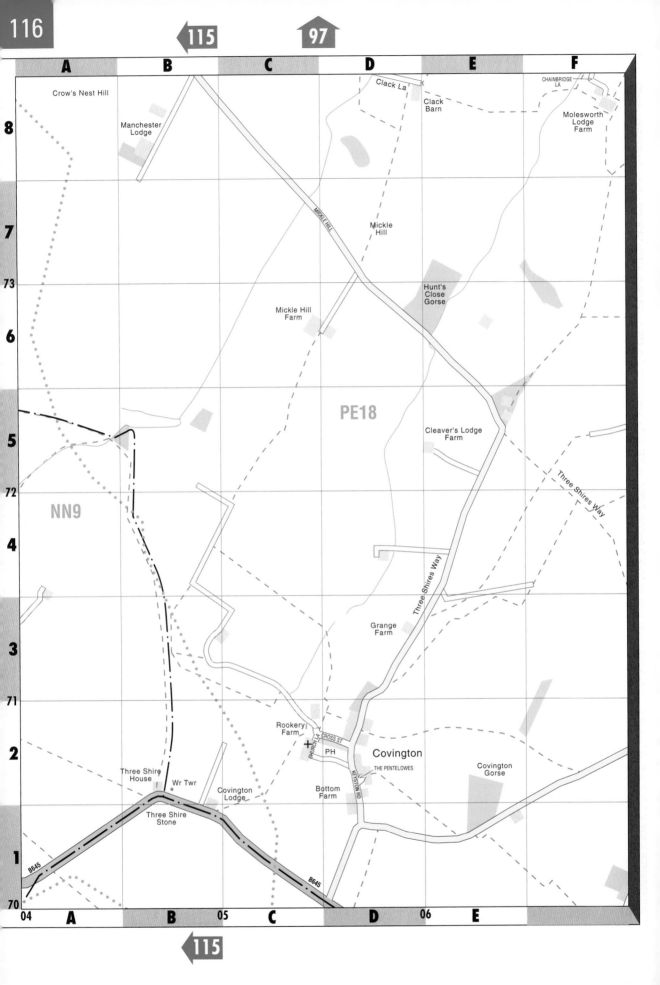

A B C D E F

8

7

73

6

5

72

4

3

71

2

1

70

Crow's Nest Hill

Manchester
Lodge

Clack La

Clack
Barn

CHAINBRIDGE
LA

Molesworth
Lodge
Farm

MICKLE HILL

Mickle
Hill

Hunt's
Close
Gorse

Mickle Hill
Farm

PE18

NN9

Cleaver's Lodge
Farm

Three Shires Way

Three Shires Way

Grange
Farm

Rookery
Farm

CROSS ST

CHURCH LA

PH

Covington

THE PENTELOWES

KEYSTON RD

Covington
Gorse

Three Shire
House

Wr Twr

Covington
Lodge

Bottom
Farm

Three Shire
Stone

B645

B645

04 A B 05 C D 06 E

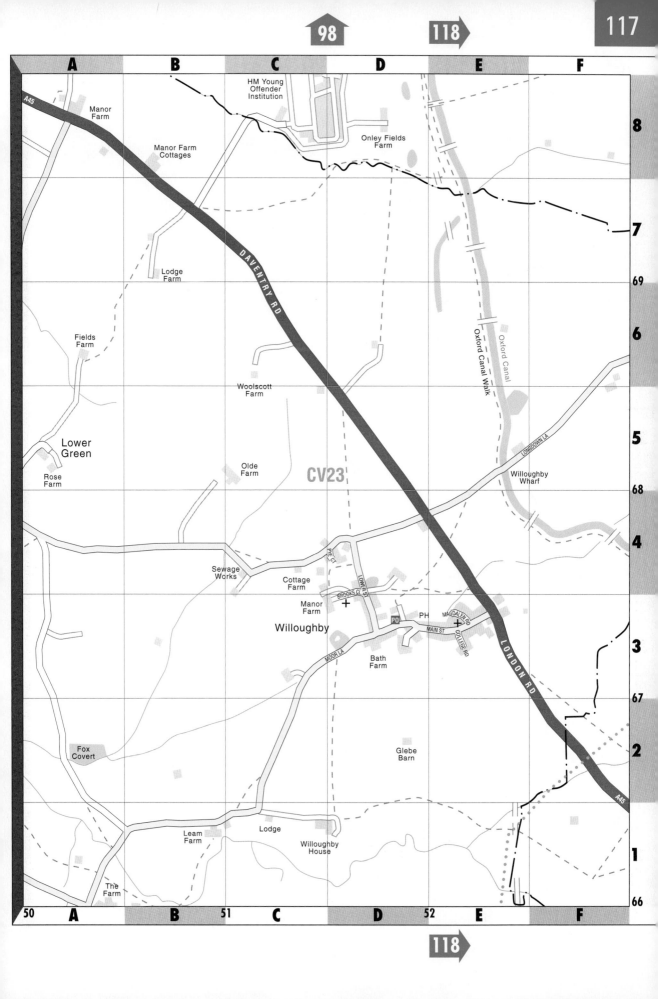

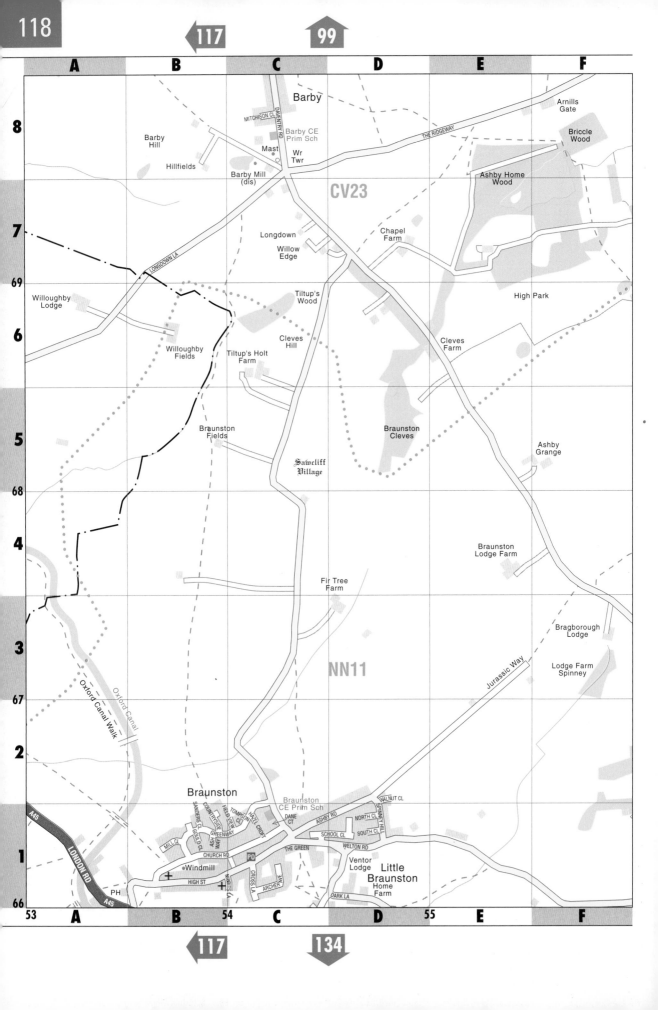

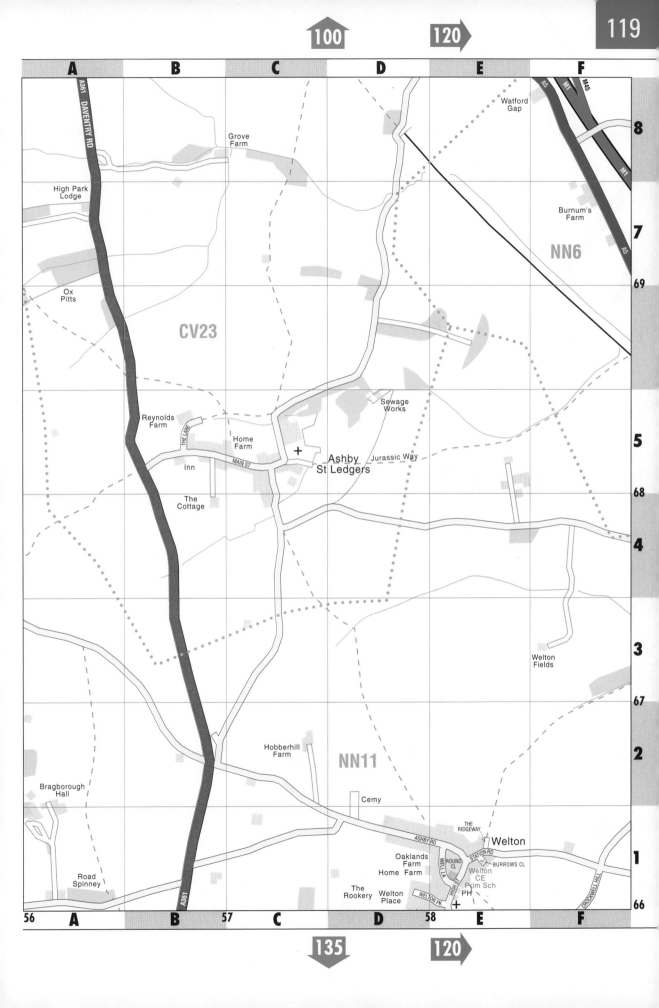

A B C D E F

8 7 69

5 68 4

3 67

2 1 66

56 57 58

DAVENTRY RD
A361

Grove Farm

High Park Lodge

Ox Pitts

CV23

Reynolds Farm

THE LANE

Home Farm

MAIN ST

Inn

The Cottage

Ashby St Ledgers

Sewage Works

Jurassic Way

Watford Gap

A5
M1
M45
M1

Burnum's Farm

NN6

A5

Welton Fields

NN11

Hobberhill Farm

Bragborough Hall

Road Spinney

A361

Cemy

ASHBY RD

THE RIDGEWAY

Welton

Oaklands Farm
Home Farm

The Rookery

Welton Place

WELTON PK

WELL LA

HIGH ST

ROUND CL

STATION RD

BURROWS CL

Welton CE Prim Sch

PH

CROCKWELL HILL

119
101

A B C D E F

8

7

69

6

5

68

4

3

67

2

1

66

M1
A5
WATFORD RD

KILSBY RD

Long Spinney

Barleypiece Spinney

Watford Lodge Farm

WEST HADDON RD

Cemy

Park House

Bluebell Spinney

Jurassic Way

WOODLANDS CT
CHURCH ST
MAIN ST

HENLEY CT

PARK LA
PARK CL
PO

Watford

Marina
Watford Locks

Grand Union Canal

Sewage Works

STATION RD

Watford Lodge

LONG BUCKBY RD

PH

Foxholes

Watford Gap Service Area

B5385

Mast

Murcott

B5385

Brockhill Lodge

Langborough Barn

Welton Lodge Farm

Mill House

Sewage Works

Welton Grange

Ryehill Lodge

White Barn Farm

Welton Hythe Marina

A5

M1

Greenhill Farm

59 A B 60 C D 61 E F

119
136

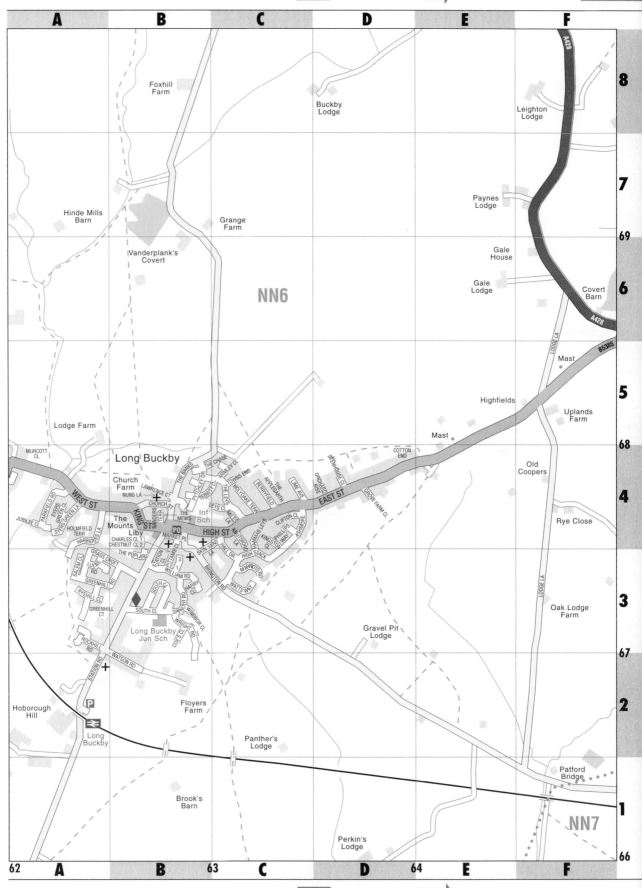

| | A | B | C | D | E | F | |

8 Foxhill Farm · Buckby Lodge · Leighton Lodge

7 Hinde Mills Barn · Grange Farm · Paynes Lodge · **69**

6 Vanderplank's Covert · NN6 · Gale House · Gale Lodge · Covert Barn · A428 · B5385

5 Lodge Farm · Mast · Highfields · Mast · Uplands Farm · **68**

4 MURCOTT CL · Long Buckby · THE CHASE · AINLEY CL · TOWNS END · PYTCHLEY DR · THE LEYS · BERRYFIELD · THE APPLEGARTH · LIME AVE · SPINNHOUSE CL · COTTON END · ORCHARD RISE · EAST ST · GROVE FARM CL · Old Coopers · LODGE LA
Church Farm · WEST ST · LAWRENCE CT · CHURCH ST · NUNS LA · KING ST · SANDERS · THE MEWS · Inf Sch · MILTON AVE · CLIFTON CL · PHILLIPS WAY · ASHMORE · Rye Close
JUBILEE CL · PARKFIELD RD · SYERS GREEN CL · HOLMFIELD TERR · The Mounts · Liby · CHARLES CL 1 · CHESTNUT CL 2 · MARKET PL · PO · HIGH ST · HAMMAS LEYS · KINGSTON CL · HIGH STACK

3 SALEM CL · GRASS CROFT · LUCY RD · GREENHILL · RYEHILL CL · GREENHILL CT · THE POPLARS · SOUTH CL · SOUTH CL · STATION RD · WILLIAMS CL · WILLIAM RD · WINDSOR CL · WRIGHT RD · COX'S CL · HARRY CL · BRINGTON RD · WATTS WAY · MARRIOTS RD · Gravel Pit Lodge · Oak Lodge Farm · LODGE LA

67 ROCKHILL RD · Long Buckby Jun Sch · WATSON RD

2 Hoborough Hill · P · Long Buckby · STATION RD · Floyers Farm · Panther's Lodge · Patford Bridge

1 Brook's Barn · NN7

Perkin's Lodge

| 62 | A | 63 | B | C | 63 | D | 64 | E | F | 66 |

A B C D E F

8

7

69

NN6

6

Steepleton
Lodge

Buckby Folly
Covert

Covert
Farm

A428

B5385

PH

Millhouse

Buckby Folly

5

Home
Farm

Brickhill
Spinney

Grovelands
Farm

TILBURY RD

TILBURY RISE

NORTHFIELD
GN
PRIESTWELL
CT

HADDON
CT

ORCHARD CL

HALL GDNS

RAVENSTHORPE RD

BARN ACRE

WHARAGE LA

East
Haddon
Prim Sch

The Dairy
Farm

CHURCH LA

PO

MAIN ST

ST ANDREW'S RD

CLIFDEN
TERR

Sewage
Works

Washbrook
Bridge

Oak
Spinney

East Haddon

Hall

LODGE
FLATS

PH

Fry's
Farm

HOLDENBY RD

Sewage
Works

Vicarage
Farm

Ryehills
Farm

68

4

Home Farm

Tire Hill
Farm

Tire Hill
Spinney

Rowell Leyes

67

3

Garretts Barn

East Haddon
Grange

2

Willow
Cottage

East Haddon
Hill

A428

The Gables

Wks

1

NN7

NN7

Althorp
Meer

Langlands
Plantation

66

65 A B 66 C D 67 E F

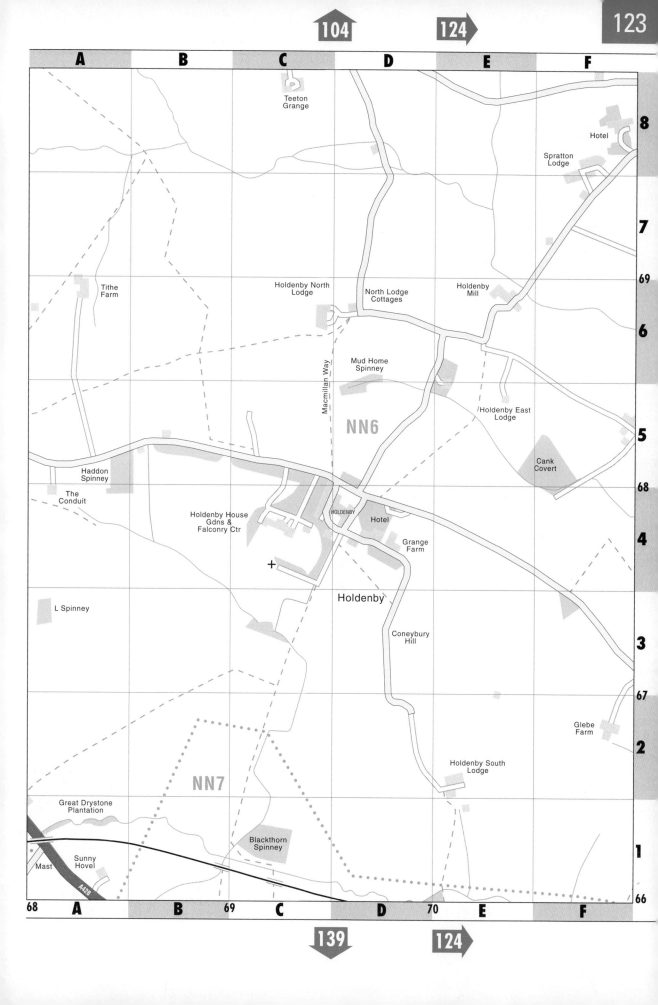

123
105

A B C D E F

8

7

Spratton Grange
Farm

Spratton
Grange

Spratton
Lodge

69

Long
Spinney

6

Cank
Farm

NN6

Midshires Way

5

Spratton
Bridge

WELFORD RD

Merry Tom
Crossing

68

Circular
Spinney

Circular
Spinney

P

4

Sander's
Covert

Hoe
Hill

MERRY TOM LA

Pitsford Lodge
Farm

Damsel's
Barn

3

Sedgebrook
Home Farm

Spinney
Farm

67

Sedgebrook
Hall

Brampton
Hill

The
Red House

2

Brampton
Hill Farm

PH

P

BRAMPTON LA

Chapel
Brampton

Humphrey
Farm

HAMILTON OT

CEDAR LA

BACK LA

Northampton & Lamport Rly

PO

Pitsford Rd

NORTHAMPTON RD

PH

1

Church
Farm

HALFWAY
THORN

HARLESTONE RD

The Bramptons
Prim Sch

A5199

66

STABLES LA

71 A B 72 C D 73 E F

123
140

A   B   C   D   E   F

STONELL WAY
FAR BROOK
POPLEY'S
SALT PIKES
HIGH SLADE
KNIGHTONS WAY
THE ASHWAY 1
WHEATENS CL 2
A508

South Lodge

Brixworth Country Park

Visitor Ctr

NORTHAMPTON RD

Pitsford Hill

Northampton Sailing Club

Pitsford Reservoir

Moulton Grange Cottages

NN6

Hill Farm

Moulton Grange

Mon

P   GRANGE LA

RESERVOIR HOS

Springhill Farm

THE DOVECOTE

CHURCH LA

ORCHARD COTTS

GLEBE LA

Pitsford

Pitsford Prim Sch

MANOR RD   BROADLANDS

THE CHASE

DRUMMOND CL

The Dairy Farm

THE SQUARE

HIGH ST

Longman's Hill   PO

PH

Northamptonshire Grammar Sch

STABLE CT

Sedgebrook Grange

BRAMPTON LA

Hillcrest

Home Farm

Mast

MOULTON RD

Stud Farm

Duke's Clump

Fox Covert Hall

PITSFORD RD

NN3

Grotto Spinney

NN2

Sedgebrook Lodge Farm

Bunkers Hill Farm

SPECTACLE LA

Butcher's Spinney

Ford

Brickhill Spinney

Boughton Park

BUTCHER'S LA

Moulton Mill

PH

SPRING CL

8   7   69   6   5   68   4   3   67   2   1   66

74   A   B   75   C   D   76   E   F

125
107

A **B** **C** **D** **E** **F**

Lower Brixworth
Lodge

8

Pitsford Reservoir

NN6

BRIXWORTH RD

RECTORY LA

WALGRAVE RD

MAIN ST

POPLARS LA

PO

PH

Manor
Farm

GLEBE CL

FARM CL

BACK LA

Holcot

SUNNY
BANK

SWELL RD

The
Hawthorns

Equestrian
Ctr

North
Fields

7

Moulton Grange
Farm

69

Hillcrest

MOULTON RD

Moulton Lodge
Farm

Tithe
Farm

6

South
Lodge

North
Farm

5

Overstone
Old Rectory

68

HOLCOT RD

Slade
Farm

Grange
Cottages

Overstone
Grange

4

Moulton
Lodge

BOUGHTON FAIR LA

NN3

A43

KETTERING RD

3

Hog Hole
Spinney

Marsh
Spinney

67

PITSFORD RD

Home
Farm

Cemy

2

Moulton

THE GROVE

CHURCH VIEW

GROVE LA

Grove
Farm

Sandy Hill
Farm

PARK VIEW

NN6

Overstone
Farm

THE HOLLIES

Sewage
Works

STEWART CL

THE LAURELS

Moulton
Coll

Moulton
Prim Sch

SCHOOL LA

WEST ST

CHURCH HILL

HILL ST

PARADE

THE BANK

HIGH ST

AL GORE CL

PYTCHLEY VIEW

HOMESTEAD CL

THE CRESCENT

SIDDONS WAY

TARRANT CL

TARRANT WAY

OVERSTONE RD

SANDY HILL

PARK VIEW

Overstone
Farm

1

ARNSBY CRES

JESSE CT

ETHON CL

HONEYSTONES

CROSS ST

BOND LA

PH

PO

DOVE ST LA

OAKLEY DR

PRINCE OF WALES ROW

ASHLEY LA

WANTAGE CL

VIEW CL

A43

PARK VIEW

OVERSTONE LA

SYWELL RD

BOUGHTON RD

CAREY CL

CAREY CT

POUND
CT

Moulton
Sch

BARLOW LA

NORTHAMPTON LA

LUNCHFIELD GDNS

LUNCHFIELD LA

ASHBY CT

Liby

1 LUNCHFIELD WLK
2 THE NURSERIES
3 ASHBY GDNS
4 WELLS CT
5 CHAPPELL HO

Libry

THE AVENUE

BILLING LA

66

77 **A** **B** 78 **C** **D** 79 **E** **F**

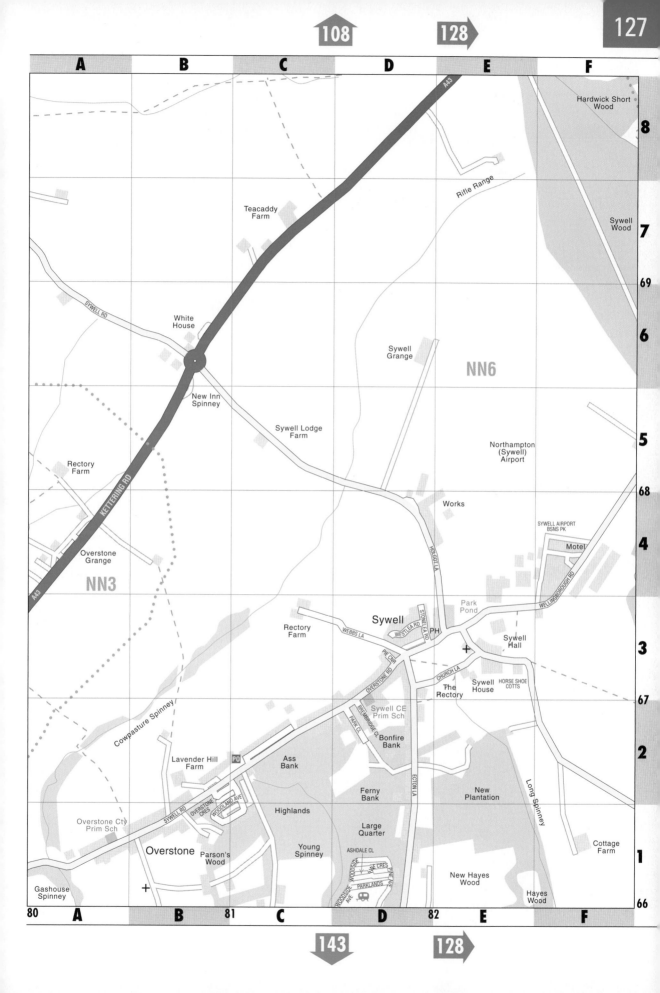

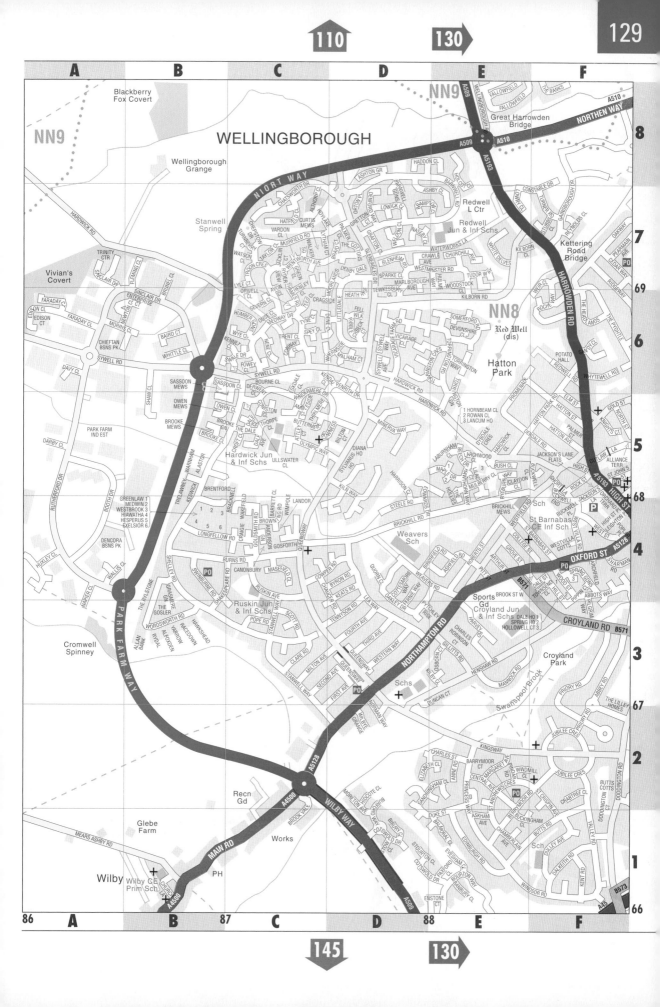

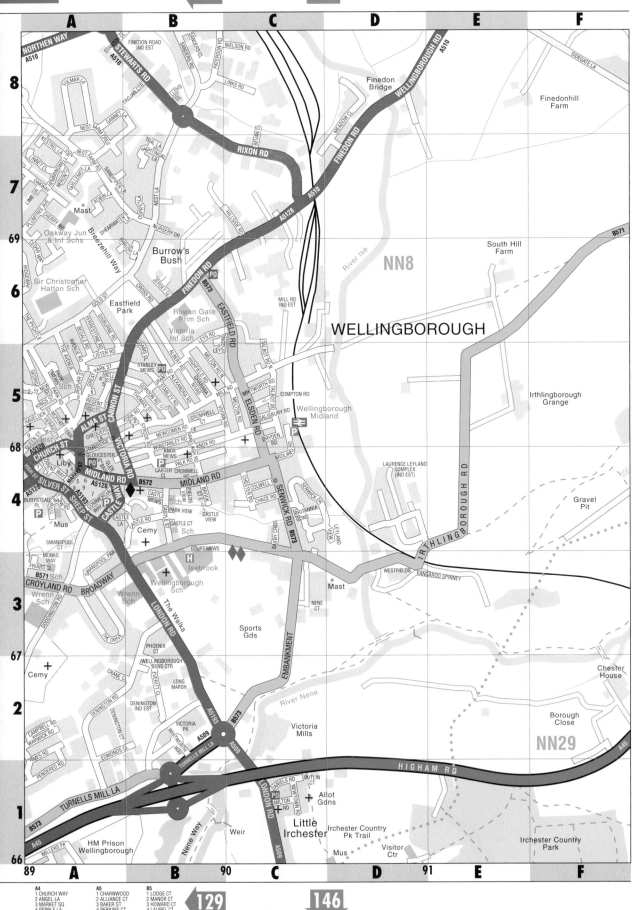

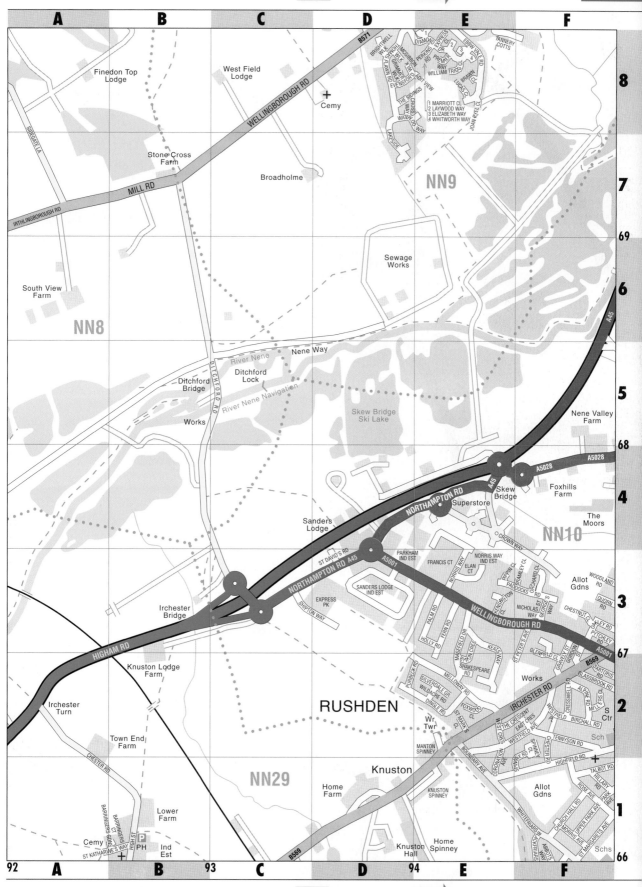

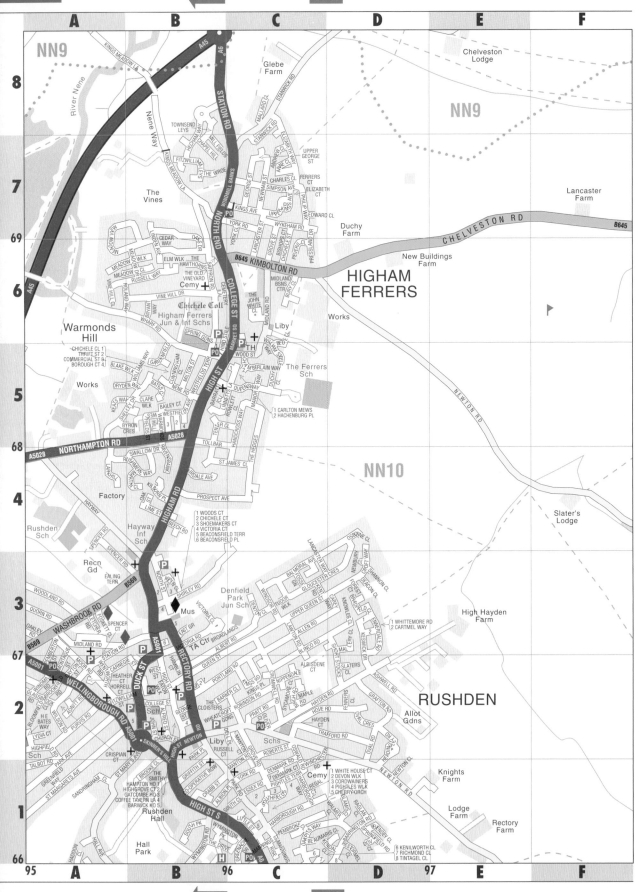

NN9

River Nene

Nene Way

KINGS MEADOW LA

A45

A6

STATION RD

Glebe Farm

Chelveston Lodge

NN9

TOWNSEND LEYS

The Vines

Warmonds Hill

CHICHELE CL 1
THRIFT ST 2
COMMERCIAL ST 3
BOROUGH CT 4

Works

NORTH END

COLLEGE ST

Cemy

Chichele Coll

Higham Ferrers Jun & Inf Schs

B645 KIMBOLTON RD

Duchy Farm

New Buildings Farm

HIGHAM FERRERS

Lancaster Farm

CHELVESTON RD

B645

THE JOHN WHITE CL

Works

Liby

TH

The Ferrers Sch

NEWTON RD

MIDLAND BSNS CTR

HIGH ST

1 CARLTON MEWS
2 HACHENBURG PL

A5028 NORTHAMPTON RD

A5028

Tollbar

ST JAMES CL

NN10

Slater's Lodge

Rushden Sch

Factory

HAYWAY

Hayway Inf Sch

HIGHAM RD

1 WOODS CT
2 CHICHELE CT
3 SHOEMAKERS CT
4 VICTORIA CT
5 BEACONSFIELD TERR
6 BEACONSFIELD PL

Recn Gd

EALING TERR

B569

SPENCER RD

P

Denfield Park Jun Sch

High Hayden Farm

1 WHITTEMORE RD
2 CARTMEL WAY

WOODLAND RD

QUORN RD

OAKLEY RD

WASHBROOK RD

B569

A5001

MIDLAND RD

RECTORY RD

Mus

SHIRLEY RD

VICTORIA CL

1 CARLTON MEWS

RUSHDEN

B569

A5001

WELLINGBOROUGH RD

DUCK ST

SKINNER'S HILL

HIGH ST

NEWTON

Liby

The Cloisters

PO

Schs

Allot Gdns

NEWTON RD

1 WHITE HOUSE CT
2 DEVON WLK
3 CORDWAINERS
4 PIGHTLES WLK
5 CHERRY ORCH

Knights Farm

Crispian CT

THE SMITHY

1 HAMPTON HO
2 HIGHGROVE CT
3 GATCOMBE HO
4 COFFEE TAVERN LA
5 BARWICK HO

HIGH ST S

Cemy

Lodge Farm

Rectory Farm

Rushden Hall

Hall Park

A6

HIGH ST S

6 KENILWORTH CL
7 RICHMOND CL
8 TINTAGEL CL

H

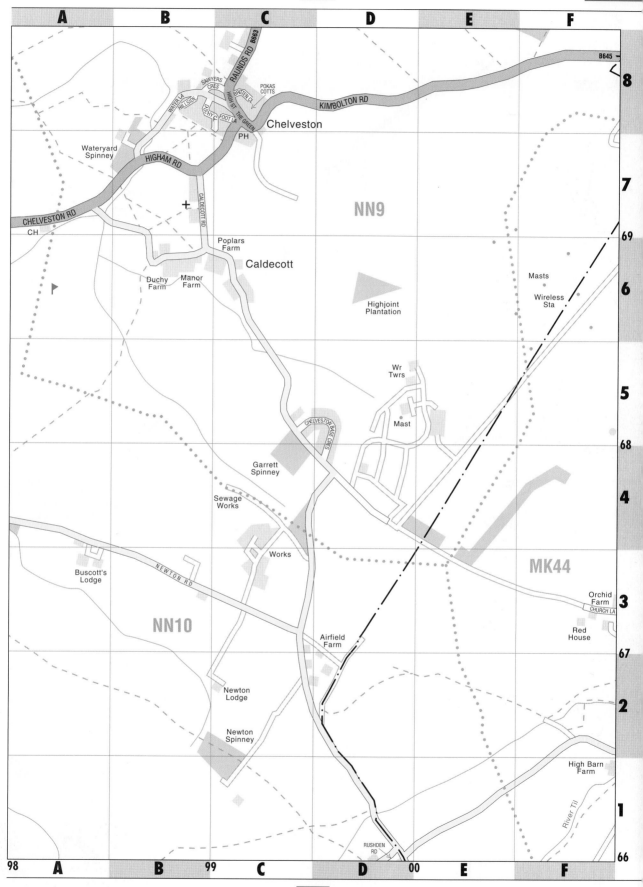

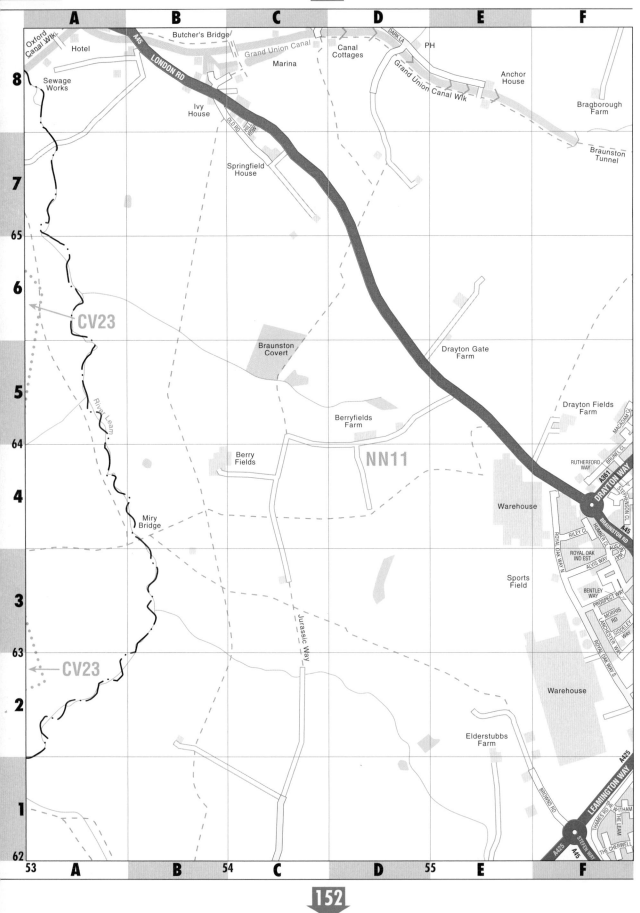

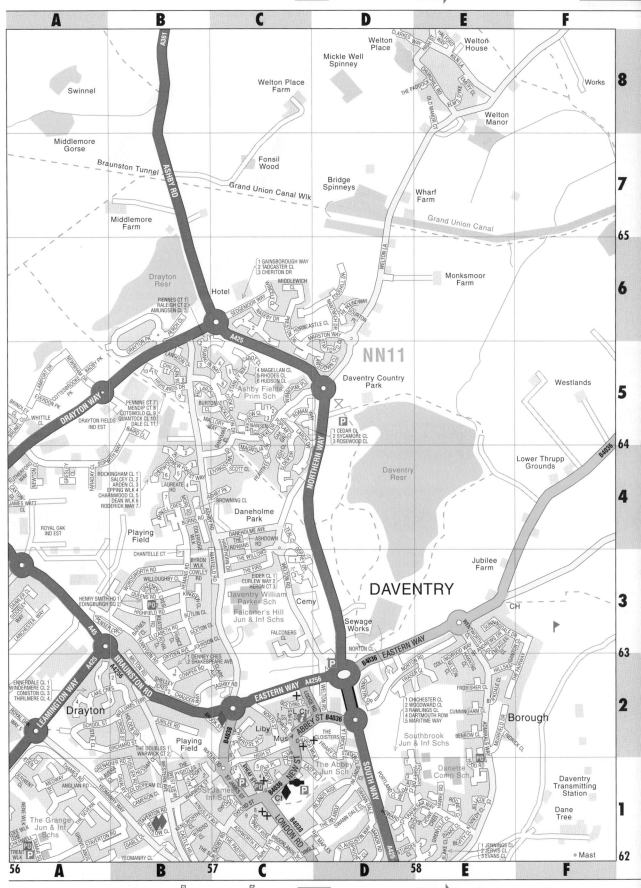

A B C D E F

8 Swinnel
Middlemore Gorse
Braunston Tunnel
Middlemore Farm
Welton Place Farm
Mickle Well Spinney
Fonsil Wood
Bridge Spinneys
Welton Place
Clarkes
The Paddock
Churchill Rd
Old Manor Rd
Kiln La
Welton House
Welton Manor
Works

7 Grand Union Canal Wlk
Grand Union Canal
Welton La
Wharf Farm
65

6 Drayton Resr
Hotel
1 GAINSBOROUGH WAY
2 TADCASTER CL
3 CHERITON DR
MIDDLEWICH CL
Evenhall Dr
Nanwich Dr
The Bourton
Pl
Monksmoor Farm
NN11

5 FIENNES CT 1
RALEIGH CT 2
AMUNDSEN CL 3
DRAYTON PK
A425
PEROH CL
SEDGEMOOR WAY
NASEBY DR
PRESTON DR
1 4 MAGELLAN CL
2 5 RHODES CL
3 6 HUDSON CL
TORNCASTLE CL
MARSTON WAY
STAFFORD CL
Daventry Country Park
Westlands
64 DRAYTON WAY
NEWNHAM RD
BAGBY PK
DRAYTON FIELDS IND EST
PENNINE CT 7
MENDIP CT 8
COTSWOLD CL 9
QUANTOCK CL 10
DALE CL 11
BAIRD CL
LANGTON CL
CHILTN
HIGHLANDS DR
FRANK II WAY
CABOT CL
STANLEY WAY
Ashby Fields Prim Sch
WIMBORNE PL
ROMAN WAY
BURTON
ERICSSON CL
NANSEN CL
OAK PK
LABOT CL
1 CEDAR CL
2 SYCAMORE CL
3 ROSEWOOD CL
Daventry Resr
Lower Thrupp Grounds
B4036

4 RUTHERFORD WAY
NEWTON CL
CAXTON CL
JAMES WATT CL
GRESLEY
FARADAY CL
SOPWITH WAY
ROCKINGHAM CL 1
SALCEY CL 2
ARDEN CL 3
EPPING WLK 4
CHARNWOOD CL 5
DEAN WLK 6
RODERICK WAY 7
SHERWOOD DR
NEW FOREST WAY
LAUREATE HO
MORE RD
ASHBY PK
LIVINGS
SCOTT CL
MAGNOLIA CL
ASH CL
ELDER CL
PEARTREE CL
NORTHERN WAY
Jubilee Farm

3 ROYAL OAK IND EST
Playing Field
CHANTELLE CT
BURNS RD
ADWELL CRES
COLERIDGE WLK
MAYFIELD RD
HAWTHORN DR
Daneholme Park
DANEHOLME AVE
THE ROWANS
ASHDOWN RD
THE WILLOWS
THE FIRS
EIDER CL
CURLEW WAY 2
HERON CT 3
WELTON RD
TEAL CL
DSPEY RD
DAMIER CL
SIDDELEY WAY
LANCHESTER WAY
BYRON WLK
WORDSWORTH RD
WILLOUGHBY CL
GREENWAY
KINGSWAY
COWLEY RD
Daventry William Parker Sch
Falconer's Hill Jun & Inf Schs
FALCONERS
Cemy
DAVENTRY
CH

63 A45
A425
A4256
JANSER CL
HENRY SMITH HO 1
EDINBURGH SQ 2
QUEENS RD
HIGHFIELD RD
BARNES CL
KEATS
ELIZABETH RD
FESTIVAL
PRINCE CL
SEXTON CL
JOHNSON CL
BUTLIN CL
PO
1 DENNEY CRES
2 SHAKESPEARE AVE
NORTON CL
Sewage Works
B4036
EASTERN WAY
NORTON RD
WENTWORTH WAY
ST ANDREWS DR
COLLINGWOOD WAY
HARTINGS
NELSON
ANGLESS
SUNNINGDALE DR
HILLSIDE
THE FAIRWAY
Borough

2 ENNERDALE CL 1
WINDERMERE CL 2
CONISTON CL 3
THIRLMERE CL 4
A4256
BRAUNSTON RD
LEAMINGTON WAY
LAKE CRES
SHELLEY CL
COWPER RD
CHAUCER
MILTON RD
TENNYSON RD
DRYDEN AVE
SPENCER CRES
ASHBY RD
Drayton
WILLIAMS TERR
SCHOOL ST
STILE CL
ORCHARD ST
JUBILEE RD
THE DOUBLES
WARWICK CT 2
Playing Field
B4038
BROOK VLW
ROSE HY
GOLDING CL
WATERLOO
CHAPEL
NORTH ST
L Ctr
Libr
Mus
NEW ST
ABBEY ST
B4036
The Cloisters
VICAR LA
STATION
1 CHICHESTER CL
2 WOODWARD CL
3 RAWLINGS CL
4 DARTMOUTH ROW
5 MARITIME WAY
FRASER CL
FROBISHER CL
CUNNINGHAM CL
BENBOW CT
ADMIRALS WAY
Southbrook Jun & Inf Schs
PO
LINDRICK CL
MAURFIELD DR
63

1 DAIMLER CL
ROYAL OAK WAY S
NENE WLK
DEE WLK
CHERWELL WLK
TRENT WLK
PO
The Grange Jun & Inf Schs
DERWENT CL
MEDWAY CL
ANGLIAN RD
THAMES RD
SEVERN CL
GROVELANDS
STAVERTON RD
GABLE CL
YEOMANRY CL
GRENADIER RD
FUSILIER RD
CAVALRY RD
COLDSTREAM WAY
WESTERN AVE
CAMERON CL
KENILWORTH DR
KINGSLEY AVE
WINDSOR
ASHWORTH DR
CASTLE HILL
WARWICK RD
THE CROFT
THE PYGHTLES
St James Inf Sch
OXFORD ST
WHEAT ST
B4038
LONDON RD
GREY RISE
ABBEY RISE
BRANDS RISE
BROOKLANDS
THE MAPLES
SWANN DALE
ST AUGUSTIN WAY
THE SLADE
THE THIMBLE
MANOR RD
PORTLAND
HOWARD
TRAFALGAR WAY
HAWKE RD
RODNEY
GRENVILLE
BLAKE CL
DRAKE CL
BEATTY CL
KENNEDY CL
JELL
COE CL
Danetre Comp Sch
PO
ROOD RD
Daventry Transmitting Station
Dane Tree
1 JENNINGS CL
2 JERVIS CL
3 EVANS CL
Mast
62

56 A 57 B C 58 D E F

C1
1 TAVERN LA
2 ST JAMES CL
3 NEWLANDS
4 FOUNDRY WLK
5 FOUNDRY CT
6 JOSEPH PRIESTLY CT
7 BOWEN SQ
8 CHARLES TERR
9 THE LIMES

C2
1 RIDLEY CT
2 WARDENS LODGE
3 BISHOPS CT
4 THE ALBANY
5 BRAMLEY HO
6 CRABTREE HO
7 BROOK ST

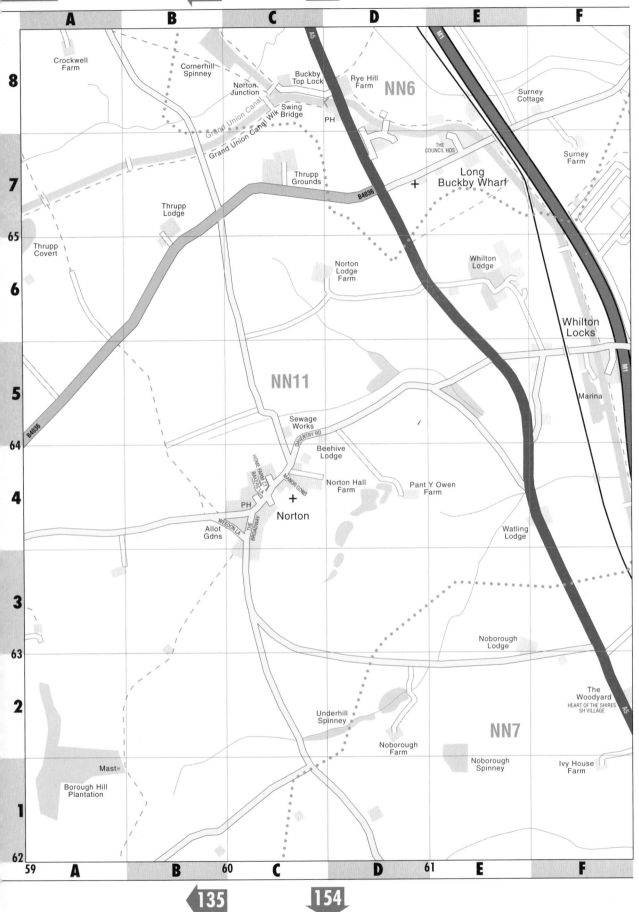

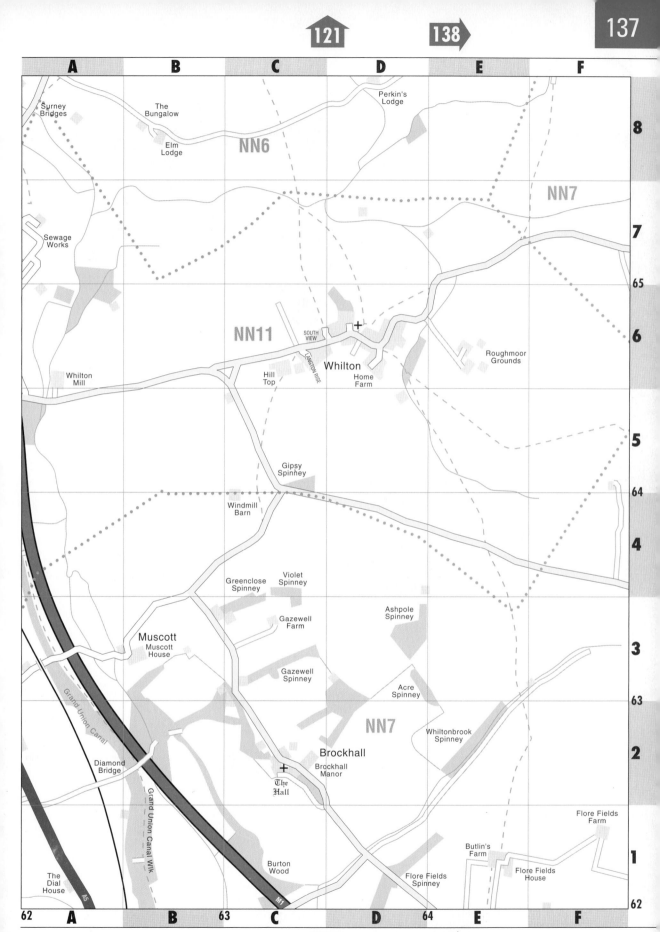

A B C D E F

Surney
Bridges

The
Bungalow

Perkin's
Lodge

Elm
Lodge

NN6

NN7

Sewage
Works

NN11

SOUTH
VIEW

Whilton

Roughmoor
Grounds

LANGTON RISE

Whilton
Mill

Hill
Top

Home
Farm

Gipsy
Spinney

Windmill
Barn

Greenclose
Spinney

Violet
Spinney

Ashpole
Spinney

Gazewell
Farm

Muscott

Muscott
House

Gazewell
Spinney

Acre
Spinney

NN7

Whiltonbrook
Spinney

Grand Union Canal

Brockhall

Brockhall
Manor

Diamond
Bridge

Grand Union Canal Wlk

The
Hall

Flore Fields
Farm

Butlin's
Farm

Flore Fields
House

The
Dial
House

A5

M1

Burton
Wood

Flore Fields
Spinney

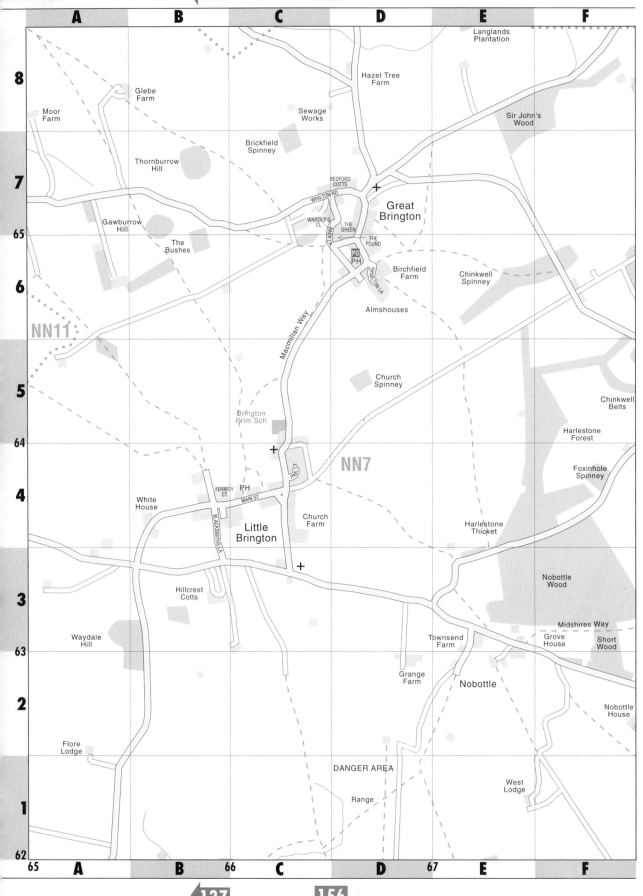

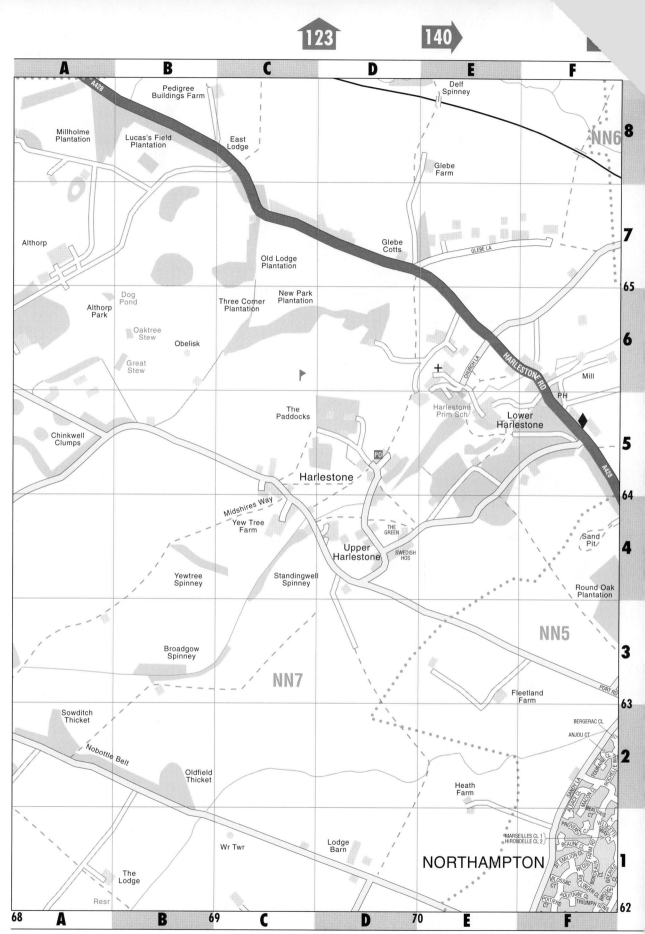

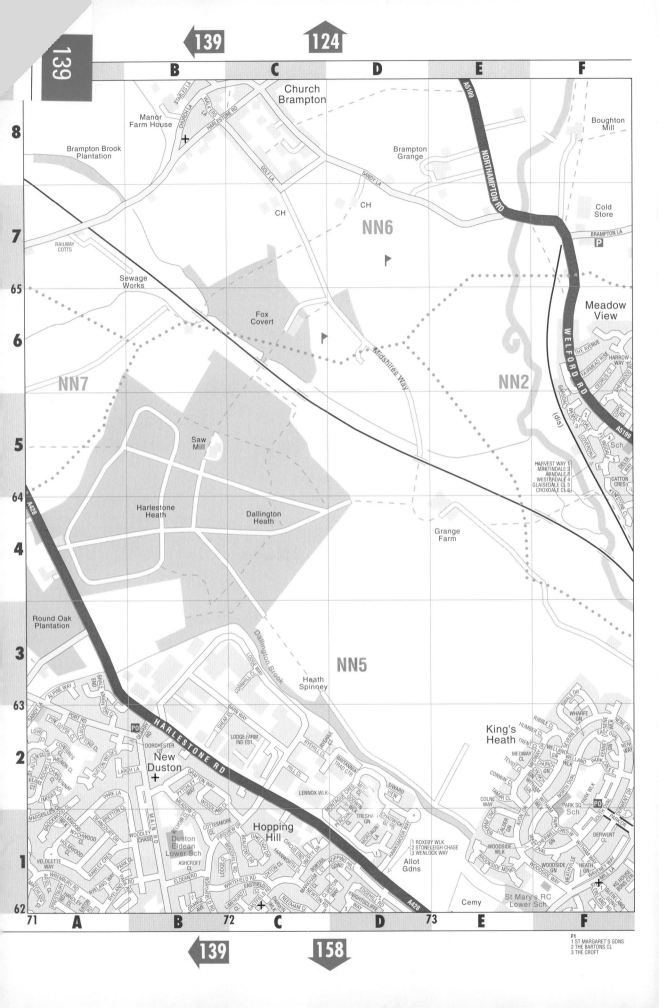

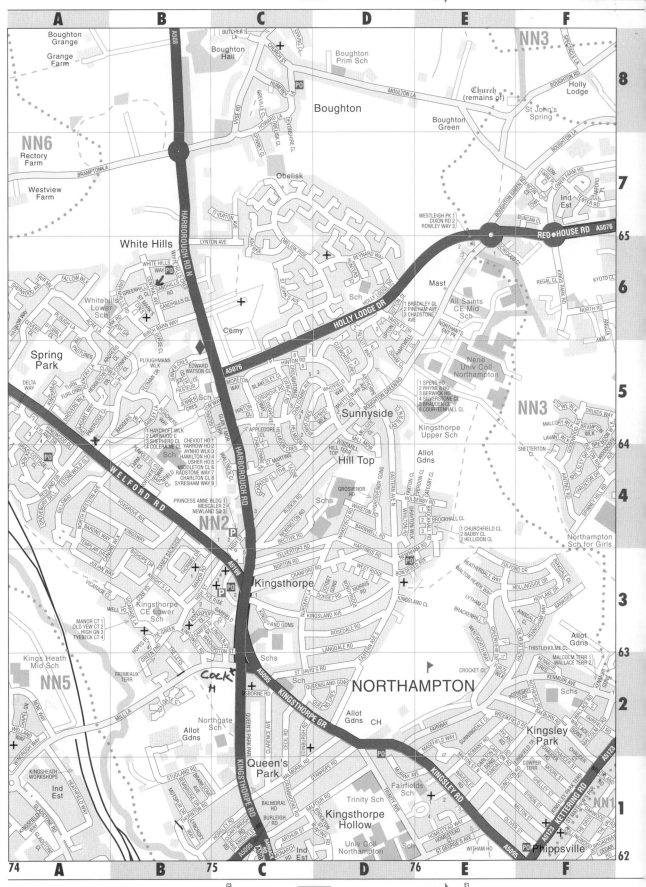

125
142
159
142

C3
1 CRANFORD HO
2 KINGSTHORPE SH CTR
3 ETON CT
4 STABLE CT
5 ALEXANDRA TERR

E1
1 BETHANY HOMESTEAD
2 DARDIS CL
3 KINGSLEY GDNS
4 METHODIST HOMESTEAD

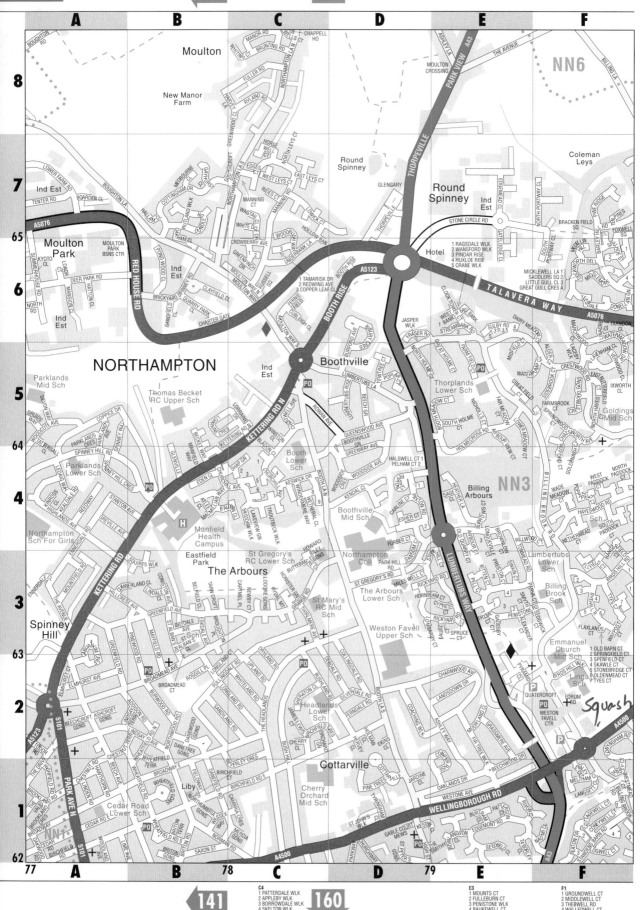

C4
1 PATTERDALE WLK
2 APPLEBY WLK
3 BORROWDALE WLK
4 SKELTON WLK
5 CALDBECK WLK
6 DALSTON WLK
7 KIRKSTONE WLK
8 LANERCOST WLK
9 AMBLESIDE CL

E3
1 MOUNTS CT
2 FULLEBURN CT
3 PENISTONE CT
4 BAUKEWELL CT

F1
1 GROUNDWELL CT
2 MIDDLEWELL CT
3 THEBWELL RD
4 WALLEDWELL CT
5 RUNNEYMEDE GDNS

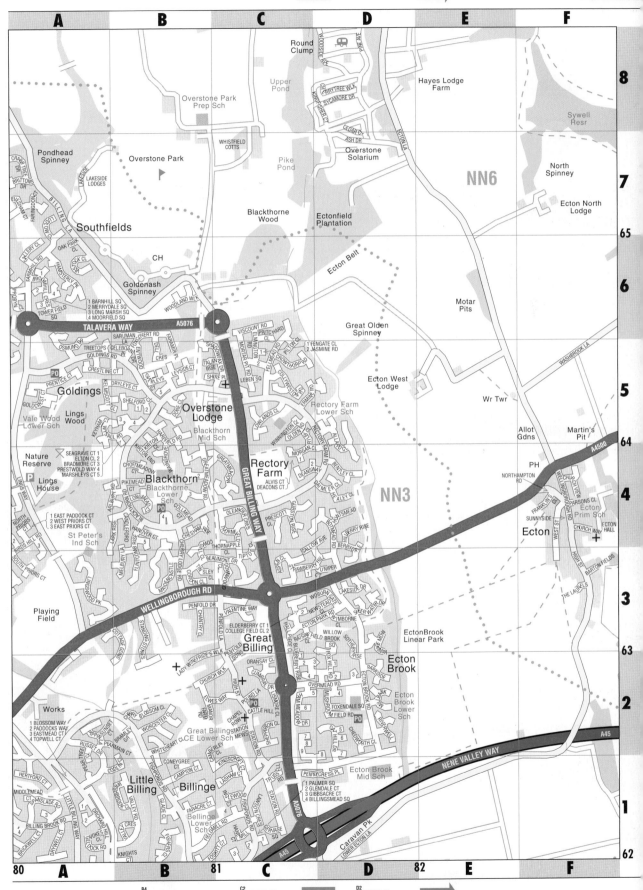

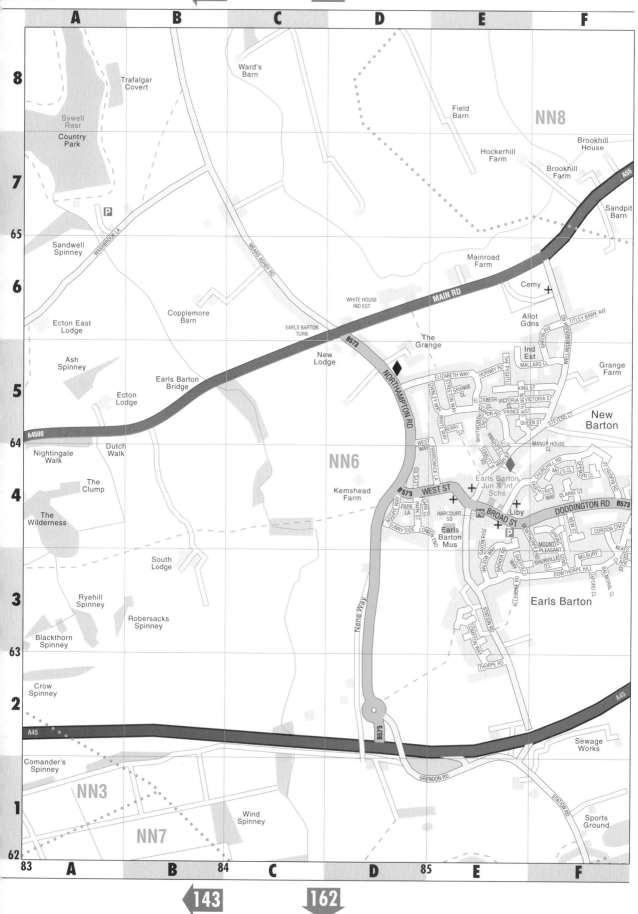

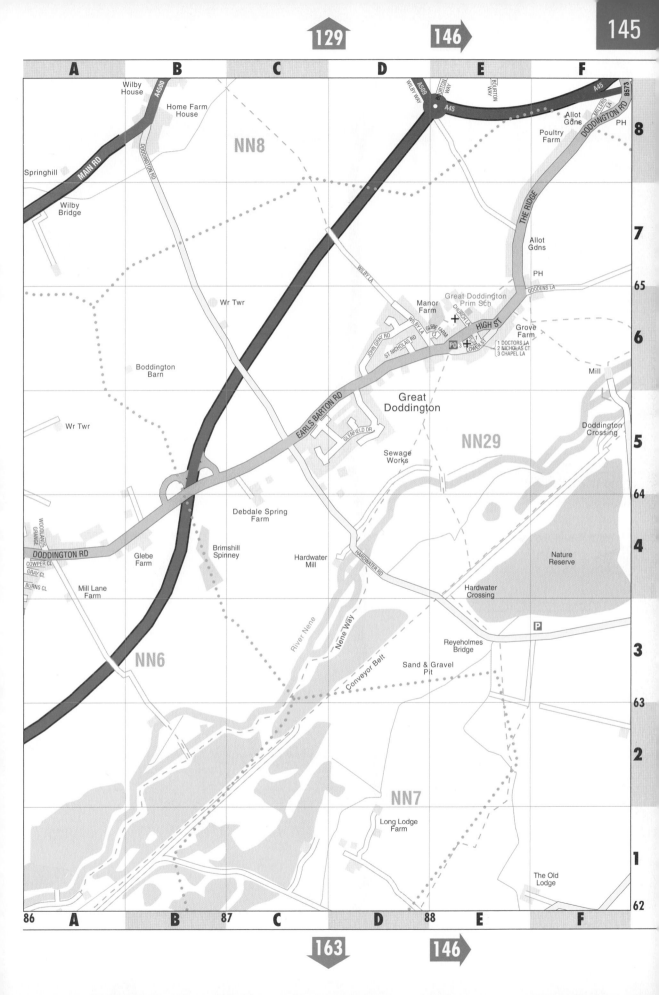

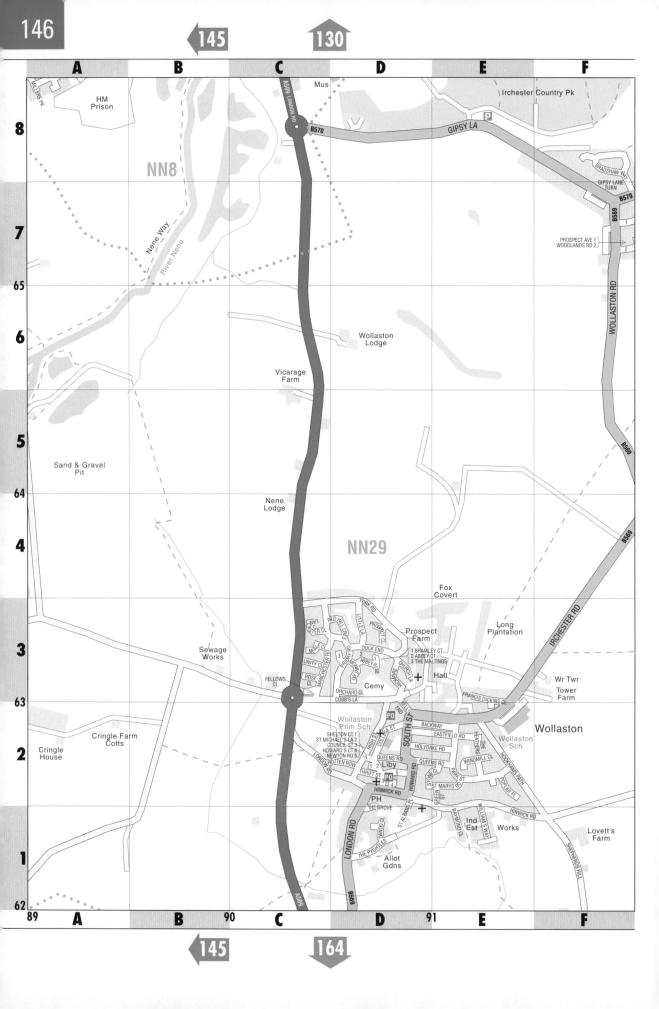

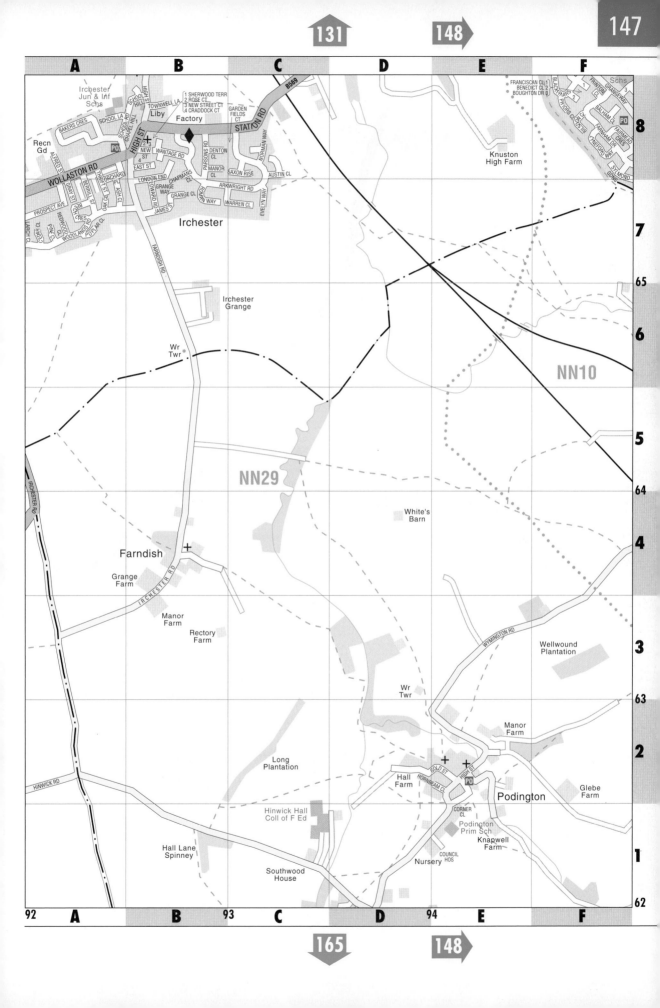

131
148
148

A **B** **C** **D** **E** **F**

Irchester Jun & Inf Schs

FRANCISCAN CL 1
BENEDICT CL 2
BOUGHTON DR 3

Schs

GRANGEWAY

FRINTON

BAKERS CRES

BLACKFRIARS CL/CRT 1B

BALHAM CL

PO

FARNHAM CRES

FARNHAM DR

THEFORD WAY

ST MOND RD

8

SCHOOL LA

CHAPEL HILL

SCHOOL HILL

TOWNWELL LA

Liby

Factory

1 SHERWOOD TERR
2 ROSE CT
3 NEW STREET CT
4 CRADDOCK CT

GARDEN FIELDS CT

STATION RD

B569

Knuston
High Farm

Recn Gd

ALFRED ST

HIGH ST

1 2 3
NEW ST

WANTAGE RD

PARSONS RD

DENTON CL

NORMAN WAY

MANOR CL

SAXON RISE

AUSTIN CL

PO

EAST ST

WOLLASTON RD

PROSPECT AVE

GRAY ST

THRIFT ST

BERRILL ST

OAK CL

ASH CL

ORCHARD

LONDON END

EDWARD RD

CHAPMANS

GRANGE WAY

GRANGE CL

JAMES ST

ROMAN WAY

ARKWRIGHT RD

WARREN CL

EVELYN WAY

TO CHELV

LARCH CL

PINE CL

REDWOOD

WOODLANDS RD

POPLAR CL

CRES

Irchester

7

FARNDISH RD

Irchester
Grange

NN10

65

Wr
Twr

6

NN29

64

Farndish

Grange
Farm

IRCHESTER RD

White's
Barn

5

4

Manor
Farm

Rectory
Farm

WYMINGTON RD

Wellwound
Plantation

3

IRCHESTER RD

Wr
Twr

Manor
Farm

63

2

HINWICK RD

Long
Plantation

Hall
Farm

HORNBEAM CL

GOLD ST

HIGH ST

PO

Podington

Glebe
Farm

Hinwick Hall
Coll of F Ed

CORNER
CL

Podington
Prim Sch

Knapwell
Farm

1

Hall Lane
Spinney

COUNCIL
HOS

Nursery

Southwood
House

62

92 **A** **B** 93 **C** **D** 94 **E** **F**

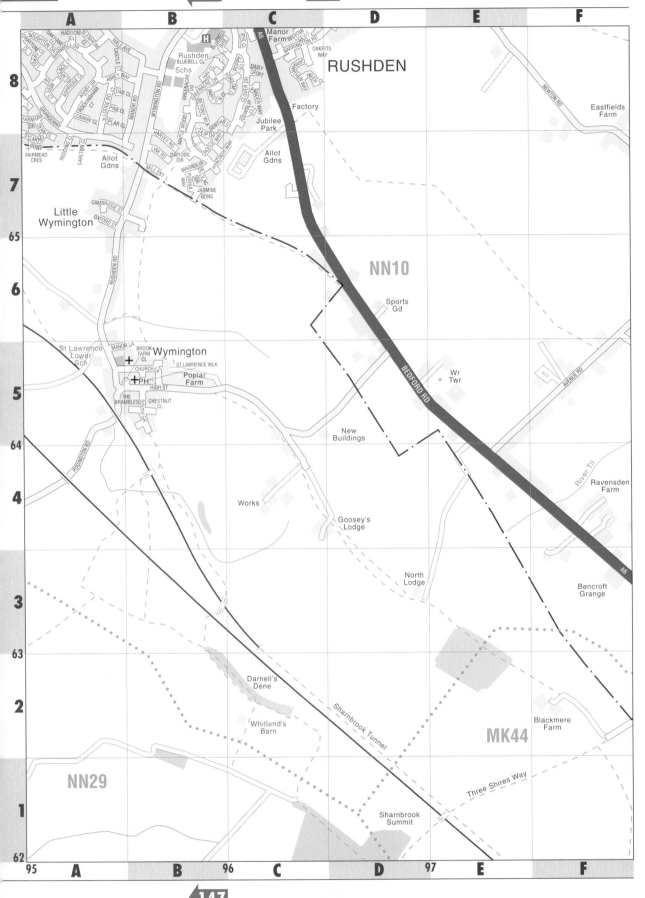

RUSHDEN

NN10

Little Wymington

Wymington

Poplar Farm

St Lawrence Lower Sch

Manor Farm

Factory

Jubilee Park

Allot Gdns

Sports Gd

Wr Twr

Avenue Rd

Eastfields Farm

New Buildings

Works

Goosey's Lodge

North Lodge

River Til

Ravensden Farm

Bencroft Grange

Darnell's Dene

Whitland's Barn

Sharnbrook Tunnel

Blackmere Farm

MK44

Three Shires Way

NN29

Sharnbrook Summit

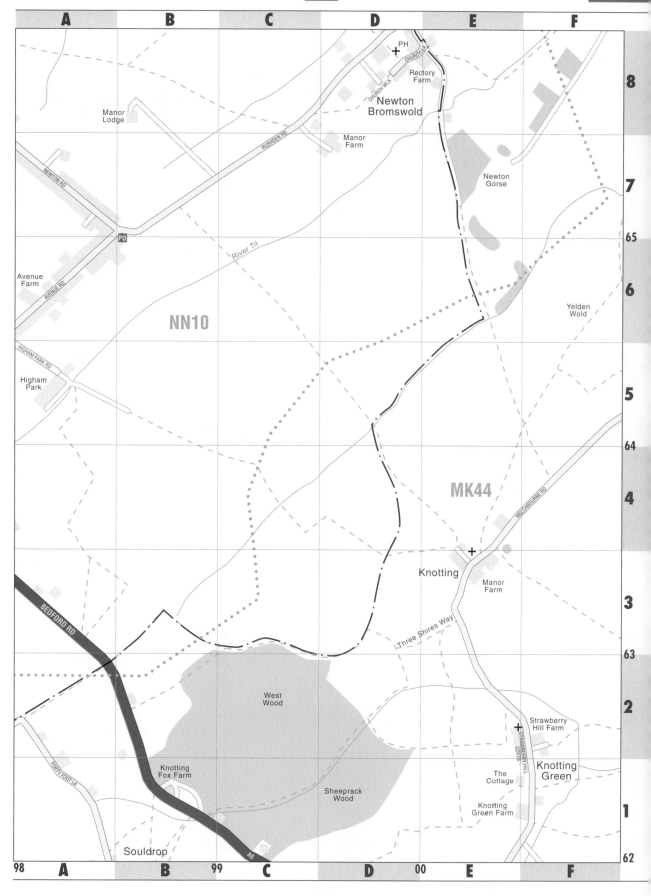

Newton Bromswold

PH

CHURCH LA

CHURCH WLK

Rectory Farm

Manor Lodge

RUSHDEN RD

Manor Farm

Newton Gorse

NEWTON RD

PO

River Til

Avenue Farm

AVENUE RD

NN10

Yelden Wold

HIGHAM PARK RD

Higham Park

MK44

MELCHBOURNE RD

Knotting

Manor Farm

BEDFORD RD

Three Shires Way

West Wood

Strawberry Hill Farm

STRAWBERRY HILL COTTS

FORTY FOOT LA

Knotting Fox Farm

Sheeprack Wood

The Cottage

Knotting Green

Knotting Green Farm

Souldrop

A6

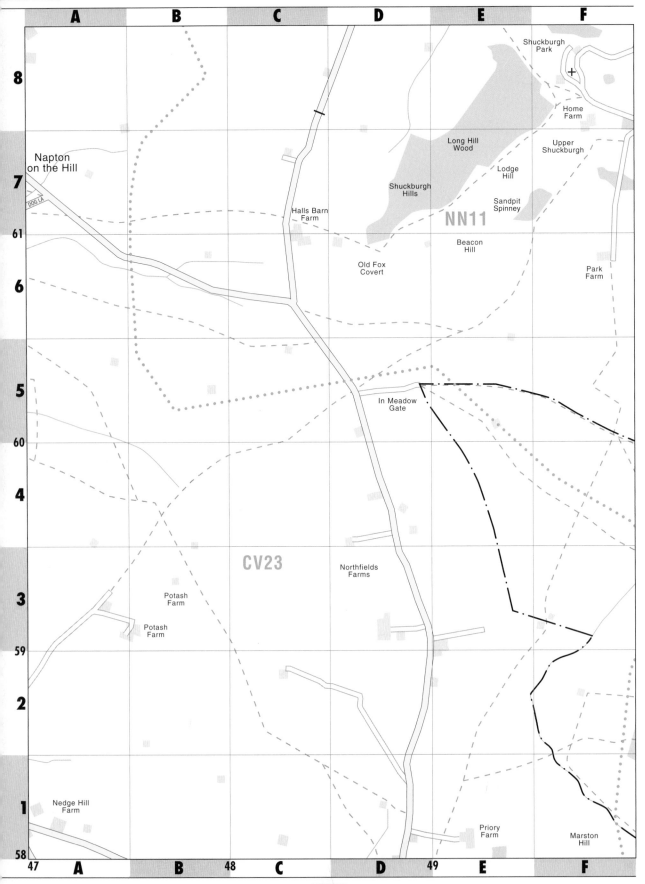

8

Shuckburgh
Park

+

Home
Farm

Napton
on the Hill

7

Long Hill
Wood

Upper
Shuckburgh

Lodge
Hill

DOG LA

Halls Barn
Farm

Shuckburgh
Hills

Sandpit
Spinney

61

NN11

Beacon
Hill

6

Old Fox
Covert

Park
Farm

5

In Meadow
Gate

60

4

CV23

Northfields
Farms

3

Potash
Farm

Potash
Farm

59

2

1

Nedge Hill
Farm

Priory
Farm

Marston
Hill

58

152

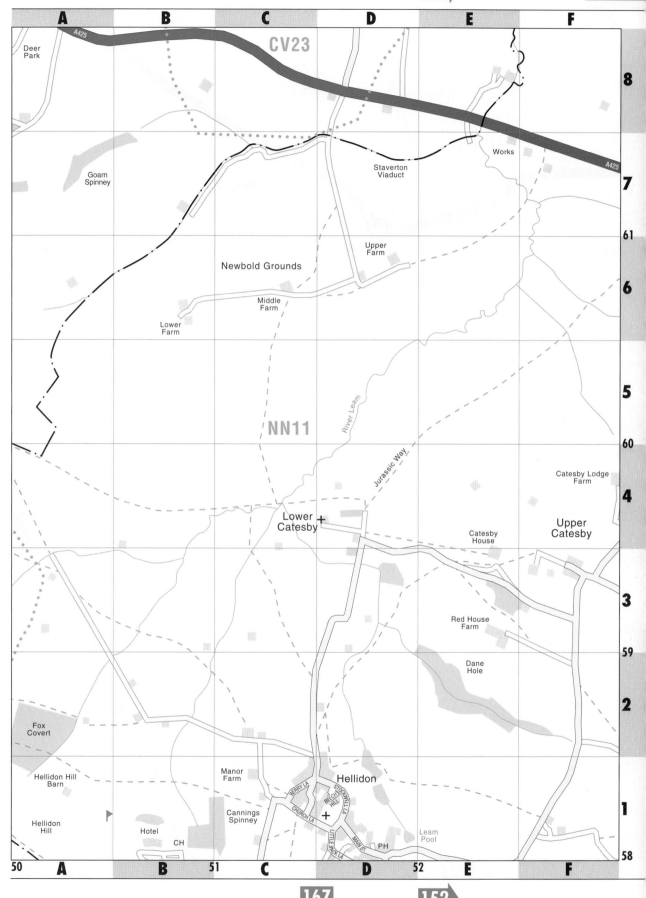

| | A | B | C | D | E | F |

8

Hall

Hall Farm

Sewage Works

Manor House

Staverton CE Prim Sch

CH

Hotel

Woodhollow Cottages

Stepnell Spinney

A425

STAVERTON RD

WELLAND CL 1
THAMES RD 2

TYNE RD

STEPNELL WAY

Drayton Lodge

A45

7

A425

THE WOODLANDS

WELL LA

MANOR RD

CROFT LA

GLEBE LA

OAKHAM LA

BRAUNSTON LA

HOME CL

DAVENTRY RD

1 WINDMILL LA
2 WINDMILL GDNS
3 CHURCHFIELDS

CHURCH ST

PH

THE ORCHARD

Staverton Acres

Oak Spinney

Compton Cottage

Staverton Clump

Whitmill Hill Farm

Mast

Staverton Wood

Big Hill

Pond Spinney

61

Staverton

Vine Tree Farm

Sports Gd

Bates Farm

Broiler Breeder Farm

Jurassic Way

Badby Lodge Farm

Staverton Fields

6

Badby Fields

NN11

5

Markleys

60

4

Studborough Hill

Studborough Clump

Bridge Hill Farm

A361

MERE SIDE CL

3

Longridge Farm

Staverton Lodge

Barehill Farm

PINFOLD GN

POUND LA

ORCHARD CL

Badby Prim Sch

PH

PO

SCHOOL LA

59

Arbury Hill

STONEWAY

MAIN ST

BUNKERS HILL

VICARAGE HILL

CHURCH HILL

2

Highfield Farm

Haycock Hill Farm

Konigssee Farm

The Beeches

Badby Plantation

1

Badby Down

A361

58

| 53 | A | B | 54 | C | D | 55 | E | F |

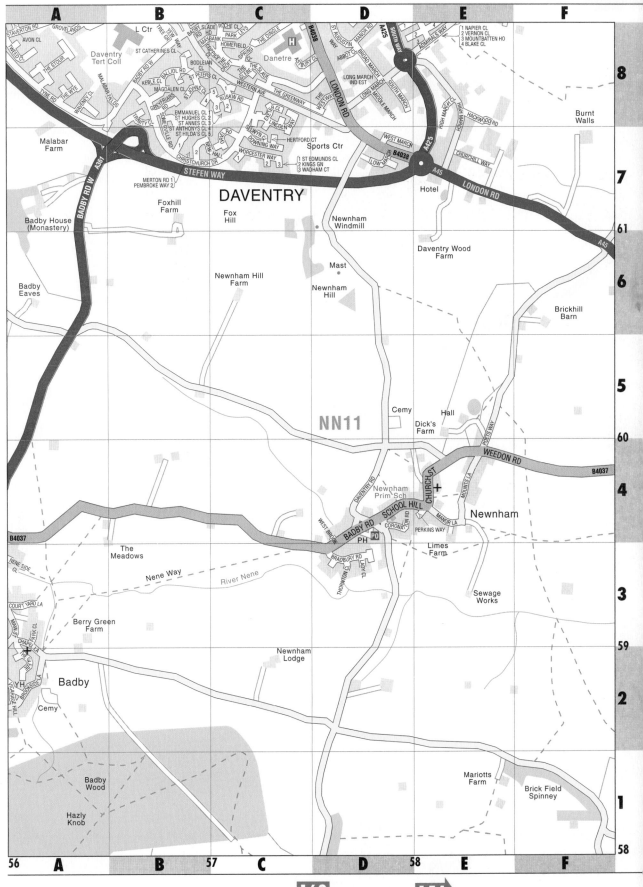

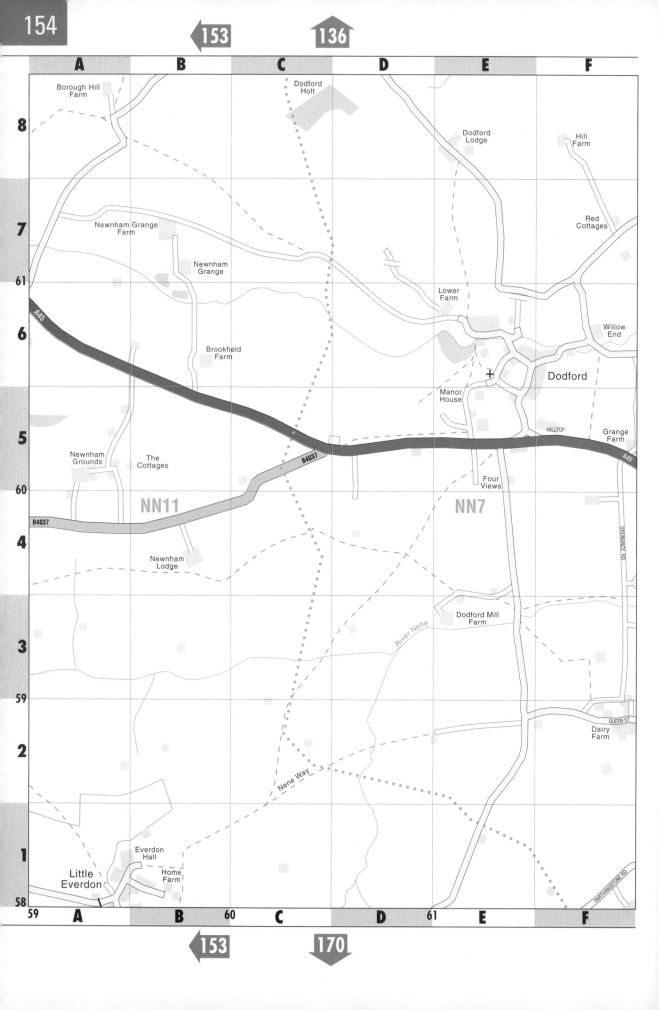

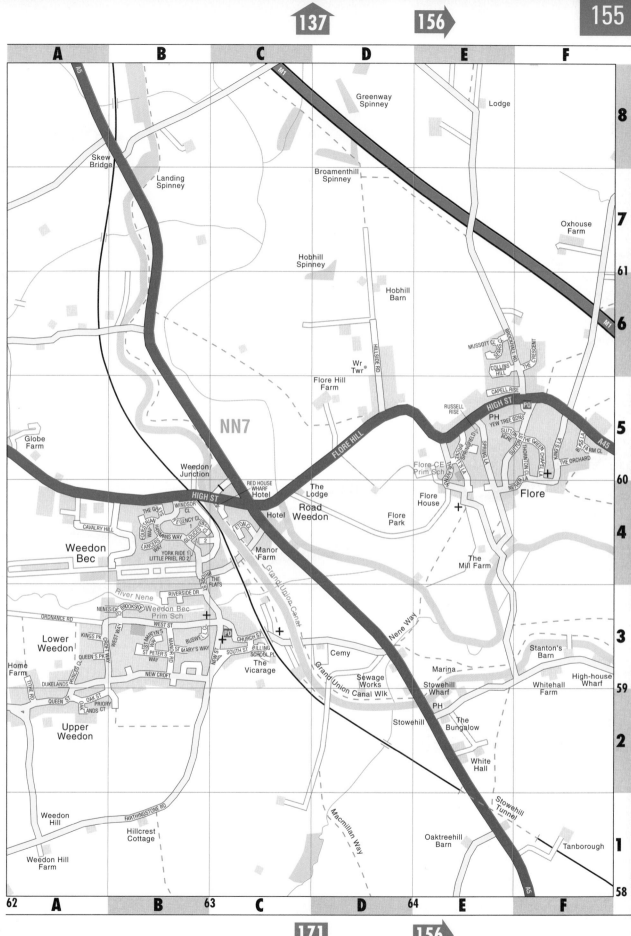

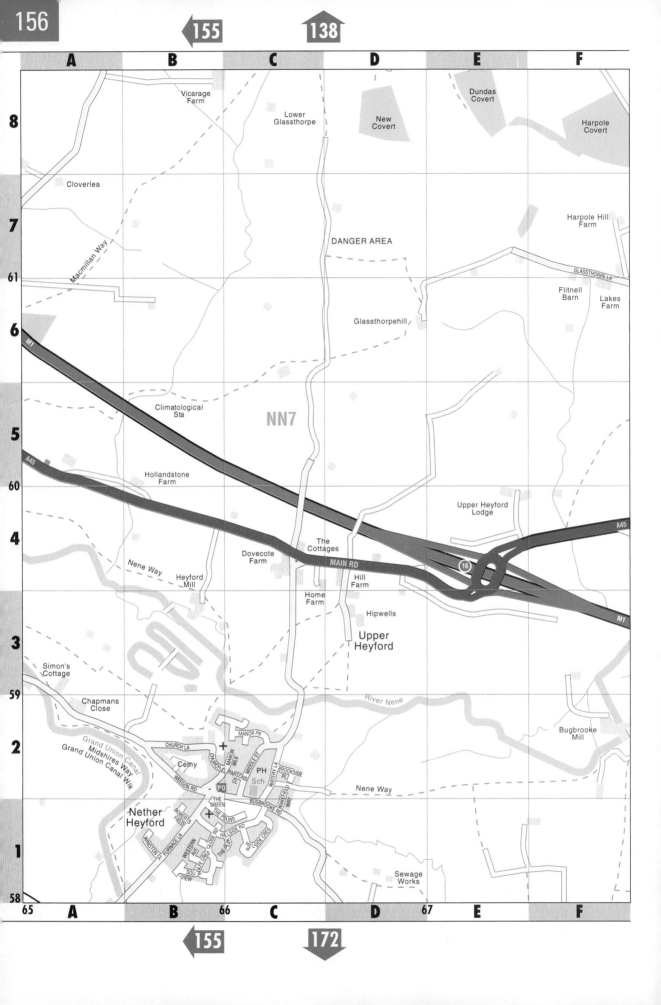

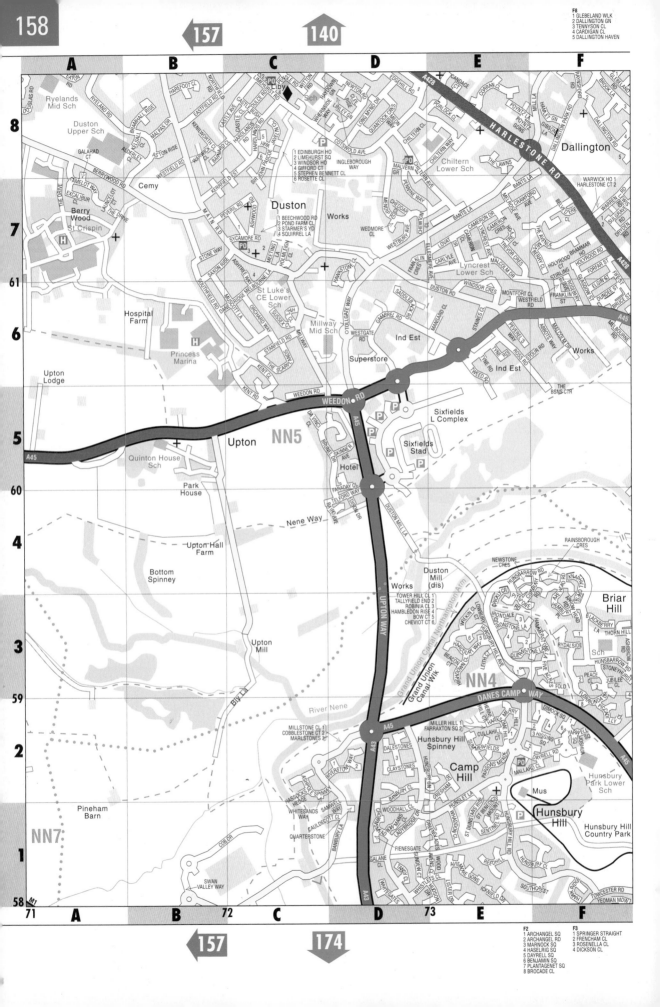

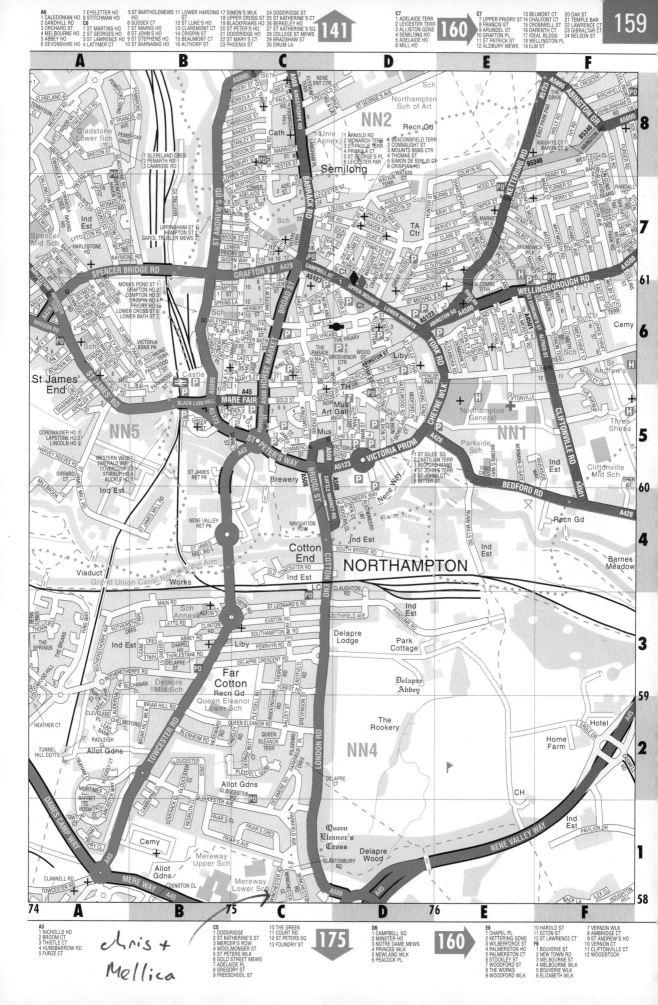

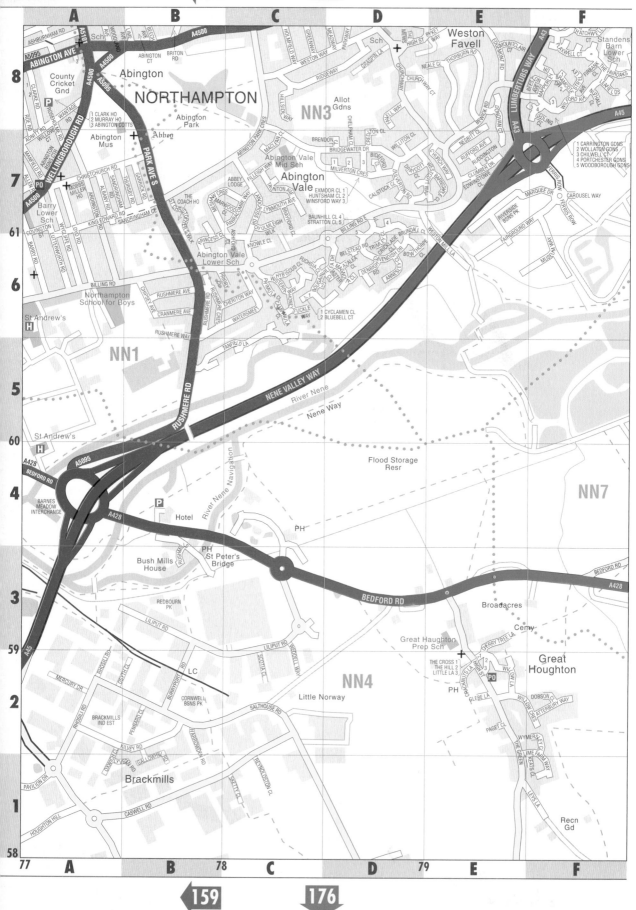

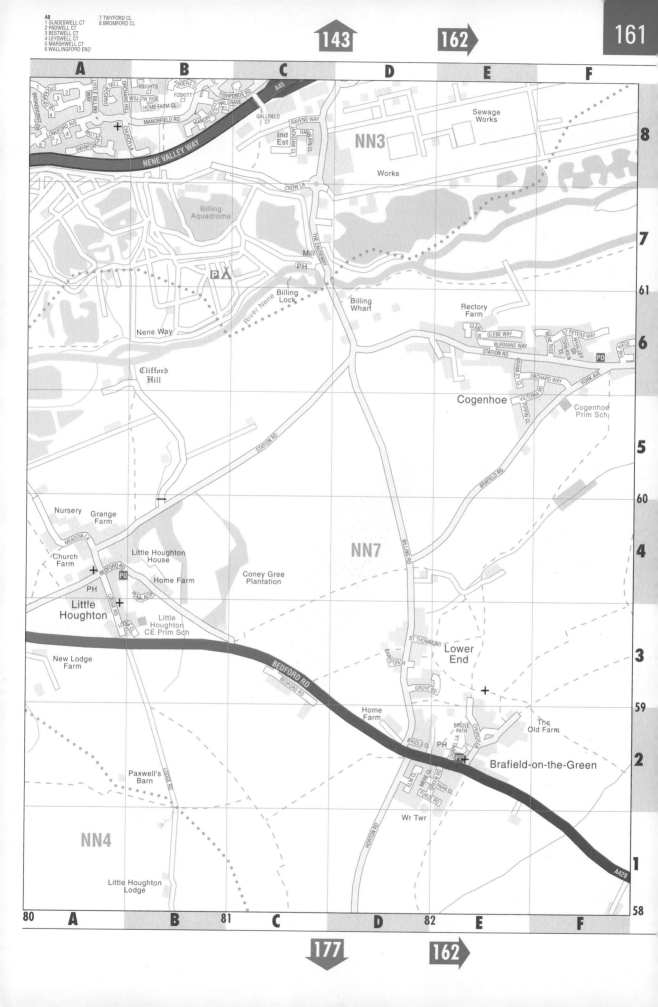

143
162
177
162

A8
1 SLADESWELL CT
2 PADWELL CT
3 BESTWELL CT
4 LEYSWELL CT
5 MARSHWELL CT
6 WALLINGFORD END
7 TWYFORD CL
8 BROMFORD CL

A B C D E F

8

7

61

6

5

60

4

3

59

2

1

58

Broadhurst Dr
Longford Ave
Swinford
Little Billing Way
Orchard Hill
Daxwell
Knights Ct
Willow Rise
Home Farm Cl
Fishers Cl
Foskitt Ct
Manorfield Rd
Church La
Fishponds Rd
Walgrave Cl
Gallfield Ct
Ind Est
Manorfield
A45
Nene Valley Way
Ravens Way
Haslburn Cl
Jackdaw Cl
Crow La

NN3

Sewage Works

Works

Billing Aquadrome

Mill
PH
The Causeway

River Nene
Billing Lock
Billing Wharf

Nene Way

Rectory Farm

Clifford Hill

Glebe Rd
Glebe Way
Burmans Way
Station Rd
Bramley Cl
Orchard Way
Victoria Rd
Pippin Cl
York Ave
St Peters Way
Whalley Gr
Corn Kiln
Nene Rise
The Piece

Cogenhoe

Cogenhoe Prim Sch

Station Rd

NN7

Billing Rd

Brafield Rd

Nursery
Grange Farm
Church Farm
Little Houghton
Meadow La
Bedford Rd
PO
PH
Lodge Rd
Home Farm
Little Houghton House
Wey Acre
Lodge Cl
Little Houghton CE Prim Sch

Coney Gree Plantation

New Lodge Farm

Bedford Rd
Bedford Rd

Paxwell's Barn
Lodge Rd

NN4

Little Houghton Lodge

St Thomas Rd
Lower End
Cares Orch
Grove Rd

Home Farm
Bridle Cl
PH
Chapel La
Church La
PO
Bridle Path
The Old Farm
Brafield-on-the-Green

Elm Cl
Mere Cl
Green Rd
Park Cl
Furze Rd
Horton Rd
Wr Twr

A428

80 A B 81 C D 82 E F

161
144

A B C D E F

8

NN6

The Gatehouse

STATION RD

River Nene

Nene Way

7

Mill

61

Cogenhoe

Roe Farm

WHISTON RD

MILL LA

Factory

SHARMANS CL

Manor Farm

6

THE PIECE

CHURCH ST

MANOR FARM CT

Combe Hill

STATION RD

Palace House

Whiston

SHORT LA

PH

The Firs

5

The Firs

NN7

60

Whistone Spinney

4

Engin Pond

PH

3

Denton Barn

Chadstone Lodge

Threefold

WHISTON RD

Whistonhill Spinney

59

Whiston Slade

Paradise Pond

2

Chadstone

Rectory

Hopyard Spinney

Castle Ashby Lodge

1

Denton

FISHPOND CL

LEYS CL

MAIN ST

Manor Farm

GRANGE CL

DOVECOTE CL

THE LEYS

PO

ORCHARD LA

COTTAGE LA

PH

Sandpit Spinney

58

A428 BEDFORD RD

83 A B 84 C D 85 E F

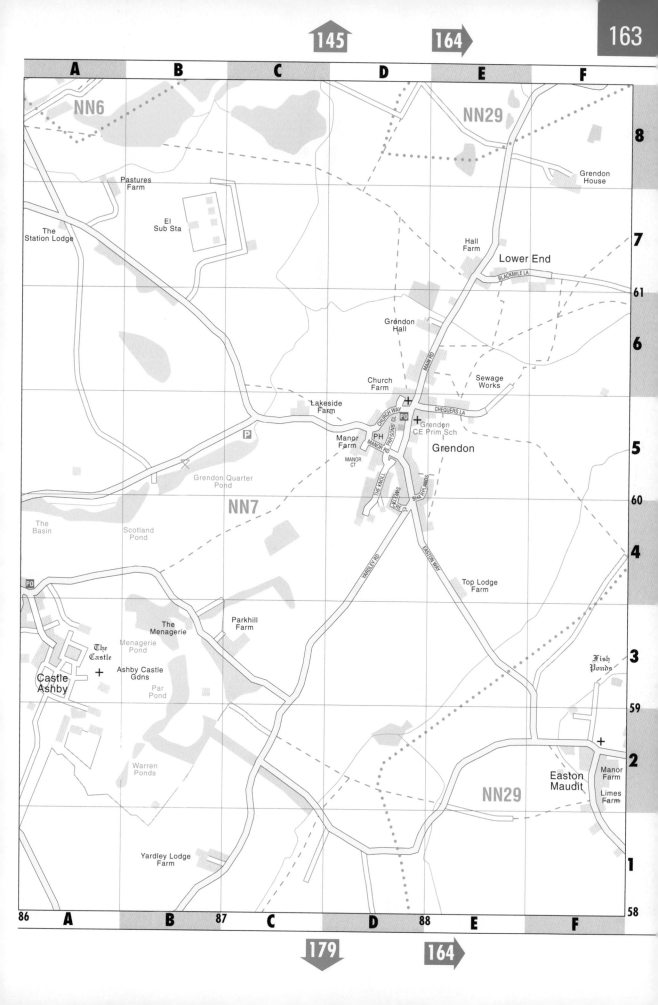

NN6

Pastures Farm

El Sub Sta

The Station Lodge

NN29

Grendon House

Hall Farm

Lower End

BLACKMILE LA

Grendon Hall

Church Farm

Sewage Works

Lakeside Farm

CHURCH WAY

PO

CHEQUERS LA

Grendon CE Prim Sch

Manor Farm

PH

MANOR RD

PARSONS CL

Grendon

MANOR CT

NN7

THE KNOLL

CRE CL

SHEARLANDS

Grendon Quarter Pond

The Basin

Scotland Pond

YARDLEY RD

EASTON WAY

Top Lodge Farm

PO

Fish Ponds

The Menagerie

Parkhill Farm

Menagerie Pond

The Castle

Ashby Castle Gdns

Castle Ashby

Par Pond

Easton Maudit

Manor Farm

Limes Farm

NN29

Warren Ponds

Yardley Lodge Farm

163
146

A | B | C | D | E | F

8

Hillmount
Spinney

Manor
Farm

Chruch
Farm

Strixton

Strixton
Plantation

Lodge
Farm

SHEPHERDS HILL

7

Poplars
Farm

61

NN7

6

Greenfield
Lodge

A509

B569

WOLLASTON RD

5

NN29

60

WOLLASTON RD

4

Red Gables
Farm

FULLWELL RD

HOPE ST

COUNCIL ST

BULL CL

Church
Farm

Bozeat

Glebe
Farm

Three Fields
Farm

PEAR
TREE
CL

ALLENS HILL

1 CHURCH FARM CL
2 PUDDING BAG LA
3 THE ORCHARD

3

Slype
Farm

Spring Vale
Farm

CHURCH WLK

HARROLD RD

HENSMANS LA

MILE ST

Bozeat
Prim Sch

Cemy

1

2

CHURCH LA

3

59

Easton La

LONDON RD

HIGH ST

PH

4

DYCHURCH LA

East Farm

Park
Farm

STONEY
PIECE
CL

ABBEY CL

MILL RD

WYMAN CL

KNIGHTS CL

5

PO

6

BROOKSIDE

Spring Hill Farm

2

DEPOT ST

ST. MARY'S RD

HEWLETTS CL

HILLSIDE CL

FIR TREE GR

CLAYLAND
CL

4 WARNERS HILL
5 CAMDEN SQ
6 WHEELWRIGHTS YD

ROBERTS ST

Easton
Low

1

White House
Farm

Home
Farm

A509

58

89 | A | B | 90 | C | D | 91 | E | F

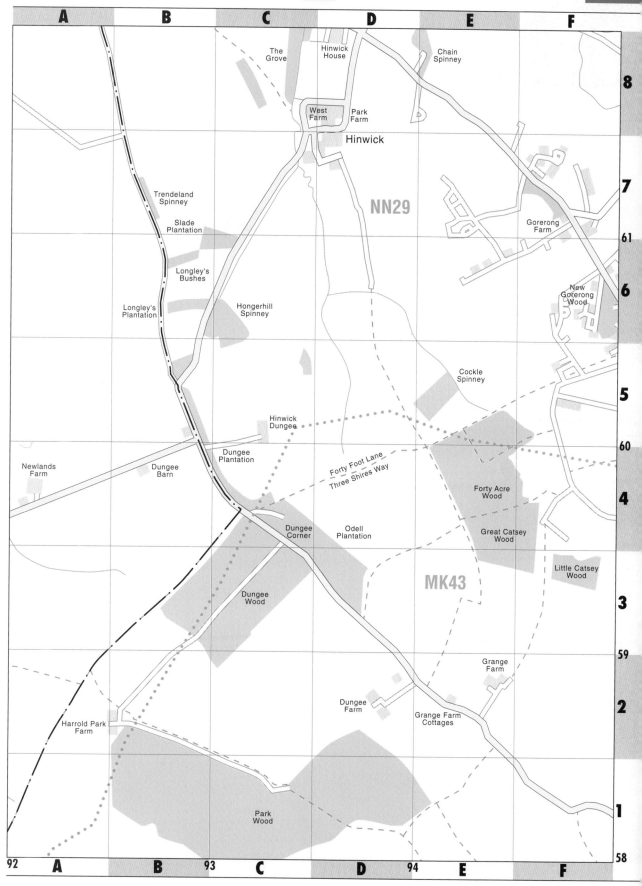

A B C D E F

The Meadows

PO

Priors
Marston

KEYS LA

Marston
Hill

Hill
Farm

The Priors
Sch

8

SHUCKBURGH RD

VICARAGE

SCHOOL LA

HOLLY BUSH LA

MARSTON HILL

Westfield
Barn

PH

THE HOLLOWAY

SOUTHAM RD

THE GREEN

HELLIDON RD

7

Westover
Farm

Chestnuts
Farm

57

Manor House
Farm

HARDWICK RD

BYFIELD RD

6

Sewage
Works

CV23

ST MARY'S CL

THE
CLOISTERS

Church
End

5

+Priors
Hardwick

Grange
Farm

PH

AGRICULTURAL
COTTS

56

London
End

WELSH RD

4

The Old
Vicarage

3

Fields
Farm

Rump
Hall

55

NN11

2

1

54

47 A 48 B C 48 D 49 E F

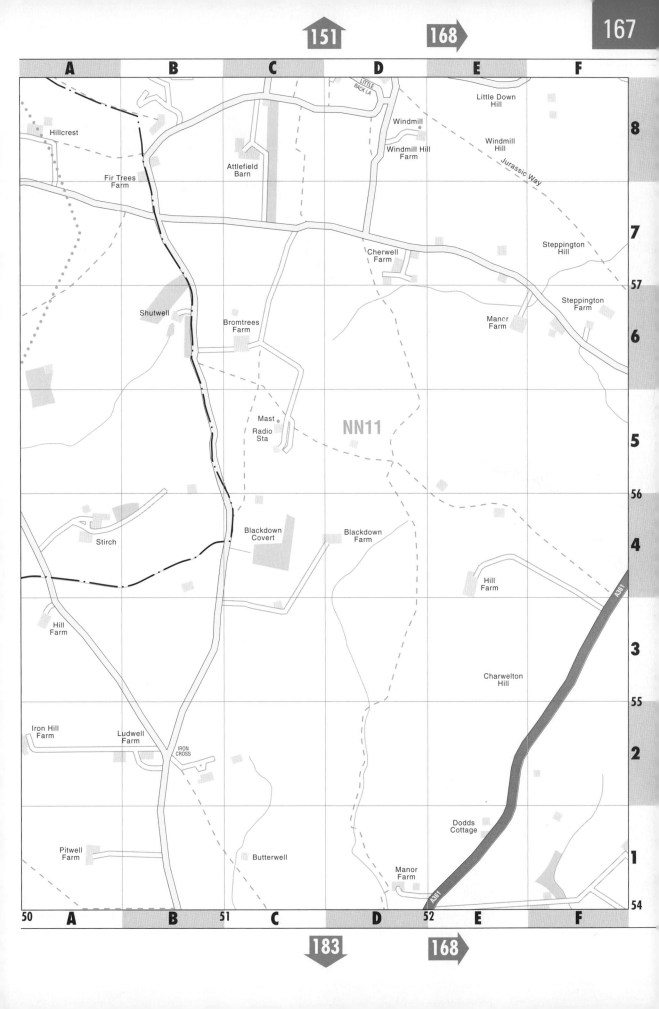

167
152

A B C D E F

8

Rytonhill
Farm

Grove
Spinney

Beeches
Farm

Sharman's
Hill

A361

7

Long Furlong
Farm

Horseground
Clump

57

Steppington
Spinney

Little
Fawsley

6

Sharmans
Farm

Fawsley
Farm

The
Dingle

Barley Field
Farm

Charwelton

5

Charwelton
Hall

NN11

56

PH

PO

COUNCIL
HQS

CHURCH ST

HIGH ST

CHAPEL ST

MANOR CL

4

Sewage
Works

Jurassic Way

The
Angles

A361

River Cherwell

Church
Charwelton

Holywell
Pool

3

55

Blindpool
Spinney

2

Preston Fields
Farm

Charwelton
Lodge

Hollingwood
House

1

54

Hinton
House

Hinton
Hill

Hintonhill
Farm

53 A B 54 C D 55 E F

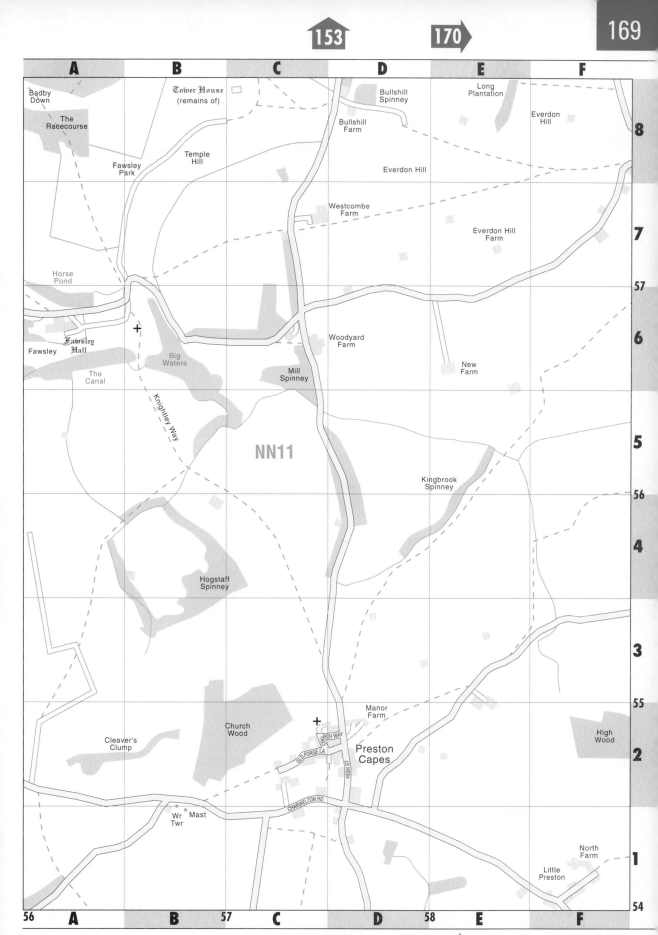

Badby Down

The Racecourse

Tower House (remains of)

Bullshill Spinney

Bullshill Farm

Long Plantation

Everdon Hill

Fawsley Park

Temple Hill

Everdon Hill

Westcombe Farm

Everdon Hill Farm

Horse Pond

Fawsley Hall

Fawsley

Big Waters

Woodyard Farm

New Farm

The Canal

Mill Spinney

Knightley Way

NN11

Kingbrook Spinney

Hogstaff Spinney

Church Wood

Manor Farm

High Wood

Cleaver's Clump

CHURCH WAY

OLD FORGE LA

HIGH ST

Preston Capes

Wr Twr

Mast

CHARWELTON RD

Little Preston

North Farm

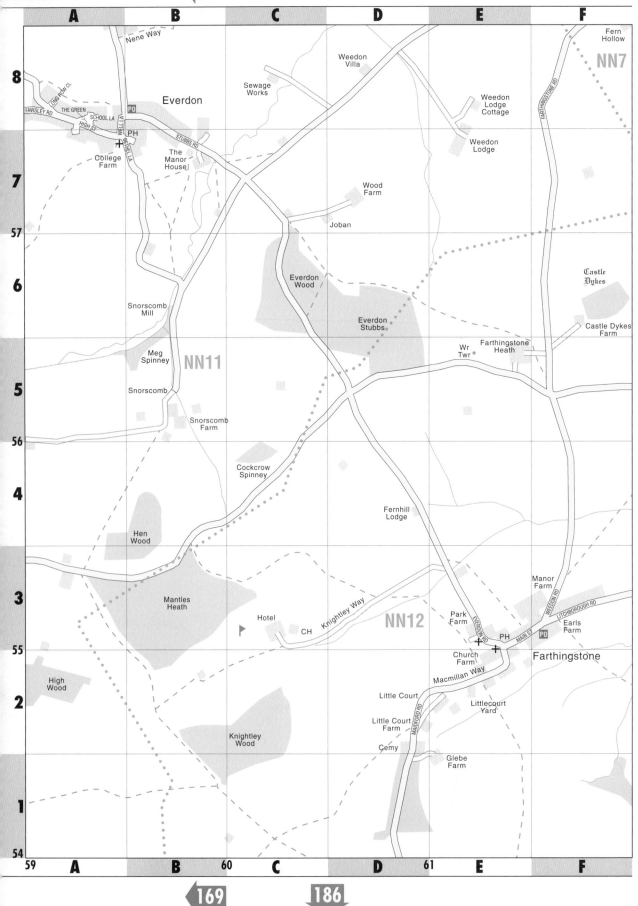

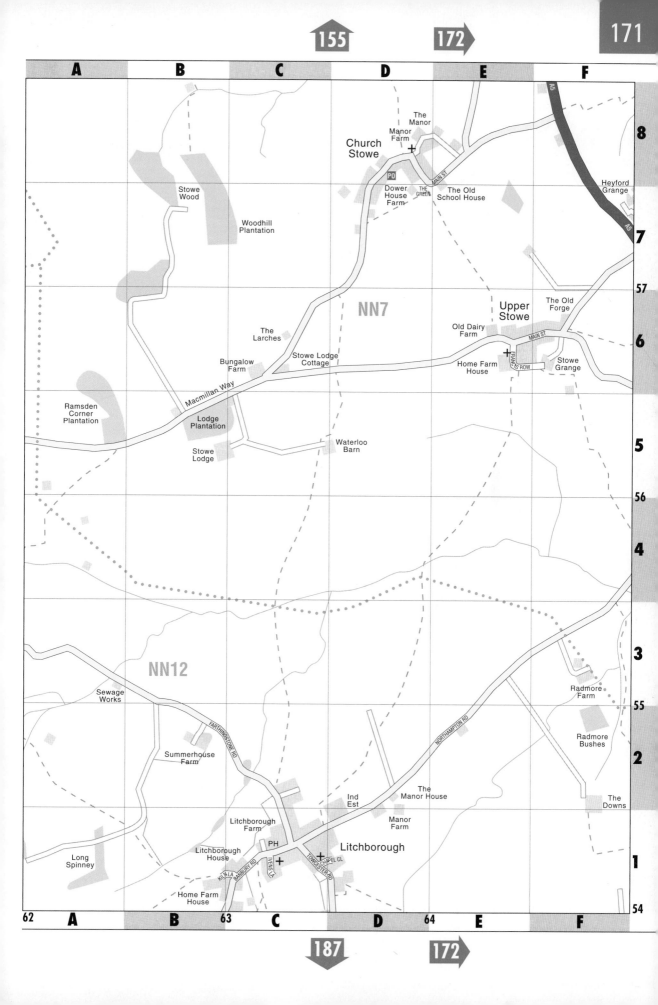

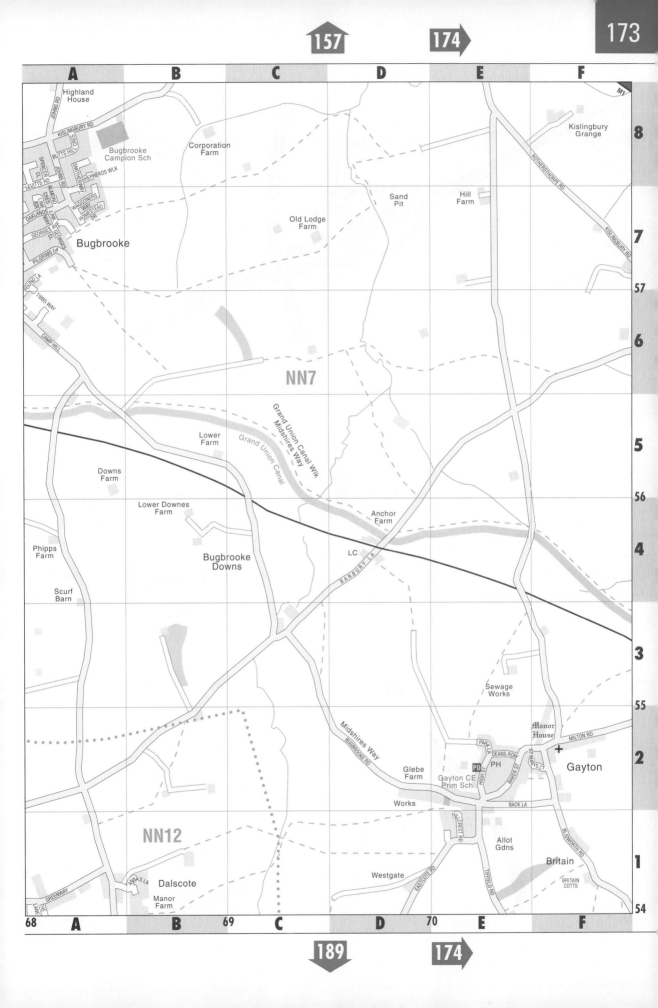

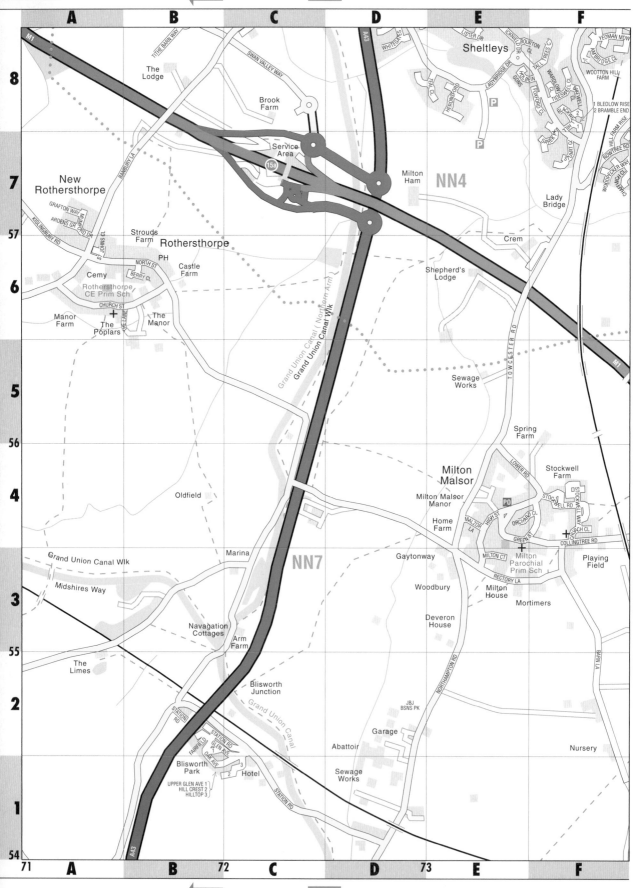

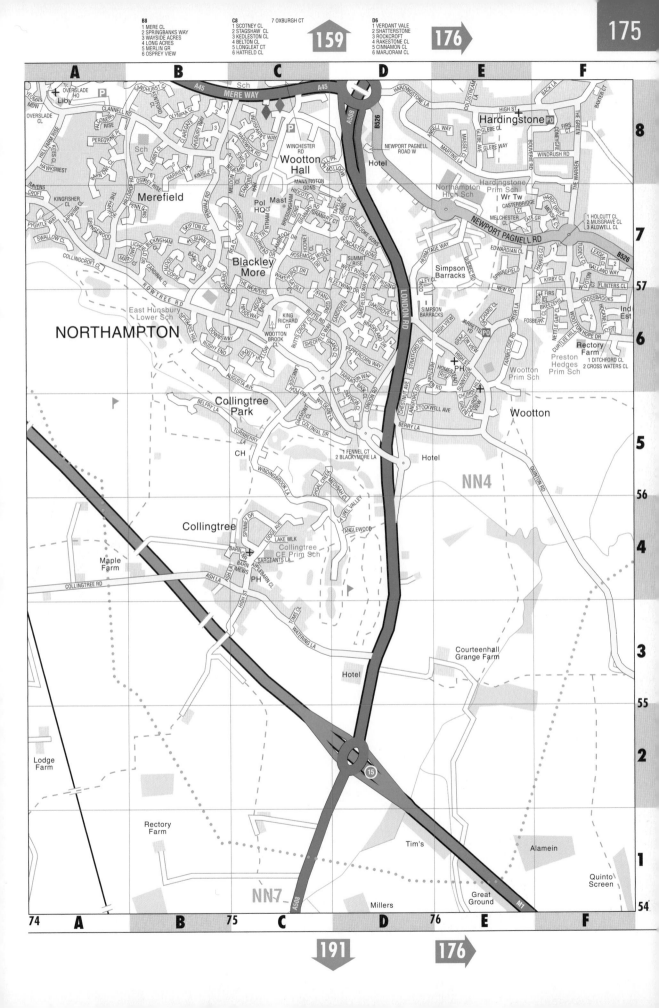

175
160

A B C D E F

8

SALTHOUSE RD

Saucebridge

NN4

7

Hardingstone
Lodge

B526

57 Ind
Est
BROOK CL
BEDDOES
CL
MORTONS BUSH
CROSSWOOD
WOLDALE RD
HIGH GREEVE
MIDDLE GREEVE
LOW GREEVE
Preston Lodge
Farm

6 WOOTTON HOPE
DR
WHITTLES CROSS
SALCROM
LADY HOLLOWS
LONG MEAD
THE ASHES
THE CHOAKLES
Preston Lodge
Cottages
THRUPP BRIDGE
MILTON BRIDGE
DENE

COPYMOOR CL 1
EARLSFIELD CL 2
LITTLE GREEVE WAY 3

NEWPORT PAGNELL RD

5
Grange
Farm
The
Grange

56

4
Hall
Woodlands
Nursery
Preston
Deanery
B526

NN7

3
Rookery Farm
Cottage
Sewage
Works

55
Lower
Farm
Fox
Field
Lower
Farm
Wood
Cottage
Rookery
Farm

2
Rookery
New Farm

WOOTTON RD
Glebe
Cottage
Rookery
Farm

Glebe
Farm
PRESTON DEANERY RD
PRESTON DEANERY RD
The
Risings
SCHOOL LA
Quinton
Preston
wood

1
The
Lodge
Park
Farm

54
77 A 78 B C 78 D 79 E F

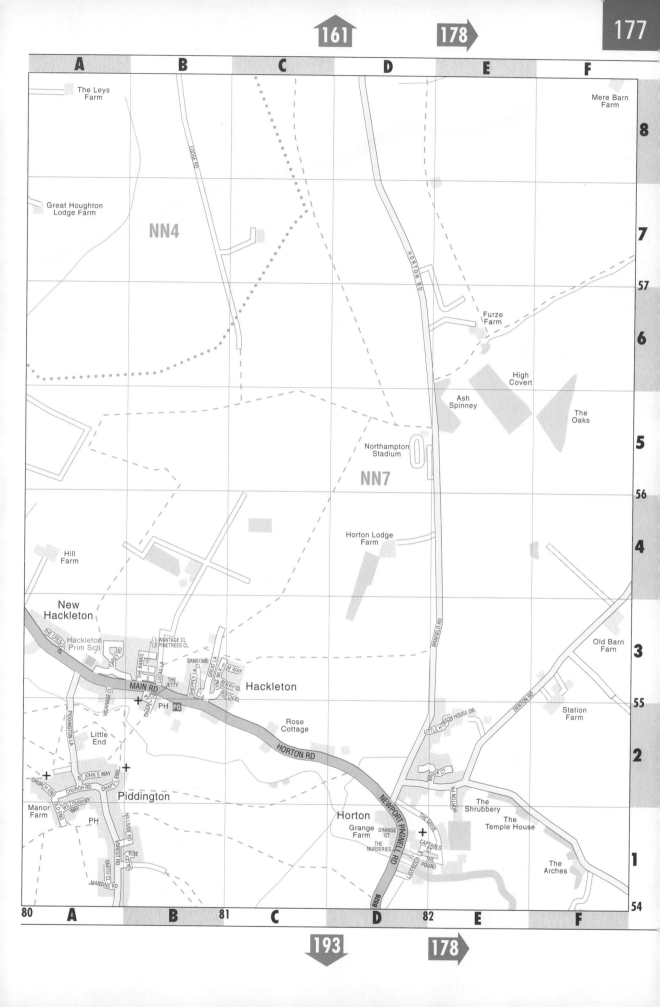

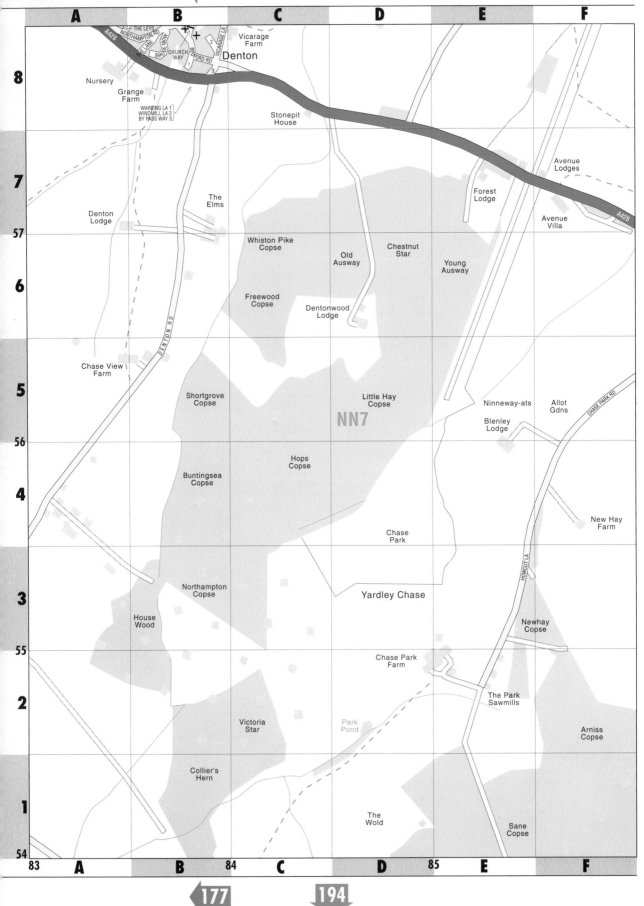

A B C D E F

8

7

57

6

5

56

4

3

55

2

1

54

THE LEYS
NORTHAMPTON RD
A428
BRICK MDW
THE LANE
CHURCH WAY
BEDFORD RD
VICARAGE LA
Vicarage Farm
Denton

Nursery
Grange Farm
WARPING LA 1
WINDMILL LA 2
BY PASS WAY 3

Stonepit House

Denton Lodge

The Elms

Whiston Pike Copse

Old Ausway

Chestnut Star

Young Ausway

Forest Lodge

Avenue Lodges

Avenue Villa

A428

DENTON RD

Freewood Copse

Dentonwood Lodge

Chase View Farm

Shortgrove Copse

Little Hay Copse

NN7

Ninneway-ats

Blenley Lodge

Allot Gdns

CHASE PARK RD

Hops Copse

Buntingsea Copse

New Hay Farm

Chase Park

Northampton Copse

Yardley Chase

HOWCUT LA

Newhay Copse

House Wood

Chase Park Farm

The Park Sawmills

Victoria Star

Park Pond

Arniss Copse

Collier's Hern

The Wold

Sane Copse

83 A 84 B C 85 D E F

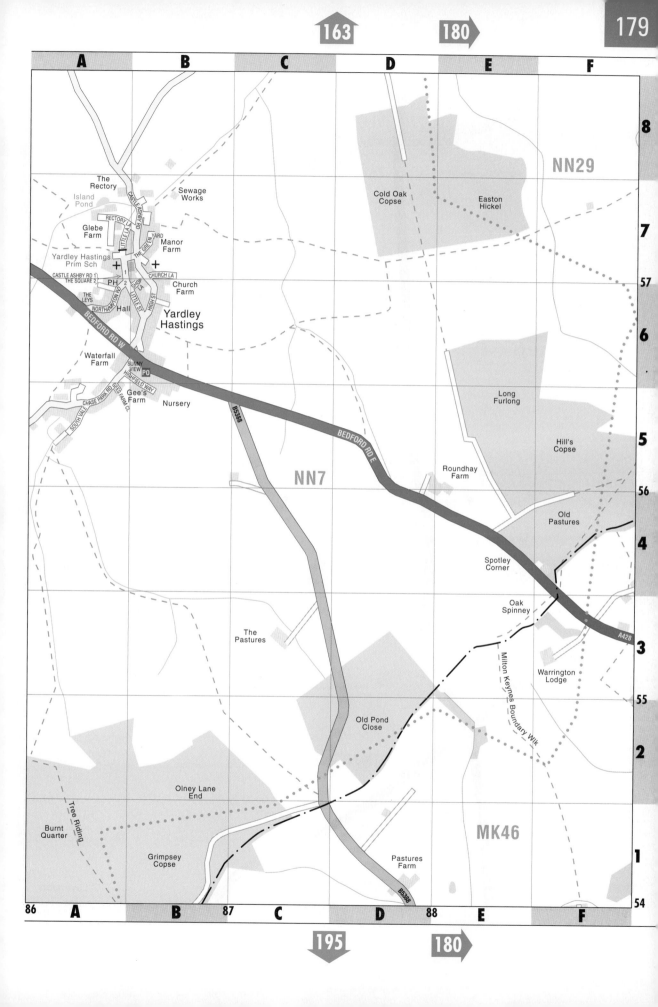

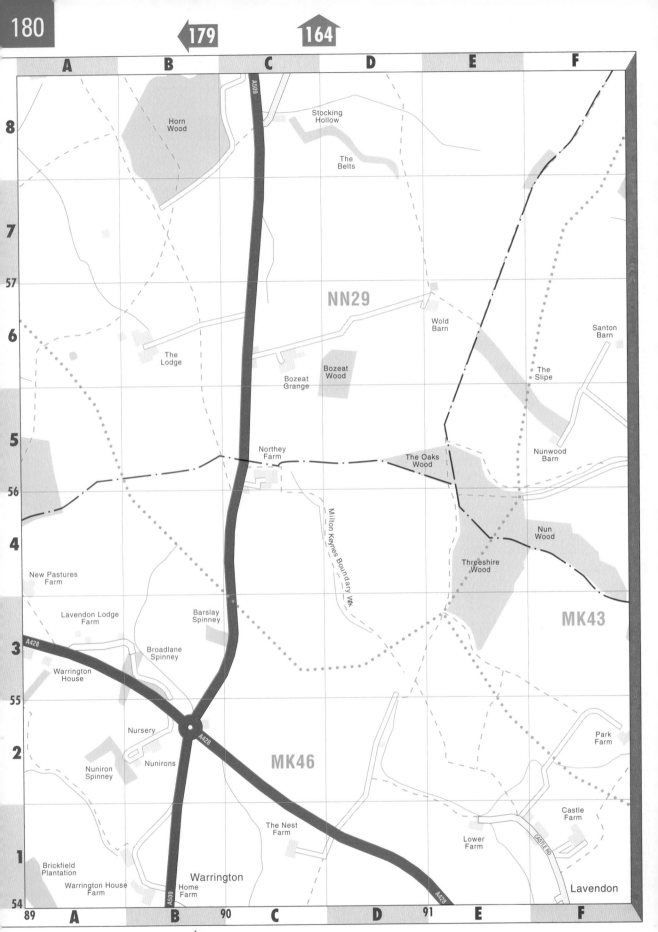

	A	B	C	D	E	F

Horn Wood

Stocking Hollow

The Belts

NN29

Wold Barn

Santon Barn

The Lodge

The Slippe

Bozeat Wood

Bozeat Grange

Northey Farm

The Oaks Wood

Nunwood Barn

Nun Wood

Milton Keynes Boundary Wk.

Threeshire Wood

MK43

New Pastures Farm

Lavendon Lodge Farm

Barslay Spinney

Broadlane Spinney

Warrington House

Nursery

Park Farm

MK46

Nuniron Spinney

Nunirons

The Nest Farm

Lower Farm

Castle Farm

Brickfield Plantation

Warrington House Farm

Warrington

Home Farm

Lavendon

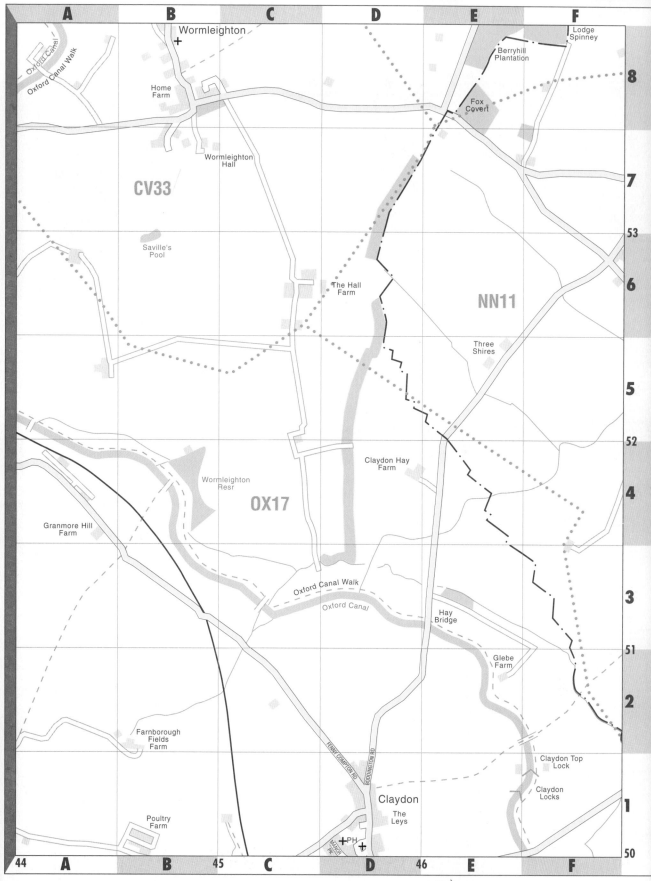

A **B** **C** **D** **E** **F**

8

Highland Farm

Townsend Farm

Upper Boddington

Playing Field

TOWNSEND LA

FARM STILE

THE LEYS

LONDON END

FROG LA

WARWICK RD

PH

PO

(Boddington)
Upper
Boddington
CE Prim Sch

CHURCH RD

Manor Farm

P

P

Boddington Resr

7

53

Spella House

6

NN11

The Manor Farm

The Grange

Sewage Works

HILL RD

OWL END
WAY

OWL END LA

PH

THE PADDOCK

MILLERS CL

BODDINGTON CT

Lower Boddington

WELSH RD

5

52

Cedars Farm

BANBURY RD

Paradise Farm

4

Springfield House

3

51

Sewage Works

BLACKSMITHS LA

SUTTON FERS CL

PO

MAIN ST

PLOWDEN CL

Aston-le-Walls
St Mary's
RC Prim Sch

Manor Farm

Aston
le Walls

APPLETREE LA

2

OX17

Lawn Hill

Field's Cottages

1

Highfurlong Brook

50

47 **A** **B** 48 **C** **D** 49 **E** **F**

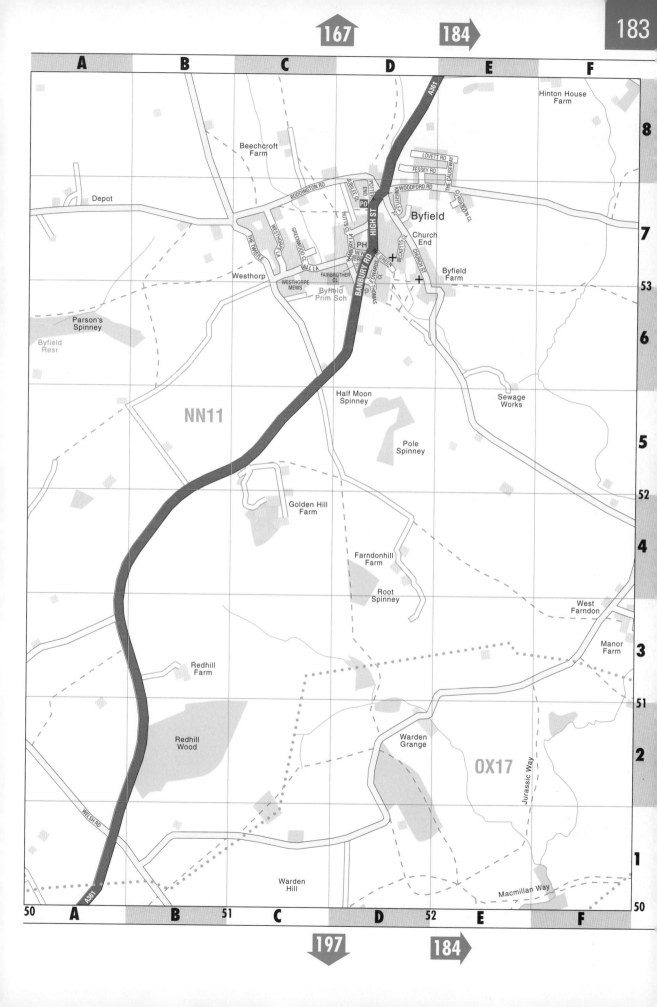

A B C D E F

8

Hinton House
Farm

Beechcroft
Farm

LOVETT RD
FESSEY RD
WOODFORD RD
THE CAUSEWAY

Depot

BODDINGTON RD

Byfield

7

Church
End

PH

THE GREEN

Westhorp

Byfield
Farm

WESTHORPE
MEWS

FAIRBROTHER
CL

Byfield
Prim Sch

53

Parson's
Spinney

6

Byfield
Resr

Sewage
Works

Half Moon
Spinney

NN11

Pole
Spinney

5

52

Golden Hill
Farm

4

Farndonhill
Farm

West
Farndon

Root
Spinney

Manor
Farm

3

Redhill
Farm

51

Redhill
Wood

Warden
Grange

OX17

Jurassic Way

2

WELSH RD

A361

Warden
Hill

Macmillan Way

1

50 51 52 50
A B C D E F

183
168

A **B** **C** **D** **E** **F**

8

7

THE BEAVER CTR
Mast
FAY CL
AVE
WHITCROFT
GORSE RD
CENTRY
DRYDEN CL
BYFIELD RD
GREAT CENTRAL WAY
53
MANOR RD
TOWNSEND
MENDIP WAY
BEECH DR
NELSON AVE
WILLOW
PRIMROSE WLK
LOVELL AVE
HIBEL
Woodford Halse
Liby
PO
SCHOOL ST
Foxhill Farm
CHESTNUT CL
SYCAMORE
BARNETT
ANSCOMBE WAY
GREBE
SWAN
HERON
MALLARD
ADAMS RD
GRES
CL
PHIPPS CL
LABURNUM
CASTLE RD
SIDNEY RD
PERCY RD
1 EBONY QT
2 WINSTON CL
MOUNT PLEASANT
SCRIVENS HILL
Woodford Halse CE Prim Sch
6
Hinton
MAPLE CL
ASH WAY
BIRCH
ROW WAY
TOP FARM
WILD
OAK
CHERRY CL
HINTON CL CT
HINTON MANOR CT
KINGFISHER CL
CHERWELL TERR
QUINTON LA
PARSONS ST
HIGH ST
SOUTH ST
PH
HAWTHORNE CL
HINTON RD
STATION RD
STATION GDNS
CHURCH ST

Woodford Hill Farm

POOL SA
FARNDON RD
BROMLEY FARM CT
Bromley's Farm
River Cherwell
Gravel Farm

Woodford Hill

5
Sewage Works
Jurassic Way

52
Gravelfield Barn
Dairy Farm
NN11

Cherry Tree

4

Eydonhill
Moors Farm

Tile Barn

3

51
Cedars Farm

Crockwell Farm

2
OX17
Ashby's Farm

BYFIELD RD
MANOR RD
WAY
WINSTON
HILL VIEW
PRESTON RD
MORETON RD
Eydon
PO
PARTRIDGE LA
LIME AVE
HIGH ST
DOCTORS LA
1
Macmillan Way
BLACKSMITHS LA
PH
Sewage Works
Cemy
HOLLOW WAY
SCHOOL LA
50

53 **A** 54 **B** **C** **D** 55 **E** **F**

183
198

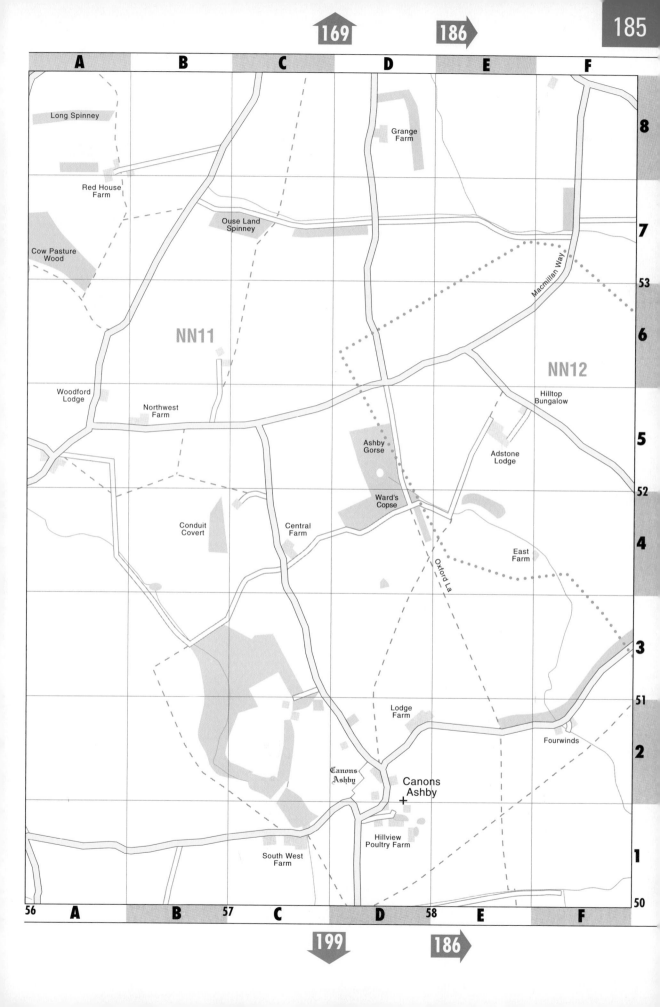

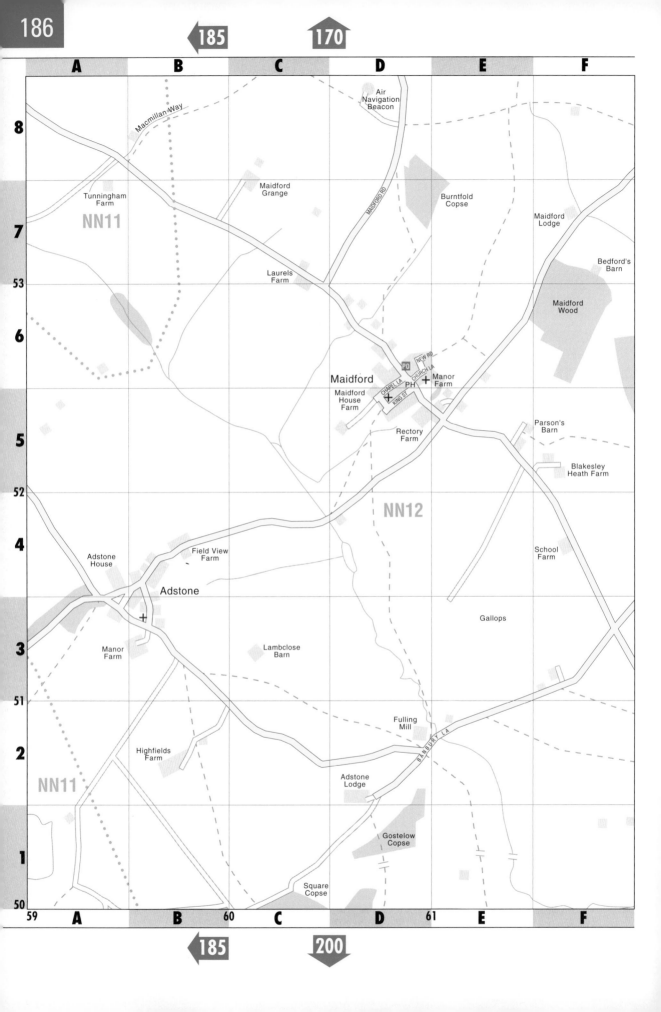

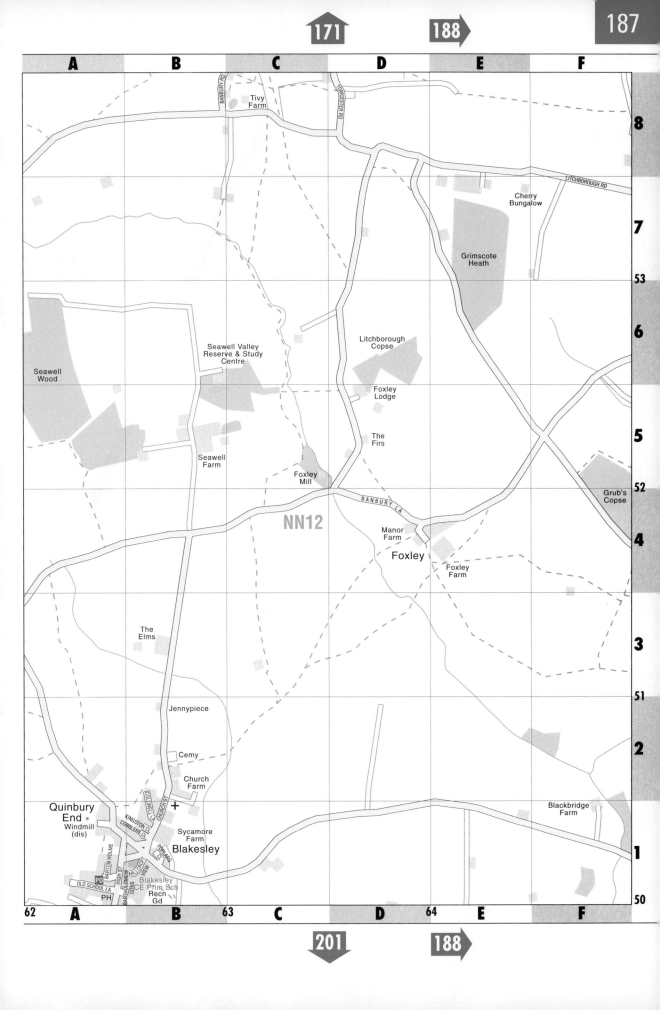

A   B   C   D   E   F

8

Litchborough Rd

Tivy Farm

Banbury Rd

Towcester Rd

Cherry Bungalow

7

53

Grimscote Heath

6

Seawell Valley Reserve & Study Centre

Litchborough Copse

Seawell Wood

Foxley Lodge

5

The Firs

Seawell Farm

52

Foxley Mill

Grub's Copse

NN12

Banbury La

Manor Farm

4

Foxley

Foxley Farm

The Elms

3

51

Jennypiece

2

Cemy

Church Farm

Blackbridge Farm

Quinbury End

Windmill (dis)

Sycamore Farm

Blakesley

Kingston Cl

Collwell La

Church St

Cobblers Cl

Poplars Cl

1

PO

High St

Bartholomew Gdns

Hallcroft View

Blakesley CE Prim Sch

Old School La

PH

Recn Gd

50

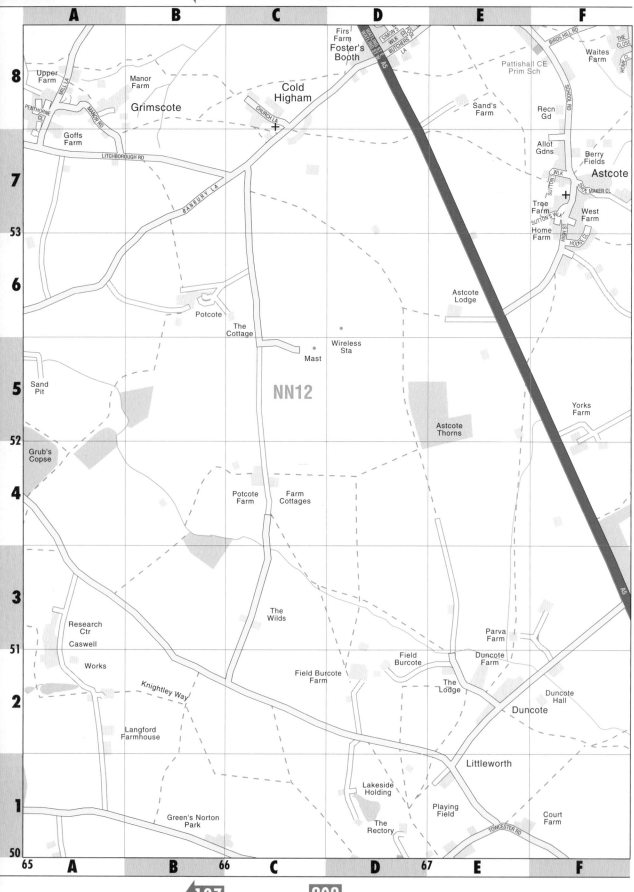

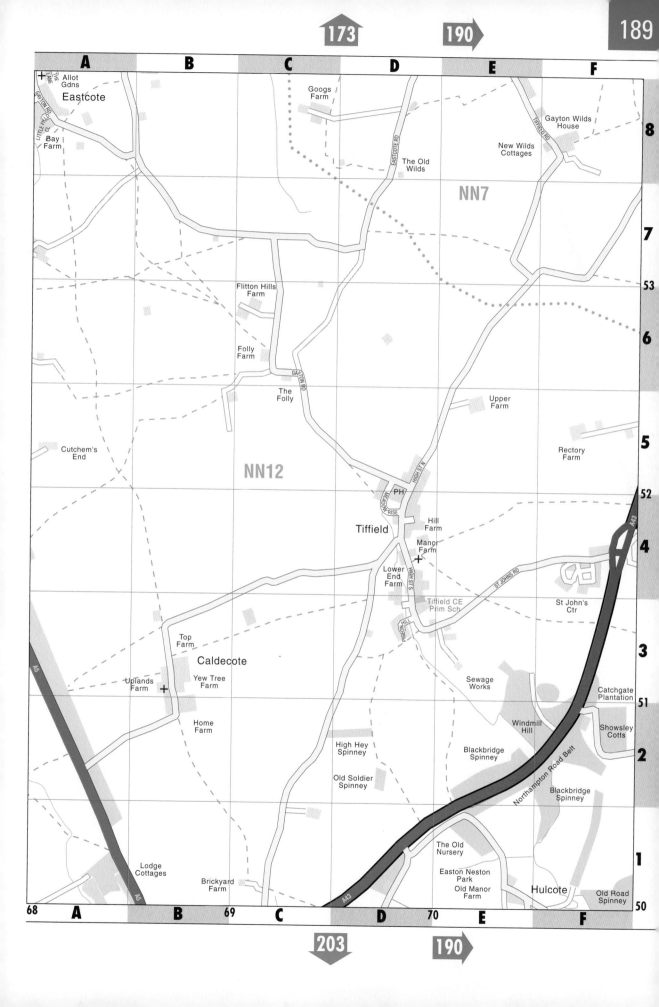

189
174

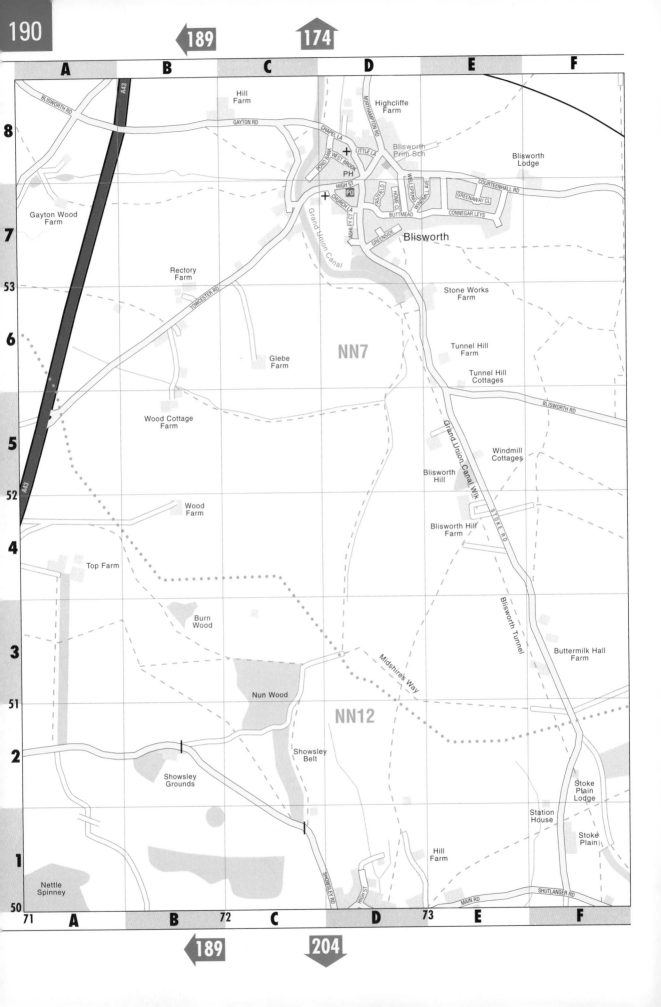

189
204

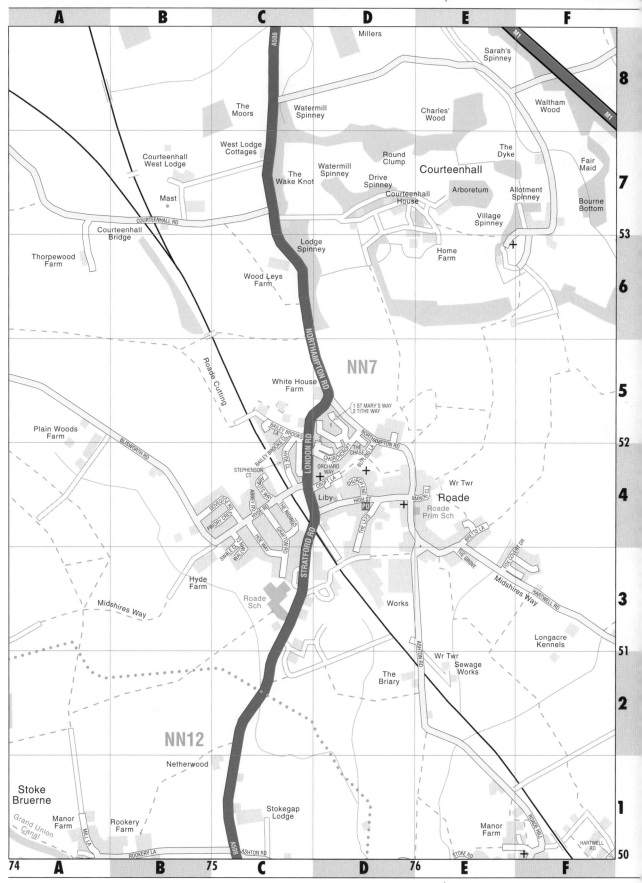

191
176

A **B** **C** **D** **E** **F**

8

Manor Farm

Manor Cottages

West Hall

M1

7

Liddell Wood

Quinton Green

Midshires Way

53

East Lodge

6

Villach

Crabtree Thick

Church Path Oak

Stoneway Copse

5

Fox Covert

Forest Close

Hollow Quarter

Shrubby Copse

52

NN7

Forest Lodge

4

Ashwood Farm

Midshires Way

Forest Wlk

Rush Copse

Hartwell Clear Copse

Seven Oaks

Pound Riding

3

Rawlesmere Copse

51

Rowley Wood

Vicarage

Ashton Lodge Farm

Woodland View Farm

Forest Glade

Sandpit Copse

2

HARTWELL RD

Colmarel Kennels

Ashton House

Meadslade

Forest View

WOOD

OAK CL

BARLEY

STONEWAY

CRABTREE CL

FOREST RD

FOREST AVE

HAZEL

SALCEY CL

RUSH CL

ROSE CL

LIME CL

ASHTON RD

CHURCH CL

MALTING

SCHOOL RD

CRAFTON CL

STOCKING CL

Hartwell CE Prim Sch

1

LOWER END

ISWYNCOMBE GM

BLACKSMITHS WAY

ROBINS CL

PARK RD

PARK LA

AMBERLEY RD 1

STONEHURST CL 2

PH Hartwell

Lower End

FOLLY LA

M1

Laythick Copse

50

77 **A** **B** **78** **C** **D** **79** **E** **F**

193
178

A   **B**   **C**   **D**   **E**   **F**

The Paddock

Manor Farm

Cross Maples

Church Slade

8

Hay Copse

NN7

Cowpers Oak Lodge

Biggin Lodge

7

Ravenstone Road Copse

Milton Keynes Boundary Wlk

53

Barnstaple Wood

Dinglederry

Ash Beds

6

Great Wood

Roadley's Brake

Hanger's Spinney

Woodlands

5

52

MK16

4

Cheyney Farm

Parkfield Farm

MK46

Northend Farm

3

NORTHEND

Parkfield Spinney

Milton Keynes Boundary Wlk

Cemy

51

Horshoe Farm

CHASEPORT CL

ABBEY WAY

2

Spring Barn

Ravenstone

WESTON RD

COMMON ST

Yew Tree Farm

1

B526

Mannings Farm

50

83   **A**   **B**   84   **C**   **D**   85   **E**   **F**

193

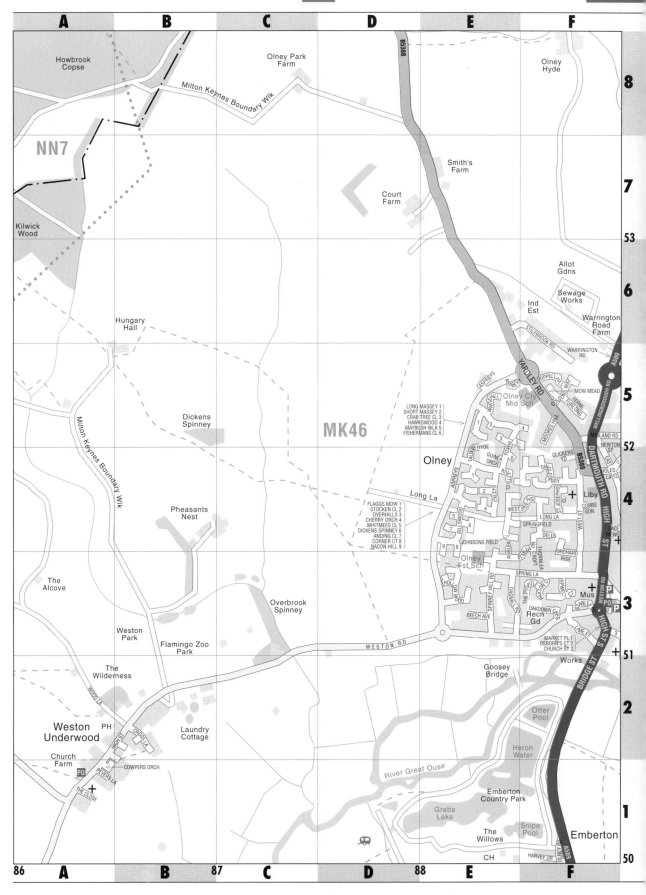

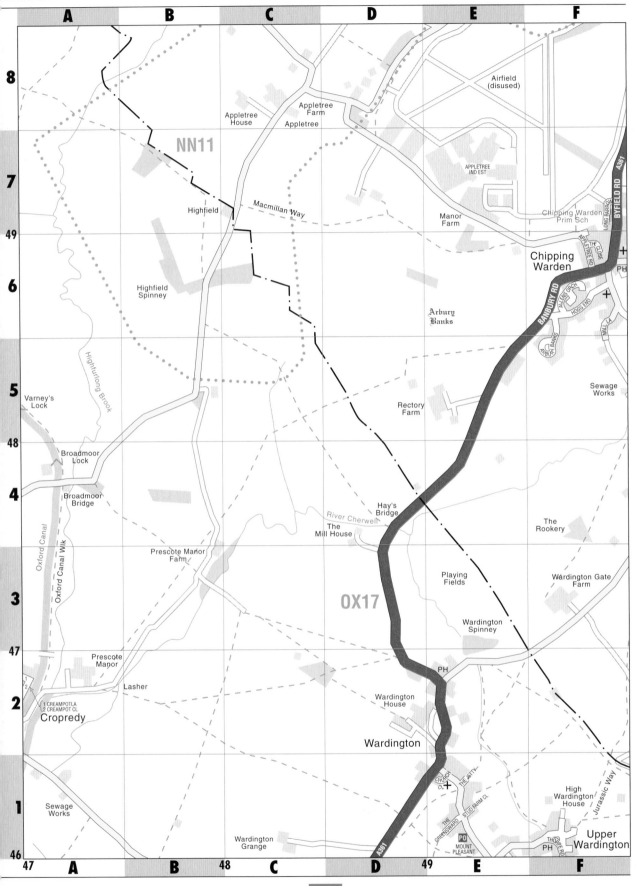

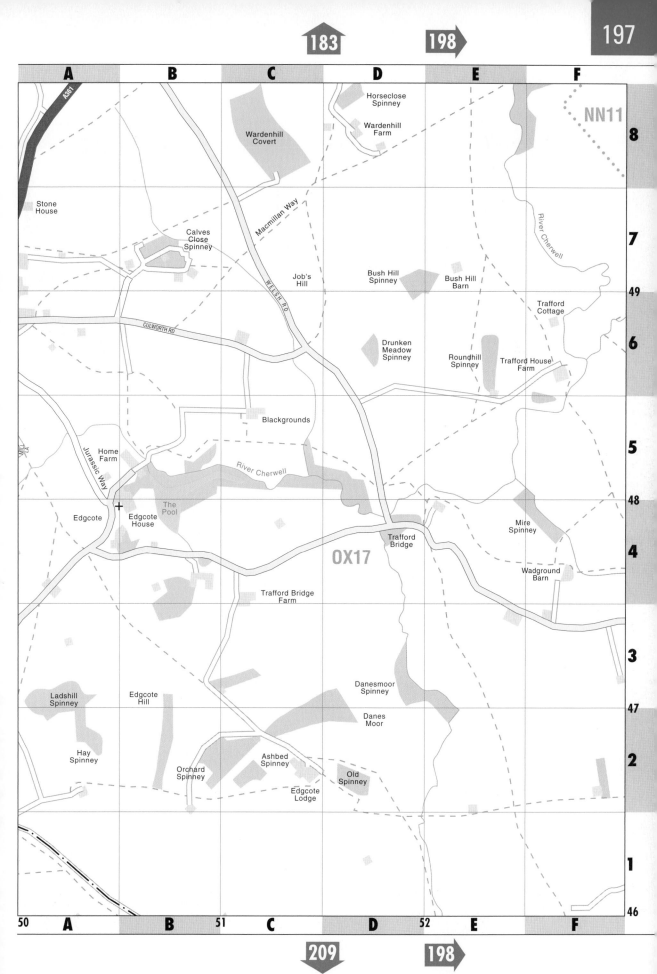

183
198

NN11

A   B   C   D   E   F

A361

Horseclose
Spinney

Wardenhill
Farm

8

Wardenhill
Covert

Stone
House

River Cherwell

7

Calves
Close
Spinney

Macmillan Way

Job's
Hill

Bush Hill
Spinney

Bush Hill
Barn

49

Trafford
Cottage

WELSH RD

CULWORTH RD

Drunken
Meadow
Spinney

Roundhill
Spinney

Trafford House
Farm

6

Blackgrounds

5

Jurassic Way

Home
Farm

River Cherwell

Mire
Spinney

48

Edgcote

Edgcote
House

The
Pool

Trafford
Bridge

OX17

4

Trafford Bridge
Farm

Wadground
Barn

3

Danesmoor
Spinney

Ladshill
Spinney

Edgcote
Hill

47

Danes
Moor

Hay
Spinney

Ashbed
Spinney

2

Orchard
Spinney

Old
Spinney

Edgcote
Lodge

1

46

50   A   B   51   C   D   52   E   F

209
198

197
184

A B C D E F

8

7

49

6

5

48

4

3

47

2

1

46

Hall Farm

Eydon Hall

Eydon Park

The Rookery

Foxhill Farm

Fox Covert

Lawnhill Farm

Macmillan Way

Little Close

Blackbird Hill Spinney

Long Spinney

NN11

Blackbird Hill Farm

Rye Hill Farm

Fulford Spinney

Zig-Zag Farm

Lodge Farm

Pewitt Farm

OX17

Fulford Farm

Adwell Farm

Culworth

HIGH ST

Culworth Hall

Banbury La

Barrow Hill

PH

THE GREEN

Culworth CE Prim Sch

QUEENS ST

TO JCT. WAY

BARL CL

PO

BUTTS CL

Sewage Works

Culworth House

Culworth Fields

BANBURY LA

SULGRAVE RD

Sulgrave Farm

Culworth Grounds Farm

53 A B 54 C D 55 E F

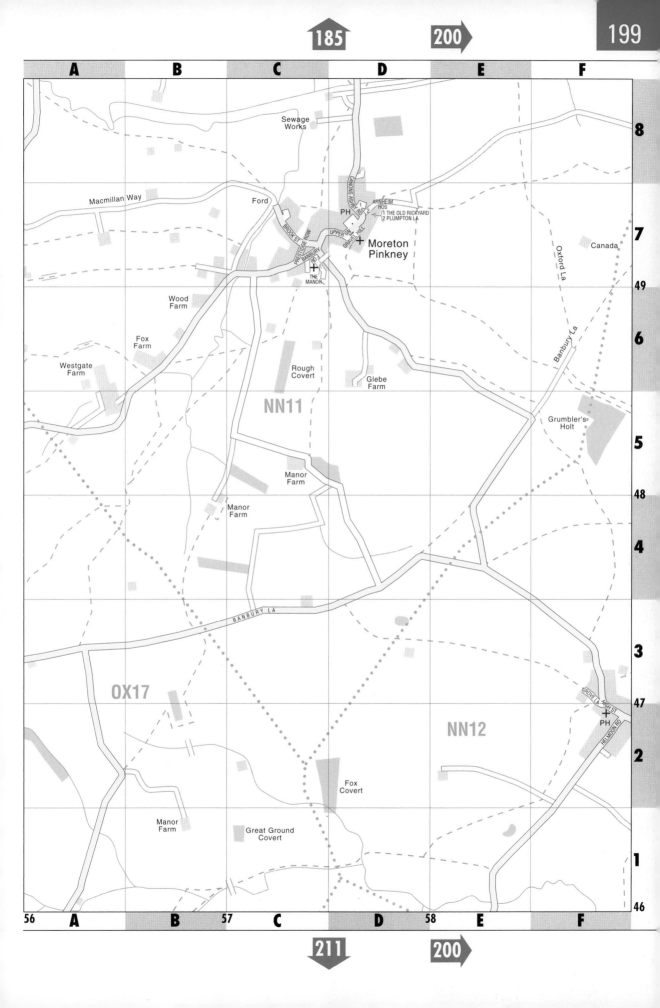

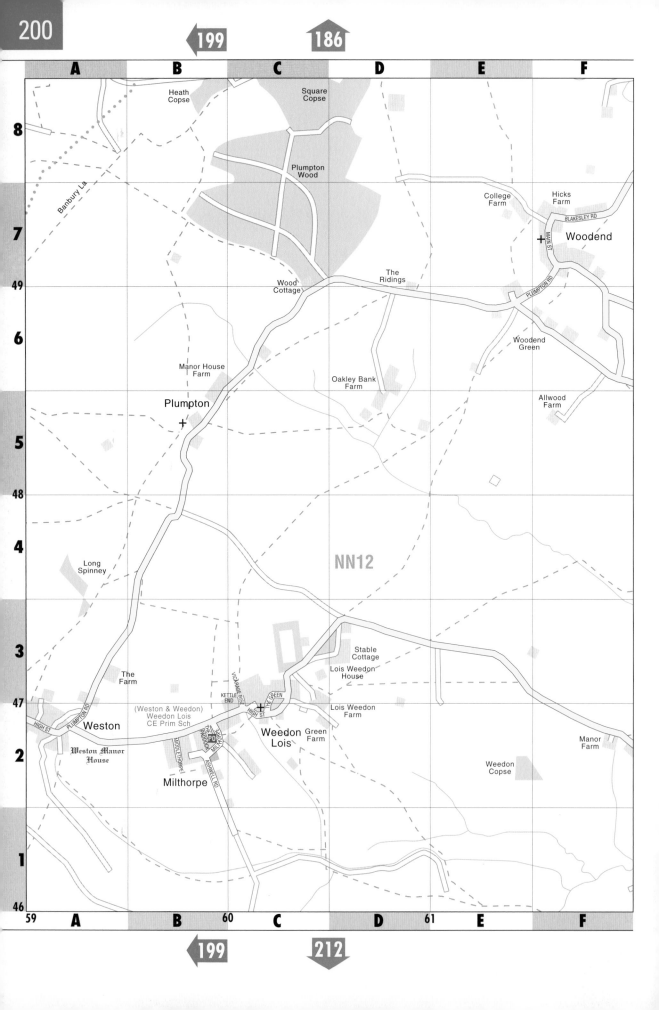

199
186

A **B** **C** **D** **E** **F**

8

Heath
Copse

Square
Copse

Plumpton
Wood

7

Banbury La

College
Farm

Hicks
Farm

BLAKESLEY RD

Woodend

MAIN ST

49

Wood
Cottage

The
Ridings

PLUMPTON RD

6

Manor House
Farm

Woodend
Green

Oakley Bank
Farm

Allwood
Farm

Plumpton

5

48

4

Long
Spinney

NN12

3

Stable
Cottage

The
Farm

Lois Weedon
House

VICARAGE RISE

THE GREEN

KETTLE
END

47

(Weston & Weedon)
Weedon Lois
CE Prim Sch

HIGH ST

Lois Weedon
Farm

HIGH ST

PLUMPTON RD

Weston

THE
PADDOCK

Weedon
Lois

Green
Farm

Manor
Farm

SCHOOL
MILL

2

Weston Manor
House

MIDDLETHORPE

ASHWELL RD

Milthorpe

Weedon
Copse

1

46

59 **A** **B** **60** **C** **D** **61** **E** **F**

A B C D E F

8

7

49

6

Blakesley
Hall Lodge

Recn
Gd

Sewage
Works

Brookside

Kirby
Grounds

Hootens
Farm

Tite's
Copse

Home
Farm

Bradden
Bradden
House

MAIN ST

WILLOWS HILL

LOWER END

Warrs Farm

Woodend
Ground

Southfields

Manor
Farm

WATER LA

Lane
Farm

5

48

4

The
Bungalow

NN12

Green's
Park

Slaptonhill
Farm

3

47

Slapton
Manor

LOCKTONS
CL

CHURCH LA

Home
Farm

CHAPEL LA

Slapton

Mill

Abthorpe
Manor

PH

Home
Farm

SILVER ST

THE GREEN

MAIN ST

2

River Tove

Abthorpe

Sewage
Works

Highfield's
Farm

WAPPENHAM RD

STANHILL ROW

BRACKLEY LA

1

Manor Farm
Cottages

Springfield
Farm

46

62 A B 63 C D 64 E F

201
188

| | A | B | C | D | E | F |

8

Langford
Farm

Falcon Manor
Sch

Green's Norton
CE Sch

BLAKESELY HILL

NEW RD

TOWCESTER RD

BENHAM RD

SCHOOL LA

CHURCH GDNS

CALVERT RD

FALCON VIEW

PH

PO

SCHOOL LA

SCHOOL CL

SOUTH
TERR

SYCAMORE
RD

CALVERT CL

WINDMILL
WAY

HOME CL

HIGH ST

CHURCH VIEW

Lodge
Farm

BRADDEN WAY

SMITHLAND CT

BENGAL VIEW

BRADDEN RD

Greens
Norton

7

Kingthorn
Mill

Bengal

BENGAL LA

The
Hall

Mill
Farm

MILL LA

49

Glebe
Farm

Kingthorn
Wood

Sewage
Works

6

Holywell
Farm

Costwell
Farm

5

48

River Tove

NN12

Rignall

4

Mileoak
Farm

Hill
Farm

3

Foxcote

Handley

Foxcote House
Farm

Park
Farm

47

Ox
Bridge

2

SCHOOL LA

WAPPENHAM RD

1

Handley
Barn

46

| 65 | A | | B | 66 | C | | D | 67 | E | | F |

201
214

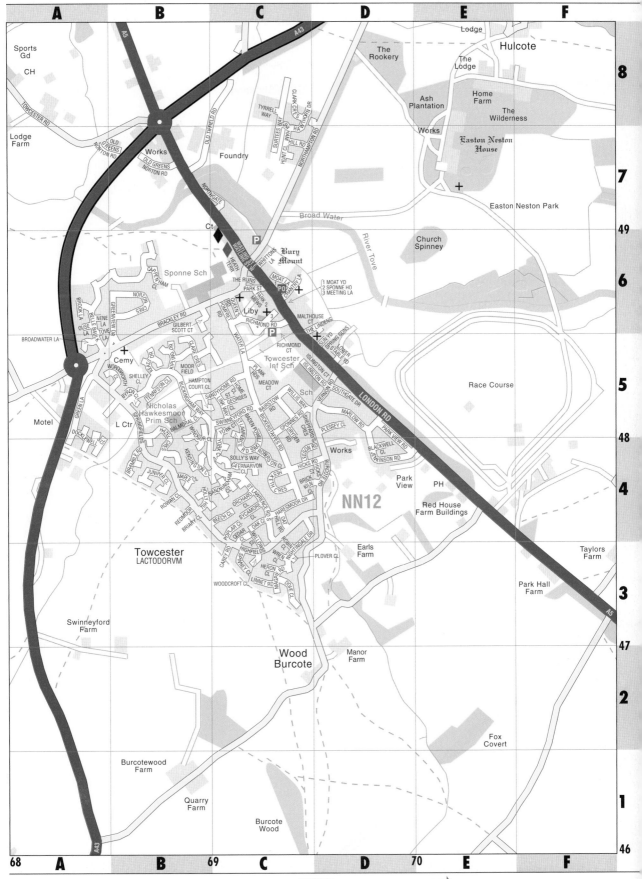

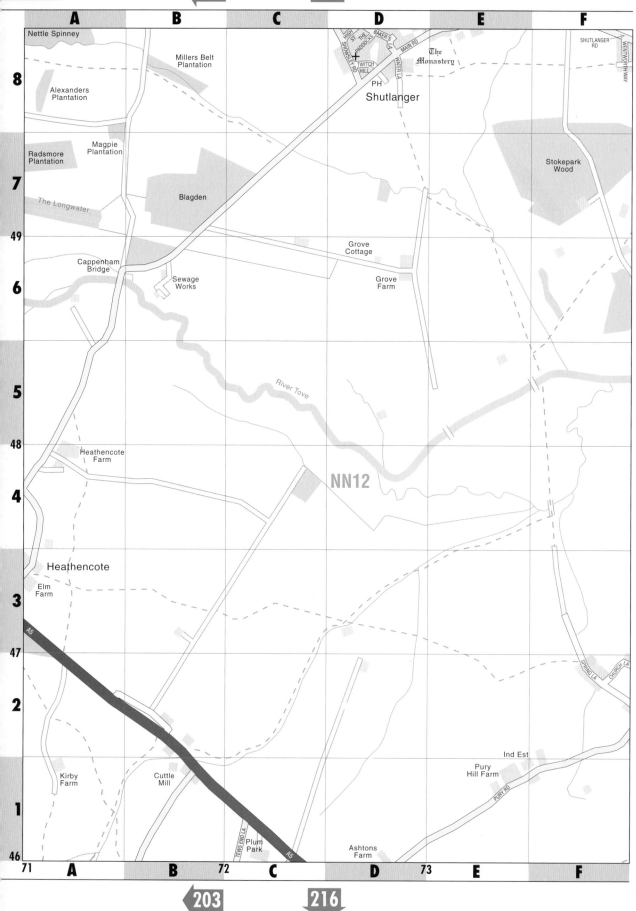

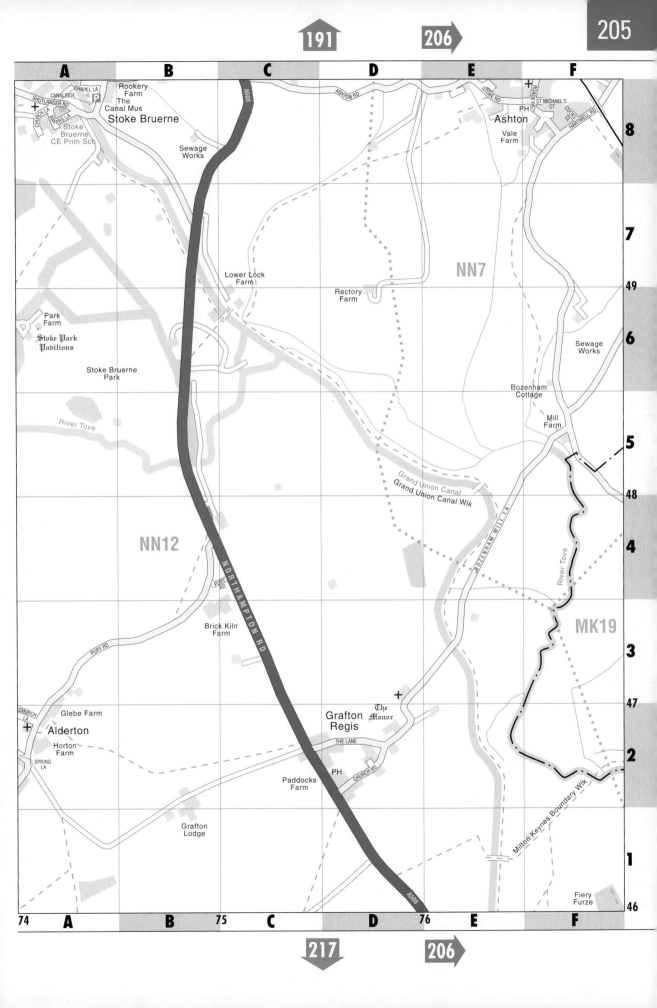

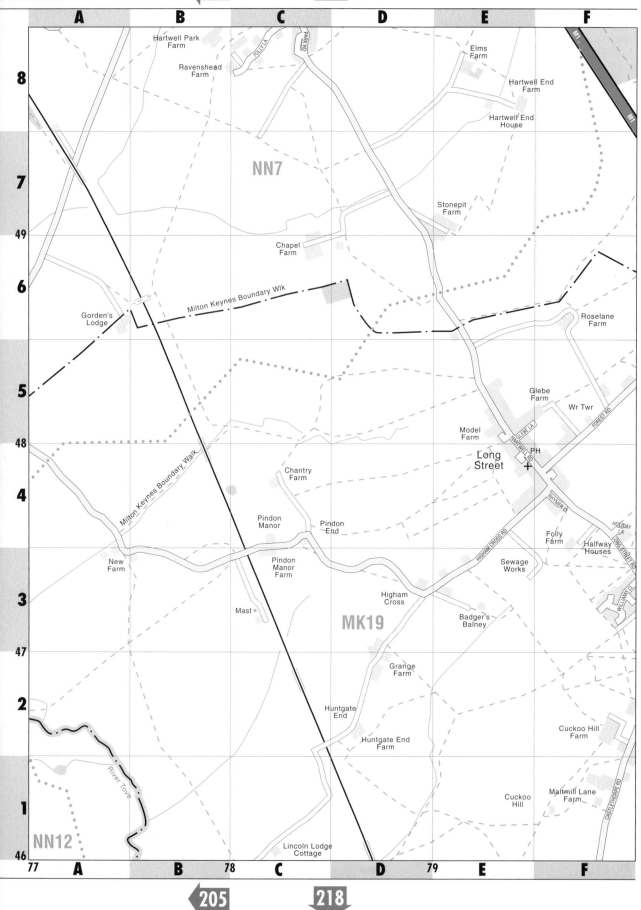

8

7

49

6

5

48

4

3

47

2

1

46

NN7

NN12

MK19

Hartwell Park Farm

Ravenshead Farm

Elms Farm

Hartwell End Farm

Hartwell End House

Stonepit Farm

Chapel Farm

Milton Keynes Boundary Wlk

Gorden's Lodge

Roselane Farm

Glebe Farm

Wr Twr

Model Farm

Long Street

PH

Milton Keynes Boundary Walk

Chantry Farm

Pindon Manor

Pindon End

Folly Farm

Halfway Houses

New Farm

Pindon Manor Farm

Sewage Works

Mast

Higham Cross

Badger's Balney

HIGHAM CROSS RD

Grange Farm

Cuckoo Hill Farm

Huntgate End

Huntgate End Farm

Cuckoo Hill

Maltmill Lane Farm

River Tove

Lincoln Lodge Cottage

FOLLY LA

PARK RD

FOREST RD

GLEBE LA

HARTWELL RD

RHYMER CL

HOLIDAY LA

LONG STREET RD

WILLIAMS CL

CASTLETHORPE RD

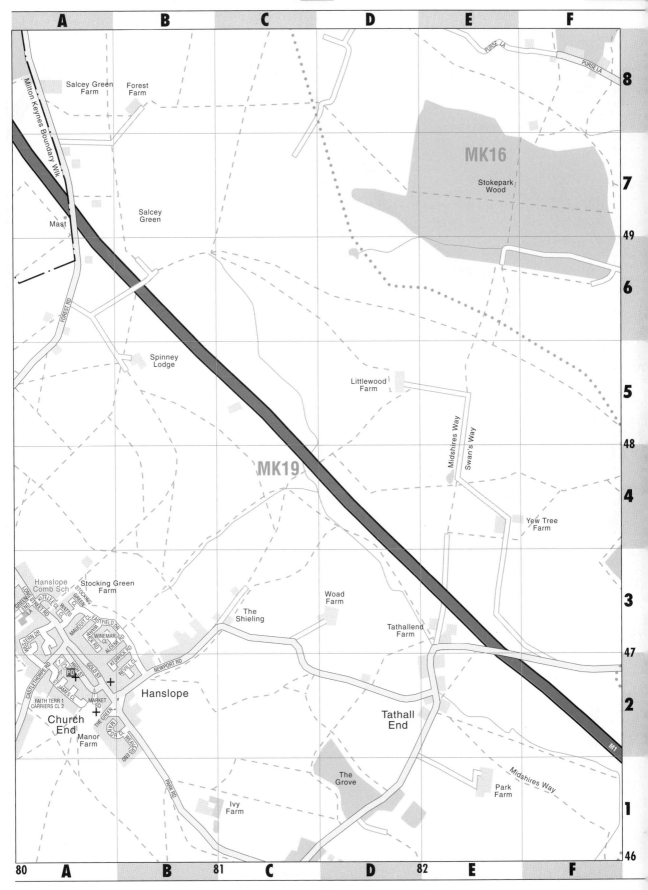

A B C D E F

8

7

49

6

5

48

4

47

3

2

1

46

MK16

Stokepark
Wood

MK19

Milton Keynes Boundary Wlk

Salcey Green
Farm

Forest
Farm

Salcey
Green

Mast

FOREST RD

Spinney
Lodge

Littlewood
Farm

Midshires Way

Swan's Way

Yew Tree
Farm

PURSE LA

PURSE LA

Hanslope
Comb Sch

Stocking Green
Farm

STOCKING
GREEN
CL

KYTE/LEE CL

WATTS
CL

LONG ST
END

GREEN'S
END

STREET RD

STERN DR

WEST

MAUDUIT CL

N'MAN
CL

WINEMAR
CL

EASTFIELD DR

ALDENE RD

STACK RD

HARTWELL RD

KESWICK RD

GOLD ST

NEVILL CL

NEWPORT RD

CASTLETHORPE RD

ST JAMES CL

PO

FAITH TERR 1
CARRIERS CL 2

MARKET
SQ

THE GREEN

TATHALL RD

Church
End

Manor
Farm

Hanslope

The Shieling

Woad
Farm

Tathallend
Farm

Tathall
End

PARK RD

Ivy
Farm

The Grove

Park
Farm

Midshires Way

M1

80 A B 81 C D 82 E F

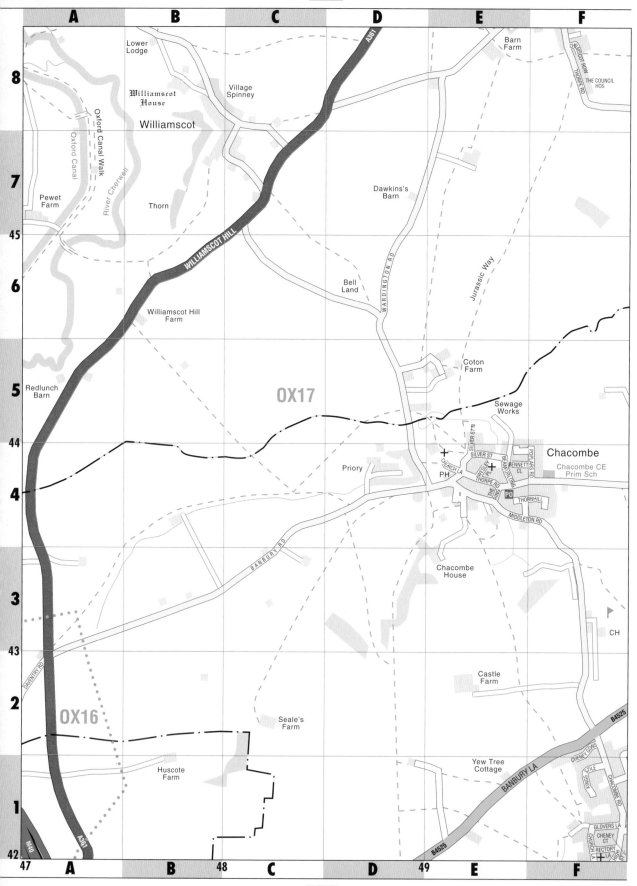

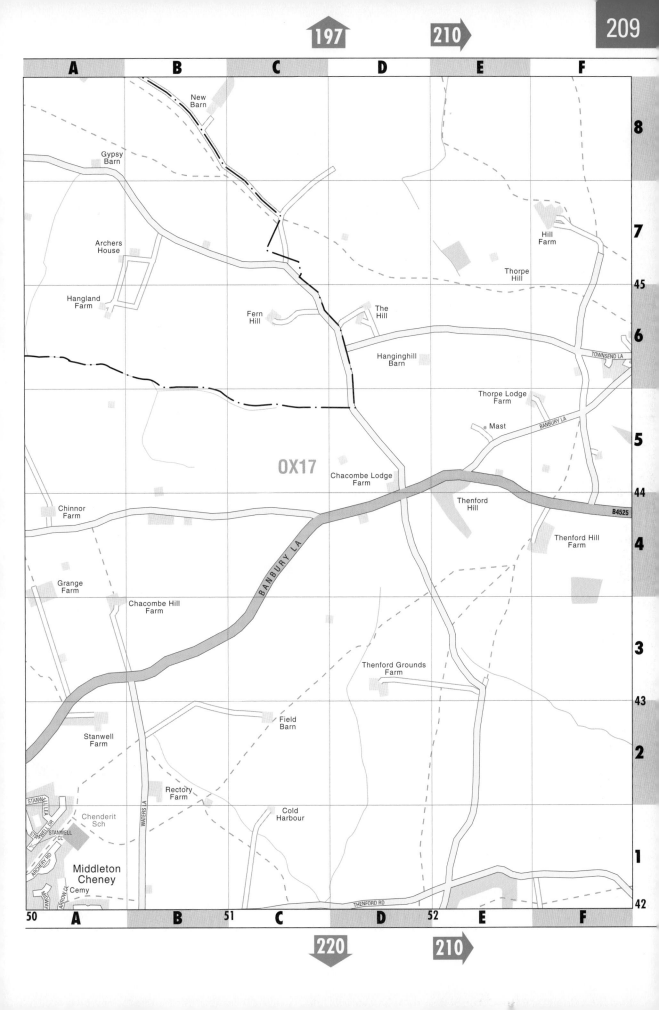

209 198

A B C D E F

8

Windmill (dis)

Happy Lands

Sulgrave
Hotel

PH
MANOR RD

STOCKWELL LA

SPINNERS COTTS

Lower Thorpe

PO

MAGPIE RD

SCHOOL ST

LITTLE ST

7

Magpie Farm

Castle Hill

PARK LA

CHURCH ST

HELMDON RD

45

Thorpe Mandeville

Manor House

Sewage Works

THE WARREN

DOVE COTTS

6

PH

Costow House

BANBURY LA

5

Dean Barn

Painter's Spinney

44

B4525

OX17

4

Woods Farm

Marston Hill Farm

Stuchbury Manor Farm

MARSTON HILL

Masts

B4525

3

43

ASTRAL ROW

HELMDON RD

WHITTON CL

PEVERIL RD

2

DERING COTTS

WESTHORP

EAST VIEW

Greatworth Prim Sch

PH

MARSTON RD

PARGETER CL

PO

Greatworth

WHITTON CL

CHURCH RD

MERESTONE HOS

FIELD VIEW

KIELDSEN CL

SOUTH CL

CHAPEL RD

THE SQUARE

Floyd's Farm

1

Marston St Lawrence

BRACKLEY RD

Sewage Works

42

53 A B 54 C D 55 E F

209 221

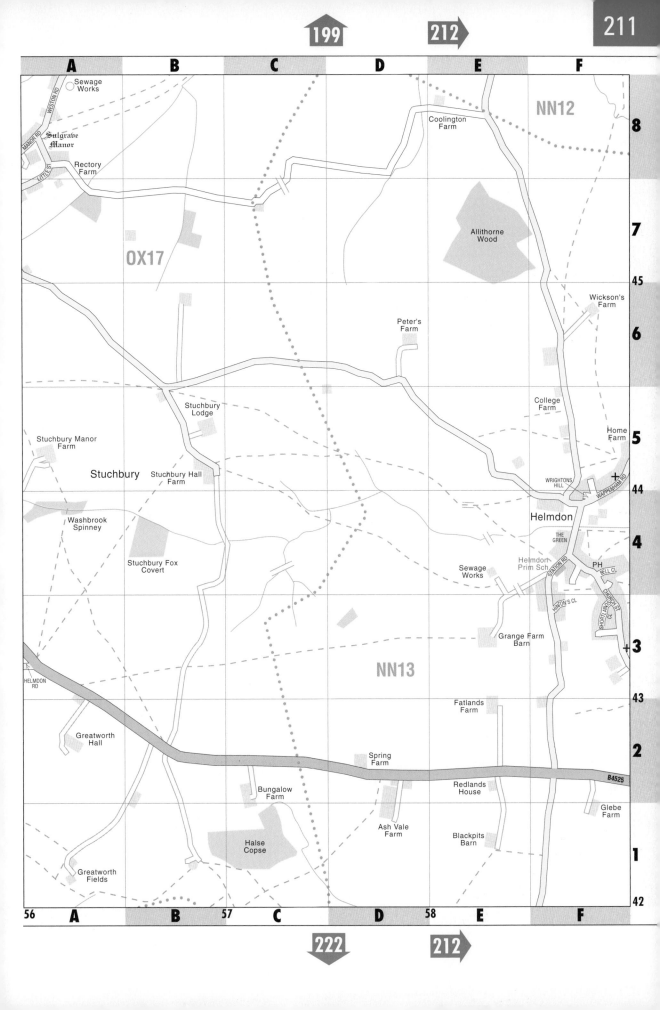

A B C D E F

8

NN12

Sewage
Works

WESTON RD

MANOR RD

Sulgrave
Manor

LITTLE ST

Rectory
Farm

Coolington
Farm

7

OX17

Allithorne
Wood

45

Wickson's
Farm

6

Peter's
Farm

Stuchbury
Lodge

College
Farm

Home
Farm

5

Stuchbury Manor
Farm

Stuchbury

Stuchbury Hall
Farm

WRIGHTONS
HILL

WAPPENHAM RD

44

Helmdon

Washbrook
Spinney

THE
GREEN

4

Stuchbury Fox
Covert

Sewage
Works

Helmdon
Prim Sch

STATION RD

PH

BELL CL

HIXON'S CL

SHORTLANDS CL

CHURCH ST

Grange Farm
Barn

3

NN13

HELMDON
RD

Fatlands
Farm

43

Greatworth
Hall

2

Spring
Farm

B4525

Bungalow
Farm

Redlands
House

Glebe
Farm

Halse
Copse

Ash Vale
Farm

Blackpits
Barn

1

Greatworth
Fields

42

56 A B 57 C D 58 E F

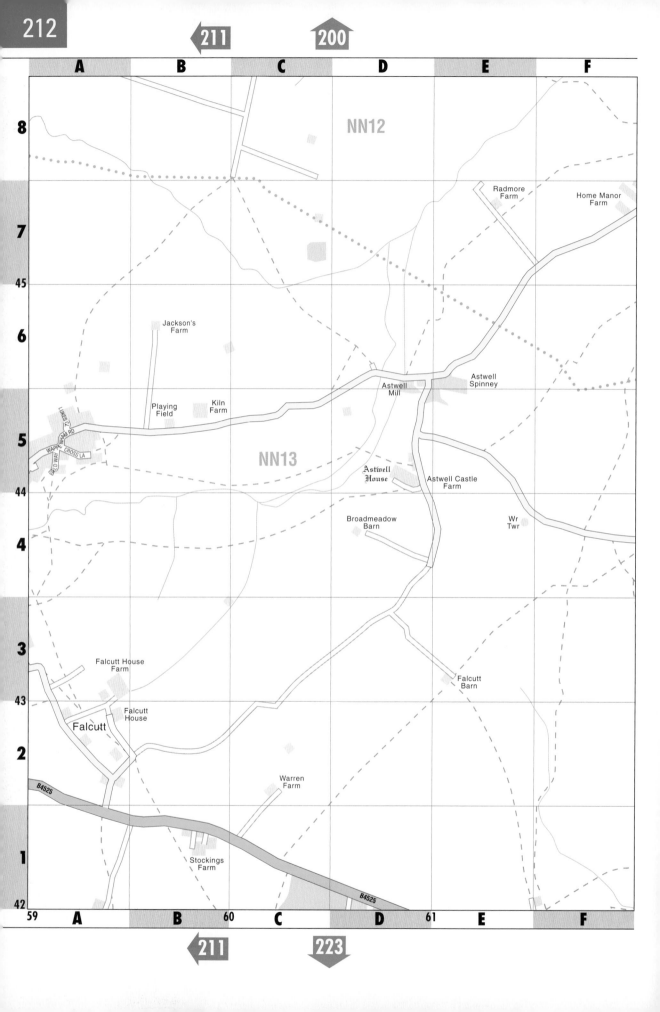

211
200

NN12

Radmore
Farm

Home Manor
Farm

Jackson's
Farm

Astwell
Spinney

Astwell
Mill

Playing
Field

Kiln
Farm

NN13

Astwell
House

Astwell Castle
Farm

LUKES CL

WAPP WNHAM RD

CROSS LA

FIELD WAY

Broadmeadow
Barn

Wr
Twr

Falcutt House
Farm

Falcutt
Barn

Falcutt
House

Falcutt

Warren
Farm

B4525

Stockings
Farm

B4525

211
223

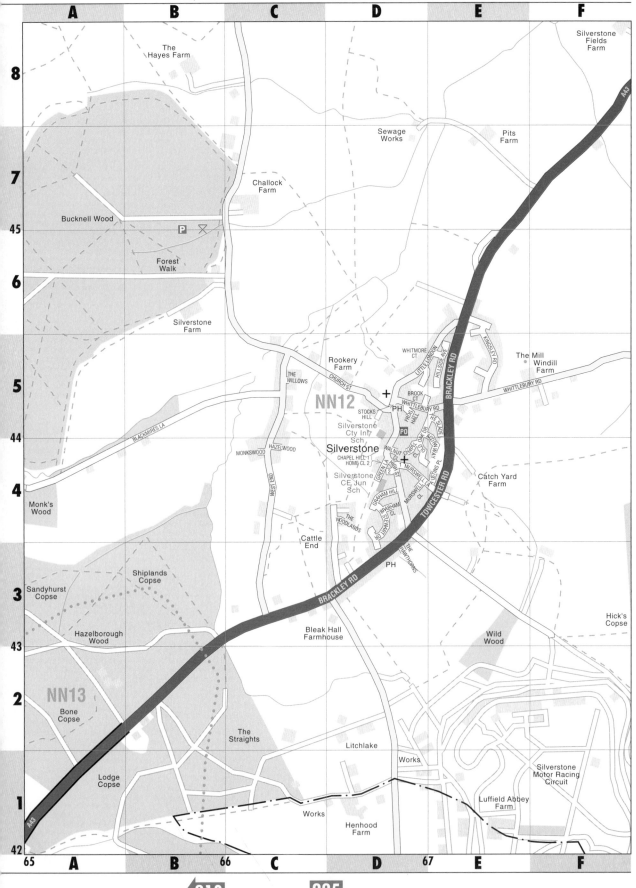

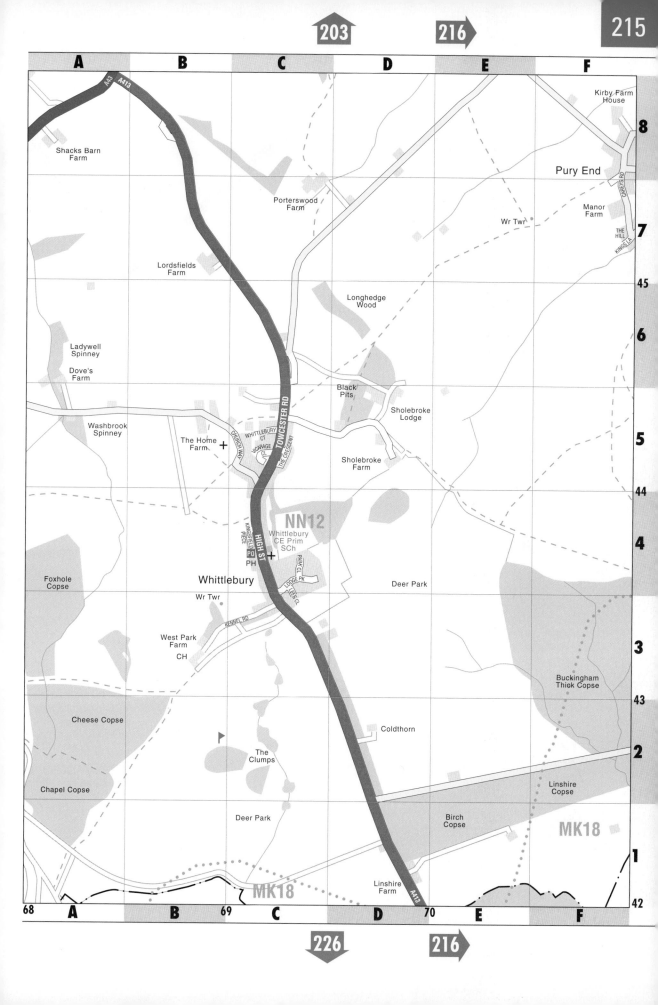

215
204

A B C D E F

8

Tew's
End
Paulerspury CE Prim Sch
Paulerspury
Plum Park
Grafton Park

Carey's Rd
Scriveners La
Lower St
PO
PH
The Green
Park La
Fairfield Rd
Lumber La
Tews End La
New Out Cl
Stony Hill
High St
Longcroft La
Grays Cl
Grays La
Plum Park La
Pury Rd
A5

7

Kingstons Farm
Plumpton End
Plum Park Farm

45

6

Park Farm
The Gullet

Stollage Farm
Bradlem Pond

5

NN12

King's Copse

44

Bear's Copse
Lady Copse

4

Say's Copse

Old Tun Copse
THE KENNELS
KENNELS DR

3

Smalladine Copse

43

Wakefield Lawn

2

MK18

Whittlewood Forest

Wakefield Lodge
MAIN DR
The Pheasantry
DEANSHANGER DR

1

Home Farm
Briary Wood
Hill Copse

42

71 A 72 B C 73 D E F

215
227

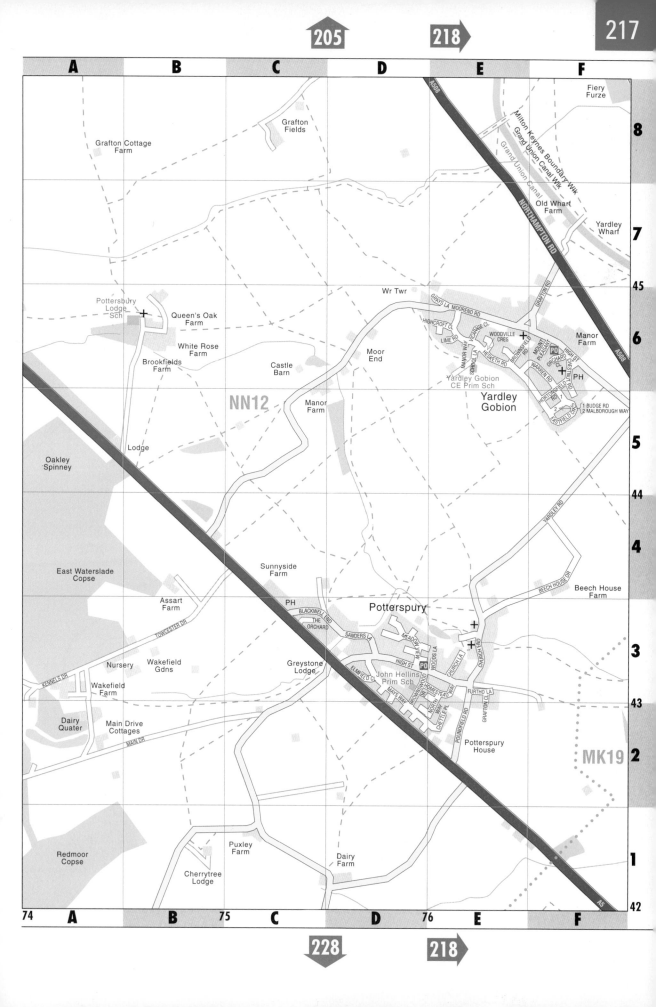

217
206

A **B** **C** **D** **E** **F**

8

Lincoln Lodge

7

Lower Balney Grounds

45

NN12

6

Milford Leys Farm

MK19

Castlethorpe Mill (dis)

Castlethorpe

Isworth Farm

Castlethorpe Fst Sch

THE CHESTNUTS PH

NORTH ST

STATION RD

SCHOOL LA

PROSPECT PL

SOUTH ST

NEW RD

PO

5

Badger's Farm

River Tove

THE CHEQUERS

SHEPPERTON CL

44

Milton Keynes Boundary Wlk
Grand Union Canal Wlk
Grand Union Canal

Sewage Works

4

Cheley Well

Thrupp Wharf

PH

Elm Tree Farm

NORTHAMPTON RD

3

Cobb's Bush Farm

The Priory

Manor Farm

Furtho

Mast

Ivy Cottage

43

Dogsmouth Brook

YARDLEY RD

Cosgrove Prim Sch

BRIDGE RD

PAGE CL

THE GREEN

2

Rectory Farm

Elms Farm

MANOR DR

BENT CL

PO

THE STOCKS

MAIN ST

LOCK LA

St Vincent's Well (chalybeate)

Hotel

Cosgrove

PH

The Little Manor

Ash Pole Spinney

Cosgrove Hall

Cosgrove Leisure Park

Broad Water

1

Knotwood Fields Farm

A508

NORTHAMPTON RD

The Quarries

STRATFORD RD

42

77 **A** **B** 78 **C** **D** 79 **E** **F**

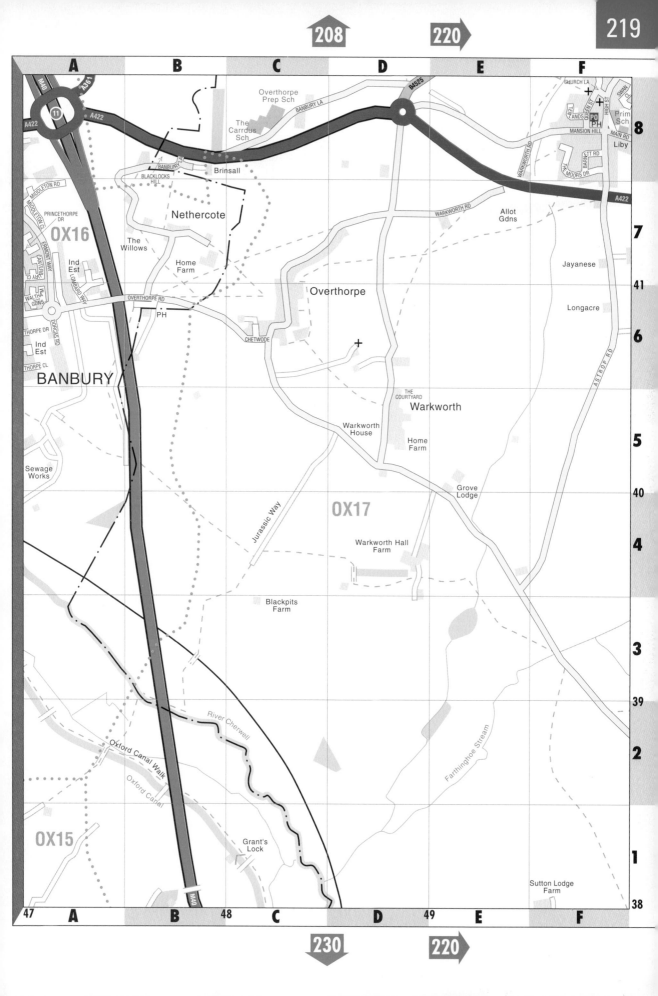

A **B** **C** **D** **E** **F**

8
7
41
6
5
40
4
3
39
2
1
38

47 48 49

M40
A361
A422
A422
11
A4525
A422

CHURCH LA
HIGH ST
SWAN
PO
PH
Prim Sch
Liby
MANSION HILL
MAIN RD
WARKWORTH RD
MOORS DR
TT RD
BARN

Overthorpe
Prep Sch
BANBURY LA
The
Carrdus
Sch
Brinsall
BANBURY LA
BLACKLOCKS
HILL

WARKWORTH RD
Allot
Gdns
Jayanese
Longacre

Nethercote
The
Willows
Home
Farm

OX16
PRINCETHORPE
DR
MIDDLETON RD
MIDDLETON CL
ERMONT WAY
CANTERB
Ind
Est
LOMBARD WAY
WALTHA
GDNS
THORPE DR
DURCAS RD
Ind
Est
THORPE CL

OVERTHORPE RD
PH

Overthorpe

CHETWODE

ASTROP RD

BANBURY

Warkworth
House

THE
COURTYARD
Warkworth
Home
Farm

Grove
Lodge

Sewage
Works

OX17

Jurassic Way

Warkworth Hall
Farm

Blackpits
Farm

River Cherwell

Oxford Canal Walk

Oxford Canal

OX15

Grant's
Lock

Farthinghoe Stream

M40

Sutton Lodge
Farm

219
209

A   B   C   D   E   F

8

MIDWAY
BOWMANS CL
PULL BAULK
ARROW CL
DANDS DR
PEACOCKS CL
NEW TREE CL
ASH TREE CT
THENFORD RD

Lower
Middleton
Cheney

DANDS CL
THE AVENUE
HORTON CRES
HORTON RD
ROSE HALL LA
POPLARS CL
OAK LA
LEYSON CL
WATERS LA
MAIN RD
STALLIONS LA
BRAGGINTONS LA
LONGBURGES
HAILSHAM CT
MANOR CL
HORTON CL
KINGSTON
NETTLE DR
ASHLADE

PH

7   A422

TULBROOK
STONES

Sewage
Works

Burgess
Farm

Thenford
House

Gardener's
Cottage

Thenford

Thenford
Lodge

+

41

OX17

6   Middleton Lodge
Farm

Thenford
Grange

5

Works

Avenue
Bridge

PURSTON
CROSS RDS

40

Farthinghoe Stream

A422

Baldwin's
Spinney

4

Great
Purston

NN13

3   Little
Purston

Farthinghoe
Park

39

Buston
Farm

Buston
Farm
Cottages

2

Farthinghoe
Lodge

Sandy La

1   Astrophill
Farm

Coldharbour

Rosamond's
Bower

38

50   A   51   B   C   52   D   E   F

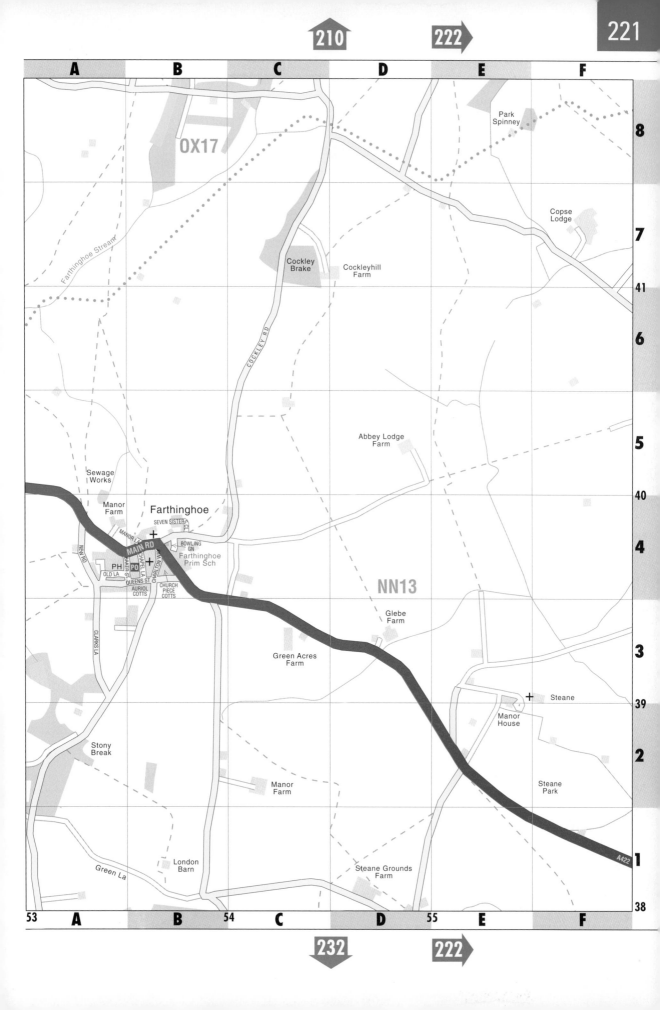

A B C D E F

8
7
41
6
5
40
4
3
39
2
1
38

OX17

Park
Spinney

Copse
Lodge

A422

Farthinghoe Stream

Cockley
Brake

Cockleyhill
Farm

COCKLEY RD

Abbey Lodge
Farm

Sewage
Works

Manor
Farm

Farthinghoe

SEVEN SISTERS

MANOR LA

MAIN RD

CHAPEL LA

JAMES ST

CHARLTON RD

NEW RD

PH

PO

OLD LA

QUEENS ST

AURIOL
COTTS

CLARKS LA

CHURCH
PIECE
COTTS

BOWLING
GN

Farthinghoe
Prim Sch

NN13

Glebe
Farm

Green Acres
Farm

Steane

Manor
House

Stony
Break

Steane
Park

Manor
Farm

Green La

London
Barn

Steane Grounds
Farm

53 A B 54 C D 55 E F 38

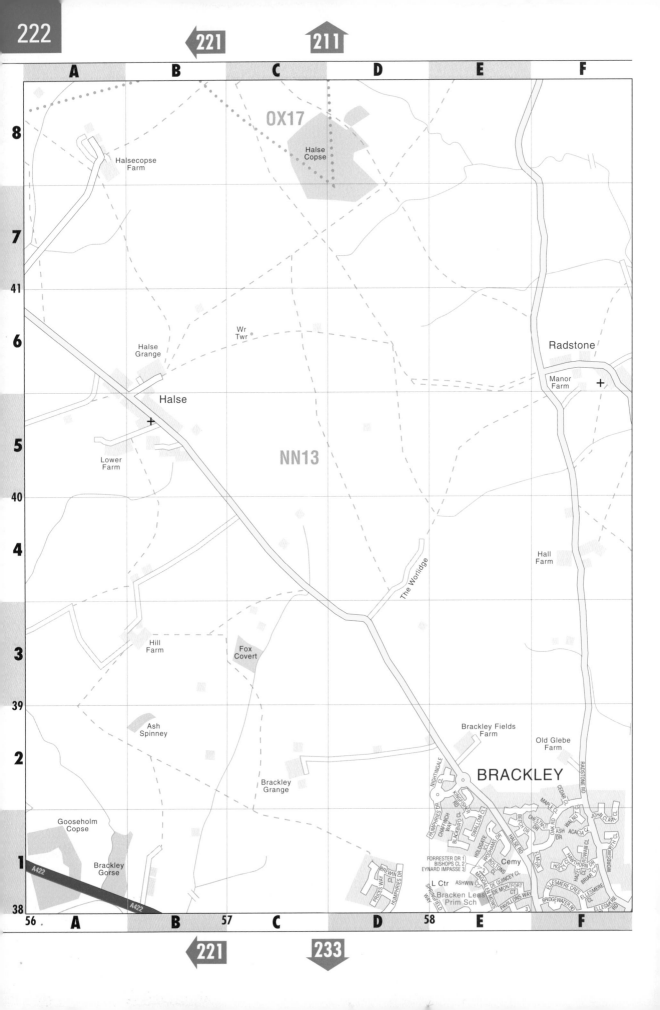

A B C D E F

8

OX17

Halse Copse

Halsecopse Farm

7

41

6

Wr Twr

Radstone

Halse Grange

Manor Farm

Halse

NN13

5

Lower Farm

40

4

Hall Farm

The Worldge

3

Hill Farm

Fox Covert

39

Ash Spinney

Brackley Fields Farm

Old Glebe Farm

2

Brackley Grange

BRACKLEY

NIGHTINGALE

Gooseholm Copse

1

A422

Brackley Gorse

FORRESTER DR 1
BISHOPS CL 2
EYNARD IMPASSE 3

Cemy

L Ctr

Bracken Leas Prim Sch

38

56 A 57 B C 57 D 58 E F

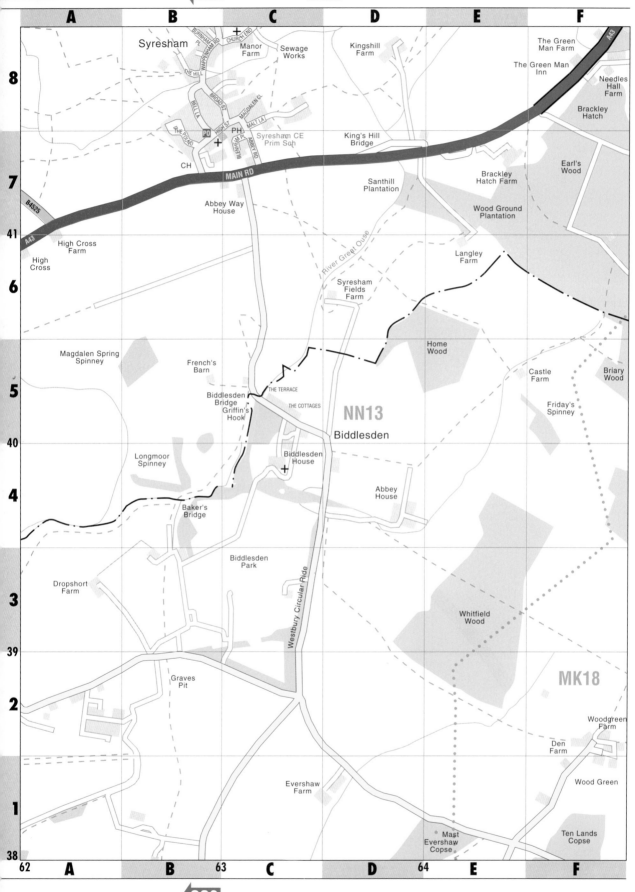

Syresham

Manor Farm

Sewage Works

Kingshill Farm

The Green Man Farm

The Green Man Inn

Needles Hall Farm

Brackley Hatch

8

BURNHAM RD
WAPPENHAM RD
CHURCH END
THE HILL
BROAD ST
BEL LA
MAGDALEN CL
MALT LA
HIGH ST
THE POUND
PO
BLENHEIM PL
ABBEY RD

PH

Syresham CE Prim Sch

King's Hill Bridge

CH

MAIN RD

7

B4525
A43

Abbey Way House

Brackley Hatch Farm

Earl's Wood

Wood Ground Plantation

Santhill Plantation

41

High Cross Farm

High Cross

River Great Ouse

Langley Farm

6

Syresham Fields Farm

Magdalen Spring Spinney

French's Barn

Home Wood

Castle Farm

Briary Wood

5

Biddlesden Bridge
Griffin's Hook

THE TERRACE

THE COTTAGES

NN13

Friday's Spinney

40

Biddlesden

Longmoor Spinney

Biddlesden House

4

Baker's Bridge

Abbey House

Biddlesden Park

Westbury Circular Ride

3

Dropshort Farm

Whitfield Wood

MK18

39

Graves Pit

2

Woodgreen Farm

Den Farm

Evershaw Farm

Wood Green

1

Mast Evershaw Copse

Ten Lands Copse

38

62 A   B   63   C   D   64   E   F

8

Airstrip

NN12

Pentimore
Wood

NN13

Farthing
Wood

7

Buttockspire
Wood

Wetley's
Wood

The
Fogs

41

Stowe
Corner

Mary
Wood

Swallowtail
Wood

Old Red
Ditch

CH

6

Red Ditches
Farm

Hollyhill
Wood

Point
Copse

Sawpit
Wood

5

Thatcham Ponds
Farm

Blackpit
Farm

40

Westbury Circular Ride

Parkfields

MK18

Woodlands
Farm

Stowe
Woods

4

Three Parks
Wood

3

39

2

Wolfe's
Obelisk

NORTH
HILL

Dadford

Gorrell
Farm

Vancouver
Lodge

1

Stowe
Park

38

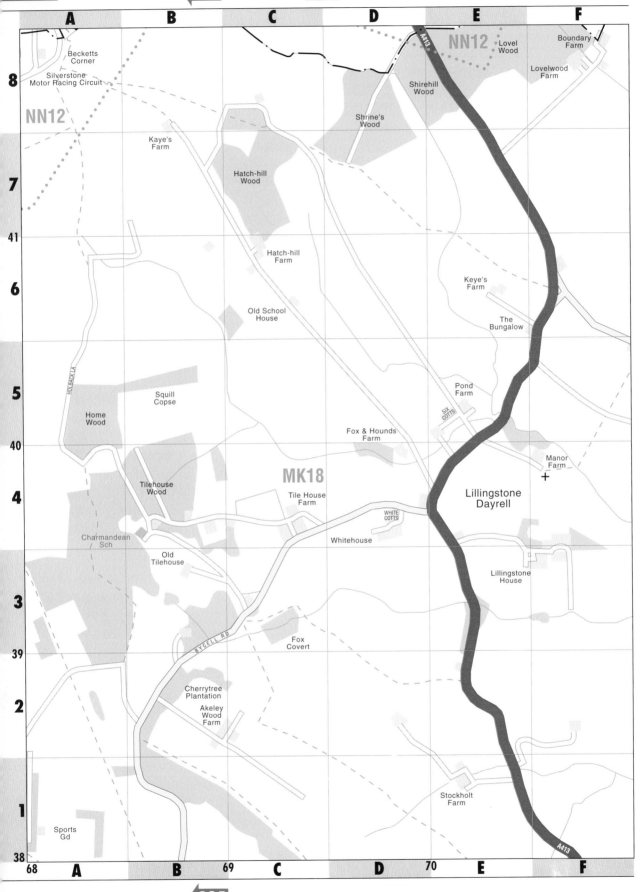

A B C D E F

8

NN12

7

41

6

5

40

4

3

39

2

1

38

68 A B 69 C D 70 E F

Becketts Corner

Silverstone Motor Racing Circuit

NN12

Kaye's Farm

Hatch-hill Wood

Shrine's Wood

Shirehill Wood

NN12

Lovel Wood

Lovelwood Farm

Boundary Farm

Hatch-hill Farm

Old School House

Keye's Farm

The Bungalow

HOLBACK LA

Home Wood

Squill Copse

Pond Farm

SIX COTTS

Fox & Hounds Farm

Manor Farm

Tilehouse Wood

MK18

Tile House Farm

WHITE COTTS

Lillingstone Dayrell

Charmandean Sch

Old Tilehouse

Whitehouse

Lillingstone House

BYCELL RD

Fox Covert

Cherrytree Plantation

Akeley Wood Farm

Stockholt Farm

Sports Gd

A413

A43

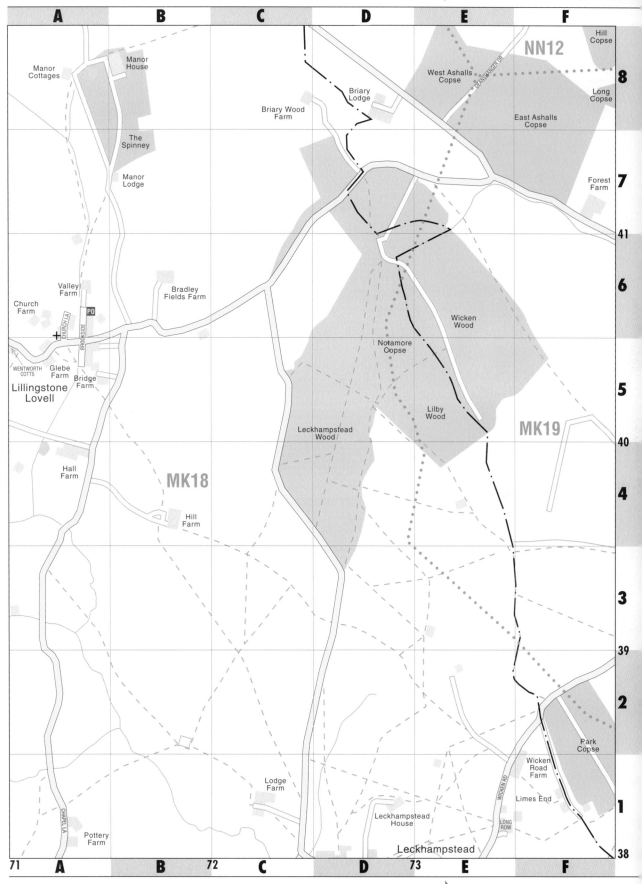

NN12

Hill Copse

Manor Cottages

Manor House

West Ashalls Copse

DEANSHANGER DR

8

The Spinney

Briary Lodge

Long Copse

East Ashalls Copse

Briary Wood Farm

Manor Lodge

7

Forest Farm

41

Valley Farm

Bradley Fields Farm

6

Church Farm

CHURCH LA

PO

BROOKSIDE

Wicken Wood

WENTWORTH COTTS

Glebe Farm

Bridge Farm

Notamore Copse

Lillingstone Lovell

Lilby Wood

MK19

5

40

Hall Farm

MK18

Leckhampstead Wood

4

Hill Farm

3

39

2

Park Copse

CHAPEL LA

Lodge Farm

WICKEN RD

Wicken Road Farm

Limes End

LONG ROW

1

Pottery Farm

Leckhampstead House

Leckhampstead

38

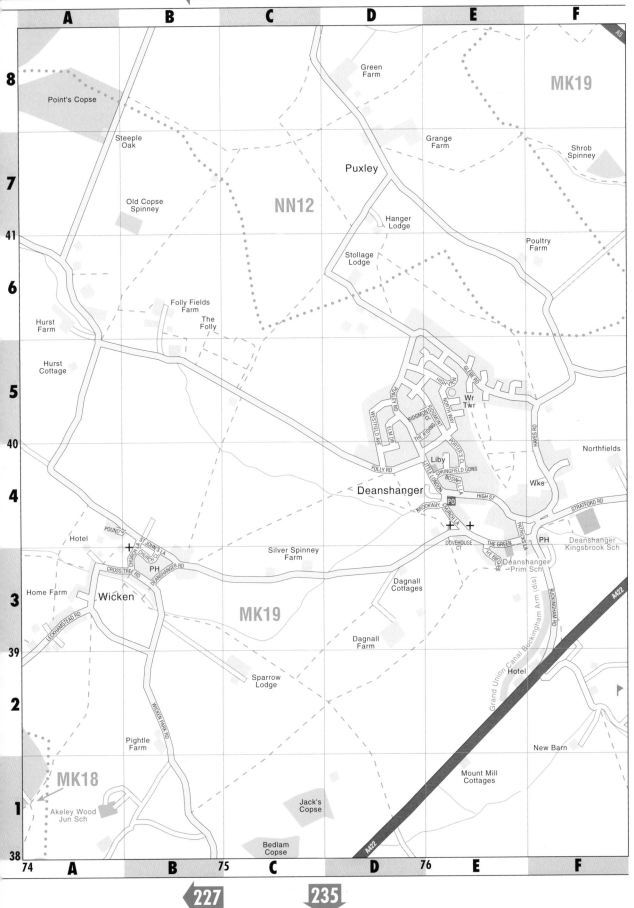

A B C D E F

8

MK19

Point's Copse

Steeple
Oak

Green
Farm

Grange
Farm

Shrob
Spinney

7

Puxley

Old Copse
Spinney

NN12

Hanger
Lodge

Poultry
Farm

41

Hurst
Farm

Stollage
Lodge

6

Folly Fields
Farm

The
Folly

Hurst
Cottage

GLEBE RD

HIGH VW

Wr
Twr

5

PIXLEY RD

NORTH WAY

ELM DR

RIDGMONT
CL

THE PLOVING

Northfields

HAYES RD

40

WESTFIELD AVE

FOLLY RD

Liby

PORTER'S CL

SPRINGFIELD GDNS

LITTLE LONDON

BOSWELL LA

Wks

4

Deanshanger

BROOKWAY

PO

ALDRICH LA

HIGH ST

STRATFORD RD

PATRICK'S LA

PH

Deanshanger
Kingsbrook Sch

POUND ST

ST JOHN'S LA

Hotel

CHURCH LA

DEANSHANGER RD

PH

CROSS TREE RD

Silver Spinney
Farm

DOVEHOUSE
CT

THE GREEN

THE BECHES

Deanshanger
Prim Sch

BUCKINGHAM RD

A422

3

Home Farm

Wicken

MK19

Dagnall
Cottages

Grand Union Canal Buckingham Arm (dis)

LECKHAMSTEAD RD

Dagnall
Farm

Hotel

39

WICKEN PARK RD

Sparrow
Lodge

2

Pightle
Farm

New Barn

MK18

1

Akeley Wood
Jun Sch

Jack's
Copse

Mount Mill
Cottages

38

Bedlam
Copse

A422

74 A B 75 C D 76 E F

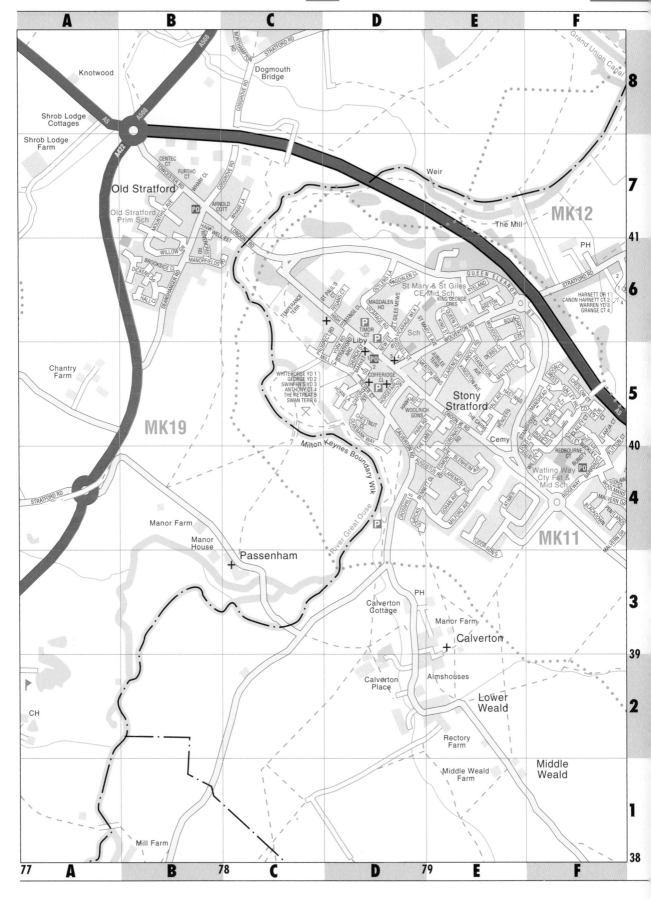

8

Knotwood

Shrob Lodge
Cottages

Shrob Lodge
Farm

Dogmouth
Bridge

NORTHAMPTON RD

STRATFORD RD

COSGROVE RD

Weir

MK12

7

41

CENTEC CT

FURTHO CT

TOWCESTER RD

WHARF CL

Old Stratford

PO

Old Stratford
Prim Sch

MOUNTHILL AVE

HAM WELL EST

COSGROVE RD

ARNOLD COTT

WHARF LA

LONDON RD

The Mill

PH

STRATFORD RD

2

1

4

HARNETT DR 1
CANON HARNETT CT 2
WARREN YD 3
GRANGE CT 4

6

WILLOW DR

BROOKSIDE CL

DICKENS DR

DEANSHANGER RD

HALL CL

RIVERCREST RD

MANORFIELDS

ST PAUL'S CT

FEGANS CT

OSTLERS LA

MAGDALEN CL

St Mary & St Giles
CE Mid Sch

KING GEORGE
CRES

NYELAND

QUEEN ELEANOR ST

BRETON

Chantry
Farm

MK19

TEMPERANCE
TERR

HIGH ST

PROSPECT RD

YORK RD

MILL LA

VICARAGE RD

CHURCH ST

Liby

P

TIMOR CT

P

PO

MAGDALEN
HO

ST GILES MEWS

NEW ST

RUSSELL ST

VICARAGE WLK

ST MARY'S AVE

WOLVERTON RD

KING ST

CLARENCE RD

JUBILEE ST

MERTON TERR

ANTILL RD

FRANKSON AVE

KINGSTON AVE

DEBBS CL

WOODSTOCK

BOUNDARY

MALLETTS CL

HASTINGS

MANSHEAD CT

GALLEY HILL

CRESTHOLME CT

COPTHORNE CT

LADYM CT

5

40

WHITEHORSE YD 1
GEORGE YD 2
SWINFEN'S YD 3
ANTHONY CT 4
THE RETREAT 5
SWAN TERR 6

COFFERIDGE
CL

P

HORN LA

OX LA

SILVER ST

HORSEFAIR

HAM RD

WOOLRICH
GDNS

CHESTNUT
CL

OSEBANK WAY

CALVERTON RD

LONDON RD

PARK RD

THE LIMES

Stony
Stratford

VALE AVE

The CARNE

MEWERS

Cemy

MIDGLEY CT

REDBOURNE
CT

BUNSTY CT

PO

SIDLAW CT

WOOLMANS

Milton Keynes Boundary Wlk

River Great Ouse

P

AUGUSTUS RD

BLENHEIM AVE

CRICKS

BENNETT CL

CROSSHILLS

CLAREMONT AVE

GORAN AVE

MILFORD AVE

EDMONT

CORONATION RD

RIDGEWAY

LATIMER

Watling Way
Cty Fst &
Mid Sch

MALVERN CL

FENTLANDS

BLACKDOWN

MALVERN DR

MK11

4

Manor Farm

Manor
House

Passenham

TUDOR GDN'S

PH

Calverton
Cottage

Manor Farm

Calverton

3

39

CH

Calverton
Place

Almshouses

Lower
Weald

2

Rectory
Farm

Middle Weald
Farm

Middle
Weald

1

38

Mill Farm

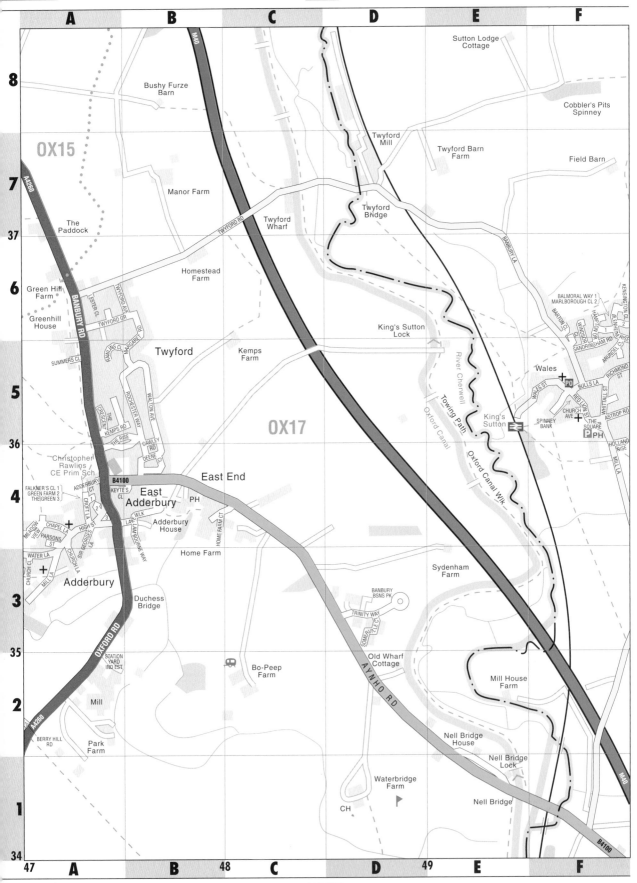

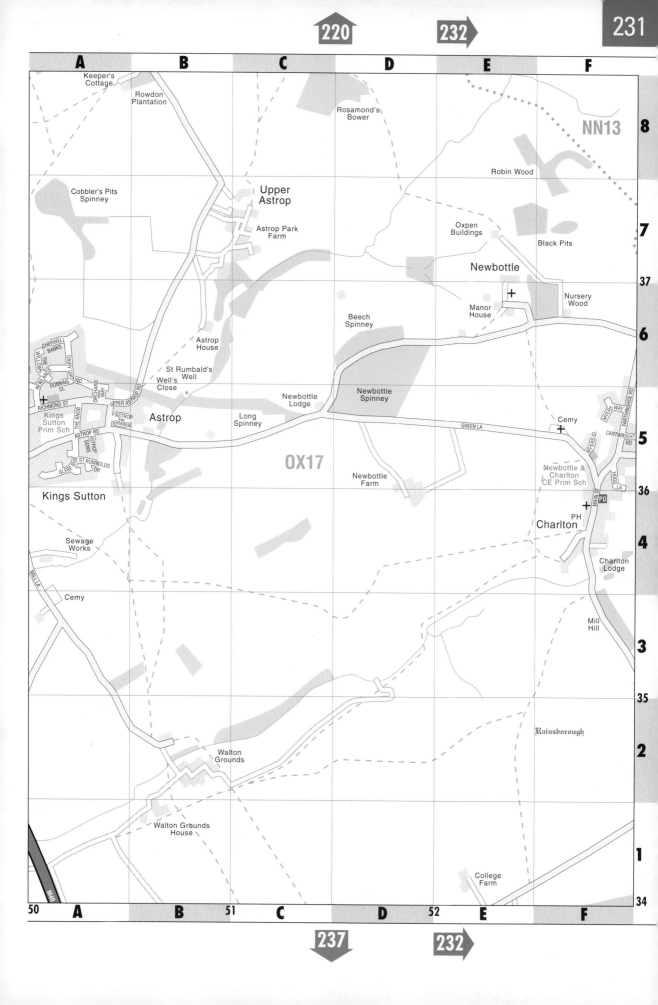

A **B** **C** **D** **E** **F**

8

Coleready
Farm

Coleready
Plantation

Hinton Grounds
Farm

7

Forceleap
Close

Walltree
Farm

THE
CHESTNUTS

37

NORRIS
ACRE

THE
GREEN

PO
PH

Airfield

6

Forceleap
Farm

Hinton-in-the-
Hedges

DUCK END

FARTHINGHOE RD

Sports
Gd

CARTWRIGHT RD

Washbrook
Farm

5

Charlton House
Farm

NN13

36

4

Charlton
Firs

3

The
Cabin

The
Dower House

College Barn
Spinney

35

Camp Farm

Rowler

OX17

2

Myers'
Copse

Rowler's
Covert

1

Cross
Stones

34

53 **A** **B** 54 **C** **D** 55 **E** **F**

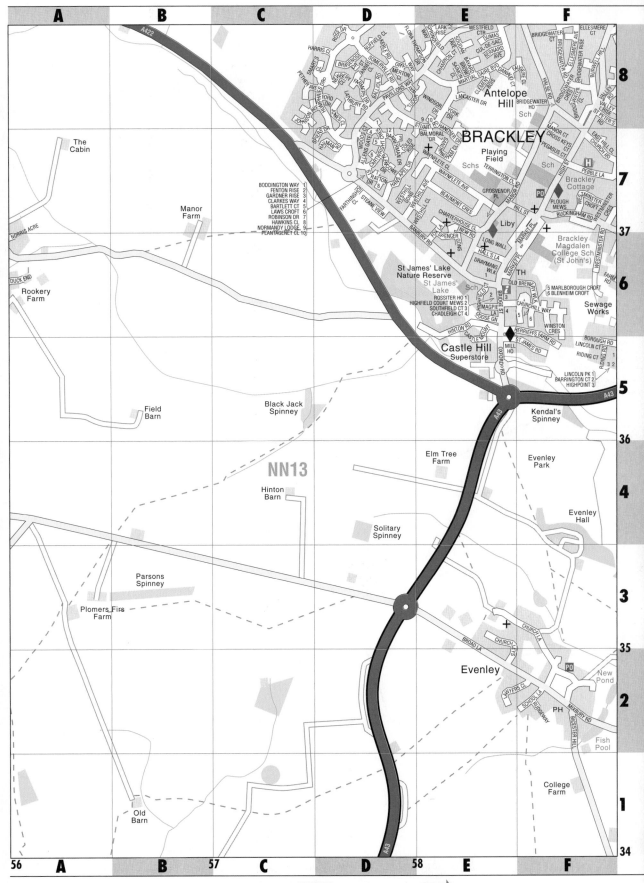

BODDINGTON WAY 1
FENTON RISE 2
GARDNER RISE 3
CLARKES WAY 4
BARTLETT CT 5
LAWS CROFT 6
ROBINSON DR 7
HAWKINS CL 8
NORMANDY LODGE 9
PLEANTAGENET CL 10

The Cabin

Manor Farm

Norris Acre

Duck End

Rookery Farm

Field Barn

Black Jack Spinney

NN13

Hinton Barn

Parsons Spinney

Plomers Firs Farm

Old Barn

Antelope Hill

BRACKLEY

Playing Field

Brackley Cottage

Brackley Magdalen College Sch (St John's)

St James' Lake Nature Reserve
St James' Lake

ROSSITER HO 1
HIGHFIELD COURT MEWS 2
SOUTHFIELD CT 3
CHADLEIGH CT 4

5 MARLBOROUGH CROFT
6 BLENHEIM CROFT

Sewage Works

Castle Hill Superstore

LINCOLN PK 1
BARRINGTON CT 2
HIGHPOINT 3

Kendal's Spinney

Elm Tree Farm

Evenley Park

Evenley Hall

Solitary Spinney

Evenley

New Pond

Fish Pool

College Farm

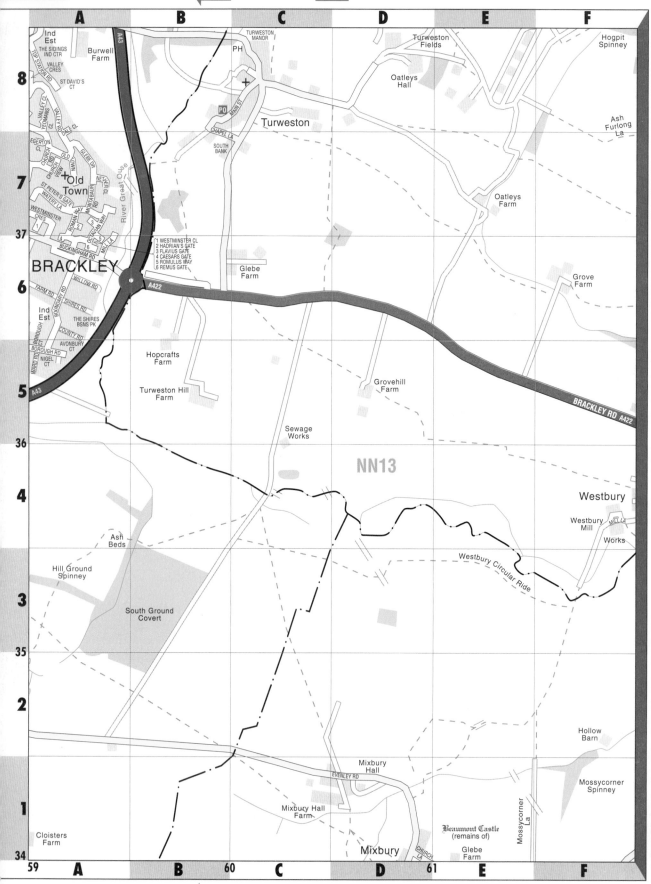

A B C D E F

8

Ind Est
THE SIDINGS IND CTR
VALLEY CRES
ST DAVID'S CT

Burwell
Farm

TURWESTON MANOR

PH

Turweston Fields

Hogpit Spinney

Oatleys Hall

Ash Furlong La

7

Old Town

St PETER'S GATE
WATERY LA
WESTMINSTER CRES

River Great Ouse

PO
MAIN ST

Turweston

CHAPEL LA
SOUTH BANK

Oatleys Farm

37

BRACKLEY

BUCKINGHAM RD

1 WESTMINSTER CL
2 HADRIAN'S GATE
3 FLAVIUS GATE
4 CAESARS GATE
5 ROMULUS WAY
6 REMUS GATE

Glebe Farm

Grove Farm

6

WILLOW RD
SHIRES RD

Ind Est

THE SHIRES BSNS PK

COUNTY RD
AVONBURY CT

A422

5

A43

Hopcrafts Farm

Turweston Hill Farm

Grovehill Farm

BRACKLEY RD A422

36

Sewage Works

NN13

4

Ash Beds

Westbury

Westbury Mill

Works

Hill Ground Spinney

Westbury Circular Ride

3

South Ground Covert

35

2

Hollow Barn

1

Cloisters Farm

Mixbury Hall

EVENLEY RD

Mossycorner Spinney

Mixbury Hall Farm

Beaumont Castle (remains of)

Glebe Farm

Mossycorner La

34

Mixbury

CHURCH LA

59 A B 60 C D 61 E F

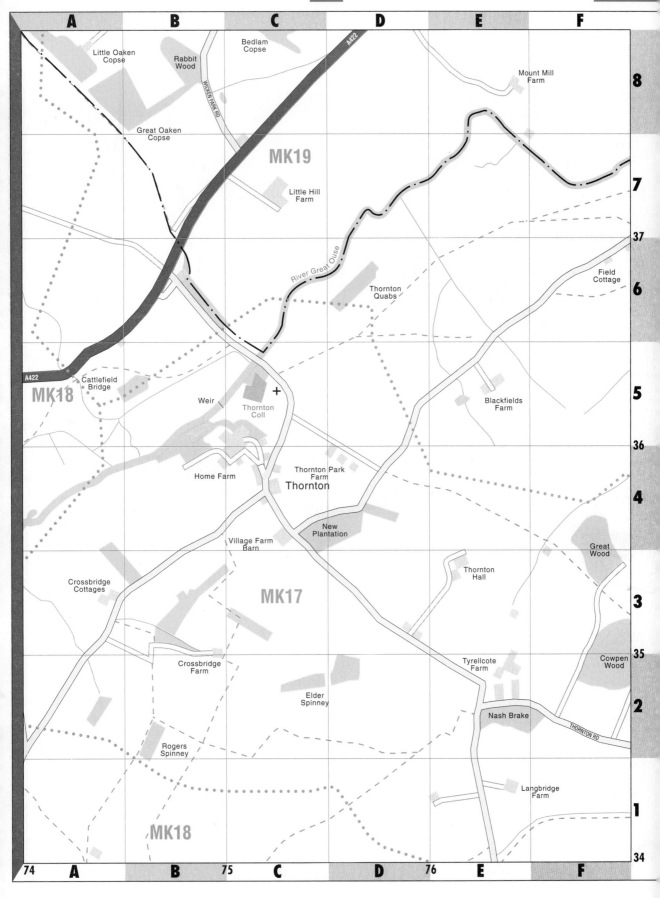

230

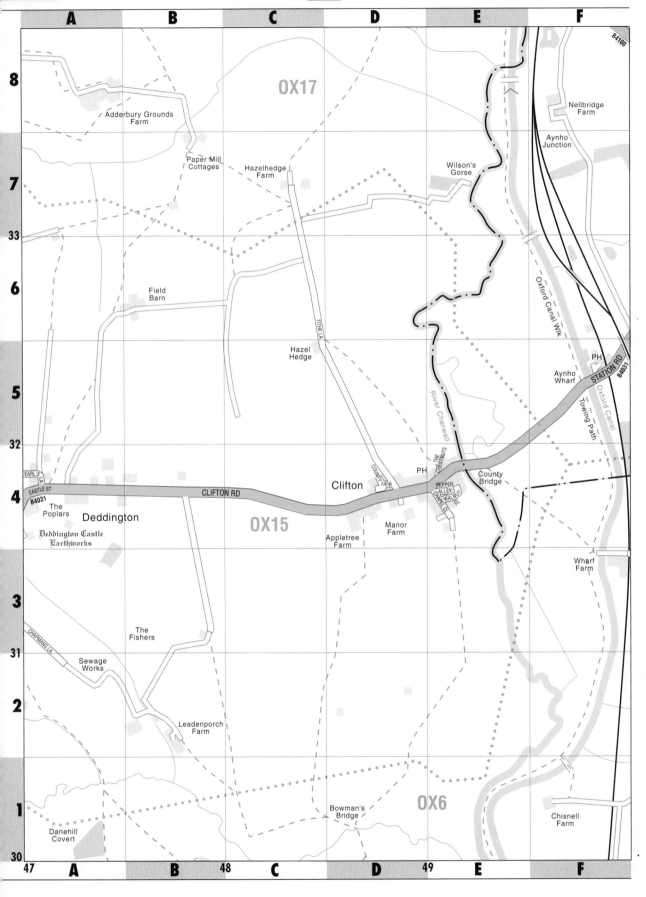

OX17

Adderbury Grounds
Farm

Paper Mill
Cottages

Hazelhedge
Farm

Wilson's
Gorse

Nellbridge
Farm

Aynho
Junction

B4100

Field
Barn

TITHE LA

Oxford Canal Wlk

Hazel
Hedge

River Cherwell

PH

Aynho
Wharf

STATION RD

B4031

EARL'S
LA

CASTLE ST

The
Poplars

B4031

CLIFTON RD

COUNTY VIEW

Clifton

PH

THE CHESTNUTS

PEPPER
ALLEY

CHAPEL CL

WALNUT
CL

County
Bridge

Oxford Canal

Towing Path

Deddington

OX15

Appletree
Farm

Manor
Farm

Wharf
Farm

Deddington Castle
Earthworks

CHAPMANS LA

The
Fishers

Sewage
Works

Leadenporch
Farm

Bowman's
Bridge

OX6

Chisnell
Farm

Danehill
Covert

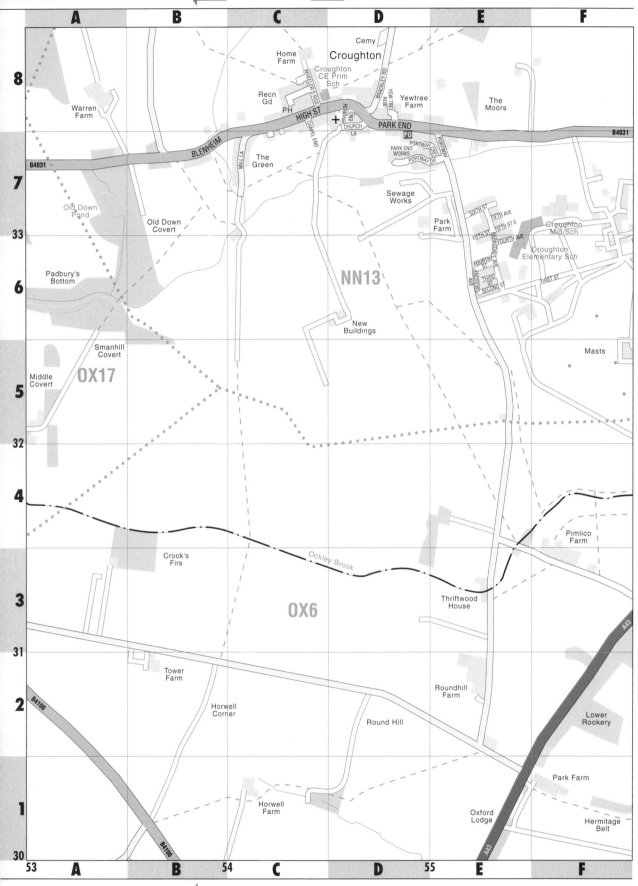

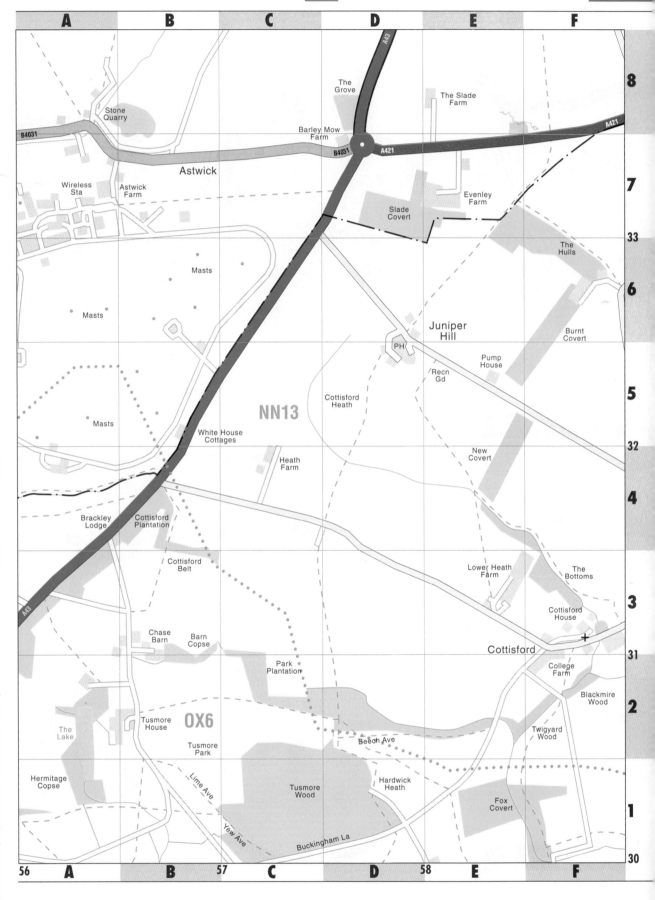

A   B   C   D   E   F

8

The Grove

The Slade Farm

Stone Quarry

B4031

Barley Mow Farm

A421

Astwick

7

Wireless Sta

Astwick Farm

Evenley Farm

33

Slade Covert

The Hulls

Masts

6

Juniper Hill

Burnt Covert

PH

Pump House

Masts

Recn Gd

Masts

Cottisford Heath

5

NN13

New Covert

32

White House Cottages

Heath Farm

4

Brackley Lodge

Cottisford Plantation

Lower Heath Farm

The Bottoms

Cottisford Belt

A43

Cottisford House

3

Chase Barn

Barn Copse

Cottisford

31

Park Plantation

College Farm

Tusmore House

OX6

Blackmire Wood

2

The Lake

Tusmore Park

Twigyard Wood

Beech Ave

Hermitage Copse

Lime Ave

Tusmore Wood

Hardwick Heath

Fox Covert

1

Yew Ave

Buckingham La

30

56   A   B   57   C   D   58   E   F

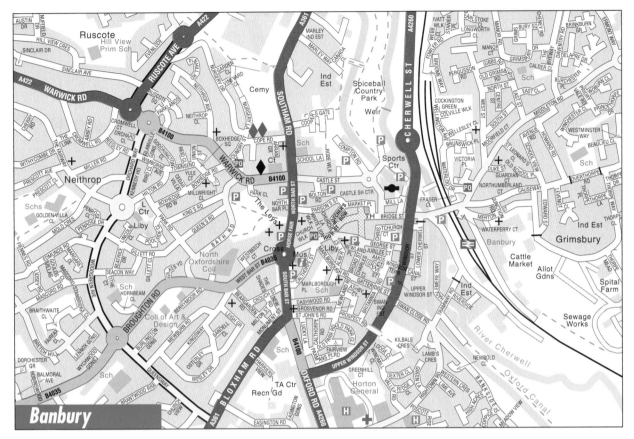

Banbury

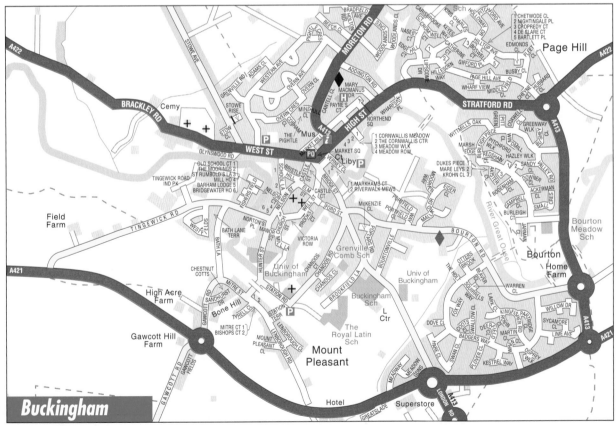

Buckingham

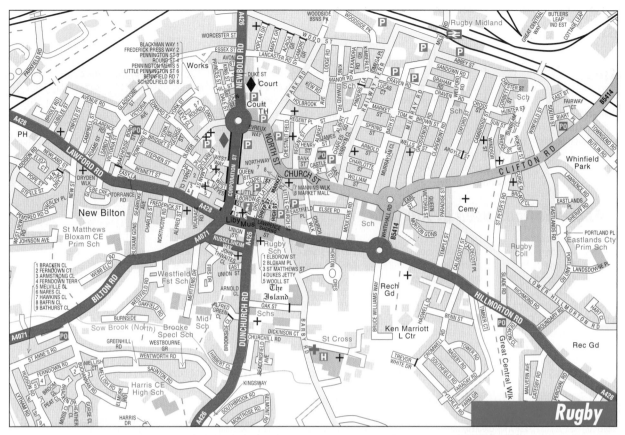

Rugby

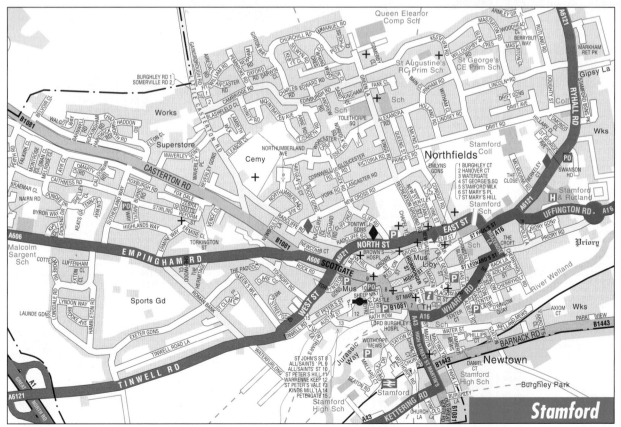

Stamford

Index

Street names are listed alphabetically and show the locality, the Postcode District, the page number and a reference to the square in which the name falls on the map page

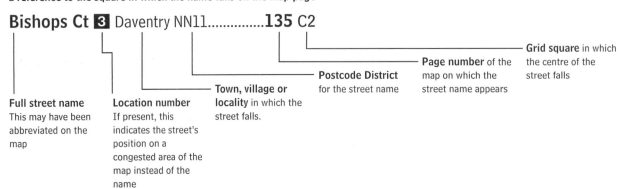

Abbreviations used in the index

App **Approach**	Cl **Close**	Espl **Esplanade**	N **North**	S **South**
Arc **Arcade**	Comm **Common**	Est **Estate**	Orch **Orchard**	Sq **Square**
Ave **Avenue**	Cnr **Corner**	Gdns **Gardens**	Par **Parade**	Strs **Stairs**
Bvd **Boulevard**	Cotts **Cottages**	Gn **Green**	Pk **Park**	Stps **Steps**
Bldgs **Buildings**	Ct **Court**	Gr **Grove**	Pas **Passage**	St **Street, Saint**
Bsns Pk **Business Park**	Ctyd **Courtyard**	Hts **Heights**	Pl **Place**	Terr **Terrace**
Bsns Ctr **Business Centre**	Cres **Crescent**	Ind Est **Industrial**	Prec **Precinct**	Trad **Trading Est**
Bglws **Bungalows**	Dr **Drive**	**Estate**	Prom **Promenade**	Wlk **Walk**
Cswy **Causeway**	Dro **Drove**	Intc **Interchange**	Ret Pk **Retail Park**	W **West**
Ctr **Centre**	E **East**	Junc **Junction**	Rd **Road**	Yd **Yard**
Cir **Circus**	Emb **Embankment**	La **Lane**	Rdbt **Roundabout**	

Town and village index

Abthorpe 201 F1	Crick 101 A5	Hartwell 192 D1	Naseby 66 B1	Swinford 62 C3
Adderbury 230 A3	Cropredy 196 A2	Hellidon 151 D1	Nassington 15 E5	Syresham 224 B8
Alderton 205 A2	Croughton 238 D8	Helmdon 211 F4	Nether Heyford 156 B1	Sywell 127 D3
Aldwincle 76 F8	Culworth 198 C3	Higham Ferrers 132 D6	New Hackleton 177 A3	Theddingworth 46 C8
Apethorpe 14 C3	Dadford 225 D1	Hinton 184 A6	Newnham 153 E4	Thornby 84 E4
Arthingworth 68 C8	Daventry 135 D3	Hinton-in-the-Hedges ...232 F6	Newton Bromswold 149 D8	Thornhaugh 7 E5
Ashby St Ledgers 119 D5	Deanshanger 228 D4	Holcot 126 E8	North Kilworth 45 A3	Thornton 235 C4
Ashley 18 E2	Deddington 236 A4	Holdenby 123 D3	Northampton 159 D4	Thorpe Langton 17 A5
Ashton 205 E8	Deene 23 F6	Hollowell 104 B5	Norton 136 C4	Thorpe Malsor 71 A3
Astcote 188 F7	Deenethorpe 24 B4	Horton 177 D1	Old 107 D7	Thorpe Mandeville 210 B7
Aston le Walls 182 F2	Denford 95 C5	Husbands Bosworth 45 D5	Old Stratford 229 B7	Thorpe Waterville 77 C8
Aynho 237 D7	Denton 178 C8	Irchester 147 B7	Olney 195 E4	Thrapston 76 E1
Badby 153 A2	Desborough 51 C2	Irthlingborough 112 D2	Orlingbury 110 B5	Thurning 60 D2
Banbury 219 A6	Dingley 33 A4	Isham 110 E8	Orton 70 A3	Tiffield 189 D4
Barby 99 D1	Dodford 154 F6	Islip 76 B3	Oundle 42 A6	Titchmarsh 77 D4
Barnwell 59 B6	Draughton 87 E6	Kelmarsh 67 F3	Overstone 127 B1	Towcester 203 B3
Barrowden 3 E5	Drayton 20 A5	Kettering 72 E3	Pattishall 172 E1	Turweston 234 C8
Biddlesden 224 D5	Duddington 5 B6	Ketton 1 A5	Paulerspury 216 C8	Twyford 230 B5
Blakesley 187 B1	Earls Barton 144 F3	Keyston 97 A4	Piddington 177 B2	Twywell 75 A1
Blisworth 190 E7	East Carlton 35 A7	Kilsby 100 B3	Pitsford 125 D5	Upper Benefield 39 F7
Boughton 141 D8	East Farndon 48 B7	King's Cliffe 13 E7	Podington 147 E2	Upper Boddington 182 D8
Bozeat 164 D3	East Haddon 122 D5	Kings Sutton 231 A4	Polebrook 43 A3	Upper Harlestone 139 D4
Brackley 233 E7	Eastcote 189 A8	Kislingbury 157 E4	Potterspury 217 D3	Upper Heyford 156 D3
Bradden 201 F6	Easton on the Hill 2 A4	Knotting Green 149 F1	Preston Capes 169 D2	Upper Stowe 171 E6
Brafield-on-the-Green ...161 F2	Ecton 143 F4	Lamport 87 D2	Priors Hardwick 166 A5	Wadenhoe 58 A4
Brampton Ash 33 E3	Elton 28 E8	Lavendon 180 F1	Priors Marston 166 E8	Wakerley 4 A3
Braunston 118 B2	Emberton 195 F1	Leckhampstead 227 E1	Pury End 215 F8	Walgrave 108 B5
Braybrooke 49 F5	Evenley 233 E2	Lilbourne 81 A6	Pytchley 90 E2	Wansford 8 B4
Brigstock 55 E7	Everdon 170 B8	Lillingstone Dayrell 226 E4	Quinton 176 B1	Wappenham 213 A8
Bringhurst 20 C5	Eydon 184 C1	Lillingstone Lovell 227 A5	Raunds 114 C6	Wardington 196 D2
Brixworth 106 A2	Farthinghoe 221 B4	Litchborough 171 D1	Ravensthorpe 103 E1	Warmington 28 C3
Broughton 90 B4	Farthingstone 170 F2	Little Addington 113 B7	Ravenstone 194 D2	Watford 120 C6
Bugbrooke 173 A7	Finedon 111 E4	Little Bowden 32 A2	Ringstead 95 B4	Weedon 155 A4
Bulwick 12 C1	Flore 155 F4	Little Brington 138 C4	Roade 191 E4	Weldon 38 C8
Burton Latimer 92 A1	Foxton 30 E8	Little Harrowden 110 B4	Rockingham 21 B4	Welford 64 E5
Byfield 183 D7	Gayton 173 F2	Little Houghton 161 A3	Rothersthorpe 174 B6	Welham 17 E5
Bythorn 97 D4	Geddington 54 B3	Little Irchester 130 C1	Rothwell 70 D8	Wellingborough 130 D6
Caldecott 21 C8	Glapthorn 26 C2	Loddington 70 C2	Rugby 99 A7	Welton 119 E1
Castlethorpe 218 F6	Grafton Regis 205 D2	Lois Weedon 200 C2	Rushden 132 E2	West Haddon 102 C4
Chacombe 208 F4	Great Addington 94 B2	Long Buckby 121 B4	Rushton 52 C2	Westbury 234 F4
Chapel Brampton 124 E2	Great Bowden 32 A6	Long Buckby Wharf 136 E7	Scaldwell 106 F6	Weston 200 A2
Charlton 231 F4	Great Brington 138 D7	Lower Benefield 40 C6	Shutlanger 204 D8	Weston by Welland 18 A3
Charwelton 168 B5	Great Doddington 145 D5	Lower Boddington 182 D5	Sibbertoft 46 F2	Weston Underwood 195 A2
Chelveston 133 C8	Great Easton 20 E7	Lower Harlestone 139 E5	Silverstone 214 D4	Whilton 137 D6
Chipping Warden 196 F6	Great Gidding 61 B3	Lowick 75 F6	Slapton 201 D2	Whitfield 223 E3
Church Brampton 140 C8	Great Harrowden 110 D2	Lubenham 30 D3	Slipton 75 A3	Whittlebury 215 B4
Church Stowe 171 D8	Great Houghton 160 F2	Lutton 44 C4	Souldern 237 E3	Wicken 228 A3
Claydon 181 D1	Great Oxendon 48 E3	Lyddington 9 C7	Souldrop 149 B1	Wilbarston 34 D5
Clifton 236 D4	Greatworth 210 E2	Maidford 186 D6	South Kilworth 63 D8	Wilby 129 A1
Clifton upon Dunsmore ...80 A6	Greens Norton 202 D8	Maidwell 87 B7	South Luffenham 3 D8	Willoughby 117 C3
Clipston 66 F8	Grendon 163 E5	Market Harborough 31 C2	Southwick 26 B5	Wittering 7 D8
Clopton 78 D5	Gretton 10 C1	Marston St Lawrence 210 A1	Spratton 105 C1	Wollaston 146 F2
Cogenhoe 162 A6	Grimscote 188 B8	Marston Trussell 47 C8	Stanion 37 F2	Woodend 200 F7
Cold Ashby 84 B5	Guilsborough 103 E6	Mears Ashby 128 C2	Stanwick 113 E4	Woodford 94 C6
Cold Higham 188 C8	Gumley 30 A8	Medbourne 18 F6	Staverton 152 C7	Woodford Halse 184 C6
Collyweston 1 D2	Hackleton 177 C3	Middleton 35 B8	Stibbington 8 D2	Woodnewton 14 F2
Corby 36 E4	Hanging Houghton 106 C8	Middleton Cheney 209 A1	Stoke Albany 34 A4	Wormleighton 181 B8
Cosgrove 218 D2	Hannington 108 D3	Milton Malsor 174 E4	Stoke Bruerne 205 B8	Wothorpe 2 D8
Cottesbrooke 104 F8	Hanslope 207 B2	Mixbury 234 D1	Stoke Doyle 41 C1	Wymington 148 B5
Cottingham 20 D1	Hargrave 115 E2	Morcott 3 A5	Stony Stratford 229 E5	Yardley Gobion 217 E5
Covington 116 D2	Harpole 157 D6	Moreton Pinkney 199 D7	Sulgrave 210 F8	Yardley Hastings 179 B6
Cranford 93 A7	Harrington 69 B4	Moulton 126 C2	Sutton 8 F2	Yarwell 16 A8
Creaton 104 E4	Harringworth 10 F7	Napton on the Hill 150 A2	Sutton Bassett 18 A1	Yelvertoft 82 C4

1

1st Drift PE9 2 D8

2

2nd Drift PE9 2 D8

A

A6 Bsns Pk NN16 71 E4
Abbey Cl NN29 164 C2
Abbey Ct NN29 146 D3
Abbey Ho 5 NN5 159 A6
Abbey Jun Sch The NN11 135 D1
Abbey Lodge NN3 160 C7
Abbey Rd
Northampton NN4 159 B3
Roade NN7 191 C4
Syresham NN13 224 C7
Wellingborough NN8 129 F3
Abbey Rise NN29 146 D3
Abbey St Daventry NN11 135 C2
Market Harborough LE16 31 E3
Northampton NN5 159 A6
Abbey Way
Ravenstone MK46 194 E2
Rushden NN10 148 A8
Abbot Cl NN11 153 D8
Abbots Way
Northampton NN5 158 F6
Roade NN7 191 C4
Rushden NN10 131 F1
Wellingborough NN8 129 F4
Abbotts Cl NN14 77 D3
Aberdare Rd NN5 159 A8
Aberdeen Terr NN5 159 A6
Abington Ave NN3 160 A8
Abington Bsns Ctr NN1 160 A7
Abington Cotts NN1 160 A8
Abington Ct NN3 160 B8
Abington Gr NN1 159 F8
Abington Mus NN1 160 A7
Abington Park Cres NN3 160 C7
Abington Rd NN17 36 B7
Abington Sq NN1 159 E6
Abington St NN1 159 D6
Abington Vale Lower Sch NN3 160 C6
Abington Vale Mid Sch NN3 160 C7
Abthorpe Ave NN2 141 D5
Acacia Cl NN13 222 F1
Ace La NN7 172 F7
Acorn Cl Islip NN14 76 B3
Lubenham LE16 30 E3
Acorn Ind Est NN14 76 B3
Acorn Pk NN15 92 D4
Acorn Way NN12 214 E4
Acre Ct NN16 72 D3
Acre La NN2 141 A6
Acre St NN16 72 D3
Acremead PE8 28 B3
Adam Bsns Pk NN16 71 F5
Adam & Eve St LE16 31 E3
Adams Ave NN1 159 F7
Adams Cl Stanwick NN9 114 A5
Wellingborough NN8 130 B5
Adams Dr NN14 70 B7
Adams Rd NN11 184 B6
Adamswood Cl LE16 31 C3
Adderbury Ct OX17 230 A4
Addington Rd
Irthlingborough NN9 113 A5
Woodford NN14 94 D6
Addison Rd
Desborough NN14 50 F3
Northampton NN3 142 B2
Addlecroft Cl NN2 141 B3
Adelaide Ho 5 NN2 159 C7
Adelaide Pl 7 NN1 159 C5
Adelaide St NN2 159 C7
Adelaide Terr 1 NN2 159 C7
Adit View NN9 131 D8
Admirals Way NN11 135 E2
Adnitt Rd
Northampton NN1 159 F7
Rushden NN10 132 A2
Afan Cl NN16 72 A5
Affleck Bridge NN9 111 F4
Aggate Way NN6 144 D4
Agnes Rd NN2 159 C8
Agricultural Cotts CV23 166 A5
Ainsdale Cl NN2 141 F3
Aintree Rd NN3 141 F4
Akeley Wood Jun Sch MK19 228 A1
Alanbrooke Cl NN15 72 E1
Alastor NN8 129 B5
Albany Gdns NN18 36 B2
Albany Rd
Market Harborough LE16 31 F4
Northampton NN1 160 A7
Albany The 4 NN11 135 C2
Albert Pl NN1 159 D6
Albert Rd Finedon NN9 111 F5
Market Harborough LE16 31 F3
Rushden NN10 132 B3
Wellingborough NN8 130 B5
Albert St NN16 72 C2
Alberta Cl NN18 36 C3
Albion Ct NN1 159 D5
Albion Pl
Northampton NN1 159 D5
Albion Pl *continued*
Rushden NN10 132 B1
Albion Rd NN16 72 B3
Albisdene Ct NN10 132 C2
Alcombe Rd NN1 159 E7
Alcombe Terr NN1 159 E7
Aldbury Mews 12 NN1 159 C7
Aldene Rd MK19 207 B3
Alder Cl NN14 51 C3
Alder Ct NN3 142 F5
Alderley Cl NN5 158 B8
Aldwell Cl NN4 175 F7
Aldwincle Rd NN14 76 A6
Aldwincle Trinity CE Lower Sch NN14 76 F8
Alexander Ct Corby NN17 22 A2
Northampton NN3 142 E3
Alexandra Pl NN9 113 A4
Alexandra Rd Corby NN17 36 E6
Desborough NN14 50 F3
Little Addington NN9 113 A4
Northampton NN1 159 E6
Wellingborough NN8 130 B5
Alexandra St
Burton Latimer NN15 92 B2
Kettering NN16 72 C2
Alexandra Terr 5 NN2 141 C3
Alfoxden NN8 129 B3
Alfred St Irchester NN29 147 A8
Kettering NN16 72 C2
Northampton NN1 159 F6
Rushden NN10 132 B2
Stanwick NN9 113 F4
Alfred Street Jun Sch NN10 132 B2
Alibone Cl NN3 126 D1
Alice Dr NN15 92 B1
Alice Gdns NN18 72 D3
Alington Cl NN9 112 A5
All Saints CE Mid Sch NN2 141 E6
All Saints' CE Prim Sch NN8 130 B4
Allan Bank NN8 129 B3
Allans Cl CV23 80 A5
Allans La CV23 80 A5
Allard Cl NN3 143 D4
Allebone Rd NN6 144 E3
Alledge Dr NN14 94 D7
Allen Rd Finedon NN9 112 A5
Irthlingborough NN9 112 E1
Northampton NN1 160 A7
Rushden NN10 132 C3
Allens Gate NN13 233 D7
Allens Hill NN29 164 D3
Allens Orch OX17 196 F6
Alliance Ct 2 NN8 130 A5
Alliance Terr NN8 129 F5
Alliston Gdns 3 NN2 159 C7
Alma St Northampton NN5 159 A6
Wellingborough NN8 130 A5
Almond Cl CV23 99 C1
Almond Cres NN7 173 A7
Almond Rd NN16 72 D4
Almshouses NN6 102 B5
Alness Cl NN15 91 E8
Alpine Rd NN10 131 F2
Alpine Way NN5 140 A3
Alsace Cl NN5 139 F2
Altendiez Way NN15 92 B4
Althorp NN7 139 A7
Althorp Cl
Market Harborough LE16 32 B3
Wellingborough NN8 129 C7
Althorp Pl NN18 36 B3
Althorp Rd NN5 159 A6
Althorp St 16 NN1 159 C6
Althorpe Pl NN16 72 D3
Alton St NN4 159 B3
Alvington Way LE16 31 D5
Alvis Ct NN3 143 C4
Alvis Way NN11 134 F3
Amber Dr NN6 108 A5
Amberley Rd NN7 192 C1
Ambleside Cl
9 Northampton NN3 142 C4
Wellingborough NN8 129 C5
Ambridge Cl NN4 174 F8
Ambridge Ct 8 NN1 159 F6
Ambush St NN5 159 B6
Amen Cnr NN14 113 C8
Amen Pl NN14 113 C8
Amundsen Cl NN11 135 B5
Ancell Rd MK11 229 E5
Anderson Ave CV22 98 A8
Anderson Dr NN15 72 F1
Anderson Gn NN8 129 C4
Anding Cl MK46 195 E4
Andrew Cl NN10 132 C7
Andrew Macdonald Cl LE16 31 F3
Andrews Ave NN13 238 E6
Andrews Way NN9 114 B5
Angel Ct LE16 31 E3
Angel La 2 NN8 130 A4
Angel St
Market Harborough LE16 31 E3
Northampton NN1 159 D5
Angel Yd 18 NN16 72 B2
Anglia Way NN3 141 F6
Anglian Rd NN11 135 B1
Angus Ho NN17 36 E6
Anjou Ct NN5 139 F2
Ann Sq NN16 72 E3
Anna's La NN12 173 B1
Annandale Rd NN17 36 E7
Anne Cl NN10 132 C7
Anne Rd NN8 129 E2
Anne St NN18 36 E5
Annesley Cl NN3 160 D6
Anscomb Way NN11 184 B6
Ansell Way NN4 175 E8
Anson Cl Corby NN17 36 B7
Daventry NN11 135 D1
Anthony Ct MK11 229 D5
Antona Cl NN9 114 B4
Antona Dr NN9 114 B4
Antona Gdns NN9 114 B4
Anvil The NN7 172 F7
Apethorpe Rd PE8 15 C6
Applebarn Cl NN4 175 C4
Appleby Cl NN9 110 F1
Appleby Wlk 2 NN3 142 C4
Appledore Cl NN2 141 C4
Applegarth Cl NN18 36 D3
Applegarth The NN6 121 C4
Appletree Ct NN9 111 F5
Appletree Ind Est OX17 196 E7
Appletree La NN11 182 F2
Appletree Rd OX17 196 F6
Aquitaine Cl NN5 139 F1
Arbour Ct NN3 142 E4
Arbour View Ct NN3 142 E5
Arbours Lower Sch The NN3 142 D3
Arbury Banks OX17 196 F5
Archangel Rd 2 NN4 158 F2
Archangel Sq 1 NN4 158 F2
Archer Ave NN11 118 C1
Archers Cl NN2 141 B5
Archers Spinney CV21 99 B8
Archery Rd OX17 209 A1
Archfield NN8 129 F4
Archfield Terr 2 NN9 112 F2
Arden Cl Daventry NN11 135 B4
Kettering NN15 91 F5
Market Harborough LE16 32 A4
Ardens Gr NN7 174 A7
Ardenway LE16 31 F5
Ardington Rd NN1 160 A7
Argyle Pk LE16 48 E8
Argyle St NN5 159 A6
Argyll Ho NN17 36 E6
Argyll St Corby NN17 36 F6
Kettering NN15 91 B8
Ariel Cl NN5 140 A1
Arkwright Rd Corby NN17 22 C1
Irchester NN29 147 C7
Arlbury Rd NN3 143 B4
Armley Cl NN6 121 C4
Armston Rd PE8 59 B8
Arndale NN2 140 F5
Arnheim Hos NN11 199 D7
Arnhill Rd NN17 10 B1
Arnills Way CV23 100 A2
Arnold Cott MK19 229 B7
Arnold Rd NN2 159 C8
Arnsby Cres NN3 126 B1
Arnsley Rd NN17 23 A1
Arnull Cres NN11 135 B4
Arran Way NN17 36 C8
Arrow Cl OX17 220 A8
Arrow Head Rd NN4 158 F3
Arthur St
Northampton NN2 141 C1
Wellingborough NN8 129 E4
Arthur's Way 9 NN16 72 C2
Artizan Rd NN1 159 F7
Arundel Cl OX17 230 F5
Arundel Ct Kettering NN15 91 F8
Rushden NN10 148 A8
Arundel St 9 NN1 159 C7
Arundel Wlk NN18 36 B5
Ash Cl Daventry NN11 135 C4
Irchester NN29 147 A7
Ash Ct NN14 76 D1
Ash Dr Brackley NN13 222 F1
Sywell NN6 143 D7
Ash Gr Bugbrooke NN7 172 F7
Desborough NN14 50 E4
Northampton NN2 141 B6
Ash La NN4 175 B4
Ash Rd NN15 72 D1
Ash Rise NN2 141 C6
Ash St NN1 159 C7
Ash Tree Ct OX17 220 B8
Ash Way Braunston NN11 118 B1
Hinton NN11 184 A6
Ashbourne Dr NN14 50 E4
Ashbrow Rd NN4 158 F3
Ashburnham Rd NN1 159 F8
Ashby Castle Gdns NN7 163 B3
Ashby Cl NN8 129 E7
Ashby Ct Guilsborough NN6 103 E7
Kislingbury NN7 157 D3
Moulton NN3 126 C1
Ashby Dr Crick NN6 100 F5
Rushden NN10 148 A8
Ashby Fields Prim Sch NN11 135 C5
Ashby Gdns NN3 126 C1
Ashby Pk NN11 135 C4
Ashby Rd Braunston NN11 118 C1
Daventry NN11 135 B4
Daventry NN11 135 B7
Daventry NN11 135 C2
Kilsby CV23 100 A2
Welton NN11 119 D1
Ashcroft Cl NN5 140 B1
Ashcroft Gdns NN3 142 A2
Ashdale Cl NN6 127 D1
Ashdown Cl NN15 92 A5
Ashdown Pl NN17 36 E7
Ashdown Rd NN11 135 C4
Ashes The NN4 176 B6
Ashfield Ave NN9 114 D6
Ashfield Rd
Market Harborough LE16 31 E4
Wellingborough NN8 129 E4
Ashfield Rise NN9 114 C6
Ashford Cl NN3 160 C6
Ashford Lea NN14 50 E4
Ashgate Ct NN14 70 C7
Ashlade OX17 220 B7
Ashlawn Rd CV22 98 C7
Ashlawn Sec Sch CV22 98 E7
Ashlea MK46 195 E3
Ashleigh Cl CV23 99 C2
Ashley Ave NN17 36 B7
Ashley Ct Blisworth NN7 190 D7
Kettering NN16 72 A3
Ashley La NN3 126 D1
Ashley Rd Medbourne LE16 18 E6
Middleton LE16 20 B2
Stoke Albany LE16 34 A5
Weston by W LE16 18 C3
Ashley Way
Market Harborough LE16 32 B3
Northampton NN3 142 E2
Ashmore NN6 121 C4
Ashpole Spinney NN4 158 C2
Ashridge Cl NN10 148 A8
Ashton Gr NN8 129 D8
Ashton Rd Hartwell NN7 192 C1
Oundle PE8 42 B5
Roade NN7 191 E2
Stoke Bruerne NN12 205 D8
Ashtree Gdns PE9 1 D2
Ashtree Way NN5 158 C7
Ashurst Cres NN18 36 B4
Ashway The
Brixworth NN6 106 C1
Brixworth NN6 125 B8
Ashwell Rd
Lois Weedon NN12 200 B2
Rushden NN10 132 D2
Ashwells La NN6 82 B4
Ashwin Cl NN13 222 E1
Ashwood Rd NN5 158 C7
Ashworth Cl NN6 101 A6
Ashworth St NN11 135 C1
Askham Ave NN8 129 E1
Aspen Cl
Northampton NN3 143 C3
Rushden NN10 132 B3
Aspreys MK46 195 E4
Astbury Cl NN11 153 C8
Aster Cl NN3 160 D6
Aster Rd NN16 72 D4
Astley Cl LE16 31 D1
Astley Pl CV21 99 B7
Aston Rise NN5 158 B8
Aston-le-Walls St Mary's RC Prim Sch NN11 182 F2
Astral Row OX17 210 E2
Astrop Gdns OX17 231 A5
Astrop Grange OX17 231 A5
Astrop Rd
Kings Sutton OX17 231 A5
Middleton Cheney OX17 219 F6
Athelstan Rd NN16 72 D2
Atlee Cl NN3 142 B4
Atterbury Cl NN6 102 D4
Atterbury Way NN4 160 F2
Attley Ct NN8 129 C5
Auctioneers Ct NN1 159 D4
Auctioneers Way NN1 159 D4
Auden Way NN17 36 C8
Audley Cl LE16 32 B2
Augusta Ave NN4 175 C6
Augustus Rd MK11 229 E4
Auriga St LE16 31 F2
Auriol Cotts NN13 221 B4
Austin Cl NN29 147 C8
Austin Ho NN14 70 D7
Austin St NN1 159 D7
Austin Way NN11 134 F4
Austins Cl LE16 31 D3
Austins Pl NN12 214 E4
Avalon Ct NN14 70 E7
Avebury Way NN4 175 B8
Avenue Cl NN9 111 E5
Avenue Inf Sch The NN8 130 A5
Avenue Rd Finedon NN9 111 E5
Rushden NN10 148 F5
Wellingborough NN8 130 A5
Avenue Terr NN16 72 E3
Avenue The Flore NN7 155 E5
Medbourne LE16 19 C8
Middleton Cheney OX17 220 A8
Moulton NN3 142 E8
Northampton NN1 159 F5
Northampton, Dallington NN5 158 F7
Northampton, Meadow View NN2 140 F6
Northampton, Spinney Hill NN3 142 A3
Rothwell NN14 70 D7
Stanwick NN9 114 A3
Wellingborough NN8 130 A5
Whitfield NN13 223 D4
Aviemore Gdns NN4 158 E1
Avignon Cl NN5 140 A2
Avon Cl Daventry NN11 153 A8
Kettering NN16 72 A5
Wellingborough NN8 129 C6
Avon Dr NN5 140 E1
Avon Fields NN6 64 E6
Avonbury Ct NN13 234 A5
Avondale Jun & Inf Schs NN16 72 D4
Avondale Mews NN16 72 D3
Avondale Rd NN16 72 D3
Axe Head Rd NN4 158 F4
Aynho Cres NN2 141 C5
Aynho Ct OX17 237 D7
Aynho Pk OX17 237 C7
Aynho Rd OX17 230 D2
Aynho Wlk NN2 141 D5
Aynsley Cl NN14 50 F3
Azalea Cl NN3 160 D6

B

Back La Brigstock NN14 55 F8
Chapel Brampton NN6 124 D1
Collyweston PE8 1 D2
Elton PE8 28 D8
Gayton NN7 173 E2
Great Brington NN7 138 C6
Holcot NN6 126 E8
Little Addington NN14 113 B8
Morcott LE15 3 A6
Northampton NN4 175 F8
Ringstead NN14 95 B3
Scaldwell NN6 106 F5
South Luffenham LE15 3 D8
Back Rd LE15 3 E5
Backway NN29 146 D2
Bacon Hill MK46 195 E4
Badby Cl NN2 141 E4
Badby Leys CV22 98 A7
Badby Pk NN11 135 A5
Badby Prim Sch NN11 152 F3
Badby Rd Daventry NN11 135 C1
Newnham NN11 153 D4
Badby Rd W
Daventry NN11 153 A7
Daventry NN11 153 B8
Baden Powell Cres NN12 203 C4
Badgers Cl NN7 172 F7
Badgers Wlk NN2 141 B5
Baffin Cl NN14 70 E7
Bailey Brooks Cl NN7 191 C5
Bailey Brooks La NN7 191 C5
Bailey Ct NN10 132 B5
Bailiff St NN1 159 D7
Baird Ave NN5 158 D4
Baird Cl NN11 135 B5
Baird Ct NN8 129 B6
Baird Rd NN17 22 D1
Bairstow Rd NN12 203 C5
Bake House La NN15 92 C3
Bakehouse Hill
Geddington NN14 54 A3
Little Addington NN14 113 B8
Bakehouse La NN6 128 B2
Bakehouse Rise NN6 85 B8
Baker Ave NN14 90 A3
Baker Ct NN14 76 D1
Baker St Farthinghoe NN13 221 B4
Gayton NN7 173 E2
Irthlingborough NN9 112 E1
Northampton NN2 159 C8
Walgrave NN6 108 A4
3 Wellingborough NN8 130 A5
Baker's La NN12 204 D8
Bakers Cres NN29 147 A8
Bakers La Norton NN11 136 C4
Spratton NN6 105 B1
Stoke Bruerne NN12 205 A8
Woodford NN14 94 D6
Bakewell Cl NN4 174 F8
Balcombe Ct CV22 98 E8
Balcombe Pl NN18 36 A5
Balcombe Rd CV22 98 D8
Baldwin Cl NN3 142 B4
Balfour Dr NN14 70 E7
Balfour Gdns LE16 31 D1
Balfour Rd NN2 141 D1
Balfour St NN16 72 C4
Balham Cl NN10 147 F8
Balland Way NN4 175 F7
Balliol Rd Brackley NN13 233 D8
Daventry NN11 153 B8
Balmoral NN18 36 C3
Balmoral Ave NN10 132 C3
Balmoral Cl
Earls Barton NN6 144 F3
Market Harborough LE16 32 B2
Towcester NN12 203 B5
Wellingborough NN8 129 E1
Balmoral Ct NN15 91 C5
Balmoral Dr NN13 233 E7
Balmoral Ho NN2 141 C1
Balmoral Rd NN2 141 C1
Balmoral Way OX17 230 F6
Baltic Cl NN18 36 A2
Bamburgh Cl NN18 36 A1
Bamburgh Ct LE16 32 B3
Bampton Ct NN18 36 F4
Banbury Bsns Pk OX17 230 D3
Banbury Cl
Northampton NN4 158 D2
Wellingborough NN8 129 E1
Banbury La Banbury OX17 219 B8
Banbury OX17 219 C8
Blakesley NN12 186 D2
Byfield NN11 183 D7
Cold Higham NN12 188 B7
Culworth OX17 198 E3
Gayton NN7 173 D4
Great Easton LE16 20 D6
Kings Sutton OX17 230 E6
Middleton Cheney OX17 209 C4
Northampton NN4 158 D1

Banbury La continued
Rothersthorpe NN7 . . . . .174 B7
Thorpe Mandeville OX17 . . .210 B8
Weston NN12 . . . . .199 C3
Banbury Rd Aynho OX17 . . .237 C7
Brackley NN13 . . . . .233 E6
Byfield NN11 . . . . .183 D7
Chacombe OX17 . . . . .208 C3
Chipping Warden OX17 . . . .196 F6
Litchborough NN12 . . . . .171 C1
Lower Boddington NN11 . . .182 C4
Moreton Pinkney NN11 . . . . .199 C7
Twyford OX17 . . . . .230 A6
Bancroft Rd LE16 . . . . .20 D1
Bangrave Rd NN17 . . . . . . .37 F8
Bank View NN4 . . . . .175 B7
Bankfield Dr LE16 . . . . .32 A5
Banks The Broughton NN14 .90 B5
Hackleton NN7 . . . . .177 B3
Kilsby CV23 . . . . .100 A2
Long Buckby NN6 . . . . .121 B4
Wellingborough NN9 . . . . . .129 F8
Bankside Corby NN18 . . . . .36 D3
Northampton NN2 . . . . .141 F3
Woodford Halse NN11 . . . . .184 C6
Bannerman Dr NN13 . . . . .233 D7
Bants La NN5 . . . . .158 E7
Barby CE Prim Sch CV23 118 C8
Barby La CV23 . . . . .99 B5
Barby Rd Kilsby CV23 . . . . .99 F3
Rugby CV22 . . . . .98 B7
Bardsley Rd NN17 . . . . .21 E3
Barford MK11 . . . . .229 F4
Baring Ho NN5 . . . . .159 A7
Baring Rd NN5 . . . . .159 A7
Barker Cl NN10 . . . . .132 C2
Barker Rd NN6 . . . . .144 E3
Barksdale Ave NN13 . . . . .238 E6
Barley Cl Hartwell NN7 . . .192 E2
Rugby CV21 . . . . .99 A8
Barley Croft NN6 . . . . .100 F6
Barley Hill OX17 . . . . .198 D2
Barley Hill Rd NN3 . . . . . .142 F6
Barley La NN2 . . . . .141 B5
Barlow Cl NN14 . . . . .70 B7
Barlow La NN3 . . . . .126 C1
Barlows La LE16 . . . . .34 C5
Barn Acre NN6 . . . . .122 D5
Barn Cl NN18 . . . . .36 B1
Barn Cnr NN4 . . . . .175 C4
Barn Ct NN9 . . . . .110 C4
Barn La NN7 . . . . .174 F2
Barn Owl Cl NN4 . . . . .175 A8
Barn Way NN5 . . . . .140 C2
Barnard NN18 . . . . .36 C3
Barnard Cl NN5 . . . . .158 B8
Barnard Gdns LE16 . . . . . .48 D8
Barnard's Way NN14 . . . . .56 A6
Kettering NN15 . . . . .91 B7
Barnes Mdw NN4 . . . . . . .159 F4
Barnes Meadow
  Interchange NN4 . . . . . .160 A4
Barneswell Cl NN6 . . . . . .106 B2
Barnet Cl NN4 . . . . .159 A2
Barnett Cres NN11 . . . . . .184 B6
Barnett Rd OX17 . . . . .219 E8
Barnfield Cl NN2 . . . . .141 B4
Barnhill Sq NN3 . . . . .143 A6
Barns The NN6 . . . . .128 C2
Barnsdale LE16 . . . . .20 D6
Barnsdale Cl LE16 . . . . . . .20 D6
Barnsley Sq NN18 . . . . . . .36 C4
Barnstaple Cl NN3 . . . . . .160 E7
Barnwell CE Prim
  Sch PE8 . . . . .59 B6
Barnwell Cl NN14 . . . . .76 E2
Barnwell Ctry Pk PE8 . . . .41 E3
Barnwell Ctry Pk Visitor
  Ctr PE8 . . . . .41 F3
Barnwell Dr NN10 . . . . . . .148 A8
Barnwell Gdns NN8 . . . . .129 D7
Barnwell Rd
  Northampton NN2 . . . . .141 D4
  Oundle PE8 . . . . .41 F3
  Wellingborough NN8 . . . . . .129 E7
Barnwell St NN16 . . . . .72 D2
Baron Ave
  Earls Barton NN6 . . . . .144 F6
  Kettering NN16 . . . . .71 E3
Baron Ct Corby NN17 . . . . .22 E1
  Northampton NN1 . . . . .159 F8
Barons Way NN2 . . . . .141 A4
Baronson Gdns NN1 . . . . .159 F8
Barrack Rd NN1, NN2 . . . .159 C7
Barratt Cl NN10 . . . . .132 B5
Barrett Cl NN8 . . . . .129 C4
Barringers Ct NN29 . . . . .131 B1
Barringers Gdns NN29 . . .131 B1
Barrington NN13 . . . . .233 F5
Barrington Rd NN10 . . . . .148 C8
Barron Cl NN15 . . . . .91 C6
Barrowden La LE15 . . . . . . .3 E8
Barrowden Rd
  Barrowden PE9 . . . . .4 C8
  Ketton PE9 . . . . .1 A4
  South Luffenham LE15 . . . . . .3 F7
Barry Green Ct NN9 . . . . .111 F5
Barry Lower Sch NN1 . . . .160 A7
Barry Rd NN1 . . . . .160 A6
Barrymoor Ct NN8 . . . . . .129 E2
Barth Cl NN18 . . . . .36 B2
Bartholomew
  Gdns NN12 . . . . .187 A1
Bartlett Ct NN13 . . . . .233 D7

Bartley Dr NN16 . . . . .71 F4
Barton Cl OX17 . . . . .230 F6
Barton Fields NN6 . . . . . . .143 F3
Barton Holme NN12 . . . . . .187 A1
Barton Rd NN15 . . . . .91 E7
Barton Seagrave Prim
  Sch NN15 . . . . .92 A6
Barton Sq NN18 . . . . .36 B6
Bartons Cl The 2 NN5 . . .140 F1
Barwick Ho NN12 . . . . .132 B2
Basil Cl NN4 . . . . .175 D6
Bassett Ford Rd PE8 . . . . .42 A4
Bassett Pl PE8 . . . . .42 A4
Bassett Way LE16 . . . . .67 A8
Bates Ave NN14 . . . . .95 B3
Bates Cl
  Higham Ferrers NN10 . . . . .132 B5
  Market Harborough LE16 . . .31 E5
Bates La OX6 . . . . .237 D3
Bath La NN16 . . . . .72 C3
Bath Rd NN16 . . . . .72 C4
Bath St LE16 . . . . .31 E1
Battle Cl NN14 . . . . .93 A6
Baukewell Ct 4 NN3 . . . . .142 E3
Baunhill Cl NN3 . . . . .160 D7
Baxter Cl NN4 . . . . .175 F8
Bayard Brow NN13 . . . . . .233 E8
Bayes St NN16 . . . . .72 A3
Baysdale Ave NN17 . . . . . .36 E6
Beacon Ct NN4 . . . . .158 E3
Beaconsfield Pl NN10 . . . .132 B3
Beaconsfield Terr
  Northampton NN1 . . . . .159 D7
  Rushden NN10 . . . . .132 B3
Beanfield Ave NN18 . . . . . .36 B5
Beanfield Jun & Inf
  Schs NN18 . . . . .36 A5
Beanfield Sch NN18 . . . . . .36 A6
Beanfurlong OX17 . . . . . . .208 E4
Beardsley Ct NN18 . . . . . . .36 D5
Beardsley Gdns NN15 . . . .92 A7
Beatrice Rd NN16 . . . . .72 B5
Beatty Ct NN11 . . . . .135 E1
Beatty Gdns NN14 . . . . . . .158 B6
Beaufort Dr Kettering NN15 92 A4
  Northampton NN5 . . . . .140 C1
Beauly St NN15 . . . . .91 E8
Beaumaris Cl NN10 . . . . . .132 C1
Beaumont Cl NN16 . . . . . . .72 B6
Beaumont Cres NN13 . . . .233 E7
Beaumont Ct 15 NN1 . . . .159 C6
Beaumont Dr NN3 . . . . . . .143 C3
Beaune Cl NN5 . . . . .139 F1
Beauvais Ct NN5 . . . . .139 F1
Beaver Ctr The NN11 . . . .184 C7
Beck Ct NN8 . . . . .129 D6
Becket Way NN3 . . . . .142 B4
Becketts Cl NN11 . . . . .183 D7
Bective Lower Sch NN2 .141 D4
Bective Rd NN2 . . . . .141 C4
Bedale Rd NN8 . . . . .130 A6
Beddoes Cl NN4 . . . . .176 A6
Bede Cl Corby NN18 . . . . . .36 A1
  Higham Ferrers NN10 . . . . .132 C5
Bede House LE15 . . . . .9 D7
Bedford Cl NN15 . . . . .91 F5
Bedford Cotts NN7 . . . . . .138 D7
Bedford Mans NN1 . . . . . .159 D5
Bedford Pl NN1 . . . . .159 D5
Bedford Rd Denton NN7 . . .178 B8
  Little Houghton NN7 . . . . . .160 F3
  Northampton NN1 . . . . .159 E4
  Rushden NN10 . . . . .148 D5
Bedford Rd E NN7 . . . . . . .179 D5
Bedford Rd W NN7 . . . . . .179 A6
Beech Ave
  Northampton NN3 . . . . .142 A1
  Olney MK46 . . . . .195 E3
Beech Cl Bugbrooke NN7 . .172 F7
  Corby NN17 . . . . .21 C1
  Desborough NN14 . . . . .51 A3
  Hackleton NN7 . . . . .177 B3
  Towcester NN12 . . . . .203 C4
Beech Cres
  Irchester NN29 . . . . .147 A7
  Kettering NN16 . . . . .72 C1
Beech Ct Rugby CV22 . . . . .98 F3
  Thrapston NN14 . . . . .76 C2
Beech Dr Brackley NN13 . .222 E1
  Hinton NN11 . . . . .184 B6
  Wellingborough NN8 . . . . . .129 C5
Beech Gr NN3 . . . . .142 D5
Beech Hill NN11 . . . . .151 D1
Beech House Dr NN12 . . . .217 A4
Beech La NN7 . . . . .157 E4
Beech Rd NN10 . . . . .132 B4
Beechcroft Gdns NN3 . . . .142 A2
Beeches Cl LE16 . . . . .46 F2
Beeches The
  Deanshanger MK19 . . . . . . .228 E3
  Pattishall NN12 . . . . .172 E1
Beechwood Dr NN3 . . . . . .142 E1
Beechwood Rd NN5 . . . . . .158 C5
Beeston Ave NN3 . . . . .160 F8
Beeston Pl NN16 . . . . .36 C5
Belfield Cl NN3 . . . . .142 B3
Belfry La NN4 . . . . .175 B5
Belgrave Cl NN15 . . . . .92 A5
Bell Cl NN13 . . . . .211 F4
Bell Ct Corby NN18 . . . . . . .36 D4
  5 Wellingborough NN8 . . . .130 A5
Bell End NN29 . . . . .146 D2
Bell Hill Finedon NN9 . . . . .111 E4
  Rothwell NN14 . . . . .70 D7
Bell La Byfield NN11 . . . . . .183 C7
  Husbands Bosworth LE17 . . .45 E5
  Syresham NN13 . . . . .224 B8
Bell St NN8 . . . . .130 A5

Bell Wlk CV21 . . . . .99 A8
Bellamy Rd PE8 . . . . .41 F7
Belle Baulk NN12 . . . . . . .203 A6
Bellfields La LE16 . . . . .32 A2
Bellfields St LE16 . . . . .32 A2
Bellfoundry La 4 NN16 . . .72 B2
Bellropes Sq 5 NN3 . . . . .143 D2
Bells Cl NN14 . . . . .55 E8
Belmont Ct 13 NN1 . . . . . .159 C7
Belmont Gdns NN9 . . . . . .114 C6
Belstead Rd NN3 . . . . .160 D6
Belton Cl 4 NN4 . . . . .175 C8
Belvedere Rd NN15 . . . . . . .72 D1
Belvoir Cl
  Northampton NN5 . . . . .140 B1
  Rushden NN10 . . . . .148 C8
Belvoir Dr NN15 . . . . .92 A6
Bembridge Dr NN2 . . . . . .141 B1
Benbow Cl NN11 . . . . .135 E2
Benedict Cl NN10 . . . . .147 F8
Benefield Rd
  Brigstock NN14 . . . . .39 B2
  Deenethorpe NN17 . . . . .24 C4
  Oundle PE8 . . . . .41 C5
Bengal La NN12 . . . . .202 E7
Bengal View NN12 . . . . . . .202 E8
Benham Rd NN12 . . . . .202 D8
Benjamin Sq 6 NN4 . . . . .158 F2
Bennett Cl
  Chacombe OX17 . . . . .208 E4
  Stony Stratford MK11 . . . . .229 D4
Bens Cl MK19 . . . . .218 F5
Bentley Cl NN3 . . . . .143 D4
Bentley Ct NN9 . . . . .111 B1
Bentley Way NN11 . . . . . . .134 F3
Bentley Wlk NN18 . . . . .36 C4
Bergen Wlk NN18 . . . . .36 A2
Bergerac Cl NN5 . . . . .139 F2
Berkeley Cl NN11 . . . . .159 F6
Berkeley Ho 20 NN1 . . . . .159 C6
Bern Links NN4 . . . . .159 A3
Bernard Ave NN13 . . . . . . .233 E8
Berneshaw Cl NN18 . . . . . .36 D3
Berridges La LE17 . . . . .45 E5
Berrill St NN29 . . . . .147 A7
Berrister Pl NN9 . . . . .114 E7
Berry Cl Earls Barton NN6 .144 E5
  Great Bowden LE16 . . . . . . .32 A5
  Hackleton NN7 . . . . .177 B3
  Rothersthorpe NN7 . . . . . . .174 B6
Berry Field Rd LE16 . . . . . .20 C1
Berry Green Pk NN14 . . . . .78 E6
Berry Green Rd NN9 . . . . .111 E5
Berry Hill Rd OX17 . . . . . .230 A2
Berry La Hellidon NN11 . . .151 C1
  Northampton NN4 . . . . .175 D5
Berry Rd LE16 . . . . .20 C1
Berrydale NN3 . . . . .143 D4
Berryfield NN6 . . . . .121 C4
Berrymoor Rd NN8 . . . . . .129 E2
Berrywood Rd NN5 . . . . . .158 A7
Bertha Way NN16 . . . . .72 E4
Berwick Ho NN2 . . . . .141 D5
Berwick Rd NN14 . . . . .37 E3
Berwick Way NN15 . . . . . . .92 A8
Bessemer Gr NN16 . . . . . . .37 B6
Bestwell Ct 3 NN3 . . . . . .161 A8
Bestwood Gn NN18 . . . . . . .36 C5
Bethany
  Homestead 1 NN2 . . . . .141 E1
Bethel La NN11 . . . . .170 B7
Betony Wlk NN10 . . . . .148 B8
Bettycroft NN6 . . . . .103 E1
Bevan Ct NN8 . . . . .130 C7
Bevan Wlk NN4 . . . . .70 B7
Beverley Cres NN3 . . . . . . .142 C1
Beverley Rd NN15 . . . . .91 D8
Beverley Wlk NN18 . . . . . . .36 C5
Bewick Cl NN18 . . . . .36 E4
Bewick Rd NN3 . . . . .160 E8
Bexhill Wlk NN18 . . . . .36 B4
Bibury Cl NN18 . . . . .129 D1
Bibury Cres NN3 . . . . .142 D6
Bicester Hill NN13 . . . . . . .233 F2
Bickerstaffes Rd NN12 . . .203 C5
Bidders Cl NN1 . . . . .159 D4
Bideford Cl NN3 . . . . .160 D7
Bideford Sq NN18 . . . . .36 F5
Big Gn PE8 . . . . .28 C3
Bignal Ct NN15 . . . . .90 E8
Billing
  Aquadrome NN7 . . . . . . .161 B7
Billing Brook Rd NN3 . . . .142 F4
Billing Brook Sch NN3 . . .142 F3
Billing La Moulton NN6 . . .126 F1
  Northampton NN3 . . . . .143 A7
Billing Rd
  Brafield-on-t-G NN7 . . . . . .161 D4
  Northampton NN1 . . . . .159 F6
Billing Rd E NN3 . . . . .160 D7
Billing School Pl NN7 . . . .155 C3
Billing Way NN3 . . . . .143 C5
Billington St NN1 . . . . .159 F7
Bilsdon Cl NN10 . . . . .147 F8
Bilton Ct NN8 . . . . .129 D5
Binbrook Wlk NN18 . . . . . .36 C4
Bingham Wlk NN18 . . . . . . .36 C4
Birch Ave NN18 . . . . .36 D4
Birch Barn Way NN2 . . . . .141 B6
Birch Cl NN11 . . . . .184 B6
Birch Rd Kettering NN16 . . .72 D3
  Rushden NN10 . . . . .132 C2
Birch Tree Gdns LE16 . . . .31 F4
Birchall Rd NN10 . . . . .131 F2
Birchfield Cres NN3 . . . . . .142 C2
Birchfield Ct NN3 . . . . .142 B1

Birchfield Rd
  Northampton NN1 . . . . .142 C1
  Wellingborough NN8 . . . . . .129 E4
Birchfield Rd E NN3 . . . . . .142 C1
Birchington Rd NN17 . . . . .22 C2
Birchvale Ct NN14 . . . . .50 E4
Bird St NN15 . . . . .92 D3
Birds Hill Rd
  Eastcote NN12 . . . . .188 F8
  Northampton NN3 . . . . .142 F3
Birds Hill Wlk NN3 . . . . . .142 F3
Birkdale Cl Daventry NN11 135 C2
  Northampton NN3 . . . . .142 F3
Birling Pl NN18 . . . . .36 E5
Birtley Coppice LE16 . . . . .31 D4
Bishop Cl LE16 . . . . .48 E8
Bishop Stopford CE
  Sch NN15 . . . . .91 B7
Bishop's Dr NN15 . . . . .91 B6
Bishops Cl NN13 . . . . .222 E1
Bishops Ct
  3 Daventry NN11 . . . . .135 C2
  Higham Ferrers NN10 . . . . .132 C7
Bishops Dr NN2 . . . . .141 B3
Bishops Way NN3 . . . . .36 A4
Bitten Ct NN3 . . . . .142 E3
Black Lion Hill NN1 . . . . . .159 B5
Black Swan Spinney PE8 . .8 A4
Blackberry Ct NN16 . . . . . .72 B6
Blackberry La NN4 . . . . . . .158 F3
Blackbird Cl NN13 . . . . . . .222 E1
Blackdown MK11 . . . . .229 F4
Blackfriars NN10 . . . . .147 F8
Blackfriars Ho 19 NN1 . . .159 C6
Blacklocks Hill OX17 . . . . .219 B8
Blackmile La NN7 . . . . .163 C7
Blackmires La NN12 . . . . .214 B5
Blackmoor Ave NN18 . . . . .36 F4
Blackpot La PE8 . . . . .42 A5
Blacksmith's Cl NN12 . . . .172 D1
Blacksmith's La
  Aston le W NN11 . . . . .182 B2
  Pytchley NN14 . . . . .90 F2
Blacksmith's Way NN7 . . .192 C1
Blacksmiths Hill OX17 . . .237 C7
Blacksmiths La
  Eydon NN11 . . . . .184 C1
  Little Brington NN7 . . . . . . .138 B4
Blackthorn Bridge
  Ct 4 NN3 . . . . .143 B4
Blackthorn Cl
  Kettering NN16 . . . . .72 C6
  Spratton NN6 . . . . .105 A1
Blackthorn Mid Sch NN3 143 C5
Blackthorn Rd NN3 . . . . . .143 B4
Blackwell Cl NN12 . . . . . . .203 D4
Blackwell End NN12 . . . . . .217 C3
Blackwell Hill NN4 . . . . . . .174 F8
Blackwell Rd NN15 . . . . . . .91 F4
Blackymore La NN4 . . . . . .175 D5
Bladon Cl NN3 . . . . .142 C4
Blake Cl NN11 . . . . .153 E8
Blake Ct NN15 . . . . .92 A8
Blake Rd NN18 . . . . .36 D4
Blake Wlk NN10 . . . . .132 A5
Blakesely Hill NN12 . . . . . .202 D8
Blakesley CE Prim
  Sch NN12 . . . . .187 B1
Blakesley Cl NN2 . . . . .141 C5
Blakesley Rd NN12 . . . . . . .200 F7
Blandford Ave NN16 . . . . . .72 B5
Blandford Ct NN18 . . . . . . .36 A6
Blatherwycke Rd PE8 . . . .13 C7
Bledlow Rise NN4 . . . . .174 F8
Blencowe Dr NN13 . . . . . . .233 D7
Blenheim NN13 . . . . .238 B7
Blenheim Ave MK11 . . . . . .229 E4
Blenheim Cl NN10 . . . . . . .148 A8
Blenheim Croft NN13 . . . .233 F6
Blenheim Ct NN3 . . . . .224 C7
Blenheim Rd
  Northampton NN4 . . . . .159 B2
  Wellingborough NN8 . . . . . .129 D7
Blenheim Rise OX17 . . . . . .230 F6
Blenheim Way
  Kettering NN16 . . . . .71 E5
  Market Harborough LE16 . . .31 E5
Blenheim Wlk NN18 . . . . . .36 C3
Blinco Rd NN10 . . . . .132 C3
Blind La LE16 . . . . .20 D1
Bliss Charity Prim
  Sch NN7 . . . . .156 C2
Bliss La NN7 . . . . .155 F5
Blisworth Prim Sch NN7 .190 D8
Blisworth Rd Gayton NN7 .173 F1
  Roade NN7 . . . . .191 B4
Bloomfield Cl NN10 . . . . . .132 C4
Blossac Ct NN5 . . . . .139 F1
Blossom Way NN3 . . . . . . .143 A1
Bluebell Cl Hinton NN11 . .184 B7
  Kettering NN16 . . . . .72 E4
  Rushden NN10 . . . . .148 C8
Bluebell Ct NN3 . . . . .160 C6
Bluebell Rise NN10 . . . . . .148 B8
Blueberry Rise 2 NN3 . . . .143 C2
Bluecoat La LE15 . . . . .9 D7
Blythe Cl NN14 . . . . .70 E6
Blyton Cl NN18 . . . . .36 C4
Board St NN9 . . . . .112 F2
Boarden Ct NN3 . . . . .142 A7
Boardman Rd NN15 . . . . . .90 F8
Boat Horse La NN16 . . . . .101 A5
Boathouse The LE16 . . . . . .31 D4
Bobtail Ct NN5 . . . . .140 C1
Boddington Ct NN11 . . . . .182 C5
Boddington Mews NN15 . . .91 C8
Boddington Rd
  Byfield NN11 . . . . .183 C7

Boddington Rd continued
  Claydon OX17 . . . . .181 D1
  Kettering NN15 . . . . .91 C8
Boddington Way NN13 . . . .233 D8
Boden Cl NN18 . . . . .36 A2
Bodiam Pl NN18 . . . . .36 A5
Bodleian Cl NN13 . . . . .153 B8
Bognor Rd NN18 . . . . .36 B4
Bollinger Cl NN5 . . . . .139 F1
Boltons Cl NN13 . . . . .222 E1
Bondfield Ave NN2 . . . . . . .141 D3
Bonham Ct NN16 . . . . .72 C3
Bonington Wlk NN18 . . . . . .36 D5
Bonnington Cl CV21 . . . . . .80 B1
Boon Wlk NN17 . . . . .37 B7
Booth Cl NN12 . . . . .172 D1
Booth Dr NN8 . . . . .129 A4
Booth La N NN3 . . . . .142 C4
Booth La S NN3 . . . . .142 D2
Booth Meadow Ct NN3 . .142 E5
Booth Rise NN3 . . . . .142 D6
Boothville Gn NN3 . . . . . . .142 D5
Boothville Mid Sch NN3 .142 D4
Bordeaux Cl NN5 . . . . .139 F1
Borough Ct Brackley NN13 234 A5
  Higham Ferrers NN10 . . . . .132 B5
Borough Rd NN13 . . . . .234 A5
Borrowdale Rd NN17 . . . . .36 D8
Borrowdale Wlk 3 NN3 . .142 C4
Bostock Ave NN1 . . . . .159 F7
Boston Ct NN4 . . . . .36 C4
Boswell La MK19 . . . . .228 E4
Bosworth Cl NN4 . . . . .159 A1
Bosworth Rd
  Husbands Bosworth LE17 . . .45 A8
  Theddingworth LE16 . . . . . . .46 C7
Bothy The OX17 . . . . .237 D2
Botmead Rd NN3 . . . . .143 D4
Bottom La LE16 . . . . .34 B5
Bougainvillea Dr NN3 . . . .160 C6
Boughton NN15 . . . . .91 D4
Boughton Cl NN18 . . . . . . .36 A4
Boughton Dr NN10 . . . . . . .148 A8
Boughton Fair La NN3 . . .126 B4
Boughton Green
  Rd NN2, NN3 . . . . .141 D5
Boughton House NN14 . . . .73 C8
Boughton La NN3 . . . . .141 F7
Boughton Prim Sch NN2 141 D8
Boughton Rd
  Boughton NN2, NN3 . . . . . .141 F8
  Moulton NN3 . . . . .126 A1
Boundary Ave NN10 . . . . . .131 E1
Boundary Cres MK11 . . . . .229 E4
Boundary Rd NN13 . . . . . . .234 A6
Bourne Cl Corby NN18 . . . . .36 D2
  Wellingborough NN8 . . . . . .129 C6
Bourne Cres NN5 . . . . .140 E1
Bourton Cl NN4 . . . . .174 E8
Bourton Way NN8 . . . . .129 E1
Bouverie Rd NN4 . . . . .175 E8
Bouverie St 1 NN1 . . . . . .159 F6
Bouverie Wlk 5 NN1 . . . . .159 F6
Bovewell OX6 . . . . .237 D3
Bow Ct NN4 . . . . .158 E3
Bowden La
  Market Harborough LE16 . . .31 E4
  Welham LE16 . . . . .17 E5
Bowden Rd
  Northampton NN5 . . . . .159 A6
  Thorpe Langton LE16 . . . . . .17 A4
Bowden Ridge LE16 . . . . . .32 A5
Bowen Rd CV22 . . . . .98 D8
Bowen Sq 7 NN11 . . . . . . .135 C1
Bowhill NN16 . . . . .72 A1
Bowland Dr NN15 . . . . .92 A5
Bowling Gn NN13 . . . . .221 B4
Bowling Green Ave NN15 .72 B1
Bowling Green Rd NN15 . .72 B1
Bowman Cl OX17 . . . . .220 A8
Bowmans Cl NN4 . . . . .158 D1
Bowmen's Lea OX17 . . . . .237 C7
Bowness NN8 . . . . .129 D5
Bowthorpe Cl NN3 . . . . . . .160 D6
Boxwood Dr CV23 . . . . .100 A3
Boyle Rd NN17 . . . . .22 C1
Bozeat Prim Sch NN29 . . .164 D3
Bozenham Mill La NN7 . . .205 E4
Brabham Cl NN12 . . . . .214 D4
Bracedale Wlk NN17 . . . . .21 C1
Bracken Borough NN6 . . . .106 C2
Bracken Cl NN16 . . . . .72 B5
Bracken Field Sq NN3 . . . .142 F7
Bracken Leas Prim
  Sch NN13 . . . . .222 E1
Brackendale Dr CV23 . . . . .99 C1
Brackenhill Cl NN2 . . . . . . .141 E3
Brackley CE Jun
  Sch NN13 . . . . .233 F8
Brackley Cl NN3 . . . . .141 D6
Brackley Cottage
  Hospl NN13 . . . . .233 F7
Brackley La NN12 . . . . .201 F1
Brackley Magdalen
  College Sch (St
  John's) NN13 . . . . .233 F6
Brackley Magdalen
  College Sch
  (Waynflete) NN13 . . . . .233 E7
Brackley Rd
  Croughton NN13 . . . . .238 D8
  Greatworth OX17 . . . . .210 E1
  Silverstone NN12 . . . . .214 D3
  Silverstone NN12 . . . . .214 E5
  Towcester NN12 . . . . .203 B4
  Westbury NN13 . . . . .234 F5
Brackley Southfield
  Prim Sch NN13 . . . . .233 E6

Brackley Waynflete Inf
Sch NN13 . . . . .233 E7
Brackmills Ind Est NN4 .160 C2
Bracknell NN8 . . . . .129 C4
Bradbury Rd NN11 . . . . . .153 D3
Bradden Cl NN2 . . . . . . .141 D5
Bradden Rd NN12 . . . . . .202 D8
Bradden Way NN12 . . . . .202 D8
Bradfield Cl
  Rushden NN10 . . . . .132 D3
  Wellingborough NN8 . . . . .111 A1
Bradfield Rd NN8 . . . . . . .111 A1
Bradmore Ct NN3 . . . . . .143 B5
Bradmore Gdns NN18 . . . .36 C6
Bradshaw St NN1 . . . . . .159 C6
Bradshaw Way NN29 . . . .146 F8
Braemar Cl NN15 . . . . . . .91 E8
Braemar Cres NN4 . . . . .175 C8
Brafield Leys CV22 . . . . . .98 A6
Brafield Rd Cogenhoe NN7 161 E5
  Horton NN7 . . . . .177 E3
Braggintons La OX17 . . . .220 B8
Braid Ct NN8 . . . . .129 D7
Braithwaite Cl NN15 . . . . .90 F8
Brakey Rd NN17 . . . . .37 F8
Bramber Ct NN18 . . . . . . .36 A5
Bramble Cl Kettering NN16 .72 B6
  Ringstead NN14 . . . . .95 A3
Bramble End NN4 . . . . . .174 F8
Bramble Rd NN12 . . . . . .203 B4
Brambleside
  Kettering NN16 . . . . .72 C6
  Thrapston NN14 . . . . .76 D1
Brambleside Com Prim
Sch NN16 . . . . .72 C6
Brambleside NN16 . . . . . .72 B6
BraMCote Dr NN3 . . . . . .160 F8
Bramhall Rise NN5 . . . . .158 B8
Bramley Cl Cogenhoe NN7 .161 E6
  Rushden NN10 . . . . .131 F3
Bramley Ct NN29 . . . . . .146 D3
Bramley Gr NN3 . . . . . . .143 B2
Bramley Ho NN11 . . . . . .135 C2
Brammar Cl NN5 . . . . . . .158 F7
Brampton Cl
  Kettering NN15 . . . . .92 A5
  Wellingborough NN8 . . . . .129 D7
Brampton Hill LE16 . . . . . .33 F4
Brampton La
  Boughton NN6, NN2 . . . . .141 A7
  Chapel Brampton NN6 . . . .125 A3
Brampton Way NN6 . . . . .106 B1
Brampton Wlk NN3 . . . . .141 F5
Brampton Wood La NN4 .50 F7
Bramptons Prim Sch
The NN6 . . . . .124 D1
Bramshill Ave NN16 . . . . .72 A6
Bramston Cl PE8 . . . . . . .42 A4
Brandenburg Rd NN18 . . .35 F2
Brangwyn Wlk NN3 . . . . .36 E5
Branksome Ave NN2 . . . .141 B1
Branksome Ct NN18 . . . . .36 A6
Branson Ct NN16 . . . . . . .72 A3
Brasenose Dr NN13 . . . . .233 D8
Brashland Dr NN4 . . . . . .175 D6
Braunston CE Prim
Sch NN11 . . . . .118 C1
Braunston La NN11 . . . . .152 C8
Braunston Pl CV22 . . . . . .98 D8
Braunston Rd NN11 . . . . .135 B2
Braunton Pl NN18 . . . . . .36 F4
Brawn Way NN9 . . . . . . .131 E8
Brawn Way PE8 . . . . .16 D1
Braybrooke Cl NN14 . . . . .95 C3
Braybrooke Prim
Sch LE16 . . . . .49 E6
Braybrooke Rd
  Arthingworth NN6 . . . . . . .68 D8
  Desborough NN14 . . . . . . .50 F4
  Dingley LE16 . . . . .33 A3
  Great Oxendon LE16 . . . . .49 A3
  Market Harborough LE16 . . .32 B1
Brayford Ave NN18 . . . . . .36 F5
Brayford Ct NN3 . . . . . . .160 C2
Breach Cl NN6 . . . . .106 C2
Breakleys Rd NN14 . . . . . .51 B2
Breck Cl NN18 . . . . .53 B8
Brecon Cl NN16 . . . . .72 B6
Brecon St NN5 . . . . .159 A8
Breedon Cl NN14 . . . . . . .36 A1
Breezehill NN4 . . . . .175 F6
Brembridge Cl NN6 . . . . .127 D2
Brendon Cl NN3 . . . . . . .160 D7
Brent Cl NN15 . . . . .92 A2
Brentford NN8 . . . . .129 B5
Brer Ct NN4 . . . . .159 F5
Bressingham Gdns NN4 .175 C7
Breton MK11 . . . . .229 E6
Bretton Cl NN5 . . . . .140 A1
Bretts La NN7 . . . . .191 E4
Brewery Ct PE8 . . . . .41 F4
Brewin Cl NN13 . . . . . . .222 F1
Briar Cl NN13 . . . . .222 F1
Briar Hill Lower Sch NN4 158 F3
Briar Hill Rd NN4 . . . . . .159 B2
Briar Hill Wlk NN4 . . . . .159 B2
Briar Rd NN16 . . . . .72 E5
Briars The NN4 . . . . .159 A3
Briary Cl NN12 . . . . .203 B4
Brick Kiln Cl NN12 . . . . .203 D4
Brick Kiln La NN2 . . . . . .159 D8
Brick Kiln Rd NN9 . . . . . .114 D8
Brickett's La NN7 . . . . . .155 E5
Brickhill Mews NN8 . . . . .129 E4
Brickhill Rd NN8 . . . . . . .129 C4
Brickwell Ct NN3 . . . . . . .143 A1

Brickyard Spinney
Rd NN3 . . . . .142 B6
Bridewell La 11 NN16 . . . .72 B2
Bridge Ct Corby NN17 . . . .37 A7
  Thrapston NN14 . . . . .76 C2
Bridge End PE8 . . . . .8 A3
Bridge Mdw NN7 . . . . . .178 B8
Bridge Rd Cosgrove MK19 .218 E2
  Desborough NN14 . . . . . . .51 A3
Bridge St Apethorpe PE8 . .14 D4
  Brackley NN13 . . . . .233 E6
  Brigstock NN14 . . . . .55 E7
  Geddington NN14 . . . . . . .54 C4
  Kettering NN16 . . . . .72 C3
  King's Cliffe PE8 . . . . .14 A7
  Northampton NN1 . . . . . .159 C5
  Olney MK46 . . . . .195 F1
  Raunds NN9 . . . . .114 D7
  Rothwell NN14 . . . . .70 D7
  Thrapston NN14 . . . . .76 C2
  Weedon NN7 . . . . .155 B4
  Weldon NN17 . . . . .38 B8
Bridgend NN6 . . . . .82 B4
Bridgewater Cl NN13 . . .233 F8
Bridgewater Cres NN13 .233 F8
Bridgewater Dr NN3 . . . .160 D7
Bridgewater Ho NN13 . . .233 F8
Bridgewater Rd NN13 . . .233 F8
Bridgewater Rise NN13 .233 F8
Bridgford Pl NN18 . . . . . .36 C6
Bridgwater Ct NN18 . . . . .36 A6
Bridle Cl
  Brafield-on-t-G NN7 . . . . .161 D2
  Wellingborough NN8 . . . . .111 A1
Bridle La NN6 . . . . .84 B6
Bridle Path NN7 . . . . . . .161 D2
Bridle Rd
  Burton Latimer NN15 . . . . .92 A2
  Hannington NN6 . . . . . . .108 C3
  Old NN6 . . . . .107 D7
Bridle Way NN14 . . . . . . .90 A6
Briery Cl NN18 . . . . .36 B1
Brigg Cl NN18 . . . . .36 C4
Brighouse Cl NN18 . . . . . .36 C4
Bright Trees Rd NN14 . . . .54 B3
Brighton Rd NN14 . . . . . .36 B4
Brightwell Wlk NN9 . . . .131 D8
Brigstock Ctry Pk NN14 . . .56 A7
Brigstock Latham's
Charity Prim Sch NN14 . .55 F7
Brigstock Rd NN14 . . . . . .38 A4
Brindley Cl NN11 . . . . . .135 A5
Brindley Rd CV21 . . . . . . .80 B1
Bringhurst Cty Prim
Sch LE16 . . . . .20 C6
Brington Dr NN15 . . . . . . .91 F5
Brington Prim Sch NN7 .138 C5
Brington Rd NN6 . . . . . . .121 C3
Brinkhill Wlk NN18 . . . . . .36 C4
Brinsley Gn NN18 . . . . . . .36 C6
Brisbane Gdns NN18 . . . . .36 B2
Britain Cotts NN7 . . . . . .173 F1
Britannia Gdns NN3 . . . .130 C4
Britannia Rd NN16 . . . . . .72 A3
Britannia Trad Ctr NN5 .140 D2
Britannia Wlk LE16 . . . . . .31 F2
British La 16 NN16 . . . . . .72 B2
Briton Gdns NN3 . . . . . .142 B1
Briton Rd NN3 . . . . .142 B1
Briton Terr NN3 . . . . . . .142 B1
Britten Cl NN9 . . . . .133 C8
Brittons Dr NN3 . . . . . . .143 A7
Brixham Wlk NN18 . . . . . .36 F5
Brixworth CE Prim
Sch NN6 . . . . .106 B1
Brixworth Country
Pk NN6 . . . . .125 C8
Brixworth Country Pk
Visitor Ctr NN6 . . . . . .125 C7
Brixworth Hall Pk NN6 .106 B2
Brixworth Rd Creaton NN6 104 F4
  Holcot NN6 . . . . .126 D8
  Spratton NN6 . . . . .105 D1
Broad La NN13 . . . . .233 E3
Broad March NN11 . . . . .153 D8
Broad St Brixworth NN6 . .106 B1
  Earls Barton NN6 . . . . . . .144 E4
  Northampton NN1 . . . . . .159 C6
  Syresham NN13 . . . . . . .224 B8
Broadgate LE16 . . . . .20 D7
Broadgate Way PE8 . . . . .28 C2
Broadhurst Dr NN3 . . . . .161 A8
Broadlands Brixworth NN6 106 A1
  Desborough NN14 . . . . . . .51 C2
  Pitsford NN6 . . . . .125 D5
  Raunds NN9 . . . . .114 E6
  Rushden NN10 . . . . .132 B3
Broadmead Ave NN3 . . . .142 B2
Broadmead Ct NN3 . . . . .142 B2
Broadstone Ct NN18 . . . . .36 A6
Broadwater La NN12 . . . .203 A5
Broadway Kettering NN15 . .91 B8
  Northampton NN3 . . . . . .142 A1
  Wellingborough NN8 . . . . .130 A3
Broadway E NN3 . . . . . . .142 B1
Broadway Terr LE16 . . . . .31 F4
Broadway The
  Market Harborough LE16 . . .31 F4
  Norton NN11 . . . . .136 C4
Brocade Cl 8 NN4 . . . . .158 F2
Brockhall Cl NN3 . . . . . . .141 E4
Brockhall Rd Flore NN7 . .155 E6
  Northampton NN3 . . . . . .141 E4
Brockhill Cl NN15 . . . . . . .72 E1
Brockton St NN2 . . . . . . .141 D1
Brockwood Cl NN5 . . . . .140 A1
Bromford Cl 8 NN3 . . . .161 A8

Bromley Farm Ct NN11 .184 B5
Bromwich Rd 11 CV21 . . . .80 A1
Bronte Cl NN16 . . . . .72 C6
Brontes The NN17 . . . . . .36 D8
Brook Cl Horton NN7 . . . .177 E2
  Silverstone NN12 . . . . . . .214 D5
Brook Farm Cl NN16 . . . .148 B5
Brook La Great Easton LE16 .20 D6
  Northampton NN5 . . . . . .158 F8
  Towcester NN12 . . . . . . .203 A6
Brook St
  7 Daventry NN11 . . . . . .135 C2
  Hargrave NN9 . . . . .115 E3
  Moreton Pinkney NN11 . . .199 C7
  Northampton NN1 . . . . . .159 B7
  Raunds NN9 . . . . .114 D6
Brook St E NN8 . . . . . . .130 B4
Brook St W NN8 . . . . . . .129 F4
Brook Terr
  1 Irthlingborough NN9 . . . .112 F2
  Medbourne LE16 . . . . .18 F6
  Rothwell NN14 . . . . .70 D7
Brook Vale NN8 . . . . . . .129 C2
Brook Wlk NN14 . . . . .95 A3
Brooke Cl Rushden NN10 .132 B1
  Wellingborough NN8 . . . . .129 B5
Brooke Gn NN8 . . . . . . .129 B5
Brooke House Sch LE16 . .31 E4
Brooke Mews NN8 . . . . .129 B5
Brooke Rd NN18 . . . . .53 B8
Brooke Weston City
Technology Coll NN18 . . .36 D1
Brookes Gr NN17 . . . . . . .21 E1
Brookfield Rd
  Market Harborough LE16 . . .31 C3
  Northampton NN3 . . . . . .141 E2
  Rushden NN10 . . . . .132 A2
Brookhaven NN14 . . . . . . .90 B4
Brookland Cres NN1 . . . .142 A1
Brookland Rd NN1 . . . . .142 A1
Brooklands Cl NN11 . . . .135 C1
Brooklands Gdns LE16 . . .31 E2
Brooks Cl
  Burton Latimer NN15 . . . . .92 C1
  Willoughby CV23 . . . . . .117 D4
Brooks Rd NN9 . . . . .114 F8
Brooksdale NN14 . . . . . . .51 B2
Brookside Bozeat NN29 . .164 D2
  Desborough NN14 . . . . . . .51 B2
  Glapthorn PE8 . . . . .26 C1
  Hinton NN11 . . . . .184 A6
  Lillingstone Lovell MK18 . .227 A6
  Stanwick NN14 . . . . .114 A3
  Wappenham NN12 . . . . . .213 C8
  Weedon NN7 . . . . .155 B3
Brookside Cl
  Old Stratford MK19 . . . . . .229 B6
  Yelvertoft NN6 . . . . .82 B4
Brookside La NN11 . . . . .153 A2
Brookside Mdws NN5 . . . .140 E1
Brookside Mews NN6 . . . .82 B4
Brookside Pl NN7 . . . . . .156 C2
Brookway MK19 . . . . . . .228 E4
Broom Ct 2 NN4 . . . . . .159 A3
Broomhill Cres NN3 . . . . .143 A6
Brough Cl NN5 . . . . .139 F1
Broughton Hill NN14 . . . . .90 A4
Broughton Pl NN3 . . . . . .142 B3
Broughton Prim
Sch NN14 . . . . .90 A4
Broughton Rd Old NN6 . .107 E8
  Pytchley NN14 . . . . .90 E2
Brown's La NN14 . . . . . . .95 C6
Brown's Way NN1 . . . . . .159 E5
Browning Ave NN16 . . . . .72 C5
Browning Cl NN11 . . . . . .135 B4
Browning Rd Rugby CV21 . .99 B8
  Wellingborough NN8 . . . . .129 C4
Browning Wlk NN17 . . . . .36 D8
Brownlow Ct NN3 . . . . . .142 E4
Browns Rd NN11 . . . . . . .134 F1
Brownsfield Rd NN10 . . . .217 E6
Brownswood Dr NN12 . . .217 D3
Bruce St NN5 . . . . .158 F6
Brundall St NN7 . . . . . . .160 D7
Brunel Cl Daventry NN11 .134 F4
  Kettering NN16 . . . . .72 A3
  Wellingborough NN8 . . . . .129 B6
Brunel Ct NN17 . . . . .22 A2
Brunel Dr NN5 . . . . .158 D5
Brunel Rd NN17 . . . . .22 A2
Brunswick Gdns NN18 . . .35 F2
Brunswick Pl NN1 . . . . . .159 E7
Brunswick Wlk NN1 . . . . .159 E7
Brunting Rd NN3 . . . . . . .142 C8
Bryant Rd NN15 . . . . .91 C7
Bryant Way NN10 . . . . . .132 B5
Buccleuch St NN16 . . . . . .72 B3
Buchanan Cl NN4 . . . . . .159 A3
Buckfast Sq NN18 . . . . . . .36 F4
Buckingham Cl
  Northampton NN4 . . . . . .175 B7
  Wellingborough NN8 . . . . .129 C1
Buckingham Rd
  Brackley NN13 . . . . .234 A6
  Deanshanger MK19 . . . . .228 F3
Buckingham Way NN12 . .203 B5
Buckle Ho NN5 . . . . .159 B5
Buckley Ct MK11 . . . . . . .229 F4
Bucknill Cres CV21 . . . . . .99 B7
Bucknills La NN6 . . . . . . .100 F5
Buckwell Cl
  Desborough NN14 . . . . . . .51 A3
  Wellingborough NN8 . . . . .129 D5
Buckwell End NN8 . . . . . .129 C5
Buckwell La CV23 . . . . . . .80 B6
Buckwell Pl NN8 . . . . . . .129 F4
Budge Rd NN12 . . . . . . .217 F5

Bugbrooke Campion
Sch NN7 . . . . .173 A8
Bugbrooke Prim
Sch NN12 . . . . .172 F7
Bugbrooke Rd
  Gayton NN7 . . . . .173 D2
  Kislingbury NN7 . . . . . . .157 D3
  Nether Heyford NN7 . . . . .156 C1
Bugby Dr NN9 . . . . .113 B5
Bull Baulk OX17 . . . . . . .220 A8
Bull Cl NN29 . . . . .164 D3
Bull La PE9 . . . . .1 A6
Bullock Rd PE7 . . . . .29 D5
Bulls La OX17 . . . . .230 F5
Bulwell Gn NN18 . . . . . . .36 C6
Bungalows The
  Theddingworth LE17 . . . . .46 D8
  Walgrave NN6 . . . . .108 A5
Bunkers Hill Badby NN11 .152 F2
  Gumley LE17 . . . . .30 A5
Bunsty Ct MK11 . . . . . . .229 F5
Bunting Cl NN15 . . . . .92 A2
Bunting Rd NN2 . . . . . . .141 D1
Bunting's La PE8 . . . . .28 B3
Burcote Rd NN12 . . . . . .203 D4
Burditt Cl NN14 . . . . .70 F6
Burford Ave NN3 . . . . . . .142 C5
Burford Cl LE16 . . . . .31 D1
Burford Way NN8 . . . . . .129 D1
Burgess Cl NN18 . . . . . . .36 A4
Burghley Cl Corby NN18 . .36 F5
  Desborough NN14 . . . . . . .51 A4
  Market Harborough LE16 . . .32 A3
Burghley Dr NN18 . . . . . .36 F5
Burghley St NN16 . . . . . . .72 C4
Burkitt Rd NN17 . . . . .21 F3
Burleigh Rd NN2 . . . . . . .141 C1
Burmans Way NN7 . . . . .161 E6
Burnell Cl NN14 . . . . .95 B3
Burnham Pl NN18 . . . . . .224 B8
Burnmill Rd LE16 . . . . . . .31 C5
Burns Dr NN17 . . . . .36 D8
Burns Rd Daventry NN11 .135 B4
  Kettering NN16 . . . . .72 C5
  Wellingborough NN8 . . . . .129 C4
Burns St NN1 . . . . .159 E7
Burrows Cl NN11 . . . . . .119 E1
Burrows Ct NN3 . . . . . . .142 E4
Burrows Farm La NN14 . .113 B8
Burrows Vale NN6 . . . . . .106 C2
Burryport Rd NN4 . . . . . .160 B2
Burton Cl NN11 . . . . . . .135 C5
Burton Ho NN15 . . . . .92 C1
Burton Rd NN9 . . . . .111 F6
Burtram Cl NN3 . . . . . . .142 E1
Burwell Hill NN13 . . . . . .233 F8
Burwell Wlk NN18 . . . . . .36 C4
Burwood Rd NN3 . . . . . .142 B2
Bury Cl Cottingham LE16 . .20 C1
  Higham Ferrers NN10 . . . .132 C6
Bury Dyke NN6 . . . . .101 A6
Burystead Pl NN8 . . . . . .130 A4
Burystead Rise NN9 . . . .114 E7
Bush Cl NN8 . . . . .129 E5
Bush Hill NN3 . . . . .142 C2
Bushacre Ct NN6 . . . . . . .71 F3
Bushey Balk Cl NN18 . . . .36 B1
Bushland Rd NN3 . . . . . .142 C2
Bushmead Rd NN7 . . . . .155 B3
Buswell Rise NN14 . . . . . .70 E7
Butcher's La
  Boughton NN6 . . . . .125 C1
  Pattishall NN12 . . . . .172 E1
  Pytchley NN14 . . . . .90 F2
Butchers Paddock NN14 . .93 A7
Bute Ct NN11 . . . . .36 B8
Butler Gdns LE16 . . . . . . .31 C3
Butlers Cl NN11 . . . . . . .182 F2
  Rothwell NN14 . . . . .70 B7
Butlin Cl Daventry NN11 . .135 B3
Butlin Ct NN8 . . . . .130 C4
Butlins La NN7 . . . . .191 D4
Butt La LE17 . . . . .45 E5
Buttermere Cl NN8 . . . . .129 C5
Buttermere Cl
  Kettering NN16 . . . . .71 E3
  Northampton NN3 . . . . . .142 C3
Butterwick Wlk NN18 . . . .36 C4
Buttmead NN7 . . . . .190 D7
Butts Cl Aynho OX17 . . . .237 C7
  Culworth OX17 . . . . .198 D2
Butts Croft Cl NN4 . . . . .175 C6
Butts Hill Cres NN7 . . . . .173 A8
Butts Rd Northampton NN4 175 C6
  Raunds NN9 . . . . .114 E6
Butts The OX17 . . . . .237 D8
Buxton Dr NN14 . . . . .50 E4
By Pass Way NN7 . . . . . .178 B8
Bycell Rd MK18 . . . . .226 F7
Byfield Prim Sch NN11 .183 C7
Byfield Rd
  Chipping Warden OX17 . . .196 F5
  Eydon NN11 . . . . .184 C2
  Hinton NN11 . . . . .184 B7
  Northampton NN5 . . . . . .159 A5
  Priors Marston CV23 . . . . .166 E2
Byron Cl NN12 . . . . .203 B5
Byron Cres
  Higham Ferrers NN10 . . . .132 A5
  Rushden NN10 . . . . .131 E2
Byron Rd Corby NN17 . . . .36 D8
  Kettering NN16 . . . . .72 C5
  Wellingborough NN8 . . . . .129 C4
Byron St NN2 . . . . .141 F1
Byron Wlk NN11 . . . . . . .135 B3

C

Cabot Cl Daventry NN11 . .135 C5
  Rothwell NN14 . . . . .70 E6
Caernarvon Cl NN12 . . . .203 C4
Caesars Gate NN13 . . . . .234 A6
Caistor Rd NN17 . . . . .10 C1
Caldbeck Wlk 5 NN3 . . .142 C4
Caldecott Rd
  Chelveston NN9 . . . . . . .133 B7
  Rockingham LE16 . . . . . . .21 B5
Calder Cl NN17 . . . . .21 D1
Calder Gn NN5 . . . . .140 E1
Caledonian Ho 1 NN5 . .159 A6
Calstock Cl NN3 . . . . . . .160 D7
Calvert Cl NN12 . . . . . . .202 E8
Calvert Rd NN12 . . . . . . .202 E8
Calverton Rd MK11 . . . . .229 D4
Cam Cl NN17 . . . . .21 C1
Camberley Cl NN3 . . . . . .143 B2
Camborne Cl NN4 . . . . . .159 B2
Cambria Cres NN3 . . . . .142 C1
Cambridge Ave NN17 . . . .36 B6
Cambridge St
  Kettering NN16 . . . . .72 C3
  Northampton NN2 . . . . . .159 C8
  Rothwell NN14 . . . . .70 D8
  Wellingborough NN8 . . . . .130 A5
  Wymington NN10 . . . . . . .148 A7
Camden Sq NN29 . . . . . .164 D2
Camelot Way NN5 . . . . . .158 A7
Cameron Cl
  Daventry NN11 . . . . .135 B3
  Northampton NN5 . . . . . .158 E7
Cameron Cres NN3 . . . . .158 E7
Cameron Ct NN17 . . . . . .36 F5
Cameron Dr NN5 . . . . . . .158 E7
Camp Hill NN7 . . . . .173 A6
Camp Hill Lower
Sch NN4 . . . . .158 E7
Camp La NN7 . . . . .157 D3
Campanula Cl NN3 . . . . .160 C6
Campbell Rd Corby NN17 . .36 F5
  Wellingborough NN8 . . . . .130 A2
Campbell Sq 1 NN1 . . . .159 D6
Campbell St NN1 . . . . . . .159 C7
Campion Cl NN10 . . . . . .148 B8
Campion Ct NN3 . . . . . . .143 B1
Camrose Rd NN5 . . . . . .159 A8
Camsdale Wlk LE16 . . . . .35 C8
Canada Sq NN18 . . . . . . .36 C3
Canal Mus The NN12 . . . .205 A8
Canalside NN12 . . . . . . .205 A8
Candace Ct NN5 . . . . . . .158 E8
Candleford NN18 . . . . . . .143 B4
Canford Gn NN18 . . . . . . .36 A6
Cannam Cl LE16 . . . . .20 B1
Cannock Rd NN17 . . . . . .36 F8
Cannon St NN8 . . . . . . .130 A5
Canon Harnett Ct MK12 .229 F6
Canon St NN16 . . . . .72 B3
Canonbury NN8 . . . . . . .129 C4
Canons Ashby NN11 . . . .185 D2
Canons Ashby Rd NN11 .199 D7
Canons Wlk NN2 . . . . . .141 B4
Canterbury Cl OX16 . . . .219 A7
Cantle Cl NN18 . . . . .36 D3
Capell Gdns NN18 . . . . . .36 E4
Capell Rise NN7 . . . . . . .155 E5
Cappenham Cl NN12 . . . .203 B6
Captain's Ct NN7 . . . . . .177 E1
Cardigan Cl 4 NN5 . . . . .158 F8
Cardigan Pl Corby NN18 . .36 C5
  Kettering NN16 . . . . .72 D2
Cardigan Rd NN14 . . . . . .37 E2
Cardinal Cl NN4 . . . . . . .175 B7
Cares Orch NN7 . . . . . . .161 D3
Carey Cl NN3 . . . . .126 B1
Carey Ct NN3 . . . . .126 B1
Carey Dr NN17 . . . . .36 C8
Carey Ho 2 NN16 . . . . . .72 B2
Carey Rd Hackleton NN7 . .177 A3
  Towcester NN12 . . . . . . .203 C3
Carey St Kettering NN16 . . .72 C2
  Northampton NN1 . . . . . .159 E7
Carey Way NN10 . . . . . . .132 D3
Careys Rd NN12 . . . . . . .215 F7
Carina Rd NN15 . . . . .91 C5
Carisbrooke Cl NN15 . . . .91 F8
Carline Ct NN3 . . . . .142 D4
Carlow Rd NN14 . . . . .95 A3
Carlow St NN14 . . . . .95 A3
Carlton Cl NN10 . . . . . . .148 A7
Carlton Gdns NN2 . . . . . .141 E2
Carlton Mews NN10 . . . . .132 C5
Carlton Pl NN18 . . . . .36 B6
Carlton Rd
  Northampton NN2 . . . . . .141 E2
  Wilbarston LE16 . . . . .34 D5
Carlton St NN16 . . . . .72 A3
Carlyle Ave NN5 . . . . . . .158 E7
Carmarthen Way NN10 . .148 C8
Carne The MK11 . . . . . . .229 E5
Carnegie St NN12 . . . . . .132 A2
Carol Trusler Mews NN2 .159 F2
Carousel Way NN3 . . . . .160 F7
Carr's Way NN7 . . . . .157 C6
Carrdus Sch
  (Overthorpe Hall)
  The OX17 . . . . .219 C8
Carriage Dr NN16 . . . . . . .72 C6
Carriers Cl NN14 . . . . . . .207 A2
Carrington Gdns NN3 . . .160 F8
Carrington St NN16 . . . . .72 B2

Carron Cl NN17 ....21 C1
Carsington Cl NN16 .....71 E3
Carter Ave NN14 ....90 A3
Carter Cl NN8 ....130 B4
Cartmel Pl NN3 ....142 C3
Cartmel Way NN10 ......132 D3
Cartrill St NN9 ....114 C6
Cartwright Cres NN13 ...233 D7
Cartwright Gdns OX17 ...237 D7
Cartwright Rd
  Charlton OX17 ....231 F5
  Northampton NN2 ....141 C1
Casterbridge Ct NN4 ....175 E7
Casterton Cl NN9 ....114 A5
Castilian St NN1 ....159 D5
Castilian Terr NN1 .....159 D5
Castle Ashby Rd NN7 ...179 B7
Castle Ave NN5 ....158 C8
Castle Bush NN5 ....158 C8
Castle Cl Corby NN18 .....36 A4
  Northampton NN5 ......158 C8
Castle Ct Rushden NN10 .148 A8
  Wellingborough NN8 ...130 B4
Castle Gdns NN14 ....54 B3
Castle Hill Daventry NN11 .135 B1
  Rothwell NN14 ....70 D7
Castle La NN8 ....130 B4
Castle Mews NN8 ....130 B4
Castle Mound CV23 ....99 C2
Castle Mount NN13 ......233 E5
Castle Rd Lavendon MK46 .180 F1
  Wellingborough NN8 ...130 B4
  Woodford Halse NN11 ..184 C6
Castle St Deddington OX15 236 A4
  Northampton NN1 ......159 C6
  Wellingborough NN8 ...130 B4
Castle Sta NN1 ....159 B6
Castle View Barnwell PE8 ..59 B7
  Wellingborough NN8 ...130 B4
Castle Way Kettering NN15 .91 F6
  Wellingborough NN8 ...130 A4
Castlethorpe Fst
  Sch MK19 ....218 F5
Castlethorpe Rd MK19 ...206 F1
Caswell Rd NN4 ....160 B1
Catchpole Cl NN18 ....36 D3
Catesby Cl NN2 ....141 C4
Catesby Rd NN14 ....70 E7
Catesby St NN16 ....72 C3
Catlow Cl NN9 ....114 C8
Cattle End NN14 ....214 C4
Cattle Hill NN3 ....143 C2
Cattle Market Rd NN1 ...159 C4
Catton Cres NN2 ....140 F5
Cauldecott Cl NN4 ......158 D1
Causeway Rd NN17 ....21 C2
Causeway The
  Byfield NN11 ....183 E8
  Northampton NN3 ......161 C7
Causin Cl NN14 ....55 F8
Causin Way PE8 ....40 C5
Cavalry Dr NN11 ....135 B1
Cavalry Hill NN7 ....155 A4
Cavendish Cl NN15 ....91 F5
Cavendish Ctyd NN17 .....22 E1
Cavendish Dr NN3 ......160 D6
Cawley Rd OX17 ....230 B5
Caxton Cl NN11 ....135 C4
Caxton St LE16 ....31 F1
Caythorpe Sq NN18 ....36 B6
Cecil Cl NN18 ....36 E4
Cecil Dr NN18 ....36 F4
Cecil Rd NN2 ....141 C2
Cecil St Kettering NN16 ...72 C4
  Rothwell NN14 ....70 D7
Cedar Cl Brackley NN13 ...222 F2
  Daventry NN11 ....135 C5
  Desborough NN14 ....51 C2
  Irchester NN29 ....147 A7
  Rushden NN10 ....148 A8
  Sywell NN6 ....143 D8
  Towcester NN12 ....203 C4
Cedar Ct NN17 ....21 E1
Cedar Dr NN14 ....76 D1
Cedar Hythe NN6 ....124 D1
Cedar Rd Kettering NN16 ...72 C4
  Northampton NN1 ......142 A1
Cedar Rd E NN1 ....142 A1
Cedar Road Lower
  Sch NN3 ....142 A1
Cedar Way
  Higham Ferrers NN10 ..132 B6
  Wellingborough NN8 ...130 A7
Cedrus Ct NN2 ....140 F6
Celeborn Pl NN3 ....143 B5
Cemetery La NN10 ......132 B6
Centec Ct MK19 ....229 B7
Central Ave Hinton NN11 .184 A7
  Kettering NN16 ....72 D3
  Northampton NN2 .....141 B6
  Wellingborough NN8 ...129 E2
Central Mus & Art
  Gall NN1 ....159 D5
Centre 2000 NN16 ....71 F4
Centre Par NN16 ....72 D4
Chace Rd NN8 ....130 C4
Chacombe CE Prim
  Sch OX17 ....208 F4
Chacombe Rd OX17 ......208 F1
Chadleigh Ct NN13 .....233 E6
Chadstone Ave NN2 .....141 D6
Chadwick Gdns NN5 .....140 D1
Chaffinch Cl NN4 ......174 F7
Chaffinch Way NN13 ....222 F2
Chainbridge La PE18 .....97 F1

Chalcombe Ave NN2 ....141 C5
Chalcombe Rd NN2 .....141 C4
Chalfont Ct ⏹ NN1 .....159 C7
Chalk La NN1 ....159 B6
Chamberlain Ave NN8 ...129 E1
Chamberlain Rd CV21 ....99 B8
Chamberlain Way
  Higham Ferrers NN10 ..132 C5
  Rounds NN9 ....114 C5
Champion Ct NN13 ......233 E8
Chancel Terr PE8 ....59 B5
Chancery La NN14 ....76 D2
Chandlers Gdns NN14 ....76 E1
Chandlers Way NN18 .....36 E5
Channing St ⏹ NN16 ....72 C4
Chantelle Cl NN11 ......135 B3
Chantry Cl NN3 ....143 B3
Chantry La NN12 ....203 C6
Chapel Cl Clifton OX15 ...236 E4
  Great Addington NN14 ...94 B2
  Litchborough NN12 ....171 C1
  Silverstone NN12 .....214 D4
Chapel Ct PE8 ....8 B2
Chapel End
  Croughton NN13 ....238 C8
  Great Gidding PE17 .....61 C1
  Piddington NN7 ....177 A2
Chapel Fields LE17 ......62 B3
Chapel Gn NN5 ....141 A2
Chapel Hill
  Higham Ferrers NN10 ..132 B7
  Irchester NN29 ....147 B8
  Little Addington NN14 .113 B7
  Silverstone NN12 .....214 D4
Chapel Hill Rd NN14 .....76 B2
Chapel Ho NN4 ....159 B3
Chapel La Adderbury OX17 230 A4
  Badby NN11 ....153 A3
  Barrowden LE15 ....3 F5
  Blisworth NN7 ....190 D8
  Brafield-on-t-G NN7 ...161 E2
  Clipston LE16 ....66 F8
  Corby NN17 ....37 B6
  Crick NN6 ....101 A5
  Daventry NN11 ....135 C2
  Denford NN14 ....95 C6
  Elton PE8 ....28 C8
  Farthinghoe NN13 .....221 B4
  Flore NN7 ....155 F5
  Geddington NN14 ....54 A2
  Great Doddington NN29 145 E6
  Hackleton NN7 ....177 B2
  Ketton PE9 ....1 A5
  Libourne CV23 ....81 A6
  Lillingstone Lovell MK18 227 A1
  Little Harrowden NN9 ..110 C4
  Maidford NN12 ....186 D6
  Old NN6 ....107 C7
  Rushton NN14 ....52 C6
  Slapton NN12 ....201 E2
  Stanion NN14 ....37 E2
  Stoke Albany LE16 .....34 B4
  Stoke Bruerne NN12 ...205 A8
  Turweston NN13 ....234 B7
  Whitfield NN13 ....223 D3
  Wilbarston LE16 ....34 C5
Chapel Pl ⏹ NN1 ....159 E6
Chapel Rd
  Greatworth OX17 ......210 E1
  Weldon NN17 ....38 A8
Chapel Row NN3 ....143 C2
Chapel St
  Charwelton NN11 .....168 A4
  Kilsby CV23 ....100 A2
  Ringstead NN14 ....95 A3
  Swinford LE17 ....62 B3
  Titchmarsh NN14 ....77 C4
  Warmington PE8 ....28 B3
Chaplins La NN14 ....51 A3
Chapman Gr NN17 ....36 E8
Chapmans Cl NN29 .....147 B8
Chapmans La OX15 .....236 A3
Chappell Ho NN3 ....126 C1
Chardonnay Cl NN5 .....140 A2
Charles Cl
  Higham Ferrers NN10 ..132 C7
  Long Buckby NN6 .....121 B3
  Old NN6 ....107 D7
Charles Robinson
  Ct NN8 ....129 E3
Charles St Corby NN17 ...36 F5
  Kettering NN16 ....72 B4
  Market Harborough LE16 .31 E3
  Northampton NN1 ......159 D7
  Rothwell NN14 ....70 C6
  Thrapston NN14 ....76 E2
  Wellingborough NN8 ...129 E2
Charles Terr ⏹ NN1 ....135 C1
Charlesfield Rd CV22 ....98 A8
Charlotte Pl NN16 ......72 E4
Charlton Cl NN2 ....141 C5
Charlton Rd OX17 ......237 C7
Charlton Way NN13 .....221 B4
Charmandean Sch MK18 226 B4
Charnwood ⏹ NN8 .....130 A5
Charnwood Ave NN3 ....142 E2
Charnwood Cl NN11 ....135 B4
Charnwood Dr NN15 .....92 A5
Charnwood Rd NN17 .....36 F7
Charter Gate NN3 ......142 B6
Charter Rd CV22 ....98 E8
Charterhouse Cl NN13 ..233 E7
Chartwell Ave NN3 .....142 C5
Charwelton Rd NN11 ...169 C2
Chase Cl NN14 ....37 E3
Chase Farm NN14 ....54 A4
Chase Hill NN14 ....54 A3
Chase Park Rd NN7 .....179 A5

Chase The
  Long Buckby NN6 .....121 B4
  Pitsford NN6 ....125 D4
  Roade NN7 ....191 D4
Chase View Rd NN14 .....54 B3
Chaseport Cl MK46 .....194 D2
Chaston Pl NN16 ....72 E5
Chatellerault Ct NN17 ...36 D8
Chater Cl LE16 ....32 A6
Chatsworth Ave
  Kettering NN15 ....91 C5
  Northampton NN3 .....142 F5
Chatsworth Dr
  Market Harborough LE16 .32 B3
  Wellingborough NN8 ...129 C7
Chaucer Cl NN2 ....141 F1
Chaucer Ho NN2 ....141 F2
Chaucer Rd Rugby CV22 ..98 A7
  Wellingborough NN8 ...129 D4
Chaucer St NN2 ....141 F1
Chaucer Way NN11 .....135 B2
Cheddar Cl NN5 ....158 D7
Cheddar Wlk NN18 ....36 A6
Chedworth Cl NN3 .....143 D2
Cheese La ⏹ NN8 ....130 A4
Chelfham Cl NN3 ....160 D7
Chelmorton Vale NN14 ...50 E4
Chelmscot Row OX17 ...208 F8
Chelmsford Cl NN4 .....159 A2
Chelveston Base
  Cres NN9 ....133 D5
Chelveston Dr NN17 .....36 B7
Chelveston Rd
  Higham Ferrers NN10 ..132 E7
  Rounds NN9 ....114 C4
  Stanwick NN9 ....114 B3
Chenderit Sch OX17 ....209 A1
Cheney Ct OX17 ....208 F2
Cheney Gdns OX17 .....208 F2
Chepstow Cl
  Kettering NN15 ....91 F8
  Northampton NN5 ......159 A7
Chepstow Dr NN8 ......129 C7
Chequers La Grendon NN7 163 E5
  Ravensthorpe NN6 .....103 D1
  Wellingborough NN8 ...130 A5
Chequers The MK19 ....218 F5
Cheriton Dr NN11 ......135 C6
Cheriton Rd NN18 ....36 F4
Cheriton Way NN1 .....160 C6
Cherry Ave NN8 ....130 A7
Cherry Blossom Cl NN3 .143 B2
Cherry Cl NN3 ....142 C2
Cherry Ct NN9 ....112 E1
Cherry Lodge Rd NN3 ..143 B3
Cherry Orch Olney MK46 195 E4
  Rushden NN10 ....132 C1
Cherry Orchard Mid
  Sch NN3 ....142 C1
Cherry Rd NN16 ....72 D4
Cherry St
  Irthlingborough NN9 ..112 E1
  Ringstead NN14 ....95 B3
Cherry Tree Cl NN14 ....51 B2
Cherry Tree La NN4 ....160 E3
Cherry Wlk NN9 ....114 B5
Cherrytree Wlk NN16 ...143 D8
Cherwell Banks OX17 ...231 A6
Cherwell Gn NN5 ....140 F1
Cherwell Terr NN11 ....184 C6
Cherwell The NN11 .....134 F1
Cherwell Wlk NN17 ......21 C1
Chesham Rise NN3 .....143 B4
Chesil Wlk NN18 ....36 A6
Chester Ave NN7 ....157 B6
Chester Rd
  Irchester NN29 ....131 A1
  Rushden NN10 ....131 F2
  Wellingborough NN8 ...130 C4
Chestnut Ave Corby NN17 .21 D1
  Kettering NN15 ....72 C1
  Northampton NN4 .....175 D5
Chestnut Cl Hinton NN11 .184 A6
  Long Buckby NN6 .....121 B3
  Rushden NN10 ....131 F3
  Stony Stratford MK11 ..229 D5
  Wymington NN10 ......148 B5
Chestnut Dr
  Brackley NN13 ....222 F1
  Desborough NN14 ......51 C2
Chestnut Gr LE16 ....67 A8
Chestnut Rd
  Northampton NN3 .....142 A1
  Yardley Gobion NN12 ..217 F6
Chestnut Terr NN3 .....142 A2
Chestnuts The
  Castlethorpe MK19 ....218 F5
  Clifton OX15 ....236 E4
Chettle Pl NN12 ....217 E2
Chetwode OX17 ....219 C6
Cheviot Cl NN16 ....72 B7
Cheviot Ct NN4 ....158 E3
Cheviot Ho NN2 ....141 C5
Chewton Cl NN5 ....158 D7
Cheyne Wlk Kettering NN15 91 E8
  Northampton NN1 ......159 E5
Chichele Cl NN10 ......132 B5
Chichele Coll NN10 ....132 B6
Chichele Cl NN10 ......132 B3
Chichele St NN10 ......132 C6
Chichester Cl
  Daventry NN11 ....135 D1
  Rothwell NN14 ....70 E6
Chieftan Bsns Pk NN8 ..129 A6
Child's St NN14 ....95 C6
Chiltern Ave NN5 ......158 D8
Chiltern Cl
  Market Harborough LE16 .31 F5

Chiltern Cl continued
  Northampton NN5 ......158 D8
Chiltern Lower Sch NN5 .158 D8
Chiltern Rd
  Daventry NN11 ....135 B5
  Kettering NN16 ....72 B6
  Northampton NN5 .....158 D8
Chilwell Ct NN3 ....160 F8
Chipping Warden Prim
  Sch OX17 ....196 F7
Chipsey Ave
  Bugbrooke NN7 ....172 F8
  Northampton NN1 .....160 B6
Choakles The NN4 .....176 B6
Christchurch Dr NN11 ..153 B7
Christchurch Rd NN1 ..160 A7
Christie Way NN15 ......90 F8
Christopher Rawlins CE
  Prim Sch OX17 ....230 A4
Chulmleigh Wlk NN3 ...160 C7
Church Ave OX17 ......230 F5
Church Bank LE16 ....20 D7
Church Cl Adderbury OX17 230 A3
  Braybrooke LE16 ....49 E6
  Caldecott LE16 ....21 B8
  Clipston LE16 ....67 A8
  Hartwell NN7 ....192 D2
  Milton Malsor NN7 ....174 F4
  Wardington OX17 ......196 E1
  West Haddon NN6 .....102 C5
  Wicken MK19 ....228 B3
Church Dr NN18 ....53 C8
Church End
  Croughton NN13 ....238 D8
  Piddington NN7 ....177 A2
  Potterspury NN12 .....217 E3
  Roade NN7 ....191 D4
  Syresham NN13 ....224 D5
Church Farm Cl NN29 ..164 D3
Church Fields NN11 ....152 E3
Church Gdns NN6 ......103 E1
Church Gn
  Northampton NN5 .....140 F2
  Woodford NN14 ....94 D6
Church Hall Rd NN10 ..131 F1
Church Hill Badby NN11 .152 F2
  Barnwell PE8 ....59 B6
  Finedon NN9 ....111 E4
  Geddington NN14 ....54 A3
  Hollowell NN6 ....104 B4
  Moulton NN3 ....126 C1
  Northampton NN4 .....175 E6
  Ravensthorpe NN6 .....103 D1
Church La Adderbury OX17 230 A3
  Alderton NN12 ....204 F2
  Barnwell PE8 ....59 B6
  Barrowden LE15 ....3 F4
  Blisworth NN7 ....190 D7
  Bozeat NN29 ....164 D2
  Brafield-on-t-G NN7 ...161 E2
  Broughton NN14 ....89 F6
  Bugbrooke NN7 ....172 E7
  Burton Latimer NN15 ...92 C2
  Bythorn PE18 ....97 D4
  Caldecott LE16 ....21 B8
  Caldecott MK44 ....133 F3
  Chacombe OX17 ....208 E4
  Church Brampton NN6 .140 B8
  Clipston LE16 ....67 A8
  Cold Ashby NN6 ....84 A5
  Cold Higham NN12 ....188 C8
  Covington PE18 ....116 C2
  Cranford NN14 ....93 B7
  Croughton NN13 ....238 D8
  Deanshanger MK19 ....228 B4
  Denford NN14 ....95 C6
  Dingley LE16 ....33 A4
  Duddington PE9 ....5 B6
  East Carlton LE16 ......35 A7
  East Haddon NN6 .....122 D4
  Evenley NN13 ....233 F3
  Great Doddington NN29 145 E6
  Harrington NN6 ....69 B6
  Hellidon NN11 ....151 C1
  Hollowell NN6 ....104 B4
  Husbands Bosworth LE17 .45 E5
  Kislingbury NN7 ......157 D3
  Lillingstone Lovell MK18 227 A6
  Lower Harlestone NN7 .139 E6
  Lyddington LE15 ....9 D6
  Maidford NN12 ....186 D6
  Middleton Cheney OX17 .208 F1
  Morcott LE15 ....3 A6
  Nether Heyford NN7 ...156 D2
  Newton Bromswold NN10 149 D8
  Northampton NN1 .....159 C6
  Northampton, Billinge NN3 161 A8
  Pitsford NN6 ....125 D5
  Potterspury NN12 .....217 E3
  Slapton NN12 ....201 E2
  Slipton NN14 ....75 A3
  South Kilworth LE17 ...63 C8
  South Luffenham LE15 ..3 E8
  Spratton NN6 ....105 B1
  Stibbington PE8 ....8 D2
  Stoke Bruerne NN12 ...205 A8
  Stoke Doyle PE8 ....41 D1
  Sywell NN6 ....127 E3
  Walgrave NN6 ....108 A4
  Warmington PE8 ....28 B3
  Welford NN6 ....64 C5
  Wicken MK19 ....228 B3
  Wilby NN8 ....129 B1
  Wollaston NN29 ......146 D3
  Wymington NN10 ......148 B5
  Yardley Hastings NN7 .179 B7
Church Leys NN13 .....233 E3
Church Mount NN6 .....103 F6

Church Piece
  Cotts NN13 ....221 B4
Church Rd Brackley NN13 .233 F7
  Braunston NN11 ......118 B3
  Grafton Regis NN12 ...205 D3
  Greatworth OX17 .....210 E1
  Hargrave NN9 ....115 F1
  Ketton PE9 ....1 A5
  Piddington NN7 ....177 A2
  Pytchley NN14 ....91 A1
  Spratton NN6 ....124 B8
  Upper Boddington NN11 182 C7
Church Sq LE16 ....31 E3
Church St Blakesley NN12 187 B1
  Boughton NN2 ....141 C8
  Brigstock NN14 ....55 F7
  Brixworth NN6 ....106 B3
  Broughton NN14 ....90 B4
  Burton Latimer NN15 ..92 C3
  Byfield NN11 ....183 D7
  Charwelton NN11 .....168 B4
  Clifton u D CV23 ....80 A5
  Cogenhoe NN7 ....162 A6
  Cottingham LE16 ......20 D1
  Crick NN6 ....100 F6
  Easton on t H PE9 ......2 A6
  Finedon NN9 ....111 E4
  Hargrave NN9 ....115 E2
  Helmdon NN13 ....211 F3
  Husbands Bosworth LE17 .45 E5
  Irthlingborough NN9 ..112 F2
  Isham NN14 ....91 F1
  Long Buckby NN6 .....121 B4
  Market Harborough LE16 .31 E3
  Mears Ashby NN6 ......128 B2
  Moulton NN3 ....126 C1
  Naseby NN6 ....85 B8
  Nassington PE8 ....15 F5
  Nether Heyford NN7 ...156 B2
  Newnham NN11 ......153 E4
  Olney MK46 ....195 F3
  Oundle PE8 ....42 A5
  Pattishall NN12 ......172 E1
  Polebrook PE8 ....42 F3
  Raunds NN9 ....114 E7
  Ringstead NN14 ....95 B3
  Rothersthorpe NN7 ...174 A6
  Rushden NN10 ....132 B2
  Sibbertoft LE16 ....47 A2
  Silverstone NN12 .....214 D5
  Stanwick NN9 ....114 A3
  Staverton NN11 ......152 C7
  Stony Stratford MK11 .229 D5
  Sulgrave OX17 ....210 F7
  Titchmarsh NN14 ......77 C4
  Wadenhoe PE8 ....58 A3
  Warmington PE8 ....28 B2
  Watford NN6 ....120 C6
  Weedon NN7 ....155 C3
  Weldon NN17 ....38 B7
  Wellingborough NN8 ...130 A4
  Wilbarston LE16 ....34 C5
  Woodford NN14 ....94 D6
  Woodford Halse NN11 .184 C6
Church View
  Brackley NN13 ....234 A7
  Broughton NN14 ....90 A4
  Burton Latimer NN15 ..92 C3
  Ecton NN6 ....143 F4
  Greens Norton NN12 ..202 E8
  Moulton NN3 ....126 C2
  Northampton NN4 .....175 E6
  Rauns NN9 ....114 D7
  Walgrave NN6 ....108 A5
Church View Rd NN14 ...51 B2
Church Way Denton NN7 .178 B8
  Ecton NN6 ....143 F4
  Grendon NN7 ....163 D5
  Northampton NN3 .....160 E7
  Preston Capes NN11 ..169 D2
  Thorpe Malsor NN14 ...71 A3
  ⏹ Wellingborough NN8 .130 A4
  Whittlebury NN12 ....215 C5
Church Way Ct NN3 ....160 D8
Church Wlk Barby CV23 ..99 C1
  Bozeat NN29 ....164 D3
  Corby NN17 ....37 B6
  Daventry NN11 ....135 C2
  Denford NN14 ....95 C6
  ⏹ Irthlingborough NN9 .112 F2
  Kettering NN16 ....72 B2
  Little Addington NN14 .113 B8
  Lubenham LE16 ....31 D3
  Market Harborough LE16 .32 A2
  Newton Bromswold NN10 149 D8
  Northampton NN3 .....143 B2
  Ringstead NN14 ....95 B3
  Weldon NN17 ....38 B7
Churchcroft NN7 ......191 D4
Churchfield Cl NN2 ....141 E4
Churchill Ave
  Irthlingborough NN9 ..113 B5
  Northampton NN3 .....142 B4
  Wellingborough NN8 ...129 E2
Churchill Cl NN14 ......70 E7
Churchill Rd
  Earls Barton NN6 .....144 F4
  Welton NN11 ....135 E8
Churchill Way
  Brackley NN13 ....233 F6
  Burton Latimer NN15 ..92 B2
  Daventry NN11 ....153 E7
  Kettering NN15 ....72 F1
Churchway NN3 ....160 D8
Cider Cl LE15 ....3 F5
Cinnamon Cl ⏹ NN4 ...175 D6
Circus End NN5 ....140 C1
Cissbury Rd NN4 ......158 F4

Clailey Ct MK11 . . . . .229 F5
Clannell Rd NN4 . . . . .175 A8
Clare Ave NN11 . . . . .135 C2
Clare Cl NN6 . . . . .144 F3
Clare Cres NN12 . . . . .203 B5
Clare Dr NN14 . . . . .76 E3
Clare Rd NN8 . . . . .129 C3
Clare St Northampton NN1 .159 E7
Rounds NN9 . . . . .114 D6
Clare Wlk NN10 . . . . .132 B5
Claregate NN4 . . . . .175 B8
Claremont Ave MK1 . . . . .229 E4
Claremont Ct **13** NN1 . . . .159 C6
Claremont Dr LE16 . . . . . . .32 A3
Clarence Ave NN2 . . . . . . .141 C2
Clarence Ct NN10 . . . . . . .148 A8
Clarence Rd
Kettering NN16 . . . . .72 C3
Stony Stratford MK11 . . . .229 E5
Clarence St LE16 . . . . .31 F3
Clark Cl NN9 . . . . .113 B4
Clark Cres NN12 . . . . .203 C8
Clark Ho NN1 . . . . .160 A8
Clarke Cl NN16 . . . . .72 A4
Clarke Ct NN6 . . . . .144 F4
Clarke Rd Corby NN17 . . . . .36 D8
Northampton NN1 . . . . . . .160 A8
Clarke St LE16 . . . . .31 D3
Clarkes Dale LE16 . . . . .20 D6
Clarkes Way
Brackley NN13 . . . . .233 D7
Welton NN11 . . . . .135 D8
Clarks La NN13 . . . . .221 A3
Claughton Rd NN4 . . . . . . .159 D3
Clay La NN17 . . . . .10 B1
Claydon Cl NN8 . . . . .129 E5
Clayfield Cl NN3 . . . . .142 B6
Clayland Cl NN29 . . . . . . .164 C2
Claystones NN4 . . . . .158 D2
Cleavers La NN6 . . . . .107 D7
Clee Rise NN5 . . . . .158 D8
Clement Bois NN13 . . . . . .233 E8
Cleveland Ave NN16 . . . . . .72 C6
Cleveland Pl NN14 . . . . . . .159 A2
Clickers Yd MK46 . . . . . . .195 F4
Clifden Terr NN6 . . . . .122 D4
Cliffe Rd PE9 . . . . .2 A3
Clifton Cl Kettering NN15 . .72 C1
Long Buckby NN6 . . . . . . .121 C4
Clifton Dr PE8 . . . . .41 E5
Clifton Gr NN15 . . . . .72 C1
Clifton Rd OX15 . . . . .236 B4
Clifton Sq NN17 . . . . .36 E8
Cliftonville NN1 . . . . .159 E5
Cliftonville Ct **11** NN1 . . .159 F6
Cliftonville Mid Sch NN1 .159 F7
Cliftonville Rd NN1 . . . . . .159 F5
Clinton Rd NN4 . . . . .159 B3
Clipston Field Pl **7** NN3 .143 C2
Clipston Prim Sch LE16 . . .67 A8
Clipston Rd
East Farndon LE16 . . . . . . .48 B4
Great Oxendon LE16 . . . . .48 D2
Clipston St LE16 . . . . .31 F1
Clipston Way NN5 . . . . . . .140 D1
Clipstone Ct NN14 . . . . .70 C6
Clive Ct NN15 . . . . .72 E1
Clock Tower Ct NN3 . . . . .142 E6
Cloisters The
Daventry NN11 . . . . .135 D2
Priors Hardwick CV23 . . . .166 A5
Rushden NN10 . . . . .132 B2
Close Rd NN7 . . . . .156 B1
Close The
Chipping Warden OX17 . . .196 F6
Eastcote NN12 . . . . .188 F8
Easton on t H PE9 . . . . .1 F4
Greatworth OX17 . . . . . . .210 E1
Irthlingborough NN9 . . . . .112 F1
Kettering NN15 . . . . .91 B8
Northampton NN2 . . . . . . .141 C4
Swinford LE17 . . . . .62 B4
Weston Underwood MK46 .195 A1
Cloutsham St NN1 . . . . . . .159 E7
Clovelly Ct NN18 . . . . .36 F4
Clover Dr NN10 . . . . .148 C8
Clover La NN2 . . . . .141 B5
Club La NN14 . . . . .94 D6
Club St NN16 . . . . .72 C3
Clumber Ct NN18 . . . . .36 B6
Clumber Dr NN3 . . . . .160 E2
Clun Wlk NN17 . . . . .21 C1
Clwyd Wlk NN17 . . . . .21 C1
Clydesdale Rd NN17 . . . . . .36 D7
Co-operative Row NN10 . .132 B1
Coach Ho The 160 B7
Coaching Wlk NN3 . . . . . .142 D2
Coalport Cl NN14 . . . . .50 F3
Cob Dr NN4 . . . . .158 B1
Cobb's La NN29 . . . . .146 D3
Cobblers Cl NN12 . . . . . . .187 B1
Cobblestone Ct NN4 . . . . .158 D2
Cobbs Gdn MK46 . . . . . . .195 F4
Cobden St NN16 . . . . .72 A3
Cockbrook La PE17 . . . . . . .79 C2
Cockerell Rd NN17 . . . . . . .37 B8
Cockerill's Mdw CV21 . . . .99 A8
Cockley Rd NN13 . . . . .221 C6
Codlin Cl NN3 . . . . .143 C5
Coffee Tavern La NN10 . . .132 B2
Cofferidge Cl MK11 . . . . . .229 D5
Cogan Cres NN14 . . . . .70 B6
Cogenhoe Prim Sch NN7 .161 F5
Cold Ashby Rd
Guilsborough NN6 . . . . . . .103 E7
Thornby NN6 . . . . .84 D4
Coldermeadow Ave NN18 .36 A3
Coldstream Cl NN11 . . . . .135 B1

Coldstream La NN4 . . . . . .175 E8
Cole Ct NN9 . . . . .114 C5
Coleman Cl NN6 . . . . .101 A6
Coleman St NN9 . . . . .114 D6
Coleraine Cl NN2 . . . . .141 A5
Coleridge Way NN17 . . . . . .36 C8
Coleridge Wlk NN11 . . . . .135 B4
Coles Rise NN13 . . . . .233 D7
College Field Cl NN3 . . . . .143 C3
College Rd CV23 . . . . .117 E3
College St
Higham Ferrers NN10 . . . .132 C6
Irthlingborough NN9 . . . . .112 F2
Northampton NN1 . . . . . . .159 C6
Rushden NN10 . . . . .132 B2
Wellingborough NN8 . . . . .129 E4
Wollaston NN29 . . . . .146 D2
College St Mews **28** NN1 .159 C6
Colley Rise LE15 . . . . .9 C7
Collingcroft Ct NN4 . . . . . .175 A7
Collingdale Rd NN3 . . . . . .142 D2
Collingham Cl NN9 . . . . . .114 A5
Collingtree CE Prim
Sch NN4 . . . . .175 B4
Collingtree Rd NN7 . . . . . .175 A4
Collingwood Ave NN4 . . . . .36 A7
Collingwood Rd NN1 . . . . .141 F1
Collingwood Way NN11 . . .135 E3
Collins Hill NN7 . . . . .155 E6
Collins St NN1 . . . . .159 F7
Collmead Ct NN3 . . . . .143 B4
Collwell La NN14 . . . . .187 B1
Collyweston Cross
Roads PE8 . . . . .6 A4
Collyweston Rd NN3 . . . . .143 C5
Colne Cl NN17 . . . . .21 C1
Colne Way NN5 . . . . .140 C1
Colonial Dr NN4 . . . . .175 C5
Colsons Way NN4 . . . . . . .195 F5
Columbus Cres NN14 . . . . .70 E6
Colwell Rd NN8 . . . . .130 C4
Colwyn Rd NN1 . . . . .159 E8
Colyers Ave NN18 . . . . .36 B3
Commercial Rd NN16 . . . . .72 B2
Commercial St
Higham Ferrers NN10 . . . .132 B5
Northampton NN1 . . . . . . .159 C5
Commercial Way NN8 . . . .130 A4
Common St MK46 . . . . . . .194 D1
Compton Gn NN18 . . . . . . .36 A6
Compton Ho NN1 . . . . . . .159 B6
Compton Pl NN16 . . . . .72 E2
Compton Rd NN8 . . . . . . .130 C5
Compton St
Desborough NN14 . . . . . . .51 A3
Northampton NN1 . . . . . . .159 B6
Compton Way NN6 . . . . . .144 E3
Coneygree NN4 . . . . .175 F8
Coneygree Ct NN3 . . . . . . .143 B1
Coneywell Ct NN3 . . . . . . .142 F1
Conifer Rise NN3 . . . . .142 F1
Coniston Ave NN3 . . . . . . .142 B3
Coniston Cl
Daventry NN11 . . . . .135 B2
Wellingborough NN8 . . . . .129 C5
Coniston Rd NN16 . . . . . . .71 F2
Connaught Rd LE16 . . . . . .31 F4
Connaught St
Kettering NN16 . . . . .72 D3
Northampton NN1 . . . . . . .159 D7
Connegar Leys NN7 . . . . . .190 E7
Connell Cl LE16 . . . . .30 F3
Connell Ct NN17 . . . . .36 F5
Connolly Dr NN7 . . . . .70 F7
Constable Dr
Kettering NN15 . . . . .92 A7
Wellingborough NN8 . . . . .129 C6
Constable Rd Corby NN18 . .36 E5
Rugby CV21 . . . . .80 B1
Constable Wlk NN14 . . . . . .94 D7
Conway Cl
Northampton NN5 . . . . . . .140 E2
Rushden NN10 . . . . .148 A8
Wellingborough NN8 . . . . .129 C6
Conway Dr NN15 . . . . .92 B2
Conway Wlk NN17 . . . . . . .21 D1
Conyngham Rd NN3 . . . . .142 F2
Cook Cl Daventry NN11 . . .135 C5
Rothwell NN14 . . . . .70 E6
Cooks Cl NN7 . . . . .205 F8
Cooks Rd NN17 . . . . .37 F8
Coomb Rd NN18 . . . . .36 D1
Cooper Ct NN14 . . . . .76 D1
Copelands Rd NN14 . . . . . .51 C3
Copenhagen Rd NN18 . . . . .36 A1
Copper Leaf Cl NN3 . . . . . .142 C6
Copperfield Cl NN16 . . . . . .72 C6
Coppice Cl
Burton Latimer NN15 . . . . .92 C4
Daventry NN11 . . . . .153 C6
Coppice Dr NN3 . . . . .142 A5
Copse Cl
Burton Latimer NN15 . . . . .92 C3
Northampton NN2 . . . . . . .140 F5
Copymoor Cl NN4 . . . . . . .176 A6
Cora Rd NN16 . . . . .72 E4
Corbieres Cl NN5 . . . . .140 A2
Corby Com Hospl NN17 . . .36 D6
Corby Gate NN17 . . . . .22 F1
Corby Gate Bsns Pk NN17 .22 F1
Corby Rd Cottingham LE16 .35 E8
Gretton NN17 . . . . .22 B6
Stanion NN14 . . . . .37 E3
Weldon NN17 . . . . .38 A7
Corby Sta NN17 . . . . .37 A6
Cordon Cl NN3 . . . . .143 B3
Cordon Cres NN6 . . . . . . .144 F4
Cordwainer Gr NN14 . . . . .76 D1

Cordwainer Ho NN5 . . . . .159 A5
Cordwainers NN10 . . . . . .132 C1
Corn Kiln Cl NN7 . . . . .161 F6
Corn La **7** NN8 . . . . .130 A4
Corner Cl NN29 . . . . .147 E1
Corner Ct MK46 . . . . .195 E4
Cornfield Cl NN2 . . . . .141 B5
Cornfield Way NN15 . . . . . .92 C1
Cornhill Cl NN5 . . . . .140 C3
Cornwall Cl NN17 . . . . .36 C6
Cornwall Rd NN16 . . . . .72 D3
Cornwell Bsns Pk NN4 . . .160 B2
Coronation Ave
Rothwell NN14 . . . . .70 D7
Rushden NN10 . . . . .131 E1
Coronation Cres PE8 . . . . . .39 E7
Coronation Rd
Newnham NN1 . . . . .153 D4
Stony Stratford MK11 . . . .229 E5
Corporation St NN17 . . . . . .36 E6
Corran Cl NN5 . . . . .158 E8
Cosgrove L Pk MK19 . . . .218 F1
Cosgrove Prim
Sch MK19 . . . . .218 E2
Cosgrove Rd
Northampton NN2 . . . . . . .141 C5
Old Stratford MK19 . . . . . .229 C7
Cosgrove Way NN2 . . . . . .141 C5
Cosy Nook NN14 . . . . .76 C2
Coton NN6 . . . . .103 E1
Coton Manor Gdns NN6 . .103 E4
Coton Rd
Guilsborough NN6 . . . . . . .103 F5
Rugby CV23 . . . . .80 A1
Cotswold Ave
Kettering NN16 . . . . .72 B5
Northampton NN5 . . . . . . .158 D8
Cotswold Cl NN11 . . . . . . .135 B5
Cotswold Cl OX6 . . . . .237 E3
Cotswold Dr NN8 . . . . .129 D1
Cottage Cl NN2 . . . . .141 A4
Cottage Gdns NN3 . . . . . .143 B3
Cottages The NN13 . . . . . .224 C5
Cottagewell Ct NN3 . . . . . .142 F1
Cottarville NN3 . . . . .142 D1
Cotterstock Rd PE8 . . . . . .41 F7
Cottesbrooke Gdns NN4 . .175 D7
Cottesbrooke
Grange NN6 . . . . .105 A8
Cottesbrooke Pk NN11 . . .135 A5
Cottesbrooke Rd NN17 . . . .36 B7
Cottesloe Ct MK11 . . . . . .229 F5
Cottesmore Ave NN15 . . . .92 A5
Cottesmore Cl NN5 . . . . . .140 B1
Cottesmore Way NN8 . . . .129 D4
Cottingham CE Prim
Sch LE16 . . . . .20 C1
Cottingham Dr NN3 . . . . . .142 B7
Cottingham Rd Corby NN16 .36 B7
Corby NN17 . . . . .36 C6
Rockingham LE16 . . . . .21 A4
Cottingham Way NN14 . . . .76 C2
Cotton End
Long Buckby NN6 . . . . . . .121 D4
Northampton NN4 . . . . . . .159 C4
Cottons The
Rockingham LE16 . . . . .21 B4
Wellingborough NN8 . . . . .129 D7
Council Ho's
East Farndon LE16 . . . . . . .48 B8
Hannington NN6 . . . . .108 C3
Council Hos
Guilsborough NN6 . . . . . . .103 F7
Podington NN29 . . . . .147 E1
Council Hos The
Long Buckby Wharf NN6 . .136 E7
Wardington OX17 . . . . . . .208 F8
Council St Bozeat NN29 . .164 D4
Wollaston NN29 . . . . .146 D2
Countess Ct NN5 . . . . .159 A7
Countess Rd NN5 . . . . .159 A7
Countryside NN11 . . . . . . .118 B1
Counts Farm Rd NN18 . . . .36 F4
County Cricket Gnd NN1 .160 A8
County Rd NN13 . . . . .234 A4
County View OX15 . . . . . . .236 D4
Courier Rd NN17 . . . . .37 B8
Court Dr NN8 . . . . .72 B6
Court House Cl NN6 . . . . .104 F4
Court La NN6 . . . . .64 D3
Court Mews NN8 . . . . .130 B4
Court Rd **11** NN1 . . . . . . .159 C5
Court Yard La NN1 . . . . . . .153 A4
Courteenhall Cl NN2 . . . . .141 D5
Courteenhall Rd NN7 . . . . .191 A7
Courtman Rd NN9 . . . . . . .114 A4
Courtwood NN3 . . . . .114 A3
Courtyard The Islip NN14 . .76 B3
Middleton Cheney OX17 . .219 D5
Courtyard
Workshops LE16 . . . . .31 E1
Coventry Rd LE16 . . . . .31 D3
Coverack Cl NN4 . . . . .159 B1
Coverdale NN2 . . . . .140 F5
Covert Cl NN2 . . . . .141 A6
Covington St NN1 . . . . . . .160 A7
Cow Yd NN14 . . . . .141 B3
Cowgill Cl NN3 . . . . .143 B3
Cowley Cl NN4 . . . . .175 D6
Cowley Rd NN11 . . . . .135 B3
Cowley Way CV23 . . . . .99 F2
Cowper Cl
Earls Barton NN6 . . . . . . .145 A4
Irthlingborough NN9 . . . . .112 D1
Cowper & Newton Mus
The MK46 . . . . .195 F3
Cowper Rd Daventry NN11 .135 B2
Wellingborough NN8 . . . . .129 C4

Cowper St Kettering NN16 . .72 B4
Cowper Terr NN2 . . . . .141 F1
Cowpers Orch MK46 . . . . .195 A1
Cowslip Cl NN10 . . . . .148 C8
Cox Gdns NN12 . . . . .202 E8
Cox's Cl NN6 . . . . .121 B3
Cox's La NN14 . . . . .90 A5
Crab Apple Way NN14 . . . .76 E1
Crab Tree Cl MK46 . . . . . .195 E5
Crabb St NN10 . . . . .132 B1
Crabtree Cl Hartwell NN7 .192 E2
Wellingborough NN8 . . . . .129 F2
Crabtree Ho **6** NN1 . . . .135 C2
Crabtree La NN6 . . . . .84 B5
Cracknuts La NN4 . . . . . . .160 E2
Craddock Ct NN29 . . . . . . .147 B8
Cragside NN8 . . . . .129 C6
Craigie NN8 . . . . .129 C4
Cranbrooke Rd NN2 . . . . . .141 C1
Crane Cl Broughton NN14 . .90 A5
Wellingborough NN8 . . . . .130 A2
Crane Wlk NN3 . . . . .142 E6
Cranford CE Prim
Sch NN14 . . . . .93 B7
Cranford Ho **1** NN2 . . . .141 C3
Cranford Rd
Burton Latimer NN15 . . . . .92 D4
Great Addington NN14 . . . .94 A4
Kettering NN15 . . . . .92 C6
Northampton NN2 . . . . . . .141 C3
Cranleigh Rd NN15 . . . . . . .91 B7
Cranmere Ave NN14 . . . . .160 B6
Cransley Gdns NN17 . . . . . .36 B7
Cransley Hill NN14 . . . . . . .90 A4
Cransley Rd NN14 . . . . .70 E1
Cranstoun St NN1 . . . . . . .159 D7
Craven St NN1 . . . . .159 D7
Crawford Ave NN5 . . . . . . .158 E7
Crawford Gr NN17 . . . . . . .36 E8
Crawley Ave NN8 . . . . .129 D7
Craxford Rd NN17 . . . . .10 B1
Creampot Cl OX17 . . . . . . .196 A2
Creampot La OX17 . . . . . . .196 A2
Creaton Rd NN6 . . . . .104 D5
Crediton Cl NN3 . . . . .160 D7
Creed Rd PE8 . . . . .41 E7
Creighton Cres NN15 . . . . .91 F6
Crescent Cl LE16 . . . . .31 F4
Crescent The
Burton Latimer NN15 . . . . .92 C4
Easton on t H PE9 . . . . .1 F1
Flore NN7 . . . . .155 F6
Hackleton NN7 . . . . .177 A3
Kettering NN15 . . . . .91 B8
Ketton PE9 . . . . .1 A7
Market Harborough LE16 . . .31 F4
Moulton NN3 . . . . .126 D1
Northampton NN1 . . . . . . .159 F8
Pattishall NN12 . . . . .172 E1
Rothwell NN14 . . . . .70 C6
Rushden NN10 . . . . .131 E2
Twyford OX17 . . . . .230 A5
Whittlebury NN12 . . . . . . .215 C5
Creslow Ct MK11 . . . . .229 F5
Cresswell Rd NN10 . . . . . .131 F2
Crestline Ct NN3 . . . . .143 A5
Crestwood Gdns NN3 . . . .142 F5
Crestwood Rd NN3 . . . . . .142 F5
Creswell Wlk NN17 . . . . . . .21 C1
Crick Cl NN11 . . . . .22 A1
Crick Prim Sch NN6 . . . . .100 F6
Crick Rd Rugby CV23 . . . . .99 D7
West Haddon NN6 . . . . . . .102 A5
Cricklade Cl NN3 . . . . .160 D6
Crickly Cres NN4 . . . . .158 E3
Crispian Ct NN10 . . . . .132 A2
Crispian Ho NN1 . . . . .159 D7
Crispin Cotts NN6 . . . . . . .108 A4
Crispin Ho NN1 . . . . .159 B6
Crispin Pl **13** NN16 . . . . .72 B2
Crispin St **14**
Northampton NN1 . . . . . . .159 C6
Rothwell NN14 . . . . .70 C6
Crispin Way St NN9 . . . . . .114 C8
Crocket Cl NN2 . . . . .141 E2
Crockwell Hill NN11 . . . . . .119 F1
Crocus Way NN10 . . . . . . .148 B7
Croft Cl NN8 . . . . .129 C5
Croft La Adderbury OX17 . .230 A4
Roade NN7 . . . . .191 D4
Staverton NN11 . . . . .152 B7
Croft The Daventry NN11 . .153 C8
Hanging Houghton NN6 . .106 C8
3 Northampton NN5 . . .140 F1
Rugby CV21 . . . . .99 A8
Croft Way Rushden NN10 .132 D3
Weedon NN7 . . . . .155 A3
Crofters Cl NN4 . . . . .175 B7
Croftmeadow Ct NN3 . . . .143 B4
Cromarty Ct NN17 . . . . . . .36 F5
Cromarty Ho NN17 . . . . . . .36 F5
Cromer Rd NN9 . . . . .111 F4
Cromwell Cl NN14 . . . . .51 A3
Cromwell Cres LE16 . . . . . .31 D1
Cromwell Ct NN8 . . . . .130 B5
Cromwell Ho NN8 . . . . . . .130 B4
Cromwell Rd
Kettering NN16 . . . . .72 A2
Rushden NN10 . . . . .132 C2
Cromwell St **15** NN1 . . . .159 C7
Cronin Ctyd NN18 . . . . .37 E7
Cronin Rd NN18 . . . . .37 E7
Crosby Rd LE16 . . . . .20 D6
Cross Bank LE16 . . . . .20 D6
Cross Ct NN16 . . . . .72 A3

Cross Hill NN6 . . . . .106 B3
Cross Keys Ct NN13 . . . . .233 F7
Cross La Aldwincle NN14 . . .57 E1
Braunston NN13 . . . . .118 C1
Helmdon NN13 . . . . .212 A5
Weston Underwood MK46 .195 B2
Cross Rd NN8 . . . . .130 B6
Cross St Covington PE18 . .116 D2
Daventry NN11 . . . . .135 B2
Kettering NN16 . . . . .72 A3
Market Harborough LE16 . . .31 F2
Moulton NN3 . . . . .126 C1
Rothwell NN14 . . . . .70 E7
Cross The NN4 . . . . .160 E2
Cross Tree Rd MK19 . . . . .228 B3
Cross Waters Cl NN4 . . . . .175 F6
Cross Way NN9 . . . . .131 D8
Crossbrooks NN4 . . . . .175 F6
Crosshills MK11 . . . . .229 D4
Crouch Rd NN9 . . . . .112 F1
Croughton CE Prim
Sch NN13 . . . . .238 D6
Croughton Cl NN2 . . . . . . .141 C5
Croughton Elementary
Sch NN13 . . . . .238 E6
Croughton Mid
Sch NN13 . . . . .238 E6
Croughton Rd OX17 . . . . .237 D7
Crow Hill Ind Est NN9 . . .113 B4
Crow La NN3 . . . . .161 C7
Crowberry Ave NN3 . . . . . .142 C6
Crown Ct Corby NN18 . . . . .36 E5
Oundle PE8 . . . . .42 A5
Crown La Barrowden LE15 . .3 F5
Rothwell NN14 . . . . .70 C7
West Haddon NN6 . . . . . . .102 C4
Crown St NN16 . . . . .72 B3
Crown Way NN10 . . . . .131 E4
Crownsmead NN4 . . . . . . .158 D1
Crowthorp Rd NN3 . . . . . .143 C5
Croxdale Cl NN2 . . . . .140 F5
Croyde Ave NN18 . . . . .36 F4
Croyland Hall Her Ctr
Mus NN8 . . . . .130 A4
Croyland Jun & Inf
Schs NN8 . . . . .129 E3
Croyland Rd NN8 . . . . .129 F3
Crucible Rd NN17 . . . . .37 B7
Cubleigh Cl NN3 . . . . .142 C6
Cuckoo Cl LE15 . . . . .3 E5
Cullahill Ct NN4 . . . . .158 E2
Culloden Ct NN17 . . . . .36 F5
Culloden Dr NN15 . . . . .91 F8
Culme Cl PE8 . . . . .41 E7
Culross Wlk NN18 . . . . .36 C3
Culworth CE Prim
Sch OX17 . . . . .198 C2
Culworth Cres NN2 . . . . . .141 D5
Culworth Rd NN17 . . . . . . .197 B6
Cumberland Ave NN9 . . . .114 A4
Cumberland Cl NN3 . . . . . .142 A3
Cumbrae Dr NN3 . . . . .143 C2
Cunliffe Dr NN16 . . . . .72 A4
Cunningham Cl
Daventry NN11 . . . . .135 E2
Higham Ferrers NN10 . . . .132 B5
Cupar Cres NN17 . . . . .36 F5
Curgenven Cl NN11 . . . . . .183 E7
Curlbrook Cl NN4 . . . . . . .176 A6
Curlew Way NN11 . . . . . . .135 C3
Currie Rd NN2 . . . . .141 C1
Curtis Mews NN8 . . . . .129 C7
Curtlee Hill NN4 . . . . .175 F6
Curver Way NN17 . . . . .22 D1
Cyclamen Cl NN3 . . . . . . .160 C6
Cypress Cl NN14 . . . . .50 F3
Cypress Ct NN3 . . . . .142 E3
Cyril St NN1 . . . . .159 E6

D

D'albini Cl LE16 . . . . .34 B4
Da Vinci Cl NN5 . . . . .158 C5
Daffodil Dr NN10 . . . . .148 B7
Dagnall Rd MK46 . . . . .195 E4
Dahlia Rd NN16 . . . . .72 D4
Daimler Cl Daventry NN11 .135 A3
Northampton NN3 . . . . . . .143 D4
Dairy Cl Brixworth NN6 . . .106 A1
West Haddon NN6 . . . . . . .102 D4
Dairy Cotts LE17 . . . . .45 A4
Dairy Field NN6 . . . . .103 D1
Dairy Ground NN7 . . . . . . .231 A6
Dairy Meadow Ct NN3 . . .142 F6
Daisy Bank Ave NN14 . . . . .70 C7
Daisy Croft NN10 . . . . .148 C8
Dakin Cl PE8 . . . . .13 F8
Dale Ave NN8 . . . . .129 C5
Dale Cl Brackley NN13 . . . .234 A7
Daventry NN11 . . . . .135 B5
Mears Ashby NN6 . . . . . . .128 C2
Wellingborough NN8 . . . . .129 C5
Dale Farm Cotts NN6 . . . .128 C2
Dale Ho NN3 . . . . .129 F4
Dale St Corby NN17 . . . . . . .36 D7
Wellingborough NN8 . . . . .129 F4
Dale The NN8 . . . . .129 C5
Dalestones NN4 . . . . .158 D2
Dalkeith Ave **19** NN16 . . .72 B2
Dalkeith Pl NN16 . . . . .72 B2
Dalkeith Rd NN8 . . . . .129 F1
Dallacre Dr LE16 . . . . .34 C4
Dallington Cl NN14 . . . . . . .54 A2
Dallington Gn **2** NN5 . . .158 F8

Dallington Haven **5** NN5 .158 F8
Dallington Park Rd NN5 .158 F8
Dallington Rd NN5 ......159 A7
Dallison Cl LE16 ....48 E8
Dalton Rd NN17 ....21 E2
Damherst Piece NN6 ...106 C2
Damson Cl NN14 ....76 E1
Damson Dell NN3 ....161 A8
Dando Cl NN29 ....146 D1
Dands Cl OX17 ....220 A8
Dands Dr OX17 ....220 A8
Dane Ct NN11 ....118 C1
Dane Ridge NN5 ....158 C6
Danefield Rd NN3 ....142 B1
Daneholme Ave NN11 ...135 C4
Danes Backside NN2 ....141 B3
Danes Camp Way NN4 ..158 E3
Danesholme Jun & Inf
  Schs NN18 ....36 A2
Danesholme Rd NN18 ...36 A2
Danetre Comp Sch NN11 135 E1
Danetre Dr NN11 ....135 D2
Danetre Hospl NN11 ....153 C8
Danetree Gdns NN3 .....142 B2
Danewood Gdns NN3 ...142 B2
Danford Cl PE8 ....41 F4
Danforths PE8 ....41 F5
Daniaud Ct NN13 ....233 E8
Daniell Wlk NN18 ....36 D5
Daniels Rd NN8 ....130 C1
Darby Cl NN8 ....129 A5
Dardis Cl **2** NN2 ......141 E1
Darenth Ct **16** NN1 ...159 C7
Darescroft LE16 ....20 B1
Dark La Braunston NN11 .118 D1
  Great Harrowden NN9 ..110 D3
Darley Cl NN16 ....72 C6
Darley Dale Rd NN17 .....36 D8
Dart Cl NN17 ....21 D2
Dartmouth Rd MK46 ....195 F4
Dartmouth Row NN11 ..135 D1
Darwin Ct NN17 ....37 C8
Darwin Rd NN17 ....37 C8
Darwin Wlk NN17 ....140 C1
Dash Farm Cl NN17 ......38 C3
Daventry Rd
  Banbury OX16 ....208 A2
  Barby CV23 ....118 C8
  Kilsby CV23 ....100 A1
  Newnham NN11 ....153 D4
  Norton NN11 ....136 C5
  Staverton NN11 ....152 B7
  Staverton NN11 ....152 C7
  Willoughby CV23 ......117 C7
Daventry Tert Coll NN11 .153 B8
Daventry William
  Parker Sch NN11 ......135 C3
Davey Rd NN17 ....37 C8
Davis Cl NN14 ....70 F6
Davis Ct NN17 ....37 A6
Davy Cl NN8 ....129 A6
Dawkins Ct NN14 ....90 A4
Dayrell Rd NN4 ....158 F2
Dayrell Sq **5** NN4 ....158 F2
Dayton St NN11 ....132 A2
De Capel Cl NN14 ....94 D6
De Ferneus Dr NN9 .....114 D7
De Lisle Cl LE16 ....31 D2
De Montfort Ct NN13 ..222 E1
De Quincey Ct NN13 ...222 E1
De Roos Way LE16 ....34 B4
De Vere Rd NN14 ....76 D2
Deacon Cl NN10 ....132 D3
Deacons Ct NN3 ....143 C4
Deal Cl NN1 ....159 D7
Deal St NN1 ....159 C7
Dean Cl NN10 ....148 A8
Dean Wlk NN11 ....135 A4
Deancourt Dr NN5 ......140 A1
Deane Par CV21 ....99 A8
Deane Rd CV21 ....99 B8
Deans Row NN7 ....173 E2
Deanshanger Dr NN12 ..216 F1
Deanshanger
  Kingsbrook Sch MK19 .228 F4
Deanshanger Prim
  Sch MK19 ....228 E3
Deanshanger Rd
  Old Stratford MK19 ...229 B6
  Wicken MK19 ....228 B3
Deansway NN3 ....143 C4
Debbs Cl MK11 ....229 E5
Debdale Rd
  Northampton NN3 .....142 D2
  Wellingborough NN8 ..129 F5
Deben Rd NN17 ....21 D1
Deddington Castle
  Earthworks OX15 .....236 A4
Dee Wlk NN11 ....135 A1
Deeble Rd NN15 ....72 F1
Deene Cl Adderbury OX17 .230 B4
  Corby NN17 ....36 E7
  Market Harborough LE16 .32 A3
Deene End NN17 ....38 C8
Deene Hall NN17 ....23 F6
Deene Rd NN17 ....10 F7
Deeneside NN17 ....38 B8
Deepdale LE16 ....20 D1
Deer Park Rd NN3 .....142 A6
Deerings Rd CV21 ....99 A8
Delamere Dr NN15 ....92 A5
Delamere Rd NN4 ......159 C2
Delapre Abbey NN4 ....159 D3
Delapre Cres NN4 ......159 C3

Delapre Crescent
  Rd NN4 ....159 C3
Delapre Ct NN4 ....159 C2
Delapre Mid Sch NN4 ..159 B3
Delapre Mid Sch
  Annexe NN4 ....159 B3
Delapre Pl NN18 ....36 A3
Delapre St NN4 ....159 B3
Dell Cres NN3 ....143 B5
Dell Pl NN10 ....132 C2
Dells MK46 ....195 F4
Dells Cl PE17 ....61 D2
Delta Way NN2 ....141 A5
Delves The NN9 ....114 C6
Dempsey Dr NN14 ....70 F6
Demswell NN6 ....106 C2
Denbigh Rd NN3 ....160 D6
Denby Dale NN3 ....129 D7
Dencora Bsns Pk NN8 ..129 A4
Dene Cl Kettering NN16 .72 A5
  Wellingborough NN8 ..129 C6
Denethorpe La NN17 ....24 B5
Denfield Park Jun
  Sch NN10 ....132 C3
Denford St NN15 ....91 F5
Denford Rd Corby NN17 .36 B8
  Ringstead NN14 ....95 C4
  Thrapston NN14 ....95 D8
Denford Way NN8 ......129 D7
Denington Ct NN8 .....130 A2
Denington Ind Est NN8 .130 B2
Denman Cl LE16 ....34 A4
Denmark Cl NN14 ....35 F3
Denmark Ct NN10 .....132 C1
Denmark Rd NN10 .....132 C1
Dennett La NN1 ....159 E6
Denney Cres NN11 .....135 B2
Denston Cl NN4 ....143 A6
Denton Cl Irchester NN29 .147 B8
  Rushden NN10 ....132 C3
Denton Ct NN15 ....92 B2
Denton Rd NN7 ....178 B6
Derby Rd NN1 ....159 F8
Dering Cotts OX17 .....210 E2
Derling Dr NN9 ....114 E6
Derngate NN1 ....159 D5
Derry The NN1 ....100 F5
Derwent Cl
  Daventry NN11 ....135 A1
  Northampton NN5 ....140 F1
  Wellingborough NN8 ..129 C6
Derwent Cres NN16 .....71 F2
Derwent Dr NN5 ....140 F2
Derwent Ho PE8 ....42 A6
Derwent Wlk NN17 ......21 D2
Drayton Fields Ind
  Est NN11 ....135 A5
Drayton Leys CV22 ......98 A7
Drayton Pk NN11 ....135 B5
Drayton Pl NN9 ....112 F3
Drayton Rd Bringhurst LE16 .20 B5
  Drayton LE16 ....19 D7
  Irthlingborough NN9 ..112 F3
  Lowick NN14 ....75 E6
  Medbourne LE16 ....19 A5
Drayton Way NN11 .....135 A5
Drayton Wlk NN2 ....141 D4
Dresden Cl NN18 ....35 F2
Driffield Gr NN17 ....36 F7
Drift The Collyweston PE9 .1 D2
  Sutton PE5 ....8 F3
Drive The Horton NN7 ..177 E1
  Kettering NN16 ....72 B1
  Northampton, Duston NN5 .158 A7
  Northampton,
  Phippsville NN1 ......141 F1
  Rushden NN10 ....132 C1
  Wellingborough NN8 ..130 A3
Drove The Collyweston PE9 .1 D1
  Nassington PE8 ....15 E5
Drovers Wlk NN2 ......141 A5
Druids Way NN3 ....141 F5
Drum La **30** NN1 ...159 C6
Drumming Well La PE8 .42 A5
Drummond Cl NN6 ....125 D4
Drydale Ave NN3 ......142 B3
Dryden Ave NN11 ......135 B2
Dryden Cl NN11 ....184 A7
Dryden Rd
  Northampton NN5 ....158 F2
  Towcester NN12 .....203 C5
  Wellingborough NN8 ..130 C5
Dryden St Kettering NN16 .72 B3
  Raunds NN9 ....114 C6
Dryden Way Corby NN17 .36 C8
  Higham Ferrers NN10 ..132 B5
Dryden's Ct NN14 ....77 C4
Dryland Rd NN3 ....142 C2
Dryland St NN16 ....72 B2
Dryleys Ct NN3 ....143 B5
Drywell Ct NN3 ....143 A1
Duchess Rd NN16 ......128 C2
Duchy Cl Chelveston NN9 .133 B8
  Higham Ferrers NN10 ..132 C5
Duck End Cranford NN14 .93 B7
  Denford NN14 ....95 D6
  Hinton-in-t-H NN13 ..232 F6
  Wollaston NN29 ......146 D3
Duck La Harpole NN7 ..157 C6
  Oundle PE8 ....42 A5
Duck St Elton PE8 ....16 D1
  Rushden NN10 ....132 B2
Duckworth Dell NN3 ..142 F6
Duckworth Rd NN3 .....36 B7
Duffy Pl CV21 ....99 A8
Duke St
  Burton Latimer NN15 ..92 B2
  Kettering NN16 ....72 B3

Donaldson Ave NN14 ....90 A3
Donellan Gn NN3 ....142 F6
Donne Cl NN16 ....72 C6
Donovan Ct NN15 ......160 E8
Dorcas Rd OX16 ....219 A6
Dorchester Ct NN5 ....140 B2
Dore Cl NN3 ....143 B5
Doris Rd NN16 ....72 E4
Dorking Wlk NN18 ......36 C3
Dorothy Rd NN16 ....72 E3
Dorset Gdns NN2 ......141 D3
Dorset Rd Corby NN17 ..36 C6
  Northampton NN2 ....141 D3
Doubles The NN11 .....135 B1
Douglas Ct NN15 ....91 E8
Douglas Rd NN15 ......157 F8
Douglass Dr LE16 ....31 F4
Doulton Cl NN14 ....50 F3
Dove Cl NN12 ....203 C3
Dove Cotts OX17 ......210 A6
Dove's La NN3 ....126 D1
Dovecote Cl Barrowden LE15 .3 C5
  Raunds NN9 ....114 E7
  Yarwell PE8 ....16 A8
Dovecote Dr Denton NN7 .162 B1
  Little Addington NN14 .113 B7
Dovecote Rd NN7 .....191 C4
Dovecote The NN6 ....125 D5
Dovedale Gr NN14 ......50 E4
Dovedale Rd NN17 ......36 E7
Dovehouse Cl NN9 ....113 F3
Dovehouse Ct MK19 ..228 E4
Dover Cl NN10 ....132 D1
Dovercourt NN5 ....159 B5
Downing Way NN11 ...153 C7
Downs The NN9 ....110 E1
Downsway NN4 ....175 B6
Downwood Cl NN3 ....143 C3
Dowthorpe End NN6 ..144 F4
Dowthorpe Hill NN6 ..144 F3
Drake Cl Corby NN17 ...36 B8
  Daventry NN11 ....135 E1
  Rothwell NN14 ....70 E7
Drake Lee Mews NN16 ..72 B2
Draper's Cl PE8 ....28 C3
Drapery NN1 ....159 C6
Draughton Rd NN6 .....87 B7
Draymans Wlk NN13 ..233 E6
Drayson La NN6 ....100 F6

Duke St continued
  Northampton NN1 ....159 D7
  Polebrook PE8 ....42 F3
Dukelands NN7 ....155 A3
Dukes Green Rd NN7 ..157 D3
Dulce Rd NN5 ....158 C8
Dulley Ave NN8 ....129 F1
Duncan Rd NN17 ....160 D7
Dumas
  Cul-De-Sac NN13 ....233 E8
Dumble Cl NN18 ....36 D2
Dunbar Cl NN15 ....91 F8
Duncan Cl NN3 ....141 F7
Duncan Ct NN3 ....129 D3
Duncan Rd NN17 ....36 B7
Dundee St NN5 ....158 F6
Dunedin Rd NN18 ....36 C2
Dunkirk Ave NN14 ......51 B3
Dunn Cl NN6 ....101 A6
Dunslade Cl LE16 ....32 B2
Dunslade Gr LE16 ....32 B2
Dunslade Rd LE16 ......32 A2
Dunsmore Ave CV22 ....98 E8
Dunster St NN1 ....159 D6
Durban Rd NN16 ....72 D2
Durham Cl NN11 ....135 D6
Durham Ct NN17 ....36 B6
Durness Cl NN15 ....91 E8
Dusthill Rd NN14 ....55 D8
Duston CE Lower
  Sch NN5 ....158 C7
Duston Eldean Lower
  Sch NN5 ....140 B1
Duston Mill La NN5 ....158 D4
Duston Rd NN5 ....158 E6
Duston Upper Sch NN5 .158 A8
Duston Wildes NN5 ....140 A2
Dybdale Cres NN8 .....129 E5
Dychurch La Bozeat NN29 .164 E3
  Northampton NN1 ....159 D6
Dyson Cl CV21 ....80 A1
Dyson Dr NN16 ....72 A4

E

Eady Rd NN15 ....92 B1
Eady's Row NN14 ....94 D7
Eagle Dr NN4 ....159 F2
Eagle La NN14 ....71 B1
Eaglehurst NN6 ....106 C2
Eaglethorpe PE8 ....28 B3
Ealing Terr NN10 ......132 A3
Earl St NN1 ....159 D7
Earl's La OX15 ....236 A4
Earls Barton Inf
  Sch NN6 ....144 E4
Earls Barton Jun
  Sch NN6 ....144 E4
Earls Barton Mus NN6 144 E4
Earls Barton Rd
  Great Doddington NN29 .145 C5
  Mears Ashby NN6 ....128 C2
Earlsfield Cl NN4 ......176 A6
Earlstrees Ct NN17 .....21 E2
Earlstrees Ind Est NN17 .21 E2
Earlstrees Rd NN17 .....21 F2
East Ave
  Burton Latimer NN15 ..92 B3
  Corby NN17 ....36 F5
  Kettering NN15 ....72 D2
East Bank NN3 ....142 E6
East Butterfield Ct NN3 .142 F5
East Carlton Park LE16 ..35 B8
East Cl NN15 ....72 D2
East Cres Rushden NN10 .131 F2
  Weldon NN17 ....38 C8
East Dr NN15 ....72 E2
East End NN6 ....106 F5
East Gr NN10 ....132 B3
East Haddon CE Prim
  Sch NN6 ....122 D5
East Haddon Rd NN6 .122 D8
East Hill Cl NN13 .....233 F7
East Hunsbury Lower
  Sch NN4 ....175 B6
East Langham Rd NN9 .114 D7
East Leys Ct NN15 .....142 C7
East Oval NN5 ....140 F2
East Paddock Ct NN3 ..143 A4
East Park Par NN1 ....159 F8
East Pl NN15 ....135 C1
East Priors Ct NN3 ....143 A4
East Rd PE8 ....42 A5
East Rising NN4 ......175 D7
East St Irchester NN29 .147 B8
  Long Buckby NN6 ....121 D4
  Market Harborough LE16 .31 D3
  Northampton NN1 ....159 F6
  Olney MK46 ....195 F6
  Stanwick NN9 ....114 A3
East View OX17 ....210 E2
East Wlk NN15 ....72 E2
Eastbourne Ave NN18 ..36 B5
Eastbrook NN14 ....36 B4
Eastbrook Hill NN14 ....51 C3
Eastcote Rd NN7 .....189 D8
Eastern Ave N NN2 ...141 D4
Eastern Ave S NN2 ...141 D3
Eastern Way NN11 ....135 C2
Eastfield NN7 ....190 D7
Eastfield Cl NN5 ......140 C1
Eastfield Cres
  Finedon NN9 ....112 A5
  Yardley Gobion NN12 .217 F5
Eastfield Dr MK19 ....207 A3
Eastfield Lower Sch NN3 142 B3

Eastfield Rd
  Brixworth NN6 ....106 B1
  3 Irthlingborough NN9 .112 F2
  Northampton, Duston NN5 .158 B8
  Northampton, Far
  Cotton NN4 ....159 C3
  Wellingborough NN8 ..130 C6
  Wollaston NN29 ......146 E2
Eastfields Cres PE8 .....15 E6
Eastlands Rd NN9 ......112 A5
Eastleigh Rd NN15 ......91 D7
Eastmead Ct NN3 .....143 A1
Easton Garfords Charity
  Prim Sch PE9 ....2 A5
Easton La NN29 ....164 C3
Easton Way NN7 ......163 E4
Easton Wlk NN17 ....37 B6
Eastwood Gr CV21 .....99 C8
Eastwood Rd PE8 ....42 A5
Eaton Rd NN15 ....158 A8
Eaton Wlk NN10 ......132 B2
Ebbw Vale Rd NN9 ....131 E8
Ebenezer Pl **13** NN16 .72 B2
Ebony Ct NN11 ....184 D5
Eccles Rd PE8 ....7 D8
Ecton Brook Lower
  Sch NN3 ....143 C2
Ecton Brook Rd NN3 ..143 D2
Ecton Hall NN6 ....143 F4
Ecton La NN6 ....127 D2
Ecton Leys CV22 ....98 A7
Ecton Park Rd NN3 ...143 C3
Ecton Prim Sch NN6 ..143 F4
Ecton St **11** NN1 ...159 E6
Edale Gn NN14 ....50 E4
Eden Cl Daventry NN11 .135 A1
  Northampton NN3 ....142 B4
Eden St NN16 ....72 B2
Edgar Rd NN16 ....72 D3
Edgehill Dr NN11 ......135 D6
Edgehill Rd NN5 ......140 D1
Edgell St NN16 ....72 C2
Edgemead Cl NN3 .....142 E2
Edgemont Rd NN3 ....142 E1
Edges Ct NN3 ....142 C7
Edinburgh Cl
  Market Harborough LE16 .31 F4
  Rothwell NN14 ....70 C6
Edinburgh Ho NN5 ....158 C8
Edinburgh Rd
  Kettering NN16 ....72 D3
  Northampton NN2 ....141 C2
  Wellingborough NN8 ..129 E1
Edinburgh Sq NN11 ...135 B3
Edison Cl NN8 ....129 A6
Edison Ctyd NN17 ......21 F3
Edison Dr NN5 ....158 D4
Edith Rd NN16 ....72 E4
Edith St NN1 ....159 E6
Edmonds Cl NN8 ......130 A2
Edmund St NN16 ....72 D2
Edmunds Dr PE9 ....1 A5
Edward Cl
  Higham Ferrers NN10 .132 C7
  Kettering NN15 ....91 C7
Edward Rd Irchester NN29 .147 B7
  Kettering NN15 ....91 C7
  Market Harborough LE16 .31 D5
Edward Watson Cl NN2 .141 B5
Edwardian Ct NN4 ....175 E7
Edwards Cl NN11 .....183 D7
Edwards Dr NN8 ......129 D5
Edwinstowe Cl NN3 ...160 E7
Egerton Cl NN13 .....234 A7
Egmont Ave MK11 ....229 E4
Eider Cl
  Burton Latimer NN15 ..92 A2
  Daventry NN11 ....135 C3
Eismann Way NN17 .....37 C2
Ekins Cl NN3 ....142 D2
Elan Ct NN10 ....131 E3
Eldean Rd NN5 ....140 B1
Elder Dr NN11 ....135 C4
Elderberry Ct NN3 ....143 C3
Eldon Cl NN16 ....100 E6
Eldon Way NN6 ....100 E6
Eleanor Ct NN6 ......102 C4
Elgin St NN5 ....158 F6
Eliot Cl NN16 ....72 C6
Elizabeth Cl
  Earls Barton NN6 ....144 E5
  Wellingborough NN8 ..129 D2
Elizabeth Ct NN10 ....132 C7
Elizabeth Dr
  Daventry NN11 ....135 B3
  Kettering NN16 ....72 D3
  Rothwell NN14 ....70 C6
  West Haddon NN6 ....102 C5
Elizabeth St Corby NN17 .36 E6
  Northampton NN1 ....159 F6
Elizabeth Way
  Earls Barton NN6 ....144 E5
  Higham Ferrers NN10 .132 C7
  Irthlingborough NN9 ..131 E8
  Irthlingborough NN9 ..159 F6
Elkington La CV23 ......99 B1
Elkington Rd NN6 ......82 B4
Elkins Cl NN14 ....82 B4
Ellen Cl NN6 ....100 F6
Ellesmere Ave
  Brackley NN13 ....233 F8
  Northampton NN5 ....158 E7
Ellesmere Cl NN13 ...222 F1
Ellesmere Cres NN13 .222 F1
Ellesmere Dr NN13 ...233 F8
Ellesmere Rd NN13 ...222 F1
Ellfield Ct NN3 ....142 F3

Ellison Cl NN9 . . . . 114 C7
Elm Cl Brafield-on-t-G NN7 .161 D2
Hargrave NN9 . . . . 115 F2
Elm Ct NN14 . . . . .76 D1
Elm Dr Brackley NN13 . . . . 222 F1
Deanshanger MK19 . . . . . 228 D5
Hinton NN11 . . . . 184 A6
Market Harborough LE16 . .31 C2
Elm Rd Burton Latimer NN15 92 C4
Kettering NN15 . . . . .72 D1
Elm St 19
Northampton NN1 . . . . . . 159 C7
Wellingborough NN8 . . . . 129 F5
Elm Way NN7 . . . . 177 C3
Elm Wlk Corby NN17 . . . . . .21 D1
Higham Ferrers NN10 . . . 132 B6
Elmfield Cl NN12 . . . . 217 D3
Elmhurst Ave NN14 . . . . . 142 A4
Elmhurst Cl NN3 . . . . 142 A4
Elmington Rd NN3 . . . . . . 143 C5
Elmlea Dr MK46 . . . . 195 F4
Elms Dr CV22 . . . . .98 F8
Elms Dyke NN15 . . . . 135 E8
Elmwood Wlk NN5 . . . . . 140 A1
Elsden Rd NN16 . . . . 130 C5
Elton CE Sch PE8 . . . . .28 D8
Elton Cl NN3 . . . . 143 B5
Elton Hall PE8 . . . . .28 D6
Elton Rd PE8 . . . . .16 C7
Elwes Way NN3 . . . . 143 B2
Elysium Terr NN2 . . . . . . 159 C8
Embankment NN3 . . . . . . 130 C2
Emberton Ctry Pk MK46 . 195 E1
Emerald Way NN1 . . . . . . 159 B5
Emerton Gdns MK11 . . . . 229 D5
Emery Cl NN11 . . . . 135 E8
Emley Cl NN3 . . . . 142 F1
Emmanuel Church Mid
Sch NN3 . . . . 142 F2
Emmanuel Cl NN11 . . . . . 153 C8
Encon Cl NN3 . . . . 141 F7
Enfield Cl NN5 . . . . 157 C7
English Martyrs RC Comb
Sch CV21 . . . . .99 A7
Ennerdale Cl
Daventry NN11 . . . . 135 A2
Kettering NN16 . . . . .72 A4
Northampton NN3 . . . . . 142 A3
Ennerdale Rd Corby NN17 .21 E1
Northampton NN3 . . . . . 142 A4
Rushden NN10 . . . . 132 D3
Ensleigh Cl NN15 . . . . . . .92 C1
Enstone Ct NN3 . . . . 129 E1
Enterprise Cl NN16 . . . . . .71 F4
Enterprise Ct NN9 . . . . . 129 B6
Enterprise Ind Pk NN17 . .22 C1
Enterprise Rd NN9 . . . . . 114 D7
Entwood Dr NN3 . . . . 143 B5
Epping Cl NN15 . . . . .92 A5
Epping Wlk NN11 . . . . . . 135 B4
Epsom Wlk NN18 . . . . .36 C3
Equestrian Way NN7 . . . . 155 B4
Ericsson Cl NN11 . . . . . . 135 C5
Ermine Rd NN3 . . . . 143 C5
Ermont Way OX16 . . . . . . 219 A7
Esher Ct NN3 . . . . 142 D4
Eskdaill Pl NN16 . . . . .72 B3
Eskdaill St NN16 . . . . .72 B3
Eskdale Ave Corby NN17 . .36 E7
Northampton NN3 . . . . . 142 B3
Eskdale Cl NN8 . . . . 129 C6
Essen La CV23 . . . . 100 A3
Essendon Ct MK11 . . . . . 229 F5
Essex Cl NN17 . . . . .36 B6
Essex Gdns LE16 . . . . .31 D1
Essex Pl NN15 . . . . .91 D6
Essex Rd NN10 . . . . 132 C1
Essex St NN3 . . . . 159 C8
Ethel St NN1 . . . . 159 C6
Eton Cl NN7 . . . . 155 C4
Eton Ct 3 NN4 . . . . 141 C3
Ettrick Cl NN16 . . . . .72 A4
Euro Bsns Pk LE16 . . . . . .32 B4
Euston Rd NN4 . . . . 159 C3
Eva Rd NN16 . . . . .72 E3
Evans Cl NN11 . . . . 135 E1
Evelyn Way NN29 . . . . . . 147 C7
Evenley Rd Mixbury NN13 .234 D1
Northampton NN2 . . . . . 141 E5
Evensford Wlk NN9 . . . . . 131 D8
Everard Ct CV23 . . . . .80 A5
Everdon Cl
Northampton NN2 . . . . . 141 E4
Rugby CV22 . . . . .98 E8
Everdon Pk NN11 . . . . . . 135 A5
Everdon Rd NN12 . . . . . . 170 E3
Everest La NN17 . . . . .36 E6
Evergreen Dr NN14 . . . . . 113 B7
Everitt Cl NN8 . . . . 130 B2
Evesham Cl NN8 . . . . 129 E1
Evesham Ct NN3 . . . . 143 A7
Evison Rd NN14 . . . . .70 C6
Ewenfield Rd NN9 . . . . . . 111 F4
Excalibur Cl NN5 . . . . . . 158 A7
Excelsior Cl NN9 . . . . 112 C2
Excelsior Gdns NN5 . . . . 157 F8
Exelsior NN8 . . . . 129 E4
Exeter Cl NN11 . . . . 153 C8
Exeter Jun & Inf
Schs NN17 . . . . .36 F5
Exeter Pl NN1 . . . . 159 C7
Exeter St NN16 . . . . .72 C5
Exmoor Cl NN18 . . . . 160 D7
Exmouth Ave NN18 . . . . . .36 C7
Express Cl NN9 . . . . 131 E8
Express Pk Kettering NN16 .71 F3
Rushden NN10 . . . . 131 D3
Eyeletter Ho 7 NN5 . . . . 159 A6

Eynard Impasse NN13 . . . 222 E1
Eynon Cl NN3 . . . . 126 B1

F

Factory La LE16 . . . . .31 E3
Fair La NN14 . . . . .76 E3
Fair Mile NN7 . . . . 141 A6
Fairfax Rd LE16 . . . . .31 E1
Fairfax Rise NN6 . . . . .85 B8
Fairfield NN7 . . . . 174 B2
Fairfield Rd Isham NN14 . .91 E1
Market Harborough LE16 . .31 D4
Northampton NN2 . . . . . 141 F2
Paulerspury NN12 . . . . . 216 B7
Fairfields Sch NN2 . . . . . 141 E1
Fairground Way NN13 . . . 160 E7
Fairhurst Way NN6 . . . . . 144 F4
Fairlight Ct 3 NN18 . . . . .36 B5
Fairmead Cres NN10 . . . . 147 F8
Fairmead Rise NN2 . . . . . 140 F6
Fairoaks Dr NN9 . . . . 114 C7
Fairoaks The NN3 . . . . . . 160 F8
Fairway
Market Harborough LE16 . .31 D4
Northampton NN2 . . . . . 141 E2
Fairway The
Daventry NN11 . . . . 135 F2
Wellingborough NN9 . . . 110 E1
Faith Terr MK19 . . . . 207 A2
Falcon Manor Sch NN12 .202 D8
Falcon View NN3 . . . . 202 D8
Falconer's Hill Jun &
Inf Schs NN11 . . . . 135 C3
Falconers Cl NN11 . . . . . 135 C3
Falconers Rise NN4 . . . . . 175 A8
Falcutt Way NN3 . . . . 141 D5
Falkner's Cl OX17 . . . . . . 230 A4
Fallow Fields NN6 . . . . . . 101 A6
Fallow Wlk NN2 . . . . 141 A6
Fallowfield NN9 . . . . 129 E8
Falmer Wlk NN18 . . . . . . .36 B4
Falster Ct NN18 . . . . .36 A2
Far Brook NN6 . . . . 125 B8
Far Meadow Ct NN3 . . . . 142 E5
Faracre Ct NN3 . . . . 143 B1
Faraday Cl Daventry NN11 135 A4
Northampton NN8 . . . . . 158 D5
Wellingborough NN8 . . . 130 B6
Faraday Ct Thrapston NN14 .76 E2
Wellingborough NN8 . . . 129 A6
Faraday Gr NN17 . . . . .37 A8
Faramir Pl NN3 . . . . 143 B6
Fareham Ave CV22 . . . . . .98 E8
Faringdon Ct NN3 . . . . . . 143 A7
Farm Cl Brigstock NN14 . .55 F7
Flore NN7 . . . . 155 F5
Holcot NN6 . . . . 126 E8
Northampton NN2 . . . . . 141 B4
Farm Field Ct NN3 . . . . . 142 E5
Farm Rd NN3 . . . . 234 A6
Farm Stile NN11 . . . . 182 C8
Farmbrook Ct NN3 . . . . . 142 F5
FarMClose Rd NN4 . . . . . 175 E6
Farmers Dr NN13 . . . . . . 233 D8
Farmfield Cl NN15 . . . . . .91 F4
Farmhill Rd NN3 . . . . 143 A6
Farmstead Rd NN18 . . . . .36 A5
Farnborough Ct NN15 . . . .91 D5
Farndale Ave NN17 . . . . . .36 E7
Farndale View LE16 . . . . . .31 C2
Farndish Rd NN29 . . . . . . 147 B7
Farndon Cl NN3 . . . . 142 F6
Farndon Ct LE16 . . . . .31 D2
Farndon Rd
Great Oxendon LE16 . . . .48 D4
Hinton NN11 . . . . 184 A5
Lubenham LE16 . . . . .30 F2
Market Harborough LE16 . .31 D1
Marston Trussell LE16 . . .47 D7
Farnham Rd NN10 . . . . . . 147 F8
Farnworth Ct NN5 . . . . . . 140 C1
Farraxton Sq NN4 . . . . . . 158 E2
Farrer Cl NN13 . . . . 223 D4
Farthinghoe Cl NN13 . . . . 233 D7
Farthinghoe Prim
Sch NN13 . . . . 221 B4
Farthinghoe Rd OX17 . . . 231 F5
Farthingstone Rd
Litchborough NN12 . . . . 171 B2
Weedon NN7 . . . . 155 A1
Faugere Ct NN13 . . . . . . 233 F8
Favell Way NN3 . . . . 160 D8
Fawsley Leys CV22 . . . . . .98 A7
Fawsley Rd Everdon NN11 170 A8
Northampton NN4 . . . . . 159 C2
Faxton Cl NN2 . . . . 141 D4
Faxton End NN6 . . . . 107 D7
Fay Cl NN11 . . . . 184 A7
Featherbed La
Geddington NN14 . . . . . .37 B1
Rugby CV21 . . . . .80 A1
Federation Ave NN14 . . . . .50 F2
Fegans Ct MK11 . . . . 229 D6
Fell Wlk NN8 . . . . 129 D6
Fellmead Rd NN3 . . . . . . 143 C5
Fellows Cl NN29 . . . . 146 C3
Fellows Way CV21 . . . . . . .98 F8
Fengate Ct NN3 . . . . 143 C5
Fenn Cl PE8 . . . . .15 E5
Fennel Ct NN4 . . . . 175 D5
Fenners Cl NN10 . . . . 148 C8
Fenny Compton Rd OX17 181 D1
Fenton Rise NN13 . . . . . . 233 D7
Fenwick Dr CV21 . . . . .99 A8
Ferguson's Cl PE8 . . . . . . .43 A3
Fermoy Ct NN7 . . . . 138 B4

Fermyn Pl NN18 . . . . .36 A3
Fern Dale Ct NN14 . . . . . .54 B3
Fern Rd NN10 . . . . 131 E3
Ferndale Rd NN3 . . . . 142 D2
Ferne Furlong MK46 . . . . 195 F5
Fernie Chase LE16 . . . . . . .17 A6
Fernie Field NN3 . . . . 142 C6
Fernie Rd LE16 . . . . .31 F3
Fernie Way NN8 . . . . 129 D4
Ferrers Ct NN10 . . . . 132 C7
Ferrestone Rd NN8 . . . . . 130 A6
Ferris Row NN3 . . . . 160 F7
Ferro Fields NN6 . . . . 106 C3
Fessey Rd NN11 . . . . 183 D8
Festival Cl NN9 . . . . 113 B5
Festival Rd NN12 . . . . . . 172 D1
Fetter St NN1 . . . . 159 D5
Fettledine Rd NN9 . . . . . . 113 B5
Field Cl NN6 . . . . 102 C4
Field Cotts NN18 . . . . .53 B8
Field Rose Sq 4 NN3 . . . 143 C2
Field St NN16 . . . . .72 B3
Field Street Ave NN16 . . . .72 B3
Field View
Braunston NN11 . . . . . . 118 C1
Marston St L OX17 . . . . . 210 B2
Field Way NN13 . . . . 212 A5
Fieldhead Cl LE16 . . . . . . .31 C3
Fieldmill Rd NN3 . . . . 143 B1
Fields View NN8 . . . . 130 B4
Fieldway NN3 . . . . 142 B1
Fienesgate NN4 . . . . 158 D1
Fiennes Ct NN11 . . . . 135 B6
Fife St NN5 . . . . 158 F7
Fifth Ave NN13 . . . . 238 E7
Fifth St NN13 . . . . 238 E7
Fifth St E NN13 . . . . 238 E7
Filleigh Way NN3 . . . . . . 160 C7
Finch Dr NN15 . . . . .92 A6
Finch-Hatton Dr NN17 . . . .10 C1
Finedon Inf Sch NN9 . . . . 111 F5
Finedon Mulso CE Jun
Sch NN9 . . . . 112 A5
Finedon Rd
Burton Latimer NN15 . . . .92 A4
Irthlingborough NN9 . . . 112 C3
Irthlingborough NN9 . . . 112 C3
Wellingborough NN8 . . . 130 B6
Finedon Road Ind
Est NN8 . . . . 130 B8
Finedon St NN15 . . . . .92 B3
Finedon Station Rd NN9 . 111 A6
Fineshade Cl
Kettering NN15 . . . . .92 A5
King's Cliffe PE8 . . . . . . .13 E7
Fineshade Gr NN17 . . . . . .36 E7
Finland Way NN18 . . . . . . .36 A2
Fir Rd NN16 . . . . .72 D2
Fir Tree Gr NN29 . . . . . . 164 D2
Fir Tree La LE17 . . . . .62 C3
Fir Tree Wlk
Market Harborough LE16 . .31 E4
Northampton NN3 . . . . . 142 E4
Firbank Cl NN3 . . . . 160 F8
Firdale Ave NN10 . . . . . . 132 B4
Firs Ct NN4 . . . . 175 F4
Firs The Daventry NN11 . . 135 C3
Market Harborough LE16 . .31 C3
First Ave NN8 . . . . 129 D3
First St NN13 . . . . 238 F6
Firsview Dr NN5 . . . . 140 C1
Fish St NN1 . . . . 159 D6
Fisher Ave CV22 . . . . .98 E8
Fisher Cl NN14 . . . . .76 E1
Fishermans Cl MK46 . . . . 195 E4
Fishers Cl Kilsby CV23 . . . .99 F2
Northampton NN3 . . . . . 143 C5
Fishpond Cl NN7 . . . . 162 B1
Fishponds Rd NN3 . . . . . 143 B1
Fishton Cl NN15 . . . . .91 C7
Fitzroy Pl NN1 . . . . 159 B6
Fitzwilliam Dr NN15 . . . . .92 A5
Fitzwilliam Leys NN12 . . . 132 B7
Fitzwilliam Rd NN9 . . . . . 112 F3
Fitzwilliam St NN10 . . . . . 132 A2
Five Acres Fold NN4 . . . . 158 F3
Fjord Wlk NN18 . . . . .36 A2
Flaggs Mdw NN4 . . . . 158 D1
Flamingo Zoo Pk MK46 . . 195 B3
Flatlets The NN9 . . . . 112 F2
Flats The NN7 . . . . 155 C4
Flavius Gate NN13 . . . . . 234 A7
Flaxland Cl LE16 . . . . .32 B3
Flaxlands Rd NN3 . . . . . . 142 F3
Flaxwell Ct NN3 . . . . 160 F8
Fleet St NN16 . . . . .72 A2
Fleetwind Dr NN4 . . . . . . 175 D7
Fleetwood Cl LE16 . . . . . . .31 D1
Fleetwood Gdns LE16 . . . .31 D1
Fleming Cl NN8 . . . . 129 B7
Fleming Rd NN12 . . . . .22 B7
Flensburg Cl NN18 . . . . . . .36 B2
Fletcher Rd NN10 . . . . . . 132 B3
Fletchers Gdns NN14 . . . . .76 D1
Fletton Way PE8 . . . . .41 F6
Flintcomb Rise NN3 . . . . 143 B3
Flinters Cl NN4 . . . . 175 F7
Flitton Ct MK11 . . . . 229 F5
Flora Thompson
Dr NN13 . . . . 233 E8
Flore CE Prim Sch NN7 . 155 E5
Flore Hill NN7 . . . . 155 E5
Florence Rd NN1 . . . . 159 F7
Floribunda Dr NN3 . . . . . 158 F2
Folly La NN7 . . . . 206 C8
Folly Rd MK19 . . . . 228 D4

Foot La NN9 . . . . 133 C8
Ford Dr NN13 . . . . 233 D8
Ford St NN16 . . . . .72 C2
Forest App PE8 . . . . .13 F7
Forest Cl NN15 . . . . .92 D3
Forest Ct NN10 . . . . 132 D3
Forest Gate Rd NN17 . . . . .36 E7
Forest Glade
Hartwell NN7 . . . . 192 D2
Kettering NN16 . . . . .72 C6
Forest Rd Hanslope MK19 207 A6
Hartwell NN7 . . . . 192 D2
Northampton NN4 . . . . . 159 C3
Piddington NN7 . . . . 177 A1
Forest View NN7 . . . . 192 D2
Foresters Pl NN21 . . . . . . .99 B7
Foresters The NN9 . . . . . 114 D5
Forfar St NN5 . . . . 158 F7
Forge Ho NN4 . . . . .70 D7
Forrester Dr NN13 . . . . . . 222 E1
Forrester Gr NN14 . . . . . . .76 E1
Forstal Ct NN18 . . . . .36 D3
Fort Pl NN1 . . . . 159 B6
Forty Foot La MK44 . . . . 149 D1
Fosberry Cl NN4 . . . . 175 F6
Foskett Cl NN10 . . . . 132 A3
Foskitt Ct NN3 . . . . 143 B1
Fosse Gn NN10 . . . . 132 C3
Foster Ct NN18 . . . . .36 E5
Foster's Booth NN12 . . . . 172 C1
Fotheringhay PE8 . . . . . . .27 D7
Fotheringhay Ct NN14 . . . .76 E2
Fotheringhay Rd
Corby NN17 . . . . .36 B8
Nassington PE8 . . . . .15 F4
Foundry St 5 NN1 . . . . . 135 C1
Foundry Pl NN11 . . . . . . 135 C1
Foundry St 16 NN1 . . . . . 159 C5
Foundry Wlk 4 NN11 . . . 135 C1
Fourth Ave
Croughton NN13 . . . . . . 238 E6
Wellingborough NN8 . . . 129 E4
Fourth St NN13 . . . . 238 E6
Fowey Cl NN8 . . . . 129 C6
Fox Cl CV21 . . . . .80 B1
Fox Covert Dr NN7 . . . . . 191 E3
Fox Hill Rd NN3 . . . . 143 D2
Fox La Brackley NN13 . . . 233 E7
Souldern OX6 . . . . 237 E3
Fox St NN14 . . . . .70 C7
Foxcovert Rd NN3 . . . . . . 143 B6
Foxendale Sq NN3 . . . . . 143 D2
Foxford Cl NN4 . . . . 174 F8
Foxglove Ave NN11 . . . . . 184 B6
Foxglove Ct NN10 . . . . . . 148 C8
Foxgrove Ave NN2 . . . . . 141 B4
Foxhill NN46 . . . . 195 E5
Foxhill La OX6 . . . . 237 E3
Foxhill Rd NN6 . . . . 102 B3
Foxlands NN12 . . . . .51 B2
Foxton Ct NN15 . . . . .72 A1
Foxton Locks LE16 . . . . . .30 C8
Foxton Rd Gumley LE16 . .30 D5
Lubenham LE16 . . . . .30 D5
Foxwell Sq NN3 . . . . 142 F7
Foxwood Cl NN10 . . . . . . 131 E2
Francis Cl NN10 . . . . 131 E3
Francis Dickins Cl NN29 . 146 B3
Francis Row NN7 . . . . . . 171 E6
Francis St
8 Northampton NN1 . . 159 C7
Raunds NN9 . . . . 114 B4
Francis Terr NN9 . . . . 114 B4
Franciscan Ct NN10 . . . . . 147 F8
Franklin Cres NN5 . . . . . 158 D7
Franklin Fields 37 A8
Franklin St NN5 . . . . 158 F6
Franklin Way NN11 . . . . . 135 B5
Franklin's Cl NN6 . . . . . . 143 F4
Frankston Ave MK11 . . . . 229 E5
Fraser Cl NN1 . . . . 135 C1
Fraser Rd NN3 . . . . 142 D6
Freehold St NN2 . . . . 159 C8
Freeman Way NN9 . . . . . 112 B5
Freeman's Endowed CE
Jun Sch NN8 . . . . 129 E4
Freeman's La NN14 . . . . . .95 C6
Freeschool St 9 NN1 . . . 159 C5
Fremeaux Terr NN1 . . . . . 141 B2
French Dr NN15 . . . . .72 F1
Frencham Cl 2 NN4 . . . . 158 F2
Friar's Cl NN4 . . . . 159 B1
Friar's Cres NN4 . . . . 159 C1
Friars Cl NN8 . . . . 130 A3
Friars Sch NN8 . . . . 130 A3
Friary Cl NN11 . . . . 135 D2
Friary The NN1 . . . . 159 D2
Frinton Cl NN10 . . . . 147 F8
Frisby La LE15 . . . . .3 D8
Frobisher Cl NN11 . . . . . . 135 E2
Frog Hall Brixworth NN6 . 106 A2
Silverstone NN12 . . . . . . 214 D5
Frog La NN15 . . . . 182 C7
Front St NN14 . . . . .95 C6
Frosty Hollow NN4 . . . . . 175 C6
Froxhill Cres NN6 . . . . . . 106 A1
Froxhill Wlk NN6 . . . . . . 106 A1
Fuchsia Cl NN3 . . . . 160 C6
Fulford Dr NN2 . . . . 141 E3
Fulleburn Ct 2 NN4 . . . . 142 E3
Fullen Cl NN11 . . . . .22 D8
Fuller Rd NN3 . . . . 142 C8
Fuller St NN16 . . . . .72 C2
Fullers Cl NN14 . . . . .76 F8
Fullingdale Rd NN3 . . . . . 142 B2
Fullwell Rd NN29 . . . . . . 164 C2
Fulmar La NN8 . . . . 130 A8

Fulwell Ave NN17 . . . . . . .10 C1
Furber Ct NN3 . . . . 142 D4
Furlong Rd NN14 . . . . .51 C3
Furlongs The LE16 . . . . . . .32 B3
Furnace Cotts NN9 . . . . . 111 A5
Furnace La Finedon NN9 . 111 B5
Kettering NN16 . . . . .72 A5
Nether Heyford NN7 . . . 172 A8
Furnace Lane Ind
Est 111 A5
Furnells Cl NN9 . . . . 114 D7
Furtho Ct MK19 . . . . 229 B7
Furtho La NN12 . . . . 217 E3
Furze Ct 5 NN4 . . . . 159 A3
Furze Rd NN7 . . . . 161 D2
Furze Wlk NN2 . . . . 141 E2
Fushia Way NN10 . . . . . . 148 B7
Fusilier Rd NN11 . . . . 135 B1
Fyfe Rd NN17 . . . . .36 B8
Fylingdale NN2 . . . . 140 F5

G

Gable Cl NN11 . . . . 135 B1
Gable Court Mews NN3 . 142 D1
Gables The NN3 . . . . .72 B1
Gadesby Ct NN3 . . . . 142 E3
Gains La PE17 . . . . .61 D2
Gainsborough Ave NN15 . .92 A7
Gainsborough Cres CV21 . .80 B1
Gainsborough Ct NN8 . . . .36 D5
Gainsborough Dr NN8 . . . 129 F3
Gainsborough Rd NN18 . . .36 C4
Gainsborough Way NN11 135 C6
Galahad Ct NN5 . . . . 158 A8
Galane Cl NN4 . . . . 158 D1
Galley Cl NN13 . . . . 143 A6
Galley Hill MK11 . . . . 229 F5
Gallfield Ct NN3 . . . . 161 C8
Galliard Ct NN1 . . . . 159 F7
Gallow Field Rd LE16 . . . .30 E7
Gallowhill Rd NN4 . . . . . 160 B1
Gambrel Rd NN5 . . . . 158 D6
Gamston Wlk 5 NN18 . . . .36 B6
Gander Cl NN17 . . . . .38 A7
Gannet La NN8 . . . . 130 A8
Ganton Cl NN11 . . . . 135 F3
Garden Fields Ct NN29 . . 147 C8
Gardenfield NN10 . . . . . . 132 B5
Gardens The
East Carlton LE16 . . . . . .35 A4
Kettering NN16 . . . . .72 A4
Gardiner St LE16 . . . . .31 C3
Gardner Cl NN9 . . . . 114 C7
Gardner Rise NN13 . . . . . 233 D7
Garfield Ct NN3 . . . . 143 C1
Garfield St Kettering NN15 .91 B8
Northampton NN2 . . . . . 141 B3
Garners Way NN7 . . . . . . 157 C7
Garrard Way NN16 . . . . . .71 F3
Garrick Rd NN1 . . . . 160 B7
Garrow Cl NN9 . . . . 112 E3
Garsdale 140 F5
Garston Rd NN18 . . . . . . .36 C1
Gatcombe Rd NN10 . . . . . 132 B2
Gate La NN14 . . . . .90 B5
Gateford St NN18 . . . . . . .36 B6
Gatehouse Cl CV21 . . . . . .99 A8
Gatehouse La LE16 . . . . . .20 F6
Gatelodge Cl NN3 . . . . . . 142 E6
Gaydon Ho NN17 . . . . . . .22 C1
Gayhurst Cl NN3 . . . . 142 B2
Gayton CE Prim Sch NN7 173 E2
Gayton Rd Blisworth NN7 .190 C8
Eastcote NN12 . . . . 172 F1
Tiffield NN12 . . . . 189 C6
Geddington CE Prim
Sch NN14 . . . . .54 B2
Geddington Rd NN18 . . . . .37 D5
Gedling Ct NN3 . . . . 160 F8
Gees Farm Cl NN7 . . . . . 179 A5
Geldock Rd NN17 . . . . . . 143 A1
Genner Rd NN17 . . . . .22 B1
Gentian Ct NN10 . . . . 148 C8
George Blackall Ct NN17 . .36 C8
George Nutt Ct NN4 . . . . 159 C2
George Row NN1 . . . . . . 159 C5
George St
Burton Latimer NN15 . . . .92 D3
Corby NN17 . . . . .36 E6
Higham Ferrers NN10 . . . 132 C7
Irthlingborough NN9 . . . 112 D1
Kettering NN16 . . . . .72 B1
Rushden NN10 . . . . 132 B2
Wellingborough NN8 . . . 130 A5
George Yd MK11 . . . . 229 D5
Georges Ave NN7 . . . . . . 173 A4
Georges Ct NN7 . . . . 173 A7
Gerandria Ct CV22 . . . . . .98 E8
Gerrard Gdns LE16 . . . . . .48 D8
Gervase Sq NN3 . . . . 143 C1
Gharana Nivas NN8 . . . . 130 B5
Gibbons Dr NN14 . . . . . . .70 E7
Gibbsacre Ct NN3 . . . . . . 143 C1
Gibraltar Ct 23 NN1 . . . . 159 C7
Gibson Dr Rugby CV21 . . . .80 A1
Upper Benefield PE8 . . . .39 F7
Gibson La NN5 . . . . 158 F8
Giffard Ct
Market Harborough LE16 . .31 D3
Northampton NN5 . . . . . 159 A5
Gifford Ct NN5 . . . . 158 C8
Gilbert Scott Ct NN12 . . . 203 B6
Gilbey Cl NN9 . . . . 110 E1

Gilchrist Ave NN17 . . . . . . .37 A8
Gillingham Rd NN15 . . . . . .90 F8
Gillitts Rd NN8 . . . . .129 E3
Gillsway NN2 . . . . .141 A4
Gingles Ct CV21 . . . . .99 A8
Gipsy La Irchester NN29 . . .146 E8
  Kettering NN16 . . . . .71 E2
Gipsy Lane Turn NN29 . . . .146 F7
Gisburne Rd NN8 . . . . . . .130 A6
Glade Cl
  Burton Latimer NN15 . . . . .92 C3
  Northampton NN3 . . . . . . .143 B1
Glade The NN9 . . . . .110 E1
Gladstone Cl NN5 . . . . . . .141 A1
Gladstone Ct 5 NN16 . . . . .72 C2
Gladstone Lower
  Sch NN5 . . . . .159 A8
Gladstone Rd NN5 . . . . . . .159 A8
Gladstone St
  Desborough NN14 . . . . . . .51 A4
  Kettering NN16 . . . . .72 C2
  Market Harborough LE16 . . .31 F2
  Raunds NN9 . . . . .114 D6
  Ringstead NN14 . . . . .95 C3
  Rothwell NN14 . . . . .70 D7
Glaisedale Cl NN2 . . . . . .140 F5
Glaister Pl NN16 . . . . .72 D2
Glamis Cl NN10 . . . . .132 D1
Glan y Mor Terr NN2 . . . .141 C5
Glapthorn CE Prim
  Sch PE8 . . . . .26 B2
Glapthorn Rd PE8 . . . . . . .41 F4
Glasgow St NN5 . . . . .158 F6
Glassbrook Rd NN10 . . . . .132 A2
Glassthorpe La NN7 . . . . .157 A6
Glaston Rd LE15 . . . . .3 A5
Glastonbury Cl NN15 . . . . .91 F8
Glastonbury Rd
  Corby NN18 . . . . .36 A6
  Northampton NN4 . . . . . . .159 C1
Glebe Ave Broughton NN14 . .90 B4
  Kettering NN15 . . . . .91 B8
  Northampton NN4 . . . . . . .175 E8
Glebe Cl Holcot NN6 . . . . .126 E8
  Northampton NN4 . . . . . . .175 E8
Glebe Ct PE8 . . . . .58 A4
Glebe Dr NN13 . . . . .234 A7
Glebe Farm Ct NN29 . . . . .145 E6
Glebe La
  Great Houghton NN4 . . . . .160 E2
  Hanslope MK19 . . . . .206 E5
  Lower Harlestone NN7 . . . .139 E7
  Pitsford NN6 . . . . .125 D5
  Staverton NN11 . . . . .152 C7
Glebe Rd
  Burton Latimer NN15 . . . . .92 A2
  Cogenhoe NN7 . . . . .161 E6
  Deanshanger MK19 . . . . . .228 C5
  Market Harborough LE16 . . .32 A2
  Mears Ashby NN6 . . . . . . .128 B2
Glebe Rise OX17 . . . . . . .231 A5
Glebe The Aynho OX17 . . .237 D7
  Badby NN11 . . . . .153 A2
  Daventry NN11 . . . . .153 C8
Glebe Way Cogenhoe NN7 .161 E6
  Northampton NN4 . . . . . . .175 E8
Glebeland Cres NN5 . . . . .159 A8
Glebeland Gdns NN5 . . . . .140 F1
Glebeland Rd NN5 . . . . . .158 F8
Glebeland Wlk 1 NN5 . . . .158 F8
Glebelands NN6 . . . . .105 B1
Glen Ave NN7 . . . . .174 B2
Glen Bank NN8 . . . . .130 A4
Glen Baulk Rd NN14, NN16 .71 C4
Glencoe Dr NN15 . . . . .91 E8
Glendale Ct NN3 . . . . . . .143 C1
Glendon Rd NN14 . . . . . . .70 E7
Gleneagles Cl
  Daventry NN11 . . . . .135 E3
  Kettering NN15 . . . . .91 F8
Gleneagles Dr NN8 . . . . . .129 D7
Glenfield Cl NN10 . . . . . . .131 F2
Glenfield Dr NN29 . . . . . .145 D5
Glengary NN3 . . . . .142 D7
Glenshee Cl NN15 . . . . . . .91 E8
Glenville NN3 . . . . .142 B4
Gloucester Ave NN4 . . . . .159 B1
Gloucester Cl
  1 Kettering NN16 . . . . . . .72 C2
  Northampton NN4 . . . . . . .159 B2
  Weedon NN7 . . . . .155 B4
Gloucester Cres
  Northampton NN4 . . . . . . .159 B2
  Rushden NN10 . . . . .132 C3
Gloucester Ct NN14 . . . . . .70 C6
Gloucester Ho NN4 . . . . . .159 C2
Gloucester Pl NN4 . . . . . .130 A4
Glovers La OX17 . . . . . . .208 F1
Glyndebourne Gdns NN18 .36 A4
Goadby's Yd 9 NN16 . . . . .72 B2
Gocker Wood Cl NN18 . . . .36 B1
Godwin Rd NN17 . . . . .21 F3
Godwin Wlk NN5 . . . . . . .140 D2
Gold St Clipston LE16 . . . . .66 F8
  Desborough NN14 . . . . . . .51 A3
  Hanslope MK19 . . . . .207 A2
  Kettering NN16 . . . . .72 B2
  Northampton NN1 . . . . . . .159 C5
  Podington NN29 . . . . .147 E2
  Walgrave NN6 . . . . .108 A5
  Wellingborough NN8 . . . . .130 A6
Gold Street
  Mews 6 NN1 . . . . .159 C5
Goldcrest Ct NN3 . . . . . . .143 A6
Goldenash Ct NN3 . . . . . .142 F5

Golding Cl NN11 . . . . . . .135 C2
Goldings Mid Sch NN3 . . .142 F5
Goldings Rd NN3 . . . . . . .143 A5
Goldsmith Dr NN17 . . . . . .36 D8
Goldsmith Rd NN8 . . . . . .129 C4
Golf La NN6 . . . . .140 C8
Good Shepherd RC
  Lower Sch The NN2 . . . . .141 C3
Goodacre Cl CV23 . . . . . . .80 A5
Goodens La NN29 . . . . . . .145 F6
Goodwood Ave NN3 . . . . .141 F5
Goodwood Cl LE16 . . . . . . .32 B3
Goose Gn NN13 . . . . .233 B6
Goran Ave MK11 . . . . .229 E4
Gordon Cl Oundle PE8 . . . . .42 A6
  Wellingborough NN8 . . . . .130 B5
Gordon St Kettering NN16 . .72 C2
  Northampton NN2 . . . . . . .159 C8
  Rothwell NN14 . . . . .70 D6
  Rushden NN10 . . . . .131 F2
Gordon Terr NN14 . . . . . . .74 F2
Gores La LE16 . . . . .32 A3
Gorricks MK11 . . . . .229 D4
Gorse Cl NN2 . . . . .141 B6
Gorse Rd Hinton NN11 . . .184 B7
  Kettering NN16 . . . . .72 E4
Gorseholm Ct 10 NN9 . . . .112 F2
Gosforth NN8 . . . . .129 C4
Gosler The NN8 . . . . .129 B3
Gotch Cl NN15 . . . . .91 F4
Gotch Rd NN15 . . . . .91 F5
Gough Cl NN15 . . . . .72 E1
Gould Cl NN11 . . . . .118 B1
Goward St LE16 . . . . .31 E3
Gower Cl NN15 . . . . .91 C6
Grace Ct NN15 . . . . .92 B1
Gracelands LE16 . . . . .31 C2
Graeme Rd PE5 . . . . .3 F7
Grafton Cl Hartwell NN7 . .192 D2
  Pottersbury NN12 . . . . . . .217 E3
  Wellingborough NN8 . . . . .129 D7
Grafton Dr NN17 . . . . .36 B8
Grafton Ho NN11 . . . . . . .159 B6
Grafton Pl 10 NN1 . . . . . .159 C7
Grafton Rd Brigstock NN14 .53 A4
  Cranford NN14 . . . . .93 A7
  Geddington NN14 . . . . . . .54 B2
  Roade NN7 . . . . .191 C4
  Rushden NN10 . . . . .132 D2
  Yardley Gobion NN12 . . . . .217 E6
Grafton St Kettering NN16 . .72 A4
  Northampton NN1 . . . . . . .159 C7
Grafton View NN4 . . . . . . .175 E6
Grafton Way
  Northampton NN5 . . . . . . .140 B2
  Rothersthorpe NN7 . . . . . .174 A7
Graham Hill NN14 . . . . . . .214 D4
Graham Hill Rd NN12 . . . .203 C7
Granary Ct NN4 . . . . .175 C7
Granary Rd NN4 . . . . .175 C7
Granby Cl NN18 . . . . .36 B6
Grandborough Way NN6 . .106 C1
Grange Ave NN5 . . . . .140 B1
Grange Cl Denton NN7 . . .162 B1
  Earls Barton NN6 . . . . . . .144 E5
  Irchester NN29 . . . . .147 B7
Grange Ct Brixworth NN6 . .106 B2
  Horton NN7 . . . . .177 D1
  Stony Stratford MK12 . . . . .229 F6
Grange Jun & Inf Schs
  The 135 A1
Grange La Pitsford NN6 . . .125 E6
  Thorpe Langton LE16 . . . . .17 A5
Grange Pl NN16 . . . . .72 E4
Grange Prim Sch NN16 . . . .72 E3
Grange Rd Broughton NN14 .90 B5
  Geddington NN14 . . . . . . .53 F2
  Islip NN14 . . . . .76 B1
  Kettering NN16 . . . . .72 A3
  Northampton NN3 . . . . . . .142 C3
  Stanion NN14 . . . . .37 E2
  Stanwick NN9 . . . . .114 A3
  Wellingborough NN9 . . . . .110 E1
Grange Way NN29 . . . . . . .147 B7
Grangeway NN10 . . . . . . .148 A8
Grangewood NN4 . . . . . . .175 A7
Grant Rd NN8 . . . . .130 B5
Granta Ho PE8 . . . . .42 A6
Grantham Wlk NN16 . . . . . .36 B4
Grantown Cl NN15 . . . . . . .91 E8
Granville St Kettering NN16 .72 C2
  Market Harborough LE16 . . .31 F2
Grasmere Gn NN8 . . . . . . .129 B4
Grasmere Rd NN16 . . . . . . .71 F2
Graspin La NN3 . . . . .160 D8
Grass Croft NN6 . . . . .121 A3
Grass Slade NN6 . . . . .106 C2
Grasscroft NN2 . . . . .141 A4
Grassmere Ave NN3 . . . . .142 E2
Gravel Hill NN11 . . . . .199 D7
Gravely St NN10 . . . . .131 F2
Gray Cl NN6 . . . . .145 A4
Gray St Irchester NN29 . . .147 A7
  Northampton NN5 . . . . . . .159 E7
Gray's Cl NN17 . . . . .36 E5
Grays Cl NN12 . . . . .216 D8
Grays Dr NN14 . . . . .37 E3
Grays La Paulerspury NN12 216 D8
  Yardley Gobion NN12 . . . . .217 E6
Greasley St 6 NN16 . . . . . .36 B5
Great Addington CE Prim
  Sch NN14 . . . . .94 B3
Great Billing CE Lower
  Sch NN3 . . . . .143 C2
Great Billing Way NN3 . . .143 C4
Great Bowden CE
  Sch LE16 . . . . .32 A6

Great Bowden Hall LE16 . .31 F7
Great Bowden Rd LE16 . . . .32 A4
Great Central Walk
  Nature Trail CV22 . . . . . . .98 C6
Great Central Way NN11 . .184 C7
Great Cl NN3 . . . . .124 D1
Great Creaton Prim
  Sch NN6 . . . . .104 F4
Great Doddington Prim
  Sch NN29 . . . . .145 E6
Great Easton Rd
  Bringhurst LE16 . . . . .20 C6
  Caldecott LE16 . . . . .21 A7
  Drayton LE16 . . . . .20 A5
  Great Easton LE16 . . . . . . .20 F6
Great Field Cl NN3 . . . . . .142 E5
Great Folds Rd NN18 . . . . .35 F1
Great Gidding CE Prim
  Sch PE17 . . . . .61 D3
Great Gull Cres NN3 . . . . .142 F6
Great Haughton Prep
  Sch NN4 . . . . .160 E3
Great Holme St NN3 . . . . .142 E5
Great La Bugbrooke NN7 . .172 F2
  Hackleton NN7 . . . . .177 B3
Great North Rd
  Stibbington PE8 . . . . .8 C2
  Wothorpe PE9 . . . . .2 B8
Great Park St NN8 . . . . . .130 A5
Great Russell St NN1 . . . . .159 D7
Greatmeadow NN3 . . . . . .143 C4
Greatmeadow Rd NN3 . . . .143 B4
Greatworth Prim
  Sch OX17 . . . . .210 E2
Greaves Cl NN5 . . . . .139 F1
Grebe Cl Hinton NN11 . . . .184 B6
  Thrapston NN14 . . . . .76 E3
Green Cl NN8 . . . . .129 C5
Green End NN6 . . . . .141 B2
Green End La MK19 . . . . . .207 A3
Green Farm OX17 . . . . . . .230 A4
Green Farm Cl CV23 . . . . . .81 A5
Green La Ashley LE16 . . . . .18 F2
  Braybrooke LE16 . . . . .49 F5
  Charlton OX17 . . . . .231 B5
  Desborough NN14 . . . . . . .50 D3
  Duddington PE9 . . . . .5 B6
  Husbands Bosworth LE17 . . .45 E5
  Kettering NN16 . . . . .72 B2
  Market Harborough LE16 . . .31 E1
  Northampton NN4 . . . . . . .175 E5
  Silverstone NN12 . . . . . . .214 D5
  Stanwick NN9 . . . . .113 F3
  Stoke Albany LE16 . . . . . . .34 B4
  Thrapston NN14 . . . . .76 D2
  Towcester NN12 . . . . .203 A5
  Weston by W LE16 . . . . . . .18 C6
Green Rd NN7 . . . . .161 E2
Green St
  Milton Malsor NN7 . . . . . .174 E4
  Northampton NN1 . . . . . . .159 B3
  Wollaston NN29 . . . . .146 E2
Green The Abthorpe NN12 .201 E4
  Adderbury OX17 . . . . .230 A4
  Barby CV23 . . . . .99 C1
  Braunston NN11 . . . . .118 C1
  Byfield NN11 . . . . .183 D7
  Caldecott LE16 . . . . .21 B8
  Chelveston NN9 . . . . .133 C8
  Church Stowe NN7 . . . . . .171 D7
  Cosgrove MK19 . . . . .218 F2
  Cranford NN14 . . . . .93 A6
  Culworth OX17 . . . . .198 C3
  Deanshanger MK19 . . . . . .228 E4
  Everdon NN11 . . . . .170 A8
  Flore NN7 . . . . .155 F5
  Great Bowden LE16 . . . . . .32 B6
  Great Brington NN7 . . . . . .138 D7
  Great Houghton NN4 . . . . .160 E2
  Hanslope MK19 . . . . .207 A2
  Helmdon NN13 . . . . .211 F4
  Hinton-in-t-H NN13 . . . . . .232 D7
  Husbands Bosworth LE17 . . .45 E5
  Kislingbury NN7 . . . . .157 D3
  Lilbourne CV23 . . . . .81 A4
  Little Addington NN14 . . . .113 B8
  Lois Weedon NN12 . . . . . .200 D3
  Lubenham LE16 . . . . .30 E3
  Lyddington LE15 . . . . .9 D7
  Nether Heyford NN7 . . . . .156 B1
  10 Northampton NN1 . . . . .159 C5
  Northampton,
    Hardingstone NN4 . . . . . .175 F8
  Northampton,
    Kingsthorpe NN2 . . . . . .141 B3
  Orlingbury NN14 . . . . . . .110 A5
  Paulerspury NN12 . . . . . . .216 B7
  Priors Marston CV23 . . . . .166 D7
  Titchmarsh NN14 . . . . .77 C4
  Twywell NN14 . . . . .75 A1
  Upper Harlestone NN7 . . . .139 D4
  Wadenhoe PE8 . . . . .58 A4
  West Haddon NN6 . . . . . .102 B4
  Weston by W LE16 . . . . . . .18 B3
  Woodford NN14 . . . . .94 D6
Green's Norton CE
  Sch NN12 . . . . .202 E8
Greenacre Dr NN10 . . . . . .148 B8
Greenaway Cl NN7 . . . . . .190 E7
Greenbank Ave NN15 . . . . .72 C1
Greenbank Terr NN14 . . . . .95 B3
Greendale Sq 8 NN3 . . . . .143 C2
Greenfield Ave
  Kettering NN16 . . . . .71 F1
  Northampton NN3 . . . . . . .142 B3
Greenfield Rd NN3 . . . . . .142 A2
Greenfield Way NN10 . . . .132 A1
Greenfields Sch NN2 . . . . .141 B5

Greenfinch Dr NN3 . . . . . .142 C6
Greenglades NN4 . . . . . . .158 E2
Greenhill Cres NN11 . . . . .135 B3
Greenhill Rd Elton PE8 . . . .28 F8
  Elton PE7 . . . . .29 B6
  Kettering NN15 . . . . .91 A8
Greenhill Rise 36 B5
Greenhills Cl NN2 . . . . . . .141 B6
Greenhills Rd NN2 . . . . . .141 B6
Greening Rd NN14 . . . . . . .70 C7
Greenland Wlk NN18 . . . . .36 A2
Greenlaw NN8 . . . . .129 B4
Greenside
  Blisworth NN7 . . . . .190 D7
  Wappenham NN12 . . . . . .213 B8
Greensward The OX17 . . . .196 E1
Greenview Dr
  Northampton NN2 . . . . . . .141 E3
  Towcester NN12 . . . . .203 B6
Greenway
  Braunston NN11 . . . . .118 B1
  Eastcote NN12 . . . . .173 A1
  Northampton NN3 . . . . . . .160 C8
Greenway Ave NN3 . . . . . .142 D4
Greenway The NN11 . . . . .153 C8
Greenwood Cl
  Byfield NN11 . . . . .183 C7
  Moulton NN3 . . . . .142 C8
Greenwood Rd NN5 . . . . .159 A6
Greenyard The NN7 . . . . . .179 B7
Greeve Ct NN15 . . . . .36 C1
Gregory St 8 NN1 . . . . . .159 C5
Gregory Wlk NN18 . . . . . . .36 D4
Grenadier Rd NN11 . . . . . .135 B1
Grendon Ave NN3 . . . . . . .36 B7
Grendon CE Prim
  Sch 163 D5
Grendon Rd NN6 . . . . . . .144 E1
Grendon Wlk NN3 . . . . . . .141 F5
Grenville Cl Corby NN17 . . .36 A8
  Daventry NN11 . . . . .135 E1
  Rothwell NN14 . . . . .70 E6
Grenville Gdns LE16 . . . . . .31 D1
Gresley Cl NN11 . . . . .135 A4
Gretton Brook Rd
  Corby NN17 . . . . .21 E3
  Corby NN17 . . . . .22 C4
Gretton Ct NN8 . . . . .129 D7
Gretton Prim Sch NN17 . . .22 C8
Gretton Rd Corby NN17 . . .22 C3
  Harringworth NN17 . . . . . .10 E7
  Lyddington LE15 . . . . .9 B5
  Rockingham LE16 . . . . . . .21 B5
  Weldon NN17 . . . . .38 A8
Greville Ct NN3 . . . . .142 A4
Greville Cl NN2 . . . . .141 C8
Greyfriars NN1 . . . . .159 C6
Greyfriars Rd NN11 . . . . . .153 B8
Greys The NN7 . . . . .155 B4
Grieg Wlk NN18 . . . . .36 A2
Griffin Rd LE16 . . . . .49 E4
Griffith St NN10 . . . . .132 B1
Grimmer Wlk NN9 . . . . . .131 D8
Grimsby Cl NN18 . . . . .36 C4
Grombold Ave NN9 . . . . . .114 C6
Grooms La NN6 . . . . .105 A4
Grosvenor Cl NN15 . . . . . .92 A5
Grosvenor Ctr NN1 . . . . . .159 D6
Grosvenor Gdns NN2 . . . .141 D4
Grosvenor Ho NN2 . . . . . .141 D4
Grosvenor Pl NN13 . . . . . .233 E7
Grosvenor Rd NN15 . . . . . .92 A5
Grosvenor St NN15 . . . . . .91 F5
Groundwell Ct 1 NN3 . . . .142 F1
Grove Farm Cl NN6 . . . . . .121 D4
Grove La Moulton NN3 . . .126 D2
  Weston NN12 . . . . .199 F3
Grove Pl NN9 . . . . .114 D5
Grove Rd
  Brafield-on-t-G NN7 . . . . .161 D3
  Northampton NN1 . . . . . . .159 E7
  Rushden NN10 . . . . .132 C2
  Thrapston NN14 . . . . .76 D1
Grove St
  Higham Ferrers NN10 . . . .132 C6
  Raunds NN9 . . . . .114 D5
  Wellingborough NN8 . . . . .129 E4
Grove The Corby NN18 . . . .37 C6
  Kettering NN15 . . . . .72 B1
  Moulton NN3 . . . . .126 C2
  Ringstead NN14 . . . . .95 A3
  Roade NN7 . . . . .191 E3
  Wollaston NN29 . . . . .146 D1
Grove Way NN9 . . . . .111 E3
Grovebury Dell NN2 . . . . .141 A4
Grovelands NN11 . . . . . . .153 A8
Grundy Ct NN15 . . . . .91 B8
Guildhall Rd NN1 . . . . . . .159 D5
Guillemot La NN8 . . . . . . .130 A7
Guilsborough CE Prim
  Sch NN6 . . . . .103 E7
Guilsborough Hill NN6 . . .104 D5
Guilsborough Rd
  Ravensthorpe NN6 . . . . . .103 D1
  West Haddon NN6 . . . . . .102 C5
Guilsborough
  Sch NN6 . . . . .103 D8
Guinea Orch MK46 . . . . . .195 E4
Gullet La LE16 . . . . .18 F2
Gumley Rd LE16 . . . . .30 C7
Gunnell Cl NN15 . . . . .90 F8
Gunnsbrook Cl LE16 . . . . . .32 A6
Gunthorpe Pl NN18 . . . . . .36 B6
Gurston Rise NN3 . . . . . . .143 C4
Gynwell NN6 . . . . .85 B8

H

H E Bates Way NN10 . . . .132 A2
Hachenburg Pl NN10 . . . . .132 C5
Hackleton Prim Sch NN7 177 A3
Hackwood Rd NN11 . . . . . .153 E8
  Wellingborough NN8 . . . . .129 D8
Haddon Cl Rushden NN10 .148 A8
Haddon Ct NN6 . . . . .122 C5
Hadfield Cl CV23 . . . . .80 A5
Hadrian's Gate NN13 . . . .234 A7
Hagley Cl LE16 . . . . .32 B3
Haigh Dr NN15 . . . . .72 E1
Hailsham Ct OX17 . . . . . .220 B8
Haines Rd NN4 . . . . .159 C3
Hale Ave MK11 . . . . .229 E5
Halford St NN14 . . . . .76 C1
Halford Way NN11 . . . . . .135 E8
Halfway Thorn NN6 . . . . . .124 C1
Halifax Sq NN18 . . . . .36 B5
Hall Ave NN10 . . . . .132 A1
Hall Cl Arthingworth LE16 . .68 C7
  Harpole NN7 . . . . .157 B6
  Kettering NN15 . . . . .90 F8
  Kilsby CV23 . . . . .100 A3
  Kislingbury NN7 . . . . .157 D4
  Northampton NN5 . . . . . . .158 C6
  Old Stratford MK19 . . . . . .229 B6
  Spratton NN6 . . . . .105 B1
Hall Dr Finedon NN9 . . . . .111 E4
  Long Buckby NN6 . . . . . . .121 C4
Hall Farm Finedon NN9 . . .106 B3
Hall Gdns
  East Haddon NN6 . . . . . . .122 D5
  Loddington NN14 . . . . . . .70 C1
  Polebrook PE8 . . . . .43 A3
Hall Hill NN14 . . . . .55 F7
Hall La Harrowden LE16 . . .18 E2
  Drayton LE16 . . . . .20 A5
  Kettering NN16 . . . . .90 F8
  South Luffenham LE15 . . . .3 E8
  Welford NN6 . . . . .64 D5
  Wittering PE8 . . . . .7 C8
Hall Piece Cl NN3 . . . . . . .143 C3
Hall Yd Collyweston PE9 . . .1 C2
  King's Cliffe PE8 . . . . .13 F7
Hall's Cl Geddington NN14 .54 B3
  Weldon NN17 . . . . .38 A8
Hall's La NN13 . . . . .233 E6
Hallam LE16 . . . . .31 D5
Hallaton Rd LE16 . . . . .18 F7
Halls Cl NN14 . . . . .18 B4
Hallwood Rd NN16 . . . . . . .72 C5
Halse Rd NN13 . . . . .222 F1
Halswell Ct NN3 . . . . .142 D4
Ham La NN14 . . . . .95 A4
Ham Meadow Dr NN3 . . . .143 C2
Hambledon Rise NN4 . . . .158 E3
Hamblin Ct NN10 . . . . . . .132 B2
Hamilton Ho Corby NN18 . .36 E5
  Northampton NN2 . . . . . . .141 C5
Hamilton La NN7 . . . . . . .138 D6
Hamlet Gn NN5 . . . . .158 F8
Hammas Leys NN6 . . . . . .121 C4
Hammerstone La NN4 . . . .158 F3
Hammond Way LE16 . . . . .31 E4
Hampden Cres NN16 . . . . .72 D3
Hampton Court Cl NN12 . .203 B5
Hampton Dr OX17 . . . . . . .230 F6
Hampton Ho NN10 . . . . . .132 B2
Hampton St NN1 . . . . .159 B7
Hamsterly Pk NN3 . . . . . .143 A6
Handcross Ct NN18 . . . . . .36 B4
Handcross Way NN10 . . . .132 C5
Handley Cl NN5 . . . . .140 A1
Hanemill Ct NN3 . . . . .143 C1
Hangerfield Ct NN3 . . . . . .142 F4
Hanover Ct NN3 . . . . .143 B4
Hanover Dr NN13 . . . . . . .233 E7
Hans Apel Dr NN13 . . . . . .233 D7
Hansbury Ironstone
  Railway Mus NN4 . . . . . . .158 E2
Hanslope Comb
  Sch MK19 . . . . .207 A3
Hanslope Rd MK19 . . . . . .218 F7
Harbidges La NN6 . . . . . . .121 A4
Harborough Rd
  Braybrooke LE16 . . . . .49 D7
  Brixworth NN6 . . . . .106 C3
  Clipston LE16 . . . . .48 A2
  Desborough NN14 . . . . . . .50 D7
  Dingley NN14 . . . . .32 D5
  Dingley LE16 . . . . .32 D5
  East Farndon LE16 . . . . . . .48 C8
  Great Oxendon LE16 . . . . .48 F4
  Great Oxendon LE16 . . . . .48 F4
  Kelmarsh NN6 . . . . .67 F5
  Lubenham LE16 . . . . .31 A3
  Maidwell NN6 . . . . .87 B4
  Market Harborough LE16 . . .31 C7
  Northampton NN2 . . . . . . .141 C4
  Rushden NN10 . . . . .132 C1
  Stoke Albany LE16 . . . . . . .34 B4
  Theddingworth LE17 . . . . . .30 A1
  Theddingworth LE17 . . . . . .46 E8
Harborough Rd N NN2 . . .141 B6
Harborough Way NN10 . . .132 C1
Harcourt Sq NN16 . . . . . . .72 C2
Harcourt St
  7 Kettering NN16 . . . . . . .72 C2
  Market Harborough LE16 . . .31 D3
  Raunds NN9 . . . . .114 D6
Harcourt Way NN4 . . . . . .158 E3
Hardays La NN6 . . . . .102 B4
Harden Cl NN18 . . . . .53 A8
Harding Cl NN15 . . . . .72 F1
Harding Terr NN1 . . . . . . .159 C7

Hardingstone La NN4 . . .175 D8
Hardingstone Prim
  Sch NN4 . . . . .175 E7
Hardlands Rd NN5 . . . . . .158 C8
Hardwater Rd NN29 . . . .145 D4
Hardwick Cl NN8 . . . . . . .129 E5
Hardwick Jun & Inf
  Schs NN8 . . . . .129 C5
Hardwick Rd Gretton NN17 . .10 B1
  Little Harrowden NN9 . . . .110 B3
  Northampton NN4 . . . . . .175 C8
  Priors Marston CV23 . . . .166 D7
  Wellingborough NN8 . . . .129 A7
  Wellingborough, Hatton
  Park NN8 . . . . .129 E5
Hardy Driive NN4 . . . . . .175 F7
Harebell Sq ▌ NN3 . . . . .143 D2
Harefield Rd NN3 . . . . . .143 B5
Harefoot Cl NN5 . . . . . . .158 B8
Harksome Hill NN4 . . . . .158 E2
Harlech NN18 . . . . .36 C3
Harlech Ct NN14 . . . . .76 F2
Harlestone Ct NN5 . . . . .158 F7
Harlestone Ho NN5 . . . . .159 A7
Harlestone Prim
  Sch NN7 . . . . .139 E5
Harlestone Rd
  Church Brampton NN6 . . .124 D1
  Lower Harlestone NN7 . . .139 F6
  Northampton NN5 . . . . . .140 B2
Harley Way Brigstock NN14 .56 D3
  Lower Benefield PE8 . . . . .40 D3
Harmans Way NN7 . . . . .155 B4
Harnett Dr MK12 . . . . . . .229 F6
Harold St ▌ NN1 . . . . . .159 E6
Harper's Ct NN14 . . . . . . .55 F7
Harpers Cl NN18 . . . . . . .53 B8
Harpole Prim Sch NN7 . .157 D6
Harrier Pk NN4 . . . . .175 B8
Harrington Aviation
  Mus NN6 . . . . .68 F3
Harrington Rd
  Desborough NN14 . . . . . .50 F3
  Loddington NN14 . . . . . . .70 D1
  Old NN6 . . . . .107 D7
  Rothwell NN14 . . . . .70 C6
Harringworth Rd NN17 . . . .10 C2
Harris Cl Brackley NN13 . .233 D8
  Northampton NN4 . . . . . .175 F7
  Raunds NN9 . . . . .114 D7
Harris Rd NN17 . . . . .21 C1
Harrison Cl
  Market Harborough LE16 . .48 D8
  Rugby CV21 . . . . .99 B8
  Wellingborough NN8 . . . .129 D5
Harrison Ct NN7 . . . . . . .172 F7
Harrod Dr LE16 . . . . .32 A4
Harrogate Ct NN18 . . . . . .36 B4
Harrold Rd NN29 . . . . . .164 D3
Harrow Way NN2 . . . . . .140 F6
Harrowden Rd
  Finedon NN9 . . . . .111 D3
  Northampton NN4 . . . . . .160 B2
  Orlingbury NN14 . . . . . . .110 A5
  Wellingborough NN8 . . . .129 F6
Harrowick La NN6 . . . . . .144 E4
Harry Cl NN6 . . . . .121 B3
Harry Potter Ho NN15 . . . .72 B1
Hartburn NN3 . . . . .161 C8
Hartley Dr NN15 . . . . .92 A7
Hartwell Cl NN2 . . . . . . .141 D5
Hartwell Rd Ashton NN7 . .205 F8
  Hanslope MK19 . . . . .206 E4
  Roade NN7 . . . . .192 A2
Harvest Cl NN15 . . . . .92 C2
Harvest Way NN2 . . . . . .140 F5
Harvey Cl NN9 . . . . .114 B5
Harvey Dr MK46 . . . . . . .195 F1
Harvey La NN3 . . . . .142 B8
Harvey Rd Rushden NN10 .148 B2
  Wellingborough NN8 . . . .129 C3
Harvey Reeves Rd NN5 . .159 A5
Haselrig Sq ▌ NN4 . . . . .158 F2
Hassocks Hedge NN4 . . .158 C2
Hastings MK11 . . . . .229 C6
Hastings Rd NN2 . . . . . . .141 D3
Hastings Wlk ▌ NN18 . . . .36 B5
Hatchdoyle La PE8 . . . . . .41 D1
Hatfield Cl
  ▌ Northampton NN4 . . . .175 C8
  Wellingborough NN8 . . . .129 C7
Hathersage Cl NN14 . . . . .50 E4
Hatton Ave NN8 . . . . . . .129 F5
Hatton Cl NN3 . . . . .142 A6
Hatton La NN17 . . . . .10 D1
Hatton Park Rd NN8 . . . .129 F5
Hatton St NN8 . . . . .129 F5
Hautboy La PE8 . . . . .28 B3
Havelock Cotts PE8 . . . . . .42 A5
Havelock Inf Sch NN14 . . . .51 A3
Havelock Jun Sch NN14 . .51 A3
Havelock St
  Desborough NN14 . . . . . .51 A3
  Kettering NN16 . . . . .72 C3
  Wellingborough NN8 . . . .130 A5
Haven Cl NN5 . . . . .159 A4
Haweswater Rd NN16 . . . .71 E3
Hawk Esbeard Pl ▌ NN3 .143 C4
Hawk Ridge NN4 . . . . . . .158 F1
Hawke Rd NN11 . . . . . . .135 C1
Hawkins Cl Brackley NN13 233 D7
  Corby NN17 . . . . .21 B1
  Daventry NN11 . . . . .135 C2
  Rothwell NN14 . . . . .70 E7
  Stony Stratford MK11 . . .229 D5
Hawkshead NN8 . . . . . . .129 B3

Hawksmoor Way NN5 . . .140 D1
Hawksnest NN4 . . . . .175 A8
Hawkstone Cl NN5 . . . . . .158 D7
Hawkswood MK46 . . . . . .195 F5
Hawkwell Est MK19 . . . . .229 B7
Hawson Cl NN15 . . . . .91 C7
Hawthorn Cl NN15 . . . . . .92 B1
Hawthorn Dr
  Brackley NN13 . . . . .222 F1
  Daventry NN11 . . . . .135 C3
  Thrapston NN14 . . . . .76 D1
  Towcester NN12 . . . . . . .203 C8
Hawthorn Prim Sch NN15 .91 B8
Hawthorn Rd
  Burton Latimer NN15 . . . .92 B1
  Kettering NN15 . . . . .91 B8
  Northampton NN3 . . . . . .142 A1
Hawthorn Way NN6 . . . . .129 E5
Hawthorne Cl NN11 . . . . .184 B6
Hawthorne Rd NN9 . . . . .112 A4
Hawthorns The
  Desborough NN14 . . . . . .51 C2
  Higham Ferrers NN10 . . .132 B6
  Silverstone NN12 . . . . . .214 D3
Hay Cl Corby NN18 . . . . . .53 B8
  Rushden NN10 . . . . .148 B8
Hay La NN9 . . . . .112 E1
Haycroft Wlk NN7 . . . . . .141 A5
Hayden Ave NN9 . . . . . . .112 A5
Hayden Ct NN10 . . . . . . .132 C2
Haydown Gn NN5 . . . . . .158 D8
Hayes Rd MK19 . . . . .228 F5
Hayeswood Rd NN3 . . . . .142 F4
Hayman Rd NN13 . . . . . . .233 D7
Haynes La NN6 . . . . .105 B1
Haynes Rd NN16 . . . . .72 D2
Hayride The NN4 . . . . . . .175 A7
Hayway
  Irthlingborough NN9 . . . .112 E1
  Rushden NN10 . . . . .132 A4
Hayway Inf Sch NN10 . . .132 B3
Hazel Cl Brackley NN13 . .222 F1
  Hartwell NN7 . . . . .192 E2
Hazel Cres NN12 . . . . . . .203 B5
Hazel Croft NN11 . . . . . . .118 C1
Hazel Leys Prim
  Sch NN18 . . . . .36 D4
Hazel Rd NN15 . . . . .72 C1
Hazeland Ho NN14 . . . . . .51 A3
Hazeldene Rd NN2 . . . . . .141 F3
Hazelwood NN12 . . . . . . .214 C4
Hazelwood Ct ▌ NN16 . . .72 B1
Hazelwood La NN16 . . . . .72 B1
Hazelwood Rd Corby NN17 .36 F4
  Northampton NN1 . . . . . .159 D5
Headingley Rd NN10 . . . .132 D2
Headlands
  Desborough NN14 . . . . . .51 C3
  Kettering NN16 . . . . .91 B8
Headlands Lower
  Sch NN14 . . . . .142 C2
Headlands The
  Market Harborough LE16 . .31 F4
  Northampton NN3 . . . . . .142 C2
  Wellingborough NN8 . . . .129 F6
Headway NN18 . . . . .53 A8
Healey Cl NN3 . . . . .143 D4
Heart Of The Shires Sh
  Village NN7 . . . . .136 F2
Hearth St LE16 . . . . .31 D3
Heath Gn NN5 . . . . .140 F1
Heath Rise NN8 . . . . .129 D6
Heath Terr NN12 . . . . . . .203 C6
Heath Way
  Burton Latimer NN15 . . . .92 C3
  Rugby CV22 . . . . .98 D8
Heathcote Gr NN14 . . . . . .50 E4
Heather Ct
  Northampton NN4 . . . . . .159 A2
  Rushden NN10 . . . . .132 A2
Heather La NN3 . . . . .142 E4
Heather Rd NN16 . . . . . . .72 D4
Heatherdale Way NN2 . . .141 E3
Heathers The NN29 . . . . .146 E2
Heathfield Way NN5 . . . .141 A1
Heathfield Wlk NN18 . . . .36 B4
Heathville NN5 . . . . .140 F1
Hecham Way NN10 . . . . .132 B7
Hedge End NN4 . . . . .175 C6
Hedgely Ct NN4 . . . . .159 A2
Hedgerow Dr NN2 . . . . . .141 A5
Hedges The NN10 . . . . . .132 C4
Hedgeway NN4 . . . . .175 C6
Heights The LE16 . . . . .32 B2
Hellidon Cl NN11 . . . . . . .141 E4
Hellidon Rd CV23 . . . . . . .166 D7
Helmdon Cres NN2 . . . . .141 C4
Helmdon Prim Sch NN13 211 F4
Helmdon Rd
  Greatworth OX17 . . . . . .210 E2
  Northampton NN2 . . . . . .141 C5
  Sulgrave OX17 . . . . .210 F5
  Wappenham NN12 . . . . .213 A8
  Weston NN12 . . . . .199 F2
Helmsley Way NN18 . . . . .36 B5
Hemans Rd NN11 . . . . . . .135 B3
Hembury Pl NN4 . . . . . . .158 F3
Hempland Cl NN18 . . . . . .53 B8
Hemmingwell Rd NN8 . . .130 A7
Hempland Dr NN6 . . . . . . .64 B2
Henders MK11 . . . . .229 E5
Henley Cl Kettering NN15 . . .91 C7
  Wellingborough NN8 . . . .129 C6
Henley Rd NN16 . . . . .120 C6
Henry Gotch Sec Jun &
  Inf Schs NN15 . . . . .72 D1

Henry Smith Ho NN11 . . .135 B3
Henry St NN1 . . . . .159 E7
Henshaw Rd NN8 . . . . . . .129 E3
Hensmans La NN29 . . . . .164 D3
Henson Cl NN16 . . . . .71 F5
Henson Way NN16 . . . . . . .71 E4
Herbert St NN1 . . . . .159 C6
Hereford Cl NN14 . . . . . . .51 C4
Hereward Rd NN14 . . . . . .159 B2
Herford Cl NN18 . . . . .36 A2
Heritage Way Corby NN17 . .22 B2
  Raunds NN9 . . . . .114 E7
Hermitage Rd LE16 . . . . . .33 E3
Hermitage Way NN4 . . . .175 D7
Herne Hill Ct NN4 . . . . . .158 E2
Herne Rd PE8 . . . . .42 B4
Heron Ave NN4 . . . . .76 E3
Heron Cl
  Burton Latimer NN15 . . . .92 A2
  Hinton NN11 . . . . .184 B6
  Towcester NN12 . . . . . . .203 C3
  Wellingborough NN8 . . . .130 A3
Heron Ct NN11 . . . . .135 C3
Heronsford NN4 . . . . .174 E8
Herrieffs Farm Rd NN13 .233 F6
Herriotts La NN6 . . . . . . .130 A5
Hertford Ct
  Daventry NN11 . . . . .153 C7
  Northampton NN3 . . . . . .143 A1
Hertford Rd NN15 . . . . . . .91 C6
Hervey Cl NN3 . . . . .142 D2
Hervey St NN1 . . . . .159 E7
Hesketh Cres NN12 . . . . .203 C4
Hesketh Rd NN12 . . . . . .217 E6
Hesperus NN8 . . . . .129 B4
Hester St NN2 . . . . .159 C8
Hever Cl NN10 . . . . .148 C8
Hewlett's Cl NN29 . . . . . .164 D2
Hexham St NN2 . . . . .159 A2
Heygate St LE16 . . . . .31 E4
Hiawatha NN8 . . . . .129 B4
Hickmire NN29 . . . . .146 D3
Hicks Ct NN12 . . . . .203 D4
Hicks Rd NN12 . . . . .203 C4
Hidcote Cl
  Northampton NN4 . . . . . .175 C7
  Wellingborough NN8 . . . .129 D2
Hield Cl NN18 . . . . .36 C1
Higgins Sq NN4 . . . . .158 F2
High Gn NN2 . . . . .141 B3
High Greene NN4 . . . . . . .176 A6
High Hill Ave NN14 . . . . . .70 C7
High Leys The NN6 . . . . .100 F4
High March NN11 . . . . . . .153 E8
High March Cl NN11 . . . . .153 E8
High Slade NN6 . . . . .125 C8
High St Adderbury OX17 . .230 A4
  Astcote NN12 . . . . .188 F7
  Blakesley NN12 . . . . .187 A1
  Blisworth NN7 . . . . .190 D7
  Bozeat NN29 . . . . .164 D2
  Brackley NN13 . . . . .233 F7
  Braunston NN11 . . . . . . .118 B1
  Brixworth NN6 . . . . .106 B3
  Broughton NN14 . . . . . . .90 A4
  Bugbrooke NN7 . . . . . . .172 F7
  Burton Latimer NN15 . . . .92 C2
  Byfield NN11 . . . . .183 D7
  Charwelton NN11 . . . . . .168 A4
  Chelveston NN9 . . . . . . .133 C8
  Clipston LE16 . . . . .67 A8
  Collyweston PE9 . . . . .1 D2
  Corby NN17 . . . . .37 A6
  Cottingham NN6 . . . . .20 C1
  Cranford NN14 . . . . .93 A6
  Creaton NN6 . . . . .104 F4
  Crick NN6 . . . . .100 F5
  Croughton NN13 . . . . . . .238 C8
  Culworth OX17 . . . . .198 C3
  Daventry NN11 . . . . .135 C2
  Deanshanger MK19 . . . . .228 E4
  Denford NN14 . . . . .95 C6
  Desborough NN14 . . . . . .51 A3
  Duddington PE9 . . . . .5 B6
  Earls Barton NN6 . . . . . .144 E4
  Easton on t H PE9 . . . . . . .2 A5
  Ecton NN6 . . . . .143 F3
  Everdon NN11 . . . . .170 A8
  Eydon NN11 . . . . .184 C1
  Finedon NN9 . . . . .111 F5
  Flore NN7 . . . . .155 E5
  Gayton NN7 . . . . .173 E2
  Great Doddington NN7 . .145 E6
  Great Easton LE16 . . . . . .20 D7
  Great Houghton NN4 . . .160 E2
  Greens Norton NN12 . . .202 D8
  Gretton NN17 . . . . .10 B1
  Guilsborough NN6 . . . . . .103 F6
  Harpole NN7 . . . . .157 C6
  Higham Ferrers NN10 . . .132 B5
  Husbands Bosworth LE17 . .45 E5
  Irchester NN29 . . . . .147 B8
  Irthlingborough NN9 . . . .112 A2
  Islip NN14 . . . . .76 B2
  Kettering NN16 . . . . .72 B2
  Ketton PE9 . . . . .1 A5
  Ketton PE9 . . . . .1 A5
  Kislingbury NN7 . . . . . . .157 D4
  Lamport NN6 . . . . .87 D2
  Little Addington NN14 . . .113 B8
  Lois Weedon NN12 . . . . .200 C2
  Long Buckby NN6 . . . . . .121 C4
  Market Harborough LE16 . .31 E3
  Middleton Cheney OX17 . .219 F8
  Milton Malsor NN7 . . . . .174 C4
  Morcott LE15 . . . . .3 A6

High St continued
  Moulton NN3 . . . . .126 C1
  Naseby NN6 . . . . .85 B8
  Northampton,
  Collingtree NN4 . . . . . . .175 C4
  Northampton, Great
  Billing NN3 . . . . .143 C2
  Northampton,
  Hardingstone NN4 . . . . .175 F8
  Northampton,
  Kingsthorpe NN2 . . . . . .141 B3
  Northampton, Weston
  Favell NN3 . . . . .142 D1
  Northampton, Wootton NN4 175 E6
  Olney MK46 . . . . .195 C6
  Paulerspury NN12 . . . . . .216 C8
  Pitsford NN6 . . . . .125 C4
  Podington NN29 . . . . . . .147 E2
  Pottersbury NN12 . . . . . .217 D3
  Preston Capes NN11 . . . .169 D2
  Pytchley NN14 . . . . .90 F2
  Raunds NN9 . . . . .114 D7
  Ringstead NN14 . . . . .95 B3
  Roade NN7 . . . . .191 D4
  Rothwell NN14 . . . . .70 C7
  Rugby CV21 . . . . .99 A8
  Rushden NN10 . . . . .132 B2
  Rushton NN14 . . . . .52 C2
  Scaldwell NN6 . . . . .106 F5
  Shutlanger NN12 . . . . . .190 D1
  Silverstone NN12 . . . . . .214 D4
  Souldern OX6 . . . . .237 E3
  Spratton NN6 . . . . .105 B1
  Stanion NN14 . . . . .37 E2
  Stanwick NN9 . . . . .113 F3
  Stony Stratford MK11 . . .229 C6
  Swinford LE17 . . . . .62 B3
  Syresham NN13 . . . . . . .224 B8
  Thrapston NN14 . . . . .76 D2
  Titchmarsh NN14 . . . . . . .77 D4
  Twywell NN14 . . . . .74 F1
  Walgrave NN6 . . . . .108 A5
  Wappenham NN12 . . . . .213 B8
  Weedon NN7 . . . . .155 B4
  Weldon NN17 . . . . .38 B8
  Welford NN6 . . . . .64 E6
  Wellingborough NN8 . . . .129 F5
  Welton NN11 . . . . .119 E1
  West Haddon NN6 . . . . . .102 C4
  Weston NN12 . . . . .199 F2
  Weston Underwood MK46 .195 B2
  Whittlebury NN12 . . . . . .215 C4
  Wollaston NN29 . . . . . . .146 D2
  Woodford NN14 . . . . .94 D7
  Woodford Halse NN11 . . .184 C6
  Wymington NN10 . . . . . .148 B5
  Yardley Gobion NN12 . . .217 F6
  Yardley Hastings NN7 . . .179 B6
  Yelvertoft NN6 . . . . .82 B3
High St N NN12 . . . . .189 D5
High St Pl NN8 . . . . .129 F4
High St S Olney MK46 . . .195 F3
  Rushden NN10 . . . . .132 B1
  Tiffield NN12 . . . . .189 D4
High St The NN6 . . . . . . .103 D1
High Stack NN6 . . . . .121 C3
High View
  Deanshanger MK19 . . . . .228 E5
  Northampton NN4 . . . . . .175 E6
Higham Cross Rd MK19 . .206 E4
Higham Ferrers Jun &
  Inf Schs NN10 . . . . .132 B6
Higham Park Rd NN10 . . .149 A5
Higham Rd
  Burton Latimer NN15 . . . .92 C1
  Chelveston NN9 . . . . . . .133 B7
  Little Irchester NN8 . . . . .130 E1
  Rushden NN10 . . . . .132 B4
  Stanwick NN9 . . . . .113 F3
Highbridge Rd NN12 . . . .213 A8
Highbrook NN18 . . . . .36 A4
Highcroft LE17 . . . . .45 E6
Highcroft NN12 . . . . .217 E6
Highcross St LE16 . . . . . . .31 C3
Highdown Cl NN4 . . . . . .158 E3
Highfield Duddington PE9 . .5 B7
  Woodford NN14 . . . . .94 C7
Highfield Cotts LE15 . . . . . .3 E8
Highfield Court
  Mews NN13 . . . . .233 E6
Highfield Cres NN15 . . . . .91 C6
Highfield Ct NN13 . . . . . .233 E6
Highfield Gr NN17 . . . . . . .36 F7
Highfield Pk NN6 . . . . . . .104 D4
Highfield Rd
  Daventry NN11 . . . . .135 B3
  Irthlingborough NN9 . . . .112 F2
  Kettering NN15 . . . . .91 B7
  Mears Ashby NN6 . . . . . .128 C4
  Northampton NN1 . . . . . .142 A1
  Rushden NN10 . . . . .131 F1
  Thrapston NN14 . . . . .76 E2
  Wellingborough NN8 . . . .130 B5
Highfield Sch NN2 . . . . . .140 F5
Highfield St Finedon NN9 .112 B5
  Market Harborough LE16 . .31 D3
Highfield Way NN7 . . . . .179 B6
Highfields Polebrook PE8 . .42 F3
  Towcester NN12 . . . . . . .203 B8
Highfields Prim Sch NN15 91 B7
Highgate Gn PE8 . . . . .28 D8
Highgrove Ct NN10 . . . . .132 B2
Highlands Ave NN3 . . . . .142 A4
Highlands Dr NN11 . . . . .135 B5
Highpoint NN13 . . . . .233 F5
Hilda Cl NN16 . . . . .72 E4
Hill Cl NN5 . . . . .140 C1
Hill Crest NN7 . . . . .174 C1

Hill Farm Est NN14 . . . . .113 C8
Hill Farm Rise NN4 . . . . .175 A8
Hill Gdns LE16 . . . . .31 C3
Hill House Gdns NN9 . . . .113 F3
Hill Rd NN11 . . . . .182 C5
Hill Row NN11 . . . . .134 C8
Hill St Brackley NN13 . . . .233 F7
  Kettering NN16 . . . . .72 A3
  Raunds NN9 . . . . .114 D6
  Wellingborough NN8 . . . .129 F4
Hill The Aynho OX17 . . . . .237 C5
  Great Houghton NN4 . . . .160 E2
  Middleton NN18 . . . . .35 B8
  Pury End NN12 . . . . .215 F7
  Syresham NN13 . . . . . . .224 B8
Hill Top NN2 . . . . .141 D4
Hill Top Rd NN9 . . . . .110 D4
Hill View NN11 . . . . .184 C1
Hillary Cl NN11 . . . . .135 B5
Hillary Rd NN10 . . . . .131 F1
Hillberry Rise NN3 . . . . . .143 D4
Hillcrest Ave
  Burton Latimer NN15 . . . .92 B1
  Kettering NN15 . . . . .72 D1
  Market Harborough LE16 . .31 D4
  Northampton NN3 . . . . . .142 A3
Hillcrest Cl NN14 . . . . .76 E3
Hillcrest La LE17 . . . . .45 E5
Hillcrest Rd NN7 . . . . . . .173 E1
Hillcroft View NN12 . . . . .187 B1
Hilldrop Rd NN4 . . . . . . .175 B7
Hillfield Rd PE8 . . . . .41 E6
Hillmorton La
  Clifton u D CV23 . . . . . . .80 A4
  Lilbourne CV23 . . . . .80 F5
  Yelvertoft NN6 . . . . .82 A4
Hillside Chelveston NN9 . .133 B8
  Daventry NN11 . . . . .135 E2
Hillside Ave Kettering NN15 91 C8
  Silverstone NN12 . . . . . .214 E5
Hillside Cl NN29 . . . . .164 D2
Hillside Cotts PE18 . . . . . .97 A4
Hillside Cres
  Nether Heyford NN7 . . . .156 C1
  Weldon NN17 . . . . .38 A7
Hillside Rd Flore NN7 . . . .155 D6
  Market Harborough LE16 . .31 F4
  Nether Heyford NN7 . . . .156 C1
  Piddington NN7 . . . . .177 B1
  Wellingborough NN8 . . . .130 C7
Hillside Terr NN4 . . . . .72 A2
Hillside Way NN3 . . . . . . .160 C8
Hillstone Ct NN9 . . . . . . .113 F3
Hilltop Blisworth NN7 . . . .174 C1
  Dodford NN7 . . . . .154 F5
Hilltop Ave
  Desborough NN14 . . . . . .50 F4
  Kettering NN15 . . . . .91 F5
Hilltop Cl NN14 . . . . .50 F4
Hilmorton Rd CV22 . . . . . .98 F8
Hind Stile NN18 . . . . .36 B5
Hinton Ave NN18 . . . . . . .36 A4
Hinton Cl Hinton NN11 . . .184 B6
  Northampton NN2 . . . . . .141 C5
Hinton Manor Ct NN11 . . .184 B6
Hinton Rd Brackley NN13 .233 E6
  Hinton NN11 . . . . .184 B5
  Northampton NN2 . . . . . .141 C5
Hinton's Cl NN13 . . . . . . .211 F3
Hinwick Cl NN15 . . . . .91 D1
Hinwick Hall Coll of F
  Ed NN29 . . . . .147 C1
Hinwick Rd NN29 . . . . . . .146 E1
Hipwell Ct MK46 . . . . . . .195 F3
Hirondelle Cl NN15 . . . . .139 F1
Historical Transport
  Mus NN10 . . . . .132 B3
Hobbs Hill NN14 . . . . .70 C6
Hobby Cl NN4 . . . . .175 B8
Hocknell Cl NN4 . . . . . . .175 F6
Hockney Ave NN15 . . . . . .92 A7
Hodge Cl NN12 . . . . .188 F6
Hodge Way NN16 . . . . . . .72 D2
Hodges La NN7 . . . . .157 C6
Hodnet Cl NN4 . . . . .175 C7
Hoe Way NN7 . . . . .191 C4
Hogarth Wlk NN18 . . . . . .36 E5
Hogg End OX17 . . . . .196 F6
Hogg La OX17 . . . . .231 F5
Holback La MK18 . . . . . . .226 A5
Holbein Gdns NN4 . . . . . .174 E8
Holbein Wlk NN18 . . . . . . .36 D5
Holbush Way NN9 . . . . . .112 E3
Holcot Cl NN8 . . . . .129 E8
Holcot La Scaldwell NN6 . .107 A5
  Sywell NN6 . . . . .127 E4
Holcot Leys CV22 . . . . . . .98 A7
Holcot Rd Brixworth NN6 .106 D2
  Moulton NN3 . . . . .126 C5
  Walgrave NN6 . . . . .107 F4
Holcutt Cl NN4 . . . . .175 F7
Holden Gr NN11 . . . . .135 B2
Holdenby Cl NN16 . . . . . . .32 B3
Holdenby House Gdns &
  Falconry Ctr NN6 . . . . . .123 C4
Holdenby Rd
  East Haddon NN6 . . . . . .122 C5
  Northampton NN2 . . . . . .141 E4
  Spratton NN6 . . . . .124 B8
Holdings The NN18 . . . . .222 C1
Holes La MK46 . . . . .195 F4
Holiday La MK19 . . . . . . .206 F4

Holland Rise OX17 ....230 F4
Hollands Dr NN15 ....92 C2
Hollies The Moulton NN3 ..126 B2
Wellingborough NN8 ....129 E5
Hollingside Dr NN2 ....141 F3
Hollington Rd NN9 ....114 D6
Hollow The NN6 ....103 E1
Hollow Bank NN3 ....142 E6
Hollow Way Aynho OX17 ...237 D7
Eydon NN11 ....184 B1
Hollow Wood MK46 ....195 E3
Holloway The CV23 ....166 D7
Hollowell Ct NN8 ....129 F4
Hollowell Rd NN6 ....104 D7
Holly Bush La CV23 ....166 D7
Holly Cl Brackley NN13 ....222 F1
Market Harborough LE16 ...31 E4
Holly Hill NN12 ....203 B4
Holly La NN14 ....90 A6
Holly Lodge Dr NN2 ....141 D6
Holly Rd Kettering NN16 ...72 C4
Northampton NN1 ....159 F8
Rushden NN10 ....131 E3
Holly Wlk NN9 ....111 D4
Holman Cl NN3 ....142 D2
Holme Cl
Wellingborough NN9 ....110 E1
Wilbarston LE16 ....34 D8
Holme Way CV23 ....99 D1
Holmecross Rd NN3 ....142 E6
Holmes Ave NN9 ....114 E5
Holmfield Dr NN9 ....114 E6
Holmfield Way NN6 ....121 A4
Holmfield Way NN3 ....160 C8
Holmfirth Wlk NN18 ....36 C4
Holmleigh Cl NN5 ....158 C7
Holmwood Cl NN5 ....140 A4
Holt Rd LE16 ....19 C8
Holyoake Rd NN29 ....146 D2
Holyoake Terr NN6 ....121 C4
Holyrood Ct NN5 ....158 F7
Holyrood Wlk NN18 ....36 C3
Home Acre NN7 ....161 B4
Home Cl Blisworth NN7 ....190 D7
Corby NN18 ....36 B1
Dingley LE16 ....33 A3
Eastcote NN12 ....188 F8
Greens Norton NN12 ....202 B2
Middleton Cheney OX17 ....220 B8
Silverstone NN12 ....214 D4
Staverton NN11 ....152 C8
Towcester NN12 ....203 C5
Home Farm Cl Corby NN18 .53 B8
Creaton NN6 ....104 F5
Northampton NN3 ....161 B8
Home Farm Ct
Adderbury OX17 ....230 B4
Norton NN11 ....136 C4
Home Farm Rd NN14 ....37 E2
Homefarm Gr LE16 ....68 C7
Homefield NN11 ....153 C8
Homestead Cl NN3 ....126 D1
Homestead Ct NN3 ....141 E1
Homestead Dr NN7 ....173 A4
Homestead Rise NN4 ....175 E6
Homestead The NN14 ....74 F1
Homestead Way
Northampton NN2 ....141 E1
Pottispury NN12 ....217 E3
Honey Holme NN6 ....106 A1
Honeypot La LE17 ....45 E5
Honeystones NN3 ....126 C1
Honeysuckle Way NN3 .....160 C6
Honiton Gdns NN18 ....36 E4
Hood Ct NN17 ....36 B8
Hood Rd NN11 ....135 E1
Hood St NN1 ....159 E7
Hood Wlk NN15 ....91 D8
Hookhams Path NN29 ....146 E2
Hope St NN29 ....164 E4
Hopes Pl NN2 ....141 B4
Hopmeadow Ct 2 NN3 ......143 B4
Hoppet Cl NN3 ....53 A8
Hopping Hill Gdns NN5 ...140 D1
Hopping Hill Lower
Sch NN5 ....158 C8
Hopton Fields LE16 ....48 D8
Horn La MK11 ....229 D5
Hornbeam Cl
Podington NN29 ....147 E2
Wellingborough NN8 ....129 E5
Hornbeam Ct
Desborough NN14 ....51 D3
Northampton NN3 ....142 D3
Hornby Rd NN6 ....144 E5
Horncastle Cl NN11 ....135 C6
Horne Cl CV21 ....99 B8
Horrell Ct NN10 ....132 A2
Horrock's Way NN15 ....72 F1
Horse Market
Kettering NN16 ....72 C2
Northampton NN1 ....159 C6
Horse Shoe La LE16 ....32 B6
Horse Well Ct NN3 ....142 C4
Horsefair Cl LE16 ....31 D4
Horsefair Gn MK11 ....229 D5
Horselease Cl NN8 ....53 A8
Horsemoor Sq 6 NN3 ......143 C4
Horsepool The CV23 ....81 A7
Horseshoe
Brixworth NN6 ....106 C2
Creaton NN6 ....104 F5
Horseshoe St NN1 ....159 C5
Horsham Wlk NN18 ....36 B5

Horsley Rd NN2 ....141 C1
Horton Cl OX17 ....220 A7
Horton Cres OX17 ....220 A8
Horton Dr OX17 ....220 A8
Horton Pk OX17 ....177 E2
Horton Rd
Hackleton NN7 ....177 D7
Hackleton NN7 ....177 C2
Middleton Cheney OX17 ...220 A7
Hortons' La NN14 ....76 D2
Hortonsfield Rd NN12 .....77 F5
Hoskyn Cl CV21 ....98 F8
Hospital Hill NN14 ....70 D7
Hothorpe Rd LE17 ....46 D8
Houghton Hill NN4 ....160 A1
Hove Rd NN10 ....132 C2
Hove St NN18 ....36 B4
Howard Ave NN17 ....36 B7
Howard Biley Gdns NN3 ..142 C3
Howard Cl NN11 ....135 D1
Howard Ct 3 NN8 ....130 B5
Howard La NN2 ....141 C8
Howard Rd NN29 ....146 D2
Howard St NN16 ....72 A2
Howard Way LE16 ....31 D1
Howard's Ct NN29 ....146 D2
Howards Mdw PE8 ....13 F7
Howcut La NN7 ....178 E3
Howden Gn NN14 ....50 E4
Howe Cres Corby NN17 ....36 A7
Daventry NN11 ....135 C1
Hoy Wlk NN17 ....21 C1
Hoylake NN8 ....129 C7
Hoylake Dr NN2 ....141 F3
Hudson Cl Corby NN18 ....53 D6
Daventry NN11 ....135 C5
Hudson Dr NN4 ....158 E1
Hulcote NN12 ....203 E8
Hulme Way NN8 ....53 C8
Humber Cl Daventry NN11 134 F4
Northampton NN5 ....140 F2
Humber Gdns NN8 ....129 C6
Humber Wlk NN17 ....21 C6
Humfrey La NN2 ....141 C8
Humphries Dr NN13 ......233 D8
Hunsbarrow Rd NN4 ......158 E4
Hunsbury Cl NN4 ....158 F1
Hunsbury Gn NN4 ....158 D2
Hunsbury Hill Ave NN4 ..158 E3
Hunsbury Hill Ctry
Pk NN4 ....158 F2
Hunsbury Hill Rd NN4 ...158 E1
Hunslet La NN4 ....158 E2
Hunt Cl Brixworth NN6 ...106 B2
Towcester NN12 ....203 C7
Hunt St NN16 ....36 D5
Hunter St NN1 ....159 D7
Hunters Cl
Husbands Bosworth LE17 ..45 E6
Northampton NN2 ....141 D6
Hunters Rd NN17 ....22 C1
Hunters' Way NN6 ....106 B2
Hunting Way PE8 ....14 C4
Huntingdon Gdns LE16 ...31 C1
Huntingdon Rd NN14 .....76 F2
Huntsham Cl NN3 ....160 D7
Huntsmead NN3 ....143 D4
Hurst Cl NN15 ....92 C4
Husbands Bosworth CE
Prim Sch LE17 ....45 E5
Hussar NN11 ....135 B1
Hutchinson Ave NN14 .....90 B3
Hutts Cl NN11 ....183 D7
Huxley Cl NN8 ....129 A4
Huxloe Pl 12 NN16 ....72 B2
Huxloe Rise NN3 ....142 E6
Hyacinth Way NN10 ......148 B7
Hybiscus Cl NN3 ....160 C6
Hyde Cl NN7 ....191 C4
Hyde Dr NN9 ....112 A5
Hyde Rd NN7 ....191 C4

Ibsen Wlk NN18 ....36 A2
Ibstock Cl NN3 ....143 A6
Icknield Dr NN4 ....158 E1
Ideal Bldgs 17 NN1 ......159 C7
Ilex Cl NN4 ....159 F1
Independent St CV23 .....100 A3
Ingleborough Way NN5 ...158 D8
Inglewood Ct NN3 ....143 C1
Inham Cl NN18 ....36 C2
Inkerman Way PE8 ....41 F5
Inlands Cl NN11 ....135 D1
Inlands Rise NN11 ....135 D1
Inlands The NN11 ....135 D1
Inn Yard Ct LE16 ....68 C7
Inwood Cl NN18 ....36 C2
Iona Rd NN17 ....36 C8
Irchester Country
Pk NN29 ....130 F1
Irchester Country Pk
Trail NN8 ....130 D1
Irchester Country Pk
Visitor Ctr NN29 ....130 D1
Irchester Jun & Inf
Schs NN29 ....147 A4
Irchester Narrow Gauge
Rly Mus NN29 ....130 D1
Irchester Rd
Podington NN10 ....147 B4
Rushden NN10 ....131 F2
Wollaston NN29 ....146 F3
Ireton Rd LE16 ....31 D2
Iron Cross NN7 ....167 B2
Iron Pikes NN6 ....106 C1

Irondale Cl NN4 ....158 E3
Ironstone Ct NN9 ....111 F4
Ironstone La NN4 ....158 E3
Ironstone Way NN6 ....106 C3
Irthlingborough Cty Inf
Sch NN9 ....112 E2
Irthlingborough Cty Jun
Sch NN9 ....112 E2
Irthlingborough Huxlow
Sch NN9 ....112 E3
Irthlingborough Rd
Finedon NN9 ....112 B4
Little Addington NN14 ...113 B7
Wellingborough NN8 ......130 E4
Irving Gr NN17 ....36 E8
Ise Rd NN15 ....72 D1
Ise Vale Ave NN15 ....51 B3
Ise View Rd NN14 ....51 B3
Isebrook Ct NN15 ....92 A2
Isebrook Hospl NN8 ......130 B3
Isebrook Sch NN15 ....91 E7
Isham Cl NN2 ....141 D5
Isham Rd Orlingbury NN14 110 A5
Pytchley NN14 ....91 B3
Isley Wlk NN17 ....36 C8
Islington Ct NN12 ....203 D5
Islington Rd NN12 ....203 D5
Ivens La NN12 ....171 C1
Ivy La NN9 ....111 F4
Ivy Rd Kettering NN16 ...72 D4
Northampton NN1 ....159 F8
Ivydene Terr NN14 ....90 A4
Ixworth Cl NN3 ....142 F5

Jackdaw Cl NN3 ....161 C8
Jacklin Ct NN8 ....129 C7
Jackson Cl LE16 ....48 E8
Jackson Rd CV21 ....80 A1
Jackson Way NN15 ....90 F8
Jackson's La NN8 ....129 F5
Jackson's Lane
Flats NN8 ....129 F5
Jamb The NN7 ....37 A6
James Lewis Ct NN3 .....142 C2
James Rd NN8 ....130 A2
James St NN7 ....147 B7
James Watt Ave NN17 ...37 A8
James Watt Cl NN11 .....135 A4
Jardine Cl NN3 ....142 D1
Jarretts Yd NN4 ....175 E6
Jasmine Ct NN16 ....72 D5
Jasmine Gdns NN10 .....148 B7
Jasmine Rd Kettering NN16 72 D4
Northampton NN3 ....143 C5
Javelin Cl NN5 ....158 C8
Jean Rd NN16 ....72 E3
Jellicoe Cl NN11 ....135 E1
Jenkins Rd CV21 ....80 A1
Jenkinson Rd NN12 ......203 D4
Jenner Cres NN2 ....141 B5
Jennings Cl NN11 ....135 D1
Jersey Cl NN8 ....130 B6
Jersey Ct NN3 ....142 F1
Jervis Cl NN11 ....135 E1
Jerwood Way LE16 ....31 F2
Jetty The Creaton NN6 ..104 F4
Hackleton NN7 ....177 B3
Wappenham NN12 ....213 B8
Wardington OX17 ....196 E1
Jeyes Cl NN3 ....126 B1
Joan Pyel Cl NN9 ....131 E8
Job's Yd NN16 ....72 B2
John Beverly Mews NN14 .70 C6
John Clare Cl NN13 ......222 F1
John Clare Ct NN16 .....72 C6
John Clare Way NN17 ....36 D8
John Eagle Cl NN9 ....113 F4
John Gray Rd NN29 ......145 D6
John Pyel Rd NN9 ....112 E1
John Smith Ave NN17 ...70 E7
John St Rushden NN10 ..132 B2
Thrapston NN14 ....76 E2
John White Cl The NN10 .132 C6
Johnhellins Prim
Sch NN12 ....217 D3
Johns Rd NN7 ....157 A1
Johnson Ave NN13 ....233 C8
Johnson Cl NN11 ....135 B4
Jones Cl NN13 ....233 D8
Jordan Cl LE16 ....32 A3
Joseph Priestly
Ct 6 NN11 ....135 C1
Joshua Sq NN4 ....158 F2
Jowett Cl NN15 ....92 A8
Jubilee Ave NN18 ....36 B5
Jubilee Cl Byfield NN11 .183 D7
Islip NN14 ....76 B3
Long Buckby NN6 ....121 A4
Northampton NN4 ....158 F3
Jubilee Cres NN8 ....129 F2
Jubilee Dr NN6 ....108 B5
Jubilee Gdns LE16 ......31 F4
Jubilee Rd NN11 ....135 B2
Jubilee St
Irthlingborough NN9 ....112 E1
Rothwell NN14 ....70 D6
Jubilee Terr Isham NN14 110 F8
Stony Stratford MK11 ...229 C5
Judges Ct NN6 ....104 F4
Judith Rd NN16 ....72 E4
Julian Way NN2 ....141 A3
Junction Rd NN12 ....141 E1
Juniper Cl NN12 ....203 B4
Juniper Ct NN3 ....143 D3

Juniper Thorn NN6 ......106 C1
Jura Cl NN17 ....36 E8
Justin Park LE16 ....48 F7
Jutland Way NN16 ....72 A2

Kane Wlk NN17 ....36 E8
Kangaroo Spinney NN8 ..130 E3
Karlstad Cl NN16 ....36 A2
Kathleen Dr NN16 ....72 E4
Katrine Cl NN17 ....21 B1
Kealdale Rd NN13 ....142 A4
Keating Cl NN15 ....92 A8
Keats Cl Earls Barton NN6 144 F4
Great Houghton NN4 .....160 F1
Keats Dr Kettering NN16 .72 C6
Towcester NN12 ....203 B5
Keats Rd Daventry NN11 .135 B3
Wellingborough NN8 ......129 D4
Keats Way Corby NN17 ...36 C8
Higham Ferrers NN10 ....132 A5
Rushden NN10 ....131 E3
Keble Cl NN11 ....153 B8
Keble Rd NN13 ....233 D8
Kedleston Cl 3 NN4 ....175 C8
Keebles Cl NN14 ....37 E2
Kelburn Cl NN4 ....175 B7
Keld Cl NN10 ....36 D2
Kelmarsh Hall NN6 ......67 F4
Kelmarsh Rd
Arthingworth LE16 ....68 C7
Clipston LE16 ....67 A7
Corby NN17 ....36 C7
Kelmscott Cl NN3 ....143 A5
Kelsall Cl NN15 ....158 B8
Kelthorpe Cl PE9 ....1 A4
Kelvin Gr NN17 ....37 A7
Kemp Ho NN17 ....21 F3
Kemps Rd OX17 ....230 A5
Kenchley Cl NN3 ....142 D4
Rushden NN10 ....132 D1
Wellingborough NN8 ......129 D6
Kendalls Cl LE16 ....34 D5
Kenilworth NN18 ....36 C3
Kenilworth Cl
Daventry NN11 ....135 B1
Northampton NN5 ....158 B8
Rushden NN10 ....132 C1
Kenilworth Dr NN15 ....91 E8
Kenmore Dr NN14 ....51 B2
Kenmuir Ave NN2 ....141 F2
Kenmuir Cres NN2 ......141 F2
Kenmuir Gdns NN2 ......141 F2
Kenmuir Rd NN9 ....111 F4
Kennedy Cl NN11 ....135 E1
Kennel Hill NN14 ....55 F7
Kennel Rd NN12 ....215 C3
Kennel Terr NN6 ....106 D3
Kennels Dr NN12 ....216 E3
Kennels The NN12 ....216 C3
Kennet Cl NN8 ....129 C6
Kennet Gn NN5 ....140 F2
Kensington Cl
Kings Sutton OX17 ......230 F6
Rushden NN10 ....131 E3
Towcester NN12 ....203 B4
Kensington Gdns NN15 ..91 B8
Kensington Wlk NN18 ...36 C3
Kent Cl Corby NN17 .....36 C7
Northampton NN5 ....158 C4
Kent Pl NN15 ....91 D6
Kent Rd Northampton NN5 .140 F1
Rushden NN10 ....132 C3
Wellingborough NN8 ......129 F1
Kent The CV21 ....80 A2
Kentford Cl NN4 ....175 B8
Kentstone Cl NN2 ....140 F4
Kerley Cl NN14 ....90 A3
Kerrfield Est NN5 ......158 C4
Keston Way NN9 ....114 B5
Kestrel Cl NN3 ....142 D1
Kestrel La NN8 ....130 A2
Keswick NN18 ....36 B5
Keswick Dr
Northampton NN3 ....142 C4
Rushden NN10 ....132 C3
Keswick Rd MK19 ....207 B2
Ketco Ave PE9 ....1 B7
Kettering Gdns 2 NN1 ..159 E6
Kettering General
Hospl NN16 ....71 F2
Kettering Parkway NN15 .91 D5
Kettering Rd
Broughton NN14 ....90 B5
Burton Latimer NN15 ....92 B3
Geddington NN14 ....54 A1
Great Harrowden NN9 ...110 E4
Isham NN14 ....91 E1
Islip NN14 ....75 E1
Market Harborough LE16 ..32 B2
Moulton NN3 ....126 F2
Northampton NN1 ....159 E6
Northampton,Spinney
Hill NN3 ....142 A3
Pytchley NN14 ....90 F2
Rothwell NN14 ....70 E5
Stanion NN14 ....37 E2
Walgrave NN6 ....108 C6
Weldon NN17 ....38 B7
Woodford NN14 ....94 B8
Wootherpe PE9 ....2 C8
Kettering Rd N NN3 ....142 C5
Kettering Sta NN16 .....72 A1
Kettle End NN12 ....200 C3
Ketton CE Prim Sch PE9 .1 A5

Ketton Rd PE9 ....1 C3
Kettonby Gdns NN15 ....91 B8
Keyham Ct NN3 ....143 A5
Keys Cl NN11 ....135 D1
Keys La CV23 ....166 E8
Keyston Rd PE18 ....116 D2
Keyte's Cl NN13 ....230 A4
KG House Bsns Ctr NN5 .140 F1
Kielder Ct NN15 ....92 A4
Kieldsen Cl OX17 ......210 B1
Kigston Way LE16 ......31 E6
Kilborn Cl NN8 ....129 E7
Kilborn Rd NN8 ....129 E6
Kilburn Pl NN10 ....132 B4
Kilby Cl NN8 ....129 E3
Killworth Rd CV21 ......99 B7
Kiln La Litchborough NN12 171 C1
Welton NN11 ....135 E8
Kiln Way NN8 ....129 D4
Kilsby CE
Prim Sch CV23 ....100 A3
Kilsby La CV21 ....99 C7
Kilsby Rd Barby CV23 ...99 C1
Crick NN6 ....100 F2
Watford NN6 ....120 B7
Kilvey Rd NN4 ....160 B2
Kilworth Rd
Husbands Bosworth LE17 .45 D4
Swinford LE17 ....62 C4
Kimble Cl NN4 ....175 B8
Kimbolton Ct NN14 .....76 E2
Kimbolton Rd
Chelveston NN9 ....133 D8
Higham Ferrers NN10 ....132 C6
Kinewell Cl NN14 ....95 A3
King Edward Rd NN1 ....159 D6
King George Cres MK11 .229 E6
King John Sch NN14 ....76 D1
King Richard Ct NN4 ...175 C6
King St Desborough NN14 .51 B3
Earls Barton NN6 ....144 E5
Kettering NN16 ....72 C3
Long Buckby NN6 ....121 B4
Maidford NN12 ....186 D5
Northampton NN1 ....159 C6
Stony Stratford MK11 ...229 C6
King Style Cl NN6 ......100 F6
King's Cliffe Endowed
Prim Sch PE8 ....13 F7
King's Ct LE16 ....31 E4
King's Forest PE8 ......13 F7
King's Head Pl LE16 ....31 E3
King's Heath Lower
Sch NN5 ....140 F2
King's La Flore NN7 ....155 F5
Little Harrowden NN9 ...110 B3
King's Rd LE16 ....31 E4
King's Sutton Sta OX17 230 E5
Kingfisher Cl Hinton NN11 184 B6
Northampton NN4 ....175 A7
Kingfisher Ct NN6 ......143 D8
Kingfisher Rd NN13 ....222 E2
Kingfisher Way NN15 ...92 A2
Kings Arms La PE8 .....42 F3
Kings Ave NN10 ....132 C7
Kings Cliffe Rd PE8 ....14 C4
Kings Ct NN14 ....51 B3
Kings Gn NN11 ....153 C7
Kings Heath Mid
Sch NN5 ....141 A2
Kings La Barrowden LE15 .3 F5
Pury End NN12 ....215 F7
Yelvertoft NN6 ....82 B4
Kings Meadow La NN10 .132 B7
Kings Park Rd NN3 ......141 F6
Kings Pk NN7 ....155 A3
Kings Pl NN10 ....132 C2
Kings Rd Oundle PE8 ...42 A6
Rushden NN10 ....132 C2
Kings St NN18 ....130 A6
Kings Stile OX17 ....208 F1
Kings Sutton Prim
Sch OX17 ....231 A5
Kingsbrook NN18 ....36 B3
Kingscroft Ct NN3 .....143 C1
Kingsfield Cl NN5 ......141 A1
Kingsfield Piece NN12 .215 C4
Kingsfield Way NN5 ....141 A1
Kingsland Ave NN2 .....141 D3
Kingsland Cl NN2 ......141 D3
Kingsland Gdns NN2 ...141 C3
Kingsley Ave
Daventry NN11 ....135 B1
Kettering NN16 ....72 B6
Rugby CV21 ....98 F8
Kingsley Dr NN17 ......36 D8
Kingsley Gdns 3 NN4 ..175 C6
Kingsley Lower Sch NN2 141 F2
Kingsley Park Mid
Sch NN2 ....141 D1
Kingsley Park Terr NN2 141 F1
Kingsley Rd
Northampton NN2 ....141 E1
Rothwell NN14 ....70 C7
Silverstone NN12 ....214 E5
Kingsley Sch NN15 .....141 E1
Kingsmead King's Cliffe PE8 13 F8
Northampton NN2 ....141 A5
Kingsmith Dr NN9 ....114 E6
Kingsthorne Distribution
Pk NN16 ....71 E4
Kingsthorpe Ave NN17 ..36 B7
Kingsthorpe CE Lower
Sch NN2 ....141 B3
Kingsthorpe Grove
Lower Sch NN2 ....141 C2

Kingsthorpe Mid
  Sch NN2 . . . . .241 B4
Kingsthorpe Rd NN2 . . . .241 C1
Kingsthorpe Sh
  Ctr **2** NN2 . . . . .241 C1
Kingsthorpe Upper
  Sch NN2 . . . . .241 E5
Kingston Ave MK11 . . . . .229 E5
Kingston Cl
  Blakesley NN12 . . . . .187 B1
  Daventry NN11 . . . . .135 B3
  Long Buckby NN6 . . . . . .121 C4
  Middleton Cheney OX17 . .220 A7
Kingsway
  Northampton NN2 . . . . . .141 B4
  Wellingborough NN8 . . . .129 E2
Kingswell Rd NN2 . . . . . .141 B3
Kingswell St NN1 . . . . . . .159 C5
Kingswood Jun & Inf
  Schs NN18 . . . . .36 C3
Kingswood Pl NN18 . . . . . .36 A3
Kingswood Sch NN18 . . . . .36 A3
Kinross Cl NN3 . . . . .142 A4
Kipling Dr NN12 . . . . .203 B5
Kipling Rd Corby NN17 . . . .36 D8
  Kettering NN16 . . . . .72 C5
Kippell Hill MK46 . . . . . . .195 F5
Kipton Cl NN14 . . . . .70 E7
Kipton Field NN14 . . . . . . .70 E7
Kirby Cl Corby NN18 . . . . . .36 A3
  Northampton NN4 . . . . . .175 F7
Kirby Ct NN15 . . . . .91 C5
Kirby Hall NN17 . . . . .23 C5
Kirby Rd NN17 . . . . .10 C1
Kirkhams Cl NN6 . . . . .82 C3
Kirkstone Wlk **7** NN3 . . .142 C4
Kirkwall NN17 . . . . .21 C1
Kirton Cl NN3 . . . . .143 B5
Kirton End NN3 . . . . .143 B4
Kislingbury CE Prim
  Sch NN7 . . . . .157 D4
Kislingbury Rd
  Bugbrooke NN7 . . . . . . .173 A8
  Rothersthorpe NN7 . . . . .174 A7
Kitchen Gdns NN14 . . . . . .89 F6
Kitelee Cl MK19 . . . . .207 A3
Kites Cl NN4 . . . . .175 A8
Knaphill Cres NN4 . . . . . .158 F4
Knibb Pl NN15 . . . . .91 F6
Knibb St NN16 . . . . .72 C2
Knight's End Rd LE16 . . . . .32 B6
Knight's La NN1 . . . . .141 B3
Knightlands Rd NN9 . . . . .112 F3
Knightley Cl NN11 . . . . . . .183 D7
Knightley Rd NN2 . . . . . . .141 C1
Knighton Cl NN5 . . . . .140 A3
Knightons Way NN6 . . . . .106 C1
Knights Cl Bozeat NN29 . . .164 D2
  Corby NN18 . . . . .36 A5
  Earls Barton NN6 . . . . . .144 E4
Knights Ct
  Northampton NN1 . . . . . .159 F8
  Northampton, Little
   Billing NN3 . . . . .143 B1
  Wellingborough NN8 . . . .129 F5
Knightscliffe Way NN5 . . .140 C4
Knob The OX17 . . . . .231 A5
Knoll St LE16 . . . . .31 C3
Knoll The Brixworth NN6 . .106 C2
  Grendon NN7 . . . . .163 D5
Knowle Cl NN3 . . . . .160 C6
Knowles Cl NN10 . . . . . . .132 D3
Knox Mews NN8 . . . . .130 B4
Knox Rd NN3 . . . . .130 B5
Knuston Spinney NN10 . . .131 C4
Knutsford La NN6 . . . . . . .121 C4
Kylesku Cres NN15 . . . . . .91 E8
Kyoto Cl NN3 . . . . .142 A6

L

Laburnham Cl NN8 . . . . . .129 E5
Laburnum Ct NN11 . . . . . .184 B4
Laburnum Cres
  Kettering NN16 . . . . .72 D4
  Northampton NN3 . . . . . .142 A6
Lace Mews MK46 . . . . . . .195 F4
Laceby Wlk NN3 . . . . .142 F5
Laddermakers Yd NN7 . . .172 E7
Lady Cl NN11 . . . . .153 D3
Lady Croft NN11 . . . . .135 C5
Lady Hollows Dr NN4 . . . .176 A6
Lady Winefride's
  Wlk NN3 . . . . .143 B2
Lady's La
  Mears Ashby NN6 . . . . . .128 B2
  Northampton NN1 . . . . . .159 C6
Ladybower Cl NN16 . . . . . .71 C3
Ladybridge Dr NN4 . . . . . .174 E8
Lake Ave NN15 . . . . .90 F8
Lake Cres NN11 . . . . .135 A2
Lake Wlk Adderbury OX17 . .230 B4
  Northampton NN4 . . . . . .175 C4
Lakeside
  Irthlingborough NN9 . . . .131 D7
  Northampton NN3 . . . . . .143 A4
Lakeside Bglws NN15 . . . . .91 B6
Lakeside Cl NN14 . . . . .76 D3
Lakeside Dr NN3 . . . . .143 B7
Lakeside Lodges NN3 . . . .143 A7
Lakeview Gn NN3 . . . . . . .142 C4
Lambourne Way OX17 . . . .230 B4
Lambrook Dr NN4 . . . . . . .175 C4
Lammas Cl
  Husbands Bosworth LE17 . . .45 E5

Lammas Cl continued
  Orlingbury NN14 . . . . . . .110 A5
Lammas Ctyd NN17 . . . . . .23 A1
Lammas Rd NN17 . . . . . . .23 A1
Lamport Dr NN11 . . . . . . .135 A5
Lamport Hall NN6 . . . . . . .87 D2
Lamport Rd NN6 . . . . .87 E6
Lamva Ct MK11 . . . . .229 F5
Lancaster Cl NN29 . . . . . .146 C3
Lancaster Dr
  Brackley NN13 . . . . .233 E8
  Thrapston NN14 . . . . . . .76 F2
Lancaster Rd
  Kettering NN16 . . . . .72 C3
  Rothwell NN14 . . . . .70 E7
Lancaster St NN10 . . . . . .132 C7
Lancaster Way
  Northampton NN4 . . . . . .159 A1
  Rushden NN10 . . . . .132 C3
Lancers Way NN7 . . . . . . .155 B4
Lanchester Way NN11 . . . .134 C3
Lancum Ho NN8 . . . . .129 E5
Landcross Dr NN3 . . . . . . .160 C7
Landor NN8 . . . . .129 C4
Landor Cl NN11 . . . . .21 D1
Landsdown Dr NN3 . . . . . .142 E2
Landseer Cl CV21 . . . . . . .80 B1
Lane The Ashby St L CV23 . .119 B5
  Denton NN7 . . . . .178 B8
  Eastcote NN12 . . . . .173 A1
  Easton on t H PE9 . . . . . . .2 A5
  Grafton Regis NN7 . . . . . .205 D2
  Rothersthorpe NN7 . . . . .174 B6
  Wappenham NN12 . . . . .213 B8
  Weston by W LE16 . . . . . .18 B4
Lanercost Wlk
  7 Northampton NN3 . . .142 C4
  8 Northampton NN3 . . .142 C4
Laneside Hollow NN4 . . . .175 C6
Langdale Gr NN17 . . . . . . .36 D8
Langdale Rd
  Desborough NN14 . . . . . .50 F3
  Northampton NN2 . . . . . .141 D3
Langdale Wlk LE16 . . . . . .31 E1
Langford Dr NN4 . . . . .175 D5
Langham Pl
  Northampton NN2 . . . . . .159 C8
  Walgrave NN6 . . . . .108 A5
Langham Rd NN6 . . . . . . .114 D7
Langley Cres NN9 . . . . . . .113 B3
Langley Ct NN15 . . . . .92 B2
Langley Way NN15 . . . . . .91 C6
Langport Gn **4** NN18 . . . .36 B6
Langsett Cl Kettering NN16 .71 E3
  Northampton NN3 . . . . . .142 F1
Langton Ct NN18 . . . . .36 B6
Langton Pl NN14 . . . . .91 E1
Langton Rd LE16 . . . . .32 A7
Langton Rise NN17 . . . . . .137 C6
Lansdown Cl NN11 . . . . . .135 D5
Lapford Rd NN18 . . . . .36 E4
Lapland Wlk NN18 . . . . . . .36 B2
Lapstone Ho NN5 . . . . . . .159 A5
Lapwing Cl NN4 . . . . .175 A7
Larch Cl Hinton NN11 . . . .184 A6
  Irchester NN29 . . . . .147 A4
Larch Dr NN11 . . . . .135 C5
Larch La NN5 . . . . .140 B2
Larch Rd Corby NN17 . . . . .21 D1
  Kettering NN16 . . . . .72 C1
Larchwood Cl NN8 . . . . . .129 E5
Lark Rise Brackley NN13 . . .233 E8
  Northampton NN3 . . . . . .143 B4
Larkhall La NN7 . . . . .157 D6
Larkhall Way NN7 . . . . . . .157 C7
Larkhill NN10 . . . . .132 A4
Larkwood Cl NN16 . . . . . . .72 C6
Larratt Rd NN17 . . . . .38 A8
Larwood Ct NN2 . . . . .141 A5
Lasham Ct NN3 . . . . .143 C1
Latham Rd PE8 . . . . .41 F7
Latham St NN14 . . . . .55 F7
Latham's Hospl PE8 . . . . .59 B6
Lathbury Rd NN13 . . . . . . .233 D8
Lathkill St LE16 . . . . .31 F1
Latimer MK11 . . . . .229 E4
Latimer Cl
  Burton Latimer NN15 . . . . .92 C2
  Gretton NN17 . . . . .10 C1
Latimer Cres LE16 . . . . . .31 F2
Latimer Rd NN17 . . . . . . .36 E8
Latimer Sch NN15 . . . . . . .92 A6
Latymer Cl LE16 . . . . .49 E5
Latymer Ct **4** NN1 . . . . .159 C6
Laud's Rd NN6 . . . . .101 A5
Lauderdale Ave NN4 . . . . .159 A2
Laughton Rd LE16 . . . . . . .30 C4
Launcelot Cl NN5 . . . . . . .158 A7
Launde Pk LE16 . . . . .32 A2
Laundry Rd PE8 . . . . .14 C4
Laureate Ho NN11 . . . . . .135 B4
Laurel Ct
  Northampton NN3 . . . . . .142 E3
  4 Wellingborough NN8 . .130 B5
Laurel Rd NN16 . . . . .72 C4
Laurel Valley NN4 . . . . . . .175 D4
Laurels The Ecton NN6 . . . .143 F3
  Moulton NN3 . . . . .126 B2
Laurence Leyland
  Complex (Ind Est) NN8 .130 D4
Lavant Wlk NN3 . . . . .141 F5
Lavender Way NN10 . . . . .148 C8
Lavendon Ct NN15 . . . . . .92 A5
Lavenham Ct NN3 . . . . . . .142 F5
Lavery Ct NN18 . . . . .36 D5

Law's La PE8 . . . . .13 F7
Lawns The Corby NN18 . . . .36 A4
  Kettering NN15 . . . . .72 A1
  Kilsby CV23 . . . . .100 A2
  Northampton NN5 . . . . . .158 E8
Lawrence Cl
  Kettering NN15 . . . . .92 A8
  Raunds NN9 . . . . .114 B5
Lawrence Ct Corby NN18 . . .36 D5
  Long Buckby NN6 . . . . . .121 B4
  22 Northampton NN1 . . .159 C7
Laws Croft NN13 . . . . .233 D7
Laws La NN9 . . . . .111 F4
Lawson Cres NN3 . . . . . . .143 C1
Lawson St Kettering NN16 . .72 C3
  Raunds NN9 . . . . .114 D6
Lawton Rd NN10 . . . . .132 C3
Lawyers Cl NN13 . . . . .233 E2
Laxton Ct NN15 . . . . .92 A5
Laxton Gram Sch PE8 . . . .42 A5
Laxton Jun Sch PE8 . . . . . .42 A5
Laywood Cl NN9 . . . . .114 C7
Laywood Way NN9 . . . . . .131 B8
Lea Rd NN1 . . . . .159 F8
Lea Way NN8 . . . . .129 D3
Leafields NN3 . . . . .160 F8
Leah Bank NN4 . . . . .159 A2
Leah Cl NN18 . . . . .53 A8
Linacre Cl NN3 . . . . .142 F6
Lealand The LE16 . . . . . . .48 B8
Leam The NN11 . . . . .134 F1
Leamington Way NN11 . . . .135 A2
Leatherland Ct **17** NN16 . .72 B2
Leben Sq NN3 . . . . .143 C5
Leckhamstead Rd MK19 . . .228 A3
Ledaig Way NN3 . . . . .142 A4
Ledbury Rd NN15 . . . . . . .91 F5
Lee Way NN9 . . . . .114 D7
Lees Cl NN12 . . . . .215 C4
Lees St NN9 . . . . .112 E1
Leeson Cres NN15 . . . . . . .91 F6
Leeson Rd NN12 . . . . .203 C4
Legg Rd PE8 . . . . .7 D8
Legion Cres NN16 . . . . . . .71 F3
Leicester Cl NN16 . . . . . . .72 A3
Leicester La LE16 . . . . . . .31 D7
Leicester Par NN2 . . . . . . .159 C8
Leicester Rd
  Husbands Bosworth LE17 . . .45 D7
  Market Harborough LE16 . .31 D5
Leicester St Kettering NN16 72 A3
  Northampton NN1 . . . . . .159 C7
Leicester Terr **2** NN2 . . .159 C7
Leighton Pl NN8 . . . . .129 F4
Leighton Rd NN18 . . . . . . .36 E5
Leith Ct NN4 . . . . .158 E3
Lely Ct NN18 . . . . .36 D5
Lennon Cl CV21 . . . . .99 C8
Lennox Wlk NN5 . . . . .140 D2
Lenthall Sq LE16 . . . . .31 E1
Lenton Cl NN14 . . . . .90 A3
Leonardo Ct NN18 . . . . . . .36 D5
Lerwick Way NN17 . . . . . . .36 C8
Leslie Rd NN2 . . . . .159 B7
Lesson Rd NN6 . . . . .106 B1
Lester Ct OX17 . . . . .230 A6
Letts Rd NN3 . . . . .159 B3
Leven Way NN17 . . . . .21 B1
Lever Rd CV21 . . . . .80 A1
Levitts Rd NN7 . . . . .173 A8
Lewin Cl NN14 . . . . .70 B7
Lewin Rd NN18 . . . . .36 E1
Lewis Ho NN14 . . . . .91 E1
Lewis Rd Kettering NN15 . . .91 C7
  Northampton NN5 . . . . . .159 A7
Lexden Cl NN4 . . . . .175 F7
Lexton Cl NN17 . . . . .36 B8
Lexton Gdns OX17 . . . . . .220 B8
Leyland Dr NN2 . . . . .141 A5
Leyland View NN8 . . . . . . .130 D4
Leys Ave Desborough NN14 .51 C3
  Rothwell NN14 . . . . .70 C7
Leys Cl Denton NN7 . . . . . .162 B1
  Long Buckby NN6 . . . . . .121 C4
Leys Gdns NN8 . . . . .130 B6
Leys La NN4 . . . . .160 F1
Leys Rd Earls Barton NN6 . .144 D4
  Pattishall NN12 . . . . . . .172 D1
  Rugby CV21 . . . . .99 C2
  Wellingborough NN8 . . . .130 B6
Leys The Bugbrooke NN7 . .172 E6
  Denton NN7 . . . . .162 B1
  Long Buckby NN6 . . . . . .121 C4
  Orlingbury NN14 . . . . . . .110 A5
  Roade NN7 . . . . .191 D4
  Upper Boddington NN11 . .182 C8
  Welford NN6 . . . . .64 E5
  Woodford NN14 . . . . .94 D7
  Yardley Hastings NN7 . . . .179 A6
Leyside CI NN3 . . . . .143 B5
Leyswell Ct **4** NN3 . . . . .161 A8
Liberty Dr NN5 . . . . .140 C1
Lichfield Cl NN17 . . . . . . .157 D3
Lichfield Dr NN4 . . . . .175 B7
Liddington Way NN2 . . . . .141 B5
Light Foot La LE16 . . . . . . .20 B1
Lilac Cl NN18 . . . . .129 E5
Lilac Gr NN10 . . . . .148 B7
Lilac Pl NN15 . . . . .72 D1
Lilbourne La LE17 . . . . . . .62 B3
Lilbourne Rd CV23 . . . . . . .80 C5
Lilford Pl NN18 . . . . .72 D3
Liliput Rd NN4 . . . . .160 C3
Lilley Homes The NN8 . . . .129 F2
Lilley Terr NN9 . . . . .112 F2
Lillington Ct NN18 . . . . . . .36 B6
Lime Ave Eydon NN11 . . . .184 C1
  Long Buckby NN6 . . . . . .121 C4

Lime Ave continued
  Northampton NN3 . . . . . .142 A1
  Oundle PE8 . . . . .41 F7
Lime Cl Broughton NN14 . . .90 B4
  Hartwell NN7 . . . . .192 C2
Lime Ct NN9 . . . . .112 F2
Lime Farm Way NN4 . . . . .160 F2
Lime Gr Bugbrooke NN7 . . .173 A7
  Wellingborough NN8 . . . .130 A7
Lime Rd Kettering NN16 . . . .72 D6
  Yardley Gobion NN12 . . . .217 E6
Lime St
  Irthlingborough NN9 . . . .112 F2
  Olney MK46 . . . . .195 F3
  Rushden NN10 . . . . .132 B4
Lime Terr NN9 . . . . .112 F2
Lime Tree Mews NN15 . . . .72 B1
Limefields Way NN4 . . . . .175 D6
Limehurst Cl NN5 . . . . . . .140 C1
Limehurst Rd NN5 . . . . . . .158 C8
Limehurst Sq NN5 . . . . . . .158 C8
Limes The
  9 Daventry NN11 . . . . .135 C1
  11 Irthlingborough NN9 . .112 F2
  Stony Stratford MK11 . . . .229 E5
  Thorpe Langton LE16 . . . .17 A5
Limoges Ct NN5 . . . . .140 A2
Lincoln Ct Brackley NN13 . .233 F5
  Market Harborough LE16 . .31 F5
Lincoln Ho NN5 . . . . .159 A5
Lincoln Pk NN13 . . . . .233 F5
Lincoln Rd NN5 . . . . .159 A5
Lincoln St NN2 . . . . .141 C3
Lincoln Way Corby NN18 . . .36 C4
  Daventry NN11 . . . . .153 C8
Lincoln Wlk NN18 . . . . . . .36 C4
Lindale Cl NN3 . . . . .142 B3
Linden Ave
  Higham Ferrers NN10 . . . .132 B6
  Kettering NN16 . . . . .72 C1
Linden Cl NN15 . . . . .72 C1
Linden Rd NN3 . . . . .142 A1
Lindens The NN12 . . . . . . .203 C6
Lindisfarne Dr NN15 . . . . .91 F8
Lindisfarne Rd NN11 . . . . .21 C1
Lindisfarne Way
  Northampton NN4 . . . . . .175 C8
  Thrapston NN14 . . . . . . .76 F2
Lindrick Cl NN11 . . . . .135 E2
Lindsay Ave NN3 . . . . .142 B2
Lindsay Terr NN16 . . . . . . .72 B3
Lindsey Cl PE8 . . . . .14 F1
Lindsey Gdns LE16 . . . . . .48 D8
Lingfield Terr NN2 . . . . . . .141 F2
Lingfield Wlk NN18 . . . . . .36 C1
Lings Lower Sch NN3 . . . . .142 F4
Lings Sch NN3 . . . . .142 F2
Lings Way NN3 . . . . .143 A4
Lingswood Pk NN3 . . . . . .143 A3
Link Rd Northampton NN2 . .141 B6
  Rushden NN10 . . . . .148 B2
Link Way Bugbrooke NN7 . .173 A7
  Towcester NN12 . . . . . . .203 C5
Links Rd NN8 . . . . .130 C6
Links The NN15 . . . . .91 B8
Linley Dr NN14 . . . . .50 F4
Linley Gn NN5 . . . . .158 D8
Linnell Way NN16 . . . . . . .71 F4
Linnet Cl NN8 . . . . .130 A7
Linnet Dr NN15 . . . . .92 A6
Linnet Rd NN12 . . . . .203 C3
Linnetts La NN10 . . . . . . .132 B5
Lismore Cl NN3 . . . . .143 C2
Lismore Wlk NN17 . . . . . . .21 C1
Lister Cl NN17 . . . . .22 A1
Lister Dr NN4 . . . . .158 E1
Lister Rd NN4 . . . . .130 A5
Litchborough Rd
  Farthingstone NN12 . . . . .170 F3
  Grimscote NN12 . . . . . . .169 C8
Litchfield Cl NN16 . . . . . . .72 C6
Little Back La NN11 . . . . . .151 D1
Little Billing Way NN3 . . . .143 A1
Little Bowden Cty Prim
  Sch LE16 . . . . .31 F2
Little Bowden Manor LE16 31 F3
Little Cl NN4 . . . . .124 D1
Little Cross St NN1 . . . . . .159 B6
Little Field NN12 . . . . .189 A8
Little Green PE8 . . . . .28 B3
Little Greeve Way NN4 . . . .176 A6
Little Gull Cl NN3 . . . . . . .142 F6
Little Harrowden Prim
  Sch NN9 . . . . .110 C4
Little Horton House
  Dr NN7 . . . . .177 E2
Little La Aynho OX17 . . . . .237 C2
  Blisworth NN7 . . . . .190 D8
  Great Houghton NN4 . . . .160 E2
  Ravensthorpe NN6 . . . . .103 D1
  Stanion NN14 . . . . .37 E3
  Wollaston NN29 . . . . . . .146 D3
  Yardley Hastings NN7 . . . .179 A7
Little London
  Deanshanger MK19 . . . . .228 E4
  Silverstone NN12 . . . . . .214 D5
Little Mdw NN18 . . . . .36 B1
Little Park St **6** NN8 . . . .130 A5
Little Priel Rd NN7 . . . . . .155 B4
Little St Rushden NN10 . . . .132 C1
  Sulgrave OX17 . . . . .211 A8
  Yardley Hastings NN7 . . . .179 B6
Littledale NN8 . . . . .129 D6
Littlewood Cl NN15 . . . . . .159 A8
Littlewood St NN14 . . . . . .70 E7
Livingstone Cl NN14 . . . . . .70 F7

Livingstone Rd NN11 . . . . .135 C4
Llewellyn Wlk NN18 . . . . . .36 D5
Lloyd Cl NN8 . . . . .130 B8
Lloyd's Rd NN17 . . . . .37 B7
Loach Ct NN3 . . . . .142 A6
Loatland St NN14 . . . . .50 F3
Loatlands Prim Sch NN14 . .50 F3
Lobelia Rd NN16 . . . . .72 C4
Lock La MK19 . . . . .218 E2
Lockcroft Sq **6** NN3 . . . .143 D2
Locks Gn PE8 . . . . .16 A8
Locks The CV21 . . . . .80 B1
Locktons Cl NN12 . . . . . . .201 E2
Lockwood Cl NN2 . . . . . . .141 C4
Loddington CE Prim
  Sch NN14 . . . . .70 D1
Loddington Rd NN14 . . . . .89 F7
Lodge Ave NN4 . . . . .175 C4
Lodge Cl
  Little Houghton NN7 . . . .161 B3
  Northampton NN5 . . . . . .140 B1
Lodge Ct **8** NN18 . . . . . .130 B5
Lodge Farm Ct MK19 . . . . .218 F6
Lodge Farm Ind Est NN5 . .140 C2
Lodge Flats NN16 . . . . . . .122 D5
Lodge Green Rd NN17 . . . .36 E8
Lodge La NN16 . . . . .121 F3
Lodge Park Sch NN17 . . . . .21 B1
Lodge Pk NN12 . . . . .215 C4
Lodge Rd Daventry NN11 . . .135 C2
  Little Houghton NN7 . . . .161 B3
  Rushden NN10 . . . . .148 A8
Lodge Way NN5 . . . . .140 C3
Lodore Gdns NN3 . . . . . . .142 C3
Logan Cres LE16 . . . . .31 C4
Logan Ct LE16 . . . . .31 D4
Logan St LE16 . . . . .31 D3
Logwell Ct NN3 . . . . .142 F1
Loire Ct NN5 . . . . .140 A2
Lombard Way OX16 . . . . .219 A6
Lombardy Ct NN3 . . . . . . .142 D3
Lomond Cl NN17 . . . . .21 C1
Lomond Dr NN15 . . . . .91 F8
London End
  Earls Barton NN6 . . . . . .144 D4
  Irchester NN29 . . . . .147 B8
  Titchmarsh NN14 . . . . . .77 D3
  Upper Boddington NN11 . .182 C8
London Rd Bozeat NN29 . . .164 C3
  Braunston NN11 . . . . . . .118 A1
  Daventry NN11 . . . . .153 D8
  Kettering NN15 . . . . .91 C8
  Little Irchester NN8 . . . . .130 C1
  Northampton, Far
   Cotton NN4 . . . . .159 C2
  Northampton, Wootton NN4 175 D5
  Old Stratford MK19 . . . . .229 C6
  Raunds NN9 . . . . .114 C6
  Roade NN7 . . . . .191 C4
  Stony Stratford MK11 . . . .229 E5
  Towcester NN12 . . . . . . .203 D5
  Wansford PE8 . . . . .8 B3
  Wellingborough NN8 . . . .130 B3
  Willoughby CV23 . . . . . . .117 E3
  Wollaston NN29 . . . . . . .146 D1
Lone Pine Ct NN6 . . . . . . .106 B2
Long Acres **4** NN4 . . . . .175 B8
Long Acres Dr NN9 . . . . . .112 E3
Long Barrow OX17 . . . . . .196 F7
Long Brimley Cl LE16 . . . . .32 B3
Long Buckby Inf
  Sch NN6 . . . . .121 B4
Long Buckby Jun
  Sch NN6 . . . . .121 B3
Long Buckby Rd NN6 . . . . .120 E5
Long Buckby Sta NN6 . . . .121 A2
Long Cl NN18 . . . . .36 B1
Long Croft Rd NN14 . . . . . .37 C3
Long Furlong CV22 . . . . . .98 A8
Long La Olney MK46 . . . . .195 F4
  Warmington PE8 . . . . . . .28 B2
Long Mallows
  Rise **9** 143 C2
Long March NN11 . . . . . . .153 D8
Long March Ind
  Est NN11 . . . . .153 D8
Long Marsh NN8 . . . . .130 B2
Long Marsh Sq NN3 . . . . .143 A6
Long Massey MK46 . . . . . .195 E5
Long Mdw NN4 . . . . .176 B6
Long Mynd Dr NN5 . . . . . .158 D8
Long Row
  Leckhampstead MK18 . . .227 E1
  Woodford NN14 . . . . .94 D7
Long Row Cl NN11 . . . . . .170 A8
Long Street Rd MK19 . . . . .207 A3
Long Wall NN13 . . . . .233 E6
Longburges OX17 . . . . . . .220 B8
Longcroft La LE16 . . . . . . .216 C8
Longdown La CV23 . . . . . .118 B7
Longfellow Dr NN16 . . . . . .72 C6
Longfellow Rd NN8 . . . . . .129 B4
Longford Ave NN3 . . . . . . .161 A8
Longland Ct NN3 . . . . .142 B2
Longland Rd NN3 . . . . . . .142 C2
Longleat Cl LE16 . . . . .32 B3
Longleat Ct **5** NN4 . . . . .175 C8
Longleat Gr NN15 . . . . . . .91 C5
Longmead Ct NN3 . . . . . . .143 B4
Longueville Ct NN4 . . . . . .176 A6
Lonsborough Dr NN15 . . . .90 E8
Lonsdale Rd NN15 . . . . . . .91 B7
Loop Rd PE18 . . . . .97 A3
Lordswood Cl NN4 . . . . . .176 A6
Lorne Ct NN17 . . . . .36 F6

Lorne Rd NN1 ....159 C7
Lorraine Cres NN3 ....142 B5
Lorraine Dr NN3 ....142 C5
Loseby Cl NN10 ....148 A8
Louisa Dr NN16 ....72 E4
Louisa Lilley Homes
  The NN9 ....112 F2
Louise Rd NN1 ....159 D7
Lounts Cres LE16 ....20 D7
Lovap Way NN18 ....36 B1
Lovat Dr NN5 ....158 E7
Lovell Cl NN9 ....114 A4
Lovell Ct 12 NN9 ....112 F2
Lovers La PE5 ....8 F2
Lovett Rd NN11 ....183 D8
Low Farm Pl NN3 ....141 F7
Low Greeve NN4 ....176 A6
Low March NN11 ....153 D7
Lowbury Ct NN4 ....158 E3
Lower Adelaide St NN2 ..159 C7
Lower Bath St NN1 ......159 B6
Lower Cross St NN1 .....159 B6
Lower Ecton La NN3 .....143 D1
Lower End Bradden NN12 ..201 F5
  Hartwell NN7 ....192 C1
  Pytchley NN14 ....91 A1
Lower Farm Rd NN3 ......141 F7
Lower Harding
  St 11 NN1 ....159 C6
Lower Hester St NN2 ....159 C8
Lower Hilmorton
  Rd 5 CV21 ....80 A1
Lower King St NN14 ......51 B3
Lower Meadow Ct NN3 ..142 E5
Lower Mounts NN1 ......159 D6
Lower Pastures NN18 .....53 A8
Lower Priory St NN1 ....159 B7
Lower Rd
  Milton Malsor NN7 ....174 E4
  Stoke Albany LE16 .....34 B5
Lower St
  Desborough NN14 ......51 A3
  Great Addington NN14 ..94 B2
  Great Doddington NN29 .145 E6
  Kettering NN16 ....72 A2
  Pury End NN12 ....216 A7
  Rugby CV21 ....99 C8
  Twywell NN14 ....75 A1
  Willoughby CV23 ......117 D4
Lower Stable Yd NN12 ..203 D5
Lower Steeping NN14 .....51 B2
Lower Thrift St NN1 .....159 F6
Lowick Cl NN8 ....129 C7
Lowick Ct NN3 ....142 C7
Lowick La NN14 ....76 F7
Lowick Rd Aldwincle NN14 .76 E7
  Islip NN14 ....76 B3
Lowlands Cl NN3 ....143 C5
Lowry Cl NN8 ....129 E7
Loxton Cl NN5 ....140 C1
Loyd Rd NN1 ....160 A6
Lubenham CE Sch NN11 ..30 F3
Lubenham Hill LE16 ......31 C2
Lubenham Rd
  East Farndon LE16 ......31 B1
  Marston Trussell LE16 ...30 D1
Lucas Cl NN9 ....131 E8
Lucas La NN7 ....177 B3
Lucas Rd NN4 ....121 A3
Luddington Rd PE8 ......61 C3
Ludlow Cl NN3 ....143 A7
Luffenham Rd LE15 ......3 F6
Lukes Cl NN13 ....212 A5
Lulworth Wlk NN18 ......36 A6
Lumber La NN12 ....216 B7
Lumbertubs La NN3 .....142 D5
Lumbertubs Lower
  Sch NN3 ....142 F3
Lumbertubs Rise NN3 ...142 E3
Lumbertubs Way NN3 ...142 E3
Lunchfield Ct NN3 ......126 C1
Lunchfield Gdns NN3 ...126 C1
Lunchfield La NN3 ......126 C1
Lunchfield Wlk NN3 ....126 C1
Lundie Cl NN3 ....114 D7
Lundy Ave NN18 ....36 E4
Lupin Cl NN16 ....72 D4
Lutterworth Rd
  Northampton NN1 .....160 A6
  Swinford LE17 ....62 B6
Lutton Rd PE8 ....43 C3
Lyddington Rd
  Caldecott LE15, L16 ......9 D2
  Gretton NN17 ....10 A1
Lydia Ct NN10 ....132 A2
Lyle Ct NN8 ....129 C7
Lyncrest Ave NN5 ......158 E7
Lyncrest Lower Sch NN5 .158 E7
Lyncroft Way NN1 ......141 B1
Lyndhurst Rd CV21 ......98 F8
Lyne Wlk NN7 ....177 B3
Lyneford Way NN10 .....147 F8
Lynmouth Ave NN3 .....160 C2
Lynmouth Pl NN18 ......36 E4
Lynton Ave NN2 ....141 C6
Lynton Gr NN7 ....36 F4
Lynwood Cl NN16 ....72 B5
Lytham Cl NN2 ....141 E3
Lytham Ct NN8 ....129 C7
Lyttleton Rd NN5 ....159 A7
Lyveden New Bield PE8 ..57 A7
Lyveden Pl NN16 ....72 D3
Lyveden Rd Brigstock NN14 .55 F7
  Northampton NN4 .....160 A1
Lyveden Way NN18 .....36 C2

M

Macadam Cl NN11 ....134 F5
Macadam Rd NN17 ....22 A1
Mackenzie Rd NN9 ......114 C5
Mackworth Dr NN9 .....111 E4
Mackworth Gn NN9 ....111 F4
Maclean Cl NN3 ....160 C7
Macmillian Way NN3 ...142 B4
Macon Cl NN5 ....139 F2
Madams Gdn NN14 ......70 D7
Madams Hill NN14 ......70 D7
Madeline Cl LE16 ....32 A5
Magdalen Cl
  Daventry NN11 ....153 B8
  Stony Stratford MK11 ..229 D6
  Syresham NN13 ....224 C8
Magdalen Ho MK11 ....229 D6
Magdalen Mdws NN11 ..222 E1
Magdalen Rd CV23 ......117 E3
Magdalene Cl NN14 ......54 B3
Magee St NN1 ....159 F7
Magellan Cl
  Daventry NN11 ....135 C5
  Rothwell NN14 ....70 E6
Magnolia Cl NN3 ......160 D6
Magnolia Dr
  Daventry NN11 ....135 C4
  Rushden NN10 ....148 B7
Magpie La NN13 ....233 E6
Magpie Rd Sulgrave OX17 .210 E2
  Towcester NN12 ......203 C3
Maidencastle NN3 ......143 B3
Maidford Rd Corby NN17 .36 C7
  Farthingstone NN12 ..170 D1
Maidwell Hall (Prep Sch
  for Boys) NN6 ....87 B6
Maidwell Prim Sch NN6 ..87 B6
Maidwell Rd NN6 ....87 D7
Main Dr NN12 ....217 B2
Main Rd Collyweston PE9 ..1 D2
  Crick NN6 ....100 F5
  Dingley LE16 ....33 A3
  Earls Barton NN6 .....144 E6
  Farthinghoe NN13 ....221 B4
  Grendon NN7 ....163 D6
  Kilsby CV23 ....99 F3
  Lowick NN14 ....75 F6
  Middleton Cheney OX17 .220 A8
  New Hackleton NN7 ...163 B8
  Northampton, Duston NN5 .158 B7
  Northampton, Far
   cotton NN4 ....159 B3
  Shutlanger NN12 .....204 D8
  Syresham NN13 ....224 C7
  Upper Heyford NN7 ...156 D4
  Wilby NN8 ....129 B1
Main St Abthorpe NN12 ..201 F2
  Aldwincle NN14 ....76 F8
  Apethorpe PE8 ....14 C4
  Ashby St L CV23 ......119 C5
  Ashley LE16 ....18 E7
  Aston le W NN11 ......182 F2
  Badby NN11 ....152 F2
  Barnwell PE8 ....59 B5
  Barrowden LE15 ....3 F5
  Bradden NN12 ....201 F5
  Bythorn PE18 ....97 D4
  Caldecott LE16 ....21 B8
  Charlton OX17 ....231 F4
  Church Stowe NN7 ....171 E8
  Clifton u D CV23 ....80 A5
  Cold Ashby NN6 ....84 B5
  Cosgrove MK19 ....218 E2
  Cottesbrooke NN6 ....105 A8
  Denton NN7 ....162 B1
  Drayton LE16 ....20 A5
  East Farndon LE16 .....48 B7
  East Haddon NN6 .....122 D5
  Farthingstone NN12 ..170 D3
  Great Addington NN14 ..94 B2
  Great Bowden LE16 .....32 A6
  Great Gidding PE17 .....61 D3
  Great Oxendon LE16 ...48 E3
  Gumley LE16 ....30 A8
  Hannington NN6 ......108 C3
  Hellidon NN11 ....151 D1
  Holcot NN6 ....126 E8
  Little Brington NN7 ...138 C4
  Little Harrowden NN9 .110 C4
  Loddington NN14 ......70 C1
  Lubenham LE16 ....30 F3
  Lyddington LE15 ....9 A7
  Lyddington LE15 ....9 C7
  Medbourne LE16 ....19 A7
  Middleton LE16 ....35 C8
  Orton NN14 ....70 A3
  Polebrook PE8 ....43 A3
  Rockingham LE16 ......21 B4
  Slipton NN14 ....75 A3
  Southwick PE8 ....26 B5
  Sutton Bassett LE16 ...18 A1
  Theddingworth LE17 ...46 D8
  Thurning PE8 ....60 D3
  Turweston NN13 ......234 C8
  Upper Stowe NN7 ....171 F6
  Wadenhoe PE8 ....58 A4
  Wakerley LE15 ....4 A4
  Watford NN6 ....120 C6
  Willoughby CV23 .....117 E3
  Woodend NN12 ....200 F7
  Woodnewton PE8 ......14 E1
  Yarwell PE8 ....15 F8
Malabar Fields NN11 ...153 B8
Malborough Way NN17 ..217 F5
Malcolm Dr NN5 ....158 E7

Malcolm Rd NN2 ....141 F2
Malcolm Terr NN2 ......141 F2
Malham Ct NN8 ....129 D6
Mall The NN16 ....72 B2
Mallard Cl
  Earls Barton NN6 .....144 F5
  Higham Ferrers NN10 ..132 C8
  Northampton NN4 ....158 F2
  Thrapston NN14 ....76 D3
Mallard Dr
  Burton Latimer NN15 ...92 A2
  Hinton NN11 ....184 B6
Mallery Cl NN10 ....132 D3
Malletts Cl MK11 ......229 E5
Mallory Way NN11 .....135 C5
Mallory Wlk NN11 .....141 F5
Mallows Dr NN9 ....114 C7
Malmo Cl NN10 ....36 A2
Malpas Dr NN5 ....158 B8
Malt La NN13 ....224 C8
Malt Mill Cl CV23 ......100 A2
Malthouse Ct NN12 ....203 C6
Malting La NN14 ....54 A3
Malting Way NN7 ......192 D1
Maltings PE8 ....42 A6
Maltings Rd NN17 ......10 B1
Maltings The Ashley LE16 ..18 F3
  Rothwell NN14 ....70 C7
  Wollaston NN29 ......146 D3
  Wothorpe PE9 ....2 E8
Malton Wlk NN18 ......36 B5
Malvern Cl NN16 ....72 B7
Malvern Dr MK11 ......229 F4
Malvern Gr NN5 ....158 D8
Malzor La NN7 ....174 E4
Manchester Rd NN29 ..146 C3
Manfield Health
  Campus NN3 ....142 B4
Manfield Rd NN1 ......160 A7
Manfield Way NN3 .....142 A7
Manitoba Cl NN18 ......36 B3
Manitoba Pl NN11 .....184 C1
Manitoba Way NN11 ...184 C1
Manning Ct NN3 ......142 C7
Manning Rd NN3 ......142 C7
Manningham Rd NN9 ..114 A4
Mannings Rise NN10 ...132 C1
Mannings St NN1 ......132 C1
Mannington Gdns NN4 .175 C7
Mannock Rd NN8 ......129 E3
Manor Cl
  Charwelton NN11 ....168 A4
  Cosgrove MK19 ......218 E2
  Great Addington NN14 ..94 B2
  Great Harrowden NN9 .110 D2
  Hanslope MK19 ......207 A2
  Harpole NN7 ....157 C6
  Irchester NN29 ......147 B8
  Isham NN14 ....110 F8
  Middleton Cheney OX17 .220 B7
  Roade NN7 ....191 E4
  Thrapston NN14 ......76 D2
Manor Ct Brackley NN13 .233 E8
  Cottingham LE16 ......20 C1
  Little Harrowden NN9 .110 C4
  Northampton NN2 ....141 B3
  2 Wellingborough NN8 .130 B5
Manor Dr Corby NN18 ..36 A4
  Irthlingborough NN9 ..113 A2
Manor Farm PE8 ....14 E2
Manor Farm Cl CV23 ...99 C2
Manor Farm Ct
  Cogenhoe NN7 ....162 A6
  Titchmarsh NN14 ......77 C4
Manor Farm Rd
  Northampton NN3 ....143 B2
  Rauns NN9 ....114 E6
Manor Gdns Norton NN11 .136 C4
  Pytchley NN14 ....90 F2
  Stanwick NN9 ....114 A3
Manor Ho The NN14 ....76 D2
Manor House Cl NN6 ..144 E5
Manor House Mus NN16 ..72 B1
Manor La
  Farthinghoe NN13 ....221 B4
  Newnham NN11 ......153 A4
  Wymington NN10 .....148 A5
Manor Pk Claydon OX17 .181 D1
  Nether Heyford NN7 ..156 C2
Manor Pl NN15 ....91 B8
Manor Rd Brackley NN13 .233 E7
  Daventry NN11 ....135 D1
  Earls Barton NN6 .....144 E5
  Great Bowden LE16 ...32 A6
  Grendon NN7 ....163 D5
  Grimscote NN12 .....188 A8
  Hanging Houghton NN6 .106 C8
  Hinton NN11 ....184 B6
  Kilsby CV23 ....100 A3
  Mears Ashby NN6 ....128 B2
  Medbourne LE16 ......19 A7
  Moulton NN3 ....142 C8
  Northampton NN2 ....141 B3
  Pitsford NN6 ....125 D5
  Rothwell NN14 ....70 B7
  Rushden NN10 ....148 B8
  Rushton NN14 ....52 C2
  Spratton NN6 ....105 B1
  Stanion NN14 ....37 E2
  Staverton NN11 ......152 B7
  Sulgrave OX17 ....210 F8
  Sutton PE5 ....8 F2
  Weedon NN7 ....155 B3
Manor St NN9 ....114 D6
Manor The NN11 ......199 C7
Manor View PE9 ....1 A6
Manor Way
  Higham Ferrers NN10 ..132 C5

Manor Way continued
  Yardley Gobion NN12 ..217 E6
Manor Wlk
  Hanging Houghton NN6 .106 C8
  Market Harborough LE16 .31 E3
  Nether Heyford NN7 ..156 C2
Manorfield Cl NN3 .....161 B8
Manorfield Rd NN3 ....161 B8
Manorhouse Gdns NN9 .114 D6
Mansard Cl NN5 ....158 E6
Manse Cl MK11 ....229 D6
Mansel Cl NN3 ....142 A6
Mansion Hill OX17 ....219 F8
Mansfield Rd NN18 .....36 B6
Manton Cl NN10 ....132 C2
Manton Rd Corby NN11 ..22 A2
  Irthlingborough NN9 ..112 E2
  Rushden NN10 ....132 C1
Manton Spinney NN10 .131 C8
Maple Cl Brackley NN13 .222 F1
  Bugbrooke NN7 ......172 F7
  Hinton NN11 ....184 A6
  Towcester NN12 .....203 B4
Maple Ct NN17 ....21 E1
  Rushden NN10 ....132 C2
Maple Dr NN8 ....129 E5
Maple Rd Kettering NN16 .72 D4
  Rushden NN10 ....132 C2
Maple Wood NN10 ....148 B7
Maples The NN11 .....135 D1
Mapletoft St NN9 .....114 C5
Mapperley Dr NN3 ....160 F8
Marchwood Cl NN3 ...142 F6
Marconi Ctyd NN17 .....22 B1
Mare Fair NN1 ....159 C5
Marecroft LE16 ....66 F7
Margaret Ave NN8 ....129 E2
Margaret Rd
  Kettering NN16 ....72 E3
  Twyford OX17 ....230 B5
Margaret St NN1 ......159 D7
Marion Sq NN11 ....72 E3
Maritime Way NN11 ..135 E1
Marjoram Cl NN4 .....175 D6
Market Cross NN9 ....112 F2
Market Harborough CE
  Prim Sch LE16 ....31 D3
Market Harborough
  District Hospl LE16 ...31 D2
  Farndon Fields Prim
   Sch LE16 ....48 E8
Market Harborough
  Mus LE16 ....31 E3
Market Harborough
  Ridgeway Prim Sch LE16 .31 F5
Market Harborough
  Sta LE16 ....32 A3
Market Hill NN14 ....70 D7
Market Pl Brackley NN13 .233 E6
  Kettering NN16 ....72 B1
  Long Buckby NN6 ....121 B4
  Olney MK46 ....195 F3
  Oundle PE8 ....42 A5
Market Rd NN16 ....76 D2
Market Sq Hanslope MK19 .207 A2
  Higham Ferrers NN10 ..132 C6
  Northampton NN1 ....159 C6
  Stony Stratford MK11 ..229 D5
  3 Wellingborough NN8 .130 A4
Market St Kettering NN16 .72 B2
  Northampton NN1 ....159 E7
  Wellingborough NN8 ..130 A4
Market Street
  Mews 10 NN16 ....72 B2
Market Wlk NN1 ......159 E7
Markham Cl NN5 ......140 C1
Markham Wlk NN18 ....36 B5
Marks Cl NN3 ....114 A3
Marlborough Ave NN9 .129 D7
Marlborough Cl
  Kettering NN15 ....72 F1
  Kings Sutton OX17 ..230 F6
Marlborough Croft NN13 .233 F6
Marlborough Rd NN5 ..159 A6
Marlborough Way LE16 .31 E5
Marlow Cl NN11 ......135 C5
Marlow Ct Corby NN18 ..36 B5
  Medbourne LE16 ......19 A8
Marlow Rd NN12 .....203 D5
Marlowe Cl NN4 ......175 B7
Marlstones NN4 ......158 D2
Marnock Sq 3 NN4 ...158 F2
Marquee Dr NN3 ......160 F7
Marriots Rd NN6 .....121 C3
Marriott Cl NN9 ......131 E8
Marriott St NN2 ......159 C8
Marseilles Cl NN5 ....139 F1
Marsh Cl NN6 ....101 A5
Marsh La NN9 ....113 A2
Marsh The NN6 ....101 A5
Marshall's Dr NN6 ....114 C6
Marshleys Ct NN3 ....143 B5
Marshwell Ct 5 NN3 ..161 A8
Marsons Dr NN6 ......100 F5
Marston Hill
  Marston St L OX17 ...210 B3
  Priors Marston CV23 ..166 F7
Marston Rd
  Greatworth OX17 ....210 E2
  Lubenham LE16 ....30 D2
Marston Trussell Rd LE16 .47 F7
Marston NN11 ....135 C1
Martel Cl NN5 ....157 F8

Martha Wallis Ct 11 NN16 .72 B2
Martial Daire Bvd NN13 .233 E8
Martin Cl NN10 ....132 B4
Martin Rd NN15 ....91 C7
Martindale NN2 ....140 F5
Martins La NN7 ....175 E8
Martins Rd NN7 ......177 A1
Marwood Cl NN3 .....160 C7
Masefield Cl NN8 .....129 C4
Masefield Dr NN10 ...131 E3
Masefield Rd NN16 ....72 C5
Masefield Way Corby NN17 .36 E2
  Northampton NN2 ...141 D2
Mason Cl Oundle PE8 ...42 A5
  Thrapston NN14 ......76 D1
Massey Cl NN3 ....175 E8
Matchless Cl NN5 ....140 A1
Matlock Way NN14 .....50 E4
Matson Cl NN14 ....70 B6
Matson Ct NN9 ....114 E7
Matthews Cl NN14 .....52 C2
Mauduit Cl MK19 ....207 A3
Maunsell Rise NN14 ...70 B6
Mauntley Ave NN14 ...55 F7
Maurice Rd LE16 ....48 D8
Mawsley La NN14 ......89 C8
Maxwell Wlk NN18 .....36 E5
Maybank NN11 ....153 B8
Maybush Wlk MK46 ..195 E5
Mayfield Rd
  Daventry NN11 ......135 C3
  Desborough NN14 ....51 C3
  Northampton NN3 ...142 B3
  Ringstead NN14 ....95 A3
  Wellingborough NN8 .130 D8
Maylan Rd NN17 ....21 F3
Mays Way NN12 ......217 D3
Mazewood Gate PE8 ...13 E7
Mazewood Gate PE8 ...13 E7
MCgibbon Wlk NN9 ...131 D8
MCinnes Way NN9 ....114 D7
Meacham Cl NN14 ......90 A3
Mead Rd NN15 ....90 F8
Meadow Cl
  Higham Ferrers NN10 ..132 B6
  Market Harborough LE16 .31 F4
  Northampton NN5 ...140 E2
  Ringstead NN14 ....95 A3
  Wellingborough NN8 .130 D8
Meadow Ct
  6 Kettering NN16 ......72 B2
  Towcester NN12 .....203 C5
Meadow Dr NN10 ......132 B6
Meadow Gate PE8 .....14 E2
Meadow La Denford NN14 ..95 C6
  Little Houghton NN7 .161 A4
  Rauns NN9 ....114 A6
  Thornhaugh PE8 ....7 F5
Meadow Rd Kettering NN16 .72 A2
  Rothwell NN14 ....70 C6
Meadow Rise NN12 ...189 D4
Meadow St LE16 ....31 E4
Meadow View
  Adderbury OX17 ....230 A4
  Great Addington NN14 ..94 C3
  Higham Ferrers NN10 ..132 A6
  Potterspury NN7 .....217 D3
Meadow Way NN9 ....112 F1
Meadow Wlk
  Higham Ferrers NN10 ..132 B6
  9 Irthlingborough NN9 .112 F2
Meadowlands NN9 ....110 B3
Meadows The NN15 ..110 E1
Meadowside Inf Sch .92 B2
Meadowside Jun
  Sch 92 B2
Meadslade NN7 ......192 D2
Meadway Bugbrooke NN7 .172 F7
  Northampton NN3 ...160 D8
Meadway NN15 ....91 D8
Mears Ashby Prim
  Sch NN6 ....128 B2
Mears Ashby Rd
  Earls Barton NN6 ....144 C6
  Wilby NN8 ....129 A1
Medbourne Cl NN3 ...142 B7
Medbourne Rd Ashley LE16 .18 E4
  Drayton LE16 ....19 E4
  Medbourne LE16 ......18 C8
Medellin Hill NN3 ....142 F6
Medina Rd NN17 ....21 C1
Medinah Cl NN4 ......175 D5
Medlicott Cl NN18 ....53 A8
Medway Cl
  Market Harborough LE16 .32 A3
  Northampton NN5 ...140 E2
Medway Dr
  Northampton NN5 ...140 F2
  Wellingborough NN8 .129 C6
Medway Ho PE8 ....42 A6
Medway The NN11 ...135 A1
Medwin Cl NN3 ....129 B4
Meeting La
  Burton Latimer NN15 ...92 C2
  Corby NN17 ....37 B7
  Irthlingborough NN9 .112 F2
  14 Kettering NN16 .....72 B2
  Northampton NN5 ...158 C2
  Rothwell NN14 ....70 C6
  Towcester NN12 .....203 C6
Meissen Ave NN14 .....50 F3
Melbourne Ho 4 NN5 .159 A6
Melbourne La NN5 ...158 C6
Melbourne Rd NN5 ...158 F6
Melbourne St 3 NN1 ..159 F6
Melbourne Wlk 4 NN1 .159 F6
Melbury La NN3 ......143 B3
Melbury Pl NN3 ......143 B3
Melchbourne Rd MK44 .149 F4
Melchester Cl NN4 ...175 E7

Meldon Cl NN4 ....175 C8
Mellor Rd CV21 ....99 B8
Melloway Rd NN10 ....131 E2
Melrose Ave NN5 ....158 E7
Melrose Cl NN15 ....91 F8
Meltham Cl NN3 ....142 F1
Melton Rd NN8 ....130 C5
Melton Rd N NN8 ....130 B5
Melton St NN16 ....72 B3
Melville St NN1 ....159 F7
Membris Way NN11 .....184 A6
Mendip Cl NN16 ....72 B5
Mendip Ct NN11 ....135 B5
Mendip Rd NN5 ....158 D7
Meon Cl NN17 ....21 C1
Meon Way NN5 ....158 D8
Mercer Ct CV22 ....98 F8
Mercer's Row 3 NN1 ...159 C5
Mercia Gdns NN3 ....142 C1
Mercury Dr NN4 ....160 A2
Mere Cl
  Brafield-on-t-G NN7 ...161 D2
  1 Northampton NN4 ...175 B8
Mere Way NN4 ....175 C8
Merefields NN9 ....112 E3
Merestone Hos OX17 ...210 B1
Merestone Rd NN18 .....36 D3
Mereway Lower
  Sch NN4 ....159 C1
Mereway Mid Sch NN4 ..175 C8
Mereway Upper Sch NN4 159 B1
Merlin Gr 5 NN4 ....175 B8
Merry Hill NN4 ....158 E2
Merry Tom La NN6 .....124 D4
Merrycot La NN6 ....82 B4
Merrydale Sq NN3 ......143 A6
Mersey Gn NN17 ....21 C1
Mershe Cl NN4 ....175 F7
Merthyr Rd NN5 ....159 A8
Merton Cl NN13 ....233 D8
Merton Rd NN11 ....153 B7
Mescalero NN4 ....141 C4
Meshaw Cres NN3 ......160 B7
Methodist
  Homestead NN2 ......141 E1
Mews Cotts LE16 ....48 E3
Mews The
  Great Bowden LE16 ....31 E7
  Long Buckby NN6 .....121 B4
  Northampton NN3 .....160 D8
  4 Rugby CV21 ....80 A1
Mickle Hill PE18 ....116 D7
Mickleborough Cl LE16 ..18 B3
Micklewell La NN3 .....142 F6
Middle Grass NN9 .....112 E3
Middle Greeve NN4 ....176 A6
Middle La LE16 ....34 B4
Middle March NN11 ....153 D8
Middle St Elton PE8 .....28 D8
  Foxton LE16 ....30 E8
  Isham NN14 ....110 F8
  Kilsby CV23 ....100 A3
  Nether Heyford NN7 ...156 C2
Middledale Rd LE16 ....32 A3
Middlemarch 5 NN3 ...143 B4
Middlemead NN3 ......143 A1
Middlemore NN3 ......142 F6
Middlethorpe NN12 ...200 B2
Middleton Cheney Cty
  Prim Sch OX17 ....219 F8
Middleton Cl
  Banbury OX16 ....219 A7
  Northampton NN2 .....141 C5
Middleton Rd Ashley LE16 .19 B3
  Banbury OX16 ....219 A7
  Bringhurst LE16 ....20 C4
  Chacombe OX17 ......208 E4
Middlewell Ct 2 NN3 ..142 F1
Middlewich Cl NN11 ...135 C6
Midfield Ct NN3 ....142 E5
Midland Bsns Ctr NN10 .132 C6
Midland Rd
  Higham Ferrers NN10 ..132 C6
  Olney MK46 ....195 F5
  Raunds NN9 ....114 E7
  Rushden NN10 ....132 A3
  Thrapston NN14 ....76 C1
  Wellingborough NN8 ..130 B4
Midway OX17 ....209 A1
Milbury NN6 ....144 F3
Milby La NN14 ....54 A2
Mildmay Cl PE8 ....41 E5
Mile St NN29 ....164 D3
Miles Cl NN9 ....114 B5
Miles La NN6 ....121 C4
Miles Well Ct NN3 .....142 D3
Milford Ave MK11 .....229 E4
Military Rd NN1 ....159 D7
Military Road Lower
  Sch NN1 ....159 D7
Milking Slade Rd PE17 ..61 F3
Mill Cl Braunston NN11 ..118 B1
  Corby NN18 ....36 B1
  Raunds NN9 ....114 C6
Mill Dale Rd NN15 ......91 D8
Mill Est NN10 ....148 B7
Mill Fields NN10 ......132 B7
Mill Hill Corby NN18 ....53 B7
  Lubenham LE16 ....30 E3
Mill Hill Rd LE16 ......31 F3
Mill Ho Brackley NN13 ..233 E6
  6 Northampton NN2 ..159 C7
Mill La Adderbury OX17 ..230 A3
  Barrowden LE15 ....4 A5
  Brackley NN13 ....234 A6
  Brigstock NN14 ....55 F7
  Caldecott LE16 ....21 B8
  Chipping Warden OX17 .196 F6

Mill La continued
  Cogenhoe NN7 ....162 A7
  Croughton NN13 ......238 C7
  Greens Norton NN12 ..202 E7
  Grimscote NN12 ......172 B1
  Isham NN14 ....91 F1
  Islip NN14 ....76 C3
  Ketton PE9 ....1 A5
  Kings Sutton OX17 ....230 F4
  Kislingbury NN7 ......157 D3
  Lowick NN14 ....75 F6
  Northampton NN2 .....159 B7
  Northampton,
   Kingsthorpe NN5 .....141 B2
  Old NN6 ....88 E3
  Oundle PE8 ....27 B1
  Stoke Bruerne NN12 ..191 A1
  Stony Stratford MK11 .229 D5
  Wadenhoe PE8 ....58 A3
  Westbury NN13 ....234 F4
  Yarwell PE8 ....16 A7
Mill Mdw NN2 ....141 D5
Mill Rd Bozeat NN29 ...164 C2
  Cottingham LE16 ....20 C2
  Great Gidding PE17 ....61 E3
  Gretton LE15, NN17 ....9 F2
  Islip NN14 ....76 B3
  Kettering NN16 ....72 C2
  Kislingbury NN7 ......157 D3
  Northampton NN2 .....159 C7
  Oundle PE8 ....41 F5
  Wellingborough NN8 ..130 B5
  Wellingborough NN8 ..131 B7
  Whitfield NN13 ....223 E4
  Woodford NN14 ....94 C7
Mill Rd Ind Est NN8 ...130 C6
Mill Road Pas 3 NN16 ..72 C2
Mill St PE9 ....5 B6
Millais Rd NN18 ....36 E5
Millbank NN3 ....143 D2
Millbrook Cl NN5 .....159 A4
Millbrook Jun & Inf
  Schs NN15 ....91 F8
Milldale Gdns NN15 ....91 D8
Miller Hill NN4 ....158 E2
Miller Rd NN15 ....92 B1
Miller Way NN17 ....36 C8
  Market Harborough LE16 .31 D3
Miller's Cl Finedon NN9 .112 A5
Miller's Yd LE16 ....31 E3
Millers Cl
  Lower Boddington NN11 182 C5
  Rushden NN10 ....131 F2
Millers La NN8 ....145 F8
Millers Pk NN8 ....130 A1
Millfield Ave LE16 ......20 D1
Millfields PE8 ....41 F6
Millfields Ave CV21 .....98 F8
Millglade The NN11 .....91 F1
Millholme Rd NN14 .....51 B2
Mills Cl NN6 ....144 F4
Millside NN2 ....141 D5
Millstone Cl NN4 ......158 D2
Millway NN5 ....158 C6
Millway Mid Sch NN5 ..158 D6
Milner Rd NN9 ....111 F4
Milthorpe NN2 ....200 B2
Milton Ave NN8 ....129 C3
Milton Bridge NN4 ....176 A6
Milton Ct Kettering NN16 ..72 C5
  Milton Malsor NN7 ...174 E3
Milton Parochial Prim
  Sch NN7 ....174 E4
Milton Rd Corby NN17 ..36 C8
  Daventry NN11 ....135 B2
  Gayton NN7 ....173 F2
  Little Irchester NN8 ...130 C1
  Oundle PE8 ....41 F5
Milton St
  Higham Ferrers NN10 ..132 B5
  Northampton NN2 .....141 F1
  Milton St N NN2 ......141 E1
Milton Terr PE8 ....44 C4
Milverton Cres NN3 ...160 D7
Minden Cl NN18 ....35 F2
Minehead Cl NN18 .....36 A6
Minerva Way NN8 .....129 D5
Minster Ho 2 NN1 ....159 D6
Minton Cl NN14 ....50 F3
Mirfield Cl NN18 ....36 C5
Mitchell Cl NN5 ....140 D2
Mitchell Rd NN17 ......22 B2
Mitchell St NN16 ....72 C5
Mitchison Cl CV23 ....118 C3
Mixbury Rd NN13 ......233 F2
Moat Farm Dr CV21 ....99 A7
Moat La NN12 ....203 C6
Moat Pl NN1 ....159 B6
Moat Yd NN12 ....203 C6
Mobbs Miller Ho NN1 .160 A7
Moffatt Terr NN1 ......130 A5
Molesworth Bglws PE9 ..1 A6
Monarch Rd NN2 ......141 C1
Monarch Terr NN2 ....159 C8
Monk's Hall Rd NN1 ...159 F7
Monks Park Rd NN1 ...159 F7
Monks Pond St NN1 ...159 B6
Monks Rd NN29 ....146 D3
Monks Way Corby NN18 ..36 A4
  Crick NN6 ....101 A4
  Wellingborough NN8 ..130 A3
Monkswood NN12 .....214 C4
Monmouth Rd NN5 ....159 A7
Monson Way PE8 ....41 E2
Montabaur Rd NN13 ...234 A7
Montagu Ct NN15 ......91 D5

Montagu Sch NN16 .....72 D5
Montagu St NN16 ......72 C2
Montagu Terr PE8 ......59 B6
Montague Cres NN5 ...140 D2
Montague Ct NN4 ....76 D2
Montague Dr CV23 ....100 A3
Montague St NN10 ....132 A2
Montcalm Cl NN15 .....72 F1
Montfort Cl NN5 ......158 E6
Montgomery Cl NN15 ..72 E1
Montrose Cl LE16 ......31 D1
Montrose St NN16 ......36 F6
Montsaye Sch NN14 ....70 B7
Moonshine Gap NN6 ..128 D6
Moor End PE8 ....60 D3
Moor Field NN12 ......203 B5
Moor La CV23 ....117 D3
Moor Rd NN10 ....132 A2
Moore Cl Corby NN17 ..36 D8
  Kettering NN15 ....92 A7
Moore St NN7 ....141 F1
Moorehouse Way NN15 ..90 E8
Moorend Rd NN12 .....217 E6
Moores Cl NN7 ....172 F7
Moores Hill MK46 .....195 F5
Moorfield Gn NN6 ......70 B6
Moorfield Rd NN14 .....70 B6
Moorfield Sq NN3 .....143 A6
Moorings The NN14 ....94 E6
Moorland Cl NN3 .....142 E2
Moorlands NN8 ....129 D7
Moors Dr The OX17 ...219 F8
Morcott Rd LE15 ....3 D5
Mordaunt La NN5 ....140 D1
More Rd NN11 ....135 B4
Morehay La
  King's Cliffe PE8 ....13 E6
  King's Cliffe PE8 ....13 F7
Moreton Ave NN6 .....129 D2
Moreton Rd NN11 .....184 C1
Moreton Way NN2 ....141 C5
Morgan Cl NN3 ....143 C4
Morgans Cl PE8 ....43 A3
Morgaunt Cl NN14 .....75 E6
Moriston Cl NN17 ......21 C1
Morland Rd NN18 ......36 E5
Morley St Kettering NN16 ..72 C4
  Market Harborough LE16 .31 D3
Morley Wlk NN17 ......36 C8
Morris Ave NN10 ......131 F1
Morris Cl NN8 ....129 A6
Morris Rd Daventry NN11 ..134 F3
  Northampton NN1 ....141 D3
Morrison Park Rd NN6 ..102 C5
Mortar Pit Rd NN3 ....143 C5
Mortimer Cl NN4 .....159 A2
Morton Ct CV22 ....98 F8
Mortons Bush NN4 ....176 A6
Moss Wlk NN18 ....36 A2
Motala Cl NN18 ....36 A2
Motherwell Ho NN17 ...37 A8
Motspur Rd NN2 ......141 B1
Motts The NN7 ....157 B6
Moulton Coll NN3 ....126 C1
Moulton Crossing NN3 .142 E8
Moulton La NN6 ......141 D8
Moulton Park Bsns
  Ctr NN3 ....142 A6
Moulton Prim Sch NN3 126 C2
Moulton Way Holcot NN6 126 D7
  Pitsford NN6 ....125 D3
Moulton Sch NN3 .....126 B1
Moulton Way NN3 ....142 C6
Moulton Way N NN3 ..142 C6
Moulton Way S NN3 ..142 C6
Mount Pleasant
  Earls Barton NN6 .....144 F4
  Harpole NN7 ....157 C7
  Wardington OX17 ....196 E1
  Woodford Halse NN11 .184 D6
  Yardley Gobion NN12 ..217 F6
Mount Pleasant Rd LE15 ..3 A6
Mountbatten Dr NN14 ..95 C3
Mountbatten Ho NN11 .153 E8
Mountbatten Way NN9 .114 E6
Mountclair Ct NN3 ....160 E8
Mountfield Rd
  Irthlingborough NN9 ..112 F3
  Northampton NN3 ....142 A3
Mounthill Ave MK19 ..229 B7
Mounts Bsns Ctr NN1 .159 D7
Mounts Ct 1 NN3 .....142 E3
Mounts La NN11 ......153 E4
Mow Mead MK46 .....195 F5
Mowsley Ct LE17 ....45 E6
Mowsley Rd
  Husbands Bosworth LE17 ..45 E6
  Theddingworth LE16 ..46 C8
Moyeady Ave CV22 .....98 E8
Muirfield Dr NN11 .....135 E2
Muirfield Rd NN14 ....129 C7
Mulberry Cl
  Northampton NN5 ....158 F7
  Wellingborough NN8 ..129 E5
Mull Dr NN17 ....36 C8
Mulso Rd NN9 ....112 A4
Mumford Dr NN7 .....174 A7
Muncaster Gdns NN4 .175 D7
Muncaster Way NN6 ..102 C5
Murcott Cl NN6 ......121 A4
Murray Ave NN2 .....141 D1
Murray Ho NN1 ......160 A8
Murray Wlk NN18 .....36 E5
Mursley St MK11 .....229 F6
Murswell Cl NN12 ....214 D4
Murswell La NN12 ....214 D4
Muscott La NN5 ......158 C6
Muscott St NN5 ......159 A6

Museum Way NN3 ....160 F6
Musgrave Rd NN4 ....175 F7
Mushroom Field Rd NN3 143 D2
Musk Cl LE16 ....20 D7
Musson Cl NN9 ....112 E2
Mussott Cl NN7 ......155 E6
Myers Cl NN15 ....231 F5
Myers Rd CV21 ....99 C8
Myers Way OX17 ......231 F5
Myrtle Rd NN16 ....72 D4

N

Nags Head La NN9 ....115 F2
Nansen Cl Daventry NN11 135 C5
  Rothwell NN14 ....70 E6
Nansen Wlk NN18 ......36 B2
Nantwich Dr NN11 ....135 D6
Naomi Cl NN3 ....142 F1
Napier Cl Daventry NN11 153 D8
  Wellingborough NN8 ..129 A4
Narvik Rd NN18 ....36 A2
Naseby Battle & Farm
  Museum 85 B7
Naseby CE Prim Sch NN6 66 B1
Naseby Cl
  Market Harborough LE16 31 E2
  Wellingborough NN8 ..129 C5
Naseby Dr NN11 ......135 C6
  Corby NN17 ....36 C7
  Kettering NN16 ....72 C2
  Sibbertoft LE16 ....46 F2
  Thornby NN6 ....84 E4
  Welford NN6 ....65 C5
Naseby Sq LE16 ....31 E2
Naseby St NN2 ....159 C8
Nash Cl NN15 ....92 A8
Nasmith Ave NN17 .....37 A8
Nassington Manor
  House PE8 ....15 E5
Nassington Prim Sch PE8 15 F5
Nassington Rd
  Woodnewton PE8 .....14 F1
  Yarwell PE8 ....15 F7
National Dragonfly Mus
  The PE8 ....42 C5
Navigation Row NN1 ..159 C4
Navisford Ct NN14 .....76 D1
Neale Ave NN16 ....72 B5
Neale Cl Northampton NN3 160 E8
  Wollaston NN29 ......146 C3
Needham Rd NN9 .....113 F4
Nelson Ave NN11 .....184 B6
Nelson Dr NN14 ....70 E7
Nelson Rd NN17 ....36 B8
Nelson Cl NN11 ......135 E2
Nelson St Kettering NN16 .72 C3
  Market Harborough LE16 ..31 D3
  24 Northampton NN1 .159 C7
Nene Cl Kettering NN15 ..92 A5
  Raunds NN9 ....114 D7
  Wansford PE8 ....8 A3
  Wellingborough NN8 ..129 C6
Nene Cres NN17 ....21 C1
Nene Ct Thrapston NN14 ..76 D2
  Wellingborough NN8 ..130 C3
Nene Dr NN5 ....140 F2
Nene Ent Ctr NN2 ....159 C8
Nene La NN12 ....203 A6
Nene Rd
  Burton Latimer NN15 ..92 A2
  Higham Ferrers NN10 .132 B5
Nene Rise NN7 ....161 F6
Nene Side Cl NN11 ....152 F3
Nene Univ Coll
  Northampton NN2 ....141 E5
Nene Valley Bsns Pk PE8 ..42 B5
Nene Valley Ret Pk NN1 .159 B4
Nene Valley Way NN3 .160 C5
Nene View
  Irthlingborough NN14 .112 F2
  Islip NN14 ....76 B3
  Oundle PE8 ....41 F6
Nene Way Kislingbury NN7 157 C3
  Northampton NN5 ....141 A2
  Oundle PE8 ....41 F7
  Sutton PE5 ....8 C2
Nene Wlk Daventry NN11 135 A1
  Northampton NN5 ....140 F2
Neneside Cl NN7 .....155 B3
Nepcote Cl NN15 ....91 D8
Nesbitt Cl NN3 ....160 E8
Nest Farm Cres NN8 ..130 A8
Nest Farm Rd NN8 ...130 A7
Nest La NN8 ....130 B7
Nether Cl NN13 ......234 A7
Nether Jackson
  Ct 3 NN3 ....143 B4
Nether La NN7 ....155 F4
Netherfield Gr NN17 ...36 F8
Netherfield Rd NN15 ..91 C7
Nethermead Ct NN3 ..142 F4
Nettle Gap Cl NN4 ...175 D6
Neuville Way NN14 ....50 F3
Nevill Cl MK19 ......207 B2
Nevill Holt Prep Sch LE16 19 D8
Nevill Holt Rd LE16 ...19 F6
Neville Day Cl PE9 .....1 F5
Nevis Cl NN17 ....21 C1
New Buildings 7 NN16 ..72 B2
New Croft NN7 ....155 B3
New Forest Way NN11 .135 B4
New Hall NN11 ....153 B7
New La PE8 ....42 A6
New Post Office Sq NN17 36 E6
New Rd Brackley NN13 .233 E6

Mel–Noo 255

New Rd continued
  Castlethorpe MK19 ...218 F5
  Collyweston PE9 ....1 C2
  Easton on t H PE9 .....2 A5
  Farthinghoe NN13 ....221 A4
  Geddington NN14 ......54 A2
  Greens Norton NN12 ..202 D8
  Maidford NN12 ....186 D6
  Northampton NN4 ....175 D6
  Oundle PE8 ....42 A6
New St Brixworth NN6 .106 A2
  Daventry NN11 ....135 C1
  Desborough NN14 .....51 A3
  Earls Barton NN6 .....144 F4
  Irchester NN29 ....147 B8
  Irthlingborough NN9 ..112 F2
  Oundle PE8 ....42 A5
  Rothwell NN14 ....70 D7
  Weedon NN7 ....155 C3
  Wellingborough NN8 ..130 A5
New Street CE NN29 ..147 B8
New Terr NN11 ....183 D7
New Town PE9 ....2 A5
New Town Rd 2 NN1 .159 F6
Newark Dr NN18 ......36 C6
Newberry Cl NN13 ...233 D8
Newbolt Cl NN12 ....216 B8
Newbottle & Charlton
  CE Prim Sch OX17 ...231 F5
Newbridge La NN9 ...114 A3
Newbury Cl NN10 ....132 C3
Newby Ct NN3 ....142 C3
Newcombe Rd NN5 ..159 A7
Newcombe St LE16 ...31 E2
Newcomen Rd NN8 ..130 B5
Newell Rd NN14 ....95 B3
Newham Cl NN14 .....70 C7
Newington Rd NN2 ..141 C4
Newland NN1 ....159 C6
Newland Rd NN6 ....108 A5
Newland Sq NN2 ....141 C4
Newland St
  Braybrooke LE16 .....49 E5
  Kettering NN16 ....72 B2
Newland Wlk 5 NN1 ..159 D6
Newlands Brixworth NN6 106 B2
  3 Daventry NN11 .....135 C1
  Kings Sutton OX17 ...231 A6
  Naseby NN6 ....66 C1
Newlands Ctr NN16 ...72 B2
Newlands Rd NN6 .....64 E5
Newman St
  Burton Latimer NN15 ..92 B2
  Higham Ferrers NN10 ..132 C7
  4 Kettering NN16 .....72 C2
Newnham Dr NN11 ...135 A5
Newnham Prim
  Sch NN11 ....153 D4
Newnham Rd NN2 ....141 D3
Newport Pagnell Rd
  Horton NN7 ....177 D1
  Northampton NN4 ....176 A7
Newport Pagnell Road
  W NN4 ....175 D8
Newport Rd
  Hanslope MK19 ......207 B2
  Northampton NN5 ....159 A7
Newstead Cl NN15 .....91 F8
Newstead Ct NN15 .....91 F8
Newstone Cres NN14 ..158 E4
Newton Cl Daventry NN11 135 A4
  Rushden NN10 ....132 D1
  Wellingborough NN8 ..129 B6
Newton Gr NN17 ....22 A1
Newton Rd Clifton u D CV23 80 A7
  Geddington NN14 .....54 A3
  Higham Ferrers NN10 ..132 E5
  Kettering NN15 ....91 F5
  Northampton NN8 ....158 D8
  Rushden NN10 ....132 E1
  Wollaston NN29 ......146 D2
Newton Road Jun & Inf
  Schs NN14 ....132 C2
Newton St MK46 .....195 F4
Newton Way LE16 .....49 F6
Newtown Brigstock NN14 .55 E8
  Woodford NN14 ....94 E8
Newtown Rd
  Little Irchester NN8 ..130 C1
  Raunds NN9 ....114 C6
  Wellingborough NN14 ..94 D7
Nibbits La NN11 ......118 C1
Nicholas Hawkesmoor
  Prim Sch 203 B5
Nicholas La NN9 .....112 E1
Nicholas Rd NN9 .....112 E1
Nicholas Way NN10 ..131 F3
Nicholls Ct NN3 ......142 E5
Nicholls Ho 1 NN4 ...159 A3
Nichols St NN14 ....51 A4
Nichols Way NN9 ....114 C7
Nielson Rd NN14 ......94 D7
Nigel Ct NN13 ....234 A5
Nightingale Cl NN13 .222 B3
Nightingale Dr NN2 ..203 C3
Nightingale La NN8 ..130 B7
Niort Way NN8 ....129 C8
Nippendale NN10 ....132 C2
Nithsdale Ave LE16 ...31 F2
Nithsdale Cres LE16 ..31 F2
Nithsdale Rd NN17 ....36 D7
Noble Ave NN9 ....113 A5
Nobold Ct LE16 ....66 F8
Nook The Corby NN17 .37 B6

Nook The continued
Cottingham LE16 . . . .**20** D1
Easton on t H PE9 . . . .**2** A5
Norbury Cl LE16 . . . .**31** D3
Norfolk Cl NN17 . . . .**36** C7
Norfolk St NN2 . . . .**159** C8
Norfolk Terr NN2 . . . .**159** C8
Norman Rd NN3 . . . .**142** B1
Norman Way
Irchester NN29 . . . .**147** E8
Wellingborough NN8 . . . .**129** D2
Norman-D-Gate NN1 . . . . . .**159** E5
Normandy Lodge NN13 . .**233** E8
Normead Sq 4 NN3 . . . .**143** D2
Norris Acre NN13 . . . .**232** F6
Norris Cl NN15 . . . .**92** A8
Norris Way NN10 . . . .**131** E3
Norris Way Ind Est NN10 .**131** E3
Norse Wlk NN18 . . . .**36** A2
North Ave NN15 . . . .**92** B3
North Cape Wlk NN18 . . . . . .**36** A2
North Cl NN11 . . . .**118** D1
North End NN10 . . . .**132** B7
North Field La NN16 . . . .**72** A4
North Folds Rd NN18 . . . .**35** F1
North Hayes Ct NN3 . . . . . .**142** F5
North Hill MK18 . . . .**225** D2
North Holme Ct NN3 . . . . . .**142** D5
North La LE16 . . . .**30** D8
North Lea LE16 . . . .**18** B3
North Leys Ct NN3 . . . .**142** C7
North Luffenham Rd LE15 . .**3** B8
North Oval NN5 . . . .**140** F2
North Paddock Ct NN3 . .**142** F4
North Park Dr NN16 . . . .**72** C5
North Portway Cl NN3 . . . .**142** F4
North Priors Ct NN3 . . . . . .**143** A4
North Rd
Clifton u D CV23 . . . .**80** A6
Earls Barton NN6 . . . .**144** E5
Northampton NN3 . . . .**141** F6
South Kilworth LE17 . . . .**63** D8
North St
Castlethorpe MK19 . . . .**218** F5
Daventry NN11 . . . .**135** C2
Kilsby CV23 . . . .**99** F3
Mears Ashby NN6 . . . .**128** B2
Oundle PE8 . . . .**42** A5
Rothersthorpe NN7 . . . .**174** B6
Rushden NN10 . . . .**132** B3
Swinford LE17 . . . .**62** B4
Titchmarsh NN14 . . . .**77** C4
Wellingborough NN8 . . . .**129** F5
North Way
Deanshanger NN12 . . . .**228** E5
Pottersbury NN12 . . . .**217** E2
North Western Ave NN2 .**141** A4
Northall NN6 . . . .**108** A5
Northall Mews NN16 . . . . . .**72** A2
Northall St NN16 . . . .**72** B3
Northam Ct NN16 . . . .**72** B4
Northampton Christian
Sch NN1 . . . .**160** A8
Northampton Coll NN3 . .**142** D3
Northampton General
Hospl NN1 . . . .**159** E5
Northampton High
Sch NN4 . . . .**175** E7
Northampton La N NN3 .**142** C8
Northampton La S NN3 .**142** C7
Northampton Mid Sch
Northampton NN2 . . . .**141** D4
Northampton NN1 . . . .**159** D7
Northampton Rd
Blisworth NN7 . . . .**174** D1
Brackley NN13 . . . .**223** A1
Brixworth NN6 . . . .**106** B1
Broughton NN14 . . . .**90** A3
Chapel Brampton NN6 . . . . .**124** E1
Cosgrove MK19 . . . .**217** F7
Denton NN7 . . . .**178** B8
Earls Barton NN6 . . . .**144** D5
Ecton NN6 . . . .**143** F4
Harpole NN7 . . . .**157** C5
Kettering NN15 . . . .**71** F1
Litchborough NN12 . . . .**171** E2
Market Harborough LE16 . . . .**31** F3
Orlingbury NN14 . . . .**109** F5
Roade NN7 . . . .**191** D5
Rushden NN10 . . . .**131** E4
Towcester NN12 . . . .**203** C7
Welford NN6 . . . .**64** E4
Wellingborough NN8 . . . .**129** D3
West Haddon NN6 . . . .**102** C4
Yardley Hastings NN7 . . . . . .**179** A6
Northampton Sch For
Girls NN3 . . . .**142** A4
Northampton Sch of
Art NN2 . . . .**159** D8
Northampton School
for Boys NN1 . . . .**160** A6
Northampton (Sywell)
Airport NN6 . . . .**127** E5
Northamptonshire
Grammar Sch NN6 . . . . .**125** D4
Northamton & Lamport
Rly NN6 . . . .**124** F1
Northants Ent Pk NN2 . .**141** E6
Northbank LE16 . . . .**31** E3
Northbrook NN18 . . . .**36** B4
Northcote St NN2 . . . .**159** C7
Northen Way NN6 . . . .**129** F8
Northend MK46 . . . .**194** E3
Northern Way NN11 . . . . .**135** D4

Northfield Ave
Kettering NN16 . . . .**72** A3
Ringstead NN14 . . . .**95** B3
Northfield Gn NN6 . . . .**122** D5
Northfield La PE8 . . . .**15** E5
Northfield Rd
Broughton NN14 . . . .**71** C1
Northampton NN5 . . . .**140** B1
Northfield Way NN2 . . . . .**141** B4
Northgate NN12 . . . .**203** C7
Northgate Sch NN2 . . . . . .**141** C2
Northleigh Gr LE16 . . . .**31** D4
Northumberland Cl NN15 .**91** D6
Northumberland Rd NN15 **91** D6
Northumbria Gdns NN3 . .**142** B1
Northwood Rd NN3 . . . . . .**142** B2
Nortoft NN6 . . . .**103** F7
Norton Cl NN11 . . . .**135** D2
Norton Cres NN12 . . . .**203** B6
Norton Leys CV22 . . . .**98** A6
Norton Rd Corby NN17 . . . . .**36** C7
Daventry NN11 . . . .**135** D2
Northampton NN2 . . . .**141** C3
Norton St NN14 . . . .**70** E7
Norway Cl NN18 . . . .**36** A3
Notre Dame
Mews 3 NN1 . . . .**159** D6
Nuffield Cl NN13 . . . .**233** D8
Nunn Mills Rd NN1 . . . . . .**159** E4
Nunneley Way LE16 . . . .**31** F5
Nunnery Ave NN14 . . . .**70** C7
Nuns La NN6 . . . .**121** B4
Nurseries The
Horton NN7 . . . .**177** D1
Moulton NN3 . . . .**126** C1
Nursery Cl NN6 . . . .**128** B2
Nursery Dr NN8 . . . .**130** B7
Nursery End LE16 . . . .**31** C2
Nursery Gdns NN9 . . . .**112** E2
Nursery La NN2 . . . .**141** C3
Nutcote NN6 . . . .**85** B8
Nuthall Cl NN3 . . . .**160** F8**

O

Oak Ave NN7 . . . .**174** B1
Oak Cl Broughton NN14 . . . . .**90** A4
Hartwell NN7 . . . .**192** E2
Irchester NN29 . . . .**147** A7
Market Harborough LE16 . . . .**31** F4
Towcester NN12 . . . .**203** C4
Oak Dr NN11 . . . .**184** B6
Oak Gr NN11 . . . .**135** C5
Oak La NN6 . . . .**100** F6
Oak Park Cl NN3 . . . .**143** A6
Oak Rd Brackley NN13 . . . . .**222** F1
Kettering NN15 . . . .**72** D1
Oak St
20 Northampton NN1 . . . . . .**159** C7
Rushden NN10 . . . .**132** B4
Weedon NN7 . . . .**155** A2
Oak Terr 6 NN9 . . . .**112** C4
Oak Tree Cl NN14 . . . .**50** F3
Oak View NN9 . . . .**110** F1
Oak Way NN9 . . . .**112** F2
Oakdown Cres MK46 . . . . .**195** F3
Oakgrove Pl NN4 . . . .**175** D6
Oakham Cl
Northampton NN3 . . . .**142** B7
Rushden NN10 . . . .**148** A8
Oakham La NN14 . . . .**152** B7
Oaklands Bugbrooke NN7 . .**173** A7
Weedon NN7 . . . .**155** A2
Oaklands Dr NN3 . . . .**142** E1
Oaklands Pk LE16 . . . .**31** F2
Oakleas Rise NN14 . . . .**76** D1
Oakleigh Cl NN9 . . . .**114** C7
Oakleigh Dr NN5 . . . .**140** C1
Oakley Ct NN18 . . . .**36** A1
Oakley Dr Moulton NN3 . . . .**126** D1
Wellingborough NN8 . . . .**129** D3
Oakley Hay Ind Est NN18 . .**36** A1
Oakley Mews LE16 . . . .**31** D3
Oakley Rd Corby NN18 . . . . .**36** C3
Rushden NN10 . . . .**131** F3
Oakley St Kettering NN16 . . .**72** B4
Northampton NN1 . . . .**159** D7
Oakmont Cl NN4 . . . .**175** C5
Oakpits Way NN10 . . . .**132** C1
Oaks Dr NN10 . . . .**132** B6
Oaktree Ct Aldwincle NN14 .**76** F8
2 Kettering NN16 . . . .**72** B1
Oakway NN8 . . . .**129** F7
Oakway Jun & Inf
Schs NN8 . . . .**130** A7
Oakwood Rd NN1 . . . .**142** A1
Oat Hill Dr NN3 . . . .**143** D2
Oat Hill Rd NN12 . . . .**203** C4
Oathill Cl NN6 . . . .**106** B1
Oathill Rise NN15 . . . .**92** C2
Oban Cl NN15 . . . .**91** E8
Obelisk Cl NN2 . . . .**141** C8
Obelisk Rd NN9 . . . .**112** A5
Obelisk Rise NN2 . . . .**141** C6
Occupation Rd Corby NN17 .**36** F7
Middleton NN16 . . . .**20** B2
Octagon The NN17 . . . .**37** A8
Octavian Way NN13 . . . . . .**234** A7
Odeon Bldgs NN17 . . . .**37** A7
Old Barn Ct NN3 . . . .**142** F3
Old Brewery Wlk NN13 . .**233** F6
Old Dairy Farm NN7 . . . . .**171** B3
Old Dry La NN14 . . . .**55** F8
Old End NN7 . . . .**177** A1
Old Forge Dr NN6 . . . .**102** C4
Old Forge La NN6 . . . .**169** C2
Old Gn LE16 . . . .**18** F6

Old Grammar School
The NN6 . . . .**103** F6
Old Great North Rd
Stibbington PE8 . . . .**8** C2
Stibbington PE8 . . . .**8** D1
Wothorpe PE9 . . . .**2** F7
Old Greens Norton
Rd NN12 . . . .**203** B7
Old Hall La LE16 . . . .**30** F3
Old Holt Rd LE16 . . . .**19** A7
Old La NN3 . . . .**221** A4
Old Leicester Rd PE8 . . . . . .**8** A3
Old Manor Ct NN11 . . . . . .**135** E8
Old North Rd PE8 . . . .**8** A4
Old Oundle Rd PE8 . . . .**7** A4
Old Post Office Cl NN17 . . .**37** B6
Old Quarry Ct NN14 . . . . . .**142** E4
Old Rd Braunston NN11 . . . .**134** C7
Scaldwell NN6 . . . .**107** A7
Stanion NN14 . . . .**37** E2
Walgrave NN6 . . . .**107** F5
Old Rectory Dr PE8 . . . .**8** A6
Old Rickyard The NN11 . .**199** D7
Old School Cotts NN6 . . . .**105** A8
Old School La NN7 . . . .**187** A1
Old Stratford Prim
Sch MK19 . . . .**229** B6
Old Tiffield Rd NN12 . . . . .**203** C8
Old Towcester Rd NN4 . . .**159** C4
Old Town NN13 . . . .**234** A7
Old Vineyard The NN10 . .**132** B6
Old Yew Ct NN7 . . . .**141** B3
Olde Hall Cl NN6 . . . .**105** B1
Olden Rd NN3 . . . .**143** C6
Oldenburg Rd NN18 . . . .**35** F3
Oldenmead Ct NN3 . . . . . .**142** B7
Oldland Rd NN18 . . . .**36** D3
Oleander Cres NN3 . . . . . .**143** C4
Oliver Cl NN10 . . . .**132** C2
Oliver St NN2 . . . .**141** E1
Ollerton Wlk NN18 . . . .**36** C5
Ollis Cl NN17 . . . .**36** E8
Olney Cty Mid Sch MK46 .**195** E4
Olney Fst Sch MK46 . . . . . .**195** E3
Olney Rd MK46 . . . .**195** F1
Olympia Cl NN4 . . . .**175** B8
Olympic Way NN8 . . . .**129** C5
Onley Cl CV22 . . . .**98** D6
Oransay Cl NN3 . . . .**143** C2
Orchard Cl Badby NN11 . . .**152** F3
East Haddon NN6 . . . .**122** D5
Finedon NN9 . . . .**111** F5
Hannington NN6 . . . .**108** C3
Hollowell NN6 . . . .**104** B5
Milton Malsor NN7 . . . .**174** E4
Northampton NN4 . . . .**175** E6
Rushden NN10 . . . .**131** F3
Spratton NN6 . . . .**124** B8
Towcester NN12 . . . .**203** C4
Warmington PE8 . . . .**28** B3
Weldon NN17 . . . .**37** B8
Wilbarston LE16 . . . .**34** C5
Wollaston NN29 . . . .**146** D3
Yardley Gobion NN12 . . . . . .**217** F6
Yelvertoft NN6 . . . .**82** B4
Orchard Cotts NN6 . . . . . .**125** C5
Orchard Cres
Kettering NN16 . . . .**72** C4
Woodnewton PE8 . . . .**14** E2
Orchard Ct
Pattishall NN12 . . . .**172** D1
Woodford NN14 . . . .**94** C7
Orchard Dr NN14 . . . .**90** F2
Orchard Field NN14 . . . . . .**93** A6
Orchard Gn NN3 . . . .**142** C2
Orchard Hill NN3 . . . .**143** A1
Orchard Ho NN17 . . . .**38** B8
Orchard La Denton NN7 . . .**162** B1
Gretton NN17 . . . .**10** C1
King's Cliffe PE8 . . . .**13** E7
Woodnewton PE8 . . . .**14** E2
Orchard Pl NN29 . . . .**147** A8
Orchard Rd Finedon NN9 . .**111** F5
Raunds NN9 . . . .**114** B5
Orchard Rise
Long Buckby NN6 . . . .**121** D4
Olney MK46 . . . .**195** F3
Orchard Sch The NN16 . . .**72** B5
Orchard St Daventry NN11 .**135** B2
Market Harborough LE16 . . . .**31** F4
3 Northampton NN5 . . . . . .**159** A6
Orchard Terr Finedon NN9 .**111** F5
Welford NN6 . . . .**64** E6
Wellingborough NN8 . . . .**129** F5
Orchard The Apethorpe PE8 **14** C4
Bozeat NN29 . . . .**164** D3
Flore NN7 . . . .**155** F5
Kislingbury NN7 . . . .**157** D3
Pottersbury NN12 . . . .**217** C3
Staverton NN11 . . . .**152** B7
Orchard Way
Cogenhoe NN7 . . . .**161** F6
Easton on t H PE9 . . . .**1** F6
Harpole NN7 . . . .**157** C6
Kings Sutton OX17 . . . .**231** A5
Northampton NN5 . . . .**158** C6
Roade NN7 . . . .**191** D4
Thrapston NN14 . . . .**76** E1
Orchards The NN6 . . . .**103** D1
Ordnance Rd NN7 . . . .**154** F4
Oriel Cl NN11 . . . .**153** C7
Oriel Way NN13 . . . .**233** D8
Orient Way NN8 . . . .**130** A4
Orion Way NN15 . . . .**91** C5
Orkney Wlk NN17 . . . .**36** B8
Orlingbury Rd
Great Harrowden NN9 . . . . .**110** D2

Orlingbury Rd continued
Isham NN14 . . . .**110** C7
Little Harrowden NN9 . . . . . .**110** B4
Pytchley NN14 . . . .**90** F1
Ormond Pl NN14 . . . .**110** E8
Orson Leys CV22 . . . .**98** A7
Orton Pl NN8 . . . .**129** C6
Orton Rd Kettering NN15 . . .**91** F5
Loddington NN14 . . . .**70** D2
Orwell Cl Clifton u D CV23 . .**80** A5
Raunds NN9 . . . .**114** D7
Wellingborough NN8 . . . .**129** C6
Osborn Ct NN8 . . . .**129** E3
Osborn's Ct MK46 . . . .**195** F3
Osborne Cl NN10 . . . .**132** D4
Osborne Rd NN2 . . . .**141** C2
Osier Bed La NN17 . . . .**24** B5
Osiers The NN14 . . . .**51** D2
Osler Cl NN2 . . . .**141** B5
Oslo Gdns NN18 . . . .**36** A3
Osmund Dr NN3 . . . .**143** A5
Osprey Dr NN11 . . . .**135** C3
Osprey La NN8 . . . .**130** B7
Osprey Rise NN4 . . . .**175** B8
Osprey View NN4 . . . .**175** B8
Ostlers La MK11 . . . .**229** D6
Oswald Rd NN10 . . . .**132** C2
Osyth Cl NN4 . . . .**160** B2
Oulton Rise NN3 . . . .**141** F4
Oundle CE Prim Sch PE8 . .**42** A5
Oundle Dr NN3 . . . .**142** B7
Oundle & King's Cliffe
Mid Sch PE8 . . . .**13** F7
Oundle & Kings Cliffe
Mid Sch PE8 . . . .**41** E7
Oundle Mus PE8 . . . .**41** F5
Oundle Rd Elton PE8 . . . . . .**16** F1
Thrapston NN14 . . . .**76** E2
Weldon NN17 . . . .**38** E7
Woodnewton PE8 . . . .**14** F1
Oundle Sch PE8 . . . .**42** A5
Our Lady & Pope John
XXIII RC Sch NN18 . . . . .**36** A4
Our Lady's Convent Prep
Sch NN15 . . . .**71** F1
Our Lady's Jun & Inf
Schs NN17 . . . .**36** F7
Our Lady's RC Jun & Inf
Schs NN3 . . . .**129** D3
Ouse Cl NN8 . . . .**129** C6
Ouse La NN10 . . . .**203** A6
Ousebank Way MK11 . . . . .**229** D5
Outlaw La NN6 . . . .**129** F5
Oval Cres NN10 . . . .**132** D2
Oval Rd Rugby CV22 . . . .**98** D8
Rushden NN10 . . . .**132** D2
Oval The Kettering NN15 . . . .**91** B8
Market Harborough LE16 . . . .**31** E4
Overdale Cl LE16 . . . .**32** A3
Overend PE8 . . . .**28** D7
Overfield Ave LE16 . . . .**31** F5
Overhills MK46 . . . .**195** E4
Overleys CV3 . . . .**143** B5
Overmead Rd NN3 . . . .**143** D2
Overslade Cl NN4 . . . .**175** A8
Overslade Ho NN4 . . . .**175** A8
Overstone Cres NN6 . . . . .**127** B1
Overstone Cty Prim
Sch NN6 . . . .**127** A1
Overstone La NN6 . . . .**126** F1
Overstone Park Prep
Sch NN6 . . . .**143** B8
Overstone Rd
Moulton NN3 . . . .**126** C1
Northampton NN1 . . . .**159** D7
Sywell NN6 . . . .**127** D3
Overthorpe Prep
Sch OX17 . . . .**219** C8
Overthorpe Rd OX16 . . . . .**219** B6
Ovett Cl NN15 . . . .**90** F8
Owen Cl NN8 . . . .**129** B5
Owen Mews NN8 . . . .**129** B5
Owl Cl NN3 . . . .**141** F7
Owl End La NN9 . . . .**182** C5
Owl End Way NN11 . . . . . .**182** C5
Oxburgh Ct 7 NN4 . . . . . .**175** C8
Oxendon Hall LE16 . . . .**48** E3
Oxendon Rd
Arthingworth LE16 . . . .**49** A1
Braybrooke LE16 . . . .**49** D5
Clipston LE16 . . . .**48** B1
East Farndon LE16 . . . .**48** B5
Oxford Cl Daventry NN11 . .**135** C1
Earls Barton NN6 . . . .**144** F3
Oxford Rd Adderbury OX17 .**230** A3
Corby NN17 . . . .**36** C6
Evenley NN13 . . . .**233** E5
Oxford St Daventry NN11 . .**135** C1
Finedon NN9 . . . .**112** B5
Kettering NN16 . . . .**72** A3
Northampton NN4 . . . .**159** B3
Rothwell NN14 . . . .**70** D8
Stony Stratford MK11 . . . . . .**229** D5
Wellingborough NN8 . . . .**129** F4
Wymington NN10 . . . .**148** A7
Oxleys MK46 . . . .**195** E4
Oxwich Cl NN4 . . . .**160** A1

P

Packwood Ave CV21 . . . . . .**99** C8
Paddock Cl NN6 . . . .**103** D1
Paddock Cl LE16 . . . .**31** E3
Paddock La
Desborough NN14 . . . .**51** A3
Mears Ashby NN6 . . . .**128** B2
Medbourne LE16 . . . .**19** D8

Paddock Mill Ct 1 NN3 .**143** B4
Paddock The Crick NN6 . . .**100** F5
Lois Weedon NN12 . . . .**200** B2
Lower Boddington NN11 . . . .**182** C5
Raunds NN9 . . . .**114** C4
Welton NN11 . . . .**135** E8
Woodnewton PE8 . . . .**14** E2
Paddocks Rd NN10 . . . . . .**131** F3
Paddocks The
Brixworth NN6 . . . .**106** B3
Bugbrooke NN7 . . . .**172** F4
Orlingbury NN7 . . . .**109** F5
Shutlanger NN12 . . . .**204** D8
Souldern OX6 . . . .**237** E3
Paddocks Way NN3 . . . . . .**143** A1
Paddox Cl CV22 . . . .**98** F8
Paddox Ct CV23 . . . .**100** A3
Paddox Prim Sch
Rugby CV22 . . . .**98** D8
Rugby CV22 . . . .**98** E8
Padwell Ct 2 NN3 . . . .**161** A8
Pages Wlk NN17 . . . .**37** B6
Paget Cl NN4 . . . .**160** E2
Paget Rd LE16 . . . .**30** E3
Palk Rd NN8 . . . .**130** B4
Palm Rd NN10 . . . .**131** E3
Palmer Ave NN9 . . . .**113** B4
Palmer Cl NN8 . . . .**129** D7
Palmer Ct NN8 . . . .**129** C5
Palmer Sq NN3 . . . .**143** C1
Palmer's Cl CV21 . . . .**99** B8
Palmerston Ct 5 NN1 . . . .**159** E6
Palmerston Ho 4 NN1 . . . .**159** E6
Palmerston Rd NN1 . . . . . .**159** E6
Parade Bank NN3 . . . .**126** C1
Parade The NN1 . . . .**159** C6
Paradise Ave NN15 . . . .**91** D6
Paradise La NN15 . . . .**91** D6
Pargeter Cl OX17 . . . .**210** E2
Park Ave Kettering NN16 . . . .**72** B4
Northampton NN5 . . . .**140** A1
Raunds NN9 . . . .**114** E5
Rushden NN10 . . . .**132** A2
Park Ave N NN3 . . . .**142** A1
Park Ave S NN3 . . . .**160** B7
Park Cl Badby NN11 . . . . . .**153** A3
Brafield-on-t-G NN7 . . . . . .**161** D2
Cosgrove MK19 . . . .**218** F2
Earls Barton NN6 . . . .**144** D4
Isham NN14 . . . .**110** F8
King's Cliffe PE8 . . . .**14** A8
Northampton NN5 . . . .**140** A1
Sywell NN6 . . . .**127** D2
Watford NN6 . . . .**120** C6
Whittlebury NN12 . . . .**215** C4
Park Cres 8 NN8 . . . .**130** A5
Park Cres E NN5 . . . .**140** F2
Park Cres W NN5 . . . .**140** F1
Park Dr
Market Harborough LE16 . . . .**31** E4
Northampton NN5 . . . .**140** F1
Park End NN13 . . . .**238** D8
Park End Works NN13 . . .**238** D7
Park Farm Ind Est NN8 . .**129** A5
Park Farm Way NN8 . . . . .**129** A3
Park Hill Rd NN3 . . . .**142** D3
Park Ho LE16 . . . .**31** E4
Park Inf Sch NN9 . . . .**114** E6
Park Jun & Inf Schs NN16 **72** C4
Park La Earls Barton NN6 . .**144** D4
Gayton NN7 . . . .**173** E2
Harpole NN7 . . . .**157** C6
Hartwell NN7 . . . .**192** C1
Northampton NN5 . . . .**140** A2
Paulerspury NN12 . . . .**216** B7
Sulgrave OX17 . . . .**210** F7
Watford NN6 . . . .**120** C6
Park Leys NN11 . . . .**135** C1
Park Lodge NN17 . . . .**36** E6
Park Mews
Market Harborough LE16 . . . .**31** E4
Towcester NN12 . . . .**203** C6
Park Pl NN10 . . . .**132** B2
Park Rd
Burton Latimer NN15 . . . . . .**92** B2
Hanslope MK19 . . . .**207** B3
Hartwell NN7 . . . .**192** C1
Irthlingborough NN9 . . . . . .**112** F1
Kettering NN16 . . . .**72** C4
Raunds NN9 . . . .**114** E6
Rushden NN10 . . . .**132** C1
Stony Stratford MK11 . . . . . .**229** D5
Titchmarsh NN14 . . . .**77** C4
Wellingborough NN8 . . . .**130** A5
Park Spinney Cl NN6 . . . . . .**84** A5
Park Sq NN5 . . . .**140** F2
Park St Earls Barton NN6 . .**144** D4
King's Cliffe PE8 . . . .**13** F7
Raunds NN9 . . . .**114** E6
Towcester NN12 . . . .**203** C6
Wollaston NN29 . . . .**146** E2
Park The PE8 . . . .**97** A3
Park View Kettering NN16 . . .**72** B4
Moulton NN3 . . . .**142** E8
Thrapston NN14 . . . .**76** D2
Wellingborough NN8 . . . .**130** B4
Park View Rd NN12 . . . . . .**203** D5
Park Wlk Brigstock NN14 . . .**55** E7
Easton on t H PE9 . . . .**2** A6
Northampton NN5 . . . .**140** F2
Parker Rd PE8 . . . .**7** D8
Parkers Terr NN7 . . . .**111** F4
Parkfield Ave NN4 . . . .**159** C1
Parkfield Cres NN4 . . . . . .**159** C6
Parkfield Rd
Brixworth NN6 . . . .**106** A1
Long Buckby NN6 . . . .**121** A4
Parkham Ind Est NN10 . . .**131** D3

Parklands Stanwick NN9 ..113 F3
Sywell NN6 ....127 C1
Parklands Ave NN3 ....142 A5
Parklands NN14 ......70 D1
Parklands Cres NN3 ...142 A5
Parklands Lower
 Sch NN3 ....142 A4
Parklands Mid Sch NN3 .142 A5
Parkside NN3 ....143 D2
Parkside Sch NN1 .....159 E5
Parkway Nassington PE8 ...15 F5
 Northampton NN3 .....142 D1
Parkway Cl PE8 ....15 F5
Parkwood St NN5 .....159 B5
Parracombe Way NN3 ..160 C7
Parsons Cl NN6 ....143 F4
Parsons' Cl NN7 ......163 D5
Parsons Cl NN7 ....156 C2
Parsons Gr NN17 ......22 A1
Parsons Meade NN4 ...158 E2
Parsons Rd NN29 .....147 B8
Parsons St
 Adderbury OX17 .....230 A4
 Woodford Halse NN11 .184 C4
Partridge Cl NN2 .....141 A5
Partridge La NN11 ....184 C5
Parva Ct NN3 ....142 E3
Pashler Gdns NN14 ....76 D2
Pasteur Cl NN2 ....141 A5
Pasteur Ctyd NN17 ....37 B8
Pasture The NN11 .....135 C1
Pastures The
 Market Harborough LE16 .31 C3
 Northampton NN2 .....141 A5
 Wellingborough NN9 ...110 A1
Paterson Rd NN8 .....130 B8
Patrick Cl NN15 ....91 C6
Patrick Rd NN15 ......91 C6
Patrick St LE16 ....31 F2
Patrick's Rd NN18 ....36 D4
Patricks La MK19 .....228 E4
Patterdale Wlk [1] NN3 .142 C4
Patterson Rd NN3 ....142 E1
Pattishall CE Prim
 Sch 188 F8
Paulerspury CE Prim
 Sch NN12 ....216 B8
Pavilion Dr NN4 ......159 F1
Pavilions Way NN13 ...233 E8
Paxford Cl NN8 ....129 C1
Paxton Cl MK46 ......195 F3
Paxton Rd NN3 ....142 D4
Payne's La LE16 ....18 F7
Peace Cl NN4 ....158 F3
Peace Hill NN7 ....172 E7
Peacock Pl [6] NN1 ....159 D6
Peacock's Cl OX17 ....220 A8
Peak The NN7 ....156 C1
Pear Tree Cl Bozeat NN29 .164 D3
 Northampton NN3 .....143 A4
Pear Tree Gdns LE16 ..31 D2
Pearmain Ave NN8 ....129 F7
Pearmain Ct NN3 .....143 A4
Peartree Cl NN11 .....135 C4
Peaselands NN14 .....50 F4
Pebble Cott LE17 .....46 D8
Pebble La Brackley NN13 .233 F7
 [4] Wellingborough NN8 .130 A4
Pebbleford Rd NN15 ...91 D8
Peg's La Clipston LE16 ..66 F8
 Denford NN14 ....95 C6
Pegasus Ct NN13 .....233 F7
Pelham Ct NN3 ....142 D4
Pell Ct NN3 ....142 E3
Pells Cl NN6 ....103 C4
Pemberton St NN10 ...132 A3
Pembroke Cl
 Rushden NN10 ....132 C1
 Thrapston NN14 ......76 C2
Pembroke Cres NN5 ...159 B8
Pembroke Gdns NN5 ..159 A8
Pembroke Rd NN5 ....159 B8
Pembroke Way NN11 ..153 B7
Pen Ct NN1 ....159 D4
Pen Green La NN17 ...37 A8
Penarth Rd NN5 ......159 A8
Pendered Rd NN8 ....130 A1
Pendle Ave NN6 ......72 A6
Pendle Rd NN5 ....158 C8
Penfold Cl NN2 ....141 B4
Penfold Dr NN3 ......143 B3
Penfold Gdns NN3 ....143 C3
Penfold La NN3 ......143 C3
Penistone Rd NN3 ....142 E3
Penistone Wlk [3] NN3 .142 E3
Penn Gdns NN4 ......175 E6
Pennard Cl NN4 ......160 B2
Pennine Cl NN11 .....135 B5
Pennine Way
 Kettering NN16 ......72 B6
 Northampton NN5 ....158 D7
Pennycress Pl NN3 ...143 D1
Penrhyn Cl NN14 .....76 C2
Penrhyn Rd NN4 .....159 C3
Penrith Dr NN8 ......129 C6
Pentelowes The PE18 .116 D2
Penthorne Cl NN12 ...188 A8
Pentlands MK11 ......229 F4
Penvale Rd NN4 ......175 B7
Pepper Alley OX15 ....236 E4
Peppercorn Way NN4 .175 D6
Perch Cl NN11 ....135 B6
Percival Cl NN5 ......140 D1
Percival Rd CV22 .....98 D8
Percy Rd Northampton NN1 159 F7
 Woodford Halse NN11 .184 C6
Peregrine Pl NN4 .....175 A8
Perkins Cl LE16 ......31 F4

Perkins Ct [4] NN8 ....130 A5
Perkins Rd NN9 ......131 E8
Perkins Way NN11 ....153 E8
Perry St NN1 ....159 F7
Peterborough Rd
 Morcott LE15 ....3 D6
 Wansford PE8 ....8 A3
 Warmington PE8 .....28 C4
Peters La NN6 ....106 F5
Petherton St NN10 ....72 B3
Pettiver Cres [2] CV21 .80 A1
Petworth Dr LE16 ....32 B2
Petworth Gdns NN18 ..36 B5
Pevensey NN10 ....132 C1
Pevensey Wlk [2] NN18 .36 B5
Peverel's Way NN5 ...158 E6
Peveril Cl NN10 ......132 C6
Peveril Rd
 Greatworth OX17 ....210 E2
 Northampton NN5 ....158 C7
Pevers La MK46 ......195 A1
Pevrel Pl NN14 ......50 E4
Pexley Ct PE8 ....41 E5
Pheasant Way NN14 ..141 A5
Phoenix Parkway NN17 .37 B8
Philip Way NN10 .....132 C7
Phillips Way NN6 .....121 C4
Phipps Rd NN11 .....184 B6
Phoenix Cl NN8 ......130 B3
Phoenix Parkway NN17 .22 B2
Phoenix St [8] NN1 ...159 C6
Piccadilly Bldgs [3] NN16 .72 B1
Piccadilly Cl NN4 .....158 F2
Pickerings The NN6 ...106 C1
Piddington La NN7 ...177 A2
Pie Cnr NN6 ....127 D3
Piece The Cogenhoe NN7 .161 F6
 Spratton NN6 ....105 B1
Pierce Cres PE8 ......28 C3
Pigeon Hill NN12 .....189 D3
Pightles Terr NN10 ...132 C1
Pightles Wlk NN10 ...132 C1
Pigott's La NN15 .....92 C2
Pike Cl NN6 ....101 A6
Pike La NN1 ....159 C6
Pike Rd NN18 ....36 A1
Pikemead Ct NN3 ....143 B4
Pilgrim Way NN8 .....129 F3
Pilgrims La NN7 .....173 A7
Pilgrims Pl NN4 ......159 C2
Pilot Rd NN17 ....37 C8
Pilton Cl NN3 ....143 C5
Pilton Rd PE8 ....58 A4
Pincet La LE17 ....45 A6
Pindar Rd NN8 ....129 E2
Pindar Rise NN3 .....142 E6
Pine Ave NN6 ....127 D1
Pine Cl Desborough NN14 .51 C2
 Irchester NN29 .....147 A7
 Rushden NN10 ......148 A8
Pine Copse Cl NN5 ...140 A2
Pine Cres NN3 ....127 D1
Pine Ct NN7 ....138 C4
Pine Gr CV21 ....80 A1
Pine Rd NN15 ....72 D1
Pine Ridge NN3 ......142 F7
Pine Trees NN3 ......142 D1
Pine Wlk NN17 ......21 E1
Pineham Ave NN2 ....141 D6
Pines The LE16 ......32 A6
Pinetrees Cl NN17 ...177 B3
Pinewood Cl NN16 ...72 B6
Pinewood Rd NN3 ...142 B3
Pinfold Cl LE15 ......3 B8
Pinfold Gn NN11 .....152 F3
Pingle La LE15 ......3 B6
Pioneer Ave
 Burton Latimer NN15 ..92 B2
 Desborough NN14 ....50 F2
Piper's Hill Rd NN15 ..91 C8
Pipers Cl
 Irchester NN29 .....112 F2
 Kettering NN15 .....72 C1
Pipewell Rd
 Desborough NN14 ....51 C4
 East Carlton LE16 ....35 B3
Pippin Cl Cogenhoe NN7 .161 E5
 Rushden NN10 ......131 E3
 Wellingborough NN8 .129 F4
Pippin La NN3 ....143 A2
Pit La PE9 ....1 A7
Pitchers La LE16 .....20 D7
Pitsford Rd
 Chapel Brampton NN6 .124 E1
 Moulton NN3 ....126 B2
Pitstone Rd NN4 .....158 E3
Pitt St NN8 ....129 E4
Pittams La NN6 ......121 B3
Pittams La NN12 .....213 B8
Pittoms La CV23 .....99 C1
Plank Hos NN10 .....203 C5
Plantagenet Cl NN13 .233 E8
Plantagenet Sq [7] NN4 .158 F2
Playford Cl NN14 .....70 F7
Pleasant Row NN14 ..94 D7
Plessey Cl NN12 .....203 D5
Pleydell Gdns NN4 ...159 C2
Pleydell Ct NN4 ......159 C2
Plough Cl NN14 ......70 D7
Plough La NN2 ......141 A6
Plough Mews NN13 ..233 F7
Ploughmans Wlk NN2 .141 B5
Plover Cl NN12 ......203 C5
Plum Park La NN12 ..216 D8
Plumpton Ct NN18 ...36 B5

Plumpton La NN11 ...199 D7
Plumpton Rd
 Weston NN12 ....200 A2
 Woodend NN12 .....200 F6
Plumtree Ave NN8 ...130 A7
Poachers Way NN2 ..141 B5
Pochin Cl LE16 ......31 F5
Podington Rd NN10 ..148 A4
Podmore Way NN14 ..90 A3
Poets Way NN11 .....153 E5
Poitiers Cl NN5 ......139 F1
Pokas Cotts NN9 .....133 C8
Polebrook Airfield
 Nature Reserve PE8 ..43 F3
Polebrook CE Prim
 Sch PE8 ....43 A3
Polebrook Ct PE8 ....42 F3
Polegate Cl NN18 ....36 B5
Police Flats NN17 ....36 E6
Pollard St NN16 .....72 B4
Polwell La NN15 .....92 A4
Pomfret Rd NN12 ....203 C6
Pond Bank NN7 .....190 D8
Pond Farm Cl NN5 ..158 C7
Pond Wood Cl NN3 ..142 B6
Ponder St NN14 .....70 D7
Ponds Cl NN9 ....114 D6
Pool Cl NN12 ....188 D8
Pool St NN11 ....184 B5
Poole St NN1 ....159 D7
Pope Rd NN8 ....129 C3
Popham Ct NN9 .....114 C7
Poplar Cl Daventry NN11 .135 C5
 Irchester NN29 .....147 A7
 Rushden NN10 ......148 A8
 Towcester NN12 .....203 C4
Poplar Ct NN3 ....142 D5
Poplar Pl
 Wellingborough NN8 ..129 F4
 Wollaston NN29 .....146 E2
Poplar Rd
 Burton Latimer NN15 ..92 C4
 Corby NN17 ....21 D1
 Finedon NN9 ....112 A5
 Kettering NN16 .....72 D2
Poplar Rise NN12 ....213 B8
Poplar St NN8 ....130 A5
Poplar's Farm Rd NN15 .92 B8
Poplars Cl Blakesley NN12 .187 B1
 Middleton Cheney OX17 .220 A8
 Raunds NN9 ....114 C6
Poplars Ct LE16 .....31 D4
Poplars La NN6 .....126 E8
Poplars Rd OX17 ....208 F4
Poplars The
 Guilsborough NN6 ...103 E7
 Long Buckby NN6 ...121 B3
Poppy Cl NN10 .....148 C8
Poppy Leys NN15 ...125 B8
Poppyfield Ct
 Northampton NN3 ...142 F4
 Thrapston NN14 ....76 D3
Porlock Cl NN5 ......158 E8
Port Rd NN5 ....140 A2
Porthchester Gdns NN3 .160 F8
Porter's Cl MK19 ....228 E4
Porter's La PE9 .....2 A5
Portland Cl NN11 ....135 C1
Portland Pl NN1 ....159 C6
Portland Rd
 Irthlingborough NN9 .112 F3
 Rushden NN10 .....132 B2
Portlow La NN6 .....100 F6
Portree Wlk NN17 ...36 C8
Portstone Cl NN5 ...140 A2
Portway Aynho OX17 .237 D7
 Croughton NN13 ...238 E7
Portway Cres NN13 ..238 E7
Portway Dr NN13 ...238 D7
Portway Gdns OX17 .237 D7
Postle Cl CV23 .....99 F2
Potato Hall NN8 ....129 F6
Potters End NN11 ...183 D7
Pottersbury Lodge
 Sch NN12 ....217 A6
Pound Cl Corby NN18 .36 B2
 Ringstead NN14 ....95 B3
 Wicken MK19 ......228 A4
Pound Ct NN3 ......126 B1
Pound La Badby NN11 .152 F3
 Bugbrooke NN7 ....173 A7
 Eastcote NN12 .....172 F1
 Moulton NN3 ......126 C1
 Northampton NN3 ...143 C2
Pound Pl NN9 ......111 F4
Pound The
 Great Brington NN7 ..138 D6
 Horton NN7 ....177 D1
 Nether Heyford NN7 .156 B1
 Syresham NN13 ....224 B7
Poundfield Rd NN12 .217 D2
Poyntz Gdns NN5 ...158 E8
Poyntz La NN5 .....158 E8
Pratt Rd NN10 .....132 C2
Premier Way NN9 ...131 E8
Prentice Ct NN3 ....143 A5
Prentice Wlk NN17 ..37 A6
Prescott Cl NN3 ....143 C4
Pressland Dr NN10 .132 C6
Prestbury Rd NN5 ..140 A1
Prestidge Row NN11 .199 D7
Preston Ct
 Burton Latimer NN15 ..92 C3
 Northampton NN3 ...142 F6
Preston Deanery Rd NN7 176 B1
Preston Dr NN11 ....135 C6
Preston Hedges Prim
 Sch NN4 ....175 F6

Preston Rd NN11 ....184 C2
Prestwold Way NN3 ..143 B5
Prices Way NN13 ....222 D1
Pride Pl LE16 ....31 D2
Pridmore Cl PE8 ....14 E2
Priestley Ct NN17 ...22 D1
Priestwell Ct NN6 ...122 D5
Primrose Cl NN16 ...72 D4
Primrose Gdns NN9 .114 D5
Primrose Hill
 Daventry NN11 .....135 C2
 Northampton NN2 ..159 C8
 Raunds NN9 ......114 D6
Primrose Wlk NN11 .184 B6
Primula Cl NN3 .....160 C6
Primula Cl NN2 .....159 C8
Prince Cl NN11 .....135 B3
Prince Of Wales
 Row NN3 ....126 D1
Prince Rupert Ave NN14 .50 F3
Prince St NN6 ......144 E5
Prince William Rd PE8 .41 E5
Prince William Upper
 Sch PE8 ....42 B4
Princes Cl NN7 .....155 A3
Princes St NN16 ....72 C5
Princes Wlk [4] NN1 .159 D6
Princess Anne Bldg NN2 141 C4
Princess Ave NN14 ..51 B3
Princess Cl NN3 ....160 B6
Princess Marina
 Hospl NN5 ....158 B6
Princess Way NN8 ..129 E2
Princethorpe Dr OX16 .219 A7
Princewood Rd NN17 .21 E3
Priors Cl NN10 .....147 F8
Priors Ct NN17 .....23 A1
Priors Haw Rd NN17 .23 A1
Priors Sch The CV23 .166 D8
Priory Cl Daventry NN11 .135 C1
 Northampton NN3 ...160 B6
Priory Cres NN7 ....191 C4
Priory Ct Geddington NN14 .54 C3
 Weedon NN7 ......155 A2
Priory Ho NN1 .....159 B6
Priory Rd
 Wellingborough NN8 .129 F3
 Wollaston NN29 ...146 D3
Pritchard Cl NN3 ...143 C6
Probyn Cl NN3 .....143 A6
Promenade NN8 ....129 C6
Prospect Ave
 Irchester NN29 ....147 A7
 Rushden NN10 ....132 B4
Prospect Cl NN29 ..146 D3
Prospect Pl MK19 ..218 F5
Prospect Rd MK11 ..229 C5
Prospect Way NN11 .134 F3
Provence Ct NN5 ...139 F1
Pudding Bag La NN29 .164 D3
Purbeck Rd NN10 ..131 D2
Purse La MK16 .....207 F8
Purser Rd NN1 .....159 F8
Purston Cross Rds OX17 220 D6
Purvis Rd NN10 ....132 A2
Pury Rd NN12 .....205 A3
Puxley Rd MK19 ...228 D5
Pye Ct CV23 ....117 D3
Pyghtle The
 Earls Barton NN6 ..144 E5
 Olney MK46 ......195 F3
 Wellingborough NN8 .129 F6
Pyghtle Way NN4 ...175 A4
Pyghtles The
 Daventry NN11 ....135 B1
 Wollaston NN29 ...146 D1
Pyket Way NN3 ....160 B8
Pyramid Cl NN3 ....142 E4
Pytchley CE Sch NN14 .90 F2
Pytchley Cl NN6 ...106 B2
Pytchley Cl Corby NN17 .36 B8
 West Haddon NN6 .102 C4
Pytchley Dr NN6 ...121 B4
Pytchley La NN15 ..91 C5
Pytchley Lodge Rd NN15 .91 C5
Pytchley Rd Kettering NN15 .91 C6
 Orlingbury NN14 ..109 F5
 Rugby CV22 ......98 C8
 Rushden NN10 ....131 F3
Pytchley Rise NN8 ..129 D3
Pytchley St NN1 ...159 E6
Pytchley View NN3 .126 D1
Pytchley Way
 Brixworth NN6 ....106 B2
 Northampton NN5 .140 B2
Pywell Ct NN17 ....22 E2
Pywell Rd NN17 ...22 E2

Q

Quakers Cl NN7 ....172 F7
Quantock Cl
 Daventry NN11 ....135 B5
 Kettering NN15 ...92 A5
Quantock Cres NN5 .158 D8
Quarry Park Cl NN3 .142 B6
Quarry Rd Brixworth NN6 .106 C3
 Northampton NN5 .140 B2
Quarterstone NN4 ..158 C1
Quatercroft NN3 ...142 E2
Quebec Cl NN18 ...36 C2
Quebec Rd NN4 ....175 E7
Queen Eleanor Lower
 Sch NN4 ....159 B2
Queen Eleanor Rd
 Geddington NN14 ...54 A3
 Northampton NN4 ..159 C2

Queen Eleanor St MK11 .229 E6
Queen Eleanor Terr NN4 .159 C2
Queen Elizabeth
 ....36 F5
Queen St Bozeat NN29 .164 C2
 Desborough NN14 ...51 B3
 Earls Barton NN6 ...144 E5
 Geddington NN14 ...54 A2
 Irthlingborough NN9 .112 E2
 Kettering NN16 ....72 B2
 Market Harborough LE16 .32 A2
 Middleton Cheney OX17 .219 B8
 Rushden NN10 ....132 B2
 Stony Stratford MK11 .229 E6
 Thrapston NN14 ...76 D4
 Weedon NN7 ......155 A2
 Wellingborough NN8 .130 A5
Queen's Park Par NN2 .141 C2
Queen's Pk NN7 ....155 A3
Queen's Rd
 Northampton NN1 ..159 E7
 Towcester NN12 ...203 C6
Queen's Sq NN18 ...36 B5
Queens Cl LE16 ....34 C5
Queens Cres NN11 .141 D2
Queens Rd Daventry NN11 135 B3
 Wilbarston LE16 ...34 D5
 Wollaston NN29 ...146 D2
Queens St Culworth OX17 .198 D2
 Farthinghoe NN13 .221 B4
Queensberry Rd NN15 .72 B1
Queensbury Ct NN15 .72 B1
Queensland Gdns NN2 .141 D2
Queensway
 Burton Latimer NN15 .92 B1
 Higham Ferrers NN10 .132 C5
 Wellingborough NN8 .129 C4
Queenswood Ave NN3 .142 D5
Quernstone La NN14 .158 E3
Quinton House Sch NN5 .158 B5
Quinton La NN11 ...184 C6
Quinton Rd NN4 ...175 F5
Quorn Cl Kettering NN15 .92 A5
 Wellingborough NN8 .129 C4
Quorn Rd NN10 ....132 A3
Quorn Way NN1 ...159 B7

R

Racecourse Rd PE9 ..2 D5
Racedown NN8 ....129 B3
Radleigh Cl NN4 ...159 A2
Radnor Way NN15 ..92 A5
Radstone Rd NN13 .222 F6
Radstone Way NN4 .141 C5
Raeburn Rd NN2 ...141 F2
Raeburn Sch NN2 ..141 F2
Raglan Cl NN10 ....132 C1
Raglan St NN1 .....159 E6
Ragsdale Ct NN14 ..70 E7
Ragsdale St NN14 ..70 E7
Ragsdale Wlk NN3 .142 E6
Railway Cotts
 Church Brampton NN6 .140 A7
 Nether Heyford NN7 .172 A8
Railway View NN16 .72 A2
Raincliffe Cl OX17 ..237 C7
Rainsborough Cres NN4 .158 F4
Rainsborough Gdns LE16 .48 D8
Rainsbrook Ave CV22 .98 E8
Rainsbrook Valley
 Railway CV22 ......98 C6
Raisins Field Cl NN3 .143 C3
Rakestone Cl [4] NN4 .175 D6
Raleigh Cl Corby NN17 .36 A8
 Rothwell NN14 ....70 E7
Raleigh Ct NN11 ...135 B5
Ramsay Cl NN9 ....114 C2
Randall Ho NN1 ...159 F7
Randall Rd NN2 ...141 E1
Rands Way NN9 ...114 E5
Ranelagh Rd NN3 .130 B4
Rankine Ho NN17 ..36 D8
Rannoch Cl NN15 .91 E8
Rannoch Way NN17 .21 C1
Ransome Rd NN4 ..159 D3
Rathbone Cl CV21 ..99 A8
Rathlin Cl NN17 ...36 C8
Raunds Manor Sch
 The NN9 ....114 E6
Raunds Rd
 Chelveston NN9 ...133 C8
 Stanwick NN9 ....114 A4
Raven Dr NN15 ....92 A6
Ravens Croft NN4 ..175 A7
Ravens Way NN3 ..161 C8
Ravensbank NN10 ..132 B4
Ravenscourt NN17 .36 F8
Ravensthorpe Rd NN6 .122 D5
Rawley Cres NN5 ..140 A1
Rawlings Cl NN11 ..135 D1
Rawlins Cl OX17 ...230 A5
Raymond Cl NN29 .146 E1
Raymond Rd NN5 ..159 A7
Raynsford Rd NN5 .158 F8
Rea Cl NN4 ....175 C7
Rectory Cl Barby CV23 .99 C1
 Crick NN6 ....100 F5
 Stanwick NN9 ....113 F4
Rectory Farm Ct PE8 .28 D8
Rectory Farm Lower
 Sch NN3 ....143 C5
Rectory Farm Mews PE8 .28 D8

Rectory Farm Rd NN3 ....**143** D4
Rectory Hill NN14 ....**93** A7
Rectory La Barby CV23 ......**99** C1
　Holcot NN6 ....**126** E8
　Market Harborough LE16 ...**32** A2
　Medbourne LE16 ....**19** A7
　Middleton Cheney OX17 ...**208** F1
　Milton Malsor NN7 ....**174** E3
　Orlingbury NN14 ....**110** A5
　Walgrave NN6 ....**108** A4
　Woodford NN14 ....**94** D6
　Yardley Hastings NN7 .....**179** A7
Rectory Rd NN10 ....**132** B2
Rectory Way NN12 ....**213** B8
Rectory Wlk NN11 ....**91** F7
Red Hill Cres NN29 ....**146** D3
Red House La NN6 ....**108** E4
Red House Rd NN14 ......**142** B7
Red House Wharf NN7 ...**155** C4
Red Lion St OX17 ....**230** F5
Red Lodge Rd NN17 ....**12** A1
Red Row NN6 ....**114** D6
Red Wood Cl NN14 ....**51** C2
Redbourn Pk NN4 ....**160** B3
Redbourne St MK11 ......**229** F5
Redding Cl NN10 ....**148** A7
Redgrave Cl NN15 ....**90** F7
Redhill Way NN9 ....**110** E1
Redhouse Rd NN14 ......**109** C4
Redland Cl LE15 ....**3** F5
Redland Dr NN2 ....**141** A4
Redliech Cl LE16 ....**32** B3
Redmile's La PE9 ....**1** A5
Redmoor NN12 ....**203** B4
Redruth Cl NN4 ....**159** B1
Redwell Jun & Inf
　Schs NN8 ....**129** E7
Redwell L Ctr NN8 ....**129** E7
Redwell Rd NN8 ....**129** F6
Redwing Ave NN3 ....**142** C6
Redwood Cl NN29 ....**147** A7
Reedham Cl NN5 ....**140** C1
Reedhill NN4 ....**158** C1
Reedway NN3 ....**142** A4
Regal Cl NN3 ....**141** F6
Regal Ct NN10 ....**132** C1
Regal Dr NN16 ....**72** C6
Regency Cl NN7 ....**155** B4
Regent Cl NN15 ....**92** A2
Regent Rd NN15 ....**92** A2
Regent St Desborough NN14 **51** B3
　Finedon NN9 ....**111** F4
　Kettering NN16 ....**72** C3
　Northampton NN1 ....**159** C6
　Wellingborough NN8 .....**130** A5
Reigate Wlk NN18 ....**36** B3
Reims Ct NN5 ....**140** A2
Remus Gate NN13 ....**234** A6
Rendelsham Cl NN16 ......**72** A6
Rennishaw Way NN2 ....**141** F3
Repton Ct NN3 ....**142** D4
Reservoir Cl NN7 ....**37** E3
Reservoir Hos NN6 ......**125** D5
Reservoir Rd NN6 ....**72** B4
Resthaven Rd NN4 ......**175** D6
Restormel Cl NN10 ......**132** D1
Retford Ct NN3 ....**142** F4
Retreat The Easton on t H PE9 **1** F5
　Stony Stratford MK11 ....**229** D5
Reynard Way NN2 ....**141** D6
Reynolds Cl Kettering NN15 **92** A8
　Rugby CV21 ....**80** B1
　Wellingborough NN8 ...**129** F7
Reynolds Rd NN18 ....**36** E5
Rhodes Cl Daventry NN11 .**135** C5
　Market Harborough LE16 ..**31** C2
Rhosili Rd NN4 ....**160** A2
Rhymer Cl MK19 ....**206** F4
Rhymer Ho NN2 ....**141** D5
Ribble Cl
　Northampton NN5 ....**140** F2
　Wellingborough NN8 .....**129** D6
Ribblesdale Ave NN17 ......**36** E7
Richard Cl NN15 ....**91** C6
Richardson Way NN9 ....**114** E7
Richardsons La NN14 ......**70** D7
Richmond Ave NN15 ......**91** F8
Richmond Cl NN10 ......**132** C1
Richmond Ct NN12 ......**203** C5
Richmond Rd Corby NN17 ..**36** E6
　Towcester NN12 ....**203** C4
Richmond St OX17 ......**231** A5
Richmond Terr NN5 ......**159** B6
Rickyard Rd NN3 ....**142** E3
Ridding Cl NN18 ....**36** D3
Rides Ct NN3 ....**142** C7
Ridge Rd NN14 ....**76** C4
Ridge The NN29 ....**145** E7
Ridgeway
　Northampton NN3 ......**160** D8
　Stony Stratford MK11 ....**229** F4
　Wellingborough NN8 ...**129** F7
Ridgeway The Barby CV23 **118** E8
　Kilsby CV23 ....**100** A1
　Market Harborough LE16 ...**31** F5
　Welton NN11 ....**119** E1
Ridgeway W LE16 ....**31** F5
Ridgmont MK19 ....**228** E5
Ridgmont Cl MK19 ......**228** E5
Ridgway Rd NN15 ....**92** B8
Riding Cl NN13 ....**233** F5
Riding Rd NN13 ....**233** F5
Riding The MK19 ....**228** D5
Ridings The
　Brixworth NN6 ....**106** C2

Ridings The continued
　Desborough NN14 ....**50** E4
　Northampton NN1 ....**159** D6
　Roade NN7 ....**191** C4
Ridley Ct **1** NN11 ....**135** C2
Ridley St Daventry NN11 ..**135** C2
　Kettering NN16 ....**72** A4
Riggall Cl NN14 ....**90** A3
Riley Cl Daventry NN11 ...**134** F4
　Northampton NN3 ....**143** C5
Riley Rd NN16 ....**71** E4
Rillwood Ct NN3 ....**142** E4
Ring The OX17 ....**208** E4
Ring Way NN4 ....**159** A3
Ringstead Cl Corby NN17 ..**36** B8
　Kettering NN16 ....**91** F5
Ringstead Rd
　Denford NN14 ....**95** C5
　Great Addington NN14 ...**94** C2
Ringwood Cl NN2 ....**141** A5
Ripley Cl LE16 ....**32** B3
Ripley Rd LE16 ....**20** D1
Ripley Wlk NN18 ....**36** C3
Ripon Cl NN4 ....**159** A2
Rise The Northampton NN2 **141** B3
　Twyford OX17 ....**230** A5
Ritchie Pk LE16 ....**48** E8
River La PE8 ....**28** C8
Rivercrest Rd MK19 ......**229** B6
Riverside
　Market Harborough LE16 ..**32** A4
　Oundle PE8 ....**42** A6
Riverside Cl PE8 ....**42** A4
Riverside Ct NN7 ....**157** D4
Riverside Dr NN7 ....**155** B3
Riverside Ind Est LE16 ....**32** A4
Riverside Spinney PE8 ......**8** A3
Riverside Way Islip NN14 ..**76** E7
　Northampton NN1 ....**159** F5
Riverstone Way NN4 ....**158** D2
Riverwell NN3 ....**143** D2
Rivetts Cl MK46 ....**195** E4
Rixon Cl NN3 ....**142** E1
Rixon Rd NN8 ....**130** C7
RNIB Rushton Hall
　Sch NN14 ....**52** B2
Roade Hill NN7 ....**191** F1
Roade Sch NN7 ....**191** C3
Robb's La NN14 ....**75** F6
Robbins Ct CV22 ....**98** F8
Roberson Cl NN12 ......**203** C4
Robert Hill Cl CV21 ......**80** A1
Robert Smyth Sch
　The LE16 ....**31** E5
Robert St NN1 ....**159** D7
Roberts Field NN7 ......**156** B1
Roberts St Bozeat NN29 ..**164** C2
　Rushden NN10 ....**132** C2
　Wellingborough NN8 ...**129** E4
Robertson Cl CV23 ....**80** A5
Robin Cl Kettering NN15 ...**92** A6
　Towcester NN12 ....**203** C3
Robin La NN8 ....**130** A7
Robinia Cl NN7 ....**158** E3
Robins Cl NN7 ....**192** C1
Robins Field NN8 ....**8** A4
Robins Wood PE8 ....**8** A4
Robinson Cl NN16 ....**71** F4
Robinson Dr NN13 ......**233** D7
Robinson Rd NN10 ......**132** C2
Robinson Way NN16 ......**71** F4
Roche Cl NN11 ....**153** C8
Roche Way NN8 ....**129** F6
Rochelle Way NN5 ......**140** A2
Rochester Gdns LE16 ......**31** D1
Rochester Way OX17 ....**230** E5
Rock Hill NN14 ....**70** D7
Rock Rd Finedon NN9 ...**112** A5
　Oundle PE8 ....**41** F6
Rock St NN8 ....**129** F5
Rockcroft **3** NN4 ......**175** D6
Rockhill Rd NN6 ....**121** A3
Rockingham Castle &
　Gdns LE16 ....**21** B3
Rockingham Cl
　Daventry NN11 ....**135** B4
　Thrapston NN14 ....**76** B2
Rockingham Ct NN10 ...**148** A8
Rockingham Hills PE8 .....**41** E7
Rockingham Ind Est LE16 .**32** B3
Rockingham Mews NN17 ..**37** A7
Rockingham
　Paddocks NN16 ....**72** B6
Rockingham Prim
　Sch NN17 ....**37** A8
Rockingham Rd
　Caldecott LE16 ....**21** B6
　Corby NN17 ....**21** E2
　Corby NN14 ....**52** F5
　Cottingham LE16 ....**20** E2
　Gretton LE16 ....**21** E7
　Kettering NN14 ....**53** A3
　Kettering NN16 ....**72** A5
　Market Harborough LE16 ..**32** B4
　Northampton NN4 ......**159** C2
Rockleigh Cl NN9 ......**112** A5
Roderick Way NN11 ....**135** B4
Rodney Cl NN11 ....**135** C1
Rodney Dr NN17 ....**36** B8
Roe Rd NN1 ....**159** A7
Rokeby Cty Fst Sch CV22 ..**98** A8
Rokeby Mid Sch CV22 ....**98** A8
Roland Way NN10 ......**132** B6
Rolfe Cres NN7 ....**156** B1
Rolleston Cl LE16 ....**32** A3
Roman Cl NN17 ....**38** B8
Roman Dr PE8 ....**8** D2

Roman Way
　Brackley NN13 ....**234** A6
　Daventry NN11 ....**135** C5
　Desborough NN14 ....**51** B2
　Irchester NN29 ....**147** B3
　Market Harborough LE16 ..**31** E4
　Raunds NN9 ....**114** F6
　Thrapston NN14 ....**76** E3
Romany Rd NN2 ....**141** E2
Romney Rd NN18 ....**36** C5
Romulus Way NN13 ....**234** A6
Rookery La
　Northampton NN2 ......**141** A5
　Stoke Bruerne NN12 ...**191** B1
Rookwell Dr LE16 ....**31** F1
Roper Cl CV21 ....**99** A8
Rose Ave Rushden NN10 .**131** F1
　Weldon NN17 ....**38** B8
Rose Cl Broughton NN14 ...**90** B5
　Hartwell NN7 ....**192** E2
　Rothwell NN14 ....**70** E6
　Wollaston NN29 ....**146** C3
Rose Cres Irchester NN29 .**147** B8
　Weldon NN17 ....**38** B8
Rose Dr NN13 ....**233** D8
Rose Hall La OX17 ......**220** A8
Rose Hill NN9 ....**112** A5
Rose Paddock NN14 ......**94** D7
Rose Terr NN14 ....**94** D7
Rosebery Ave NN5 ......**158** F6
Rosebery St
　Burton Latimer NN15 ....**92** B1
　8 Kettering NN16 ......**72** C1
　Ringstead NN14 ....**95** B3
Rosedale Ave NN17 ....**36** E6
Rosedale Rd NN2 ....**141** D3
Roseholme Rd NN1 ......**160** A8
Rosemoor Cl LE16 ....**32** B3
Rosemoor Dr NN4 ......**175** C7
Rosemount Dr NN15 ......**91** C7
Rosenella **3** NN4 ......**158** F3
Rosette Cl NN5 ....**158** C8
Rosewood Ave CV22 ......**98** A8
Rosewood Cl NN11 ......**135** C5
Rosewood Pl NN16 ....**72** C4
Rosgill Pl NN3 ....**142** B2
Ross Rd NN5 ....**158** C6
Rossendale Dr NN15 ......**92** A5
Rossetti Rd NN18 ....**36** E5
Rossiter Ho NN13 ......**233** E6
Rothersthorpe
　Ave NN4 ....**159** A3
Rothersthorpe CE Prim
　Sch NN7 ....**174** A6
Rothersthorpe Cres NN4 **159** A3
Rothersthorpe Rd
　Kislingbury NN7 ....**157** E2
　Northampton NN4 ......**159** A3
Rothesay Rd NN2 ....**141** F2
Rothwell Inf Sch NN14 ....**70** E6
Rothwell Jun Sch NN16 ...**70** D7
Rothwell Rd
　Desborough NN14 ....**51** A2
　Harrington NN6 ....**69** B5
　Kettering NN16 ....**71** D4
　Kettering NN16 ....**71** F3
Rotten Row NN29 ......**146** D2
Rotton Row NN9 ....**114** D7
Roughton Cl NN15 ....**91** B6
Round Cl NN11 ....**119** E1
Roundhill Rd NN15 ....**91** C8
Roundtown OX17 ......**237** C7
Roundway The NN11 ....**135** D6
Roveley Ct MK11 ......**229** F5
Rowan Ave
　Market Harborough LE16 ..**31** E4
　Northampton NN3 ......**142** C5
Rowan Cl Brackley NN13 .**222** F1
　Towcester NN12 ....**203** B4
　Wellingborough NN8 ...**129** E5
Rowan Ct NN17 ....**21** E4
Rowan Gate Prim
　Sch NN8 ....**130** B6
Rowan Way NN11 ......**184** B6
Rowans The NN11 ......**135** C4
Rowden La LE16 ....**17** D4
Rowell Way NN8 ....**42** B4
Rowlandson Cl NN3 ....**142** E1
Rowlett Cl NN10 ....**132** C5
Rowlett Prim Sch NN17 ...**37** B6
Rowlett Rd NN17 ....**36** D8
Rowley Way NN17 ....**36** D6
Rowtree Rd NN4 ....**175** B6
Roxeby Wlk NN5 ....**140** D1
Roxton Cl NN15 ....**92** A5
Royal Cl NN11 ....**135** B3
Royal Oak La OX17 ......**220** A8
Royal Oak Way N NN11 ..**134** F3
Royal Oak Way S NN11 ..**134** F2
Royal Terr NN1 ....**159** C7
Royce Cl NN17 ....**21** F1
Rubens Wlk NN18 ....**36** E5
Ruddington Cl NN3 ....**160** E2
Rudge Mews NN5 ......**157** F8
Rudgeway NN13 ....**233** F2
Rufford Ave NN3 ....**160** E2
Rufford Cl NN15 ....**92** A5
Rufford Wlk NN18 ....**36** C6
Rugby Cl LE16 ....**31** C2
Rugby Rd Barby CV23 ....**99** C1
　Kilsby CV23 ....**99** C5
　Lilbourne CV23 ....**80** F6
　South Kilworth LE17 .....**62** E6
　Swinford LE17 ....**62** B3
Rugby Way NN9 ....**114** D7
Ruins The NN12 ....**203** C6
Runnell La PE8 ....**15** F5

Runneymede
　Gdns **5** NN3 ....**142** F1
Rupert Rd LE16 ....**31** E1
Rush Cl NN7 ....**192** E2
Rushden Hospl NN10 ....**148** B8
Rushden Rd
　Newton Bromswold NN10 **149** C7
　Wymington NN10 ....**148** A6
Rushden Sch NN10 ......**132** A4
Rushes La LE16 ....**30** F3
Rushmere Ave NN1 ......**160** B6
Rushmere Ct NN14 ....**76** B3
Rushmere Cres NN1 ....**160** B6
Rushmere Rd NN1 ......**160** B5
Rushmere Way
　Northampton NN1 ......**160** B6
　Rushden NN10 ....**132** B4
Rushmills NN1 ....**160** B3
Rushmills Prim Sch NN14 .**52** C2
Rushton Rd
　Desborough NN14 ....**51** C3
　Rothwell NN14 ....**70** E8
　Wilbarston NN14 ....**34** C5
Rushton Triangular
　Lodge NN14 ....**52** A2
Rushwell Cl NN14 ....**94** B3
Rushy End NN4 ....**175** B6
Ruskin Ave NN8 ....**129** C4
Ruskin Jun & Inf
　Schs NN8 ....**129** C3
Ruskin Rd Daventry NN11 **153** C8
　Northampton NN2 ......**141** C4
Russell Cl LE16 ....**31** F5
Russell Fst Sch MK11 ....**229** D5
Russell Hill PE8 ....**8** A6
Russell Rise NN7 ....**155** C5
Russell St Kettering NN16 .**72** C2
　Stony Stratford MK11 ...**229** D5
Russell Way NN10 ......**132** B6
Russet Dr NN3 ....**143** A2
Russett Cl LE16 ....**31** F5
Ruth Gdns NN16 ....**72** E3
Rutherford Ct NN17 ......**22** B1
Rutherford Dr NN8 ....**129** A5
Rutherford Way NN11 ...**134** F4
Rutherglen Rd NN17 ......**36** F7
Rutland Cl NN17 ....**36** B7
Rutland St NN14 ....**50** F4
Rutland St NN16 ....**72** C3
Rutland Wlk
　Market Harborough LE16 ..**31** F5
　Northampton NN3 ......**142** B7
Rydal NN8 ....**129** B3
Rydal Mt NN3 ....**142** C3
Rydalside Kettering NN15 .**92** D1
　Northampton NN4 ......**158** F3
Ryder Ct NN18 ....**52** F8
Ryder View NN18 ....**36** C7
Rye Cl NN10 ....**148** C8
Ryeburn Way NN8 ......**129** E5
Ryebury Hill NN8 ....**111** E2
Ryefields NN6 ....**124** B8
Ryehill Cl Isham NN14 ....**91** E1
　Long Buckby NN6 ......**121** A3
　Northampton NN5 ......**140** C2
Ryehill Ct NN5 ....**140** C2
Ryehill Rd NN3 ....**142** F3
Ryeland MK11 ....**229** E6
Ryeland Rd NN5 ....**158** A8
Ryeland Way NN5 ......**140** A1
Ryelands Mid Sch NN5 ..**158** A8
Ryland Rd Moulton NN3 ..**142** C8
　Northampton NN1 ......**141** E2
Rylands Cl LE16 ....**32** B3
Rylstone The NN8 ......**129** B4

S

Sackville St Kettering NN16 **72** A4
　Raunds NN9 ....**114** D6
　Thrapston NN14 ....**76** D2
Sacrewell Farm & Ctry
　Ctr PE8 ....**8** B5
Saddleback Rd NN5 ....**158** D6
Saddlers Sq NN3 ....**142** F6
Saddlers Way NN9 ......**114** B5
Saffron Cl NN4 ....**175** D5
Saffron Rd NN10 ....**132** B6
Sage Cl NN3 ....**142** E4
Saimon Cl NN13 ....**233** E8
St Alban's Cl
　Kettering NN15 ....**73** A1
　Northampton NN3 ......**142** B3
St Alban's Rd NN3 ......**142** B3
St Albans Pl NN29 ......**146** D2
St Amandas Cl NN15 ......**72** F2
St Andrew's CE Prim
　Sch NN16 ....**72** A4
St Andrew's Cl NN13 ......**77** D3
St Andrew's Ct NN14 ......**90** B4
St Andrew's Ho **9** NN1 .**159** F6
St Andrew's La NN14 ......**93** A7
St Andrew's Rd
　East Haddon NN6 ......**122** D5
　Northampton NN2 ......**159** B7
St Andrew's St
　Kettering NN16 ....**72** B3
　Northampton NN1 ......**159** C6
St Andrews Cl
　Broughton NN14 ....**90** B4
　Great Easton LE16 ......**20** D7
St Andrews Cres
　Rugby CV22 ....**98** A8
　Wellingborough NN8 ...**129** E2
St Andrews Dr NN11 ...**135** E3

St Andrews La NN14 ......**77** D4
St Andrews Way NN14 ....**90** B4
St Ann's Ct PE8 ....**41** F5
St Anne's Rd NN15 ....**73** A1
St Annes Cl
　Brackley NN13 ....**233** D8
　Daventry NN11 ....**153** C8
St Anthony's Hill NN14 ....**51** A2
St Anthony's Rd NN15 ....**72** F1
St Anthonys Cl NN11 ...**153** B8
St Augustin Way NN11 ..**135** D1
St Augustine's Cl NN15 ...**73** A1
St Barnabas CE Inf
　Sch NN16 ....**129** F4
St Barnabas' Cl NN15 ....**73** A1
St Barnabas Ho **10** NN1 **159** C6
St Barnabas St NN8 ....**129** F4
St Bartholomews
　Ho **6** NN1 ....**159** C6
St Bartholomew's
　Cl NN15 ....**73** A1
St Benedicts Mount NN4 **158** E2
St Bernards Ct NN15 ......**72** F1
St Boltoph Gr PE8 ....**28** E7
St Botolph's Rd NN15 ....**91** F7
St Brendan's Jun & Inf
　Schs NN18 ....**36** B6
St Catharine's Rd NN15 ..**73** A1
St Catherines Cl NN11 ..**153** B8
St Cecilia's Cl NN15 ......**72** F1
St Chad's Cl NN15 ....**73** A1
St Christopher's Cl NN13 .**73** A1
St Christopher's Dr PE8 ..**42** B4
St Christopher's
　Wlk NN3 ....**160** B7
St Crispin Ave NN8 ......**129** F2
St Crispin Cl NN15 ....**92** C3
St Crispin Hospl NN5 ....**158** A7
St Crispin Rd NN6 ......**144** F4
St David's Cl NN13 ......**234** A8
St David's Ct NN13 ......**234** A8
St David's Rd
　Brixworth NN6 ....**106** A1
St David's Rd
　Northampton NN2 ......**141** C2
　Rushden NN10 ....**131** D3
St Davids Cl NN6 ......**106** B1
St Davids RC Mid
　Sch NN1 ....**141** C3
St Dunstan's Cl NN15 ....**91** F8
St Dunstans Rise NN4 ..**158** C1
St Edmund's Hospl NN1 **159** E7
St Edmund's Rd NN11 ..**159** E6
St Edmund's St NN1 ....**159** E6
St Edmunds Cl NN11 ...**153** C7
St Edward's RC Prim
　Sch NN15 ....**91** E7
St Emilion Cl NN5 ......**139** F1
St Francis Ave NN5 ....**159** A8
St Francis' Cl NN15 ......**73** A1
St George's Ave NN2 ..**159** D8
St George's Pl NN2 ....**159** C8
St George's St NN1 ....**159** C7
St George's Way NN10 .**131** F3
St Georges Ave CV22 ....**98** A8
St Georges Cl NN12 ....**203** C5
St Georges Ho **2** NN1 .**159** C6
St Giles' Cl NN15 ....**73** A1
St Giles Mews MK11 ...**229** D6
St Giles' Sq NN1 ....**159** D5
St Giles' St NN1 ....**159** D6
St Giles' Terr NN1 ......**159** D6
St Giles's Cl NN14 ....**51** A3
St Gregory's RC Lower
　Sch NN3 ....**142** C3
St Gregory's Rd NN3 ...**142** D3
St Helens Cl NN6 ....**84** D4
St Hilda's Cl NN11 ......**153** C8
St Hughes Cl NN11 ....**153** C8
St James' CE Lower
　Sch NN5 ....**159** A6
St James Cl
　2 Daventry NN11 ....**135** C1
　Hanslope MK19 ....**207** A2
St James' Cl
　Kettering NN15 ....**92** A8
　Rushden NN10 ....**132** C4
St James' Cres NN14 ......**76** C2
St James Inf Sch NN11 ..**135** C1
St James' Lake Nature
　Reserve NN13 ....**233** E6
St James' Mill Rd NN5 ..**159** A4
St James Mill Rd E NN1 **159** B4
St James' Park Rd NN5 .**159** A6
St James Rd
　Brackley NN13 ....**233** F5
　Corby NN17 ....**37** A6
St James' Rd NN5 ......**159** A5
St James Ret Pk NN1 ..**159** B5
St James St NN11 ......**135** C1
St James' St NN1 ......**159** C5
St John's Ave NN2 ......**141** C6
St John's Ho **8** NN1 ..**159** C6
St John's La MK19 ......**228** B4
St John's Pl NN17 ....**37** B6
St John's Rd NN15 ....**91** F8
St John's Sq NN11 ....**135** C2
St John's St
　Northampton NN1 ......**159** D5
　Wellingborough NN8 ...**129** F5
St John's Terr NN1 ....**159** D5
St John's Way NN7 ....**177** A2
St John's Wlk NN3 ....**142** D1
St Johns Ave CV22 ....**98** E8
St Johns Cl
　Daventry NN11 ....**153** B8
　Rothersthorpe NN7 ....**174** A6
St Johns Ct NN1 ....**159** D5

St Johns Rd NN12 ....189 E4
St Joseph's Cl NN15 ......73 A1
St Joseph's RC Prim
　Sch LE16 ....31 E3
St Josephs Cl MK46 ......195 F4
St Julien Cl NN5 ....140 A2
St Katharine's Way NN29 131 B1
St Katharine's Ct 25 NN1 .159 C6
St Katharine's Sq 27 NN1 .159 C6
St Katharine's St 2 NN1 .159 C6
St Laurence Way NN9 ....113 F4
St Lawrence CE
　Sch NN12 ....203 C5
St Lawrence Ct 12 NN1 ...159 E6
St Lawrence Ho 3 NN1 ...159 C6
St Lawrence Lower
　Sch NN10 ....148 A5
St Lawrence Rd NN12 ....203 C5
St Lawrence Rd S NN12 ..203 D4
St Lawrence Wlk NN10 ...148 B5
St Leonard's Cl NN15 .....72 F1
St Leonard's Rd NN4 .....159 C3
St Leonards Cl CV23 .....166 D8
St Luke's Cl NN15 ....92 A8
St Luke's Ho 12 NN1 .....159 C6
St Luke's Hospl LE16 .....31 D5
St Luke's Rd NN18 ....37 A5
St Lukes Cl NN6 ....105 B1
St Magdalenes Rd NN15 ..72 F2
St Margaret's
　Gdns 1 NN5 ....140 F1
St Margarets Ave NN10 ..132 A1
St Mark's Cl Kettering NN15 73 A1
　Rushden NN10 ....131 E2
St Mark's Cres NN18 ....141 B6
St Mark's Rd NN18 ....37 A5
St Marks Ho 7 NN1 ......159 C6
St Martins Cl NN2 ....141 C4
St Martins Ho 1 NN1 ....159 C6
St Martins Yd LE16 ......31 E3
St Martyn's Way NN7 ....155 B3
St Mary & St Giles CE
　Mid Sch MK11 ....229 E6
St Mary's Ave
　Finedon NN9 ....111 F5
　Rushden NN10 ....132 B1
　Stony Stratford MK11 ...229 E6
St Mary's CE Prim
　Sch NN16 ....72 C2
St Mary's Cl Nassington PE8 15 E5
　Priors Hardwick CV23 ...186 A5
St Mary's Ct Finedon NN9 .111 E5
　Market Harborough LE16 ..32 A4
　22 Northampton NN1 ...159 C6
St Mary's Hospl NN15 ....72 C1
St Mary's Pl LE16 ....31 F3
St Mary's RC Lower
　Sch NN5 ....140 F1
St Mary's RC Mid
　Sch NN3 ....142 C3
St Mary's Rd Bozeat NN29 164 D2
　Kettering NN15 ....72 C1
　Market Harborough LE16 .31 F3
St Mary's St NN1 ....159 C6
St Mary's Way
　Nassington PE8 ....15 E5
　Roade NN7 ....191 D5
　Weedon NN7 ....155 B3
St Marys Cl Thrapston NN14 76 F3
　Woodnewton PE8 ....14 E2
St Marys Ct NN7 ....173 E4
St Marys Hill PE8 ......14 E2
St Marys Rd NN29 ......146 E2
St Matthew's Par NN2 ..141 F1
St Matthew's Rd NN15 ...73 A1
St Michael's Ave NN1 ...159 E7
St Michael's Ct NN7 ....205 F8
St Michael's La NN29 ...146 D2
St Michael's Mount NN1 .159 E6
St Michael's Rd
　Kettering NN15 ....91 C4
　Northampton NN1 ......159 C6
St Michaels Gdns NN15 ..91 C4
St Nicholas Cl
　Kettering NN15 ....72 F2
　Market Harborough LE16 .31 F2
St Nicholas Rd NN29 ....145 C6
St Nicholas Way Islip NN14 76 B3
　Market Harborough LE16 .31 F2
St Oswald's Cl NN15 ....91 F8
St Osyths La PE8 ....42 A5
St Patrick St 11 NN1 ....159 C7
St Patrick's RC Prim
　Sch NN18 ....36 D4
St Paul's CE Lower
　Sch NN2 ....159 C8
St Paul's Rd Kettering NN15 72 B1
　Stony Stratford MK11 ..229 E6
St Paul's Rd NN2 ....159 C8
St Paul's Terr NN2 .....159 C8
St Peter's Ave
　Kettering NN16 ....72 C1
　Rushden NN10 ....131 E7
St Peter's CE Jun
　Sch NN9 ....114 E6
St Peter's Cl NN14 ......37 F2
St Peter's Gate NN1 ....234 A7
St Peter's Gdns NN3 ....142 D1
St Peter's Ho 20 NN1 ...159 C6
St Peter's Ind Sch NN3 ..143 A3
St Peter's Rd NN13 ....233 F8
St Peter's Sch NN15 ....91 B8
St Peter's St NN1 ......159 B5
St Peter's Way Corby NN17 37 A6
　Irthlingborough NN9 ....112 F2
　Northampton NN1 ......159 C6
　Weedon NN7 ....155 B3
St Peters Cl NN11 ......153 B8

St Peters Ct NN9 ....114 D6
St Peters Rd PE8 ....41 F7
St Peters Sq 12 NN1 ....159 C5
St Peters Way NN7 .....161 F6
St Peters Wlk 5 NN1 ....159 C5
St Philip's Cl NN15 ......73 A1
St Rumbolds Dr OX17 ...231 A6
St Saviour's Rd NN15 ....73 A1
St Simon's Cl NN15 .....73 A1
St Stephen's Rd NN15 ...73 A1
St Stephens Ho 9 NN1 ..159 C6
St Swithins Cl NN15 .....72 F2
St Theresa's Cl NN15 ....72 F1
St Thomas More RC Prim
　Sch NN16 ....71 F1
St Thomas Rd NN7 .....161 D3
St Valentine's Cl NN15 ..72 F1
St Vincents Ave NN15 ...72 F2
St Wilfrids Rd PE8 ......41 F7
Salcey Ave NN7 ....192 D2
Salcey Cl Daventry NN11 .135 B4
　Hartwell NN7 ....192 E4
　Kettering NN15 ....92 A5
Salcey Rise NN7 ....177 B1
Salcey St NN4 ....159 C2
Salcombe Rd NN18 .....36 E4
Salem Cl NN6 ....121 A3
Salem La 9 NN8 ....130 A5
Salen Cl NN15 ....92 B5
Salford Cl NN6 ....64 E6
Salisbury Rd NN8 ......130 C5
Salisbury St Kettering NN16 72 C4
　Northampton NN2 ......159 C8
Sallow Ave NN3 ....143 C3
Sallow Rd NN17 ....22 C1
Salmons La OX17 ......220 B8
Salt Pikes NN11 ....125 B8
Salthouse Rd NN4 .....160 C2
Saltwell Sq 5 NN3 .....143 C2
Samuel Pl NN7 ....37 A8
Samwell Way NN4 .....158 D1
Sandby Rd NN18 ....36 E4
Sanders Cl
　Braunston NN11 ....118 B1
　Wellingborough NN8 ...111 B1
Sanders La NN12 ......217 D3
Sanders Lodge Ind
　Est NN10 ....131 D3
Sanders Rd NN8 ....111 B1
Sanders Terr NN6 .....121 B4
Sanderson Cl NN15 .....91 A8
Sandfield St NN3 ....142 B6
Sandhill Rd 2 NN5 .....159 A6
Sandhills NN6 ....105 A1
Sandhills Cl NN12 .....141 B6
Sandhills Rd NN2 ......141 B6
Sandhurst Cl NN4 .....175 B8
Sandiland Rd NN15 ....142 B2
Sandlands Ave NN14 ...55 F7
Sandlands Cl NN14 ....55 F7
Sandover NN4 ....175 D6
Sandpiper Cl NN15 .....92 A2
Sandpiper La NN8 .....130 A7
Sandringham Cl
　Brackley NN13 ....233 E7
　Northampton NN1 .....160 B7
　Rushden NN10 ....132 A1
　Towcester NN12 ......203 C4
　Wellingborough NN8 ...129 E2
Sandringham Ct NN15 ..91 D5
Sandringham Rd
　Kings Sutton OX17 ....230 F5
　Northampton NN1 .....160 A7
Sandringham Way LE16 ..32 B3
Sands Cl NN12 ....172 D1
Sandy Cl NN8 ....129 F6
Sandy La
　Church Brampton NN6 .140 D8
　Harpole NN7 ....157 E7
　Northampton NN5 ....139 F2
Sandyhome Rd NN12 ...203 C5
Saneco La NN6 ....106 B3
Sansom Ct NN3 ....142 D4
Sansome Rd NN7 ......177 B3
Sapphire Cl NN15 ......72 C1
Sarek Pk NN17 ....174 F7
Sargeants La NN4 .....175 C4
Sargent Rd NN18 ......36 E4
Sarrington Rd NN17 ....36 F8
Sartoris Rd NN10 .....131 F2
Saruman Cl NN3 ......143 B6
Sassoon Cl NN8 ......129 C6
Sassoon Mews NN8 ...129 B6
Saunders Cl NN16 .....72 B1
Savill Cl NN4 ....175 C7
Sawyers Cres NN9 ....133 B8
Saxby Cres NN8 ....130 C4
Saxilby Cl NN18 ....36 C4
Saxon Cl Desborough NN14 51 A3
　Market Harborough LE16 .31 F4
Saxon Dale NN16 ......72 C6
Saxon Rise
　Earls Barton NN6 .....144 E3
　Irchester NN29 ....147 C8
　Northampton NN5 ....158 B7
Saxon St NN3 ....142 B1
Saxon Way NN9 ......114 E6
Saxon Way E NN18 ....53 A8
Saxon Way W NN18 ....52 F8
Scaldwell Rd
　Brixworth NN6 ....106 D4
　Old NN6 ....107 C7
Scapa Cl NN17 ....36 C8
Scarborough Rd NN17 ..112 E2
Scarborough Wlk NN18 ..36 B4
Scarletwell St NN1 .....159 B6
Scarplands The NN5 ...158 C6
Scharpwell NN9 ....112 E3

Scholars Ct NN1 ......159 D5
School Cl Braunston NN11 118 D1
　Greens Norton NN12 ..202 D8
　Yelvertoft NN6 ....82 A4
School End OX17 ......237 C7
School Gdns CV21 .....80 A1
School Hill Irchester NN29 147 B8
　Middleton LE16 ....35 C8
　Newnham NN11 ....153 D4
School La Abthorpe NN12 .202 A2
　Badby NN11 ....152 F3
　Barrowden LE15 ....3 F5
　Braybrooke LE16 ......49 F5
　Bythorn PE28 ....97 D4
　Castlethorpe MK19 ...218 F5
　Cottingham LE16 ......20 C1
　Denford NN14 ....95 C6
　Elton PE8 ....28 D8
　Evenley NN13 ....233 F2
　Everdon NN11 ....170 A8
　Eydon NN11 ....184 C1
　Greens Norton NN12 ..202 D8
　Hannington NN6 ......108 C2
　Harpole NN7 ....157 B6
　Hartwell NN7 ....192 D2
　Husbands Bosworth LE17 .45 E5
　Irchester NN29 ....147 A8
　Islip NN14 ....76 B2
　Kettering NN16 ....72 B2
　Kislingbury NN7 ......157 D4
　Little Harrowden NN9 ..110 C4
　Lubenham LE16 ......30 F3
　Market Harborough LE16 31 E3
　Morcott LE15 ....3 A6
　Moulton NN3 ....126 C1
　Naseby NN6 ....85 B8
　Priors Marston CV23 ..166 D8
　Quinton NN7 ....176 B1
　Rothwell NN14 ....70 D7
　Scaldwell NN6 ....106 F6
　Swinford LE17 ....62 B4
　Titchmarsh NN14 .....77 C4
　Wappenham NN12 ....213 B8
　Warmington PE8 ......28 B3
　Weldon NN17 ....38 B8
　Wilbarston LE16 ......34 C5
School La
　Yardley Gobion NN12 ..217 E6
　Yelvertoft NN6 ....82 B4
School Pl NN18 ....36 D5
School Rd Gretton NN17 .10 B1
　Irchester NN29 ....147 A8
　Pattishall NN12 ......188 F8
　Spratton NN6 ....105 B1
School St Daventry NN11 .135 A2
　Rugby CV21 ....80 A1
　Sulgrave OX17 ....210 F7
　Woodford Halse NN11 .184 C6
Scirocco Cl NN3 ......141 E6
Scoborough Rd LE16, LE17 30 A1
Scotgate NN17 ....10 C7
Scotia Cl NN4 ....160 C2
Scotland End LE16 .....31 F1
Scotland Rd LE16 ......32 A2
Scotland St NN16 .....72 C3
Scotney Cl 1 NN4 ......175 C8
Scots Mere NN9 ....112 D3
Scott Ave NN14 ......70 D7
Scott Cl Daventry NN11 .135 C4
　Market Harborough LE16 .31 E5
　Ravensthorpe NN6 ....103 D1
Scott Rd Corby NN17 ....37 A6
　Kettering NN16 ....72 C5
　Wellingborough NN8 ..129 C3
Scotter Wlk NN18 .....36 C4
Scotts La LE16 ....34 C5
Scriveners La NN12 ...216 A8
Scrivens Hill NN11 ....184 D6
Seaford Wlk NN18 .....36 B5
Seagrave Ct NN3 ......143 B5
Seagrave St NN15 .....91 C8
Sears Cl NN7 ....155 E6
Sears Ho NN1 ....159 F7
Seaton Cres NN18 .....36 E4
Seaton Dr NN3 ....142 F1
Seaton Rd Barrowden LE15 .3 C4
　Harringworth NN17 ....10 E8
Second Ave NN8 ......129 D3
Second St NN13 ......238 E6
Sedbergh Rd NN18 ....36 C4
Sedgemoor Way NN11 .135 C6
Sedgwick Ct NN3 .....142 F3
Sedlescombe Pk CV22 ..98 A8
Seedfield Cl NN3 ......142 E1
Selby Cl LE16 ....48 E8
Selby Rd NN15 ....91 F8
Selby Wlk NN18 ....36 C4
Selsey Rd NN18 ....36 B5
Selwyn Cl NN11 ....153 C7
Semilong Ho 4 NN2 ...159 C7
Semilong Rd NN2 .....159 C8
Sentinel Rd NN4 ......158 E1
Senwick Dr NN8 ......130 C4
Senwick Rd NN8 ......130 C4
Setchells Yd PE8 ......41 F5
Seven Sisters Cl NN13 .221 B4
Severn Cl NN8 ....129 C6
Severn Ct NN15 ....92 B2
Severn Dr NN5 ....140 F2
Severn Ho PE8 ....42 A6
Severn The NN11 ......135 A1
Severn Way NN16 .....72 A5
Severn Wlk NN17 .....21 C1
Sexton Cl NN11 ....135 B3
Seymour Pl PE8 ....41 E7
Seymour St NN5 ......159 A6
Shackleton Cl NN14 ...70 D7
Shackleton Dr NN11 ...135 C5

Shadowfax Dr NN3 ....143 C5
Shaftesbury Rd NN18 ..36 B6
Shaftesbury St NN16 ...72 C2
Shakespeare Ave NN11 .135 B2
Shakespeare Dr NN15 ..92 A2
Shakespeare Rd
　Kettering NN16 ....72 B5
　Northampton NN1 .....159 E7
　Rushden NN10 ....131 E2
　Wellingborough NN8 ..129 C6
Shakespeare Way NN17 ..36 D8
Shale End NN5 ....140 A3
Shannon Cl NN10 .....132 D3
Shannon Ct NN18 .....36 E4
Shannon Way NN15 ...92 B2
Shap Gn NN3 ....142 C4
Shard Cl NN4 ....175 D6
Sharman Cl
　Daventry NN11 ....135 C5
　Rothwell NN14 ....70 F7
Sharman Rd
　Northampton NN5 ....159 A5
　Wellingborough NN8 ..129 F4
Sharmans Cl NN7 .....162 A6
Sharplands NN7 ......163 D5
Sharrow Pl 7 NN3 .....143 C2
Shatterstone 2 NN4 ..175 D6
Shaw Cl NN3 ....129 B5
Shawell Rd LE17 ......62 A4
Sheaf Cl NN15 ....140 B2
Sheaf St NN11 ....135 C1
Shearwater La NN8 ...130 A7
Shedfield Way NN4 ...175 C6
Sheep St Kettering NN16 .72 B1
　Northampton NN1 ....159 C6
　Wellingborough NN8 ..130 A4
Sheerwater Dr NN3 ...143 D3
Sheffield Cl NN9 ......114 C5
Sheffield Way NN6 ....144 E3
Sheffield Wlk NN18 ....36 C4
Sheldons La NN6 .....108 A5
Shelford Cl NN3 ......143 B5
Shelia Pl NN16 ....72 E4
Shelley Cl NN12 ......203 B5
Shelley Cres NN11 ....135 B2
Shelley Dr Corby NN17 ..21 D1
Shelley Dr
　Higham Ferrers NN10 ..132 B2
　Kettering NN16 ....72 B5
　Wellingborough NN8 ..129 B4
Shelley St NN2 ....141 F1
Shelleycotes Rd NN6 ..106 A1
Shelmerdine Rise NN9 ..114 D6
Shelsley Dr NN4 ......141 F4
Shelton Ct Corby NN17 ..22 E2
　Wollaston NN29 ......146 D2
Shelton Rd Corby NN17 ..22 C4
　Raunds NN9 ....114 C4
Shepherd Cl NN2 .....141 A5
Shepherds Hill NN29 ..146 F1
Shepherds Wlk
　Bugbrooke NN7 ......173 A8
　Harpole NN7 ....157 C6
Sheppard Way NN12 ..213 B8
Shepperton Ct
　Castlethorpe MK19 ...218 F5
　Northampton NN3 ....143 C2
Sheppey La NN7 ......177 B3
Shepton Ct NN18 .....36 A6
Sheraton Ct NN3 .....142 C2
Sherborne Way NN14 ..76 C2
Sherborne Wlk NN18 ..36 A6
Sheriff Rd NN1 ....159 F7
Sherrard Rd LE16 ....31 E5
Sherwood Ave NN4 ...140 F6
Sherwood Cl NN17 ....36 E8
Sherwood Dr
　Daventry NN11 ......135 B4
　Kettering NN15 ......91 F5
Sherwood Terr NN29 ..147 B8
Shetland Way NN17 ...21 C1
Shieling Ct NN18 ......36 A1
Ship La PE8 ....41 F4
Shipton Way NN3 .....131 C3
Shire Pl NN3 ....143 C5
Shire Rd NN17 ....21 C1
Shires Bsns Pk
　The NN13 ....234 A6
Shires Rd NN13 ......234 A6
Shirley Rd NN10 ......132 B3
Shoal Creek NN4 .....175 C5
Shoe Maker Cl NN12 ..188 F7
Shoemakers Ct NN10 ..132 B3
Shop La NN7 ....179 B6
Shoreham St NN18 ...36 B5
Short La Cogenhoe NN7 .162 A6
　Thorpe Malsor NN14 ..71 B3
　Wellingborough NN8 ..129 F5
Short Massey MK46 ...195 E6
Short Stocks NN10 ...132 D2
Shortlands Cl NN13 ..211 F3
Shortlands The NN9 ..113 B5
Shortwoods Cl NN9 ...114 D5
Shotwell Mill La NN14 ..70 D8
Showsley Rd NN12 ...204 D8
Shrewsbury Ave LE16 ..32 B2
Shropshire Cl LE16 ....31 E4
Shropshire Pl LE16 ....31 E4
Shrubberies The NN14 ..94 D7
Shrubfield Gr NN17 ....36 F6
Shuckburgh Cres CV22 ..98 D8
Shuckburgh Rd CV23 ..166 D8
Shurville Cl NN6 ......144 F3
Shutlanger Rd NN12 ..190 F1
Sibbertoft Rd Clipston LE16 47 E1
　Husbands Bosworth NN6 ..45 F2
　Marston Trussell LE16 ..47 B6
Sibley Rd NN9 ....112 B4

Siddeley Way NN11 ...134 F3
Siddons Cl PE8 ....41 E7
Siddons Way NN3 ....126 D1
Sidebrook Ct NN3 ....142 F5
Sidegate La NN8 .....130 F8
Sidings Ind Ctr
　The 234 A8
Sidings The NN9 .....131 D8
Sidlaw Cl MK11 ......229 F4
Sidmouth Wlk NN18 ...36 F4
Sidney Rd Rugby CV22 ..98 D8
　Woodford Halse NN11 .184 C6
Sillswood MK46 ......195 E4
Silver St Abthorpe NN12 .201 D4
　Brixworth NN6 ....106 B3
　Broughton NN14 .....90 A5
　Chacombe OX17 .....208 E4
　Kettering NN16 ......72 B2
　Northampton NN1 ...159 C6
　Stony Stratford MK11 .229 D5
　Walgrave NN6 ......108 A5
　Wellingborough NN8 ..130 A4
Silver St N OX17 .....208 E4
Silverdale Gr NN10 ..131 E2
Silverdale Rd NN3 ...142 D2
Silverstone CE Jun
　Sch NN12 ....214 D4
Silverstone Cl NN2 ..141 D5
Silverstone Cty Inf
　Sch NN12 ....214 D5
Silverstone Motor
　Racing Circuit NN12 .214 F1
Silverwood Ct NN15 ..91 C8
Silverwood Rd NN15 ..91 C8
Simon de Senlis Ct NN1 .159 D7
Simon de Senlis Lower
　Sch NN4 ....175 B8
Simon's Wlk
　17 Northampton NN1 .159 C6
　Pattishall NN12 ......172 D1
Simpson Ave NN10 ...132 C7
Simpson Barracks NN4 .175 D6
Sinclair Dr NN18 .....129 B6
Sir Christopher Hatton
　Sch NN18 ....130 A6
Sir Georges La OX17 ..230 A4
Sir John Brown Ct NN16 .72 A2
Sir John Pascoe
　Way NN5 ....158 C8
Siward View NN5 .....140 D2
Six Cotts MK18 ......226 E5
Six Willows NN9 .....110 B3
Sixth St NN13 ....238 E7
Skagerrak Cl NN18 ...36 A2
Skawle Ct NN3 ....142 F3
Skeffington Cl NN14 ..54 A2
Skegness Wlk NN18 ..36 C4
Skelton Wlk 4 NN3 ...142 C4
Sketty Cl NN4 ....160 C1
Skiddaw Wlk NN3 ....142 C4
Skin Yard La NN6 ....121 B4
Skinner Ave NN5 .....158 D5
Skinner's Hill NN10 ...132 B2
Skippon Cl LE16 .....31 D2
Skipton Cl Corby NN18 ..36 B4
　Northampton NN4 ...175 B7
Skittle Alley OX17 ...237 C7
Skye Rd NN17 ....36 B8
Slade Cl NN14 ......54 E3
Slade Cres NN15 .....91 B7
Slade Ho NN11 ......153 C8
Slade The Daventry NN11 153 C8
　Silverstone NN12 ....214 E5
Slade Valley Ave NN14 .70 F7
Sladeswell Ct 1 NN3 ..161 A8
Slate Drift PE9 ....1 C1
Slaters Cl NN11 .....132 D2
Slawston Rd
　Medbourne LE16 .....18 E7
　Welham LE16 ....17 F6
Slim Cl NN15 ....72 F1
Slip The NN6 ....106 C2
Slips The NN7 ....110 E2
Slipton La NN14 .....75 A3
Smart's Cl NN13 ....233 D8
Smarts Est CV23 ....100 A3
Smith Cl NN7 ....177 A1
Smith Ct NN9 ....114 D5
Smith St NN6 ....105 A1
Smitherway NN7 .....173 A8
Smithfield Pl NN9 ...114 D6
Smithland Ct NN12 ..202 D8
Smithy The
　Northampton NN3 ...142 D1
　Rushden NN10 ......132 B1
Smyth Cl LE16 ......31 E5
Smyth Ct NN3 ......142 E3
Snetterton Cl NN3 ...141 F4
Snowball Sq 1 NN3 ..143 C2
Soar Gn NN11 ....21 C1
Solly's Way NN12 ....203 C5
Somerford Rd NN8 ..129 E6
Somerset St NN1 ....159 E7
Somerton Cl NN18 ...36 A6
Somerville Ct OX17 ..230 D3
Somerville Rd
　Brackley NN13 ......233 D8
　Daventry NN11 .....153 B8
Sondes Cl PE8 ......41 E7
Sondes Rd NN17 ....22 E2
Sopwith Way NN11 ..135 B5
Sorrel Cl NN14 ......91 F1
Sorrel The NN14 .....91 F1
Sotheby Rise NN3 ...143 D3
Soudan Ave NN13 ...233 E8

Sourton Pl NN11 . . . .**135** D6
South Ave NN15 . . . .**92** B3
South Bank NN13 . . . .**234** B7
South Bridge Cl PE8 . . . . . .**41** F4
South Bridge Rd NN4 . . . .**159** D4
South Cl Braunston NN11 . .**118** D1
  Greatworth OX17 . . . .**210** D1
  Long Buckby NN6 . . . .**121** B3
  Rushden NN10 . . . .**132** C1
South Copse NN4 . . . .**175** B7
South End Jun & Inf
  Schs NN10 . . . .**148** B8
South Fields Dr NN6 . . . .**101** A5
South Folds Rd NN18 . . . . .**35** F1
South Gr NN10 . . . .**148** B5
South Holme NN3 . . . .**142** E5
South Kilworth CE Prim
  Sch LE17 . . . .**63** C8
South Kilworth Rd NN6 . . .**64** B5
South March NN11 . . . . . .**153** D8
South Oval NN5 . . . .**140** F1
South Paddock Ct NN3 . .**142** F4
South Pk NN10 . . . .**132** B1
South Portway NN3 . . . . .**142** F6
South Priors Ct NN3 . . . . .**143** A3
South Rd Clifton u D CV23 . .**80** A5
  Corby NN17 . . . .**37** B6
  Oundle PE8 . . . .**42** A4
South St
  Castlethorpe MK19 . . . . . .**218** F5
  Isham NN14 . . . .**110** F8
  Northampton NN1 . . . .**159** F6
  Weedon NN7 . . . .**155** C3
  Wollaston NN29 . . . .**146** D2
  Woodford Halse NN11 . . . .**184** C6
South Terr
  Greens Norton NN12 . . . . .**202** E8
  Northampton NN1 . . . .**159** F6
South Vale NN7 . . . .**179** A5
South View Brixworth NN6 **106** B1
  Harpole NN7 . . . .**157** E5
  Nether Heyford NN7 . . . . .**156** B1
  Whilton NN11 . . . .**137** C6
South Way NN11 . . . .**135** D1
Southall Rd NN17 . . . .**37** B6
Southam Rd CV23 . . . .**166** D2
Southampton Rd NN4 . . .**159** C3
Southbrook NN18 . . . .**36** B3
Southbrook Jun & Inf
  Schs NN11 . . . .**135** D1
Southcrest NN4 . . . .**158** F1
Southcroft NN3 . . . .**142** C2
Southfield Ave NN4 . . . . .**159** D3
Southfield Ct NN13 . . . . . .**233** E6
Southfield Dr NN15 . . . . . .**91** F4
Southfield Rd
  Gretton NN17 . . . .**10** C1
  Northampton NN5 . . . .**158** B6
Southfield Sch for
  Girls NN15 . . . .**91** C7
Southfields NN10 . . . .**132** C1
Southgate Dr
  Kettering NN15 . . . .**72** D2
  Towcester NN12 . . . .**203** D5
Southlands NN15 . . . .**72** B1
Southleigh Gr LE16 . . . . . .**31** D4
Southwood Hill NN4 . . . .**159** A4
Sovereign Pk LE16 . . . .**31** F1
Sovereigns Ct NN16 . . . . . .**72** C6
Sower Leys Rd NN18 . . . . .**36** C4
Spalding Rd NN18 . . . .**36** C4
Spanslade Rd NN3 . . . . . .**143** A1
Sparke Cl NN8 . . . .**129** D7
Spectacle La NN3 . . . . . .**125** F1
Speke Dr NN11 . . . .**135** C5
Spelhoe St NN3 . . . .**142** F6
Spencer Bridge
  Rd NN5 . . . .**159** A7
Spencer Cl
  Bugbrooke NN7 . . . .**173** A4
  Earls Barton NN6 . . . .**144** F4
Spencer Ct Corby NN17 . . .**36** E6
  Rushden NN10 . . . .**132** A3
  West Haddon NN6 . . . .**102** C4
Spencer Gdns NN13 . . . . .**233** E6
Spencer Haven NN5 . . . . .**159** A7
Spencer Mid
  Sch NN5 . . . .**159** A7
Spencer Par
  Northampton NN1 . . . .**159** D6
  Stanwick NN9 . . . .**113** F3
Spencer Rd
  Irthlingborough NN9 . . . . .**112** E1
  Long Buckby NN6 . . . .**121** B3
  Northampton NN1 . . . .**159** E7
  Rushden NN10 . . . .**132** A3
  Stanion NN14 . . . .**37** C3
Spencer St
  Burton Latimer NN15 . . . . .**92** B2
  Kettering NN16 . . . .**72** B4
  Market Harborough LE16 . . .**31** D3
  Northampton NN5 . . . .**159** A5
  Raunds NN9 . . . .**114** E6
  Ringstead NN14 . . . .**95** B3
  Rothwell NN14 . . . .**70** D8
Spencer Wlk NN18 . . . .**36** E5
Spendlove Dr NN17 . . . . . .**10** C1
Spenfield Ct NN3 . . . .**142** F3
Spens Ho NN2 . . . .**141** D5
Spenser Cres NN11 . . . . .**135** A3
Spey Cl NN8 . . . .**129** C6
Spiers Dr NN13 . . . .**233** D7
Spilsby Cl NN18 . . . .**36** C4
Spinners Cotts OX17 . . . .**210** F7
Spinney Bank OX17 . . . .**230** F5

Spinney Cl Boughton NN2 .**141** C7
  Market Harborough LE16 . .**31** C3
  Rushden NN10 . . . .**131** F2
  Thrapston NN14 . . . .**76** D1
  Towcester NN12 . . . .**203** C3
  Warmington PE8 . . . .**28** B2
Spinney Dr Kettering NN15 .**91** D7
  Northampton NN4 . . . .**175** C4
Spinney Gr NN17 . . . .**36** E7
Spinney Hill NN11 . . . . . .**118** A5
Spinney Hill Cres NN3 . .**142** A4
Spinney Hill Rd
  Northampton NN3 . . . .**142** A4
  Olney MK46 . . . .**195** E3
Spinney La NN15 . . . .**91** D7
Spinney Rd
  Burton Latimer NN15 . . . . .**92** C3
  Irthlingborough NN15 . . . .**112** F2
  Rushden NN10 . . . .**131** F1
  Weldon NN17 . . . .**38** C7
Spinney Rise
  Daventry NN11 . . . .**135** C1
  Denford NN14 . . . .**95** C6
Spinney St NN9 . . . .**114** D6
Spinney Terr NN9 . . . . . .**112** F2
Spinney Way NN3 . . . . . .**142** A5
Sponne Ho NN12 . . . .**203** C6
Sponne Sch NN12 . . . . . .**203** B6
Sponnes Rd NN12 . . . . . .**203** C5
Spratton CE Prim
  Sch NN6 . . . .**105** B1
Spratton Hall Sch NN6 . .**105** B1
Spratton Rd NN6 . . . .**106** A2
Spring Bank LE16 . . . .**18** F7
Spring Cl Boughton NN2 . .**125** C1
  Daventry NN11 . . . .**153** C8
  Hollowell NN6 . . . .**104** B4
  Kilsby CV23 . . . .**100** A2
Spring Gdns
  Burton Latimer NN15 . . . . .**92** C3
  Earls Barton NN6 . . . .**144** F4
  Higham Ferrers NN10 . . . .**132** B6
  Northampton NN1 . . . .**159** D5
  Rothwell NN14 . . . .**70** D7
  Towcester NN12 . . . .**203** D5
  Wellingborough NN8 . . . .**129** F4
Spring Ho NN8 . . . .**129** F4
Spring La Alderton NN12 . .**204** F2
  Flore NN7 . . . .**155** E5
  Northampton NN1 . . . .**159** B6
  Olney MK46 . . . .**195** F3
  Wellingborough NN8 . . . .**130** A4
Spring Lane Lower
  Sch NN1 . . . .**159** B6
Spring St NN9 . . . .**112** F2
Spring Terr NN9 . . . .**112** F2
Springbanks Way NN4 .**175** B8
Springer Straight NN4 .**158** F3
Springfield Flore NN7 . . . .**155** E5
  Northampton NN4 . . . .**175** E7
  Olney MK46 . . . .**195** F4
Springfield Ave NN14 . . . .**76** E3
Springfield Cl NN15 . . . . . .**91** C7
Springfield Ct NN3 . . . . . .**142** F3
Springfield Gdns MK19 . .**228** E4
Springfield Gr NN17 . . . . . .**36** F8
Springfield Rd
  Kettering NN15 . . . .**91** C7
  Oundle PE8 . . . .**41** F7
  Rushden NN10 . . . .**132** D1
  Walgrave NN6 . . . .**107** F5
  Wilbarston LE16 . . . .**34** C4
Springfield St LE16 . . . . . .**31** F2
Springfield Way NN13 . . .**233** E8
Springfields NN12 . . . . . .**203** B5
Springhill Hos CV22 . . . . .**98** C8
Springs The
  Northampton NN4 . . . .**159** A3
  Swinford LE17 . . . .**62** C4
Springwood Ct NN3 . . . .**142** F5
Spruce Ct NN3 . . . .**142** E3
Spurlings PE8 . . . .**41** F5
Spy Glass Hill NN4 . . . . .**175** B6
Square The Aynho OX17 . .**237** C7
  Greatworth OX17 . . . .**210** E1
  Kings Sutton OX17 . . . . . .**230** F5
  Market Harborough LE16 . .**31** E3
  Pitsford NN6 . . . .**125** C4
  Raunds NN9 . . . .**114** D6
  South Luffenham LE15 . . . . .**3** D8
  Thorpe Malsor NN14 . . . . .**71** B3
  Welford NN6 . . . .**64** E6
  Yardley Hastings NN7 . . . .**179** A6
Squire Cl NN18 . . . .**36** A4
Squires Wlk NN3 . . . .**142** B3
Squirrel La NN5 . . . .**158** C7
Stable Ct
  Northampton NN2 . . . . . .**141** C3
  Pitsford NN6 . . . .**125** D4
Stable Yd NN14 . . . .**70** C1
Stablegate Way LE16 . . . . .**32** A3
Stables La NN6 . . . .**140** B8
Stables The PE8 . . . .**8** A3
Stadtpeine Cl NN17 . . . . . .**36** C7
Staff Hos NN16 . . . .**71** F2
Staffa Wlk NN17 . . . .**36** B8
Stafford Cl NN11 . . . .**135** D5
Stafford Pl NN3 . . . .**141** F7
Stafford Rd NN11 . . . .**22** C8
Staffords La NN6 . . . .**102** B4
Stagshaw Cl NN4 . . . . . .**175** C8
Staines Cl NN5 . . . .**158** C6
Stamford Cl LE16 . . . .**31** E2
Stamford La PE8 . . . .**28** B3
Stamford Rd Duddington PE9 .**5** C7
  Easton on t H PE9 . . . .**2** B5

Stamford Rd continued
  Geddington NN14 . . . .**54** A1
  Geddington NN14 . . . .**54** C7
  Kettering NN16 . . . .**72** E5
  Ketton PE9 . . . .**1** C8
  South Luffenham LE15 . . . . .**3** D7
  Weldon NN17 . . . .**23** E2
  Weldon NN17 . . . .**38** A6
Stamford Wlk NN18 . . . . . .**36** C4
Stanbridge Ct MK11 . . . .**229** F5
Standens Barn Lower
  Sch NN3 . . . .**160** F8
Standens Barn Rd NN3 .**142** F1
Standing Stones NN3 . . .**143** B3
Stanfield Rd NN5 . . . .**158** C6
Stanford Cl NN6 . . . .**84** A5
Stanford Rd
  Cold Ashby NN6 . . . .**84** A5
  Swinford LE17 . . . .**62** D3
Stanford Way NN4 . . . . . .**175** C8
Stanhill Row NN12 . . . . . .**201** F1
Stanhope Rd NN2 . . . . . .**141** D1
Stanier Rd NN17 . . . .**21** F1
Stanion CE Prim
  Sch NN14 . . . .**37** D4
Stanion La Corby NN18 . . . .**37** B6
  Corby NN18 . . . .**37** D5
Stanion Rd NN14 . . . .**38** C1
Stanley Boddington
  Ct NN15 . . . .**91** C8
Stanley Ct MK46 . . . .**195** F3
Stanley Mews NN8 . . . . .**130** B5
Stanley Rd
  Northampton NN6 . . . .**159** A6
  Wellingborough NN8 . . . .**130** B5
Stanley St
  Northampton NN2 . . . .**159** C8
  Rothwell NN14 . . . .**70** E7
Stanley Way NN11 . . . . . .**135** C5
Stannard Way NN6 . . . . .**106** B2
Stanton Ave NN3 . . . .**142** A4
Stanton Cl NN8 . . . .**111** B1
Stanway Cl NN14 . . . .**32** A3
Stanwell Cl OX17 . . . .**209** A1
Stanwell Dr OX17 . . . . . .**209** A1
Stanwell Lea OX17 . . . . .**209** A2
Stanwell Way NN8 . . . . .**129** C3
Stanwick Rd
  Higham Ferrers NN10 . . . .**132** C8
  Raunds NN9 . . . .**114** B4
Star Cnr CV23 . . . .**99** C1
Starmer's Yd NN5 . . . . . .**158** C7
Starmers La NN7 . . . .**157** D4
Starvold Cl NN7 . . . .**105** A1
Station Cl Daventry NN11 .**135** D2
  Long Buckby NN6 . . . .**121** B3
Station Gdns NN11 . . . . .**184** C6
Station Mews NN3 . . . . .**143** C2
Station Rd
  Aynho OX17, OX17 . . . . . .**237** A6
  Blisworth NN7 . . . .**174** B2
  Brixworth NN6 . . . .**106** A4
  Burton Latimer NN15 . . . . .**92** A2
  Castlethorpe MK19 . . . . . .**218** F5
  Cogenhoe NN7 . . . .**161** E6
  Corby NN17 . . . .**37** A6
  Cottesbrooke NN6 . . . .**105** A7
  Desborough NN14 . . . .**51** A4
  Earls Barton NN6 . . . .**144** E3
  Earls Barton NN6 . . . .**144** F1
  Finedon NN9 . . . .**111** D6
  Great Bowden LE16 . . . . . .**32** A6
  Great Easton LE16 . . . .**20** E6
  Gretton NN17 . . . .**10** B1
  Helmdon NN13 . . . .**211** F4
  Husbands Bosworth LE17 . .**45** D3
  Irchester NN44 . . . .**147** D3
  Irthlingborough NN9 . . . . .**113** A2
  Kettering NN15 . . . .**72** B1
  Ketton PE9 . . . .**1** A5
  Kilsby CV23 . . . .**100** A3
  King's Cliffe PE8 . . . .**13** F7
  Lilbourne CV23 . . . .**81** A7
  Little Houghton NN7 . . . . .**161** C5
  Long Buckby NN6 . . . .**121** A2
  Morcott LE15 . . . .**3** B6
  Nassington PE8 . . . .**15** F5
  North Kilworth LE17 . . . . . .**45** A4
  Northampton NN3 . . . .**143** C1
  Oundle PE8 . . . .**42** A6
  Raunds NN9 . . . .**115** B4
  Ringstead NN14 . . . .**94** F2
  Rushden NN10 . . . .**132** A3
  Rushton NN14 . . . .**52** C2
  Theddingworth LE17 . . . . . .**46** C8
  Watford NN6 . . . .**120** C5
  Welton NN11 . . . .**119** E1
  West Haddon NN6 . . . .**102** B4
  Woodford Halse NN11 . . . .**184** C6
Station Yard Ind
  Est OX17 . . . .**230** A2
Stavanger Cl NN18 . . . . . .**36** A2
Staveley Way NN6 . . . . . .**106** C3
Staverton CE Prim
  Sch NN11 . . . .**152** C7
Staverton Leys CV22 . . . . .**98** A7
Staverton Rd NN11 . . . . .**135** A1
Steadfold La PE9 . . . .**1** C8
Steane View NN13 . . . . . .**233** D7
Steel Rd NN17 . . . .**22** E2
Steele Rd NN8 . . . .**129** D4
Steene St NN5 . . . .**159** A6
Stefen Way NN11 . . . .**153** B7
Stenhouse Cl NN6 . . . . . .**121** D4
Stenson St NN5 . . . .**159** A6
Stephen Bennett NN5 .**158** C8
Stephenson Cl NN11 . . . .**134** F4
Stephenson Ct Kilsby CV23 .**99** F2

Stephenson Ct continued
  Roade NN7 . . . .**191** C4
Stephenson Way NN17 . . .**37** A8
Sterling Cl NN14 . . . .**70** C1
Sterndale Cl NN14 . . . .**50** E4
Stevens Cl NN6 . . . .**144** F5
Stevens St LE16 . . . .**31** D3
Stevenson St NN4 . . . . . .**159** C2
Stewart Cl NN3 . . . .**126** B2
Stewart Dr NN12 . . . .**214** D4
Stewarts Rd NN8 . . . .**130** B8
Steyning Cl NN18 . . . .**36** A5
Stile Cl NN11 . . . .**135** A2
Stilebrook Rd MK46 . . . . .**195** F6
Stimpson Ave NN1 . . . . . .**159** F7
Stimpson Avenue Lower
  Sch NN1 . . . .**159** F7
Stirling St NN5 . . . .**158** F6
Stirrup Ho NN5 . . . .**159** B5
Stitchman Ho NN5 . . . . . .**159** A6
Stock's Hill PE9 . . . .**1** A5
Stock's La NN17 . . . .**37** B6
Stockbridge Rd NN17 . . . .**22** A1
Stocken Cl MK46 . . . .**195** E4
Stockerston La LE16 . . . . .**20** D8
Stockholme Cl NN3 . . . . . .**36** A2
Stocking Cl NN7 . . . .**192** D1
Stocking Green Cl MK19 .**207** A3
Stockley St NN1 . . . .**159** E6
Stockmead Rd NN1 . . . . .**163** A8
Stocks Hill Finedon NN9 .**111** E4
  Silverstone NN12 . . . .**214** D5
Stocks The MK19 . . . .**218** E2
Stockwell Hill NN5 . . . . . .**175** D5
Stockwell Cl LE16 . . . .**32** B3
Stockwell La
  Hellidon NN11 . . . .**151** D1
  Sulgrave OX17 . . . .**210** F8
Stockwell Rd NN7 . . . . . .**174** F4
Stockwell Way NN7 . . . . .**174** F4
Stockwood Dr NN17 . . . . . .**21** F1
Stoke Albany Rd LE16 . . . .**18** D4
Stoke Bruerne CE Prim
  Sch NN12 . . . .**205** A8
Stoke Doyle Rd PE8 . . . . .**41** D4
Stoke Firs Cl NN4 . . . .**175** F6
Stoke Hill Oundle PE8 . . . . .**41** F5
  Stoke Albany NN14 . . . . . .**34** A4
Stoke Rd Ashton NN7 . . . .**205** D6
  Blisworth NN7 . . . .**190** E4
  Desborough NN14 . . . .**51** A7
  Lyddington LE15 . . . .**9** C7
Stokes Rd NN18 . . . .**36** D4
Stone Circle Rd NN3 . . . .**142** F3
Stone Cl NN29 . . . .**146** D2
Stone Hill Ct NN3 . . . .**142** E4
Stone House Mews NN6 .**84** C4
Stone Way NN5 . . . .**158** B7
Stonebridge Ct NN3 . . . .**142** F3
Stonehill Way NN15 . . . . .**125** B8
Stonehouse Ct CV23 . . . . .**81** A6
Stonehurst Cl NN17 . . . . .**192** C1
Stonelea Rd NN6 . . . .**127** D3
Stoneleigh Chase NN5 . .**140** D1
Stonepit Dr LE16 . . . .**20** D1
Stoneway Badby NN11 . . .**152** F2
  Hartwell NN7 . . . .**192** E2
Stonewold Cl NN2 . . . . . .**141** A4
Stoney Piece Cl NN29 . . .**164** C2
Stoneyhurst NN4 . . . .**158** F3
Stony Hill NN12 . . . .**216** C8
Stornoway Rd NN17 . . . . . .**21** C1
Stotfold Ct MK11 . . . .**229** E4
Stour Rd Corby NN17 . . . . .**21** D1
  Northampton NN5 . . . .**158** F6
Stour The NN11 . . . .**153** A8
Stourhead Dr NN4 . . . . . .**175** C7
Stourton Cl NN4 . . . .**129** D1
Stow Cl NN8 . . . .**129** D1
Stowe Wlk NN3 . . . .**141** F5
Stratford Arc MK11 . . . . .**229** D5
Stratford Dr NN4 . . . .**175** D6
Stratford Rd
  Cosgrove MK19 . . . .**218** D1
  Deanshanger MK19 . . . . .**228** F4
  Roade NN7 . . . .**191** C3
  Stony Stratford MK12 . . . .**229** F6
Strath Cl CV21 . . . .**99** A7
Strathay Wlk NN17 . . . . . .**21** C1
Stratton Cl
  Market Harborough LE16 . .**31** D1
  Northampton NN3 . . . .**160** D7
Stratton Dr NN13 . . . .**233** D7
Strawberry Hill NN3 . . . . .**143** C3
Strawberry Hill
  Cotts MK44 . . . .**149** F2
Straws Cl NN9 . . . .**112** E1
Streambank Rd NN3 . . . .**142** E6
Streatfield Rd NN5 . . . . . .**159** A8
Streather Ct NN14 . . . . . .**114** C5
Streather Dr NN17 . . . .**36** E7
Street The LE15 . . . .**3** E8
Streeton Way NN6 . . . . . .**144** E5
Strelley Ave NN3 . . . .**160** F8
Stringer's Hill NN14 . . . . .**90** F2
Strode Rd NN8 . . . .**130** B5
Stronglands PE8 . . . .**41** F6
Stuart Cl Kettering NN16 . . .**72** C2
  Northampton NN4 . . . .**174** F7
Stuart Cres LE16 . . . .**30** F7
Stuart Rd Brackley NN13 . .**233** C3
  Corby NN17 . . . .**36** F6
  Market Harborough LE16 . .**31** E2
Stubbing End NN18 . . . . . .**53** B8
Stubble Cl NN2 . . . .**141** A6
Stubbs La NN15 . . . .**92** A8
Stubbs Rd NN11 . . . .**170** B7

Stud Farm Cl OX17 . . . . .**196** E1
Studfall Ave NN17 . . . .**36** E8
Studfall Inf Sch NN17 . . . .**36** E8
Studfall Jun Sch NN17 . . .**36** D8
Studland Rd NN2 . . . .**141** B1
Sturdee Cl NN11 . . . .**135** D1
Sturminster Way NN14 . . .**36** A6
Sturton Wlk NN18 . . . .**36** C4
Styles Pl NN16 . . . .**82** B3
Sudborough Rd
  Brigstock NN14 . . . .**56** A4
  Slipton NN14 . . . .**75** A6
Suffolk Pl NN15 . . . .**91** D6
Sulby Hall Old Dr NN6 . . . .**46** B1
Sulby Rd Northampton NN3 **142** E6
  Welford NN6 . . . .**65** A8
Sulehay Rd PE8 . . . .**7** C1
Sulgrave Rd NN17 . . . .**36** C7
Sulgrave Manor OX17 . . .**211** A8
Sulgrave Rd
  Culworth OX17 . . . .**198** D1
  Northampton NN5 . . . .**158** F7
Summerfield Rd NN15 . . .**91** C8
Summerfields NN4 . . . . . .**158** E2
Summerhouse Rd NN3 . .**142** A4
Summerlee Mews NN9 . .**111** F4
Summerlee Rd NN9 . . . . .**111** F4
Summers Cl OX17 . . . . . .**230** A5
Summit Rise NN4 . . . .**175** D7
Sun Yd NN12 . . . .**203** D5
Sunderland St NN5 . . . . .**159** A6
Sundew Ct NN4 . . . .**158** D1
Sunningdale Ct NN12 . . . .**141** E2
Sunningdale Dr NN11 . . .**135** E3
Sunny Bank NN6 . . . .**126** E8
Sunny Side NN6 . . . .**144** D4
Sunny View NN7 . . . .**179** B6
Sunnyside Ecton NN6 . . . .**143** F4
  Northampton NN5 . . . .**175** E6
  Woodford NN14 . . . .**94** D7
Sunnyside Lower
  Sch NN2 . . . .**141** D6
Sunset Cl NN3 . . . .**143** A2
Surfleet Cl NN18 . . . .**36** C4
Surrey Cl NN17 . . . .**36** C6
Surrey Rd NN15 . . . .**91** D6
Surtees Way NN12 . . . . . .**203** C2
Sussex Cl NN5 . . . .**158** C6
Sussex Ct NN1 . . . .**159** C6
Sussex Rd NN15 . . . .**91** C6
Sutcliffe Rd PE8 . . . .**7** D8
Sutherland Rd NN18 . . . . . .**36** D4
Sutton Acre NN7 . . . .**155** E5
Sutton Cl Aston le W NN11 **182** F3
  Northampton NN2 . . . .**141** D6
Sutton Ct LE16 . . . .**31** E1
Sutton Rd
  Great Bowden LE16 . . . . . .**32** B6
  Little Bowden LE16 . . . .**32** E7
  Oundle PE8 . . . .**42** B4
  Weston by W LE16 . . . .**18** B3
Sutton St NN7 . . . .**155** F5
Sutton's Wlk NN12 . . . . .**188** F7
Swain Cl NN3 . . . .**142** E3
Swale Cl Corby NN17 . . . . .**21** D1
  Roade NN7 . . . .**191** C3
Swale Dr
  Northampton NN5 . . . .**140** F3
  Wellingborough NN8 . . . .**129** C6
Swallow Cl Brackley NN13 **222** E1
  Kettering NN15 . . . .**92** B6
  Northampton NN4 . . . .**175** A7
Swallow Dr NN10 . . . .**132** B5
Swan Ave NN14 . . . .**55** E8
Swan Cl
  Burton Latimer NN15 . . . . .**92** A2
  Hinton NN11 . . . .**184** B6
  Middleton Cheney OX17 . .**219** F8
  Thrapston NN14 . . . .**76** D3
Swan St NN1 . . . .**159** D5
Swan Terr MK11 . . . .**229** D5
Swan Valley Way NN4 . .**174** C8
Swanage Ct NN18 . . . .**36** A6
Swanhill PE8 . . . .**8** A4
Swann Dale NN11 . . . . . .**135** D1
Swann Dale Cl NN11 . . . .**135** D1
Swans La NN8 . . . .**130** A4
Swansea Cres NN5 . . . . .**159** A7
Swansea Rd NN5 . . . .**159** A8
Swansgate Ctr
  The NN8 . . . .**130** A3
Swanspool Par NN8 . . . .**130** A4
Swedish Hos NN7 . . . . . .**139** D4
Sweetacre Cl NN7 . . . . . .**163** D4
Swinburne Cl NN16 . . . . . .**72** C6
Swinburne Rd NN8 . . . . .**129** B4
Swinen's Yd MK11 . . . . . .**229** D5
Swinford CE Sch LE17 . . . .**62** B4
Swinford Cnr LE17 . . . .**62** A8
Swinford Hollow NN3 . . .**161** A8
Swinford Rd LE17 . . . .**62** A8
Swingbridge St LE16 . . . . .**30** E8
Swinnertons La NN6 . . . . .**82** B4
Swinneyford Rd NN12 . . .**203** C5
Swyncombe Gn NN7 . . . .**192** C1
Sycamore Ave NN11 . . . .**184** B6
Sycamore Cl Corby NN17 . .**21** E1
  Daventry NN11 . . . .**135** C5
  Kettering NN16 . . . .**72** D4
  Rushden NN10 . . . .**132** C2
  Towcester NN12 . . . .**203** C4
Sycamore Dr
  Desborough NN14 . . . .**51** D2
  Sywell NN6 . . . .**143** D8
Sycamore Rd
  Greens Norton NN12 . . . . .**202** E8
  Northampton NN5 . . . .**158** C7

Sydney St NN16 ....72 D2
Syers Green Cl NN6 ....121 A4
Syers Green La NN6 ....121 A4
Syke The NN14 ....55 F7
Sykes Ct NN17 ....37 A8
Syles Cl NN6 ....102 B5
Sylmond Gdns NN10 ....148 A7
Sylvanus Ho NN8 ....129 D5
Symington St NN5 ......159 A7
Symington Way LE16 .....31 E3
Syresham CE Prim
  Sch NN13 ....224 C7
Syresham Way NN2 .....141 C5
Sywell Airport Bsns
  Pk NN6 ....127 F4
Sywell Ave NN8 ....129 D6
Sywell CE Prim Sch NN6 127 D3
Sywell Dr Holcot NN6 ..126 F8
  Mears Ashby NN6 .....128 A1
  Overstone NN6 ....127 B1
  Wellingborough NN8 ..129 B1
Sywell Way NN8 ....129 D6

T

Taborley Cl NN3 ....142 E1
Tadcaster Cl NN11 .....135 C6
Taggies Yd NN14 ......109 F5
Tainty Cl NN9 ....111 E5
Talan Rise NN3 ....143 C5
Talavera Cl NN11 ......135 B1
Talavera Way NN3 .....142 E6
Talbot Rd
  Northampton NN1 .....159 E7
  Rushden NN10 ....131 F1
  Wellingborough NN8 ..130 C5
Talbot Rd N NN8 ....130 C5
Talbot Yd LE16 ....31 E3
Talbots Hyde MK46 ....195 E4
Tall Trees Cl NN4 .....174 F8
Tallyfield End NN4 .....158 E3
Tamar Cl NN5 ....140 E2
Tamar Gn NN17 ....21 D1
Tamar Sq NN11 ....135 A1
Tamarisk Dr NN3 ......142 C6
Taney Ct PE8 ....42 A5
Tanfield La NN1 ....160 C5
Tanfields Gr NN17 .....36 E8
Tanglewood NN4 ......175 D4
Tann Rd NN9 ....111 F5
Tanner St NN1 ....159 C6
Tanner's La NN16 ......72 B2
Tansor Cl NN17 ....36 B8
Tansy Cl NN4 ....158 D1
Tantree Way NN6 .....106 C2
Tapeley Gdns NN4 .....175 D7
Tarn Croft NN3 ....142 B3
Tarrant Cl NN3 ....126 D1
Tarrant Way NN3 .....126 D1
Tarrys End NN6 ....82 B4
Tasman Way NN14 ....70 E6
Tate Gr NN4 ....175 F7
Tattersall Cl NN3 .....142 A5
Taunton Ave Corby NN18 ..36 B6
  Northampton NN3 .....160 C7
Tavern La ① NN11 .....135 C1
Tavern Wlk NN16 ......36 A4
Tavistock Cl ③ NN3 ...143 C2
Tavistock Rd NN15 ....92 A5
Tavistock Sq NN18 ....36 F4
Tay Cl NN17 ....21 D1
Taylor Cl NN8 ....129 C2
Taylors Gn PE8 ....28 B2
Teal Cl Burton Latimer NN15 ..91 F2
  Daventry NN11 ....135 C4
  Northampton NN4 .....174 E8
Teal La NN8 ....130 B7
Tebbitt Cl NN6 ....121 B4
Tebbutt Cl NN14 ......70 F7
Tebbutt's Yd NN6 .....144 E4
Tees Cl NN8 ....129 C6
Teesdale NN3 ....142 F6
Teesdale Rd NN17 .....36 D7
Teeton La NN6 ....104 E3
Teeton Rd
  Guilsborough NN6 ....103 F1
  Ravensthorpe NN6 ....103 E1
Telford Way Kettering NN16 71 F4
  Northampton NN5 .....158 D4
Telfords La NN17 ......37 A8
Temperance Terr MK11 .229 D6
Templar Dr NN2 ......141 A4
Templar Rd NN15 ......72 F1
Temple Bar ㉑ NN1 ....159 C7
Ten Pines NN3 ....142 F7
Tenbury Way NN14 ....70 F7
Tenby Rd NN5 ....159 A8
Tenlands OX17 ....219 F8
Tennyson Cl
  ③ Northampton NN5 ..158 E4
  Towcester NN12 ......203 B5
Tennyson Dr NN17 .....36 D8
Tennyson Rd
  Daventry NN11 ....135 B3
  Kettering NN16 ....72 B2
  Rothwell NN14 ....70 C7
  Rushden NN10 ....131 F2
  Wellingborough NN8 ..129 D3
Tennyson Road Inf
  Sch NN10 ....131 F2
Tenter Cl NN10 ....132 B5
Tenter La NN9 ....111 F5
Tenter Rd NN3 ....141 F7
Terrace The NN3 .....224 C6
Terrington Cl NN13 ....233 D7
Test Gn NN17 ....21 D1

Tettenhall Cl NN18 ....36 A1
Teviot Cl Corby NN17 ..21 D1
  Northampton NN5 ....140 E2
Tewkesbury Cl
  Northampton NN4 ....159 A1
  Wellingborough NN8 ..129 D6
Tews End La NN12 .....216 C8
Thackers Cl PE8 ......8 A4
Thames Cl NN15 ......92 B2
Thames Rd Daventry NN11 135 A1
  Northampton NN4 ....175 C7
  Wellingborough NN8 ..129 C6
Thames Rise NN6 .....72 A4
Thames Wlk NN17 .....21 D1
Thatch Meadow Dr LE16 .32 B3
Thatchwell Cl NN3 ....160 F8
Thebwell Rd ③ NN3 ...142 F7
Theddingworth Rd
  Husbands Bosworth LE17 ..46 A6
  Lubenham LE16 ......30 C2
  Marston Trussell LE16 ..47 B8
Thenford Rd OX17 ....209 C1
Thenford St NN1 .....159 E6
Thetford Cl NN18 .....36 B1
Third Ave NN8 ....129 D3
Third St NN13 ....238 E6
Thirlestane Cres NN14 .159 B3
Thirlestane Rd NN4 ...159 B3
Thirlmere NN8 ....129 C5
Thirlmere Ave NN3 ...142 C3
Thirlmere Cl
  Daventry NN11 ....135 A4
  Kettering NN16 ......71 E3
Thirlmere Flats NN16 ..71 E3
Thirsk Rd NN18 ......36 C5
Thistle Ct ③ NN4 ....159 A3
Thistleholme Cl NN2 ..141 E3
Thoday Cl NN14 ......90 A3
Thomas Becket RC
  Upper NN3 ....142 B5
Thomas Cl Byfield NN11 ..183 D7
  Corby NN18 ....36 D4
Thomas Flawn Rd NN9 131 D8
Thomas Rd NN15 ......91 C7
Thomas St
  Northampton NN1 ....159 E6
  Wellingborough NN8 ..130 B5
Thompson Way NN15 ..90 F8
Thor Wlk NN18 ....36 A2
Thorburn Rd NN3 .....160 E8
Thoresby Ct NN18 ....36 C5
Thorn Cl NN16 ....72 B6
Thorn Hill NN4 ....159 A3
Thornapple Cl NN3 ...143 C4
Thornborough Cl PE16 .32 A2
Thornby Dr NN2 ......141 B3
Thornby Rd NN6 .....84 B5
Thorne Cl NN18 ......36 C5
Thornfield NN3 ....143 C4
Thorngate St NN16 ...72 C2
Thornhill OX17 ....208 F4
Thornlea Croft NN6 ..195 F3
Thornton Cl Flore NN7 ..155 F5
  Newnham NN11 ....153 D3
Thornton Coll MK17 ..235 C5
Thornton Rd
  Northampton NN2 ....141 B1
  Thornton MK17 ......235 D2
Thoroughsale Rd NN18 .36 C6
Thorpe Banbury OX16 .219 A6
  Wellingborough NN8 ..129 C5
Thorpe Cl NN14 ......77 C7
Thorpe Dr OX16 ......219 A6
Thorpe Langton Rd LE16 .17 D6
Thorpe Rd
  Chacombe OX17 ......208 E4
  Earls Barton NN6 ....144 E4
  Lyddington LE15 ......9 D6
  Northampton NN5 ....159 C3
  Wardington OX17 ....208 F8
Thorpe St NN9 ....114 D5
Thorpeville NN3 ......142 D7
Thorplands Lower
  Sch NN3 ....142 E5
Thrapston Prim Sch NN14 76 D1
Thrapston Rd
  Finedon NN9 ....112 B7
  Woodford NN14 ......94 D8
Three Shires Hospl NN3 .159 F5
Thrift St
  Higham Ferrers NN10 .132 B5
  Irchester NN29 ......147 A4
  Wollaston NN29 .....146 D2
Thrupp Bridge NN4 ...176 A6
Thrush La NN8 ....130 B6
Thruxton Dr NN3 .....141 F4
Thurburn Cl NN14 ....90 B5
Thursby Rd NN1 ......160 B7
Thurso Wlk NN17 .....21 D1
Thurspit Pl ③ NN3 ...143 D2
Thurston Dr NN15 ....91 A8
Thyme Ct NN3 ....142 E3
Tibbs Way NN7 ....173 A6
Tideswell Cl NN4 .....174 F8
Tiffany Gdns NN4 ....175 C6
Tiffield CE Prim
  Sch NN12 ....189 D3
Tiffield Rd NN7 ......189 E8
Tilbury Rd NN16 ......122 C5
Tilbury Rise NN6 .....122 C5
Tilley Hill Cl PE8 .....41 E7
Timor Ct MK11 ....229 D6
Timpson Cl NN16 ....72 C5
Tingdene Rd NN9 ....111 F5
Tinkers Cres NN6 ....128 B2
Tinsley Dr NN3 ......143 B3
Tintagel Cl NN10 ....132 D1
Tintern Ave NN5 .....159 A7

Tintern Cl NN15 ......91 F8
Tippings La LE15 .....3 F5
Tiptoe Cl NN3 ....143 C3
Titchmarsh CE Prim
  Sch 77 C4
Tithe Barn Cl NN9 ...114 E7
Tithe Barn Rd NN8 ..130 A4
Tithe Barn Way NN4 .174 B8
Tithe Cl NN4 ....95 A3
Tithe La OX15 ....236 C6
Tithe Rd NN7 ....155 A2
Tithe Way NN7 ......191 D5
Titley Bawk Ave NN6 .144 F6
Titty Ho NN9 ....114 C5
Tiverton Ave NN2 ...141 C7
Tixover Grange PE9 ..4 F8
Todd's Hill PE9 ......5 B6
Todmorden Cl NN18 ..36 C5
Tofts Cl NN14 ....77 D4
Toll Bar La PE18 ....97 B4
Toll Bar Rd NN14 ...76 B2
Toll Gate Pl NN18 ...37 B6
Tollbar NN10 ....132 B5
Toller Pl NN15 ......91 F6
Toller St NN16 ......72 C3
Tollgate Cl NN2 .....141 B2
Tollgate Way NN5 ..158 D6
Tompson Cl NN11 ...118 C1
Toms Cl Northampton NN4 175 C3
  Theddingworth LE17 ..46 D8
Tonmead Rd NN3 ...142 E3
Top Cl NN14 ....76 F3
Top Dysons NN14 ...92 F7
Top End
  Little Addington NN14 .113 B7
  Pytchley NN14 ....90 F2
Top Farm Cl NN11 ...184 B6
Top Station Rd NN13 .234 A8
Topwell Cl NN3 ......143 A1
Tordoff Pl NN16 .....72 B2
Torksey Cl NN18 ....36 A1
Torridge Cl NN16 ....71 F4
Torridon Cl NN17 ....21 C1
Torrington Cres NN8 .129 D6
Torrington Gn NN8 ..129 E6
Torrington Rd NN8 ..129 E6
Torrington Way NN8 .129 E6
Torville Cres NN15 ..91 A8
Totnes Cl NN18 .....36 F4
Touraine Cl NN5 ....139 F2
Tove La NN12 ......203 A6
Tovey Dr NN11 .....135 D1
Towcester Inf Sch NN12 203 C5
Towcester Rd
  Blisworth NN7 ......190 B6
  Greens Norton NN12 .188 E1
  Litchborough NN12 ..171 C1
  Milton Malsor NN7 ..174 E5
  Northampton NN4 ...159 B2
  Old Stratford MK19 ..229 B7
  Silverstone NN12 ...214 E4
  Towcester NN12 ....203 A8
  Whittlebury NN12 ...215 C5
Tower Ct NN9 ......112 A4
Tower Ct LE16 ......30 F3
Tower Field Sq NN3 .143 A6
Tower Hill NN4 .....158 E3
Tower Hill Rd NN18 ..36 A4
Tower St NN1 ....159 C6
Town Ct NN9 ......110 C3
Townley Way NN6 ..144 E5
Towns End NN6 .....121 C4
Townsend NN11 ....184 B6
Townsend Cl
  Hanging Houghton NN6 ..106 C3
  Wellingborough NN8 .129 F4
Townsend Ct PE8 ...39 E7
Townsend La
  Thorpe Mandeville OX17 ..209 F6
  Upper Boddington NN11 ..182 B8
Townsend Leys NN10 .132 B8
Townsend Rd NN6 ..107 F5
Townson Cl NN6 ....107 D7
Townwell La NN29 ..147 B8
Towrise OX17 ......210 F8
Towton Ct NN4 ....159 A1
Trafalgar Rd NN6 ...72 A2
Trafalgar Way NN11 .135 D1
Trafford Rd NN10 ...132 D2
Treen Cl NN14 .....76 F2
Treetops NN3 ......143 A5
Trelawney NN8 ....129 B5
Trengothal Ct NN13 .223 D4
Trent Cl Northampton NN5 140 F2
  Wellingborough NN8 ..129 C6
Trent Cres NN15 ....92 B1
Trent Rd Corby NN17 ..21 D1
  Kettering NN16 .....72 A5
  Wittering PE8 ......7 D8
Trent Wlk NN11 ....135 A1
Trentham Cl NN4 ...175 C2
Tresham Gn NN5 ...140 D1
Tresham Inst Corby NN17 ..36 E6
  Kettering NN16 .....72 C1
  Rushden NN15 .....91 D8
  Wellingborough NN8 .130 A5
Tresham St Kettering NN16 .72 C3
  Rothwell NN14 .....70 D7
Trevithick Rd NN17 ..37 C8
Trevor Cl NN5 .....158 E7
Trevor Cres NN5 ...158 E7
Trimley Cl NN3 ....160 D6
Trinity Ave NN1 ....141 D1
Trinity Cl NN11 ....153 B8
Trinity Cl NN14 ...70 C6
Trinity Ct NN8 ....129 A7
Trinity Rd NN14 ...70 C6

Trinity Sch NN2 ......141 D1
Trinity Way OX17 ....230 D3
Trinity Wlk NN18 .....36 E4
Triumph Gdns NN5 ...139 F1
Trojan Ctr NN8 ......130 B8
Tromso Cl NN18 .....36 A1
Troon Cres NN3 ....129 C7
Troutbeck Wlk NN3 ..142 C4
Trussell Cl NN3 ....143 C1
Tudely Cl NN4 ......175 F7
Tudor Ct ② NN1 ....159 C7
Tudor Gdns MK11 ..229 E4
Tudor Rd NN1 ......142 A2
Tudor Way Brackley NN13 ..233 E8
  Wellingborough NN8 .129 E7
Tudor Wlk NN10 ....132 C3
Tulbrook Stones OX17 ..220 B7
Tulip Dr NN10 ......148 B7
Tunnel Hill Cotts NN4 ..159 A2
Tunwell La NN17 ....37 B7
Turn Furlong NN3 ..141 A5
Turnberry Ct NN8 ..129 C6
Turnberry La NN4 ..175 C5
Turnells Mill La NN8 .130 A1
Turner Cl Kettering NN15 ..92 A8
  Rugby CV21 ....99 B8
Turner Rd Corby NN17 ..36 E5
  Wellingborough NN8 .129 F7
Turner St NN1 ......159 F7
Turners Yd PE8 ....41 F5
Turturaine Manor NN13 ..234 A8
Turweston Rd NN13 .223 A1
Tweed Cl
  Burton Latimer NN15 ..92 B2
  Daventry NN11 .....153 A8
Tweed Rd NN5 .....158 E6
Twickenham Ct ③ NN18 ..36 B5
Twigden Rd NN7 ...157 D3
Twistle The NN11 ...183 C7
Twitch Hill NN12 ...204 D8
Twyford Ave Raunds NN9 ..114 C7
Twyford Cl ⑦ NN3 .161 A8
Twyford Gr OX17 ...230 A6
Twyford Rd OX17 ...230 C7
Tyebeck Ct NN2 ....141 B3
Tyes Ct NN3 ....142 F3
Tyler Way NN14 ....76 C1
Tymecrosse Gdns LE16 ..31 D5
Tynan Cl NN15 .....92 A8
Tyne Cl NN29 ......129 C6
Tyne Ho PE8 ......42 A6
Tyne Rd Corby NN17 ..21 D1
  Daventry NN11 .....153 A8
  Northampton NN5 ..158 E6
Tyringham Cl NN3 ..142 D1
Tyrrell Way NN12 ..203 C8
Tyson Ctyd NN18 ..37 E7

U

Uist Wlk NN17 ....21 C1
Ullswater Cl NN8 ....129 C5
Ullswater Rd NN16 ...71 E2
Underbank La NN3 ..142 C6
Underwood Rd NN14 ..70 C7
Union St Desborough NN14 ..51 B8
  Finedon NN9 ....112 A5
  Kettering NN16 ....72 A3
Unity Cl NN29 .....146 C3
Unity St NN14 .....51 A2
Univ Coll
  Northampton NN2 ..141 D1
Univ of Leicester
  (Annexe) NN2 .....159 C8
Upland Rd NN3 .....142 C2
Upper Astrop Rd OX17 ..231 A5
Upper Bath St NN1 ..159 C6
Upper Boddington CE
  Prim Sch NN11 ....182 C7
Upper Cross St ⑱ NN1 ..159 C6
Upper Dane NN14 ..50 E3
Upper George St NN10 ..132 C7
Upper Glen Ave NN7 .174 B2
Upper Gn NN11 ....199 D7
Upper Green Pl LE16 ..32 A6
Upper Havelock
  St ⑦ NN8 ....130 A5
Upper High St NN7 ..157 C7
Upper Kings Ave NN10 ..132 C7
Upper Mounts NN1 ..159 D6
Upper Park Ave NN10 .131 F1
Upper Priory St ⑦ NN1 ..159 C7
Upper Queen St NN10 ..132 C3
Upper St NN16 .....72 A2
Upper Steeping NN14 .51 B2
Upper Thrift St NN1 ..159 F6
Upperfield Gr NN17 ..36 E8
Uppingham Rd
  Caldecott LE16 .....9 B2
  Corby NN17 ......36 A7
  Medbourne LE16 ...19 A8
Uppingham St NN1 ..159 B7
Upton Cl NN2 .....141 D6
Upton Way NN4, NN5 ..158 D3
Usher Ho NN2 ....141 C5

V

Vale Cl CV21 ....99 A8
Vale St NN16 ....72 A3
Valentine Way NN3 ..143 C3
Valley Cres Brackley NN13 234 A8
  Northampton NN3 ..143 B1

Valley End NN12 .....172 D1
Valley Rd Brackley NN13 ..234 A8
  Northampton NN3 ...143 B1
  Wellingborough NN8 .129 F1
  Weston by W LE16 ..18 B3
Valley Rise Brackley NN13 ..51 B2
  Desborough NN14 ..51 B2
Valley Way NN14 ...32 B4
Valley Wlk NN16 ...72 E2
Vancouver Cl NN18 .36 B2
Vantage Mdw NN3 ..143 D3
Vara Cl NN18 ....36 B2
Vardon Cl NN4 .....129 C7
Vaughan Cl LE16 ...48 E8
Vaux Rd NN4 ......111 A1
Velbert Ho NN17 ...21 E1
Velocette Way NN5 .140 A1
Verdant Vale ① NN4 .175 D6
Vernon Ave CV22 ...98 E8
Vernon Cl NN11 ....153 E8
Vernon Ct ⑩ NN1 ..159 F6
Vernon Rd NN12 ...203 D5
Vernon St NN1 .....159 F6
Vernon Terr NN1 ...159 F6
Vernon Terrace Lower
  Sch NN1 ....159 F6
Vernon Wlk ⑦ NN1 .159 F6
Verwood Cl NN3 ...142 F5
Vian Way NN17 ....36 B8
Vicar La NN11 .....135 D2
Vicarage Cl
  Hackleton NN7 ....177 A3
  Northampton NN2 ..141 A3
  Wellingborough NN8 .129 D6
  Whittlebury NN12 ..215 C5
  Yardley Gobion NN12 ..217 E6
Vicarage Farm Rd NN8 ..129 D6
Vicarage Hill NN11 ..153 A2
Vicarage La Denton NN7 ..178 B8
  East Haddon NN6 ..122 D5
  Mears Ashby NN6 ..128 B2
  Northampton NN2 ..141 B3
  Priors Marston CV23 ..166 E8
Vicarage Rd
  Northampton NN5 ..159 A7
  Stony Stratford MK11 ..229 D6
Vicarage Rise NN12 ..200 C3
Vicarage Wlk MK11 ..229 D6
Viceroy Cl NN9 ....114 E6
Vickers Cl NN14 ...70 F7
Victoria Ave LE16 ..31 D5
Victoria Bsns Pk NN5 ..159 B6
Victoria Ct
  Earls Barton NN6 ..144 E5
  Rushden NN10 ....132 B3
  West Haddon NN6 ..102 C5
Victoria Ct Rothwell NN14 ..70 D7
  Rushden NN10 ....132 B3
  Woodford NN14 ...94 C7
Victoria Gdns NN1 ..159 D5
Victoria Inf Sch NN8 ..130 B6
Victoria Jun Sch NN8 ..130 B5
Victoria Pk NN8 ...130 B2
Victoria Prom NN1 ..159 D5
Victoria Ct Cogenhoe NN7 161 E5
  Finedon NN9 ......111 F5
  Northampton NN1 ..159 E6
  Oundle PE8 ....42 A6
  Rushden NN10 ....132 B3
  Wellingborough NN8 ..130 B4
Victoria St
  Burton Latimer NN15 ..92 B2
  Desborough NN14 ..51 A3
  Earls Barton NN6 ..144 F5
  Irthlingborough NN9 ..112 E1
  Kettering NN16 ....72 B2
  Northampton NN1 ..159 D6
Victoria Yd PE8 ...41 F5
Vienne Cl NN5 ....157 F8
View Cl NN3 ......126 E1
Vigo Cres NN3 ....159 E5
Viking Cl NN16 ...72 C6
Viking Way Corby NN18 ..36 A2
  Corby NN18 ......36 B1
Villa Gdns NN15 ..92 B1
Villa La NN9 ......113 F3
Vincent Cl NN5 ...157 F8
Vinco Terr PE8 ...28 D8
Vine Cl PE8 ......42 A5
Vine Hill Cl NN10 ..132 A6
Vine Hill Dr NN10 ..132 B6
Violet La Creaton NN6 ..104 F4
  Rothwell NN14, NN16 ..71 C6
Viscount Rd NN3 ..143 C6
Vivian Rd NN8 ...130 B5
Vokes Cl NN3 ....143 A1
Vyse Rd NN2 ....141 C5

W

Wadcroft ③ NN16 ..72 B2
Wade Meadow Ct NN3 ..142 F4
Wadenhoe La PE8 ..57 F4
Wades Cl PE8 ....14 F1
Wadham St NN11 ..153 C7
Waggoners Way NN7 ..173 A7
Wagtail Cl NN3 ...142 C7
Waingrove NN3 ..143 B4
Wainwright Ave NN14 ..76 D1
Wakefield NN8 ...129 C4
Wakefield Dr NN6 ..64 D5
Wakefield Rd NN4 ..141 D4
Wakefield Way NN7 ..156 C1
Wakehurst Dr NN4 ..175 C7

Wakerley Great Wood
  Forest Trail LE15 ....4 C2
Wakerley Great Wood
  Orienteering Course LE15 .4 B2
Wakerley Rd Barrowden LE15 4 A4
  Harringworth NN17 ....10 F7
Walcot Rd LE16 ....31 E2
Walcote Rd LE17 ....63 C8
Wales St
  Kings Sutton OX17 ....230 F5
  Rothwell NN14 ....70 C7
Walford Pl CV22 ....98 F8
Walgrave Cl NN3 ....161 B8
Walgrave Prim Sch NN6 .108 A5
Walgrave Rd Holcot NN6 .107 E1
  Old NN6 ....107 E6
  Walgrave NN6 ....108 B4
Walk The NN6 ....124 B8
Walker Sq NN8 ....129 C7
Walker's La 5 NN6 ......72 B2
Walker's Way NN9 ....111 F4
Walkers Acre NN6 ....108 A5
Walkers Field PE8 ....13 F8
Walkers La NN6 ....140 B8
Walks The PE9 ....1 D2
Wallace Gdns NN2 ......141 F2
Wallace Rd NN2 ....141 F2
Wallace Terr NN2 ....141 F2
Wallbeck Cl NN4 ....141 C4
Walledwell Ct 4 NN3 ...142 F1
Wallingford End 6 NN3 .161 A8
Wallis Cl NN8 ....129 A4
Wallis Cres NN15 ....91 C8
Wallis Rd NN15 ....91 C8
Wallwin Cl NN7 ....191 C4
Walmer Cl NN10 ....132 D1
Walnut Cl Brackley NN13 .222 F1
  Braunston NN11 ....118 D2
  Clifton OX15 ....236 B4
  Culworth OX17 ....198 D2
  Silverstone NN12 ....214 D4
Walnut Cres NN16 ....72 D4
Walsingham Ave NN15 ...91 F8
Waltham NN17 ....36 D8
Waltham Gdns LE16 .....219 A6
Walton Ave OX17 ....230 D5
Walton Heath Way NN2 .141 E3
Walton Pl NN18 ....36 B6
Wansford Pl NN11 ....36 B8
Wansford Rd Elton PE8 ...16 E3
  Yarwell PE8 ....7 F2
Wansford Sta PE8 ....16 E8
Wansford Wlk NN3 ......142 E6
Wantage Cl
  Hackleton NN7 ....177 B3
  Moulton NN3 ....126 E1
Wantage Rd
  Irchester NN29 ....147 B8
  Northampton NN1 ......160 A8
Wappenham Rd
  Abthorpe NN12 ....201 F1
  Helmdon NN13 ....212 A5
  Syresham NN13 ....213 C2
Ward Rd NN13 ....234 A5
Wardens Lodge NN11 ...135 C2
Wardington Rd OX17 ...208 D6
Wardle Ct NN16 ....72 B3
Wardle's Cl NN7 ....138 C7
Wardlow Cl NN4 ....174 F8
Wards La NN6 ....82 C3
Ware Orch CV23 ....99 C2
Ware Rd CV23 ....99 C2
Wareham Gn 1 NN18 ...36 B6
Warehouse The LE16 .....31 D4
Wareing La NN7 ....178 B8
Warkton La NN15 ....73 B1
Warkton Way NN17 ......36 B8
Warkworth Rd OX17 ....219 E7
Warmington Prim
  Sch PE8 ....28 B3
Warminster Cl NN18 .....36 A7
Warmonds Hill NN10 ...132 B5
Warners Hill NN29 ......164 D2
Warnham NN8 ....129 B5
Warren Bridge PE8 ....41 E5
Warren Cl NN29 ....147 C7
Warren Hill NN16 ....71 E3
Warren La Bythorn PE18 ..97 D4
  Clopton NN14 ....78 F1
Warren Rd
  Northampton NN5 ......158 F7
  Stanion NN14 ....37 E3
  Wothorpe PE9 ....2 E7
  Yardley Gobion NN12 ...217 F6
Warren The
  Northampton NN4 ......175 F4
  Thorpe Mandeville OX17 .210 A6
Warren Yd MK12 ....229 F6
Warrens Cl NN9 ....112 F2
Warrington Rd MK46 ...195 F5
Wartnaby St LE16 ....31 E5
Warwick Ave NN14 ......37 E3
Warwick Cl
  Market Harborough LE16 ...31 F5
  Northampton NN5 ......158 B8
  Raunds NN9 ....114 D5
Warwick Ct
  Daventry NN11 ....135 B1
  Kettering NN15 ....91 F8
Warwick Gdns NN14 .....76 E5
Warwick Ho NN5 ....158 F7
Warwick Prim Sch NN8 .129 F1
Warwick Rd
  Hanslope MK19 ....207 A3

Warwick Rd continued
  Upper Boddington NN11 .182 C7
  Wellingborough NN8 ...130 A2
Warwick St NN11 ....135 B1
Warwick Way NN17 ......36 C6
Washbrook Cl NN3 ......143 B1
Washbrook La NN6 .....143 F5
Washbrook Rd NN10 ...132 A3
Washingley La PE7 ......44 F6
Washington Ct NN14 .....76 E3
Washington Sq NN16 ....72 D3
Washington St NN2 ....141 C3
Washle Dr OX17 ....220 B7
Water La
  Adderbury OX17 ....230 A3
  Bradden NN12 ....201 F5
  Chelveston NN9 ....133 B8
  Cottingham LE16 ....35 D8
  Northampton NN4 ......175 E6
  Shutlanger NN12 ....204 D8
  Towcester NN12 ....203 C5
  Weldon NN17 ....38 A8
Water Meadow Cl NN18 .36 B1
Water St NN16 ....72 C2
Waterfall Way LE16 .....18 F6
Waterfield Pl LE16 ....31 E5
Waterhouse Gdns NN15 .92 A7
Watering La NN4 ....175 C3
Waterloo NN11 ....135 C1
Waterloo Way NN9 .....131 D8
Watermeadow Dr NN3 .142 F6
Watermill Cl NN14 ....51 D3
Waterpike NN6 ....106 C2
Waterpump Ct NN3 .....142 F5
Waters La OX17 ....209 B1
Watersmeet NN1 ....160 C6
Waterworks La NN8 ....129 E7
Waterworks Way LE17 ...45 F5
Watery La Brackley NN13 .234 A7
  Nether Heyford NN7 ...156 C2
Watford Rd Crick NN6 ..101 A2
  West Haddon NN6 .....102 B3
Watkin Cl NN1 ....159 D7
Watkin Terr NN1 ....159 D7
Watling St CV23 ....100 A3
Watling St E
  Pattishall NN12 ....172 D1
  Towcester NN12 ....203 C6
Watling St W
  Pattishall NN12 ....172 D1
  Towcester NN12 ....203 C6
Watling Way Cty Fst
  Sch MK19 ....229 F4
Watling Way Cty Mid
  Sch MK19 ....229 F4
Watson Ave LE16 ....48 D8
Watson Cl Oundle PE8 ...41 E7
  Wellingborough NN8 ...129 C7
Watson Rd NN16 ....121 B2
Watts Cl MK19 ....207 A3
Watts La CV21 ....99 B8
Watts Way NN6 ....121 C3
Wavell Cl NN15 ....72 E1
Waveney Cl NN11 ......153 A8
Waveney Way NN5 .....140 F1
Waver Cl NN18 ....36 D3
Waverley Ave NN17 .....37 A6
Waverley Rd
  Kettering NN15 ....91 D8
  Northampton NN2 .....141 E1
  Rugby CV21 ....80 A1
Waynflete Ave NN13 ...233 E7
Waynflete Cl NN13 .....233 E7
Waypost Cl NN3 ....142 F3
Wayside Acres 3 NN4 .175 B8
Weares Cl LE15 ....3 B5
Weaver Cl NN16 ....72 B6
Weavers End MK19 .....207 B2
Weavers Rd NN8 ....129 D4
Weavers The NN4 ......175 C6
Webb Cl PE8 ....42 B5
Webb Rd NN9 ....114 C7
Webbs La NN6 ....127 D3
Webster Cl NN7 ....114 D7
Weddell Way NN4 .....160 C2
Wedmore Cl NN5 ......158 D7
Wedmore Ct 3 NN8 .....36 B6
Weedon Bec Prim
  Sch NN7 ....155 B3
Weedon La NN11 ......136 C4
Weedon Lois CE Prim
  Sch NN12 ....200 B2
Weedon Rd
  Farthingstone NN12 ...170 F3
  Kislingbury NN7 ....157 D5
  Nether Heyford NN7 ...156 B2
  Newnham NN11 ....153 E4
  Northampton NN5 ......158 D5
Weekley Glebe Rd NN16 .72 D5
Weekley Wood La NN16 ..72 E6
Weggs Farm Rd NN5 ...139 F1
Weinahr Cl LE16 ....34 C5
Weir Cl NN8 ....129 F7
Welbeck Ct Corby NN18 ..36 C5
  Kettering NN15 ....91 F8
Welbourne Cl NN9 .....114 C6
Weldon CE Prim
  Sch NN17 ....38 A8
Weldon Cl NN8 ....129 D7
Weldon North Ind
  Est NN17 ....22 F1
Weldon Rd NN17 ....37 C5
Weldon St NN16 ....72 C3
Welford Ave NN9 ....113 B5
Welford Gr NN17 ....36 C7

Welford Rd
  Husbands Bosworth LE17 ...45 E3
  Northampton NN2 .....141 B4
  Sibbertoft LE16 ....46 D2
  South Kilworth LE17 ....63 D7
  Spratton NN6 ....124 A8
  Thornby NN6 ....84 D4
  Welford NN6 ....64 E7
Welford Sibbertoft &
  Sulby Sch 64 E5
Welham La LE16 ....17 E8
Welham Rd
  Great Bowden LE16 ....32 B8
  Thorpe Langton LE16 ...17 B5
  Welham LE16 ....18 A8
  Weston by W LE16 ......18 A8
Well Hill Cl NN6 ....100 F5
Well La Barnwell PE8 ....59 B7
  Everdon NN11 ....170 A8
  Guilsborough NN6 .....103 F6
  Rothwell NN14 ....70 D7
  Staverton NN11 ....152 B7
  Welton NN11 ....119 E1
Well St NN9 ....111 F5
Well Yd NN3 ....141 B3
Welland Ave LE16 ....30 E7
Welland Cl Caldecott LE16 .21 C8
  Daventry NN11 ....152 F8
  Raunds NN9 ....114 C7
Welland Ct
  Burton Latimer NN15 ...92 B2
  Desborough NN14 ......51 A3
  Market Harborough LE16 .31 F2
Welland Gn NN5 ....140 F2
Welland Ind Est LE16 ...32 B4
Welland Park Com
  Coll 31 E2
Welland Park Rd LE16 ...31 E2
Welland Rd NN16 ....72 A5
Welland Rise LE16 ......46 F2
Welland Vale Rd NN17 ..21 E1
Welland View Rd LE16 ...20 D1
Welland Way NN5 ......141 A2
Welland Wlk NN5 ......140 F2
Wellingborough Bsns
  Ctr NN8 ....130 B2
Wellingborough Jun
  Sch NN8 ....130 B3
Wellingborough
  Midland Sta NN8 .....130 C5
Wellingborough Park
  Inf Sch NN8 ....130 A5
Wellingborough Rd
  Broughton NN14 ....90 B3
  Earls Barton NN6 .....144 F6
  Finedon NN9 ....111 F4
  Great Harrowden NN9 .110 E1
  Irthlingborough NN9 ...131 C8
  Isham NN14 ....110 F8
  Little Harrowden NN9 ..110 B3
  Mears Ashby NN6 .....128 C2
  Northampton NN3 .....142 E1
  Olney MK46 ....195 F5
  Rushden NN10 ....131 F3
  Sywell NN6 ....127 F4
  Wellingborough NN8 ...111 E1
Wellingborough Sch
  Wellingborough NN8 ...130 B3
  Wellingborough NN8 ...130 B4
Wellington Pl 18 NN1 .159 C7
Wellington Rd NN9 ....114 C5
Wellington St
  Kettering NN16 ....72 C3
  Northampton NN1 .....159 D6
Wellington Terr NN14 ...76 B2
Wells Cl
  Husbands Bosworth LE17 ..45 E5
  Kettering NN15 ....90 F8
Wells Ct NN3 ....142 C8
Wells Gn NN18 ....36 B6
Wells The NN9 ....111 F5
Wellspring NN7 ....190 D7
Welsh Rd Aston le W NN11 182 C8
  Chipping Warden OX17 .197 C6
Welton CE Prim
  Sch NN11 ....119 E1
Welton La NN11 ....135 D6
Welton Pk NN11 ....119 E1
Welton Pl CV22 ....98 D8
Welton Rd
  Braunston NN11 ....118 D1
  Daventry NN11 ....135 C3
Wenlock Way NN5 .....140 D1
Wensleydale NN2 ......140 F5
Wensleydale Pk NN17 ...36 D8
Wentworth Ave NN6 ...129 C7
Wentworth Cl NN11 ...135 E3
Wentworth Cotts MK18 .227 A5
Wentworth Dr PE8 ......41 E7
Wentworth Rd
  Finedon NN9 ....112 A5
  Rushden NN10 ....132 A2
Wentworth Way
  Northampton NN2 .....141 E3
  Stoke Bruerne NN12 ...204 F8
Weskers Cl LE16 ....67 A7
Wesley Cl NN7 ....114 D6
Wesley Pl OX17 ....208 E4
Wesley Rd CV21 ....99 A8
Wessex Cl NN16 ....72 B6
Wessex Way NN3 ......142 B1
West Ave NN15 ....92 B3
West Bank NN3 ....142 E6
West Brook Blisworth NN7 190 D8
  Newnham NN11 ....153 D4
West Cres NN10 ....131 E2
West Ct NN11 ....135 C1
West End Bugbrooke NN7 .172 E7

West End continued
  Scaldwell NN6 ....106 F5
  Silverstone NN12 ....214 C4
  Welford NN6 ....64 D4
  West Haddon NN6 .....102 B4
West Farm Cl NN3 .....108 C3
West Furlong NN15 .....71 F1
West Glebe Rd NN17 ....36 F7
West Haddon Prim
  Sch 102 B4
West Haddon Rd
  Cold Ashby NN6 ....84 A5
  Crick NN6 ....101 B6
  Guilsborough NN6 .....103 D7
  Ravensthorpe NN6 ....103 C1
  Watford NN6 ....120 D7
West Leys Ct NN3 .....142 C7
West March NN11 .....153 D7
West Mill PE9 ....1 F4
West Oval NN5 ....140 F1
West Paddock Ct NN3 .142 F4
West Priors Ct NN3 ...143 A4
West Ridge NN2 ....141 D3
West Rising NN4 ......175 D7
West Side Rise MK46 ...195 F4
West St Broughton NN14 .90 A5
  Earls Barton NN6 .....144 E4
  Easton on t H PE9 ......2 A5
  Ecton NN6 ....143 F4
  Geddington NN14 ....54 A3
  Kettering NN16 ....72 B1
  King's Cliffe PE8 ....13 E7
  Long Buckby NN6 ......121 A4
  Moulton NN3 ....126 C1
  Northampton NN1 ......159 F6
  Olney MK46 ....195 F4
  Oundle PE8 ....41 F5
  Raunds NN9 ....114 D6
  Rushden NN10 ....132 B2
  Stanwick NN9 ....113 E3
  Weedon NN7 ....155 B3
  Welford NN6 ....64 E6
  Wellingborough NN8 ...129 F4
  Woodford NN14 ....94 C7
West View Corby NN17 ...37 B7
  Daventry NN11 ....135 B1
West Villa Rd NN8 .....129 F4
West Way
  Earls Barton NN6 .....144 D5
  Weedon NN7 ....155 B3
Westbrook NN8 ....129 B4
Westbury Ave NN5 .....158 D7
Westcott Way Corby NN18 .36 D5
  Northampton NN3 .....160 E7
Westerdale NN2 ....140 F5
Western Ave
  Daventry NN11 ....153 B8
  Easton on t H PE9 ......1 F5
  Market Harborough LE16 ..31 E2
  Nether Heyford NN7 ...156 B1
Western Dr MK19 ......207 A3
Western View NN1 .....159 B5
Western Way NN8 .....129 D3
Westfield Ave
  Deanshanger MK19 ...228 D5
  Raunds NN9 ....114 B4
  Rushden NN10 ....131 F2
Westfield Barn CV23 ...166 D7
Westfield Cl LE16 ....31 C3
Westfield Cres NN16 ....64 E6
Westfield Ctr NN13 ....233 E8
Westfield Dr NN9 ......114 B4
Westfield Ho 8 NN16 ...72 B2
Westfield Pl NN11 .....131 F2
Westfield Rd
  Northampton NN5 .....158 F6
  Northampton, Duston NN5 .158 B8
  Wellingborough NN8 ...129 E4
Westfields Easton on t H PE9 .1 F5
  Little Harrowden NN9 ..110 B3
  Wellingborough NN8 ...130 D3
Westfields Ave NN10 ...132 B5
Westfields Cl NN17 ......36 E8
Westfields St NN10 ....132 B5
Westfields Terr NN10 ..132 B5
Westgate La LE16 ....30 E3
Westgate Rd NN5 .....158 D6
Westhaven PE9 ....2 A5
Westhill Ave NN13 .....233 E7
Westhill Cl Brackley NN13 .233 E7
  Kettering NN15 ....71 F1
Westhill Dr NN15 ....71 F1
Westhill Gdns NN13 ...233 D7
Westhorp OX17 ....210 E2
Westhorpe Ashley LE16 ...18 E2
Westhorpe La NN11 ...183 C7
Westland Cl LE16 ....30 E3
Westlea Rd NN6 ....127 D3
Westleigh Cl NN1 ......159 F8
Westleigh Pk NN16 ....141 E6
Westleigh Rd NN15 .....92 B8
Westmead St NN3 .....142 F1
Westminster Cl NN13 ..234 A7
Westminster Cres NN13 .234 A7
Westminster Croft NN13 .233 F7
Westminster Rd
  Brackley NN13 ....233 A7
  Wellingborough NN8 ...129 E2
Westminster Wlk NN3 ...36 D3
Westmoreland Cl PE8 ...15 E5
Westmorland Dr NN14 ..51 C4
Weston Favell CE
  Lower Sch NN3 ....160 D8
Weston Favell Ctr NN3 .142 F2
Weston Favell Upper
  Sch NN3 ....142 D3

Weston Mill La NN3 ...160 E6
Weston Rd Ashley LE16 ..18 D3
  Olney MK46 ....195 D3
  Ravenstone MK46 .....194 E2
  Sulgrave OX17 ....211 A8
  Sutton Bassett LE16 ....18 A2
  Welham LE16 ....17 F5
Weston Way NN3 ......160 C6
Weston Wlk NN18 ......36 C6
Westone Ave NN3 .....142 E1
Westonville NN1 ....1 D2
Westover Rd NN15 ......71 F1
Westvilla Cotts NN8 ...129 F4
Westway NN15 ....71 F1
Westway The NN11 ....153 D8
Westwood Rd CV22 .....98 F7
Westwood Wlk NN18 ...36 C5
Wetenhall Rd NN9 .....114 A4
Wetheral Cl NN3 ......142 C4
Weymouth Cl NN18 .....36 B6
Whaddon Cl NN4 ......158 E1
Whaddon Field NN6 ...106 C1
Whalley Gr NN7 ....161 F6
Wharf Cl MK19 ....229 B7
Wharf La
  Old Stratford MK19 ...229 C7
  Souldern OX6 ....237 B4
Wharf Rd NN10 ....132 B6
Wharfe Gn NN5 ....140 F2
Wharfedale Rd NN17 ...21 E1
Wheatcroft Gdns NN10 .132 C2
Wheatens Cl NN6 .....125 C8
Wheatfield Dr NN15 ....92 C2
Wheatfield Gdns NN3 ..142 B1
Wheatfield Rd NN3 ....142 B1
Wheatfield Rd N NN3 ..142 B2
Wheatfield Rd S NN3 ..142 B1
Wheatfield Terr NN3 ...142 B1
Wheatley Ave NN17 .....36 F6
Wheel La LE15 ....3 F5
Wheeler's Rise NN13 ..238 C8
Wheelwright Cl NN9 ...114 E7
Wheelwright Ho NN14 ...70 D7
Wheelwrights Yd NN29 .164 D2
Whernside NN8 ....129 D6
Whernside Way NN5 ..158 C8
Whilton Rd
  Great Brington NN7 ...138 C2
  Northampton NN2 .....141 D4
Whistfield Cotts NN6 ..143 B4
Whistlets Cl NN4 ......158 D1
Whiston Rd
  Cogenhoe NN7 ....162 C6
  Denton NN7 ....162 B2
  Northampton NN3 .....141 D4
Whitby Cl NN15 ....91 F8
White Cotts MK18 .....226 D4
White Delves NN3 .....129 E7
White Doe Dr NN3 ....142 C7
White Hills Cres NN2 ..141 B6
White Hills Way NN2 ..141 B6
White House Ct NN10 .132 C1
White House Ind
  Est NN6 ....144 D6
White Post Ct NN17 ....21 E2
White Way NN6 ....144 E5
Whitecroft Gdns NN11 .184 B7
Whitefield Rd NN3 ....140 C1
Whitefield Way NN6 ...114 C7
Whiteford Dr NN15 .....91 C7
Whitefriars NN11 ......131 F1
Whitefriars Jun & Inf
  Schs NN10 ....147 F8
Whitegates NN3 ....158 E1
Whiteheart Cl NN3 ....143 B2
Whitehill NN5 ....195 E5
Whitehills Lower
  Sch NN2 ....141 A6
Whitehorse Yd MK11 ..229 D5
Whiteland Rd NN3 ....142 C2
Whiteman La NN14 .....70 C7
Whites Rise NN9 ......112 E1
Whitesands Way NN4 .158 C2
Whitfield Way NN2 ....141 D5
Whiting Ct NN3 ....142 C8
Whitmees Cl MK46 ....195 E4
Whitmore Ct NN12 ....214 D5
Whitney Rd NN15 ......92 B1
Whitsundale Cl NN9 ...111 F4
Whittall St OX17 ......230 F5
Whittam Cl NN9 ....114 C7
Whittemore Rd NN10 .132 D3
Whittle Cl Daventry NN11 .135 A5
  Wellingborough NN8 ...129 B6
Whittle Rd NN17 ....37 B8
Whittlebury CE Prim
  Sch NN12 ....215 C4
Whittlebury Cl NN12 ..141 D5
Whittlebury Ct NN12 ..215 C5
Whittlebury Rd NN12 .214 E5
Whittles Cross NN14 ..176 A6
Whittlesea Terr NN14 ...94 D6
Whitton Cl OX17 ......210 E2
Whittons La NN12 ....203 C6
Whitwell Cl PE8 ....41 E5
Whitworth Ave NN17 ...37 A8
Whitworth Cres NN6 ..144 E5
Whitworth Rd
  Northampton NN1 .....159 F7
  Wellingborough NN8 ...130 C5
Whitworth Way
  Irthlingborough NN9 ..131 B8
  Wellingborough NN8 ...130 B2
Whytewell Rd NN8 ....129 F6
Wick Cl NN18 ....36 D3
Wicken Park Rd MK19 .228 B1
Wicken Rd MK18 ......227 E1

Wickery Dene NN4 .....176 A6
Wicksteed Cl NN15 .....91 C6
Wicksteed L Pk NN15 ...91 D6
Wigston Rd 3 CV21 .....80 A1
Wilbarston CE Prim
  Sch LE16 ....34 C5
Wilbarston Rd LE16 .....34 B4
Wilberforce St 8 NN1 ..159 E6
Wilby CE Prim Sch NN8 .129 B1
Wilby Cl NN17 ....36 B8
Wilby La NN29 ....145 D6
Wilby Rd NN6 ....128 D2
Wilby St NN1 ....159 F6
Wilby Way NN8 ....129 D1
Wilbye Grange NN8 ....129 D2
Wild Cherry Cl NN11 ...184 B6
Wildacre Rd NN10 .....131 E2
Wildern La NN4 ....175 C5
Wilford Ave NN3 ......160 F8
Willetts Cl NN17 ....36 E8
Willey Ct MK11 ....229 F4
William Rd NN6 ....121 B3
William St
  Burton Latimer NN15 ..92 B2
  Finedon NN9 ....112 A4
  Kettering NN16 ....72 B4
  Northampton NN1 ....159 D7
William Steele
  Way NN10 ....132 C5
William Trigg Cl NN9 ..131 E8
William's Way NN29 ...146 E1
Williams Cl MK19 .....206 F3
Williams Terr NN11 ...135 B2
Williams Way NN10 ...132 B5
Williamscot Hill OX17 .208 B6
Willis Way NN12 ......203 C5
Williton Cl NN3 ....160 D7
Willoughby Cl NN11 ...135 B3
Willoughby Pl CV22 ....98 D7
Willoughby Rd LE15 .....3 A6
Willoughby Way NN7 ..177 A1
Willow Brook Rd NN17 ..36 C8
Willow Brook Sq NN3 ..143 D2
Willow Cl Desborough NN14 51 C3
  Hinton NN11 ....184 A6
  Spratton NN6 ....124 A8
  Towcester NN12 .....203 C3
Willow Cres
  Great Houghton NN4 ..160 F2
  Market Harborough LE16 .31 C2
Willow Ct NN1 ....160 A7
Willow Gr MK19 ......229 B6
Willow La
  Great Houghton NN4 ..160 E2
  King's Cliffe PE8 ......13 F7
  Stanion NN14 ....37 F2
Willow Rd Brackley NN13 234 A6
  Kettering NN15 ....72 C1
Willow Rise NN3 ......161 B8
Willow Tree Gdns CV21 ..99 A8
Willow View NN7 .....157 C3
Willowbrook East Ind
  Est NN17 ....22 E2
Willows Hill NN12 ....201 F5
Willows The
  Daventry NN11 ......135 C3
  Kings Sutton OX17 ...231 A6
  Little Harrowden NN9 .110 B3
  Silverstone NN12 ....214 C5
Wills Cl NN6 ....103 E7
Wilson Cl LE16 ....32 A3
Wilmington Wlk 1 NN18 .36 B5
Wilson Cres NN9 .....112 E1
Wilson Rd NN10 ......132 A2
Wilson Terr NN16 .....72 B4
Wilson Way NN6 .....144 E3
Wilton Cl NN14 ....51 A2
Wilton Rd NN15 ....91 F8
Wimbledon St NN5 ...159 A6
Wimborne Cl NN3 ....143 D3

Wimborne Pl NN11 ...135 C5
Wimborne Wlk NN18 ...36 A7
Wimpole NN8 ....129 C4
Wincanton Ct NN18 ....36 B6
Wincely Cl NN11 .....135 C5
Winchester Cl NN4 ...159 C1
Winchester House
  Sch NN13 ....233 F7
Winchester Rd
  Northampton NN4 ...159 C1
  Rushden NN10 ......132 C1
Winchilsea Dr NN17 ...10 B1
Windermere Cl NN11 ..135 B2
Windermere Dr NN8 ..129 C6
Windermere Rd NN16 ..71 F2
Windflower Pl 2 NN3 .143 D2
Windgate Way PE8 .....8 A6
Winding Way NN14 ....76 E2
Windingbrook La NN4 .175 C5
Windmill Ave
  Blisworth NN7 ....190 E7
  Raunds NN9 ....114 D6
Windmill Banks NN10 .132 C7
Windmill Cl
  Cottingham LE16 ......20 D1
  Wellingborough NN8 ..129 E2
  Wollaston NN29 .....146 E2
Windmill Gdns NN11 ..152 C7
Windmill Glade NN6 ..106 A1
Windmill Gr NN9 .....114 D6
Windmill La Denton NN7 .178 B8
  Raunds NN9 ....114 D7
  Staverton NN11 .....152 B4
Windmill Prim Sch NN9 .114 C7
Windmill Rd
  Irthlingborough NN9 ..112 E1
  Rushden NN10 ......132 A2
Windmill Rise LE16 ....20 D1
Windmill Terr NN2 ...141 D4
Windmill Way
  Greens Norton NN12 ..202 D8
  Lyddington LE15 ......9 D6
Windmill Wlk NN15 ....72 D1
Windrush Rd NN4 .....175 F8
Windrush Way NN5 ...141 A2
Windsor Ave NN14 .....50 F2
Windsor Cl Daventry NN11 135 B1
  Kings Sutton OX17 ...230 F6
  Long Buckby NN6 ....121 B3
  Towcester NN12 .....203 B4
  Weedon NN7 ....155 B4
Windsor Cres NN5 ....158 E6
Windsor Ct LE16 ....31 D4
Windsor Dr Brackley NN13 233 E8
  Thrapston NN14 ......76 E2
Windsor Gdns NN16 ...72 A2
Windsor Ho NN5 .....158 C8
Windsor Pl NN18 ......36 E5
Windsor Rd
  Rushden NN10 ......132 C3
  Wellingborough NN8 .129 F1
Windyridge NN2 ......141 D3
Winemar Cl MK19 ....207 A3
Wing Rd LE15 ....3 A6
Wingate Cl NN15 ......72 E1
Winnington Cl NN3 ...143 C5
Winsford Way NN3 ...160 D7
Winstanley Rd NN8 ...130 B5
Winston Cl
  Nether Heyford NN7 ..156 B1
  Northampton NN3 ...142 C5
  Woodford Halse NN11 .184 D5
Winston Cres NN3 ....233 F6
Winston Dr NN14 ......91 D1
Winterbourne Ct NN18 ..36 B6
Winthorpe Way NN18 ..36 C6
Winwick Rd PE17 .....61 D1

Wire La LE16 ....19 D2
Wisley Cl NN4 ....175 C7
Wisteria Way NN3 ....160 C6
Witham Gn NN5 ......140 E2
Witham Ho NN2 .....141 E1
Witham The NN11 ....134 F1
Witham Way NN5 ....140 F1
Witham Wlk NN5 ....140 F2
Witton Rd NN5 ......158 C8
Woburn Cl LE16 ....32 A3
Woburn Gate NN3 ...143 D3
Wodhams Dr NN13 ...222 E1
Wold Rd NN15 ....92 E2
Wolfe Cl NN15 ....72 F1
Wollaston Rd
  Bozeat NN29 ....164 C5
  Irchester NN29 .....146 F6
Wollaston Sch NN29 ..146 E2
Wollaton Gdns NN3 ..160 F8
Wolsey Cl NN6 ....101 A6
Wolverton Rd MK11 ..229 E6
Wood Avens Cl NN4 ..158 E1
Wood Hill NN1 ....159 D5
Wood La
  Hartwell NN7 ....192 E2
  King's Cliffe PE8 .....13 E7
  Oundle PE8 ....41 D4
  Weston Underwood MK46 .195 A2
Wood Rd PE8 ....13 F7
Wood St
  Corby NN17 ....36 E6
  Geddington NN14 .....54 B3
  Higham Ferrers NN10 .132 C5
  Kettering NN16 ....72 C4
  Northampton NN1 ...159 D6
  Wellingborough NN8 .129 F4
Woodborough Gdns NN3 160 F8
Woodbreach Dr LE16 ..32 B3
Woodcock St NN15 ....92 D3
Woodcote Ave NN3 ..142 A5
Woodcroft Cl NN12 ..203 C3
Woodfield PE9 ....1 D1
Woodfield Gr NN17 ....36 E7
Woodford St NN15 ....91 F5
Woodford Glebe NN6 ..64 E5
Woodford Halse CE
  Prim Sch NN14 .....184 D6
Woodford La NN14 ....75 E6
Woodford Rd
  Byfield NN11 ....183 D7
  Great Addington NN14 ..94 C1
  Great Addington NN14 ..94 C3
Woodford St 7 NN1 ...159 E6
Woodford (Thrapston)
  CE Prim Sch NN14 ...94 C3
Woodford Wlk 9 NN1 .159 E6
Woodgate LE16 ....30 E8
Woodgate Cl LE16 .....32 B2
Woodhall Cl NN4 .....158 D1
Woodhill Rd NN5 .....140 C1
Woodland Ave
  Kettering NN15 ....92 A5
  Northampton NN3 ...142 A1
  Overstone NN6 ......127 B1
Woodland Cl
  Brigstock NN14 ....55 F7
  Northampton NN5 ...140 B1
Woodland Dr NN15 ....92 C4
Woodland Hospl
  The NN14 ....71 B5
Woodland Rd NN10 ..132 A3
Woodland Wlk NN3 ..143 B6
Woodlands Ave NN17 ..21 F1
Woodlands Ct
  Kettering NN16 ....72 C4
  Watford NN6 ....120 C6
Woodlands Grange NN6 .145 A4
Woodlands La NN18 ...53 C8
Woodlands Rd
  Irchester NN29 .....147 A7

Woodlands Rd continued
  Weldon NN17 ....38 C7
Woodlands The
  Geddington NN14 .....54 B3
  Market Harborough LE16 .31 C4
  Silverstone NN12 ....214 D4
  Staverton NN11 .....152 B7
Woodley Chase NN5 ..140 B1
Woodnewton CE
  Sch PE8 ....14 E1
Woodnewton Jun & Inf
  Schs NN17 ....36 C8
Woodnewton Rd PE8 ..15 D4
Woodnewton Way NN17 .36 C7
Woodpecker Way NN4 .174 F7
Woodroffe Rd PE8 .....7 D8
Woodrush Way NN3 ..142 C7
Woods Ct
  Brackley NN13 ......233 D7
  Rushden NN10 ......132 B3
Woods La NN12 ......217 E3
Woodside
  Stony Stratford MK11 .229 E6
  Sywell NN6 ....127 D1
Woodside Ave
  Northampton NN3 ...142 D8
  Sywell NN6 ....143 D8
Woodside Cres NN3 ..142 D4
Woodside Way NN5 ..140 F1
Woodside Gn NN5 ....140 F1
Woodside Wlk NN5 ...140 E1
Woodstock 12 NN1 ...159 F6
Woodstock Cl NN8 ...129 C4
Woodville Cres NN12 .217 E6
Woodward Cl NN11 ..135 C1
Woodwell Hill NN14 ...50 F2
Wooldale Rd NN4 ....176 A6
Woolmans MK11 .....229 E4
Woolmonger St 4 NN1 .159 C5
Woolrich Gdns MK11 .229 E5
Woolston Ct NN17 ....10 C1
Wooton Ct NN4 ......175 E8
Wooton Hope Dr NN4 .175 F7
Wootton Brook Cl NN4 .175 C6
Wootton Hill Farm NN4 .174 F8
Wootton Hope Dr NN4 .175 F6
Wootton Prim Sch NN4 .175 E6
Wootton Rd NN4 .....176 A2
Worcester Cl NN3 ....143 C4
Worcester Dr LE16 ....31 E5
Worcester Way NN11 .153 C7
Wordsworth Ave NN17 ..21 D1
Wordsworth Cl
  Brackley NN13 ......222 F1
  Towcester NN12 ....203 B5
Wordsworth Rd
  Daventry NN11 ......135 B3
  Kettering NN16 ....72 C5
  Wellingborough NN8 .129 B3
Works The 8 NN1 .....159 E6
Wormleighton CV23 ..181 B8
Worthing Rd NN18 ....36 B5
Wrekin Cl NN4 ......158 E3
Wren Cl Kettering NN15 ..92 A6
  Towcester NN12 ....203 C3
Wren Spinney
  Sch NN15 ....71 F1
Wrenbury Rd NN5 ....140 A1
Wrendyke Cl LE15 .....3 A6
Wrenn Sch NN8 ......130 A3
Wright Rd NN6 ......121 B3
Wrightons Hill NN13 .211 F4
Wroe The NN10 ......132 B7
Wyatt St NN16 ....72 C2
Wyatt Way PE8 ....41 E6
Wychwood Cl NN5 ...140 A1
Wycliffe Rd NN1 .....160 A6
Wye Cl NN8 ....129 C6
Wye The NN11 ......153 A8

Wic–Zio 263

Wykeham Rd NN10 ...132 C7
Wyman Cl NN29 .....164 D2
Wymersley Cl NN4 ...160 F2
Wymington Pk NN10 .132 B1
Wymington Rd
  Podington NN29 ....147 E3
  Rushden NN10 .....148 B3
Wyndham Way NN16 ..71 E4
Wysall Rd NN3 ......143 B5

Y

Yardley Cl NN17 ......21 D1
Yardley Dr NN2 ......141 D6
Yardley Gobion CE Prim
  Sch NN12 ....217 E6
Yardley Hastings Prim
  Sch NN7 ....179 A7
Yarrow NN8 ....129 B3
Yarrow Ho NN2 .....141 C5
Yarwell Mill PE8 ......16 A7
Yarwell Sq NN4 .....158 F2
Yateley Dr NN15 ......92 A5
Yeldon Ct NN8 ......111 B1
Yelvertoft Prim
  Sch NN6 ....82 B4
Yelvertoft Rd
  Crick NN6 ....101 A8
  Lilbourne CV23 ......81 D6
  Northampton NN2 ..141 C3
Yelvertoft Rd NN6 ...102 B5
Yeoman Cl NN14 ......95 A3
Yeoman Dr NN2 .....141 B5
Yeoman Mdw NN4 ...174 F8
Yeomanry Cl NN11 ...135 B1
Yeomanry Way NN11 .135 B1
Yeomans Cl NN13 ...234 A8
Yeomans Ct NN15 ....92 C2
Yew Cl NN17 ....21 E1
Yew Tree Cl OX17 ...220 A8
Yew Tree Gdns NN7 .155 F5
Yew Tree Gr NN15 ...153 B8
Yew Tree La NN6 ....124 B8
Yew Tree Rise NN13 .238 D8
Yewtree Ct NN3 .....142 D5
York Ave NN7 ....161 F6
York Cl
  Higham Ferrers NN10 .132 C7
  Towcester NN12 ....203 C4
York Ct NN12 ....203 C5
York Dr NN13 ......233 E8
York Rd
  Corby NN18 ....36 C5
  Higham Ferrers NN10 .132 C7
  Kettering NN16 ....72 B2
  Northampton NN1 ...159 E6
  Rushden NN10 .....132 C1
  Stony Stratford MK11 .229 D5
  Wellingborough NN8 .130 B5
  Wollaston NN29 ....146 D3
York Ride NN7 ......155 B4
York St LE16 ....31 F3
York Way NN9 ......114 C9
Yorke Cl NN9 ....111 E5

Z

Zion Hill NN6 ....108 A5

Also available in various formats

- Berkshire
- Birmingham and West Midlands
- Bristol and Avon
- Buckinghamshire
- Cannock, Lichfield, Rugeley
- Cardiff, Swansea and Glamorgan
- Cheshire
- Derbyshire
- Derby and Belper
- Durham
- Edinburgh and East Central Scotland
- North Essex
- South Essex
- Glasgow and West Central Scotland
- North Hampshire
- South Hampshire
- Hertfordshire
- East Kent
- West Kent
- Lancashire
- Greater Manchester
- Merseyside
- Northwich, Winsford, Middlewich
- Nottinghamshire
- Oxfordshire
- Peak District Towns
- Staffordshire
- Stafford, Stone, Uttoxeter
- Surrey
- East Sussex
- West Sussex
- Tyne and Wear
- Warrington, Widnes, Runcorn
- Warwickshire
- South Yorkshire
- West Yorkshire

- Colour regional atlases (hardback, spiral, wire-o, pocket)   Colour local atlases (paperback)
- Black and white regional atlases (hardback, softback, pocket)

◆ Paperback

'Very clear mapping. Great in scope and value'
BEST BUY, AUTO EXPRESS

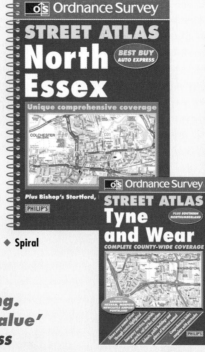

◆ Spiral

◆ Pocket

◆ Hardback